# IMPROVING READING
## IN
# SECONDARY SCHOOLS

# IMPROVING READING IN SECONDARY SCHOOLS

## Selected Readings

**LAWRENCE E. HAFNER**

Associate Professor of Education
University of Georgia
Athens, Georgia

71695

THE MACMILLAN COMPANY
COLLIER-MACMILLAN LIMITED, LONDON

Sixth Printing, 1970

Library of Congress catalog card number: 67–16688


THE MACMILLAN COMPANY
866 THIRD AVENUE, NEW YORK, NEW YORK 10022
COLLIER-MACMILLAN CANADA, LTD., TORONTO, ONTARIO

Printed in the United States of America

TO
Becky Jean and Katie Jane
and in appreciation
TO
A. Sterl Artley

# PREFACE

It becomes increasingly apparent that the successful teacher in grades seven to twelve is the one who can help his students master the materials of his subject by helping them do a better job of reading. Occasionally a teacher asks why reading should be taught in the secondary schools if the elementary schools have taught reading well. Part of the answer to this question lies in the fact that the elementary schools cannot provide in the sixth grade all of the reading-study skills and conceptual background the student will need in the tenth, eleventh, and twelfth grades. As one goes through high school the reading materials present an increasingly difficult challenge to the reader—concepts are more difficult, the sentences and paragraphs become more involved, more figurative language is used, the topics are broader in scope, and purposes for reading in the various subjects become more varied and demanding. Therefore, the teachers in the secondary schools must continue the guidance in reading instruction begun by the teachers in the elementary schools.

Why does the concept "teacher" imply the role of "teacher of reading skills"? When the student reads, he is thinking, for reading is a thinking process that involves the use of several kinds of reasoning. The teacher's task, and privilege, is to help the student think more effectively about the ideas in reading materials; therefore, the teacher in the secondary school is a teacher of reading. He becomes a good teacher of reading through worthwhile study, training, and experience.

This does not mean that every high school teacher need assume the task of providing the basic core of reading instruction as the elementary school teacher does. It does mean that he will learn how to help his students to read better. He should know how to help the students apply to the subject he teaches the general reading skills taught by the developmental reading teacher. And he should know how to teach the specific reading skills that are germane to his subject.

One must remember that implicit in our definition of teaching is the concept of helping students, of stimulating and *guiding* their efforts to learn. And there is scarcely a better way of guiding their efforts than by helping the students to sharpen their academic tools— their reading and study skills and their attitudes toward and interest in reading.

It is evident, then, that the teacher needs to be well versed in the best literature on the teaching of reading in the secondary schools. The purpose of this book of readings is to make available a sizable number of excellent articles on the important facets of teaching reading in the secondary schools.

To be included in this book, an article had to fall into one or more of the following categories:

1. A research study.
2. A review of research.
3. A critical survey.
4. A unique contribution to the literature.
5. An explanation of a teaching method or a process.
6. A penetrating analysis of a problem area.
7. A report of a worthwhile teaching practice.

Each unit is preceded by an introduction, and each selection is preceded by an introduction and several questions to guide one's reading. The person who reads to answer these questions should gain an understanding of the field not ordinarily obtained through a book of readings.

L. E. H.

# CONTENTS

ix

# THE ROLES OF READING
# IN MODERN LIFE

## INTRODUCTION

*Today we are literally engulfed by reading material. Yet record keeping is a comparatively recent development in the history of man that dates back to 4,000–6,000 B.C. Alphabetic writing in Western Civilization dates to 1400 B.C. and corresponds to the time when the first books in the Judeo-Christian heritage were written. The development of the printing press about three thousand years later made reading material available in quantity and thus served as a catalytic agent for stimulating the minds of men. Reading and writing have played an important role in the development of Western Civilization. Four Great Ages—the Age of Pericles, the Rise of Christianity, the Renaissance, and the Industrial Revolution—stand out as having drawn on and contributed to the resources communicated through reading and writing.*

*In our day men read to be informed, entertained, enlightened, stimulated, and comforted. But to attain these goals satisfactorily in this fifth great age—the Space Age—it is necessary to process much information through reading, and to process it with a reasonable degree of speed and a high degree of accuracy. If it is important to be a skillful, discriminating, active reader, then the schools must face the challenge of developing this kind of reader; for it is the schools that are charged with the responsibility of teaching the various communication skills, the tools of learning—and earning.*

*The articles in this unit illustrate the fact that reading has a role in promoting the academic and personal development of individuals; that there is a great need for the schools to help young people improve their reading skills in order to become more mature readers; and that there are specific ways, formal and informal, of helping these students to accomplish these goals.*

1

# THE USES OF READING AND THE NEED FOR READING INSTRUCTION *

Lawrence E. Hafner

*If we were to dichotomize the attitudes of people toward reading, we could say there is one group of people that always seems to be running away from books. Educators and laymen alike are concerned about whether or not more students can be taught to develop greater interest in reading as well as increased competence in reading.*

*The author of this article explores vital problems in order to establish firmly the value of reading and the need for reading instruction in our schools.*

*1. What is involved in developing true reading maturity?*

*2. How is the improvement of reading proficiency related to improvement of the individual?*

*3. What problems arise in the attempt to use literature therapeutically?*

*4. How does Spranger's theory of values help you gain perspective regarding the motivational forces in the lives of individuals?*

*5. How serious is the need for improved reading instruction?*

## USES OF READING

Ink flows. Typewriters click. Linotypes clack. Computers whirr. The presses roll . . . and roll . . . and roll . . . on and on. Homes, schools, libraries, and shops are flooded with reading matter. And people read these materials for different purposes and to satisfy different drives. On the one hand, we see a Thomas Wolfe who voraciously consumes book after book in the library stacks because of an insatiable desire for knowledge. On the other hand, we see an "Uncle Charlie" who would not be seen in a library under any circumstances and whose attitude toward books ranges from utter disdain to mild contempt.

Somewhere in-between the Thomas Wolfes and the Uncle Charlies we find countless individuals who are doing quite a bit of reading for rather admirable purposes. As we look a little closer at what these individuals are reading, we notice they are reading for some rather basic purposes. They are reading in an attempt to solve problems, to gain scholastic success, to become better informed, to earn a living, and to entertain themselves. Let us investigate these basic purposes more closely.

### Solving Problems in the World

It is an obvious fact that there are many problems in the world. Not only does printed material bring us news of today's problems, but it also recounts

---

* Written especially for this volume.

the problems of the ages and the ideas which have been offered as solutions to these problems. At least a partial solution to these problems may be obtained by gleaning clues from history, from the way similar problems have been handled in other times.

If problems can be solved through reading, it should be possible to improve problem-solving through improving reading proficiency. It is not to be thought that this reading proficiency is a mere intellectual process devoid of emotional factors. Developing true reading maturity involves the development of appropriate values, attitudes, and feelings, for these factors guide and motivate the application of ideas gained through the interpretation of reading material, as well as the interpretation itself. Before getting into the more philosophical aspects of solving problems through reading, let us discuss some more of the common uses of reading.

### Reading and Scholastic Success

Our elementary schools, high schools, and colleges are reading schools. Fay [1] shows that achievement in general reading comprehension, and in several important specific reading skills, is highly related to achievement in social studies and science in grade six. The correlations between reading achievement and marks in college vary from low, *.10*, to high, *.60*. A great problem and challenge lie in the fact that roughly thirty-five to fifty per cent of high-school students are not reading as well as their general ability indicates they should. Another challenge is found in the fact that reading skills are involved in eighty to ninety per cent of college work, yet approximately twenty-five per cent of college freshmen lack the reading skills to do their work successfully.[2] Fortunately many of these individuals can be salvaged through special instruction in the reading study skills.[3, 4]

### Building a Background of Experience

Not all one's ideas and experiences are gained directly; many are gained indirectly. These indirect experiences gained through avenues such as reading, movies, and television are called vicarious experiences. We retain an organized trace or residue of experiences in the form of concepts, facts, and generalizations, and words are "counters" of those experiences. Without going into qualifying detail, one can say that one's vocabulary reflects his experiences and how he is able to profit from these experiences. The information that one

[1] Leo C. Fay, "The Relationship Between Specific Reading Skills and Selected Areas of Sixth-Grade Achievement," *Journal of Educational Psychology*, XLIII (March 1950), p. 544.

[2] Ruth Strang, Constance M. McCullough, and Arthur E. Traxler, *The Improvement of Reading* (New York: McGraw-Hill Book Company, Inc., 1961), p. 27.

[3] Mildred B. Smith and Carl I. Brache, "When School and Home Focus on Achievement," *Educational Leadership*, XX (February 1963), pp. 314–318.

[4] Albert J. Kingston and Clay E. George, "The Effectiveness of Reading Training at the College Level," *Journal of Educational Research*, LXVIII (February 1955), pp. 467–471.

gains from reading a given piece of material can be used to enrich one's understanding and enjoyment of similar topics in other reading materials.

### Reading and Earning a Living

Any occupation requiring a college education requires one to read to prepare for the occupation. As working members of these professions, individuals depend on reading in the day-to-day exercise of their duties and in keeping up with developments in their fields: a city manager reads contracts, bulletins, proposals, books, and journals; a person in the medical profession reads case histories, charts, texts, scientific journals, and monographs; an agricultural specialist reads bulletins, building specifications, books, graphs, charts, experimental research reports, and project reports.

Studies by Dael Wolfle [5] show the variations in average mental ability among graduate and professional students specializing in different fields. Average AGCT scores range from a low of 114 for one graduate group to 133 for the highest group, psychology graduate students. Because of the high correlation between group intelligence tests and group reading tests, one can infer differences in reading achievement among various occupations from the above data. However, it is possible to cite an actual example of differences in reading achievement that exist among professions.

The Ohio State Psychological Examination is a test heavily loaded with the reading factor. Three sources provide us with information to show us differences in average OSPE scores among several professional groups and scores of comparison groups of college freshmen and college graduates.

|  | AVERAGE OSPE SCORE |
|---|---|
| College freshmen [6] | 75 |
| Male photographers (metro. newspaper) [8] | 84.2 |
| Master's degree candidates in education [7] | 98 |
| College graduates [6] | 108 |
| Small city newspapermen [6] | 115 |
| Copyreaders (metropolitan) [8] | 115.4 |
| Editors, editorial writers, and reporters [8] | 124.2 |
| Master's degree candidates in psychology [7] | 125 |
| Doctoral degree candidates in psychology [7] | 133 |

### Sheer Joy of Reading

Another important use of reading is reading for sheer pleasure. The young child reads for pleasure stories such as *Mike Mulligan, Are You My Mother?*,

[5] Dael L. Wolfle, *America's Resources of Specialized Talent* (New York: Harper and Brothers, 1954), p. 200.

[6] Robert L. Jones and Charles E. Swanson, "Small-City Daily Newspapermen: Their Abilities and Interests," *Journalism Quarterly*, XXXI (Winter 1954), p. 42.

[7] Unpublished data from a state university.

[8] Harold C. Stone, "An Objective Personnel Study of Metropolitan Newspapermen," *Journalism Quarterly*, XXX (Fall 1953), p. 451.

*Charlotte's Web, Homer Price* or any one of countless stories which can be obtained from the library, the bookstore, or the supermarket.

As people get older it becomes difficult to dichotomize their reading into job-related reading versus reading for pleasure. Perhaps such dichotomies arise in some quarters when a scientific monograph or statistical report is contrasted with a "who-done-it?" Other individuals, fortunately, can use information gained in some of the "sheer joy" reading in their professional work: the historian, the psychologist, the reading specialist, the theologian, the professional writer. Perhaps their "nonsheer joy" material would be the income tax forms and routine administrative report forms.

A given piece of reading material, then, cannot be neatly categorized. One person will perceive, value, and use the material in one way, and another person in another way.

Among people there is evidently a continuum of pleasure for reading. At one end of the continuum is the individual who detests all reading material and reads nothing with joy. At the other end is the person who likes to read everything, and who can find something satisfying and enjoyable in any kind of reading material. The latter person more likely will approximate the Renaissance ideal of the "universal man" or pansophist. He also is the person who will score in the 170's and 180's on Terman's *Concept Mastery Test*, whereas the person who reads little will be fortunate if he does not obtain a negative score.

### Solving Problems Through Reading

Already in Old Testament times a sage remarked, "Of the making of books there is no end." Many of the books that have appeared in the last thirty-two centuries have offered advice to people or solutions to their problems. The person who made the remark about the making of books also provided us with several books full of advice—Proverbs, Ecclesiastes, and the Song of Solomon. Many sages since Solomon's time have taken up the stylus, the quill or the ball-point pen to set down their words of wisdom and their solutions to problems. Yet these various solutions probably do not have equal validity.

If man is to survive and flourish, he must use the collected wisdom of the past to solve problems, to come to grips with moral and philosophic issues. He must go beyond everyday experience. He must read, study, discuss, and reflect on many writings—newspapers, quality magazines, religious writings, biographies, dramas, books, and novels.

Implicit in the foregoing discussion is the idea that for almost every problem that faces an individual—a school-age child or an adult—there is a solution or partial solution in some piece of literature. Literature, then, has a role in personal development. By literature we do not mean a number of stories, poems, and essays written by a few quaint people, but the entire range of writings of able men and women of various times. When one reads how another person solved a problem similar to his own, he has the advantage of being detached from the actual event while still identifying with the problem and being able to enter into the situation vicariously. In this way he can then analyze and solve his own problem. Literature is therefore a potential force for enlightening the individual, for enriching his life, and for aiding him in building confidence. This writer does not share the euphoric dreams of the social engineers who feel confident they can manipulate and improve large segments of the world's population. Certain individuals can be affected. We must show the individual the better way through precept and example and hope that free, responsible individuals will continue the tradition.

The British bibliophile, Sir William Haley [9] provides us with an extraordinary example of one individual's use of reading. He used reading as an aid in stress and believed that a well-chosen book can help restore one's balance and perspective. He sometimes read a book early in the morning so he could see a little clearer during the day what things really mattered. Sir William felt that to succeed at this role a book must: (1) look at life from a *higher vantage point*; (2) deal with *enduring issues*, and (3) have a *moral standpoint*.

### Developing a Philosophy of Life

Everyone lives by some set of values—those things we consider important that guide our actions and serve as motivators of behavior.

E. Spranger, in his book *Lebensformer*,[10] discusses six basic values. In each person one of these values operates as a dominant motive. The six types of persons corresponding to these value systems are (1) the theoretical; (2) the esthetic; (3) the economic; (4) the political; (5) the social; (6) the religious.

Commins and Fagin [11] discuss these types of persons and show the roles each type takes in educational circles. The *theoretical* person's highest value is truth or knowledge. He believes that ignorance is the greatest evil of society, and the chief remedy is "education which stresses information, facts, intellectual understanding of principles." "In education, the theoretical person is more often found in college teaching, particularly in the sciences." To the *esthetic* person beauty, harmony, and elegance of form and color are the most significant values. He evaluates people by their taste and degree of refinement and has much interest in artistic, literary, and musical experiences.

The *economic* person values and is motivated by efficiency and economic well-being. He often appears among members of school boards and sometimes in the ranks of teachers. For him education must pay off in economic betterment. As a teacher, he emphasizes the utilitarian value of school subjects and methods of teaching.

The *political* person is fond of discipline, order, and control. In educational circles these people range from the excellent administrator to the common martinet.

[9] Sir William Haley, A *Smallholding on Parnassus* (London: Cambridge University Press, 1954), p. 17.

[10] E. Spranger, *Lebensformer* (Halle: Niemeyer, 1927).

[11] W. D. Commins and Barry Fagin, *Principles of Educational Psychology*, 2nd ed. (New York: The Ronald Press Co., 1954), pp. 578–580.

The *social* person stresses kindness and warmth in human relations. He evaluates people according to the degree of kindness they exhibit to others. Generally teachers are of this type; particularly the elementary teacher who strives to meet the needs of children, even at the cost of personal sacrifice.

The *religious* type person, according to Commins' interpretation of Spranger, seeks to integrate "all values into a meaningful scheme or philosophy" and "all experience into a comprehensive framework." As a teacher, he would "stress character education through inculcation of moral and religious values."

Spranger assumed that no person is motivated exclusively by one kind of value. These values are considered to be equal in worth unless the religious or philosophical value that seeks integration of the values might be considered the best.

A little exercise that causes a person to reflect on his values is to ask him if he would like to sit down for fifteen minutes and commit to paper the values by which he guides his life and then have them published in the local newspaper. Do you know your values? Can you verbalize them? How did you come by them? Some serious questions a person may ask himself in order to help him reflect on his value system are: Who am I? Where did I come from? What is my purpose on this planet? What is my eventual destiny?

As a teacher or parent, one expects to guide or at least influence the destiny of others. Should one expect a person to guide others until he has answered such questions as these?

One's philosophy of life develops gradually over a period of years and many factors, including those over which the individual has little control, are involved in its development: temperament, intelligence, family values, real and vicarious experiences, religion, reward systems, etc. No matter how excellent one's philosophy or value system is, upgrading is in order and reading has a role to play in this improvement process.

Spache [12] has emphasized that "bibliotherapy, or the modification of habits and attitudes through reading, does not occur as a spontaneous result of reading. Also, if one is to implement by action the two mechanisms of identification and insight which are involved in bibliotherapy, careful nurture and guidance are necessary.

There are many personality needs which need to be met, and emotional maladjustments for which therapy is in order. Smith and Dechant [13] list books of potential therapeutic value under five broad categories of problem areas. Illustrative of the specific titles of books considered to have therapeutic value for children with emotional conflicts are Beirn's *Time for Gym* (jealousy and resentment); Cavanna's *Going on Sixteen* (shyness and loneliness); and Schneider's *While Susie Sleeps* (fear).

[12] George D. Spache, *Toward Better Reading* (Champaign, Illinois: Garrard Publishing Company, 1963), p. 160.
[13] Henry P. Smith and Emerald V. Dechant, *Psychology in Teaching Reading* (Englewood Cliffs, N. J.: Prentice-Hall, Inc., 1961), pp. 316–320.

Teachers in parochial elementary schools may wish to explore books and stories with a spiritual message and tone such as the following: Sellew's *Adventures with Abraham's Children*; K. Phillips' *Gift from a Stranger*; H. Van Laar's *Joel and the Silver Trumpet*, and A. P. Wright's *The Little Shepherd*.

High-school students have an opportunity to upgrade their attitudes by steeping themselves in the writings and/or biographies of great people such as Paul, Charlemagne, St. Francis of Assisi, Luther, Whittier, Lincoln, Anne Lindbergh, Eleanor Roosevelt, Charles Kettering, Helen Keller, and Robert Frost.

College students should profit from the works of such stimulating thinkers as Plato, Aquinas, Roger Bacon, Montaigne, Calvin, Loyola, Berkeley, Pascal, Kant, de Tocqueville, Kierkegaard, Gladstone, Dostoyevski, and modern thinkers such as Nicholas Berdyaev, Joseph Wood Krutch, Russell Kirk, Roscoe Pound, Albert Schweitzer, J. Nehru, Walter Lippmann, Jacques Maritain, Martin Niemoeller, Thomas Molnar, and John F. Kennedy.

In Albert Schweitzer we have the personification of Spranger's *religious* type and his *social* type. Schweitzer exemplified the religious type as he sought to integrate "all values into a meaningful scheme," as illustrated by his academic interests and by his volume, *The Philosophy of Civilization*. He was the epitome of the social type who stresses kindness and warmth in human relations as he devoted many years of his long life to service and compassion for his fellow men.

Schweitzer evolved this philosophy of commitment during long years of reflection on his own experiences and on ideas that he had read, and then he put them into practice as a missionary-doctor in Africa. In a special article[14] written shortly before his death, he shows how such ideas as his "reverence for life" evolved and how the latter idea can, through education, take root in people's lives:

During a short stay in Europe in 1951, I was visited by the dean of a big school in Hanover. She came to tell me that reverence for life was being taught in her school. The children, she said, showed a great understanding of it and tried to apply it in their own attitudes and behavior. Under the influence of this teaching, she said, a great spiritual change had taken place in their lives.

I kept in touch with the head of that school. During a later trip to Europe, I visited the school and took the opportunity to talk with the children. They had shed all childishness. Their awareness of the meaning of my philosophy of kindness toward all creatures had made them at once serious and gay. Today, many schools throughout the world are teaching reverence for life.

### Maintaining a Proper Balance of Tension and Confidence

Foster McMurray[15] has shown that although the ideally uneducated, simple man and the ideally intelligent man could face the world with com-

[14] Reproduced from *The World Book Year Book* with permission. Copyright © 1964 by Field Enterprises Educational Corporation. All rights reserved.
[15] Lecture notes, Dr. Foster McMurray, University of Illinois, Spring 1958.

plete confidence, actual man must live in a mixture of confidence and tension. He must learn and continue to learn. The primary purpose for learning intellectual, nonutilitarian living is to maintain life in a proper balance of tension and confidence.

Although, generally, the more a person learns, the more we might expect him to be confident, it works out, in fact, that the complex mentality will see more reasons for being tense in a given world situation or crisis. The function of intellectual instruction, then, is to keep a high and expanding level of confidence and tension. The school can help modify confidence through the intellectual instruments it helps children acquire in school. The types of confidence are:

1. Confidence of *location*.
2. Confidence of *command*.
3. Confidence of *opportunity*.

McMurray shows how these important types of confidence can be acquired by the intellectual instruments one acquires through survey knowledge and literary knowledge.

To have confidence of *location*, confidence that one is abreast of the world, one needs a literary understanding of the things that are transforming the world. For instance, teacher and student will make use of excellent survey accounts in materials such as *Reader's Digest, Science Digest*, and *U.S. News and World Report*.

Man needs confidence of *command*—what he can't do for himself he gets someone else to do for him, if it is important. We can teach people how to do this through literary knowledge.

A man who has confidence of *opportunity* is more likely to feel that he is doing the type of work best suited to his inclinations and ability, if he has had real opportunity to develop his capabilities, explore his capabilities, and learn what interests him. Survey knowledge and literary knowledge will provide students with the needed opportunity to sample—a sampling based on correct information, and reading is the key to this survey knowledge and literary knowledge.

*Unique Values of Reading*

Modern communication media such as radio and television are highly regarded in education circles. However, in comparison with such forms of communication media reading has the following unique values or uses:

1. Reading material is readily accessible.
2. Reader can react as an individual.
3. Reading allows time for reflection.
4. Information is easily rechecked.
5. Memories can be renewed.
6. One can select segments of material he wants.
7. Sources can be compared readily.

8. One can readily skim a wide range of material.
9. One can check on the credentials of the author.
10. Reading provides excellent contexts for concept development and vocabulary study.
11. Material is readily accessible.

## NEED FOR READING INSTRUCTION

One can hardly dispute the fact that reading has many vital uses. Nor can anyone who has enjoyed some success as a reader forget the stimulation and the pleasure that reading can give. But how does one learn to practice this magic? How does one learn to read?

Few individuals teach themselves to read—most are taught to read by someone else. But even among people of similar ability we find varying degrees of reading proficiency. Large numbers of students in our schools are reading as well as capacity measures indicate they should. But many students do not read up to capacity, and are not able to solve their problems through reading. Neither do they obtain much pleasure from reading. For these students excellent reading instruction is in order. In fact it is desperately necessary.

But let us switch from these hortatory remarks to some indisputable evidence of the need for reading instruction.

### Need for Readiness Instruction

Robinson [16] has discussed the need to instruct children at the beginning reading level rather than to just wait for readiness to develop:

It is clear, then, that we cannot wait for years of living to bring readiness for beginning reading. Instead, good teachers hasten children's progress in all aspects of readiness through well-planned programs to meet the specific needs of large and small groups and of individuals within the group.

### The Kentucky Reading Study

Ramsey [17] studied the reading achievement of Kentucky children at the fourth-grade and eighth-grade levels. Evidence indicated that although the fourth-grade children were reading satisfactorily compared to national norms, there was a substantial lag among the eighth-graders studied.

He points out that "for the immediate future there is a need for concentrated effort to give reading instruction in the junior and senior high schools of the state."

[16] Helen M. Robinson, "Development of Reading Skills," *Elementary School Journal*, LVIII (February 1958), pp. 269–274.

[17] Wallace Ramsey, "The Kentucky Reading Study," *The Reading Teacher*, XVI (December 1962), pp. 178–181.

### New York City Survey

A survey in the city of New York to determine reading achievement of freshmen and sophomore high school students compared with their mental ability revealed that 15.6 per cent of the students were reading at least one year above expectancy, 42.1 per cent were achieving commensurate with their ability, while 42.3 per cent were reading below expectancy.[18]

We are alarmed when we read how so many young people are failing to use their talents fully. It is apparent that the need for reading instruction in situations such as this is marked.

In this article, only representative studies have been selected to show the gap that exists between potential to achieve and actual reading achievement. These studies alone would be enough to show the need for reading instruction. However, aspects of the problem will be explored to adduce further proof of the need for the comprehensive instruction needed to develop the good reader-citizen and mature reader.

### Characteristics of Poor Readers

From elementary school through college two characteristic reading problems of poor readers are their inability to succeed in the higher level interpretation skills, and their inability to remember what they read.

These reading weaknesses often result in or are accompanied by poor attitudes toward reading, poor grades in school, vocational problems, compensating defense mechanisms, dropping out of school, feelings of failure, and a self-concept that eventually relegates reading and intellectual endeavor dependent upon reading to a low place in the hierarchy of values of such poor readers.

### My Brother's Keeper

Many of the pupils in our schools are caught up in a web of reading failure. This failure and its concomitant problems of school failure and self-concept depreciation often can be alleviated to the extent that reading problems are cleared up. The well-trained, conscientious teacher can help clear up those problems—or perhaps *George* will do it; after all, am *I* my brother's keeper?

"George will not do it" and "you *are* your brother's keeper!" The idea of taking a child when he is ready and teaching him the necessary skills and attitudes to succeed in academic life is so axiomatic as a generalization that we tend to verbalize the phrase and to forget about its implementation in the real-life, concrete, school situation with John Doe, Jr.

Pupils will not unlock the many doors of opportunity if they do not read well. The teacher represents the last opportunity for many of these pupils to learn to read well. What an opportunity and responsibility! The teacher must

[18] Bernard E. Donovan, *Survey of Abilities of Pupils Entering the Academic High Schools in September 1955* (New York Board of Education, 1955), p. 3.

give his pupils *direct instruction* in reading if they are going to master the various skills and attitudes which they need to (1) earn a living; (2) be thoughtful, critical citizens; and (3) lead a full, interesting, and useful life!

## Improving Citizenship

As we explore the need for reading instruction to help improve citizenship, we learn that reading is a complex process, that there are many mysterious facets to this process, and that there are probably fewer mature readers extant than we would like.

It has been said that the skillful, mature reader reads the lines (comprehends), reads between the lines (interprets), and reads beyond the lines (reacts to and applies ideas).

There is a positive relationship between intelligence and reading ability, and highly intelligent individuals are often quite sensitive to ethical and moral problems. However, we ask these questions: Does measured intelligence govern citizenship? Are we fighting a losing battle in our attempt to improve the individual through making him a better reader?

Many valuable citizenship practices don't require high intelligence. We get some insight into the complexity and mystery of reading if we thoughtfully reflect on this enigma: High intelligence is no guarantee that a person will fully read (react to and apply ideas) such apparently simple signs as STOP and QUIET; and stopping at stop signs and obeying quiet signs are two important social practices. If the present reader should think that reading is a simple process, he might explain why some people do not fully read (react to and apply, i.e., obey) simply-worded traffic signs such as: CITY SPEED LIMITS 35 mph!

There are various ways of being a good citizen and a mature reader. Surely the person of 130 I.Q. who elaborates on the qualification of a candidate for political office serves a useful function as a citizen. So does the person, say of "lesser" intellect, who strives to obey the traffic laws at all times instead of trying to impress someone with the quite-questionable reflected glory of his engine-powered vehicle as he drag-races down the street. His recognition should not be at the expense of the life of a fellow human being. Some people who seek glory through acceleration, reckless driving, and uncontrolled horsepower "read" the newspaper accounts but do not *fully* read them. Other people do not even bother to read the newspaper. They live outside the reading world.

It is tragic, but some people in the elementary schools and the high schools *cannot read*. Just think! The teacher who opens up the world of print to these people, and who teaches for reading maturity among those who can already attain literal comprehension, will give such individuals another chance to read, to learn, and to change their attitudes. Beneficial changes in attitudes resulting from increased maturity in reading are worth the effort required on the part of the teacher. And such teaching stems from the highest type of dedication and hard work—work that requires ingenuity and energy.

Through effective teaching of reading from elementary school through the college years we teachers can help individuals gain insights, improve attitudes, and function more adequately—in short, be mature readers. Surely such goals are worthy and attainable. As we contemplate the foregoing thoughts let these words of Horace Mann ring in our ears: "Be ashamed to die until you have won some victory for humanity."

# THE DEVELOPMENT OF READING MATURITY IN HIGH SCHOOL— IMPLICATIONS OF THE GRAY-ROGERS STUDY *

A. Sterl Artley

*Suppositions are often made about the achievements of high school students. However, it is important to know whether our schools are actually producing mature readers. In this article several astounding findings regarding the reading maturity of high school students are revealed, and the implications of the study are used as guidelines for teacher education.*

*1. State the crux of the argument found in the introductory paragraphs.*

*2. Briefly state the purpose of the Gray-Rogers study.*

*3. In what ways do you find the reading competence of the elementary and high-school-graduate groups studied by Gray and Rogers to be different from what one might expect?*

*4. What does a high level of reading competence allow a person to do?*

*5. How do you account for the findings of the study?*

*6. How can the teachers in the secondary schools cope with the problems raised in this article?*

THERE is evidence of an increased interest in reading instruction on the secondary school level. Professional magazines are devoting more columns to articles dealing with junior and senior high school reading programs. More program space is being allocated to discussions in this area in educational meetings. It is not uncommon to find a junior or senior high school actually carrying out a pilot program, while still other schools are making plans to inaugurate some type of reading program within a short period of time.

The idea of a reading program in the secondary school is by no means new. As early as 1925 the National Society for the Study of Education boldly pro-

---

* REPRINTED FROM *Educational Administration and Supervision*, XLIII (October 1957), pp. 321–328, by permission of the Abrahams Magazine Service, Inc., New York.

posed in its *Twenty-Fourth Yearbook* that reading guidance should be provided on the junior and senior high school levels. In 1937, the same organization issued its second report in the *Thirty-Sixth Yearbook*. In this report the committee proposed five important stages of reading development, the last one providing for the refinement of reading interests, habits, and tastes. This. stage, the committee contended, occurred on the junior-senior high school and junior-college levels.

By 1948, the importance of reading on the secondary levels was so widely recognized that the National Society for the Study of Education through a committee headed by Dr. William S. Gray brought out a report dealing exclusively with reading on the advanced educational levels. This report, *Reading in High School and College*, set the general tone and level of thinking that only recently has come to be implemented in pilot programs. This noteworthy report delineated the role of reading among youth and detailed the nature and scope of a sound secondary school reading program.

A significant feature of the above report was the contention that the primary attack on reading on the secondary level should be through a program designed to promote maximum reading growth among *all* students in keeping with their individual capacities and needs. This point of view was in sharp contrast to that held by many educators who conceived of a high school reading program as being primarily remedial in nature. These educators argued, as do even a minority today, that the elementary program was inadequate in developing the reading abilities and skills needed on the secondary school level, and, as a result, a short-term, stop-gap program was needed to overcome a reading handicap found among a few students. The committee preparing the *Forty-Seventh Yearbook*, however, stressed the fact that reading was a complex of abilities and understandings that could not be carried to maturity in the first five or six grades. This, the committee insisted, was not due to the inability of elementary school people to carry out their responsibility, but to the demand for a level of reading maturity that could not be achieved in the elementary grades regardless of how effectively the children were taught.

## Study of Reading Maturity

Reading maturity, though recognized as a goal of the secondary program, has been poorly defined. Though growth toward this elusive goal was assumed, there was little understanding of the specific abilities and understandings of which the goal was composed. Within the last year, however, Dr. William S. Gray and Miss Bernice Rogers have published their findings of a comprehensive study of reading maturity (1). Though the study is oriented in the direction of adult reading, with its findings and conclusions drawn from that segment of the population, its implications for secondary schools and colleges are potent, for it is on these levels that students have their last opportunity for guidance in reading.

In brief review, the Gray-Rogers study set out first to determine the nature of reading maturity and to build a scale that might measure its constituents. Having achieved this goal the authors then applied the scale to a number of adults of various social and educational levels. On the basis of the findings derived from this analysis, Gray and Rogers delineated the instructional problems that teachers face if they are to help reading make its maximum contribution to the reader's personal and social growth.

Gray and Rogers were able to identify five dimensions of which reading maturity is comprised. These five areas were interest in reading, purposes for reading, recognition and consideration of meaning (comprehension), reaction to and use of ideas apprehended, and the kinds of material read. Each of these dimensions was then analyzed into criteria by which maturity in that area might be appraised. In turn, each of the criteria was scaled to a five-point scale and verbal descriptions set down objectifying the behaviors relating to that particular criterion.

Eventually the maturity scale was applied to fifty-nine adults representing various educational and social levels as well as several occupational and vocational groups. The findings from this study were analyzed in detail to determine the degree of maturity present in these groups and to ascertain the influence on reading behavior of such factors as education and social participation. The remainder of this paper will deal with three implications of this study which the writer feels have cogent bearings on the question of reading instruction on the secondary school level.

## Reading Maturity of Elementary and High School Graduates

In the first place, the Gray-Rogers study showed in a dramatic manner that those adults in the study who had completed high school were superior in reading only to a limited extent to those who had terminated their education experience at the end of grade school. One must assume either that the secondary schools attended by these adults had no program to promote continued growth in reading, or that the program in use was ineffective in promoting growth on a level perceptibly higher than that attained at the end of the elementary grades.

Regardless of which of these two reasons apply, the implications with respect to the secondary school program are clear. No longer may one assume that the responsibility for promoting reading growth belongs solely in the elementary grades. In the words of Gray and Rogers, "It (the absence of a differential in maturity between high school and elementary school graduates) challenges the validity of the traditional assumption that high schools have little or no responsibility for developing increased competence in reading. Fortunately many high schools have recently recognized that growth in reading is a continuous process and are assuming responsibility for the organization of sound reading programs. This movement should be greatly extended . . . If the high school's responsibilities are properly conceived, it

might make a tremendous contribution to the reading interest and competence of oncoming generations" (2).

The failure to give adequate attention to reading growth on the secondary
level is verified in a study recently completed by Dr. Margaret Early into
the nature of the English programs in a group of New England high
schools (3). In the ninety-seven classrooms studied, Early found practically
no evidence of the systematic teaching of reading. Though some of the
student responses indicated that they were aware of some work being given
in vocabulary development, reading for the main idea, and developing reference skills, programs providing this help were embryonic, at the best. In
only three of the ninety-seven classrooms was the reading instruction based
on pre-testing and small group methods.

It certainly would be unfair to infer that the situations found in the Gray-
Rogers and Early studies are typical of those found in all schools in the
country. The writer is aware of many situations where real efforts are being
made to institute sound secondary programs in reading, where the same type
of continuity and systematic concern for reading growth is found as on the
elementary level. In all too many places, however, action is still on the verbal
level. This can be condoned only if words give way to practice.

## Levels of Reading Competence

In the second place, the Gray-Rogers study shows the general low level of
reading competence found among the adults studied. In applying their scale
of reading maturity to a group of thirty-eight adults in a typical mid-western
city the authors found that the low level of ability to recognize and interpret
meaning and to react to and use the ideas gained from reading was one of the
limiting factors in reading maturity among the high school-graduate group. In
other words, had the adults in the study possessed a high level of reading
enthusiasm and a variety of reading purposes normally leading to extensive
reading, they still would have lacked the competencies necessary for effective
and mature reading. The implication of this finding to the high school program is clear, since it is on this level that the basic competencies should be
raised to as high a level of proficiency as the reader's potential makes possible.

The term, reading competence, needs careful definition if it is a goal toward
which the high school program is to be directed. By many, reading competence is thought of as the utilization of skills and abilities that enable the
reader to pronounce words in a facile manner and to derive accurately the
literal meaning of the page or chapter so that its contents may be handed
back to the teacher in a "recitation." Though one must not overlook the fact
that accurate word perception and comprehension are important reading
competencies, their use alone can result in a mechanical process engaged in
by the reader in a relative passive state.

According to Gray and Rogers, a high level of competence in reading

". . . enables (the reader) to proceed with reasonable ease and understanding in grasping and interpreting meanings, in reacting rationally to the ideas apprehended, and in applying his ideas with sound judgment and discrimination" (4). In other words, the authors are describing reading competence as a four-dimensional process involving word perception, comprehension of meaning, reaction to the ideas expressed and application of these ideas to behavior. It is in these four areas that direction and training must be given if reading is to be more than a passive process of assimilation.

A detailed outline of the basic competencies may be found in the Forty-Seventh Yearbook, Part II, of the National Society for the Study of Education (5). The Commission on the Curriculum in *The English Language Arts in the Secondary School* also describes the major strands in the developmental program in reading (6), though it will be observed that particular stress is given to the assimilative proficiencies rather than to those involving reaction and integration.

## Reading Interests and Motives

In the third place, the Gray-Rogers study indicates that reading competence, as important as it is, does not in and of itself make for complete reading maturity. The mature reader sees reading as a source of pleasure, understanding, and insight. This idea is expressed well by Gray and Rogers as follows: ". . . the mere possession of skills involved in efficient reading does not insure that they will be used in adult life. Some compelling motive for their use must arise out of the problems and projects which are recognized by the individual as genuinely important" (7).

In other words the secondary school has as much a responsibility to promote the kinds of interests and motives that lead to wide personal interests as it has to develop the ability to understand and interpret what is read. To emphasize the latter at the expense of the former is to run the risk of developing skillful readers whose interests take them no further than the pulps and comics.

Properly handled, literally all areas of the curriculum may contribute to the development of reading interests and motives. Particularly is this true in an area such as literature where the student has the opportunity to experience the inspiration and exhilaration that comes from meeting and dealing with great ideas. Social studies, too, provides the context within which the student may develop his social role and become concerned with and learn to be responsible for a better life and society.

Though both literature and social studies furnish the context for developing reading interests and motives, their potential has not always been realized. Too often the study of literature has been concerned primarily with a study of types and forms, the reading of assigned pages to be discussed in an unanimated manner, the preparation of formal book reports, and the memorization of prescribed lines. Such uninspired teaching can seldom make a contribution to the developing personal and social needs of youth, to say nothing of fostering strong and abiding interests in quality material. For an excellent discussion of the values inherent in literature as a medium for developing reading maturity and the methods of organizing the program to realize these values, the reader is referred to the chapter, "Meeting Youth's Needs Through Literature," in *The English Language Arts in the Secondary School* (8).

Likewise, the teaching of social studies—history, geography, citizenship, social problems, or combinations of these—in the past has suffered from an overemphasis on learning *facts about* rather than the development of *attitudes toward*. It has failed to develop sufficiently the concept of the social role and the need for social participation, or ". . . the degree to which an individual sees himself as a responsible member of the larger community of which he is a part; the degree to which he feels himself personally involved in problems and events outside the orbit of his daily routine; the degree to which he enters into the solution of these problems through communication with others" (9). It is this close involvement in social problems that creates a demand for information as a basis for objective thinking. If social studies are taught from this frame of reference it becomes not only the context within which to encourage and develop community participation and leadership, but a high level of reading maturity as well" (10).

It is quite likely that each reader can recall situations in his own educational experience, perhaps high school, where under creative teaching he caught fire and found in reading a key that unlocked doors to exciting adventure, to realms of great ideas. Gray and Rogers report this to be true of many of the mature readers they interviewed. "In the case of most of the outstanding mature cases interviewed, there was some period in school or college where they acquired strong motives that lead to stimulating adventures in reading or when they experienced the pleasure and inspiration that acquaintance with great literature provided. In some cases this acquaintance developed gradually; in others it was a turning point—a sudden opening up of vast new horizons reaching out to worlds scarcely dreamed of before" (11).

## Conclusion

Reading on the secondary school level is not a fad or a new "educational epidemic." If we are to understand and deal intelligently with the multiplicity of problems that confront our society, we must make provision for reading growth that extends beyond the elementary level. A sound developmental reading program must give concern to the development of as high a level of competence as the reader is capable of attaining, so that he may comprehend and interpret adequately what he reads. At the same time, all areas of the curriculum should contribute to reading maturity by supplying the context within which strong and abiding interests in reading may be stimulated and developed.

REFERENCES

1. WILLIAM S. GRAY and BERNICE ROGERS, *Maturity in Reading—Its Nature and Appraisal*, Chicago, The University of Chicago Press, 1956.
2. *Ibid.*, p. 244.
3. OLIVE S. NILES and MARGARET J. EARLY, "Adjusting to Individual Differences in English," *Journal of Education*, 138:56–58, December, 1955.
4. GRAY and ROGERS, *op. cit.*, p. 237.
5. THE YEARBOOK COMMITTEE, "The Nature and Development of Reading," Chapter III, and William S. Gray, "Increasing the Basic Reading Competencies," Chapter VI, *Reading in High School and College*, Forty-Seventh Yearbook, Part II, of the National Society for Study of Education, Chicago, The University of Chicago Press, 1948.
6. THE COMMISSION ON THE ENGLISH CURRICULUM OF THE NATIONAL COUNCIL OF TEACHERS OF ENGLISH, *The English Language Arts in the Secondary School*, pp. 165–179. New York, Appleton-Century-Crofts, 1956.
7. GRAY and ROGERS, *op. cit.*, p. 172.
8. THE COMMISSION ON THE ENGLISH CURRICULUM OF THE NATIONAL COUNCIL OF TEACHERS OF ENGLISH, *op. cit.*, Ch. 5.
9. GRAY and ROGERS, *op. cit.*, p. 234.
10. ASSOCIATION FOR SUPERVISION and CURRICULUM DEVELOPMENT, *What Shall the High School Teach*, 1956 Yearbook of the Association, Washington, D. C., The Association, 1956.
11. GRAY and ROGERS, *op. cit.*, p. 233f.

# IMPACT OF READING ON THE PERSONAL DEVELOPMENT OF YOUNG PEOPLE IN SECONDARY SCHOOLS *

David H. Russell

*Some of the problems regarding reading maturity raised in the first two articles are further discussed by Russell as he explores research on the psychological factors involved in creative reading. He also gives the teacher some practical suggestions in taking his pupils beyond* the obvious facts in a literature selection to the underlying ideas with which pupils may struggle.

1. What are the implications for teaching of the fact discovered by both Sochor and Clark?

2. The author lists six research find-

* REPRINTED FROM *New Frontiers in Reading*, J. Allen Figurel, editor, International Reading Association Proceedings, V (New York: Scholastic Magazines, 1960), pp. 77–82, by permission of the International Reading Association.

*ings about interpretation of reading. One particular qualifying word (most) appears in the first and last finding. What injustices to your students might you perpetrate in your teaching if you did not take cognizance of the effect of this word?*

*3. Why did the author provide illustrations of the kinds of results obtainable from reading?*

*4. How can one prove to himself that his students are truly individuals?*

*5. Do the author's conclusions strike a responsive chord? In what ways?*

THE INTERNATIONAL Reading Association is concerned with the improvement of reading instruction. The teacher of English in secondary schools, in contrast, often works primarily with English and American literature organized historically or in thematic units. Somehow or other a bridge must be built between these two goals and activities. One means of fraternization or unification is our concern today with the impact of reading on young people. It is not enough for the elementary teacher to develop efficient word-attack skills or the English teacher to concentrate on the interpretation of figurative language. The teacher of reading is concerned with interpretation and the teacher of English develops specific reading skills. The area of common concern lies in the region of the interpretation of the impact of reading. It is at these levels that an alliance between the reading approach and the literature approach can be effected.

## FIVE LEVELS OF READING

This reciprocity can be achieved for the maximum development of young people if we review the fact that we read at five levels:

(1) At the first level we are largely concerned with the sounds of words and letters. In some school situations children are encouraged in word calling or "barking at words" without much meaning attached.

(2) At the second level we read casually for a general impression as the pupil sees what the book is about or the business man dozes over his evening newspaper. Such scanning may be useful as a preliminary device or it may leave no trace.

(3) At the third level we read for literal comprehension. We get the facts or we follow explicit directions. The children fill in the workbook blanks and the high school students answer the questions on the plot of the novel. This type of literal comprehension is most used in schools and most studied in research. Such reading may have many positive values for the child finding some facts on Africa or the suburbanite engaged in a weekend "do-it-yourself" project.

(4) At the fourth level we interpret what we read. We go beyond the literal comprehension of the fact or the main idea to read between the lines. We draw some conclusion of our own from the passage—we envisage or

predict or infer. Sometimes we reflect on the author's argument—we evaluate or analyze critically. Such reading we can roughly label creative and critical reading. We ordinarily don't do much of this in school but, as we shall see, perhaps we can do more. This and the following level are more complex and subtle.

(5) Occasionally we read at a fifth level—or depth. We go beyond thoughtful analysis, interpretation of literary devices or critical review. At the fifth level reading becomes a stirring personal experience. We recognize a new, important idea in the actions, characters or values described. We feel what Wilson called "the shock of recognition." The impact of the material is such that we see ourselves or others more clearly. In our reading we are changed, a little, as persons.

Most reading, in school and home, is done at the third, associative level and most of the writing and research in the field of reading have been done at the first and third levels. We know a lot about word perception, the teaching of phonics, and ways of developing comprehension of the printed page. Activities at these two levels make many contributions to the individual. There are worthwhile effects of this sort of reading for all people. The young child enjoys his new-found skill of working out new words and the world's work and its week end hobbies involve the use of much factual material to contribute to knowledge and skill. Reading has always been one of our most important resources for gaining knowledge. Granted a modicum of reading skill in the individual, books and libraries are storehouses of information for him. Thus, reading at the third level may have influences on personal development. It may give the twelve-year old increasing skill in making model airplanes or it may help the adolescent acquire some facts about the French Revolution or about adult life.

At the fourth level, we are not so sure of our ground as we are concerning word recognition or literal comprehension. A feature of recent research, however, has been considerable work on critical and creative reading abilities. For example, Sochor [1] has edited for the National Council on Research in English a research bulletin entitled *Critical Reading*. In a recent study at the University of California, for a second example, Clark [2] developed twenty-three lessons in reading to predict beyond the given facts and tested some ways of teaching these in the classroom. Both Sochor and Clark found that tests of critical reading and of reading to predict were relatively independent of the usual measures of vocabulary and comprehension. In going from literal comprehension to personal interpretation as in prediction, a reader puts more of himself into his reading. He thinks beyond the line of print. In critical and creative reading the perceptual process is the stimulus to many kinds

[1] E. Elona Sochor, editor, *Critical Reading: An Introduction*. Bulletin of the National Conference on Research in English. National Council of Teachers of English, 1959.

[2] Charles M. Clark, *Teaching Sixth-Grade Students to Make Predictions from Reading Materials*. Doctoral dissertation, University of California, Berkeley, 1958.

of thinking—to drawing analogies, to checking a writer's point of view, or to beginning an attack on a personal problem. As suggested below, more work needs doing in exploring this process of thoughtful reaction to an author's ideas.

It is on the fifth level, however, that our knowledge is slightest and our needs are greatest, and so it is with the effects of reading on individuals that this paper is chiefly concerned. Can literature affect the lives of children, adolescents or adults? In the words of Ciardi, can it make him "quietly passionate" about an idea or a cause? Can literature contribute to the self-concept? Can a story about courage fill a boy with courage or help him find himself? Or is this too much to ask, even of great literature? Reading may be useful at all five levels, but somehow, this fifth level of impact seems the most tantalizing and important of all.

## PREVIOUS ASSUMPTIONS

In the past, the teaching of English in the secondary school has been guided by two assumptions, depending in part on the maturity of the students and the personality of the teacher. The first assumption is the scholarly one—that adolescents should study literature as literature. This means not only that youth should know some of the great writers and literary works of our heritage but that they should be able to state why they are great. The approach has embraced, accordingly, an introduction to such fields as literary history and criticism. At its worst this teaching has been a rehashing of the instructor's college notes. At its best, it has opened new worlds to adolescents with superior verbal abilities and language interests. The second assumption, however, is our primary concern today. It is the belief that the study of good literature can influence character and behavior. It goes beyond the enjoyment of stories and poems, typical of good elementary school teaching, to the hypothesis that literature influences lives. We teach literature to add meaning to friendship, loyalty, courage, honesty, justice, faith, truth, and the other lovely words of our language.

In assuming that literature inculcates the virtues, the moral certitudes of our culture, we have followed the beliefs of the ancient Greeks and other philosophers down through the ages. On many occasions, too, good men have testified to the power of literature in their lives as when Luther Burbank declared that his whole life was changed by reading one book, *The Origin of the Species*. But such testimony, especially from literary people, does not constitute evidence in the scientific sense. What happened to Housman or de la Mare or Vachel Lindsay may not necessarily happen to the typical junior in George Washington High. We may hope that the study of literature will influence youth, but we cannot depend upon the personal affirmation of a few exceptional people. Instead, it is our duty to look at other evidence based on research, incomplete as it is. What, then, are some solid facts about the impact or effects of reading?

## SOME POSSIBLE EFFECTS OF READING

The effects of reading depend upon the kind of reading we do—upon which of the five levels we are operating. At the first two levels of word recognition and casual impression the impact on the reader's personality or life cannot be great. In elementary school or secondary school the child who is barely deciphering material much too difficult for a person of his reading ability has little opportunity to interpret at the fourth level or, at the fifth level, to find materials useful in solving his own problems. Piekarz,[3] for example, has shown that children unable to read a passage with relative ease have fewer reactions to it, with many more responses at the literal-meaning level than at the implied-meaning or evaluation levels. Accordingly, the effort we give to the making of skilful, fluent readers is worthwhile in both the elementary and the secondary school. Youth need word-attack skills and ability to follow directions, not because they are going to read only words or follow directions blindly, but so they can go into the meanings behind the words and, if necessary, to questions about the validity of the directions. Grasp of literal meaning ordinarily comes first. No student can interpret sensory appeal or symbolism if he cannot understand the literal meaning of the passage. This is one argument for occasional use of the "read-to" situation, whether in third grade or tenth grade, but it is also an argument for a sound body of literal comprehension skills as a basis for interpretation and for impact.

But teachers of elementary and of secondary classes can help young people derive both literal meanings and implied meanings. I believe the problem is not "either-or" and that teachers of fourth grade and teachers of secondary English must operate in both orbits. However, it is in the realm of imaginative literature that we usually get to the fourth and fifth levels of reading. It is here that good writing is intrepid in its approach to problems, ingenious in its solution of difficulties, in a way that the child or adolescent cannot achieve by himself. Getting the words right is not enough. It is at these fourth and fifth levels that reading can make its greatest contribution to individual development.

Fortunately, we have some research evidence beginning to be accumulated about reading at the fourth level of interpretation of printed materials. The effects, of course, will depend upon how the reader interprets.

a. Most children do not seem to respond to some of the commoner literary devices such as metaphor or personification before they are in their teens.
b. Children's interpretations are influenced by their attitudes and expectancies toward what they are reading, by their previous "set" in the reading situation.
c. When asked to respond to short stories, adolescents give interpretational reactions as a dominant type of response; other categories of response,

[3] Josephine A. Piekarz, "Getting Meaning from Reading," *Elementary School Journal*, 56:303–309, March 1956.

in order, are narrational, associational, self-involvement, literary judgments.

d. Responses to a piece of literature are largely an individual matter. Children and adolescents with different experiences, personalities, and needs see different things in the same character, story, or poem—and one interpretation may be just as "true" or "honest" as the other. Consequently, teachers of reading and literature should beware of looking for the one "correct" interpretation.

e. With adolescents, literary judgments and emotional involvements vary inversely. In other words, children and adolescents tend to suspend objectivity when emotionally involved. Conversely, if we emphasize objective judgment, we may cut down emotional response.

f. The most common emotional involvements of adolescents in fiction seem to be "happiness binding" (the desire for a happy ending) and insistence upon certainty in interpretation.

Perhaps these half-dozen samples of findings are enough to show that we are beginning to accumulate some research evidence about some of the psychological factors involved in interpretation, whether it is a good story in a third reader, a chapter or poem in a high school anthology, or an individual example of an author's work.

## THE IMPACT OF READING

Unfortunately, evidence about reading having an impact on lives is largely confined to anecdote and to case studies. Some of you remember a book, story or poem that greatly affected you. MacLeish has said that "A poem must not mean, but be." Proust has written, "Every reader reads himself. The writer's work is merely a kind of optical instrument that makes it possible for the reader to discern what, without this book, he could perhaps have never seen in himself." But we and our students are not MacLeishes or Prousts and we have trouble translating such insights into classroom practices. Elsewhere I have summarized the research on the impact of reading [4] and shown that effects depend upon the characteristics of the individual doing the reading, the content of the materials read, and the total situation in which the reading is done. Studies by Smith, Weingarten, and others have shown possible influences on values and behavior. The process of bibliotherapy as used with individuals with personality difficulties may have some lessons for us here in work with more normal adolescents. Rather than trying to quote you the ten or fifteen researches that give some evidence of the effects of reading, I should like to proceed with a few examples of what can be done in ordinary classroom situations.

[4] David H. Russell, "Some Research on the Impact of Reading," *English Journal*, 47:398–413, October 1958.

## SOME PRACTICAL SUGGESTIONS

A few lucky young people make private discoveries of the world of literature, but most children need to be helped in their explorations by the understanding parent and teacher. For generations parents and teachers have made an honest effort to go beyond the surface facts or literal ideas of a selection to some of the important, underlying ideas because they would have children or youth greatly influenced by literature. Teachers especially can be aware of the many different potentialities of the reading process corresponding, in part, to the five levels described above. Reading *may* bring at least eight kinds of results:

|  |  |
|---|---|
| Skill and Understanding | Acquisition of new skills<br>Increase of worthwhile information<br>Knowledge of how to find out more |
| Interpretation | Development of interests and appreciation<br>Improvement of problem-solving and critical thinking |
| Impact | Evolution of social and personal insights<br>Understanding of fundamental values<br>Changes in behavior and personality |

The list is hypothetical and formidable, but teachers should not stop short at the end of the first three possibilities described as literal understanding. Let me illustrate something of the last two areas because they are the most difficult. The materials I use are deliberately taken from popular basal readers and anthologies. You don't have to go to a highly selected individual piece of literature to get literary or human values. In fact, above second readers at least, most selections are put in reading materials for class use just because they have some underlying ideas and may illustrate important values.

Take for example the little poem, "Bird Talk" found in a basal third reader. Now you could teach this poem at the level, here are birds chattering together and this is what they say. Or by question and discussion you can lead the group to see that our perceptions depend upon our point of view. Birds see things in bird-ways and each of us see things in our own individual way. You might stop with this important bit of psychology. Finally, some children might be led to the climactic idea expressed elsewhere by Robert Burns

> O wad some power the giftie gie us
> To see oursels as others see us!

Because this is a third-grade poem, of course the children should do something about it besides discussing it. Perhaps they will write other poems, as one class did, from the point of view of other animals. "Think—said the rabbit,"! or "Think, said the horse," etc. Or perhaps they might write, as another group did, "How I see myself and how some other person (mother, friend) sees me." These last were personal documents to be read only by the teacher.

Or at the secondary school level take the Edwin Arlington Robinson poem "Richard Cory" found in some anthologies. The poem starts:

> Whenever Richard Cory went downtown,
>     We people on the pavement looked at him;
> He was a gentleman from sole to crown,
>     Clean favored and imperially slim.

One way to use this poem is to postpone discussion. Instead, let the students hear the poem a couple of times and then write what they think is its theme. The reactions of one group of students to this ambiguous poem varied considerably. In response to the question about its main idea one student said, "The personal problems of Richard Cory," another, "Money is not everything"; another, "contrast between rich and poor"; and still another, "All that looks perfect may not be so; deceptiveness of appearances." Here were young people reaching for the truth, each in his own way, and who is to say which answer is "correct." Perhaps, all of them deserve further discussion, writing, and searches for related literary materials.

This poem may be a bit of a shocker to the junior high school student who is "happiness bound," who has been accustomed to stories with the Hollywood ending of "all's well." Perhaps this is enough—all does not end well in this world. How would you do it? Perhaps the group can be encouraged to dig a little deeper, can be helped to understand the behavior, first of the townspeople, and then of Richard Cory himself. Here is a piece of literature whose ambiguity can stimulate discussion and writing. Thus the group moves away from the black-and-white of the Westerns and much cheap fiction to a study of some of the mixed motives and human conflicts found in all of us. Then they are on the way to some of the self insight and social insights which literature can give.

We have evidence that teen-agers want to grapple with some of these problems. For example, one English teacher in a California high school collected the opinions of an "average" ninth grade about the books labelled "teen-age books" in their school library. Here are some of the comments (these are all quotations):

1. I'd like more realism, not so much fairy stuff, with phony living happily ever after.
2. Books which present the ordinary teen-ager and his problems, so we can see how some are solved.
3. Teen-agers cuss and know cuss words, but the books I read sound as if they were written for ten-year-olds.
4. I'd like a book which would show how hard it is for a high school girl to

get to know the boy she likes. Parents always tell you that you should go with someone else.
5. A book which shows us what life is like when you grow up.
6. Most teen-age books are too childish and not real enough. Most of them sound like a little 8- or 9-year-old wrote them.
7. Authors must think that teen-agers are awfully innocent.
8. Life isn't like what you find in books. Life is hard and people are cruel and don't think of others. It's dog eat dog, and an eye for an eye, and a tooth for a tooth. (From a boy in an underprivileged family.)

Here, then, are interpretations by young adolescents not of one poem or story, but of the books labelled as written for teen-agers and usually found in high school libraries. You have noted that a few students found these books satisfying and realistic, that others regarded them as pap and fantasy. In the reactions there are, perhaps, some implications for the content of what we ask young adolescents to read. Their books should deal somehow with situations which seem important to them; the books' problems should be their problems.

I have used poems for my practical examples because they are short. You have other poems, and other stories and plays which mean a lot to you at the fourth and fifth levels of reading and which, accordingly, can be shared with young people. These may be a simple story in a primer about a family, a tale of heroism, or a well-known piece of literature. Whatever it is, teach it in depth. Give it time for thought.

To summarize what I am saying, perhaps I have been suggesting that secondary teachers can learn from elementary teachers, and elementary teachers can learn from secondary people. In the past, the elementary school has been strong on teaching reading skills; in secondary schools, some of our best teaching has been in literature. Accordingly, secondary teachers can learn from elementary people ways of teaching reading skills—not just word recognition or comprehension, but how to read a newspaper, how to handle a science chapter, how to study a short story, how to attack a play or a novel. Conversely, an elementary teacher can adopt more of the techniques of a good secondary teacher of literature. The teacher of the third or the sixth grade can assume that some reading is to be done in depth—children can be aided in the interpretation of character and in discovering social and spiritual values. Thus in years ahead, successful procedures in each part of the school system can be applied at the other level.

For three hundred years now, since the days of the *New England Primer*, some people have believed that reading can contribute to the virtuous life. Probably they are right, but we all have to work on it.

# TRANSCRIPT OF A DIRECTED READING LESSON TAUGHT ON TELEVISION *

Lawrence E. Hafner

*Many years ago the teaching of reading was a rather laissez faire, amorphous event in which the child took his book home the night before a reading "lesson" and read aloud to his mother and the next day he did the same for his teacher. In this situation little teaching was done; the teacher merely served as a hearer; and any credit for teaching went to the mother.*

*There were no provisions made for the systematic development of word recognition, interpretation, and appreciation skills; nor was much of an attempt made to develop concepts, to motivate the reading, and to guide it for the purposes of seeing relationships and drawing conclusions.*

*In the modern directed reading lesson a systematic endeavor is made to teach these skills, and to relate the ideas gained to the lives of the students. The teacher takes an active, responsible role as he interacts with the students and guides their development in reading and through reading.*

*The reading lesson reported in this article was taught by the author to a small group of above-average junior high-school students (grade eight) on a thirty-minute television program according to the suggestions of the* Teacher's Guidebook. *In the normal classroom situation a teacher could use to even better advantage the many guidebook suggestions, particularly in the section, "Extending Interests."*

*1. Why do we use a directed reading lesson when teaching reading?*

*2. List the basic steps in a directed reading lesson and explain the purpose of each step.*

*3. How did the lesson meet the theoretical expectations of a directed lesson? Explain your answer.*

*4. Expand on the importance of allowing your students to reflect on the more complex questions.*

### INTRODUCTION

*Instructor, L. E. Hafner:* Hello. This evening our topic is "Teaching the Directed Reading Lesson." In a manner of speaking, we have been working up to this lesson because we thought it was important. In some of our lessons and demonstrations we did not actually prepare our children to read by working on the vocabulary and the concepts ahead of time. There was a particular purpose in doing that. At one point (I believe it was in telecast nine) I said that we would have a lesson in which we would work on the vocabulary that would prepare the children for their reading; and this is the particular lesson in which we will do this.

---

* Broadcast published in 1963 on WSIU-TV. By permission of the Board of Trustees, Southern Illinois University.

Now we feel it is very important to direct the learning of the children and because of this we have a directed reading lesson. The students are not on their own but they are helped to get the most out of reading their material. We feel that many skills must be taught to be learned and that if they are not taught they will not be learned. Now there are four basic steps in a directed reading lesson and I would like to show you here on the chalkboard what they are.

## THE STEPS IN A DIRECTED READING LESSON

The first step is *preparation for reading*. In this step we iron out the concepts and the vocabulary difficulties. We also try to set the stage for the reading. We try to give the people a question to answer in the reading and then, in the second stage, *interpreting the story*, we read to answer questions, to build meaning, and to see relationships. And then we also have a further discussion of the story to discover what some of its implications are, etc. In the third step we try to *extend the skills and abilities* of the children through word analysis work and more comprehension exercises. Finally, in the fourth step, *extending interests*, we try to point out other things in other areas that might be related to the story—perhaps another book that the children might read on this particular topic. So we feel that it is very important to follow these steps in teaching.

Now we are going over to our studio class to start our work with them.

## TEACHING A DIRECTED READING LESSON [1]

### Preparation for Reading

Hello. We are really glad to have you here this evening. We are going to read a story about Louis Pasteur and the name of the story is "Words to Match the Occasion." [2] And we are going to find out something about Louis Pasteur by reading the author's explanation of how he happened to write this article and this is at the top of page one of your material. You can read this to find out why this man wrote the story that you will be reading after a while. Go ahead and read that now. (Pause.)

(While the students are reading this, I would like to point out that this is a good thing to do, because it creates a little interest on the part of the students and helps to get them ready to read. They are interested in who these authors are. The author of this particular story is a man by the name of Vincent Edwards. The students were asking me whether this is the man who plays the part of the doctor on television. I told them I wasn't just too sure about it but, anyway, it did create some interest. I think that the chil-

---

[1] An unrehearsed lesson.
[2] Paul V. D. Hoysradt, in *More Panoramas*, grade 8 (Chicago: Scott, Foresman, 1957).

dren enjoy this, and I don't think you should bypass this sort of thing because you do not think it is important. Actually, I think it is important.

We will be getting back to the children right now.) [3]

*Inst:* All right. What achievements made Pasteur famous? Dorothy?

*Dorothy:* He developed a method called pasteurizing milk—so it would become pure for people to drink.

[Instructor writes PASTEURIZATION on board]

*Inst:* All right, he developed pasteurization. Now in the pasteurization process we heat milk to a temperature of, I believe, about 140 degrees in order to kill the germs. Now I don't know whether any of you have had the opportunity to go to a dairy and watch them do this. But when I was a child, we had a dairy about a block away; I used to go in there. They had all kinds of funny coils running through a vat, and the milk seemed to be rather warm. I asked the man questions, and he told me that they did this to kill the germs. You probably . . . have you studied about this any place . . . this pasteurization? Have any of you been to a dairy? Yes? Well, maybe I don't have anything on you after all. Did you see the pasteurization?

*Dorothy:* Yes, it was a long time ago.

*Inst:* It was a pretty long time ago for me, too.

From what you know about the purpose and value of pasteurization, could you define one of Pasteur's fields of scientific interest? You know there are different fields of interest; you have physics and biology, geology, chemistry. What was his particular area? Do you know?

*Dorothy:* I am not sure; but was it bacteriology?

*Inst:* All right. Bacteriology. And this has to do—it is part of biology, isn't it? . . . studying very small organisms. Now this is a very important area of work. I think that you will find this out as you read it, and as you find out the words that Pasteur is going to utter. You also will be able to see something of the relationship of his work to our modern times.

There are certain words here that we would like to get straightened out before we start. We told our television audience that we like to iron out some of the difficult concepts. How many of you know how to pronounce this (carnot)? Well, look in your glossary on the second page.

We have a glossary and the students are going to look to see how to pronounce that word; and while they are looking at it, we are going to switch to this next word which we have on a card—a visual—to show you how this glossary is set up. So we will take a look now at the next word, *deprecate.*

All right. We have the word there—*deprecate;* and, as you see, we have a short sound in the first closed syllable (dep), and then the *schwa* (rə). Finally the *a* in the last syllable is long so that it is *dep′rə kāt;* and it means to express strong disapproval of or plead against. This is what our glossary looks like. (Visual for T.V. audience.) Now we are going to get back to see if we

---

[3] During the lesson proper, material in parentheses was directed to the T.V. audience.

know how to pronounce this word. How would you pronounce that (Carnot)?
*Debbie:* Kärnō.
*Inst:* Very good. We had this kind of mark over the a (ä), didn't we? This kind of mark over the o (ō), and we dropped the t, didn't we? So it is *karno* with a long mark here (ō). We were just talking with the T.V. audience, and we said that this next word *deprecate* means to. . . . What does it mean? You can look now.
*Bill:* Well, I looked before. Disapproval of something. . . . If you deprecate something, you don't think too much of it.
*Inst:* All right, it's kind of related to the word *appreciate*. We talk about appreciating people and more or less "depreciating" them; this is related to that. Do you know what a *facsimile* is? How many of you know what a facsimile is?
*Bill:* An exact copy.
*Inst:* Good. An exact copy. And we have a facsimile here. I don't know whether you will be able to see it, but it is a picture of Albert Schweitzer; and it is from the time that we had the lesson when we discussed Schweitzer with some other high-school students. We had to make facsimilies or copies by a certain process. So this is a facsimile. This is an exact copy of a particular page in one of those books. All right. Now, this word—*Lister:* We won't go into this, but you can look at your glossary there. He was a famous medical man. And next the word, *Pasteur*, of course. . . . Let's read about him, though. Who was he? What does it say there? Bill?
*Bill:* Well, it says here in the glossary that he was a French chemist who invented a way of preventing hydrophobia and a way to keep milk from spoiling.
*Inst:* What do you think about that achievement?
*Dorothy:* Wasn't hydrophobia rabies?
*Inst:* Yes, it is.
*Dorothy:* Well, rabies is a deadly disease. Once you've got it in your system, it is fatal; so since he found a way of preventing it, that saved people's lives.
*Inst:* That is a pretty good deal then, isn't it?
Who has ever heard of this word—*Sorbonne*? Have you ever heard of that? Well, how do you pronounce it? Do you want to try it again, Debbie; you had pretty good luck last time.
*Debbie:* Sorbonne.
*Inst:* Correct. And this is a university . . . where?
*Bill:* Well, this is a university in Paris.
*Inst:* All right; and it's quite a famous university, too. Now, the next expression. Do you know the meaning of *taint*. Have you ever been tainted? I hope not. Would you like to be tainted, Jim?
*Jim:* Well, it is a stain or spot or corruption.
*Inst:* All right. Jim took a real quick glance before he answered. He got his eye on that explanation; he wasn't going to let himself in for it. He said, "No!" (This is one good way to get people to look things up. Ask them if they

would like to be a certain thing. This will enlist their curiosity and often they will look it up because they want to know how to answer this. They don't want to say yes or no until they know what the word means.)

### Interpreting the Story

Now we are going to look at the story; it is on the third page of your material: "Words to Match the Occasion." The first line of the story says that there was a very distinguished audience at the University of Sorbonne at Paris. Now let's read to find out if the words that were spoken on that particular day actually did match the occasion. We are going to read the story to see if the words that were spoken by Pasteur matched the occasion that we are going to have in the story. And while you are reading that, I am going to talk to the T.V. audience. O.K., you may read to find that out.

We'll just walk over here a bit and mention to you that it is very important that this first reading is silent; and I would like to tell you why. First of all, silent reading is used more often in real life than oral reading. Much of our studying, our reading of the newspaper, etc., is silent reading. We have much greater use for it, and of course it is more rapid than oral reading. You can save a lot of time in this manner. Now some people have to read orally—such as people who give very long speeches; and television and radio announcers read some of their material, so there is a use for it. But you get this speed through your silent reading, and we know, too, that it is more versatile.

It can be more easily adapted to various purposes. Also, it's psychologically sound, because if you read fast, it means that you can get the gist of the story— the whole picture—the oneness—the unity. And it is also useful in developing habits of study. And finally, if you read silently first, this means that you have a chance to look over any words which may be difficult; then if you do have to read orally you will have prepared yourself to do a good job of the oral reading. I am not going to talk too much about this any more right now. I am going to give the people a few seconds to concentrate on their story. [Pause.]

All right, I think that most of the students have just about finished. Let's get to this main question that we had and then we will go back. I am going to do this now, because I don't want to miss out on answering the question that we first asked. Do you think the words that Pasteur used matched the occasion? Do you think they were fitting to the occasion . . . the thing that took place? What do you think about that, Billy?

*Billy:* Yes, I think they did.

*Inst:* All right, why?

*Billy:* Well, he tried to get the youth not to be discouraged in what they wanted to do in their jobs.

*Inst:* You think this is a noble thing to say? What makes you think that this was a great occasion, then? If you think this was a noble thing to say because this was a noble occasion, why do you think it was a great occasion? Anybody like to think? . . . . Somebody else . . . think about that, too. . . . You all think about that. Is there any evidence that points to this being a great occasion? Andrea?

*Andrea:* They said that they were celebrating his seventieth birthday; and they were saluting him for his work in science and for making this great discovery. Then he stood up and he talked to the students about how science and peace overrules war and hatred.

*Inst:* Good. And so it was a fine speech and a great occasion. Now let's go back and find out something about Pasteur's background. Read the first eight paragraphs again to see if you can find some biographical data, that is, some data about his life and also some information that tells how the people felt about him. Then we will ask you what these things were—these things that tell something about his life and about him. (Pause) Have you found any? O.K., let's have them. Andrea?

*Andrea:* Well, they said that he lived in poverty. (These words are written on the board.)

*Inst:* All right. He lived in poverty. Well, what does that mean . . . poverty?

*Andrea:* Well, living conditions weren't very . . . well, desirable.

*Inst:* All right. They weren't very desirable. In fact he was what we might call . . . what?

*Andrea:* Poor.

*Inst:* Poor, yes. Any other information about him? Bill?

*Bill:* Through his whole life he worked; he devoted his life to the welfare of humanity.

*Inst:* All right—to the welfare of humanity. What else, Billy? Bill, did you find something?

*Bill:* Well, it said that he was in ill health during quite a bit of this time, so really he was working for other people while he, himself, was sick.

*Inst:* All right. He was sick quite a bit of the time. What else? What nationality was he? O.K.

*Andrea:* French.

*Inst:* Yes, he was French, wasn't he? Fine. Do you agree with the president of the students association that Pasteur must have been a very great and a very good man? We kind of covered this a little bit, but let's get back to this point and reiterate. Do you agree that he was a very great and a very good man? Jim, how about that? What do you think about that?

*Jim:* He was a great man in his work in science.

*Inst:* Is there anything that would lead you to think that he was a good man? . . . Well, I'll give you a chance to look back into your material if you have to, and while you are doing that, I want to point out something to the T.V. audience.

(Now usually in this sort of thing we like to try to keep things rolling a bit, and perhaps you, too, in your teaching like to think that—well, you don't like these pauses. But these pauses are important and I'll tell you why. If you are going to ask a child when Columbus discovered America, then you would expect a quick response. This is rote memory. But if you ask a child a thought question don't be afraid to have some silence in your classroom, because the child has to have time to think about this. You don't ask a reflective question, and if he doesn't answer in five seconds then go to somebody else. Realize that time to think on a hard question should be given the student.)

All right. We've given you some time now; I don't know whether it was enough or not, but. . . . Can anybody answer this question now: Is there any evidence that Pasteur was a good man? Oh, we give you enough time, and we get an answer. Very good. O.K., see how this works? Debbie?

*Debbie:* Well, I think that just the fact that he wanted to devote his life, and give his life to helping humanity, and trying to find . . . well, things that weren't common and things that could be helpful to people . . . that that just showed he was kind and considerate of other people and wanted to help them.

*Inst:* Good. Does anyone else want to add anything to that? Bill?

*Bill:* It says on the second page that when Pasteur came in, the students were hushed. So evidently they thought very highly of him at the time.

*Inst:* All right. Now we are going to step over here a little bit and talk about another point. Pasteur thought that young people ought to have three obligations. Now what did he say these three obligations were? What were the three obligations that young people should have? O.K., Andrea?

*Andrea:* Well, he said they should believe that science and peace would triumph over ignorance and war—that nations should unite . . . and not to destroy, but build the future.

*Inst:* Well, that sort of implies that since young people are going to build the future, that this would be a responsibility. Did he say anything there about the necessity of instructing themselves? Does it say in so many words—that they would have to instruct themselves?

*Andrea:* Yes. Well, he said that the future will belong to those who have gone through the most suffering to make it a good place to live.

*Inst:* All right, and what should they do for their country? You have said it already—but let's pinpoint it. What should they do for their country?

*Andrea:* Build ideas and carry them out.

*Inst:* All right. President Kennedy said something similar in his inaugural address. He said, "It is not what my country can do for me, but what I can do for my . . . what?

*Bill:* What I can do for my country.

*Inst:* And this kind of re-echoes what Pasteur said. He thought that is was a kind of day for young people to do what?

*Debbie:* Serve their country.

*Inst:* Yes, serve their country; and also contribute to the progress of humanity. We have already said this. We have just restated it in different words.

### Extending Skills and Abilities

The next thing we are to talk about is this third point—extending skills and abilities. We want to try, first of all, to strengthen word meaning. Do you remember what a synonym is? What is a synonym?

*Dorothy*: They are two words that are the same or they mean the same . . . almost the same.

*Inst*: Well, they are synonyms then, aren't they? So it's a word having a meaning the same as another word. Now, read the first sentence in the third paragraph on page two—the one that starts out "To the famous doctors and scientists." You notice the word *famous* in there. We are going to try to find in the first paragraph of the story how the author used five synonyms for the word *famous*. Turn back to the first page of your story and see if you can find these synonyms for the word *famous* and we will list them. (Pause.) O.K.

*Dorothy*: Eminent, is one. (List on board.)

*Inst*: Eminent. All right, we talked about the eminent men. What else? Bill?

*Bill*: Distinguished.

*Inst*: What kind of distinguished? What are we talking about? Distinguished what?

*Bill*: The audience. The audience was composed of scientists.

*Inst*: All right. They were distinguished, and this has a meaning that they were set above and apart from other people; that they were especially capable people, and they had been recognized as distinguished people. And what else do you have, Billy?

*Billy*: Famous.

*Inst*: That is the thing we are finding the synonym for. Did it occur again in that first paragraph?

*Billy*: Is was in the second paragraph.

*Inst*: I see. O.K. And so famous would be a synonym for what? I'm going to put it back at you now.

*Billy*: Eminent.

*Inst*: O.K. For eminent then. Any questions, Andrea?

*Andrea*: Celebrated.

*Inst*: Celebrated. What were they talking about? Celebrated what?

*Andrea*: Scientists and scholars.

*Inst*: Celebrated scientists and scholars. All right.

### Extending Interests

(There is other work provided in the *Teacher's Guidebook* that we could be doing here, but we are running short of time, and I would like to briefly touch on one activity to help extend interests.) Have any of you read this story of Louis Pasteur that I have in my hand?

*Debbie*: Well, a few years ago I got a book; it wasn't a big book; it was a book on Louis Pasteur. I got it from the library.

*Inst*: Did you enjoy it?

*Debbie*: Yes.

*Inst*: Did this kind of recall some of the things that you had read previously? Did any of you others read it? . . . . Yes!

*Dorothy*: I didn't read it, but last summer on the late show there was an old movie about Louis Pasteur.

*Inst*: All right. Here is a booklet about Pasteur. It is in a series called *Health*

*Heroes,* and there are many such famous people discussed in this series. And I would like to say that if any of you would like to read this, I will be glad to give it to you. I think you would enjoy it because it gives a lot of details about his life that would be missing in the kind of story that we read. If anybody would like to have it to read. . . . Debbie? All right. Debbie is getting to be a kind of Pasteur expert.

(I would like to recapitulate at this point and go over what we have done today. We have tried to show you the plan that is used in basal series for guiding the reading of junior high-school students. The stories are interesting, and the children have as their purpose the enjoyment of their reading; and I think that they enjoyed it. *Our* problem, of course, is to teach skills and attitudes, but we do want them to enjoy their reading. The teacher uses the story, then, as a vehicle for teaching important interpretation skills. We know there are four important steps that are followed in the teaching of a story, and we will show them to you again on the board: (1) preparation for reading; (2) interpreting the story; (3) extending skills and abilities, and (4) extending interests.

Now we feel that this type of direction that we have given today, and have tried to demonstrate in our limited amount of time, is very important. I think that you have seen something of the value of such teaching. We might also point out that this plan may be applied to the various subject matter areas such as science, geography, and history—that you can teach a section or a chapter following this basic plan. So remember that you want to clarify your concepts, and you want to, above all, guide the reading of your students so that they get a "fair shake" and can learn these skills. This is very important. Thank you for watching and "Good evening!")

# WORDS TO MATCH THE OCCASION *

### Paul V. D. Hoysradt

T HE GREAT theater of the Sorbonne in Paris probably never held a more distinguished audience than on the morning of December 27, 1892. From all over Europe celebrated scientists and scholars had traveled to be present. Even the great Dr. Lister had come from London to represent the Royal Medical Society.

At exactly half-past ten, from a side door, President Carnot of France escorted an unassuming, bearded little man to a table in the center of the

---

* REPRINTED FROM *More Panoramas* (Chicago: Scott, Foresman, 1957), copyright 1956 by W. L. Jenkins, by permission of the author.

crowded amphitheater. At sight of him, every person present rose to his feet.

It was the seventieth birthday of Louis Pasteur!

The whole world knew his story—how from childhood his life had been devoted to the welfare of humanity. Through poverty, sorrow, ill health, and opposition, he had gone forward, carrying on his great work in bacteriology until even his bitterest critics recognized his genius.

On this memorable day, the most eminent men of that time rose, one after another, to pay their tributes.

The renowned Dr. Lister said, "You have raised the veil that for centuries covered infectious diseases." Pasteur was presented with an album containing the signatures of all the residents of his little mountain birthplace. Along with their loving sentiments was a photograph of his old home and a facsimile of his birth certificate. But the climax came with the students' greeting. The top gallery of the auditorium was filled with young people, their eager faces turned toward their spokesman, Young Monsieur Devise, the president of the students' association, as he faced the great man.

"You have been very great and very good," he said, as he concluded his tribute. "You have given students a shining example."

When it came time for Pasteur's response to all these greetings, the theater was strangely hushed. Somehow the vast audience sensed that the man whom they were honoring would have words to match the occasion.

They were not mistaken.

To the famous doctors and scientists who had come from far-off places to honor him, Pasteur brought a message of hope and optimism. "You bring me the deepest joy that can be felt by a man whose invincible belief is that science and peace will triumph over ignorance and war; that nations will unite, not to destroy, but to build; and that the future will belong to those who have done the most for suffering humanity."

But the most impressive part of Pasteur's reply was directed to young people. For the students in the crowded top gallery, for youth everywhere, the great man had inspiring counsel to give in his hour of highest acclaim.

"Whatever your careers may be, do not let yourselves become tainted by a deprecating and barren skepticism. Do not let yourselves be discouraged by the sadness of certain hours which pass over nations. Live in the serene peace of laboratories and libraries. Say to yourself first, 'What have I done for my instruction?' and as you gradually advance, 'What have I done for my country?' until the time comes when you may have the immense happiness of thinking that you have contributed in some way to the progress and good of humanity."

# PROBING PROBLEMS IN PANELS *

Albert Nissman

*Getting students to approach good literature positively, to interpret it well, and to develop insights that can be applied to solving problems and enriching lives is a difficult and elusive task. In the experiment reported in this article, Nissman provides a comprehensive model for attaining these goals. He also explains the dynamics of his adventure, and an evaluation of the experiment's effectiveness.*

*1. What learning principles did the author employ in his experiment?*

*2. What was the purpose of the experiment?*

*3. How can you overcome objectively the doubts that may be creeping into your mind regarding the efficacy of this plan in your school situation? Do you owe it to your students to try?*

*4. How might you adapt this plan to your situation?*

THERE WERE methods in my madness and goals in my grouping. This was my approach as I explained it to my ninth-grade class.[1] The results of our panel activity and its evaluations eventually verified my belief in its efficacy and justified the procedures.

The units for the entire year I had already devised. During the first eighteen weeks we had studied the following units: [2]

The Individual and His Immediate Environment.
The Individual and His Physical Environment.
The Individual and His Technological Environment.

The units were composed of many activities, resources, instructional aids, and procedures. But one thing was a constant: a reading list for each of the units which included fiction and non-fiction that dealt with the unit themes. And from these lists, the youngsters were to choose four books for each unit about which they were to write book reports according to my specifications (see Book Report form illustrated).

Thus I could plot the progress of each individual's understanding of the human problems inherent in the books and units. But it was obvious that much of the value would never be realized unless a well organized group discussion were employed.

It was then that I decided to clarify and reformulate my purposes of instruction. Such purposes need not be profound; they must only be clear.

The pupils were asked to survey the lists of books each had read during

---

* FROM the *Journal of Developmental Reading* (Winter 1961), pp. 139–144, reprinted with permission of Albert Nissman and the International Reading Association.

the three units. They were to think of these books in terms of the satisfaction, enjoyment, and enlightenment they had afforded. Then they were asked to list in order the three books that they would most enjoy discussing in a panel.

These lists were collected and we began to discuss the format of a panel discussion, the duties of the moderator and of the panelists, and the purposes of such a discussion. When we came to a lull, we decided to consult our language textbook. By employing a variety of reading skills, we scanned the index and the table of contents, hunting down all additional information on the subject of panel discussions.

BOOK REPORT

Name_____ Section_____ Date_____ Mark_____
  I. Bibliographical Information (after this model: Marquand, John P. *Sincerely, Willis Wayde*. Boston: Little, Brown and Co., 1954)
 II. Biographical notes about author
III. Type of Literature
IV. Main Characters (brief descriptions).
    1.
    2.
    3.
 V. Minor Characters (brief descriptions).
    1.
    2.
    3.
VI. Main Ideas of Book
    1. What problems was this book concerned with?
       a. Personal
       b. Family
       c. Social, moral, civic
       d. Physical and emotional
       e. Technological and economic
       f. National and global
    2. How did the main character(s) solve the problems?
    3. How would you have solved the problems?
    4. Has this book modified any of your ideas, ideals, attitudes and behavior? How? Why?
VII. What was your reaction to this book?
    1. Style of writing
    2. Characterization
    3. Plotting of story
    4. Statement of problem
    5. Character's philosophy of life or
    6. Author's philosophy of life

Thus I listed the goals and explained them to my class.

  1. To stimulate wide reading within a given unit.

2. To challenge the pupils to do some real thinking and probing about the reading.
3. To probe the similarities in themes, problems, styles, plotting and character.
4. To probe the differences in themes, problems, styles, plotting and character.
5. To generalize and conclude, to form concepts in capsule form that might help them in settling the affairs of their own lives.

While the pupils were browsing, I played a purposeful "solitaire" and placed the youngsters in groups on the basis of their choices of three books. Additional criteria for this grouping were similarity in thematic content, structure, purpose of the writing. These similarities were not always apparent on the surface and would, therefore, demand thorough discussion within the small groups. This factor also determined the ultimate structure of the panels.

This, then, was primarily a grouping which was based on book titles. Below the groups are listed as they were formed.[3]

*Group 1*
My Lord, What A Morn
Cheaper by the Dozen
Lost Horizon
Fear Strikes Out
Huckleberry Finn
Tom Sawyer

*Group 2*
Pasteur: Knight of the Laboratory
Albert Einstein
Invisible Men

*Group 3*
Clay Fingers
The Child Who Never Grew
Lost Horizon
The  Red Badge of Courage
The Citadel
Rise and Walk
Our Town
Of Human Bondage
Scarlet Letter

*Group 4*
Diary of a Young Girl
Sayonara
Jane Eyre
With A High Heart

*Group 5*
The Nun's Story
Arrowsmith
My Antonia
The Silver Pencil
The Human Comedy
Four Young Teachers

*Group 6*
Pleasant Valley
The Big Wave
Volcano
Kon-Tiki
Hiroshima

Even a cursory glance at these lists will show the reader that quite a spread of good books, fiction and non-fiction, was represented. And the concepts and the tangents that the panel discussions led to were legion. Among the principal ideas were problems of family life, idealism, problems of the scientists, professional jealousy, finding a niche in the world, professions

dedicated to serving humanity, bigotry and persecution, and scientific developments and their effects on humanity. It was illuminating and profitable to
listen to young teen-agers discuss these many somber aspects of life.

Just before the pupils became involved in the small group work, I reminded
them that a phase of *grouping* is *groping*. But eventually the haze would lift
and out of the murky confusion enlightenment and learning would arise.
The latter, however, would only happen with dedication and efficiency in
group work. Therefore, at the end of each of the four meeting periods their
group outlines were to be turned in. Each group outline or progress report
contained the following:

1. Names of the committee members.
2. Date of session.
3. Problem areas discussed.
4. Methods of research and investigation.
5. Sources of research and investigation.
6. Time still needed for research.
7. Methods of presentation.
8. Time needed for presentation.
9. Subject matter content (highlights of information).

The four-division system of evaluation was arranged at this time, too. *Class
evaluation* involved the participation of all the pupils in the class. Various
pupils and I contributed comments on the group's presentation in terms of
procedure and content. Then the group was asked to leave the room so that
the rest of the class could openly vote on a letter grade which they deemed a
just reward for their peers. And to the skeptics may I say that "A" was *not*
the only grade given.

The second division was *group evaluation*. Here, each group member
assessed every other group member's contribution to the group's effectiveness.
Let me inject here that this was more than a popularity poll. These youngsters
could spot immediately the morale builders, the efficient workers, the glib
talkers, and the "goof-offs."

The third division in this process of evaluation was *self-evaluation*. While
no youngster ever failed himself, it was significant to note that some rated
themselves with a "c". Whether they did so because of conscience pangs or
because they knew that I knew what they were actually doing in the group,
I can not determine with certainty. But the process, I feel, made them take
a good introspective look.

The last division involved *teacher evaluation* of the individuals as effective
group members. Although each of the four evaluations carried equal weight,
the teacher evaluation was done last at the insistence of the class. They felt
that any other position would unduly influence the other three judgments.
For this reason, where possible, I saved my own criticism for last, too.

Among the criteria we used in all of the evaluations were *leadership, in-*

*formation, reasoning, opinion, attitude, and speaking skill.*[4] In addition we looked for adaptability and originality. We estimated the success with which each group accomplished its stated purposes as listed on the progress reports. And finally, we asked whether the group communicated with us and in turn stimulated discussion.

As we attempt to evaluate the entire project, we can see an interesting instructional panorama. In this panorama we note concepts of considerable breadth and depth: ideas such as "All men have problems which must be solved or ignored," or "Man must learn to control the forces of nature or be overcome by them," or "Man needs a salable skill in this technological age." These and dozens more were discussed and argued. And in the end, I believe, the youngsters learned that such concepts, conclusions, generalizations, social understandings—call them what you will—are not absolute. They are relative. They can be modified. There are exceptions. There are extenuating circumstances. Life, in short, is not a rhythmical pattern with perfect symmetry. These understandings, too, were part of their instruction.

The crux of evaluating such instructional activity lies in the question, "Is such an activity with its methods valid and are the results purposeful?" My answer is a resounding YES. And I base my confident answer on direct quotations written by the youngsters anonymously on 3 x 5 cards:

"I enjoyed hearing the short summaries of the books. The discussions have encouraged me to want to read the books."

"I think that this type of work and presentation is very enjoyable and educational. I feel that the job of discovering the likenesses of certain books is a very difficult job, but all of the groups did a good job."

"It was actually fun finding out the linking parts of the book and putting them together to form panel discussions."

"I think that the unit was well worth while. It brought together many different books with similar problems."

"I would like to work on more committees of this sort."

"I think that the time was well spent." (This refers to four periods of 42 minutes of group work and six double periods of 84 minutes each, one double for each of the panel presentations.)

"I've also gotten interested in books to read. It was a clever way to bring most of the books into light. It also was a good way to stimulate the imagination."

"I liked this idea of a panel discussing books which have a similar theme. I learned a lot from just discussing with our group and more from hearing other committee reports. I think I would like to present it in this fashion again."

"It adds to your knowledge of the books that you have read, and gets you interested in the books you haven't read."

"I think the unit was refreshing in its informal air and in the oral work rather than the written work. The marking system I liked very much."

"I enjoyed searching out the problems and methods of presentation."

Of course, not all the comments were glowing tributes. Most were sincerely favorable as quoted above. A goodly number were moderate, and a few, like those quoted below, were rather negative.

"I think skits hold more interest than these 'hit or miss' discussions. But, I do highly approve of committee work as a whole and learn more from it, than from individual research."

"I think that in some committees certain persons tried to dominate the whole report."

"I don't particularly care for committee work. Too many people do nothing, piling all the responsibility on one person. It isn't entirely fair."

All comments, the favorable and the negative, are most valuable in aiding teachers to determine the effectiveness of their instructional programs. And who can really be the best judge of the efficacy of instruction? Is it not the pupils who are subjected to this instruction, and does not anonymity assure a greater degree of honesty in the expression of opinion?

I must then conclude, on the basis of my personal experience in my own classroom, that probing problems in panels is justifiable, valid, and purposeful. Of course, it need not be limited to books, or to stimulation of reading, or to the sending of pupils scurrying out to read more and better books.

It can be used in many instructional settings and new situations. It can be based on any facet of learning—the sciences, the arts, and real life situations. It can endure many mutations and adaptations.

One underlying principle serves, however, as a pillar for this activity as it does with most human endeavors: it is most effective when youngsters cooperate to achieve understanding of problems which they have agreed are worthy of serious study.

### REFERENCES

1. 15 boys and 14 girls on the junior-senior high reading levels with an I.Q. range of 113–138 in a class of English and social studies.
2. Taken from ROBERT G. CARLSEN and RICHARD S. ALM, *Social Understandings Through Literature*. Washington, D. C.: National Council for The Social Studies, 1954, p. vii.
3. Some youngsters discussed more than one book.
4. As listed and defined on the *Discussion Group Evaluation Form*, Chicago, Illinois: Blue Cross Commission.

# A MODERN DEFINITION
# OF READING

## INTRODUCTION

*In his book,* The Art of Loving, *Erich Fromm explains that there are different kinds of love and that these different kinds of love can be defined in a number of ways. The theory of love affects the practice of love: one's definition of love affects his general attitude toward love, the way he loves, whom he loves, and for what purposes he loves.*

*In a similar way a person's definition of the reading process affects his attitude toward reading: the way he reads, what he will read, and for what purposes he will read. The teacher who instructs the student in the theory and art of reading stands as the mediator of what we know about the reading process.*

*What do we know about the reading process? Briefly stated, most authorities on the subject consider reading a complex process involving the perceiving of written meanings, the interpretation of meanings, and the reaction to and applying of meanings to life. It is an active process that requires the individual to demand meaning, and to bring ideas to the printed page, so that the symbols will trigger off meanings according to the pattern of the writing and the experience and intelligence and habits of inquiry of the reader.*

*In this group of selections the authors provide further insights into the nature of the reading process and show what the implications of these insights are for teaching: what the reading process is; how we can delve more deeply into its nature; how we can identify some of the barriers to successful reading performance, and how we can take measures to help students overcome these barriers and to think effectively and interpret accurately in reading situations.*

# READING IS THINKING *

Emmett A. Betts

*The man who wrote the first compre-
hensive book in the field of reading
methodology here pinpoints the basic
needs in reading education. Using the
premise that reading is thinking, he de-
lineates a master plan to be used by competent teachers to develop these thinking skills and abilities in students. Then
he shows how these plans are used to
select teaching procedures for achieving the desired instructional goals.*

*1. What proof does the author ad-
vance to substantiate his claim that
reading is thinking?
2. What steps can be taken to teach
children how to think?
3. How can the teacher skillfully
plan the strategy for insuring the necessary conditions of learning?
4. What practices have resulted from
inadequate conceptions of the nature of
reading process?*

"MY CHILD can't read!" is a common complaint of parents. When
asked what they mean, parents explain that Johnny doesn't have the
necessary phonic skills to learn words. It is true that word (telling-the-child-
the-word) method of teaching beginning reading has produced many non-
readers and crippled readers. While phonic skills are essential in learning to
read, reading needs are not met by massive doses of isolated drill on phonics.

It is true that too many children do not know phonic and other word-
learning skills and are, therefore, handicapped in their reading. There is also
evidence that more of our pupils need help on *how to think* in a reading
situation. But too often parents believe their children can read when they are
merely pronouncing words.

Most parents can tell that a child is reading poorly or not at all when he
cannot identify written words. But it takes a competent teacher to identify
the six-year-old who repeats the exact words of an author to answer a question, the eight-year-old who does not relate names (antecedents) to pronouns, or the older student who has not learned to tell the difference between
facts and opinions. In short, professional competence is needed to assess the
learning needs of pupils and to guide their development into truly able
readers.

## STRATEGY

For developing thinking skills and abilities, highly competent teachers have
in mind a well-conceived master plan:

*How to identify and provide for individual differences in needs and levels*

---

* FROM *The Reading Teacher* (February 1959), pp. 146–151, reprinted with permission
of Emmett A. Betts and the International Reading Association.

*of achievement within the classroom* (1). Master teachers recognize the limitations of standardized tests for estimating an individual's (1) independent reading level, (2) teaching or instructional level, and (3) specific needs. For this reason, they make maximum use of systematic, informal observations of pupil behavior in reading situations. They know that a pupil cannot be taught how to think when the instructional material is so difficult he finger points his way slowly under each word or gives up in despair. They also know that the best reader in the class can realize his full potential only when he is dealing with interesting materials that challenge his thinking. Therefore, they *plan in advance* to organize their classes in different types of groups to provide equal learning opportunities for all pupils.

*How to identify and classify comprehension needs, as a basis for when and what to teach* (3, 13, 14). Competent teachers preplan—that is, map their strategy—to teach children how to think in different types of reading situations. They consider large groups of pupil needs:

1. Does the group have the necessary personal experiences for making a concept? Hal, for example, cannot estimate the distance from New York to San Francisco. During the discussion, however, he tells about a 500-mile trip to visit his grandmother, which he had helped to plan on a road map. His teacher helps him to use his personal experience with 500 miles to estimate on a map of the United States the 2600-mile airline distance. From this point, Hal continues to develop his concepts of space. Equally important, he takes new interests to reading.

2. Does the group use language effectively to deal with ideas (2)? Language serves at once to express and to shape our thoughts. In other words, we think with language. For this reason relatively simple language may be used to discuss everyday ideas, but complex language is used to discuss abstract ideas.

*Penny, ball, dictionary,* and *raccoon* are labels for things in the physical world; that is, we can point to *a ball* or *a dictionary. Roundness,* on the other hand, is a quality, or an abstraction. *Cottage, dwelling,* or *structure* can be used to represent different levels of abstraction. In life we can point to *a cottage* but not to *cottage,* to *a dwelling* but not to *dwelling,* to *a structure* but not to *structure.* At their successive levels of abstraction, *cottage, dwelling,* and *structure* are shorthand representations of increasingly complex concepts. It is with these nonverbal and verbal abstractions that we do our thinking. So, we teach pupils how to abstract and generalize, and help them develop an awareness of their use of abstractions.

*And, or, but, for,* etc., are connecting words which get their meanings from language. They connect or show relationships between ideas. The meanings of these words are taught, therefore, in their language settings.

*Ten, minute, mile,* and other definite terms can be interpreted when the pupil has certain concepts of quantity, size, etc. However, he may trip over *almost, long, soon,* and other indefinite terms, unless he has been given cause to think about their relative values.

To improve the interpretation of what he reads, the child is made aware of the important ways in which the meanings of words shift. For example, *talent* may mean "musical talent" or "the Biblical thirteen talents"; that is, two different things.

Comprehension is improved by an understanding of the structure or organization of language. Often the sentence gives a clue to the meaning of words. An appositional explanation ("Thor, the god of war,") may tip the scale of understanding. An index type of clue may explain a new term: "The *thralls* were the carpenters, the fence builders, the fagot carriers." Then again, a classification type of clue gives needed detail: "These people lived on the valley's neat farms and sowed barley, wheat, and other *grains.*" These and other types of context clues are considered in the teacher's strategy to improve thinking abilities.

Relationships between subject and predicate, between modifying and independent clauses, and between modifying phrases and other sentence elements are hazards to comprehension until the child understands them. Equally important are the meanings of different types of linking, separating, and enclosing punctuation, as, for example, when the dash is used to "direct the reader's attention backward" (15).

*How an author develops a story or presents information, as a basis for preparing a teaching plan.* Master teachers have learned that the best motivation for reading is the pupil's inner drive to learn—his questions and other expressions of purposes. Consequently, they plan to know each selection used for intensive directed reading activities with a group. This knowledge helps them take the group smoothly and promptly into the introduction of a well-written story or informational selection.

The introduction is usually a brief, stimulating setting for the story. For example, the title of Lee Wyndham's "Grandma's Ostrich" causes both children and adults to ask, "Why did Grandma have an ostrich?" This question is answered clearly and provocatively in the first few paragraphs.

When teachers *know* a selection, they can skillfully guide the pupils' reading from the introduction into the main body of it. After the pupils learn that Grandma "inherited" the ostrich from a defunct circus of which she was part owner, they always ask, "What did Grandma Jones do with the ostrich?" Reading to answer this question takes the group through the main part of the story.

When the pupils learn how Grandma Jones taught the ostrich to behave, they usually ask, "But will she be able to keep him?" As they read the conclusion of the story, they learn how a special event resolved the conflict, leaving them with a sense of satisfaction.

By *planning* their strategy before using a selection to develop skills, master teachers prepare themselves to develop (1) *interest,* (2) *phonic* and other word-learning skills, and (3) *thinking* abilities in the field of action—the guided reading of the story.

*How a teaching plan is organized as a basis for making the best use of teaching opportunities.* When competent teachers guide individualized reading they plan ahead to make accessible to their pupils (1) books at their *independent* reading levels (2) books that can be used to develop new interests and skills. When guiding a directed activity in a basic reader, however, they group the pupils so that the first reading is done at the teaching or instructional level, and the rereading can be done independently (1).

These master teachers know that a selection or a book challenges their pupils when it presents new learnings. They also know that when a child is frustrated by the difficulty of the material, interest wanes sharply and comprehension is defaulted.

When making systematic use of a basic textbook teachers familiarize themselves with the strategy of the authors—the organization of the teaching plans. First, they learn how the pupils are prepared for reading a selection, especially the attention given to developing interests and concepts to be taken to it.

Second, they note the kinds of suggestions given for guiding the first or silent reading of it. In this part of the plan they give special consideration to the ready availability of specific help on both phonic and thinking needs which may arise.

Third, they evaluate informal suggestions, study-book use, and other help given for rounding out learning experience so that growth is insured.

## TACTICS

One of the earmarks of a successful teacher is the ability to plan strategy for insuring the necessary conditions of learning. Skillful planning (1) places a premium on individual differences, (2) permits a sharp focus on the specific thinking needs of the pupils, (3) makes the most of the teaching opportunities in instructional material, and (4) gives a set for the wise selection and use of tactics or teaching procedures. Above all, the teacher is free to use the author's guide book with discretion.

Master teachers plan to help their children find out "what the author says"; that is, do literal reading. But they do much more: they plan to have the pupils learn how to "think about what the author says," to do critical reading (4).

In preparing the pupils for reading a selection in a story book, for a study-book activity, or for pursuing a major interest in some curriculum area, master teachers guide them into *thinking* about "what we know" and "what we want to know." The first step assesses their interests, attitudes, and concepts which they take to the activity. The second step heightens interest and establishes clear-cut purposes to guide their thinking. In short, the teacher uses sound tactics for starting the pupils on the road to critical thinking, to the considered evaluation of ideas and concepts.

With a general purpose and specific questions in mind, the pupils are ready to locate and evaluate sources of relevant information. This activity requires a consideration of the reputation of authors, dates of publication, etc., even when using basic readers and study books.

In surveying the materials the pupils are made aware of the difference between facts and opinions. They learn, for example, that the following are statements of fact because they are verifiable:

"In August of 1620, two vessels sailed from England, headed for the new world."

"The temperature in this room is 80 degrees Fahrenheit."

They will learn that a great many statements are opinions, or expressions of attitudes, and are not verifiable:

"You will have fun with it."

"This room is hot."

When pupils learn to discriminate between facts and opinions they tend to do less arguing and more discussing. Equally important, they are better prepared to select information *relevant* to their purposes.

In testing the relevance of material pupils learn to answer these questions: (1) What does the author say? (2) Is the statement a fact or an opinion? (3) Does the statement answer my question? (4) How can I use this statement? (5) What other help did the author give on my question?

Many kindergarten children learn to judge between highly relevant and totally irrelevant statements. As children learn how to think at succeeding school levels, they make closer judgments of the relevance between statements.

Judging the relevance of statements to purposes plays a major role in thinking. First, the pupil evaluates relevance of sub-points to each other and to the main points in an outline. Furthermore, he consistently uses questions or statements, sentences or phrases to parallel language structure with his ideas. Second, he evaluates relevance in visualizing both stories and information: sequences of important events in a story or experiment, organization of material on maps, charts, slides, etc. Third, he uses relevant facts in solving a mystery, in using the results of an experiment, in making social judgments, etc. That is, straight thinking is required for drawing conclusions from related facts or from cause-effect relationships (5, 10, 11, 12).

In following through on their strategy for teaching children how to think, teachers are confronted with a subtle, but potent, tactical situation: Attitudes. This situation can be summarized as follows.

1. The child's interpretation of a selection depends upon the attitudes he takes to it. Therefore, preparation for reading includes the assessment of attitudes toward the topic. Favorable attitudes increase comprehension, while unfavorable attitudes interfere with comprehension.
2. The child's attitudes influence recall. Favorable attitudes promote ease and vividness of recall, and unfavorable attitudes tend to produce hazy, confused ideas.

3. Favorable attitudes increase interest in a topic or a type of selection.
4. Individual attitudes are modified by peer discussions.

## In Summary

Contrary to popular opinion, children can be taught how to think. Their ability to think is limited primarily by their personal experiences and the uses they make of them in problem solving, in abstracting and generalizing to make concepts, in judging, and in drawing conclusions. Under competent teacher guidance children gradually learn to think, within the limits of their rates of maturation, or inner growth (6, 8, 9).

From available evidence it appears that children who have not learned to think far outnumber those who have not learned necessary phonic skills. (Both, of course, are crippled readers or non-readers!) Consider the number of children who can pronounce *fearless*, for example, but who think it means "afraid." How many children cannot divide ⅓ by 4 because they have merely memorized a meaningless rule about "inverting and multiplying"? Or, how many high school graduates cannot substract a minus 2 from a plus 10, because they have never related the mathematical process to the use of a thermometer? How many children can pronounce astronomical numbers and yet cannot estimate the coast-to-coast distance across the United States? How many children try to achieve variety of sentence structure by the mechanical rearrangement of sentences rather than by the careful consideration of the ideas they wish to express? The answers to these and related questions offer undisputed evidence of the need for teaching children how to think.

The mere pronunciation of words, the memorization of phonic or mathematic rules, and other emphases on rote memory and mechanics lead to the use of empty words. This false security in words leads to the acceptance of a carload of words without a single idea. The acceptance of word manipulation rather than the thinking about ideas is called *verbalism*. And verbalism can become a malignnant disease in education, dooming the would-be learner.

But there is hope, real evidence of progress in understanding the strategy and tactics of teaching children how to think. In the last ten years, four outstanding books have been published on the psychology of thinking. Writers of pedagogical textbooks in social studies, science, arithmetic, and reading have begun to apply the conclusions reached by psychologists. Lastly, it is highly significant that this issue of THE READING TEACHER is dedicated to the proposition that children can be taught how to think.

### REFERENCES

1. BETTS, EMMETT A. *Foundations of Reading Instruction.* New York: American Book Co., 1957 (Revised).
2. ——. "Reading: Semantic Approach." Reprinted from *Education*, May 1949. Ha rford, Pa.: Betts Reading Clinic.

3. ——. "Reading As a Thinking Process." Reprinted from *The National Elementary Principal*, September 1955. Haverford, Penna.: Betts Reading Clinic.
4. ——. "Research on Reading as a Thinking Process." Reprinted from *Journal of Educational Research*, September 1956. Haverford, Penna.: Betts Reading Clinic.
5. BINGHAM, ALMA. "Improving Children's Facility in Problem Solving." *Practical Suggestions for Teaching*, No. 16. New York: Teachers College, Columbia University, 1958.
6. BLAIR, ARTHUR WITT and BURTON, WILLIAM H. *Growth and Development of the Preadolescent*. New York: Appleton-Century-Crofts, 1951.
7. MORRIS, CHARLES. *Signs, Language and Behavior*. New York: Prentice-Hall, 1946.
8. PIAGET, JEAN. *The Construction of Reality in the Child*. New York: Basic Books, 1954.
9. ——. *The Language and Thought of the Child*. New York: Humanities Press, 1952.
10. RUSSELL, DAVID H. *Children's Thinking*. Boston: Ginn and Co., 1956.
11. VINACKE, W. EDGAR. *The Psychology of Thinking*. New York: McGraw-Hill, 1952.
12. WATTS, A. F. *The Language and Mental Development of Children*. Boston: D. C. Heath, 1944.
13. WESLEY, EDGAR BRUCE and ADAMS, MARY A. *Teaching Social Studies in Elementary Schools*. Boston: D. C. Heath, 1952.
14. WESLEY, EDGAR BRUCE. *Teaching Social Studies in High School*. Boston: D. C. Heath, 1950.
15. WHITEHALL, HAROLD. *Structural Essentials of English*. New York: Harcourt, Brace, 1956.

# WHY MANY CHILDREN AND YOUTH ARE RETARDED IN READING *

Anne McKillop

From time immemorial sages have warned men to develop the special talents of those individuals who have great potential. Studies of great historical figures, modern studies in the psychology of reading, and everyday observation point to such individuals who encounter real problems in developing the reading skills that help bring these talents to fruition. If teachers are to help their students who have reading problems, they must understand how

* FROM *Better Readers for Our Times*, William S. Gray and Nancy Larrick, editors, International Reading Association Conference Proceedings, I (New York: Scholastic Magazines, 1956), pp. 120–124, reprinted with permission of Anne McKillop and the International Reading Association.

these problems develop in younger children and take their toll of potential talent. McKillop explains masterfully how the characteristics of the complex reading process combine with personality and social factors to retard the reading progress of individuals.

1. Why does the author not set up an arbitrary criterion for retardation?

2. How does the author illustrate the point that reading is a complex perceptual task?

3. How would you explain to someone else the fact that reading is an abstract task?

4. Why are some children not taught to read?

5. How should the fact that reading is an interpersonal experience affect your teaching?

"RETARDED in reading" is a phrase that frightens parents and embarrasses youngsters. What does it mean and why is it being applied to so many youngsters and teen-agers today?

"Retarded in reading" means different things to different people. To some it means that a child is still reading a primer when all the other children in his class are reading a first-grade reader. To some it means that he obtained a test score a year, or a year and a half, or two years below the national norms. To others it means that "he is not reading up to his ability." To still others it means that he is not reading as well as he needs to in order to meet the demands put upon him. If we consider retardation to mean the inability to read as well as one might under certain desirable conditions, or if we think of the ever increasing demands for reading faced by citizens today, most adults could be considered retarded in reading.

Because of this uncertainty about the meaning of retardation and because of the limitations of tests, it does not seem wise to set up an arbitrary criterion for retardation. Differences in abilities or in developmental patterns make the process of learning to read too subtle to set up neat categories; and tests, at best, are crude tools which must be used with imagination and caution. A rigid criterion of retardation is not necessary. It is relatively easy to pick out those youngsters who are severely handicapped in school by their inability to read, and whose lack of ability in reading is out of line with their other abilities. Why are they having so much trouble?

Instead of seeking an answer to this question in a listing of the various environmental and personal characteristics that have been found to be associated with difficulty in learning to read, the answer can be found in an analysis of the nature of the reading process. From this analysis one can deduce the reasons why some children learn to read easily while others struggle with the process. It should be remembered, too, that there is seldom only *one* cause; usually there are several working together.

## READING IS A COMPLEX PERCEPTUAL TASK

First of all, reading is a complex perceptual task. It involves the ability to make fine visual discriminations; to focus clearly on relatively small stimuli;

to progress in a rigidly patterned sequence from left to right and from one line to the next; to take in large "eyefuls" at a glance; and, perhaps most difficult of all, to pick out certain words for emphasis, to know which ones to skip, which to note carefully. The complexity of the task was made vivid to me a few weeks ago when I participated with friends in a Seder, the Jewish passover ceremony. The *Haggadah* was in Hebrew; others at the table could read it; I could not. The symbols all looked alike to me. In my attempt to follow, I was constantly losing the place, starting on the wrong page and on the wrong side of the page. Later in the week I listened with sympathy to a six-year-old read from his reader.

Since reading is a complex perceptual task, youngsters will learn it most easily if by experience and endowment they are equipped to perceive verbal symbols accurately and quickly. Anything which might interfere with quick accurate perception of symbols may prove a handicap. Poor vision is an example. Within broad limits, the human eye is capable of amazing accommodations so that words may be seen clearly, but fatigue and distaste for the reading process may ensue.

Another interfering factor may be hearing loss which will certainly prove a handicap in learning to read by the usual methods. Most common, however, is lack of auditory discrimination. This lack of ability to hear the differences between sounds may have nothing to do with hearing loss, but may be related closely to the kind of English the child has heard at home and in his community. If, for example, he has grown up where a dialect is spoken, the language at school may sound almost as different as if it were a foreign tongue.

There are many things which we do not know about the perceptual abilities and skills involved in reading, especially in the beginning stages. We do know these abilities and skills are important.

## READING IS AN ABSTRACT TASK

A second characteristic of the reading task is that it is abstract. It involves the capacity to make generalizations, to apply knowledge learned in one situation to another, to see relationships not only between word parts but also between ideas. It is reasonable to expect that the slow learner, the child who is not so bright as the others, will have difficulty learning to read. He is handicapped in several ways. He does not catch on as quickly as the others; he needs more repetitions; he probably has a more limited vocabulary; he may have poorer speech patterns.

Most teachers expect that the slow learner, the child with an IQ on an individually administered intelligence test of 75 or 80, will have difficulty with reading. They are less likely to recognize that other children may also have trouble with the abstract aspects of reading. Difficulty is especially likely to arise if the teaching method relies heavily on abstract generalizations, or if the child is already under one or more handicaps.

## READING IS LEARNED

Another characteristic of the reading process is that it is learned. No one was born able to read. Even those bright youngsters who seem to have taught themselves to read did a lot of practicing with letters, sounds, words and pictures before they could put it all together into reading. As with many other skills, much can be learned about reading without formal instruction; but also, as with many other skills, much of this learning may be inefficient and even detrimental to a highly skilled performance. Good teaching can be an important factor in the acquisition of a high degree of reading skill; and conversely, poor teaching can be a severe handicap.

Many youngsters have not learned to read because they have not been taught. A child may have missed a great deal of school, have changed schools many times, or had many different teachers in any one year. The class may have been too large; the program too poorly organized. In the upper grades many of the more subtle reading skills such as skimming, picking out main ideas, selecting the important points to remember, may never have been demonstrated, analyzed, or practiced.

A youngster may have been exposed to enough teaching, but he may have failed to learn. The method, the materials, or the teacher may have been unimaginative, rigid, and unsuited to this child. His experiences may have been so limited that he has an inadequate fund of meanings; he may not see the connection between reading in school and anything that goes on in real life; he may not even see the relationship between the different parts of a reading program. Instruction in phonics may have been something quite apart from his reading. He may have been preoccupied with his own affairs. He may have been bored or fearful in school.

Even under the most desirable conditions, learning requires effort and concentration. If a youngster sees no use for this skill, he may fail to learn. Reading seems very important to teachers, but to many youngsters it is a rather silly business. It may be that the people the child knows and loves do little reading and they get along quite well. Why should he learn? He may be unable to concentrate on reading because he is so busy concentrating on other matters of more concern to him.

One youngster said, "My eyes go on, but my mind goes away—to my past." An eight-year-old put it this way, "Some days I'm just in a bad mood and I can't do anything. I still have a nightmare in my system."

## READING IS AN INTERPERSONAL EXPERIENCE

Reading is a complex perceptual task; it does require the ability to think abstractly; it must be learned; but there is more to it than this. Reading is an interpersonal experience. It involves a relationship between the reader and the author. It is essentially a form of communication. Communication may fail because the individual does not know the language or because he does

not care to communicate. A child may not know the language of reading if
he does not see it as important or if he does not understand the task. He may
not want to communicate if he is fearful or angry.

He may be fearful if he is sure he is "no good," if he is convinced that he
cannot do this difficult thing, cannot learn to read. One child expressed his
reaction vividly when his teacher asked what he did when he came to a word
he did not understand. "It feels bad inside," was his response. How can we
expect him to remember to break a word into syllables, to sound out each
part, or even to use a context clue when his energies are tied up in "feeling
bad"? A child who feels he is not really competent will feel even less competent before such an important and difficult task as reading.

The child may also be fearful of making mistakes, a necessary part of learning to read. This involves "taking a chance," "giving it a try." The six-year-old
must take a chance on a word—for example, is it "and" or "said"? The teen-
ager must take a chance on the main idea of the paragraph. No child ever
learned to read without taking these chances and without being wrong sometimes. And yet to some children "taking a chance" seems dangerous—you
could be wrong and being wrong is bad, and being bad is dangerous because
you might lose the affection and respect of those you love.

Being afraid to try may take other forms. Some children feel that success
achieved without effort, without making any mistakes, is the only kind that
counts in proving your worth. For them to try at all is almost equivalent to
failure. Unless you get it "first shot," it is a failure. These children cannot
really study; they either get it at once or they don't try, and they don't try
because they are so afraid of being wrong. Related to this is the tendency to
put forth the minimum effort—to study hardly at all and get a B. Then the
student feels, "If I got a B with that little work, look what would happen if
I worked!" But he never does because he might prove to himself and others
what he fears—that he couldn't really do it.

The unrealistic goals of some children are part of the picture of fear as a
barrier to communication. There is the child who will read only seventh-
grade books, nothing else; he must learn all at once without effort. This desire
for magic seems to reflect a deep fear of trying and failing. A child may have
to learn to fail before he can succeed. He has to be able to try, to take a
chance on a relationship with the printed word and thus on a relationship
with a person. He can only risk this attempt at relationship when he has had
satisfying relationships with real people.

Another aspect of taking a chance or trying involves curiosity and zest for
exploring and learning. Reading is the key to finding out about the world.
Of course, we assume that the child is curious, that he wants to find out,
wants to explore this new and exciting world, wants to learn about toads, and
rockets and knights of old. This desire to explore, this curiosity seems to be
an essential condition for learning to read. A child starts out with eager
curiosity, but sometimes he loses it. He may have asked too many questions

until adults told him to keep quiet. He may have asked questions at inappropriate times, about the wrong subjects. He may have explored too enthusiastically and been constantly warned about getting hurt. Parents may have let him know their embarrassment over his questions; they may have been abrupt, or may have laughed or may have given him untrue answers. He has become resigned to the feeling that questions don't have answers. He may have learned to feel that it isn't safe to be curious and actively exploratory—you might get hurt, or people might get angry with you. He is afraid of his own curiosity because it seems to lead to trouble. In this way he is afraid to enter into the communication process, to ask questions of the authors.

The fear of being wrong is the other side of the individual's desire to be always right and perfect. Many children have not learned to differentiate between being partly wrong and being all wrong. An eight-year-old reads "massacred" for "murdered." We say he is wrong and do not give him credit for having kept the sense of the story and been almost right. He may feel that no one credits him with his attempts to use previous knowledge, that we aren't interested in how the story turns out. Often he gives up.

In addition to being afraid of mistakes, a child may be afraid of success. This sounds impossible, but success to a child may be something to be avoided and failure something to be sought. The child who feels "bad," "wicked" or "guilty," may feel that he does not deserve success, that failure is his just punishment, that he has no right to communicate with others. Sometimes failure in reading represents a form of self-punishment.

A youngster may not wish to enter into the interpersonal experience of reading if he is angry. He may be angry at grown-ups. He may see them as people to be outwitted. One nine-year-old memorized the location of all the type bars on the typewriter rather than learn touch typing. He was outwitting the teacher! Another eighth-grade youngster said about a hated teacher, "I don't like her; she don't like me. I ain't goin' to do no work at all." It is true—this a cut-off-your-nose-to-spite-your-face technique, but it is one that children often use. Thus, failure to learn to read becomes a child's secret weapon, one he is not fully aware of using but which he may use, nonetheless, with telling effect.

A youngster may be angry, too, because he feels smothered, feels that he has no life of his own, that others would take over his life if he would let them. This may, of course, be true. Parents may have made all the decisions for him and may have fed off him emotionally, taking his achievement as their own so that he may feel he has no say in his own life. However, he must retain some autonomy and he can do it in the area of reading. Here he is boss. Perhaps he can maintain this self-integrity only by not reading. He will willingly pay the high cost of adult and peer disapproval, of inability to find out about interesting things, rather than give up his own right to determine his life, rather than capitulate to the enemy.

It is possible for a child to be so angry that he is afraid of his own anger, the roots of which are to be found in his early experiences. He has to keep a tight hold on himself or else anger would come out in violent form. Reading involves being active, making an aggressive attack on the page and this may be too much for him. He cannot do this lest his aggression get out of bounds. He dare not communicate if he is too angry.

A child's reading is as truly an expression of all that he is as his way of walking or talking, as his interests or his friendships. Anything which influences him may influence his reading. His general health, for example, or his rate of basal metabolism; his inability to attend to the task at hand, or his identification with a non-reading hero. There is seldom only one reason why any child does not read easily. It is more often a series of difficulties with one serving as the straw that broke the camel's back. Many children, for example, miss a good deal of school, need glasses, don't hear very well, and yet learn to read easily; while comparatively short absences, or a slight visual or auditory handicap may disrupt the performance of others. It is not the objective situation that is important. It is what it means to the child.

## WHY READING CAUSES SO MUCH TROUBLE

One more question remains. Why reading? Why don't any of the other tool subjects cause so much trouble? No one knows the answer, but what we know about the reading process provides some clues. Reading is the most personal and least structured of the forms of communication which depend upon printed symbols. Spelling may involve more specifically perceptual abilities and skills; arithmetic is less personal. In none of the other tool subjects do one's feelings about people and about communicating with them enter in so clearly.

Then, reading often symbolizes growing up in our society. We say to children, "Wait until you get big enough to read for yourself." Visitors to the home of a seven-year-old often ask, "Can you read yet?" The youngster soon comes to see that this is an unusually important skill, one which takes a long step toward grown-upness. This is fine if the youngster wants to grow up, but if he doesn't, and there are a few who do not, he cannot afford to learn to read. Most children cannot verbalize their fears about growing up, but one little girl said, "I don't want to learn to read. I don't want to be a mommy. I want to be a little girl. Little girls can't read." The other tool subjects do not carry this symbolic meaning.

Reading, too, is considered an unusually important skill in our society. Some of this pre-eminence is based on reality. A person who cannot read finds many doors closed in his face. But the anxiety of parents and teachers goes beyond the realistic. It is as if reading symbolizes success to the child and his parents. If he learns to read easily, it appears that his success in school and life is assured; if he fails, then, as one mother put it, "He can't never be nothing but a no-good." The mother of a three-year-old called to ask for tutoring for her child. She said, "I want her to get a good start and not be one of those retarded readers." Anything upon which so much depends is bound to be fraught with difficulty.

Why are so many children and teen-agers retarded in reading? For as many reasons as there are children.

# NEW APPROACHES TO THE STUDY OF INTERPRETATION IN READING *

William S. Gray

*Definitions of key concepts in any field guide the thinking about related concepts in the field. In the field of reading, different superstructures of teaching methodology rise from the diverse definitions of the nature of the reading process. Naïve definitions equate reading with pronunciation. It is more accurate to think of reading as understanding, as developing meaning, rather, i.e., of comprehending. Comprehension as a generic term for understanding. can be divided into (1) literal comprehension of ideas clearly stated in the text and (2) interpretation of ideas, which involves such activities as inferring (reading between the lines), drawing conclusions, and organizing ideas.*

*Gray rapidly sketches the recent history of the study of interpretation in reading, beginning with Thorndike's 1917 study. After showing the advances that have been made and then lament-*

*ing the drawbacks of the factorial studies of interpretation, he launches into the discussion of studies which aim to uncover the dynamics of interpretation through the use of retrospective and introspective research techniques.*

*1. Have factorial analysis techniques added much knowledge of the basic factors in interpretation?*

*2. Explain the values of each of the newer techniques for studying factors in interpretation.*

*3. To more fully understand the introspective technique, have someone type a 500-word news story that you have not read, leaving a blank space for every tenth word. Verbalize your thought processes as you attempt to fill in the blanks. Record your verbal responses on tape, and have them typed. Analyze your responses.*

*4. Study several of your students in a similar way.*

INTEREST in improved techniques in the study of interpretation in reading stems from three facts: the increasing demand which current life makes on readers for breadth and depth of interpretation; failure to increase ability to interpret in many recent reading improvement programs in colleges and at the adult level; and slow progress during the last two decades in securing a

---

* REPRINTED FROM the *Journal of Educational Research*, LII (October 1958), pp. 65–67, by permission of the publisher and the author.

more penetrating understanding of the nature of the interpretive process. Before describing recent approaches to the problem it may be helpful to view the problem briefly in historical perspective.

One of the earliest efforts to identify objectively the processes involved in understanding what is read was reported by Thorndike[1] in 1917 as a result of detailed studies of children's errors in sentence and paragraph reading. On the basis of the evidence secured, he concluded, first, that the understanding of a paragraph involves the same sort of "organization and analytic action of ideas as occurs in thinking of supposedly higher sorts"; second, that in effective reading the mind selects, represses, softens, emphasizes, correlates and organizes "all under the influence of the right mental set or purpose or demand"; and third, that "the fishing around in the text" for something to use in answering a question "and its use without reorganization is one of the most debased forms of reasoning—selective thinking—which school work shows."

A second milestone was established by Judd and Buswell[2] in a study of different types of silent reading. On the basis of eye movement records they concluded that the mental processes in reading vary with the kind of material read, its difficulty and the purpose for which it is read. They also distinguished between silent reading for "understanding and appreciation" and "analytical study". They pointed out that as long as instruction fails to distinguish between different types of reading "pupils will adopt a purely incidental method". Since most of them are uncritical of their methods improvement will be slow and more or less accidental unless guidance is provided.

Stimulated by such findings, teachers made vigorous efforts during the twenties and thirties to improve comprehension. At least four procedures were used widely: first, the *use of questions*, both fact and judgment; second, detailed studies of the form, organization, and structure of the passages read, which led ultimately to questions concerning the value of a knowledge of grammar and syntax; third, the procedures recommended by semanticists who pointed out that meanings of words are influenced by the context in which they are used, by the author's purpose and mood, and by the kind of material read—historical, scientific, emotive. They also differentiated sharply between literal and implied meanings and emphasized the importance of interpreting passages in the light of their broader context. A fourth procedure consisted of vigorous training in reading for various purposes.

Paralleling these developments, research specialists sought to identify through the use of various correlation techniques the factors which exert most influence on comprehension. As early as 1924, Hilliard[3] reported the results of a detailed study which showed that intelligence and meaning vocabulary are more closely related to comprehension than any other factors studied. The third factor in order of importance was ability to organize, which implied capacity to grasp relationships and to reconstruct ideas. During the next two decades many similar studies were reported. Various summaries of findings led to the conclusion that many factors are involved in comprehension which are related but not identical. As a result, pointed questions arose concerning the nature of the techniques that would discriminate more sharply among factors.

The technique which seemed most promising at the time was factorial analysis. Since 1930 more than a score of studies using this technique have been reported. A striking example was Davis' study [4] in 1944 in which the following factors were identified: "knowledge of word meaning"; "ability to reason", that is "to infer meanings and to weave together several statements"; "ability to identify the writer's intent, purpose, or point of view"; "ability to grasp the detailed statements in a passage"; and "knowledge of literary devices and techniques". Such findings appeared to be very promising until Thurstone used a different procedure on Davis' data and found only one common factor. More recent investigators also report that they found only one common factor in addition to meaning vocabulary.

On the basis of findings to date, the use of factorial analysis has not greatly advanced our knowledge of the basic factors in interpretation nor methods of improving competence in thoughtful reading. Whereas the basic methods used may be mathematically unique and valid they do not provide methods of interpreting the data on which all can agree. Furthermore, the analyses made have not gone beyond the answers to the questions in the tests used. As a result, it has become necessary to search for other techniques which are more productive. Some investigators have adopted the procedures used by Thorndike, to which reference was made earlier, and are studying the errors and difficulties of children and adults in reading assigned passages. A recent study by Black [5] of the difficulties which students who are preparing to teach in England face in understanding what they read illustrates both the technique used and the nature of the findings.

Other investigators are now making use of retrospective and introspective techniques which were first used by Huey [6] in studies of the interpretive process in reading more than a half century ago. In 1953, Swain [7] reported the results of a study among college students in which introspection was used in identifying the conscious thought processes involved in answering questions based on the passages read. She sought to find out among other things whether attention was focused primarily on the analysis of language or on the reconstruction of meaning. Her findings when compared with the results of other studies indicated that a reader, varying with his level of competence, may focus most of his attention on word perception, on the analysis of language in identifying the author's meaning, or on the restructuring of meanings in the light of his experiences, interest or specific purposes. A second study which used both introspection and retrospection was made by Piekarz.[8] She secured recordings of interviews with high level and low level readers in the sixth grade following the silent and oral reading of selected passages. During the interviews, each pupil verbalized his thoughts and feelings concerning what he had read and answered thirty questions, the answers to which involved nine aspects of interpretation.

An analysis of the responses showed that the higher level readers made a greater variety and number of responses, implying greater penetration. Their responses were more evenly divided over three broad areas, namely, literal meanings, implied meanings, and evaluations. They tended to remain objective and impersonal in their interpretations, to use their general background in enriching the author's meaning, to restrict their responses to the text, and to refer to their personal experiences only in proving a point. Finally, they seemed to be able to view the selection impersonally and to see both sides of an issue objectively. Even though they possessed strong feelings toward the ideas presented, they were able to control their reactions and to distinguish clearly between their own opinion and those of the author.

The lower level readers, on the other hand, limited their responses to literal meanings and gave only passing attention to implied meanings and critical reactions. They had difficulty in maintaining an objective attitude and in distinguishing between their own and the author's ideas. For example, many of the words read stimulated the recall of experiences that led them far beyond the author's intended meanings. The evaluations expressed stemmed from an emotional rather than an intellectual base and were highly personal in nature.

Using an interview and retrospective techniques with adults, Gray and Rogers [9] secured evidence which clearly supported the conclusions of Piekarz. Of special significance was the fact that the mature readers had mastered the skills of word recognition and those involved in a clear grasp of meaning and concentrated on the evaluation of the ideas read and their reconstruction into patterns that served their purpose. In this connection each reader exhibited compelling interests, or indeed, a central point or radix which influenced directly the nature of the interpretations made. To a surprising extent the evaluation and reconstruction of ideas were directed by their concern for efficient living and a better society.

In an effort to gain added insight concerning the processes involved in problem solving while reading, Bloom and Broder [10] made use of introspections with college students. They found, first, that success in problem solving is usually accompanied by tension followed by relaxation when a solution is found. The tension usually varies with the complexity of the problem. They found, second, that as individuals give attention to a problem, certain aspects and details appeared to stand out and to occupy the foreground of attention while other details remained in the background. Four characteristics of this foreground-background relationship were identified: the speed with which they were recognized, the strength with which they could be held, the amount of detail which could be brought to the foreground, and their degree of relevance. Finally, three major steps leading to the attack on a problem were identified. First, the reader attempts to dispose of unfamiliar items; second, he selects a point that stands out as a possible starting point; and finally he attempts to limit the problem. This last step was found to be more characteristic of superior than of poor students.

The studies to which references have been made provide clear evidence of the value of the use of retrospective and introspective techniques in studying interpretation in reading. They reveal as clearly as any technique used thus far the nature of the thinking involved. By securing recordings of the reader's responses, it is possible to analyze them in as much detail as often as may be desirable. The subject can also be re-examined at points in order to verify or extend conclusions.

The use of introspection and retrospection can be adapted to the study of various kinds of reading situations. For example, Jenkinson [11] has just completed a study in which blanks were left in the passages read, the demands made on the reader being similar to those in an expanded completion test. However, the blanks occurred at strategic points which made it possible to study the influence of selected aspects of a passage on its interpretation. Letton is now completing an illuminating Ph.D. study of the interpretative process when reading poetry. Rogers is well launched on a study at the high-school level which aims to compare the interpretative processes in a typical structured assignment situation and in free reading, using equivalent passages with respect to difficulty and human interest appeal.

The foregoing discussion should not be interpreted as critical of techniques that have been used widely in the past in the study of interpretation. As indicated earlier, the study of difficulties and failures of readers, using the Thorndike or Black techniques, can be very illuminating. The chief aim has been to call attention to another approach which merits careful considerations in planning studies of the interpretive process in reading.

### REFERENCES

1. THORNDIKE, EDWARD L. "Reading as Reasoning: A Study of Mistakes in Paragraph Reading," *Journal of Educational Research,* VIII, June 1917, pp. 323–332.
2. JUDD, CHARLES H. and BUSWELL, GUY T. *Silent Reading: A Study of Its Various Types,* Supplementary Education Monographs. University of Chicago, 1922.
3. HILLIARD, GEORGE H. *Probable Types of Difficulties Underlying Low Scores in Comprehension Tests.* University of Iowa Studies in Education, Vol. II, No. 6, 1924.
4. DAVIS, FREDERICK B. "Fundamental Factors of Comprehension in Reading," *Psychometrika,* IX, September 1944, pp. 185–197.
5. BLACK, E. L. "The Difficulties of Training College Students in Understanding What They Read," *British Journal of Educational Psychology,* XXIV, February 1954, pp. 17–31.
6. HUEY, EDMUND B. *The Psychology and Pedagogy of Reading.* New York: The Macmillan Company, 1912, Chapter VIII.
7. SWAIN, EMELIZA. *Conscious Thought Processes Used in the Interpretation of Reading Materials,* Unpublished Ph.D. dissertation. The University of Chicago, 1953.
8. PIEKARZ, JOSEPHINE A. "Getting Meaning From Reading," *Elementary School Journal,* LVI, March 1956, pp. 303–309.
9. GRAY, WILLIAM S. and ROGERS, BERNICE. *Maturity in Reading: Its Nature and Appraisal.* Chicago: University of Chicago Press, 1956.

10. BLOOM, BENJAMIN S. and BRODER, LOIS J. *Problem-Solving Processes of College Students.* Chicago: University of Chicago Press, 1950.
11. JENKINSON, MARION. *Selected Processes and Difficulties of Reading Comprehension,* Unpublished Ph.D. dissertation. University of Chicago, 1957.

# SPEED, COMPREHENSION AND POWER IN READING *

Jack A. Holmes

*In addition to supplying some cogent remarks on rates of reading, Holmes reports on one of a series of research studies based on his "Substrata-Factor Theory of Reading." This theory has evoked a considerable number of doctoral and post-doctoral studies in reading. In addition, it has evoked some criticism. One purpose of this paper is to outline his theory, and then report some experimental findings. After discussing these strata that underlie power in reading, he explains several implications of his theory for teaching.*

*1. How can a person gain a working knowledge of reading?*

*2. How is speeded reading accomplished according to the theory of the author?*

*3. Which two factors contribute most to power of reading? Which subfactor seems to be most prevalent?*

*4. (a) Many information books exist for primary level children. (b) Basal readers have specific teaching purposes. (c) Herbartian and modern psychology tell us of various teaching-learning modes. In the light of this information, explain the relevance or purpose of the statement regarding the amount of information in primary readers.*

*5. What implications for the teaching of reading do you see in this research?*

## INTRODUCTION *

SPEEDED reading is demanded by the tempo of the times, but the keen appreciation of crucial ideas, the understanding of those great concepts which have taken the human race thousands of years to evolve, need not, indeed cannot, be fully grasped as one's speed approaches its limit.

* This paper draws heavily upon a research study done by the writer and Dr. Harry Singer, "The Substrata Factor Theory: Substrata Differences Underlying Reading Ability in Known Groups." This study was a Cooperative Research Project supported by the University of California, the United States Office of Education, and the Carnegie Foundation of New York.

* FROM *Problems, Programs, and Projects in College-Adult Reading,* Emery P. Bliesmer and Ralph C. Staiger, editors, Eleventh Yearbook of the National Reading Conference (Milwaukee: The National Reading Conference, Inc., 1962), pp. 6–14, reprinted with permission of Jack A. Holmes and the National Reading Conference, Inc.

The secret of good reading lies in the ability to know when and how to change pace. The mundane material concerning the commerce of life may well be read quickly; but when one comes to the crux of the message, or when one fortuitously encounters one of those fountainhead concepts from which ideas flow, then one must deliberately drink the delightful draught until the full meaning has been drained. Even then such passages are well-springs that may be read again and again, each time affording the reader a little deeper insight, a greater understanding, a new zest for life!

Indeed, the deepest satisfactions come not when one is able to read a book in 30 minutes flat (the goal stressed by some teachers today), but rather when one chances upon a beautifully written passage carrying so much meaning, sparkle, and conviction that it verily sings—as when great poetry clarifies the meaning of life and causes one to bring his value system into closer harmony with the realities of the universe.

My first point, then, is this: If one *already knows* how to read, his *rate of comprehension* of the printed page can be increased enormously by persistent practice on easy material over an extended period of time. This is all to the good. Nevertheless, as one pushes his speed above the four to eight *hundred* words per minute mark into the next higher order of magnitude, say two to eight *thousand* words per minute, the reader simply rides in on the crest of the wave. As his eyes race down the page it is true that he may learn to catch the gist of the story; but the beauty of the syntax, the style, the sting, the twinkle, the music in the well-turned phrase, the technical explanation, or logic of a philosophical discussion cannot be truly pondered, grasped, and appreciated. One may gain a knowledge of a subject by speeded reading, but he cannot gain a *working knowledge* of it. To achieve such a working knowledge, i.e., technical mastery of scientific material, or high appreciation for the music and sense of great literature, one must read not for comprehension alone, but for *power*—and it is just this *power of reading* that I wish to discuss with you in my next go-around. That is, what *is* it that makes for power in reading; and what exactly is meant by the word "power" when used in this context?

## THE THEORY

It was my intent, a moment ago, to imply that theory and fact can be brought together to explain just what it is that makes one student differ from another in his ability to read with what I term "power." To this end, then, I will first outline the basic essentials of the Substrata-Factor Theory and, second, report some of the findings of an experiment we have recently completed in our labs at the University of California.

Figure 1 presents a diagrammatic model of a working-system for power of reading. The large ball at the apex represents power of reading, the lines-of-support umbellating out from it represent psychoeducational associations between power of reading and the substrata factors at Level I.

Holding to the same logic, the Theory hypothesizes that underlying each of the subabilities discovered at Level I, we may expect to find even more fundamental ones at Level II. Below such secondary abilities, we might further expect to find a set of tertiary elements.

The Substrata-Factor Theory of Reading is concerned with the way the mind *mobilizes* sets of *sub-abilities* (which we will refer to as elements) into an ordered arrangement or hierarchy. In varying degrees, according to their existing strengths, the elements of this hierarchy simultaneously stimulate and reinforce each other. They compare and contrast incoming information with existing knowledge leading to a new conception, a new working knowledge, gained from the reading material. This complex ability, with its various elements, we have sought to measure and have termed it "power of reading."

The Theory holds that the auditory, visual, and kinesthetic components of incoming information are ordered and stored in localized cell-assemblies in the brain. Individuals differ in the degree to which they tend to use one of these input channels over others. At the high school level approximately two-thirds of the students are predominantly visually minded; somewhat *less* than one-third will learn better through their auditory senses, and a small percentage (mostly boys) must rely heavily upon the proprioceptive or kinesthetic senses as their most efficient input channel. This part of the Theory gives us the key as to why the majority of a class learn quickly and easily by the Look and Say method, why some children appear to thrive under a system that stresses phonics, and why still others who fail to learn by either of these methods are, in fact, able to learn to read by Fernald's tracing method.

In the brain, sets of these cell-assemblies form centers, each with its distinctive function. Oversimplified:

1. The function of one center is to store the memory traces from visual impulses which arise when viewing a concrete object.

2. The function of a second visual center is to store *symbolic representations* of the *ideas about* concrete objects, relationships, or other ideational abstractions. Here, then, is where words are perceived, registered, categorized, and filed for future reference and recall.

3. A third center stores auditory impulses which carry information conveyed by *spoken* language.

4. A fourth center stores kinesthetic impressions from tactile and muscle sensations. The location of these centers in the brain is a long-established anatomical fact.

### Comprehension

According to the Substrata-Factor Theory, as a result of the on-going cerebral activity during the act of perception (as in reading), the details deposited in the separate centers are now reassociated as faithfully coded representations of the objects themselves. In other words, during reading coded audio-visual and kinesthetic impressions derived from the descriptions of concrete objects are reassembled in the mind—this is comprehension.

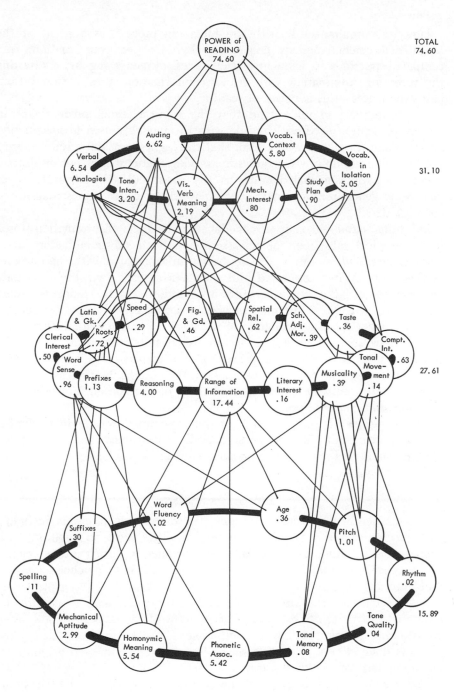

FIGURE 1.
Ping-Pong Model of Working System.

*Power*

However, simultaneously with the foregoing process, as a result of the heightened cerebral activity engendered by increased concentration, conceptual abstractions are wrought by the process of comparing and contrasting the incoming information with relevant information already stored from past experiences—this is power of reading.

It is important to understand that the input channel predominant in sensory perception need *not* coincide with the modality used in imagination and thinking. In fact, it would seem that the highest reasoning tends toward not the conjuring up of visual, auditory, or kinesthetic images, but of abstract conceptualizations mediated either as (a) subarticulated verbalizations, or (b) vague generalizations unattached to words or coded representations of concrete details.

*Substrata factors*, then, are psychoeducational subsets of information stored in neurological subsystems of cell-assemblies. Such substrata factors stand ready to be *mobilized* into a *working-system* in accordance with the purposes of the reader. When connected into such a working-system, each substrata factor exerts an influence on all other information centers. Hence, the more efficient and the greater the number of associations among the substrata factors, the higher the *interfacilitation* of the total working-system. The explanation of how speeded reading is accomplished rests, therefore, not in the persistent practice of reading easy material, but in persistent pressure forcing the individual to increase the number of the interfacilitating associations. This, in turn, results in a heightened activity of perception, integration, abstraction, and generalization.

This being the Theory, the task of the experiment was to find whether such a model could, in fact, be statistically constructed; and, if so, what abilities would be found making up such substrata levels.

## The Experiment

In the experiment, 400 students were given some 56 separate tests, including such diverse elements as primary mental abilities, linguistic abilities, perceptual abilities, study methods skills and attitudes, and such interest factors as are recorded by the Kuder interest inventory. A host of psycho-sociological problem areas were also assessed with respect to their ability to explain individual differences in the criteria, Speed and Power of Reading. These variables were analyzed by the Substrata-Factor Analysis. Time does not allow us to go into the statistical details or methodology. Suffice it to say that when this was done, a very interesting set of abilities were indicated as substrata factors underlying Power of Reading.

Figure 2 presents the results diagrammatically, and it will be seen that under Power of Reading we were able to account for 75 per cent of the variance as indicated distributed among the seven following variables: Vocabulary in

Context, 16%; Mechanical Interest, 1%; Study Planning and Deliberation, 1%; Visual Verbal Meaning, 6%; Verbal Analogies, 16%; Auding Ability, 16%; Tone Intensity, 3%; and Vocabulary in Isolation, 16%, at Level I.

It is strikingly apparent that Power of Reading is greatly dependent upon a knowledge of words and the concepts that they symbolize. Notice that Vocabulary in Isolation, Vocabulary in Context, and Visual Verbal Meaning are all different phases of the vocabulary domain. Verbal Analogies itself is reasoning through the manipulation of verbal concepts. Auding ability has to do with listening comprehension of human speech. So it is definite that at the first level the most essential element of Power of Reading is a knowledge of the meaning of words and the ability to manipulate the concepts behind these auditorily and visually perceived verbal symbols on the printed page. (This point favors the Look-Say method.)

As shown by Fig. 2 at Level II, underlying the various forms of vocabulary are a host of other factors such as Range of Information, Computational, Literary, and Clerical Interest, Word Sense, Reasoning, Prefixes, Latin and Greek Roots, School Adjustment, Speed of Addition, Spatial Relations, Figure and Ground, Musical Taste, Musicality, and Tonal Movement.

As shown by Fig. 2, Pitch, Phonetic Association, Homonyms, Age, and Mechanical Aptitude all combine to account for 38% of Range of Information at Level III. Now I think this is an important result because, of all the elements, Range of Information is the most ubiquitous. Like Reasoning, it underlies the basic verbal elements that enter into Power of Reading at Level I. For instance, it accounts for over half, 52%, of Vocabulary in Isolation; 43% of Vocabulary in Context; 36% of Auding Ability; 38% of Verbal Analogies; and 16% of Visual Verbal Meaning. And yet, we are able to account for only about 38% of Range of Information itself by the more fundamental factors in our matrix. This would lead us to believe that the information represented by this particular substrata factor is information of a specific sort and goes way beyond the mechanics of the language itself. And, if I might say so, this gives us definite proof that those who have criticized our basal readers of the last thirty years have some justification. That is to say, there has been very little real information given to the student in most of our primary readers up to the present time.

IMPLICATIONS

Most of the basal readers have been a Dick and Jane, a Bob and Barbara type of chit-chat, centered on exercises which will increase vocabulary. But that vocabulary has been of a very low order and tied to the everyday concepts the child has already learned around the house. What I am saying is that these concepts do not give the child a chance to stretch his mind. He knows nothing more in terms of information, of new knowledge, after having read through a set of primary and elementary textbooks in *reading* than he did before he started, except that he now knows how to read a certain high-

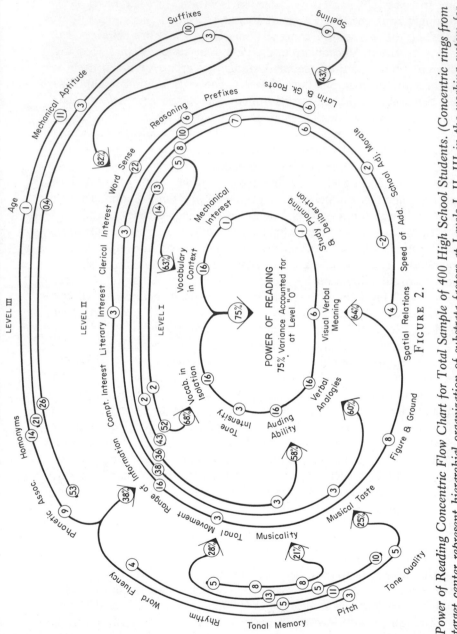

Power of Reading Concentric Flow Chart for Total Sample of 400 High School Students. (Concentric rings from target center represent hierarchial organization of substrata factors at Levels I, II, III in the working system for power of reading. The discs give per cent of variance accounted for in each substrata factor's line of support. Holmes 1961)

FIGURE 2.

frequency list of words with some fluency. This in itself is good, but the fact that he does not get those basic concepts, or ideas, or information which will help him expand his mind when he begins to read in order to learn is a valid criticism of this type of reader.

Perhaps here we can stress the difference between learning to read and reading to learn. I think that we are prolonging the initial period of learning to read beyond the time that is profitable. Learning to read must also, sooner or later, begin to take on the concepts of reading to learn, because later reading depends upon prior learning, and that prior learning is not only a matter of the right pronunciation or visual identification of words, but also (and more important) the mental manipulation of abstractions and an increased store of pertinent information.

If we were to return, as many people are now suggesting, to the *McGuffey* type of reader, we would not be much better off. There is so much in the McGuffey Readers that would be unacceptable to most moderns. For instance, a class system is definitely implied. There is the Horatio Alger type of story told over and over again, which is really not applicable today. While we admire the fortitude of the person in the story, teachers know better than to suggest that hard work on the job is a substitute for education. We know very well that times have changed and that many of the concepts expounded in the McGuffey Readers are no longer practical or tenable. Furthermore, while its code of ethics is unassailable, the manner of its presentation is effusively sentimental.

A hope for the future, in answer to this dilemma, is to introduce into our programs reading textbooks that have not only a graded list of words, but a graded list of *concepts*. And these concepts must become deeper, more difficult and more complex than we have previously thought possible for children to learn. I maintain, I think with some justification, that children are more capable than many educators would have us believe. For as they begin to understand more, as the reading material becomes more meaningful, their interest and power of reading will increase.

One bright spot in the developmental reading in the modern curriculum is the introduction of science and modern geography, history, and social studies into the elementary school classrooms. We must have, I think, more of these subjects in our *reading* textbooks; that is, we need the technical words that will carry over into the so-called solid disciplines, keyed to the major concepts that the child must know in order to read in these fields. And the reading teacher is in a strategic position to help the child expand and consolidate those substrata elements involved in power of reading, of which the most important is Range of Information.

REFERENCES

1. Holmes, Jack A. "The Substrata-Factor Theory of Reading: Some Experimental Evidence." In J. Allen Figurel, ed., *New Frontiers in Reading,*

International Reading Association Conference Proceedings, Volume 5, 1960. New York: Scholastic Magazine, 1960, pp. 115–121.

2. HOLMES, JACK, and SINGER, HARRY. *The Substrata-Factor Theory: Substrata Factor Differences Underlying Reading Ability in Known-Groups at the High School Level.* United States Office of Education Monograph Series, 1962. (Based upon final experimental reports covering Contract No. 538, SAE-8176, and No. 538A, SAE-8660. U. S. Dept. of Health, Education, and Welfare, 1961.)

# SOME THOUGHTS ON READING COMPREHENSION *

Albert J. Kingston, Jr.

A *person's definition of reading comprehension conditions his approach to the teaching of reading and to teaching in general. In this article Kingston attempts to define reading (comprehension) more accurately by relating aspects of verbal behavior to reading. In contrasting communicating through the printed word with communicating orally he shows the comparative inflexibility of the written word and, consequently, the importance of the symbols used in the transmission and reception of the printed word. Finally, Kingston discusses the type of comprehension required in reading tests compared with degrees of comprehension in an actual reading selection.*

*1. How do you interpret the author's "working definition" of reading?*

*2. What differences do you see between oral and written communication?*

*3. Why is it important to be cognizant of these differences?*

*4. What are the implications of the author's ideas on comprehension and testing for those who evaluate reading behavior?*

IN PREVIOUS reports the writer has suggested that the term "reading comprehension" is a vague and poorly defined concept. (1; 2) In a later discussion it was suggested that an analytical approach to the study of the reading act might be fruitful. (3) This paper is designed to relate certain theories and findings concerning broad aspects of verbal behavior to the concept of reading comprehension.

Perhaps a suitable starting point would be to develop a working definition of reading. The following definition seems to be sufficient for the purposes of discussion. Reading is a process of communication by which a message is

---

* FROM *Problems, Programs and Projects in College-Adult Reading,* Emery P. Bliesmer and Ralph C. Staiger, editors, Eleventh Yearbook of the National Reading Conference (Milwaukee: The National Reading Conference, Inc., 1962, pp. 20–23, reprinted with permission of Albert J. Kingston, Jr., and the National Reading Conference, Inc.

transmitted graphically between individuals. This rather simple definition implies that certain percepts are conveyed from one individual to another by use of a written, as contrasted to oral, form. With this simplified definition we can reconcile a number of the common uses of the word in educational circles. Note, for example, that we talk about "reading pictures," "reading graphs and tables," "reading maps and globes," and "reading stories." Our definition also implies that the sophisticated reader can even successfully read an abstract painting. One important condition exists and must be met, however, before communication can take place. It is axiomatic that both the transmitter and the receiver of any message agree on the meanings of any symbols employed. Perhaps the difficulties many of us have in reading abstract paintings is due to our lack of knowledge about the symbols employed by the painter.

The important role of the transmitter (i.e., the writer) is recognized by reading specialists who have utilized such concepts or methods as readibility formulas, the assessment of vocabulary difficulty, examination of the lexical nature of the writing, and the abstractness of the content of the passage. The realization that such factors may hamper message transmittal is implicit in our traditional basal reading programs with their stress on graded vocabulary and carefully introduced word recognition skills. Unfortunately the reading specialist who functions at the college or adult level tends to pay less attention to the role of the writer and the symbols he employs to encode his message. Although there remains a tendency to give lip service to awareness of the importance of the level of vocabulary and the lexical structure of the writing, reading comprehension is largely regarded as the degree to which a reader understands what has been written. Unlike ordinary oral communication between two individuals, in reading there is no feedback to the transmitter. Most of us who lecture or talk as part of our livelihood learn to adjust our deliveries and language as we become aware that our messages are not getting through. Unfortunately the writer usually has no way of being aware that his reader does not understand.

The lack of flexibility inherent in graphic methods of communication then places an added emphasis on the importance of the symbols used in transmission and reception. Symbolic logicians long have pointed out that words are symbols which have arbitrary significance. Men must agree on the meanings of words if they are to be able to communicate by using them. Shakespeare's comment that "a rose by any other name would smell as sweet" shows insight into this condition. We learn the necessary symbols and attach meaning to symbols as a result of learning, for we lack this knowledge at the time of birth. An interesting facet of verbal learning is that we learn to respond to verbal stimuli only when others reinforce our behavor. (4:5; 5:52) It is inevitable that individual differences in learning will result in certain differences of meaning being attached to any symbol. In fact it is highly debatable whether any two individuals attach the identical meaning to any word. In addition to the kind of associations developed in connection with a given symbol, the number of associations is an important condition. Some verbal stimuli are likely to elicit a number of responses while others may elicit a comparatively few responses. Another word may elicit strong emotional responses (as shown by word association tests) while others may elicit neutral or weak responses. Certainly these aspects play important roles in the discrimination of a graphic symbol and in its "comprehension." It is likely that for the mature reader every symbol elicits a number of responses depending upon his needs at the moment and the strength and number of his associations. It also seems likely that each mature reader develops a more or less stylized or habitual mode of response to graphic symbols. Skinner's statement is noteworthy in this connection. He states that "Reading is not an ability or a capacity but a tendency. When we say that an individual is 'able to read' we mean that he *will* behave in certain ways under suitable circumstances involving a verbal nonauditory stimulus." (5:66)

It is popular to talk about reading comprehension as the degree to which a reader "gets the message of the writer" or "understands what he reads." In this paper it has been suggested that rarely is the writer available to the reader so that interaction between writer and reader is necessarily limited. Because of this limitation a greater agreement on the significance of any symbols employed in encoding and decoding the transmitted message is necessary. Despite similarities in culture, it is unlikely that all persons will attach identical associations to any given word, phrase, sentence, or paragraph. In actual practice today reading comprehension means the degree to which reader's interpretations of a graphic symbol are congruent with those of some authority figure, such as a teacher or test constructor, or approximate those of the majority of his fellow men. It is perhaps a measure of conformity rather than comprehension.

We have had an unfortunate tendency to treat reading comprehension as an absolute quality. This tendency may be due to the popular type of multiple-choice test usually employed to measure comprehension in practice exercises of tests. In such cases the student who chooses an incorrect foil is marked wrong and the assumption is he has not understood the passage. In an actual reading selection it is possible to have comprehension of the message in a number of degrees. Take the following hypothetical reactions of a group of children who read the nursery rhyme.

> Jack and Jill went up the hill
> To fetch a pail of water.
> Jack fell down and broke his crown
> And Jill came tumbling after.

1. Two lads went up a hill to get some water but both fell down.
2. A boy named Jack and a girl named Jill went up a hill to get a bucket of water from the well. The boy fell down and hurt his head. Then the girl fell down too.

3. A king and queen went up a hill to get some water. The king fell and broke his crown. The queen fell too.
4. A man and a woman climbed a mountain. The man whose name was Jack fell and broke a crown the dentist had put in a tooth. The lady whose name was Jill fell down after him as she tried to help him.
5. Two people went up a hill looking for water. The man slipped and fell down to the bottom. The woman fell down on top of him.
6. A boy and a girl named Jack and Jill ascended a hill seeking water. Jack slipped and fractured his skull. Jill also slipped and rolled down the hill.

In each interpretation it will be noted that there are certain elements of correct average decoding. It also is apparent that each child's associations led to interpretations which were meaningful to him. Note for example the translation in Case 2 of bucket for pail, certainly a more meaningful concept to a southern child. Note in Cases 3 and 4 the attempt to find a meaningful referent for the word "crown." Can we assume that child Number 1 understood less than child 6? Certainly not on the evidence shown here. If we were teachers in the classroom, we would seek to elicit more information from the children by questions, discussions, and suggestions. By such means we seek to develop similar patterns of response and judge success or failure by the degree of similarity or congruency shown.

REFERENCES

1. KINGSTON, ALBERT J. "Cautions Regarding the Standardized Reading Test." In O. S. Causey and A. J. Kingston (eds.), *Fourth Yearbook of the Southwest Reading Conference.* Fort Worth, Texas: Texas Christian University Press, 1955, pp. 11–16.
2. KINGSTON, ALBERT J. "The Measurement of Reading Comprehension." In O. S. Causey and Emery P. Bliesmer (eds.), *Ninth Yearbook of the National Reading Conference.* Fort Worth, Texas: Texas Christian University Press, 1960, pp. 88–93.
3. KINGSTON, ALBERT J. "A Conceptual Model of Reading Comprehension." In Emery P. Bliesmer and Albert J. Kingston (eds.), *Tenth Yearbook of the National Reading Conference.* Milwaukee, Wisconsin: The Conference, 1961, pp. 100–107.
4. MILLER, GEORGE A. *Language and Communication.* New York: McGraw-Hill Book Company, 1957.
5. SKINNER, B. F. *Verbal Behavior.* New York: Appleton-Century-Crofts, Inc., 1957.

# DEVELOPING THE ABILITY TO DECODE WORDS

## INTRODUCTION

*An aura of mystery and excitement surrounds the word "decoding" for anyone familiar with some of the classical examples of decoding in history and literature. For years experts tried to decipher or decode the Egyptian hieroglyphics, but failed. When Champollion broke the code of the triglot inscriptions on the Rosetta Stone the riddle was solved, and scholars were able to decode the writings of the ancient Egyptians. The code in Poe's story,* The Goldbug, *was broken by a knowledge of the frequency of occurrence in writing of the letters of the English alphabet. A decided advantage accrued to the Allied forces in World War II when an American cryptographer broke the Japanese code, enabling the Allies to decode Japanese messages and thereby be informed of Japanese military plans.*

*For the person who is learning how to read, the code represented by the English language is an obstacle of no mean proportions. However, if the person is going to enjoy the mystic academic rites of the initiated, he must break this code.*

*In this section the authors discuss several methods for teaching a person how to decode printed English. One of these decoding aids is phonics. Basically, when a person learns phonics he learns to associate the appearance of a letter or letter combination with a particular sound. Hunt discusses the merits of letter-blend phonics compared to relationship phonics. Experience and research have shown the wisdom of employing other aids for decoding words besides phonics. Curry explains a five-pronged attack for decoding words. His approach at once represents a balance of decoding skills, and increases the probability that an individual will be able to decode any given word. Betts discusses what linguistics can and cannot do in helping an individual become a good reader. Finally, Lefevre caps the discussion by giving us a linguist's view of the contributions of linguistics to reading, including its contribution to the decoding process.*

# THE RIGHT QUESTIONS
# ABOUT PHONICS *

Lyman Hunt

*While it is true that most teachers agree that phonics are a useful word recognition tool, it is not true that they agree how phonics should be taught.*

*In this article Hunt contends that when the right questions are asked about phonics, the stage is set for dispelling incorrect ideas about phonics instruction. He first clarifies a basic issue by defining the two basic systems of phonics—letter-sound-blend phonics and relationship phonics. He continues by drawing on principles of educational psychology to show certain advantages*

*in teaching children relationship phonics.*

*1. What are the basic ideas upon which letter-sound-blend phonics is predicated?*

*2. State the premises of relationship phonics.*

*3. How can you differentiate the two systems?*

*4. What are the practical differences between the two phonic systems?*

*5. The author states that "l-s-bl" phonics will be detrimental in certain situations. What are those situations?*

S AY "PHONICS" and you have the setting for an educational battleground. Books, journals, and mass media, whether for professional educators or for the lay public, treat the topic of phonics with great frequency. The ignorance displayed in dealing with this inflammatory phase of reading instruction is appalling. Certainly the public is confused. Often the educator is uncertain. The teacher, the most important personage on the scene, frequently seems but slightly less bewildered. "Suffer the little children," the victims of the violent educational battle being fought over phonics.

## Issues Clarified

The most important statement that can be made about phonics is implied in this conundrum: "Phonics are, not is." The meaning is significant, "There are two kinds!"

To approach the topic intelligently two kinds of phonics must be considered. Both are currently being taught in our schools. Both kinds have been practiced for varying lengths of time with varying degrees of popularity. Most teachers teach some of each kind and are blandly unaware of the basic differences between the two. Teachers, professional educators and parents continue to discuss whether phonics is being taught.

---

* REPRINTED FROM *Education* (May 1962), pp. 540–544, copyright 1962 by The Bobbs-Merrill Company, Inc., Indianapolis, Indiana.

A false charge has been made that for a long period of time our schools did not teach phonics. This myth is a gross distortion of the truth. Actually a transition was made from one phonic system to another. The question is, which kind of phonics is better? It is important to describe and differentiate the distinguishing features and practices associated with each of the two phonic systems.

## The Two Systems Defined

First, there is letter-sound-blend phonics (l-s-bl). Secondly, there is letter-sound-relationship phonics (l-s-rel). The only feature common to both is that letters must be recognized by sight. The differences between the systems are marked.

In l-s-bl phonics sounds or letter elements must be voiced. In l-s-rel phonics likeness or differences in sounds must be heard. Basic to l-s-rel phonics is the concept that when twenty-six letters are used to create a multitude of words— each one *unique* in appearance—then it follows that certain letters or letter parts must be represented in several different words. Relationships are formed through these recurring letters or letter parts. L-s-rel phonics means teaching the child to perceive and work effectively with several types of relationships prevalent among words.

## Sequences Contrasted

A list of sequential steps for each kind of phonics has been derived from those authors on reading instruction who strongly support each system.

| L-S-BL [1] | L-S-REL [2] |
|---|---|
| 1. Five short vowels plus all single letter consonants. | 1. Rhyming elements (heard and seen). |
| 2. Two and three letter consonant combinations. | 2. All initial and final single letter consonants. |
| 3. Two and three letter vowel combinations. | 3. Initial and final consonants combinations of two or three letters. |
| 4. Five long vowels. | 4. Vowels, short or long. |
| 5. Irregular combinations. | 5. Vowel and vowel-consonant combinations. |
| | 6. Syllables. |

[1] For l-s-bl see Flesch, R., *Why Can't Johnny Read* (Harpers, 1955), p. 27.
[2] For l-s-rel see Gray, W. S., *On Their Own in Reading* (Scott Foresman and Company, 1961).

According to those who know, teaching l-s-bl phonics is simple. The child learns the letter sounds and blends them as they occur in words. As Flesch states, "every word in English contains a vowel," so you start at that point.

Advocates of relationship phonics reason otherwise. Those who have observed children closely have had an opportunity to notice their predilection for rhyming elements. Most five year olds are tickled to hear the euphonious relationships in the lines "See you soon, you old baboon." Few show much unsolicited concern for the short sound of *u*. Rhyming elements are the most obvious of all word relationships and consequently are the first the child discerns. They become the natural and logical starting point.

Relationship phonics is built upon sight recognition vocabulary, which the child has personally learned. Thus the study of initial rhyming words is based on individual words the child has learned. These gross likenesses in word forms should be the easiest first step in word analysis. This is in marked contrast to the initial step of having the child voice the sounds of the five short vowels and/or the twenty-odd consonants.

Relationship phonics continues on the premise that the next most obvious relationship to the child is that of beginning consonants. Typically a child is shown common relationships between the initial letter of his name and the initial letter of several other words familiar to him. This step of having the child see and hear similar elements in several known words is not developed in l-s-bl phonics. Instead, energy is consumed in sounding the letter elements in a particular unknown word without any particular association with known words.

As initial consonant relationships are perceived the child is guided on to more complex relationships: words ending with the same letter, double and triple letter combinations occurring in both the initial and final position, vowels long or short (alone or in combination with consonants and other vowels) recurring among words in specific relationship which can be discovered and studied. Syllables common to several words can be studied through relationships.

Obviously there are myriad relationships under each sequential step, each somewhat more complex and intricate than the previous one.

### SEQUENCES DIFFERENTIATED

The most obvious difference between the two systems is the weight attached to the vowel element. In l-s-bl phonics the vowel is central. In l-s-rel phonics the vowel is peripheral and is among the final relationships developed. It is last because typically the vowel occupies an internal position in those words which are usually selected for study in introductory work.

A more compelling reason pertains to the instability of vowel sounds. Frequently the vowel sound has such variability that the relationship is unsteady and thus difficult for children to learn (*our, pour, sour, your; do, so, to, go*). In l-s-rel phonics the teacher would stress the vowel relationship through words linked by consistency and would teach the exceptions as individual distinct words or as special cases.

The question is, do we teach phonics by starting with the innermost part of the word (vowel) and work out to the extremities, or do we build from the edges of any particular word to its center? Does the vowel have first priority or is it one of the least significant of the many relationships among words?

## Systems Compared

Several essential differences between the systems emerge from the issue of whether vowel sounds are stressed.

| L-S-BL | L-S-REL |
|---|---|
| a. Vowel sounds first, consonants follow. | a. Obvious to fine relationship. |
| b. Blending sounds of letter elements basic. | b. Sensitivity to likeness heard when words are spoken. |
| c. Oral sounds emphasized. | c. Similarity of patterns perceived. |
| d. Practice not based on meaningful material. | d. Practices developed in connection with meaningful material. |
| e. Instruction concentrated in separate phonics period. | e. Phonic instruction integrated with other activities in reading instructional period. |
| f. Instruction commences in inception of school program and continues on a daily basis for 1½ to 2 years. | f. Instruction built on auditory readiness thus appears delayed. |
| g. All steps in sequence presented in 1st year with review of first. | g. All steps of sequence distributed gradually over grades 1 to 3 or more. |
| h. Oral sounding of words as the first and only important step in reading. | h. Perceiving relationship is but one of several word study skills. |

Listing differences clearly indicates two essentially diverse concepts of phonic instruction. The (l-s-bl) school would place reading in the category of making speech sounds in response to a group of letters. The issue of a constantly developing sight vocabulary is confronted obliquely, if at all. Those teachers whose first concern is with developing a recognition vocabulary as a visual (rather than vocal) response believe that seeing letter patterns or relationships is but one of several valuable word study tools. Ultimately, is recognition blending a series of letter sounds or is it responding at sight to the *unique* appearance of the total word form? The difference is significant.

## Instructional Example

The differences between the two phonic systems are practical as well as theoretical. The procedures of instruction when analyzed mentally are substantially different. How a teacher aids a child in word study through phonics is directly involved. Take, as an example of an unrecognized word, *teachers*.

Most teachers are familiar with the application of l-s-bl phonics. The child would be coaxed into sounding the *t*, applying the double vowel rule, voicing the *ch* blend, adding the *er* and *s* endings.

Now notice the difference in teaching l-s-rel phonics. The teacher's first question as she tries to help the child is "How can I simplify the appearance of the word form?" By striking out the ending. Second "How can I build a relationship with the double consonant ending?" Then, if necessary, "How can I help with the initial consonant *t*?"

Step by step the procedure would be:

Step 1: Strike the ending in the word *teachers*. Draw a line through it or rewrite the word without it.

Step 2: Relate known words to ending. Start building by thinking of each related word most likely to be known by the child: *teach(ers)*, *each*, *reach*, *porch*, *much*.

Step 3: Stress the relationship of using oral instructions. "Do you see how the words are alike?" "Do you hear how the words are alike" (following oral repetition of the words)? Practice is repeated a sufficient number of times to ensure learning of the particular relationship.

Step 4: Should it be discovered that the initial consonant *t* was a source of difficulty, the following procedure would be utilized: *teach, ten, time, tall, tumble*.

Again the relationship is emphasized. "Do you hear; do you see the way the words are alike?"

Once the relationship is understood and learning assured, transfer of this known principle will function. When the child is studying a word he will see parts familiar to him and, by mentally substituting known for unknown parts, decipher the puzzling word confronting him. No claim is made that learning l-s-rel is easily obtained, but the base is sound and permanence is certain!

## Practical Consideration

There are many purists when phonics is discussed in the theoretical sense, yet few teachers apply either system with consistency. Similarly few educators who develop materials for classroom instruction are entirely consistent relative to one or the other phonic system.

Most classroom teachers will recognize the l-s-rel sequence as the system developed through the basal textbook programs with precise directions for instruction found in the teacher's manual. Yet many teachers, yielding to a variety of pressures, interweave a liberal amount of l-s-bl phonics along with the structured l-s-rel program.

Many pressures come from producers of materials of the l-s-bl vintage. In these teaching materials the focus is solely on l-s-bl phonics, and other word study methods are neglected.

The teacher caught in the cross fire from the battle ground of the two phonic systems emerges with an admixture of practices drawn from both systems. The result for children happily or unhappily is that they receive a double-barreled barrage of phonics instruction. Quite a few children, both able and less able, are casualities of this pedagogical conflict.

Should the teachers teach both systems? There are many loud voices clamoring "yes." Should she discard the l-s-rel phonics program of the typical basal readers, when the school system requires an intensive program of l-s-bl phonics? Again, there are loud "yeses."

Which one should form the basis of instruction? How does the teacher decide? The answer depends primarily on her view of the word recognition phase of the reading process. If she believes the ordering of facts about word recognition skills is substantially as follows she will subscribe for the most part to l-s-rel phonics:

1. A word has meaning.
2. A word form has unique appearance.
3. Ultimately every word must be recognized on sight.
4. An organized set of relationships exists among parts of many words.

If her goal is to have the child realize that each word is a combined series of letters which in turn can be uttered as a series of sounds, then her predisposition will be toward l-s-bl phonics. But to answer the question on better kinds of phonics means facing the issue of sight recognition skills.

Does it make a real difference which system is used? For most children it does not. But l-s-bl phonics will be a great detriment to those children who after the first few encounters with a word cannot substitute a visual sight response for uttering a series of letter sounds based on particular letters seen.

Any child who is observed uttering a series of letter sounds more than eight or ten times to any given word is demonstrating the ineffectiveness of the l-s-bl approach for him. Complex linguistic and l-s-bl phonic rules tend to confuse the child having difficulty with word recognition skills. Certainly in this case other more effective approaches to word learning should surely be brought into play and l-s-rel phonics would be among them.

Those who would like to make l-s-bl phonics equivalent to the total reading program—and many people still do—are doing great harm. Years of effort have gone into developing a balanced program of reading instruction which gives consideration to many complex aspects of the reading process. Reading is much more than word recognition; word recognition is much more than word study; word study is much more than phonics. Some educators, following decades of study, have learned this. Let not ignorance undo this progress! We can debate honestly the strength and weakness of each system of phonics. We must stop the absurd discussion about whether or not phonics are being taught. They are!

# TEACHING THE DECODING SKILLS *

Robert L. Curry

We hear writers, artists, surgeons, and mechanics refer to "tools of the trade." Basically these tools are the skills and instruments that enable the workers to accomplish their tasks successfully. The reader also uses tools. He uses five basic word-recognition skills as tools for developing meanings in reading.

In this article Curry explains what these word-recognition skills are, and how the high school teacher can help students acquire these skills and become more proficient in their use.

1. What is the role of word recognition skills in reading?

2. What are the more rapid means for recognizing a new word?

3. How are verbal context clues and initial letter clues used to advantage in unlocking a word?

4. Explain the role of phonics in reading.

5. How are phonics and structural analysis used together?

6. Is the ability to use the dictionary well a useful skill? Explain.

THE WORD-RECOGNITION skills are extremely important to the reading process. The role of these skills in the reading process is also quite unique. Without a high degree of proficiency in applying the word-recognition skills in the reading process an individual will never become an efficient and mature reader. On the other hand, a high degree of proficiency in the application of the word-recognition skills will not necessarily assure an individual of being an efficient and mature reader. The word-recognition skills must be thought of as an intermediary step in the reading process. They serve as an essential means to the ultimate goal—that of gaining meaning from the printed words. They are merely a means to an end, not an end in themselves. Too often individuals are capable of recognizing the words and of associating the correct sounds with them, but nevertheless are incapable of gaining the intended meanings of the writer when words are combined into sentences, paragraphs, and longer selections. Teachers must be constantly alert to the appropriate role of the word-recognition skills and keep them in their proper perspective in the reading process.

Many high-school students have learned to apply most of the word-recognition skills in the reading process, and many high-school students have gaps or deficiencies in using some of these skills. These deficiencies should be eliminated through a corrective or a developmental reading program at the high-school level which will provide the students with a higher degree of proficiency in reading. Many students who are also proficient in applying the word-recognition skills are not aware that certain skills provide

---

* Written especially for inclusion in this volume.

a more rapid means for unlocking words which they do not recognize at sight.

Students should be taught or retaught the preferred order for applying these skills. However, since a single technique will not serve as an effective means for unlocking all the words encountered, the students should be taught to use all the word-recognition skills. When a reader encounters a word in print that cannot be recognized by the application of one skill, it then becomes necessary to utilize another word-recognition skill that may be a much slower process, but which will result in the reader's unlocking the word.

There are five word-recognition skills which should be included in every program for developing reading skills. These five skills are

1. Sight words.
2. Context clues.
3. Phonics.
4. Structural analysis.
5. Dictionary usage.

Every high-school student will benefit from the instruction when these skills are developed in a logical and sequential manner. An emphasis should be placed on using the skill that provides the most rapid means for recognizing the new word before proceeding to one of the slower processes of word recognition.

## SIGHT METHOD

Most high-school students have acquired the ability to recognize a large number of words by sight. An adequate sight vocabulary is essential to proficiency in the reading process in that the words recognized instantly do not require the student to dwell on the word for a prolonged period of time. When the student has a limited number of sight words, the reading process becomes much slower. Research indicates that any factor which slows the reading process unnecessarily lowers the student's power to comprehend the materials being read.

The initial contact with learning to read is most often through learning basic service words by sight. The sight words are usually those which cannot be recognized by applying other word-attack skills. This bank of sight words provides a group of known words which can be used for teaching other word-recognition skills.

Students who become proficient readers gradually expand their sight vocabularies. This is accomplished by using other word-recognition skills such as context clues, phonics, etc., in the initial contacts with the new words. Since the student's listening and speaking vocabularies are much greater than his reading vocabularies, many of the words are known but are not recognized in printed form. After the student associates the pronunciation with the visual form of the word for a number of times, the word should then be recognized instantly and thus become a part of the sight vocabulary.

## Context Clues

The verbal context clues provide the reader with one of the most important and useful methods for recognizing new words. The reader gains meaning from the words which precede and follow the new word; and, based upon the meaning derived, the reader deduces what the new word must be to complete the thought being conveyed. Most people constantly employ the use of verbal context clues as they read. The use of verbal context clues is extremely important to the reader in that these clues provide a very rapid technique for determining new words.

The use of context clues may give the clue as to the exact word that will complete the meaning of the sentence. In the sentence:

*I wrote a long _____ to my mother.*

the reader would probably conclude that the word necessary in the missing blank is *letter*. Of course the ability to recognize or determine the word through verbal context clues is determined to a great extent on the reader's having had the background experiences necessary for determining the appropriate word. A student, who understands how the context or meaning derived from the sentence assists in identifying the unknown word, may be deficient in applying this skill in some instances because of a limited background of experience on the topic around which the selection is written. As a result, it may often be essential that the teacher prepare the students for the reading selection by providing some background information about the topic. This background information will certainly not take the place of firsthand or other vicarious experiences, but it may provide enough information to be an aid in the use of context clues and serve to minimize the deficiencies of the students.

Verbal context clues may serve only as a means for limiting the number of words which may logically fit into the meaning pattern of the sentence. In the sentence:

*I mailed a _____ to my mother.*

there are several words such as *letter, package, parcel, postcard, card,* and possibly a few other words which might logically complete the meaning of the sentence. However, the use of the verbal context clues in this sentence is extremely important in that the number of possibilities is restricted to fewer than ten words out of a possible 600,000 or more words in the English language. Often when the meaning of the sentence restricts only the number of possible choices of words that logically complete the meaning of the sentence, the reader must rely on another word recognition skill as an aid to making the final determination of the word. A quick visual inspection of the word from left-to-right may assist the student in recognizing the word as a sight word, or when the reader visualizes the first letter of the word the correct word may be selected. Again using the sentence referred to above:

*I mailed a l_____ to my mother.*

when the reader observes the first letter of the word, the word may be recognized because the word *letter* is the only word in the limited number of possible choices which begins with the consonant *l*. The use of context clues and phonics is combined when a word is recognized in this manner. If, however, the correct word in the sentence were *postcard*, the reader may, through a visual inspection of the word, recognize the two words which are combined to form the compound word and thus recognize the word and verify it by the context. Even though it may be necessary to utilize skills other than verbal context clues in recognizing an unknown word in print, it must be remembered that the verbal context clues serve as a final check on the accuracy in the application of all the other word-recognition skills.

Verbal context clues also provide the only means for determining the correct pronunciation of many words as they are used in a sentence. The appropriate pronunciation of words such as *present, read, lead,* and *bow* cannot be ascertained in isolation but only as they are used in a contextual setting. In these sentences:

John gave her a *present.*
Are you going to *read* the book?
The horse will not *lead.*
The boy was playing with a *bow* and arrow.

the appropriate pronunciations of these words are clarified.

The teacher should give attention to the level of development of each student in utilizing the verbal context clues in the reading process. Activities and exercises should be provided which include instructions for learning to apply these skills, and the opportunities to practice the usage of these skills. It is not difficult to detect the student who does not use the verbal context clues while reading, for the student will not demand sense from the materials being read and will often substitute words which are obviously incorrect and inappropriate to the meaning of the sentence. Other students may overuse the verbal context clues. This overusage becomes obvious when a student persists in substituting words which are synonyms for the word in the selection. When the student substitutes words appropriate in the sentence, it is an indication that he is deficient in applying the other word-recognition skills.

## PHONICS

The use of phonics as a skill in identifying words which are not sight words to the reader is a complex process. Phonics is the relating of the sounds to the visual symbols in the form of letters, groups of letters, syllables, and words. The reader must relate the sounds to the letters and combinations of letters, and then synthesize, or blend, the individual sounds to determine the correct pronunciation of the word. The analytical process involved in the application of phonics to the sounding out of words of necessity makes it a slower process than the use of the sight method and context clues. However, the sounding out of words is of extreme importance to the reading process because it often serves as the only or most effective means for identifying many new words.

During the past several decades there has been heated controversy between the antagonists and the advocates of phonics. The values and logical criticisms of phonics have often been overshadowed by emotional arguments in which both groups of extremists have failed to recognize that those taking either position had a valid point worthy of consideration. The more tenable position for most authorities in reading seems to be that, although there are some undesirable characteristics developed by the person who is taught only the phonics approach as a skill to identifying new words, the student will never become a mature independent reader if the skill cannot be effectively applied.

The moderates also contend that an effective reader is one who has multiple approaches to utilize in attacking new words. The multiple approach to word recognition is undoubtedly the only logical means to becoming an effective reader. This is true because no one technique will serve to unlock every new word encountered. A perusal of the literature related to the irregularities of English words indicates that an estimated 85 per cent of the words can be accurately sounded out. The application of phonics generalizations often results in the incorrect pronunciation of a word, such as *recipe*; the correct pronunciation of a word, such as *bake*; or a pronunciation that is similar to the correct pronunciation of the word. When the pronunciation derived from an application of phonics generalizations is similar to the correct pronunciation of the word, the reader often recognizes the correct pronunciation of the word because the word is in the reader's listening and/or speaking vocabularies.

The phonics generalizations must be taught, or retaught, in a planned program in the high school. This is essential even though the skills are taught in the basic reading program in the elementary grades. Many of the students have not developed proficiency in their usage, or they need assistance in applying these skills as the vocabulary becomes progressively more difficult.

The more important generalizations which should be included in the instructional program for high-school students are

1. A vowel in a syllable that ends with one or more consonants usually has the short sound.

    *hat     bet     with     hot     hut*

2. A vowel in an open syllable is usually long (an *open syllable* is a syllable in which the final letter is a vowel).

    *hero     halo     nitro*

3. The letter *i* preceding the consonant combinations *ld*, *gh*, and *nd* in a syllable is usually long.

mild    wild    find

high    sigh    bind

4. The letter *o* often has the long sound when followed by *w* or *st*.

snow    most

bowl    ghost

5. A syllable having two vowels, one of which is a final *e*, usually has the long sound for the first vowel and the final *e* is usually silent.

take    mete    bite    note    tube

6. Certain vowel digraphs (*ai, ay, oa, ee, ea*) usually have a long sound for the first vowel and the second vowel is silent.

maid    day    boat    beet    meat

7. Certain vowel digraphs (*au, aw, eu, ew, oo*) have a special sound unlike either of the vowels.

haunt    dawn    feud    new    took    gloom

8. The final *y* of monosyllabic words has a long *i* sound and the final *y* of multisyllabic words has the long *e* sound.

dry    swiftly

sky    dandy

9. Diphthongs (*oi, oy, ou, ow*) have a special blend sound of the two letters.

oil    boy    loud    brown

toil    toy    bound    gown

10. The sound of a vowel followed by the letter *r* is usually changed considerably.

star    her    stir    word    turn

bar    clerk    dirt    border    furnish

11. Some consonants are silent when placed in certain relationships with other letters in a word.

gn—*g* is silent before *n* at beginning of word    *gnat, gnaw*
gh—*h* is silent following *g* at beginning of word    *ghost, ghetto*
gh—*gh* is usually silent within a word    *sight, though*
kh—*h* is silent following *k* at beginning of word    *khaki, khan*
rh—*h* is silent following *r* at beginning of word    *rhetoric, rhombus*
kn—*k* is silent before *n* at beginning of word    *knit, knife*
lm, lk—*l* is usually silent before *m* or *k*    *calm, chalk*

| | |
|---|---|
| mb—*b* preceded by *m* is silent at end of syllable | *comb, crumb* |
| pn, ps—*p* is silent before *n* or *s* at beginning of word | *psalm, pneumonia* |
| sl—*s* is often silent following *i* | *aisle, island* |
| tch—*t* is usually silent before *ch* | *watch, pitch* |
| wr—*w* is silent before *r* | *write, wrong* |
| double consonants—second consonant usually silent | *funny, fatty* |

12. The consonants *c* and *g* have both a hard and a soft sound.

| | | | |
|---|---|---|---|
| *cite* | *can* | *gem* | *gain* |
| *cinch* | *coal* | *giant* | *goat* |

Phonics instruction should be provided on a systematic basis; the skills should be taught in a functional manner by the inductive process; and, instruction should be adapted to the individual differences found among high-school students.

## Structural Analysis

The use of structural analysis skills as an aid to the reading process is very important. Structural analysis involves the division of the structural elements of a word and deals with inflectional endings such as *s, es, est, ed, er,* and *ing;* word derivatives formed by the addition of a prefix and/or suffix such as *unhappy;* compound words such as *roadway;* and syllabication, the breaking of words into syllables such *num / ber.* Structural analysis is vital as it often breaks the words into larger elements which may be recognized by the reader. Often too the reader may recognize one or more of the structural elements and only have to apply another word recognition skill to the structural elements which are not recognized, thus providing for a more rapid recognition of unknown words. Structural analysis is also essential to the application of phonics generalizations because certain sounds, especially vowel sounds, are determined by their position in a syllable.

After many of the root words have been learned, instruction should be focused on teaching the students to scrutinize new words quickly to determine whether the words contain a root word. The students must be taught the common inflectional endings if they are to be expected to recognize them when affixed to words. As an aid to both word recognition and comprehension, the changes in meanings brought about by an inflectional ending also must be clearly understood by the students. Practice should be provided in identifying the inflected forms of words and the principles which are applied when adding inflectional endings to words.

The form and meanings of prefixes and suffixes are necessary for recognizing word derivatives. When students recognize the basic root words and the useful prefixes and suffixes, they have at their command the skills necessary for recognizing the pronunciations and meanings of many words which are not presently in their reading, listening, speaking, and writing vocabularies.

Compound words consist of two or more words which are combined to form a new word with a different meaning. Compound words are usually easily recognized when each word, which forms the compound, is part of the student's sight vocabulary. However, some students are able to recognize the words when separated, but not when they are combined. Instruction should be provided in which the students receive practice in recognizing, forming, and determining the meanings of compound words.

Syllabication is another skill that is a requisite to success in word recognition. The reader often encounters polysyllabic words the pronunciation of which is confusing until the words are divided into syllables. When the words are syllabicated, some of the syllables may be recognized and the others may require the application of phonic generalizations. As previously indicated, the sounds of letters, especially vowels, are determined by the position in a syllable. To correctly sound the word or syllables not readily identified the word must be separated into its structural elements. The generalizations should be taught inductively in that they will be more meaningful to the students. The following generalizations should be included among those for teaching syllabication:

1. A single consonant usually goes with the vowel which follows when that consonant appears between two vowels.

   | | |
   |---|---|
   | silent | si / lent |
   | minus | mi / n̄us |
   | nomad | no / mad |

2. A single consonant appearing between two vowels usually goes with the preceding vowel if that vowel is short and within an accented syllable.

   | | |
   |---|---|
   | acid | ʹac / id |
   | bigot | ʹbig / ot |

3. No syllabic division should be made between consonants that constitute a consonant blend or consonant digraph. The consonant blend may go with the vowel which precedes or the one which follows. When the preceding vowel is short and within an accented syllable the consonant blend or consonant digraph usually goes with the preceding vowel.

   | | |
   |---|---|
   | locket | ʹlock / et |
   | migrate | ʹmi / grate |
   | bishop | ʹbish / op |

4. The syllabic divisions of two consonants, which are neither blend nor digraph, and which appear between two vowels, usually comes between the two consonants.

   | | |
   |---|---|
   | mildew | mil / dew |

millet       mil / let

crescent     cres / cent

5. Prefixes usually form separate syllables.

react       re / act

defrost     de / frost

invent      in / vent

6. Suffixes usually form separate syllables.

peaceful    peace / ful

worker      work / er

7. The suffix *ed*, if immediately preceded by the letter *d* or *t*, forms a separate syllable. The suffix *ed* combines with other letters to form one syllable if *not* preceded by *d* or *t*. (One exception to the application of this principle should be noted: when the *d* or *t* appears before the suffix *ed* in double for the *d* or *t* immediately before that *ed* comprises the final syllable jointly.

shrouded    shroud / ed

posted      post / ed

forced      forced

sinned      sinned

budded      bud / ded

omitted     o / mit / ted

8. A word ending in *le*, when the *le* is preceded by a consonant forms a final syllable with that consonant and the *le*. However, *le* stands alone as the final syllable when preceded by the consonants *ck*.

uncle       un / cle

pebble      peb / ble

buckle      buck / le

freckle     freck / le

9. A syllabic division is made between words which form a compound.

pathway     path / way

flashlight  flash / light

## DICTIONARY USAGE

The proper use of the dictionary as an aid to recognizing new words is of significant importance in the reading program. When words are encountered which are not a part of the reader's listening and/or speaking vocabularies it is often necessary to rely on the dictionary to determine the correct pronunciation of the word. This is often true when the student lacks the phonic skills or when the application of phonic generalizations results in the incorrect pronunciation of the word.

There are certain dictionary skills essential to locating an entry word in a dictionary, such as using guide words, determining root words, and so on. However, for purposes of recognizing the correct pronunciation and meaning associated with a word in its particular context the skills can be limited to: using guide words, interpreting diacritical markings, syllabication, and accent. Students who do not correctly utilize guide words in locating an entry word can be provided with instruction and exercises in which they have to identify the guide words for a group of words. Students should also be taught how to interpret the diacritical markings used in the phonetical transcription of the word by using the key to pronunciation provided in the front of the dictionary, or at the bottom of the page of the dictionary.

In that different dictionaries use somewhat different phonetical transcriptions to represent sounds, the students should be made aware that the sounds represented are contingent upon the transcriptions used in a particular dictionary. Syllabication and accent are also important in determining the correct pronunciation of words. Therefore, students should be taught the procedure used in each dictionary for indicating syllabic divisions and accent.

## SUMMARY

The most effective instructional program is one that provides the students with a variety of techniques for unlocking new words. Students should be taught the different ways for identifying words; the ways in which the skills can be used in combination; and, the preferred order in which the skills should be applied to develop the highest degree of proficiency in reading. Programs must be provided which are designed to develop the skills in a logical and sequential manner. Also, corrective reading programs are essential to eliminate the deficiencies of students regardless of grade level.

## BIBLIOGRAPHY

BAMMAN, HENRY A., HOGAN, URSULA, and GREENE, CHARLES E. *Reading Instruction in the Secondary Schools.* New York: Longmans, Green and Company, 1961.

BOND, GUY L. and WAGNER, EVA BOND. *Teaching the Child to Read.* New York: Macmillan Company, 1966.

DEBOER, JOHN J. and DALLMAN, MARTHA. *The Teaching of Reading.* New York: Holt, Rinehart and Winston, 1964.

DECHANT, EMERALD V. *Improving the Teaching of Reading.* Englewood Cliffs, N.J.: Prentice-Hall, Inc., 1964.

HILDRETH, GERTRUDE. *Teaching Reading.* New York: Holt, Rinehart and Winston, 1960.

KARLIN, ROBERT. *Teaching Reading in High School.* New York: Bobbs-Merrill Company, 1964.

# A NEW AREA: READING
# AND LINGUISTICS *

Emmett A. Betts

*Is linguistics new to the field of reading? To the average teacher, yes; to the serious students of reading instruction, no. For years the latter have applied insights gained from phonemics—a facet of linguistics—to reading.*

*Linguistics has made other content contributions to reading. However, linguistics is no panacea for reading ills. It is important for the teacher to view linguistics in the proper perspective so that he uses well what linguistics has to offer and also uses, at the right time, the contributions that other disciplines have made to the teaching of reading. These are the kinds of insights that Betts shares with the readers of this article.*

*1. What specific contributions does linguistics make to the field of reading?*

*2. State in your own words the role of phoneme-grapheme relationships in word perception.*

*3. In what way have linguists served as a "balance wheel" in the teaching of word-perception skills?*

*4. Explain the expression "language as codification includes the phonemic, morphemic, and syntactic structure."*

*5. Try to illustrate each of the "possible contributions" of descriptive or generative grammar to reading.*

*6. What are the three essential steps to "teaching with vision"?*

*7. What are two "limitations" of linguistics that require the teacher to seek help from the field of psychology?*

ANOTHER high pressure center has moved into the reading instruction area: linguistics. But this pressure system has been moving in for a long time—undetected, to be sure, by those concerned more with methods than with content.

While Barrows and Cordt's *The Teacher's Book of Phonetics*, published in 1926, has been superseded by Charles K. Thomas' *Phonetics of American English*, at least one course on the sounds of speech has been available to undergraduate and graduate students for more than a generation. Although Bloomfield's descriptive grammar and Chomsky's generative grammar have put Priestly's "traditional" grammar and Jesperson's historical grammar under at least a broken cloud cover, teachers of reading and writing have had access to courses on the structure of language for several generations.

Hence, the two major facets of linguistics—phonology and grammar—have been a high pressure center for serious students of reading instruction for a considerable time.

Neither linguistics nor the teaching of reading is a new area of concern in

* REPRINTED FROM *Education* (May 1964), pp. 515–520. Copyright, 1964, by The Bobbs-Merrill Company, Inc., Indianapolis, Indiana.

94

education. That "linguistics and reading" is viewed as a new interdisciplinary area provides evidence that the house of reading may be given stronger foundations.

American reading instruction has been plagued by perpetual emotion: the alphabet method, John Russell Webb's word method (1846), phonetic and phonic methods, a sight-word method for beginning reading, a three-group plan, individualzed reading, and so on. Each exclusive method or plan offered a magic that failed. Each one equipped teachers and teachers of teachers more often with fashionable *words* rather than with fundamental *ideas*. Now, on this superstructure of progress (or of confusion), this so-called linguistic approach to reading instruction may be superimposed.

## LINGUISTICS

Reading and linguistics! What is reading? What is linguistics? "Reading and linguistics" is a mixture of hope and apprehension for some teachers, an illusory goal for a few who live on expectations, an invitation to broaden the base of reading instruction for others.

Reading is far more than a process of saying words—of relating letters of the alphabet to the sounds which they represent. Yet reading does require the automatic use of perception skills, because the reader has only one mind and, therefore, tends to give his attention either to word forms or to ideas. But, basically, reading is a thinking process—a process of reconstructing personal experiences symbolized by language. Because language itself has structure and because language, at the same time, represents structured experience, the reader learns to deal with a dyad of meaning: structural and referential.

## PHONEMICS

Linguistics offers *content*—pedagogical oxygen for teachers of reading!—rather than *methods* of teaching reading or *plans* for differentiating instruction. Linguistics is a story with a purpose; it is much ado about something worthwhile.

In the first place, linguists have identified fairly large segments of speech sounds called phonemes. These phonemes are abstractions without meaning, but they are signals or distinguishers of meaning. For example, each of the spoken words *sat* and *sad* has three phonemes; two of these, *s* and *a*, are the same in each word, but the phonemes *t* of *sat* and *d* of *sad*—along with contextual aids—signal different meanings.

Of course, a number of phoneticians have studied speech sounds; therefore, differences of opinion regarding the identity of the phonemes and their organization are par for the course. But honest differences of opinion regarding the phonemic structure of language are to be ironed out by the linguists themselves. In the meantime, teachers of reading must recognize the plurality of linguistics.

In general, most people, including teachers, are not aware of the speech sounds they use. They learned to hear and to use most of these sounds long before being admitted to school; hence, they make automatic responses to them in both listening and speaking. However, a master teacher—such as phonetician Charles K. Thomas—can help qualified graduate students to acquire a working knowledge of phonemics in a three-semester hour course.

A very substantial reduction in the time required for learning methods of teaching reading is made when prospective teachers have studied both the phonemic and grammatical structure of language as a pre-requisite. Today very few teachers have the opportunity to study either phonemics or a more comprehensive course in linguistics. No wonder there is so much despair in the air regarding the teaching of phonic skills.

Since word perception involves phoneme-grapheme relationships in perceptual settings, some linguists have concerned themselves not only with the study of phonemes but also with the letters used to represent them.

Moreover, they have gone further afield by prescribing the form of letters (*e.g.*, all capital letters or all lower case letters for beginning reading) and methods of teaching these relationships (*e.g.*, use of analogous spelling-phoneme patterns as in *hit-sit* and *hit-hip*). They offer plausible but not necessarily painless method magic. Again, however, these linguists—as outsiders rather than insiders—offer widely diverse suggestions regarding methods and materials for teaching reading.

Furthermore, some linguists tend to stereotype plans regarding the programming of phonics in today's reading instruction: (1) the time at which phonic skills are introduced, (2) the sequential and cumulative development of skills. There are, of course, a diversity of *opinions* regarding these important matters and these different opinions are reflected in different types of phonic programs.

In a well-structured program, the teaching of phonics is done systematically:

First, the pupil is taught the sounds usually represented by letters; e.g., the *ch* sound represented by *ch* in *chair*.

Second, the pupil is taught that a sound may be represented by different letters; e.g., the *sh* sound by *sh* in *she*, *s* in *sure*, *c* or *t* before *i* in *vicious* and *nation*, *ch* in *Chicago*, etc.

Third, the child is taught that different sounds may be represented by the same letter(s); e.g., the letter *s* may represent *s* in saw, *z* in *was*, *sh* in *sure*, etc.

Some educators tend to under-emphasize the consistency of spelling patterns (e.g., *at-hat-sat, eat-heat-bleat, ate-date-mate*). On the other hand, some linguists tend to overemphasize the consistency of the relationships between sounds and the letters used to represent them.

Linguists have served as a balance wheel in the teaching of word perception skills. Beginning with Bloomfield, many of them have emphasized that pupils can talk or they could not be taught to read; hence, the purpose of phonics is to teach the child the relationships between the speech sounds he already uses and the alphabet used to represent them. But some educators persist in the belief that phonics embraces "the teaching of vowel and consonant sounds." This belief is a dangerous delusion and gives the teaching of reading an air of unreality.

Then, too, very few linguists are aware of crucial factors in perception, such as *need, grouping* of letters and sounds, *feedback* between a stimulus and previous learning, *closure* of likely whole words, *referential* as well as structural meaning, and so on. Hence, they are unaware of the need not only to teach a new skill but to insure its retention by application—of teaching a phonic skill by proceeding from the spoken word to its written form and of completing the feedback when the pupil relates the written form to the spoken word during his silent reading activity.

## GRAMMAR

In some schools, educators limit their discussions of "linguistics and reading" to phonemics. This limited view of linguistics tends to distort the confusion regarding the possible contributions of linguistics to reading instruction.

Linguistics does embrace the *phonemic* structure of language. But it also embraces the *grammatical* structure of language: morphology plus syntax (word formation and sentence structure). That is, language as codification includes the phonemic, morphemic, and syntactic structure. Phonemics contributes to word perception in reading; grammar to the thinking facet of reading instruction.

Reading is thinking that results in comprehension or concept formation. It also is the use of skills for a specific purpose and a relationship with the author. But, equally important, reading is thinking in a language.

In grammar, as in phonemics, most people make automatic responses. That is, they are vaguely, if at all, aware of signals of structural meaning, e.g., word order, grammatical inflection, function words and intonation.

Bloomfield and his followers emphasize that phonemes "do not occur in isolation" or "are not uttered in isolation." With a few exceptions, such as the pronoun I (*I*), their statement appears to be true. These linguists imply that having the pupil hear the sound *a* in *at* or say the sound *a* as a part of a teaching procedure is "to create a difficulty."

Some linguists, however, have developed materials for beginning readers using *isolated* words, such as *can, Dan, fan,* to teach the "alphabetic principle." This procedure is impractical pragmatism because intonation contours are violated. That is, in ordinary speech each word is not given equal stress, but if each word is equally stressed, word-by-word reading is likely to result.

At the present time there is no substantial evidence that the study of either descriptive grammar or generative grammar increases the pupil's ability to write or to read. However, the possible contributions appear to be substantial:

1. An intonational, especially pitch and juncture, basis for understanding the use of punctuation and the structure of sentences.

2. A grammatical basis for teaching an understanding of higher level structures, especially the sentence.
3. A structural dimension for the study of context clues to words and ideas in reading situations; that is, structural as well as referential meaning.
4. A psycholinguistic approach to the assessment of language development; e.g., the seven-year-old's control over language structure.
5. A morphemic basis for teaching informative parts of words: roots and affixes.

## GOALS OF READING INSTRUCTION

Over the years a substantial amount of respectable research has been accumulated on three major goals of reading instruction:

1. The development of worthwhile *interests* which take the child to reading and which are satisfied through his increasingly effective reading-study skills—a facet of motivation.
2. The learning of *word perception skills* to the point where they are used automatically.
3. The maturing of *thinking* and related comprehension abilities needed to draw conclusions, to solve problems, etc., and to get genuine satisfaction from reading-study activities.

Guidance in the development of these attitudes, skills, and abilities begins in the kindergarten or first grade and continues as long as the individual is in school. These three "firsts" of reading instruction are indispensable and inseparable.

Other things being equal, the goals of reading instruction are achieved to the degree that each pupil is taught where he is—at his own achievement level in terms of his motivation, perception skills, and thinking abilities. But the program of systematic reading instruction rests on linguistics (the scientific study of language) and psychology (the scientific study of behavior). Interlacing these two sciences are semantics, logic, and a number of other disciplines.

In today's schools there are many classrooms of opportunity where teaching is done with vision—where there is "know why" as well as "know how." In these classrooms of quiet freedom, teachers have taken three essential steps:

First, they have estimated the independent and the instructional reading levels of their pupils and they keep this information current.

Second, they have experimented with plans for differentiating instruction at their own levels of professional competence—making optimum use of both group and individualized plans.

Third, they have managed to obtain instructional materials for a comprehensive program of differentiated instruction.

In terms of the above goals of reading instruction, it appears that linguistics does not embrace all of the essentials needed by the teacher for the improve-ment of reading instruction. In the first place, linguistics does not reduce the increasingly wide range of pupil achievement and needs at succeeding levels of instruction. A teacher with an excess of professional preparation in lin-guistics would still lack the necessary competence in the teaching of reading, especially for differentiating instruction.

In the second place, linguistics does not *per se* offer help on interest and other facets of motivation. There isn't a shred of evidence, for example, that Bloomfield's descriptive grammar or Chomsky's generative grammar has a stronger appeal to students than traditional grammar.

On the other hand, linguistics has contributed to two goals of reading instruction: word perception and thinking.

The identification of distinctive segments of speech sounds, or phonemes, has given an air of reality to the teaching of word perception skills and inter-pretation of pronunciation symbols in the dictionary. This shift of emphasis from a multiplicity of phonetic elements to approximately 38 segmental phonemes has helped to move this facet of reading instruction to today, rather than yesterday.

Phonemics has made a significant difference in the development of dic-tionaries. This science has been applied, for example, in the G. & C. Merriam dictionaries for elementary (1956) and secondary school (1959) pupils. As a result, one symbol is used to represent one phoneme and each symbol is used consistently.

For example, one pronunciation symbol, the schwa, serves in place of nine different pronunciation symbols for this phoneme. The use of one symbol rather than nine symbols to represent one phoneme gives the pupil the right to be secure. Then, again, consistent use of symbols is made; e.g., the same symbol is used to represent the vowel sound in *few* and *use*.

Although the fruits of research in phonemics have been available for some time, most phonic systems of today are based on the syllabicated vocabulary entries in dictionaries rather than on the respelling. This fact alone produces disenchanted teachers and a profusion of confusion among the learners.

For example, the vocabulary entries in *Webster's New Secondary School Dictionary* (1959) includes items to show how to break words into syllables and respellings to show how to pronounce them. Accordingly, the respelling of each word shows how to say the word and serves as a basis for word per-ception skills.

## SUMMARY

Reading instruction is being moved forward today by two significant inter-disciplinary approaches. The significance of these approaches stems from the promise they extend of fruitful future improvement.

First, linguists offer important concepts regarding the structure of language —the system of symbols with which thinking is done.

Second, psychologists offer important concepts regarding individual differences, motivation, perception and concept formation—which provide the basis for both differentiated instruction and methods of teaching.

Educators who share the responsibility for the improvement of reading instruction are not satisfied with the status quo. Instead, they are extending the cutting edges of progress by working closely with scholars in cognate disciplines: linguistics, semantics, psychology, sociology, etc. To serve as custodians of quality in reading instruction, educators are making systematic efforts today to understand the possible contributions which may be made by enlightened leaders in these important and relevant areas of learning.

# CONTRIBUTIONS OF LINGUISTICS *

Carl A. Lefevre

*At a time when much heat and little light is being generated regarding the topic of linguistics and reading, it is gratifying to read a selection that throws light on the matter. In this article Lefevre provides the needed light by presenting a clear, well-ordered discussion of the contributions linguistics can make to reading. Rather than viewing linguistics as a cure-all for reading problems, he modestly suggests how teachers can use it to improve the teaching of reading and related language arts.*

*1. What new ideas regarding the relationship between oral language and reading do you get from reading the section "A Definition of Linguistics?"*

*2. How can structural linguistics contribute to an understanding of reading?*

*3. When is phonics instruction most effective? How can a knowledge of phonemics serve as a corrective in the area of reading instruction?*

THIS ARTICLE will be an attempt to do three things:

1. Define linguistics in a usable way.
2. Outline structural linguistics with respect to ways in which it may contribute to an understanding of reading.
3. Relate phonics to the corresponding topic in linguistics (phonemics).

Since linguistics deals with language, you will find an unusual emphasis on language throughout this discussion. I hope to show how this emphasis can be helpful in teaching reading.

---

* REPRINTED FROM *Instructor* (March 1965), pp. 77; 103–105, by permission of the publisher.

## A Definition of Linguistics

Linguistics is a scientific method of studying language. Speech, using verbal symbols, is the *primary* communication system of language. Handwriting and print, using graphic symbols, are the *secondary* communication system, based upon and derived from speech. Fundamentally, alphabetical writing is a representation of speech; we cannot get meaning directly from print. We go first from print to sound, and then from sound to meaning. Thus we see that reading is a language-related process. In beginning reading, it is relatively slow, but with practice and experience reading goes like the wind.

As a language-related process, reading requires perception and interpretation of the graphic counterparts of spoken language patterns. In English, sentences are the basic building blocks of meaning, and are far more important than letters and words.

Structural linguistics provides an accurate, objective description of the *structure* of the English language—basic sounds, words, and sentences. We need this description in order to apply modern knowledge of language to reading theory and methodology.

The question for teachers of reading is, "What is the best way to read *English?*"

## An Outline of Structural Linguistics

Our concern is to teach English-speaking children to read their native language when reduced to print. Should not a knowledge of the sound patterns of this speech be helpful in learning to read it?

Structural linguistics describes English as having three interlocking levels of structure, all applicable to reading and to reading instruction:

1. The smallest sound units are *phonemes*. They do not occur singly, but they are grouped in the larger patterns of words and word parts.
2. The smallest meaning-bearing units, words and word parts, are *morphemes*. They are patterned out of phonemes and occur generally in the larger patterns of phrases, clauses, and sentences.
3. In sentences, morphemes are grouped into unitary meaning-bearing patterns which are the basic units of reading comprehension. This is *syntax*.

Information about *phonemes* is helpful in teaching phonetic word analysis, phonics, and spelling. Information about *morphemes* is helpful in teaching structural word analysis and in vocabulary development. Knowledge of *syntax* is helpful in teaching sentence sense. Reading teachers know that sentence sense is fundamental to reading comprehension.

Syntax, the analysis of sentence patterns, involves four subsystems:

1. Intonation: the systematic rhythms and melodies of English.

2. Sentence patterns: the order of words and parts of sentences.
3. Structure words (or function words): sentence joints and glue, that hold sentence parts together.
4. Word-form changes: grammatical inflections; derivational prefixes and suffixes.

In the following brief discussion, I shall relate these four subsystems to reading, taking them up in the above order. To me, this is the order of their relative importance, though of course they are interrelated.

### Intonation

American English intonation is the system of native rhythms and melodies of speech; it combines obligatory features with the optional and interpretative. The three elements of intonation are pitch, loudness (stress or accent), and pause (juncture). Native intonation gives native speech its distinctive sound; the lack of it unmistakably identifies the foreigner.

Wrong or awkward intonation in oral reading distorts language and its meaning. Good intonation combines rhythm and melody so that phrases, clauses, sentences, make sense.

The most important single element of English intonation for reading and reading instruction is the regular dropping of the voice at the end of a sentence. This dropping of the voice means, "This pattern is now complete." *It means the same thing in word-by-word reading* (word calling) or in reading by meaningless pattern fragments. The dropping of the voice after each word or after each fragment wrongly signifies the end of a pattern. This kind of reading chops up the actual meaning-bearing patterns into unintelligible pieces: each piece receives the final intonation feature reserved in English for complete sentences.

The danger to reading comprehension is that such broken oral reading may lead to similarly broken silent reading, and to the development of an internalized process of habitual word-and-fragment reading. If this happens (and it does far too often) distorted comprehension in silent reading inevitably follows.

The rising inflection that occurs within sentences, often at pauses marked by commas, is another feature of intonation important to reading. This inflection means that only one part is complete; that the pattern will soon be resumed. Such an inflection is common in counting: *one, two, three, four, five*; and in lists: *paper, pencils, ink, chalk, erasers*. Only the last item is read with a falling tone.

A rising inflection is also used to terminate certain questions, but more end with the same falling tone that terminates sentences. For example: *What time is it? Who won the game? Where is the library?* These questions are identified as questions by the question markers, *what, who,* and *where.* If a speaker or reader use a rising inflection at the end of any of these questions, he turns it into a very different question; in fact, the difference between the rising tone and the falling tone is a structural pattern signifying a different intent.

Intonation is a study in itself, but reading teachers can rely on their automatic, intuitive sense in applying it to reading. A tape recorder is an invaluable aid in sharpening the sense of intonation.

### Sentence Patterns

An infinite variety of English sentences can be generated from a few basic patterns, often called *kernel sentences.* Structural grammar provides descriptions of these patterns and suggests some of their important transformations: manipulations, expansions, inversions, and substitutions within patterns.

A grasp of these sentence processes can be very helpful to both teacher and pupil in developing reading comprehension. *The boy hits the ball* is a simple subject-verb-object sentence. The word order in this sentence is completely rigid; if a single word is moved, the sentence either has a completely different meaning, *The ball hits the boy,* or it becomes nonsense, *Boy the hits ball the,* and so on. A passive transformation, however, gives *The ball is hit by the boy.*

Also, the sentence can be expanded with adjectives: *The large boy, The very large boy, The very large overgrown boy;* with prepositional phrases: *The very large boy with the red uniform, The very large boy from our school with the red uniform;* with clauses: *The very large boy from our school with the red uniform who has never missed a single ball game;* and so on almost indefinitely.

For reading comprehension it is very helpful to understand that both *The boy* and *The very large boy from our school with the red uniform who has never missed a single ball game* are the subject, or noun part, of the sentence, and that the verb is *hits.* The verb part, hits, can be similarly expanded, as can the second noun part, or object, *the ball.*

In reading instruction, it is important to realize that pupils are often required to read language patterns in their textbooks that they have never before heard, spoken, or written themselves. Pupils can first be taught how to read the kernel patterns and their simpler variations; subsequently they can move on to reading more involved and sophisticated sentences.

In the formulas below, the capital letters stand for parts of sentences, not parts of speech: N, means Noun part; V, Verb part; A, Adjective completer; *Ad,* Adverb completer; after the Verb part, N stands for Noun completer (complement, object complement, direct and indirect object). *Lv* stands for *Linking verb.* Now, here is a summary of four common sentence patterns:

Pattern One
---
N V   John arrived.
N V A   John arrived hungry.
N V *Ad*   John stood nearby.

Pattern Two
N V N   John hit the ball.

Pattern Three
N V N N   John gave Harry a watch.
N V N N   John made Harry chairman.
N V N A   John made Harry angry.

Pattern Four
N Lv N   John is the boss.
N Lv A   John is sick.
N Lv Ad   John is here.

Following are several common inversions of kernel sentences, including patterns using the expletives *there* and *it*.

Pattern One
A V N   Loud and clear rang the bell.
Ad V N   Nearby stood John.
There V N   There came a day.
It V N   It developed that he was out.
(Here the N is a noun clause.)

Pattern Four
N Lv N   Winner by inches was Dick.
A Lv N   Cleverest was Ruth.
Ad Lv N   Nearby was her mother.
There Lv N   There was a reason.
It Lv N   It was clear.
It Lv A N   It was clear that he was out.
It Lv Ad   It was just like that.

Following are common passive transformations of kernel sentences. In these formulas, *v* represents a form of *be* marking the passive verb form.

Pattern Two
N vV by N   The party was given by John.
N vV   The party was spoiled.
There vV V N   There were developed theories.
It V N   It developed that he was out.

Pattern Three
N vV N by N   He was given a toy by John.
N vN N   He was given a toy.
N vV N by N   He was made boss by John.
N vV N   He was made boss.
N vV A by N   He was made angry by John.

N *v*V A   He was made angry.
*It v*V A N   It was considered unfortunate that he was out.

In these simple examples, as well as in more complex and sophisticated sentences, a reader who misses the total pattern will miss the total meaning too. This part of structural grammar applied to reading instruction helps significantly to develop sentence sense and thus develop the basis for skills of literacy.

### Structure Words (or Function Words)

Structure words have the unique function of showing relationships among parts of sentences. They serve as joints between structural parts, or as glue binding structural joints together. The italicized words in the following sentence are all structure words. *If* you *can* believe *it, that* small boy is *the* best pitcher *on our* team.

There are about three hundred structure words in English, and in frequency of use they far surpass all the rest of our words. They include five sets of markers, the conjunctions, and several smaller sets having limited use, such as intensifiers.

1. Noun markers: *a, an, the, their, this, my, some*
2. Verb markers: *am, are, is, was, have, has been, done, did*
3. Phrase markers: *up, down, in, out, out of, above, below*
4. Clause markers: *if, because, although, even though, that, which*
5. Question markers: *who, why, how, when, where, what*

Structure words are so important to reading comprehension that misreading just one may result in failure to comprehend an entire meaning-bearing pattern.

### Word-Form Changes

Word-form changes include two sets: (1) grammatical inflections and (2) derivational prefixes and suffixes. Thus they may (1) indicate grammatical relationships such as tense or number within or between sentences: they may (2) change a word from one part of speech to another, or otherwise alter its meaning. A knowledge of the two sets or systems can be very helpful in structural word analysis and in vocabulary development.

*Number:* The boy likes *pie.*
   The boys like *pie.*
*Tense:* The boy *eats* pie.
   The boy *ate* pie.
*Structural Word Analysis:*
   The material is *workable.* (A verb base, *work,* plus suffix, *able,* makes the adjective *workable.*)

The material is *unworkable*. (A prefix, *un*, attached to *workable*, makes it negative, *unworkable*.)

The *work* is difficult. (*Work* as a noun subject.)

Can you *work* for me today? (A question using inverted order with verb marker *can*.)

## Phonics and Phonemics

Linguistics generally agree that American English has between thirty-one and thirty-three basic consonant and vowel sound units, or phonemes, varying somewhat according to regional dialects. *Phonemics*, the study of these basic sound units, is perhaps the most completely objective aspect of structural linguistics, because phonemics derives important data from the laboratory science of phonetics and makes important structural distinctions.

In the elementary school, phonics deals with the relationships of the twenty-six letters of the Roman alphabet to the 31–33 vowel and consonant phonemes. This is an aspect of reading instruction where pertinent findings of linguistics can be valuable in contributing accurate new information and in correcting some old information.

In our English writing system, phonemes are represented by various single letters and by combinations of letters; in linguistic terminology, any unit of writing (spelling) that represents a phoneme is a *grapheme*. It is of fundamental importance for all of us to think (and to teach both reading and writing) in terms of putting first things first. That is, *phonemes are primary* and graphemes (spellings) *secondary*. *Graphemes represent sounds*. Letters cannot be said to *make* sounds, nor even to *have* sounds. Profound confusion will certainly develop if this distinction is not kept crystal clear in the minds of elementary teachers and pupils.

It is not always clear in phonics materials and phonics instruction that letters do not and cannot make any sounds. On the contrary, this confusion is sometimes part and parcel of the instructional materials issued by publishers. Also, many phonic generalizations will not bear examination; for example, "When two vowels go a-walking" is not even half true. And there are others like it. Study of phonemics would equip any teacher to handle phonics instruction effectively, compensating if necessary for errors in published phonics materials.

Exactly what is being taught is not always clear in phonics materials, both in print and on records. Only in remedial speech is it necessary to give instruction in the production of the phonemes, but if remedial speech instruction is needed, it should not be part of the reading program. *Phonics instruction is most effective when it deals as simply and clearly as possible with the relationships between spelling and sound* and does not stray off into remedial speech.

Section 4

# DEVELOPING THE ABILITY TO UNDERSTAND, TO INTERPRET, TO REACT CRITICALLY, AND TO APPLY INSIGHTS GAINED THROUGH READING

## INTRODUCTION

*In any comprehensive discussion of reading we talk about understanding, interpreting, reacting critically, and applying insights gained through reading. It is possible to illustrate similarities and differences among these concepts, and to show that the mature reader engages in all of these activities.*

*The average reader in high school will read an American history book and understand that a war was fought between the states in the 1860's, and that the precipitating cause of this conflict was the shelling of Ft. Sumter in South Carolina. If he has a skillful teacher, he may be led to read the information about the events that occurred for a number of years prior to the War; and he may be helped to interpret this information, i.e., to make inferences and draw conclusions regarding it in order to determine the real, underlying causes for this rift. In this instance he would discover that one of the more deep-seated causes of the war was an economic battle between the industrial North and the agrarian South.*

*At a higher level of maturity the reader will react critically in examining sources relating to the conflict to determine the validity and accuracy of his information, and in reflecting on the value of these insights for the life of the reader. Finally, at the highest level of maturity, the reader wisely applies the insights he has gained from this reflective reading to improve his attitudes toward other people and their needs.*

*As the authors of this section probe deeply into the meaning of thoughtful, critical reading, they develop several important ideas: Reading is a thinking process that is improved as individuals learn to use*

107

*language more constructively and to clarify concepts through discussion that is generated and guided by skillful questioning. Furthermore, academic advantages accrue to the individual who is taught to apply learning principles designed to help him set purposes for reading, to interpret meanings, and to organize these meanings efficiently and effectively. However, the reader must develop accurate meanings that are relevant to his purposes for reading. Nor is the student left to his own devices, for in a first-rate classroom the alert teacher takes steps to help the student inquire more intelligently and more effectively.*

# SECONDARY SCHOOL READING
# AS THINKING *

Ruth Strang

*In recent years various panaceas for the reading problems of children and adults have been offered the general public. Such panaceas as phonics and "whiz-bang" speed reading reflect inaccurate, poorly-conceived ideas concerning the nature of the reading process.*

*The constructive use of language requires a person to see relationships, to generalize, to draw conclusions—in short, to think. Strang shows how such aspects of thinking are used in the following facets of reading: word recognition, locating information, skimming, organizing information, and comprehending paragraphs. She finishes her discourse by showing which conditions are conducive to thoughtful reading.*

*1. Thorndike's 1917 article "Reading As Reasoning" is widely quoted in articles on reading. Why?*

*2. How might the insights that you glean from the introduction affect your*

*teaching? your own reading?*

*3. What changes can you make in your approaches to teaching word recognition?*

*4. In the light of the information in the section "Skills in Locating Information," rewrite this section heading.*

*5. a. In the section "Paragraph Comprehension" read only the quoted material following the number one. b. Before reading the discussion that follows this paragraph, answer these questions:*

*(1) Where is the main idea of the paragraph expressed?*

*(2) State the major premise of the argument.*

*(3) State the minor premise.*

*(4) What are the three things that support the minor premise?*

*(5) Restate the conclusion.*

*6. Can you add any statements to the section "Conditions Favorable to Thoughtful Reading"?*

BROADLY defined, reading involves physical factors, thinking, and feeling. Thinking is implicit in every aspect of reading. To recognize words one must perceive likenesses and differences, and must be aware of the relations between letter sounds and printed symbols. Understanding of word meaning depends on giving proper weight to each part of the word, as E. L. Thorndike pointed out in 1917 in his article, "Reading As Reasoning." For example, giving undue weight to the first two syllables of the word *majority* led one youngster to define it as "the greatest general of them all." Similarly, in order to comprehend accurately the literal meaning of a passage, one must see relationships and give proper weight to each word, phrase, and sentence.

It is important not only to find out what an author says, but also to think about why he says it. Thinking is involved in arriving at generalizations,

* FROM *The Reading Teacher* (December 1961), pp. 155–161, reprinted with permission of Ruth Strang and the International Reading Association.

109

drawing conclusions, and making inferences and applications. As the reader recognizes that a given concept is similar to ones he has encountered previously, he may arrive at a generalization. When related ideas are evaluated, a conclusion may emerge. When they are used as a basis for speculation, inferences may be formulated. When the reader relates certain concepts to his life experiences, he may apply them to his own uses. In every instance thinking brings order to the material read, or creates new patterns out of it.

All these aspects of reading involve some feeling tone. The reader may feel satisfaction in being mentally alert and in accomplishing his purpose. He may feel pleasure or displeasure, satisfaction or annoyance with the content or the style. He may approve or disapprove of the author's ideas. Sometimes he will find his emotions aroused by some incident or character that the author describes. These feelings may either facilitate or hinder the thinking process.

Both thinking and feeling are involved in an individual's personal development through reading. For example, in discussing a detective story, *Buttons*, the teacher asked, "What clues do you find to the mother's character?" Students pointed out details indicating that she was reluctant to let her son grow up, that she jumped to conclusions, that she was a quick thinker, that she was jealous of his girl friend. The teacher followed up the first point by asking, "If the mother is overprotective, how might that affect Ernie?" And one student replied, "Children don't appreciate it when the mother does all the thinking for them."

In high schools today we find that students represent a wide range of reading ability—from nonreaders to some who read as well as superior adults. Contrary to general opinion, thinking is involved in teaching all kinds of students to read.

## WORD RECOGNITION AS THINKING

That thinking is required in phonic analysis is illustrated by the experience of a group of nonreading pupils of high school age. In reading their own stories these pupils were having difficulty with certain small words.*

Teacher: Which of these words begin with *w*?

Pupils: *Went, what, when.*

Teacher: Which one of these words begins with a sound different from the two others?

Pupil: *Went.*

Teacher: Think of three words that begin with the same sound as *went*.

Pupils: *Water, wash, wish.*

The teacher wrote these words on cards and asked the pupils to analyze the way each one is built, while they listened carefully to its sound. A similar

* For some of these illustrations the author is indebted to Mr. John McInnes' demonstrations in the summer High School and College Reading Center, Teachers College, Columbia University.

study was made of *what, when,* and *they.* After the pupils had practiced these words and had reread fluently the story in which they had initially encountered difficulty with them, the teacher again called their attention to the purpose of this practice in phonic analysis by saying, "You see, it's important to know the little words that cause many people trouble in reading."

Reasoning is also involved in teaching other word recognition skills, as in the following lesson with able learners:

Teacher: You have just begun to write books about yourselves. What do we call books people write about themselves?

Pupil: *Autobiography.* (Teacher writes it on the board.)

Teacher: This is an interesting word. With what smaller word does it start?

Pupil: *Auto.*

Teacher: What other words start the same way?

Pupil: *Auto*matic.

Pupil: *Auto*mobile.

Pupil: *Auto*graph.

Teacher: What do you think the first part of the word means?

Pupil: Self.

(Teacher writes *automaton* on the board to challenge their newly acquired learning): Can you think what this word means?

Pupil: Self-starting.

Pupil: It goes by itself.

Teacher: If you know the "key" to a word, it helps you get the meaning. You recognize the same part of a word in a number of different combinations.

That every step in unlocking the meaning of unfamiliar words requires thinking is illustrated by the following teaching experience. The teacher mentioned the problem, common to good as well as to poor readers, of discovering the meaning of words one does not know. He presented the sentence: He is an *iconoclast.*

Teacher: What word would you have difficulty with?

Pupil: The fourth.

Teacher: Is there any clue in the sentence as to its meaning?

Pupil: *He.*

Teacher: What does that tell us?

Pupil: That it is a person.

Teacher: If we added a few words to the sentence we would have better clues: *He was an iconoclast who undermined the boy's belief.* What are the key words here?

Pupil: *Undermined* and *belief.*

Teacher: What does *undermined* tell you?

Pupil: That he took away the boy's foundation or faith.

Teacher: What kind of belief might it be?

Pupil: Belief in God.

Teacher: Are there any clues in the word itself that make you think it's belief in God?

Pupil: My uncle brought an icon from Russia, and it's an image of Christ.

Teacher: Do you know any other word that has clast in it? (No answers.)

Teacher: *Idoloclast* is quite similar to *iconoclast*, but is not as commonly used. Let's try the dictionary. What does it say about these two words? What does the last part, *clast*, mean? What does the whole word mean? Give us some sentences using *iconoclast*. Who are the iconclasts today?

In answering these questions the students related *clast* to the Greek *klao*, *break*. They discussed the more specific meaning of *idoloclast*, and noted how the meaning of *iconoclast* had been extended from the breaking of an image to include the destruction of almost any faith or belief. They referred to "the angry young men" as iconoclasts of today.

Each of the word recognition skills—context clues (4), structural analysis, phonic analysis, and even the use of the dictionary—requires seeing relationships and making judgments as to the relevance of similar forms or meanings to the word in question.

## Skills in Locating Information

In exploring a book of short stories with a group of seriously retarded teen-age pupils, the teacher encouraged thinking by saying: "Let's look at the index. What kind of stories are there in this book? What kind of stories do you like best?"

Pupil: Adventure stories.

Teacher: What are adventure stories?

Pupil: Something exciting happens.

Teacher: Are there adventure stories in this book? Look through the book and judging by the titles and pictures find an adventure story. Then tell us why you think it is an adventure story. You can pick out the one you'd like to read first.

This exercise gave these youngsters practice in setting up and applying a criterion for the selection of interesting reading material.

Locating sources of information on a given topic may require an amazing amount of thinking.

It is easy enough to say glibly, "Select the material relevant to your topic," but many students need specific instructions in how to do this. For these students it is helpful, as McCullough pointed out (7), to go over a passage, sentence by sentence, asking such questions as, "Has this anything to do with.......? What has it to do with it? What shall we put down as part of our answer to this question?"

Second, there are many questions concerning the authenticity and reliability of the source. Is the publication date recent enough so that the material may include new developments on the topic? Is the author's purpose to give full and impartial information or to support a preconceived conclusion? Is he an authority on the subject? Does he distinguish between fact, reasonable opinion, and unsupported conjecture? Can his statements be verified? On what basis were the judgments made? Does the author have some special bias? Does he make exaggerated claims?

Differences between opinion and fact can be brought out by having a class give their snap judgment on a current news item, and then collect, organize, and relate facts that have a bearing on the item. A second opinion poll will show how the added information has changed the first impression. This experience shows the class that there is a great difference in the quality of opinions, depending upon the nature and amount of the evidence that supports the opinions.

Certain common errors may be found in source material: generalizations that go beyond the facts, reliance on a single authority rather than a representative range of authorities, and explanation of results by reference to a single cause rather than by reference to all possible causes.

Third, critical thinking is constantly necessary in the process of extracting content that is related to the topic and the reader's purpose.

Advertisements provide excellent material for practice in critical thinking. Television commercials can be presented in class and critically analyzed: What "persuasive" or "color" words are used to give certain impressions? What attention-getting devices are used? What things or ideas are associated with the product to enhance its appeal? What claims are made but not substantiated? Pupils may do experiments to test the accuracy of some of the statements. From this analysis of relatively obvious propaganda, the students may go on to the more subtle "slanting" that occurs in newspaper headlines and editorials. They may also consider the viewpoints implicit or expressed in history books, and eventually analyze the effectiveness and appropriateness of the figures of speech used in poetry.

## SKIMMING SKILLS

In skimming one must think about the purpose for which the skimming is done: to find a specific date or fact, to survey the organization of a chapter or article, to note the main ideas, to get a general impression of the topic. The first kind of skimming requires little thinking; it is somewhat like looking for a four-leafed clover. In the other types of skimming one must select relevant ideas and relate them in the desired form or pattern. This process often requires more concentration than would be necessary in a slower, more careful reading of the same material.

## OUTLINING AND SUMMARIZING

Outlining and summarizing are exercises in thinking. Questions help to direct the pupil's attention to meaning. If the teacher finds gaps in the pupil's outline, he may take the opportunity to offer instruction in methods for identifying important ideas. As preliminary practice the students may be asked to arrange separate sentences or paragraphs in logical order; this will show their ability to grasp the relations between ideas.

## PARAGRAPH COMPREHENSION

Paragraph reading can be an exercise in logical reasoning. The main idea of the paragraph is its premise or conclusion. The reader examines the evidence given in support of the premise or conclusion. To do this he must follow the organization of the passage as he reads. Once he has exposed the framework, he must determine whether the argument is valid by appraising each bit of evidence and each opinion. When he has a clear idea of what the author has said, the reader is able to distinguish between the author's ideas and those which the passage has evoked in his mind. Consider the following:

1. "The United States today faces a serious challenge to its basic, fundamental concept. If any nation, even when there is need for caution, in a period of anxiety, displays irrational fear and loss of nerve, and ignores the denial of human rights and the sublimation of national principles, that nation is losing its moral courage. In our time, we place censorship over the free play of intelligence upon issues, we foster the urge and tendency to turn the spirit of free inquiry into indoctrination and restraint of criticism, and we tolerate without protest sweeping attacks upon education. A crisis is upon us."

The main idea of this paragraph is expressed in both the first and the last sentence; it is a conclusion that is reached by deductive thinking. The major premise of the argument is included in the second sentence and can be stated thus: "All nations which exhibit fear and restrain liberty are nations which are losing moral courage." The minor premise, found in the third sentence, is that "the United States is a nation which exhibits fear and restrains liberty." This minor premise is supported by induction: the author lists three things which, in his opinion, show that we are exhibiting fear and restraining liberty. The conclusion can now be restated: "The United States is losing moral courage."

The organization of the paragraph is now clear. What are its implications? Does "facing a serious challenge to its basic concept" mean the same thing as "losing moral courage"? The author implies that it does. If it does not, the syllogism is not valid and the conclusion is not true. The author presents acceptable evidence of fear and restraint of liberty, but what about his assumption that a nation which displays fear and restrains liberty is losing moral courage? This is questionable. The author does not, in this paragraph, propose a solution or call for action. If the reader takes this additional step, he should be aware that this is his thought, and not the author's.

2. "Loyalty, whether to country or other individuals or to ideals, is a personal thing. Most truly loyal Americans are quite rightfully offended when their loyalty is not taken for granted. The person who should be suspect is

not the reluctant oath-giver but the one who all too readily and glibly proclaims to everyone within earshot that he is impeccably loyal. The faithless husband is the one most likely to protest too much about his fidelity to his wife. But the faithful husband, badgered by a nagging wife, is more likely to affirm his loyalty only with the sort of distaste that breeds contempt." *

Here the main idea is expressed in the third sentence: "The person who should be suspect is the one who all too readily and glibly proclaims his loyalty." The author seeks to support his argument by drawing an analogy between faithfulness to one's country and fidelity to one's wife. He makes the generalization that all loyalties have one factor in common—they are personal, but he does not mention their differences. His implication that the unfaithful husband and the disloyal American will behave in the same way does not stand up under critical appraisal; therefore the argument must be rejected.

## COMPREHENSION OF THE WHOLE

Different patterns of thinking are required for different school subjects. In the social studies one must follow sequences of events and discern cause and effect relations. This kind of thinking may be stimulated by such questions as these: "How has the geography of the country influenced the character of its people?" "How have events in the history of the country affected conditions there today?" Scientific materials, as Russell (8) pointed out, "are often organized around some principle or law . . . in health [the writer] is usually making applications of known facts."

To encourage students to think while reading a story, such questions as these are helpful: "Why did this boy want a car?" "Read the part that tells what kind of a person he was. Do you think he knew much about cars? What evidence do you have of this?" "What has happened in the story up to this point?" (This question involves telling the events in the story in logical sequence.) "What do you think happened next?"

Reading an article demands reasoning from start to finish. The source of the article—editorial page, news page, advertisement, textbook, or popular magazine—gives the reader an initial clue to the purpose for which it was written. By examining the title he may get further clues as to what to expect. From the first paragraph he sometimes gets information about "who," "where," "when," and "how many." In the succeeding paragraphs the reader may find elaboration or support of the ideas introduced in the first paragraph. In a final paragraph he is likely to find the author's conclusions, which he should compare with his own conclusions as he forms them.

* These illustrations of the application of formal logic to the analysis of prose arguments were given in an unpublished paper written by Captain Philo A. Hutcheson in the author's course in the improvement of reading in high school and college at Teachers College, Columbia University. Captain Hutcheson has shown how the teaching of logic may help to improve the higher-level reading skills that are so important in our life today.

## CONDITIONS FAVORABLE TO THOUGHTFUL READING

Reading is most likely to be a thinking process under the following conditions:

1. When there is a problem to be solved, a story to be interpreted, a question to be answered; under these conditions the reader has a mind-set to read in a thoughtful, purposeful way.
2. When the reader has time to review what he already knows about the problem and to think while he is reading.
3. When the reader receives instruction and practice in the techniques of reading critically and determining the precise meanings of words.
4. When pupils have a chance to discuss what they read; group discussion alerts them to the need for critical reading and rewards their efforts to read thoughtfully.
5. When pupils are encouraged to relate their experience to their reading.
6. When pupils have not been lulled to passivity by the effortless entertainment provided by television, radio, and other mass media where the thinking, such as it is, has all been done by the producer.
7. When examination questions can be answered only by thoughtful reading.

Each reading task requires a different kind of thinking, depending on the material and the reader's purpose. Life is too short to make a detailed, logical analysis of every paragraph. Overemphasis on critical interpretation may make some meticulous pupils overmeticulous.

On the other hand, thinking makes reading exciting, and opens doors into the adventurous unknown. It enhances the delight and satisfaction that one may obtain from books.

### REFERENCES

1. BETTS, A. EMMETT. "Reading Is Thinking," *The Reading Teacher*, XII (Feb., 1959, 146–51.
2. BULLOCK, HARRISON. *Helping the Non-Reading Pupil in the Secondary School*. New York: Bureau of Publications, Teachers College, Columbia University, 1956.
3. CHERINGTON, MARIE R. "Improving Reading Skills in College Subjects." Unpublished doctoral thesis. New York: Teachers College, Columbia University, 1952.
4. "Context Aids in Reading," *The Reaching Teacher*, XI (Apr., 1958), 225–43.
5. DALE, EDGAR. "Teaching Critical Thinking," *The Newsletter*, Ohio State University, XXIV (Jan., 1959), 1–4.
6. GERRELL, ROBERT M., and LAIRD, CHARLTON. *Modern English Handbook*. Englewood Cliffs, New Jersey: Prentice-Hall, 1956.
7. McCULLOUGH, CONSTANCE C. "Conditions Favorable to Comprehension," *Education*, LXXIX (May 1959), 533–36.

8. RUSSELL, DAVID H. *Children Learn to Read*, pp. 233–34. Boston: Ginn, 1949.
9. STAUFFER, RUSSELL G. "A Directed Reading-Thinking Plan," *Education*, LXXIX (May 1959), 527–32.

(*From Vol. 13, No. 3, February 1960.*)

# IMPROVING COMPREHENSION-INTERPRETATION SKILLS *

Joseph A. Fisher

*There is a definition of mind control that has a negative connotation to many teachers. Fortunately, there is a definition of mind control in education which implies benevolent guidance of students, and the activities that are a part of this kind of mind control are not negative or objectionable.*

*Donald O. Hebb has stated in the* Control of the Mind (*Farbes and Wilson, eds.*) *that an important consideration in controlling the mind is man's insatiable activity which, although environmentally initiated, is self-paced. Fisher recognizes a related problem in teaching comprehension-interpretation skills: although stimulation and guidance are necessary in teaching children, the subject matter teacher should help these children develop into independent, inquiring readers. In this article Fisher presents many practical suggestions for attaining this goal through learning how to interpret and organize ideas gained through reading.*

*1. What distinction does the author make between learning to read and reading to learn? What are the implications of this distinction for teaching?*

*2. How can the secondary teacher help his students develop into independent readers?*

*3. According to the author, what academic advantages can accrue to the student who learns to preview material, to ask questions about the material, and to answer the questions?*

*4. Which principles of learning are involved in the exercises in "Improving skill in reading for main ideas"?*

*5. What is the value in reading to organize details?*

*6. Which learning principles are involved in the suggestions on developing a vocabulary?*

*7. Rank the twelve suggestions for "Reading to Interpret Meaning" according to (a) complexity, (b) difficulty in developing, and (c) usefulness in developing the ability to interpret meaning.*

THE MOST basic principle guiding reading instruction has been that children learn to read so that they can read to learn. It is almost impossible to find a single statement in the literature on reading which would endorse word-calling as being of any value in learning to read. Therefore, it is not

---

* Written especially for inclusion in this volume.

surprising that in one form or another methods of developing comprehension skills in readers form the essential content of all manuals concerned with reading instruction, and that this concern has always formed the ultimate basis for research in the field of reading.

Because the basic comprehension skills at the primary level are so well established, and the recognized procedures commonly employed by teachers to develop these skills are so generally effective in producing readers who can read elementary materials with understanding, it would seem incredible that we should have secondary readers who are unable to understand their reading assignments. Yet it is common knowledge that as many as one child in four in the secondary school population experiences some degree of difficulty in understanding his reading assignments.

Undoubtedly, there are children at this level who simply never learned to read for some reason or another. These must be given remedial assistance to compensate for this deficiency. But the majority of these readers did learn to read; they are able to attack and pronounce new words and are able to read certain materials with understanding. They seem to have reading problems which in some mysterious way are associated with textbooks in subject matter fields. They may be said to have learned to read but are not able to read to learn. In order to help these readers, it is important that the secondary teachers understand the meaning of the distinction between these two concepts.

In learning to read, the emphasis is on the mechanics of reading, word attack, sentence formation, etc. At this level the child is concerned with making an association between the oral language he already knows, and the written language he is learning to read. At this level, the most important skill he is required to use is his power of discrimination between the various symbols used to convey the meaning. This accounts for the necessity to control the rate of introduction of new vocabulary, and the restriction of content to concepts already in the child's experience. These things are done primarily because they make it possible for the child to focus all his energy on the discriminatory learning task. In a somewhat oversimplified form, this is the meaning of learning to read.

Eventually, as the student becomes more proficient at the discrimination task, more emphasis is placed on his grasp of the thought words convey. At this point he begins reading to learn. Reading to learn begins, to some extent, even before the child has completely learned to read in the sense that he is always required to give evidence that he has understood what he has read. But because most of the content of reading material at this lowest level is already in the reader's experience, it is possible that these comprehension checks draw upon the child's memory as much as his power to understand the reading matter.

As he progresses from the primary through the elementary levels, more and more emphasis is placed on reading to learn, and the concept load of the reading matter becomes proportionately farther and farther removed in time and place from the experience of the individual child demanding a greatly increased vocabulary. Therefore during this gradual development the child must be carefully guided in his effort to learn to read by the teacher who thoroughly prepares the child for each learning task.

Quite possibly, as a direct result of the assistance the children receive during this prolonged period of elementary reading, many come to expect this guidance to be provided in all their new reading experience. But unless the child has been made aware of the need to prepare himself for independent reading, he may find himself unable to read anything new or challenging without assistance.

It is entirely possible that a large proportion of poor secondary readers have either never been taught to prepare themselves to read, or have been unable to transfer their preparation skills to new reading assignments. We know that most poor readers are passive readers; that is, readers who expect the writer to be responsible for capturing and building their interest, explaining his terminology, and so presenting his material that they need merely gaze at it to grasp his meaning. No doubt many authors of textbooks have accepted this responsibility; this may account for the number of students in college who have reading problems, as it may be the first time such readers have actually been required to be really independent readers.

## Preparing to Read

In the last analysis, the secondary teacher has the responsibility of developing independent readers. An essential element in this development consists in making readers aware of the fact that they must always prepare themselves for reading to learn. Reading to learn is never a one-shot affair; it is a process, not a single act. Just as the writer is seldom satisfied to write his material only once but first prepares an outline or rough draft, then expands his outline and follows this with careful revision of details, so the reader should first become familiar with the general organizational pattern of what he intends to read; then identify the principal points used to develop the thought and, finally, analyze the details through which the main points are established or developed.

Unfortunately, students who still have dependent reading habits, or are passive readers, often actively resist the effort and energy required to read the way they should. The teacher must therefore take steps to insure the development of these skills. Since many of these students are motivated to read their assignments primarily so that they can answer questions about them, the teacher can control the kind of reading the students will do by giving reading assignments which require students to employ particular reading skills.

The most important step in preparing students to read independently centers on the prereading survey. An excellent way to insure that such preparation will be undertaken is to give a survey assignment at the beginning of a course, or unit, or even a chapter. To make such an assignment effective the teacher should explain to students where the most essential information of the assignment can be found, and how the unit or chapter is organized.

Approximately 80 per cent of the principal ideas of textbook assignments can be found in the first sentences of paragraphs. The introductory paragraph usually indicates the general scope of the topic covered and frequently provides background information or a very specific outline of the contents. The final paragraph often provides a summary of what has been said. Such information will not of itself do much to alter old reading habits. But if the teacher immediately gives an open-book quiz that requires the students to survey the assignment, a value is assigned to the procedure which will provide motivation.

The questions in such a quiz should obviously deal with such information as can be found in the survey if it is properly made. Examples of the types of questions for a chapter on the Civil War might include such items as:

1. What five topics are discussed in the chapter on the Civil War?
2. How does the author divide his discussion of the causes of the Civil War?
3. Which states belonged to the confederacy? (Using map provided.)
4. Name the major battles of the Civil War.
5. What does the author discuss under Reconstruction, and so on?

The teacher must always remember that the purpose of the survey is to acquaint the student with the general content and organization of the assignment before he attempts to read it. Since various types of visual aids, pictures, maps, charts, may be found in the assignment, the information they afford should be included in the questions. This kind of quiz can profitably be corrected in class and form the basis of the teacher's own introductory remarks.

As important and useful as it may be, the survey does not complete the preparation necessary for reading to learn. In order to be able to read for meaning, the student needs to be taught how to concentrate on and organize the thought content of the material. To do this it is necessary to be able to form questions which can be answered by the reading done. Because a question is easier to keep in mind than a statement and serves as a natural center for organizing details, it is a very useful learning device.

Students should be encouraged to convert major headings into organizational questions as they read each subdivision of their assignment as a technique of keeping track of the thought processes being developed. This is easily accomplished by placing words like who, what, where, when, why, how, before the topic heading. The process of converting topic sentences into questions as one reads serves as a preparation for reading each succeeding paragraph, and so gives it more meaning. By focusing the reader's attention in this way on understanding what is read, the teacher develops in the student an attitude of active response to content.

In order to insure that students develop independence in reading in the way they have been guided, the teacher can require them to make up the questions based on a survey of an assignment for themselves. These questions may then be used as the basis for class discussion of the topic they were intended to cover prior to reading the assignment.

Often students find it difficult or impossible to grasp the meaning of what they read because they do not know the meaning of certain words used. The survey step can serve as a convenient means of identifying such terms before reading begins. Many publishers italicize or use special type faces to identify such words. By calling attention to them in context, and often providing a definition as well, the publishers make it as convenient as possible for the student to learn these words before he begins reading without the bother of looking up meanings in the dictionary. The teacher can reinforce the vocabulary thus identified by including it in the preparatory discussion in class.

It also happens that students soon forget what they learn from an assignment. Learning, like writing and reading, is not complete in one act. To be remembered, material must be reviewed. For this reason the student must be taught to frequently review what he has learned. After he has once learned to make a good survey before reading, the student can be taught to use the same technique for making reviews. By viewing the headings or questions, he should attempt to recite from memory the major ideas which were included under them by the author. When he is unable to recall the content under a heading well enough to answer his question, he should reread that portion of the material.

The teacher, who has given survey assignments requiring students to convert topic headings into questions, can suggest that students use these questions in preparing for weekly quizzes and unit tests. This procedure cultivates the habit of frequent review and thus insures the permanence of learning.

The preceding suggestions will be recognized substantially as a means of developing the SQ3R study method of study in students by the classroom teacher. This means of improving comprehension skills at the secondary level has been presented as being the usual situation in which comprehension skills can generally be developed by the average classroom teacher at the secondary level, who is only incidentally a teacher of reading. The following specific suggestions for developing different types of comprehension skills discussed are all implicit in the process and approach previously described, but are intended to assist the subject matter teacher desiring to provide special help in improving particular reading skills to accommodate individual student needs.

## IMPROVING SKILL IN READING FOR MAIN IDEAS

1. Select a few paragraphs from the textbook and supply several topic sentences for each. Ask students to select the best topic sentence for the paragraph. In the beginning use the exact words of the topic sentence of the para-

graph as the correct choice. When students have become proficient at this, the correct topic sentence can be paraphrased to make it harder to identify. A very useful technique that students can be taught to use to determine whether the sentence they select is, in fact, the topic sentence, is to repeat the selected sentence after each sentence in the paragraph. If they have correctly identified the topic sentence, the paragraph thought will continue to flow smoothly.

2. Several paragraphs from the text may be presented and the students required to write a topic sentence for each. If the topic sentence is actually the first sentence of the paragraph in the beginning and then found elsewhere, or implied, in later exercises students will be able to improve their ability to formulate topic sentences with confidence.

3. The introductory paragraph of a chapter can be presented and the students required to make an outline of the chapter from it. This can be checked by actually referring to the chapter for subheadings.

4. The summary paragraph of the chapter can be read carefully and the students required to identify the major points of the chapter from it. This can be checked by referring to the chapter.

5. Students can then be asked to put the topic sentences of several paragraphs into their own words and form a summary of the contents of the material in their own words.

6. When permissible, students can be assigned the task of underlining their texts, or marking the margins, to indicate the organization of the material presented. Because underlining achieves the same purpose as outlining, and has the added advantages of requiring less time and permitting the students ready access to supplementary information they may need to review, it should not be discouraged when students own their textbook. Outlining is an alternative when state-owned books are being used.

7. When the content admits of the technique, requiring students to prepare a diagram or sketch illustrating the content of a chapter is an excellent means of forcing them to look for general organizational patterns.

## READING TO ORGANIZE DETAILS

After the student has developed sufficient skill in determining the main ideas he will recognize for himself the need for skill in reading for details, for without these the general ideas will lack depth and the degree of meaning he needs to master the subject matter.

In order to be able to remember details, the student should be taught to look for the organizational patterns by which they are related to their topic sentence. Here it is useful to call attention to the way textbooks usually organize paragraphs. Generally, the topic sentence opens the paragraph and the subsequent sentences develop this single thought. Often there is a summary sentence given. Three types of sentences are used in a paragraph; the topic sentence, the developmental sentence, and the summary sentence.

The details which the student needs to organize are found in the developmental sentences usually found in the body of the paragraph. The sentences which develop the main thought of the paragraph do this by either repeating the main idea in other words; by contrasting this idea with something else or telling what it is not; by providing illustrations or examples of the topic sentence; by justifying the topic sentence or giving reasons for it, or, finally, by describing or qualifying the topic sentence. The teacher can develop exercises to improve this ability to read for details by:

1. Providing the students with paragraphs from their texts and asking them to classify each sentence as 'T' for topic, D for detail or developmental, or S for summary.

2. Present paragraphs from their texts to the students and ask them to identify the developmental sentences as to kind using R for repetition, C for contrast, E for example, J for justification, and D for description.

3. Present several paragraphs from the text into which an irrelevant sentence has been inserted, and ask the students to identify this sentence by striking it out.

4. Have the students read a paragraph from the text, and then ask them to select from a group of prepared sentences those which would properly fit into the paragraph.

5. Have the students make a formal outline of a section of the chapter in their text places, with special emphasis on the ability to distinguish between generalization and details.

6. To assist students in recognizing the relationships between generalizations and supporting details, the teacher may present a number of generalizations and a number of details and ask the students to list the details under their proper generalization. If all this material is drawn from the text, it serves to develop understanding of the subject matter as well.

7. The teacher can call attention to certain words used by writers to indicate organization.

a. Clues to a contrasting thought:
   Although, but, however, nevertheless, rather, whereas, and yet.
b. Certain common phrases serve the same purpose:
   Even though, in spite of, on the other hand, on the contrary.
c. Additional information on the same point is often introduced by such expressions as:
   Beyond this, moreover, furthermore, and in addition.
d. Conclusions begin with such expressions as:
   As a result, consequently, hence, in conclusion, so, therefore.

The use and value of such terms can be brought to the student's attention by presenting paragraphs in which they are used and asking him to indicate the effect of the term on the thought.

## VOCABULARY BUILDING

Frequently teachers find that students have difficulty with reading assignments because they have not learned the special vocabulary for the subject area. To develop vocabulary effectively the teacher can:

1. Provide a contextual definition of a word and ask the student to underline the word defined.
2. Provide sentences with blanks to be filled with one of several words.
3. Provide for periodic review of difficult words by preparing a matching test in which the words are to be paired with their correct meaning.
4. Provide a list of words that need to be learned in a given assignment and ask the students to write the sentence in which each is used in the text when they read it in their lesson and provide a definition in their own words.
5. Have students survey an assignment and note all italicized words, or words printed in bold-faced type and discuss these or require students to define them before reading the assignment.

## SETTING READING PURPOSE

Unless the student has some specific goal in mind when he reads his assignment he is likely to simply wander through it, hoping to be impressed with a few of the more significant ideas presented. By teaching the student to take a few moments to determine what he is supposed to learn from an assignment, the teacher can assist him in making study a more rewarding experience emotionally for the student and a more effective learning experience. The following suggestions will indicate how the teacher can teach students to form their own reading purposes:

1. During the survey assignment which students do in the classroom, the teacher can point out the purpose of the day's lesson by converting the introductory paragraph into a series of questions. Since part of all assignments is to teach information, the learning task is to find answers to the questions thus formed.
2. The teacher can allow the class to make a survey and then ask them to share the reading purpose they formed for themselves with the class.
3. It is useful at times to provide the class with a problem and require them to read an assignment to find a solution. This problem should not consist of a question made by converting the chapter heading or a subhead into a question, but deal with something implied in the lesson.
4. Students should be asked what the author intended in writing a given chapter or assignment. They should be able to phrase this purpose in their own words.
5. Students may be assigned specific material to read in order to relate it

to some current problem or put it to some specific use in a report, presentation, or the preparation of a chart, illustration, or a diagram.

6. The purpose of some assignments is simply to provide enrichment for students. A chapter in another text may be assigned relating to a topic covered in class to provide background or supplement classroom work. Students who have been given such assignments should be asked to read it to share their information with the class in discussion.
7. Students can be provided with a general statement and asked to list reasons or justifications for the statement found in the text.
8. Suggestions for reading to get the general idea, organizational pattern, or specific details can also be used as purposes for reading particular assignments.

## READING TO INTERPRET MEANING

Reading for interpretation is perhaps one of the most advanced reading skills the student can learn. Essentially it involves going beyond the ideas actually expressed by the author, and determining implications, justifiable inferences, and possible applications. Only after a student has mastered the ideas expressed can he hope to cope with interpretation. The following practices will prove useful in assisting students to develop such power:

1. Have the students write a summary of an assignment in their own words.
2. Have the students read the introductory paragraph of a chapter or section of a chapter, and ask them to predict the probable organization of the chapter.
3. Present the students with a conclusion drawn from the assignment, and ask them to find justifications. After practice in this way a false generalization may be presented and students can be asked to evaluate it in terms of information given in a chapter of the text.
4. Present students with a paragraph and several conclusions and ask them to determine which conclusions appear justified.
5. Offer students a number of paragraphs out of sequence and ask them to place them in proper order.
6. Give the students a paragraph, and offer them a series of statements. Ask them to indicate which statements are consistent with the information provided in the paragraph.
7. Explain to students that deductive paragraphs begin with generalizations that are justified by details which follow, and that inductive paragraphs present a number of facts terminating in a generalization or conclusion. Then ask students to classify sample paragraphs as inductive or deductive.
8. Present students with an incomplete deductive paragraph and require them to write the conclusion.

9. Offer students an incomplete series of logical steps and ask them to supply the missing part.
10. After completing an assignment discussing a particularly complex issue, ask students to explain why it is difficult to arrive at simple clean-cut solutions.
11. Ask students to explain emotional factors which gave rise to certain complications encountered in an assignment.
12. Have the student place himself in the role of a person involved in the content of an assignment and have him explain how he would feel or think.

### INTERPRETING SYMBOLISM

In certain courses the use of figures of speech and verbal symbolism plays an important role in conveying the writer's meaning. Because these are more sophisticated forms of communication, the teacher must anticipate difficulty in the proper interpretation of such language and call attention to it as part of the preparation for reading. To foster independence in this difficult facet of reading, the teacher should encourage students to carefully skim assignments in which symbols are used. Symbolism is not regularly employed in expository writing but the following suggestions as to how to do this would include:

1. Provide students with selected paragraphs from the text and identify the symbols used perhaps by underlining them. Ask the students to tell what they think the symbol means. The meaning is usually determined by the context in which it is used.
2. Provide the students with a series of paragraphs and ask them to identify the symbolic language and interpret its meaning.
3. After students have interpreted the symbols in a series of paragraphs, call attention to the compressing power of symbols by having them write the paragraphs over and use their own interpretations instead of the symbols.

### CONCLUSION

The ultimate goal of education is to teach the student to learn for himself. Because of the role reading plays in achieving this purpose, it will only be realized if he is given assistance in developing independent reading ability in the various subject matter areas.

By calling attention to the distinction between learning to read and reading to learn, the responsibility of the subject-matter teacher has been clarified. Because such teachers are frequently subject-matter oriented, suggestions regarding reading improvement have been directly related to the process of teaching subject matter.

While the teacher who uses the suggestions given as paradigms for his own individual initiative in improving reading skills of students cannot reasonably expect to eliminate all reading learning problems, he will have done much to make the ability to read effectively in textbooks another skill his course has to offer the student. Although it is true that the degree to which many of these higher reading skills can be developed will be determined to a great extent by the student's native intelligence, the teacher must realize that most students are probably operating well below these natural limits. The teacher who incorporates reading skills into the teaching of subject matter will lessen this gap considerably and make it possible for the individual student to develop his full potential.

# SEQUENCE IN THOUGHTFUL AND CRITICAL REACTION TO WHAT IS READ *

Robert Karlin

*The truly critical reader applies himself vigorously to determining the accuracy, relevance, and worth of what he reads. The very fact that the Latin terms* ad hominem, caveat emptor, post hoc ergo propter hoc, (and cui bono?) *enjoy current usage is a grim reminder that the problem of ascertaining truth is a perennial one and a difficult one.*

*The ability to differentiate true statements from false ones is not automatically bestowed upon a person when he reaches a certain age. Karlin takes the point of view that children can be taught to read critically, but that the skills involed in critical reading must be taught sequentially and systematically—*

*if individuals are to learn to make thoughtful, critical reactions of what they read.*

*1. What are the author's assumptions in the introduction, and in the section "Needs and Problems"?*

*2. What factors are associated with the ability to do critical reading?*

*3. Relate the ability of several of your students to read critically to the abilities and backgrounds of the students in the categories listed by the author.*

*4. What steps can you take to improve the critical reading abilities of the students whom you analyzed previously?*

*5. Why is it important to teach people to read critically?*

T HE PURPOSE of this paper is to discuss the skills and abilities which should be developed to permit children and older students to react thoughtfully and critically to what they read. Before the reader can evaluate

---

* REPRINTED FROM *Sequential Development of Reading Abilities*, Helen M. Robsinson, editor, Supplementary Educational Monographs, No. 90, pp. 74–79, by permission of The University of Chicago Press. Copyright, 1960, by the University of Chicago Press.

the content of a selection, it is essential that he perceive the words accurately and secure the meanings intended by the author. Sequential development of skills and abilities in these areas have been considered in the preceding chapters. The term critical is defined in *Webster's New World Dictionary of the American Language* as characterized by careful analysis; furthermore, the term implies an attempt at objective judging so as to determine both merits and faults. Applied to reading then, to be critical means to be discriminating or evaluative. A kind of judgment based on what is known is implied.

Those who have studied the process of reading emphasize the similarities to the process of thinking. The reader deals with printed language much in the same way as the listener deals with spoken language. In reading, the element of visual symbols must be introduced but once they are known, symbols trigger the orderly processes of thinking. If we regard the reading process as similar to the thinking process, then we may conclude that critical reading involves critical thinking. Therefore, Russell's definition of critical thinking appears to be appropriate. He explains it as "the process of examining . . . verbal materials in the light of related objective evidence, comparing . . . the statement with some norm or standard, and concluding or acting upon the judgment then made." [1] He refers to the use of concrete objects as well as verbal materials since he is not limiting the discussion to reading. With this frame of reference, let us examine some of the problems associated with the teaching of critical reading.

## NEED AND PROBLEMS

Any reasonable group of educators would agree that the need for teaching critical reading is paramount. The authors of almost every modern textbook on the teaching of reading devote some space to developing this ability.

One of the problems in teaching critical reading has to do with the learner and the influence of teaching upon him. We know that children pattern their thinking and behavior upon models in whom they have confidence and with whom they feel a sense of security. These first models are their parents and other adults with whom they have some relation. When a pupil comes for the first time face to face with doubts that are cast upon his models' reliability, he has a difficult choice to make. Some children are not sufficiently mature to cope with this challenge and must not be forced by continuing pressures.

A second problem revolves around the issue of determining what kind of attitudes shall be fostered by the schools and who has the ultimate responsibility for deciding which these shall be. In some homes more than in others complete submissiveness to authority is demanded and ideas presented and pronouncements made are to be accepted without any reservations. The introduction and encouragement by the school of conflicting attitudes through

---

[1] David Russell, *Children's Thinking*, p. 285. Boston: Ginn & Co., 1956.

the teaching of critical reading can be opposed to the training carried on in such homes. Obviously the schools must assume leadership roles in such situations but at times we are blinded to the consequences of our acts by our cause. By all means, teach children to read critically but be prepared to deal with exigencies which might result from this teaching.

## INFLUENCING FACTORS

Data have been accumulated showing that many students need help in improving their abilities to read and think critically. However, several factors may limit the extent of development in this area. Intelligence may prove to be a significant factor. Just as we ordinarily expect the child of normal or superior intellectual ability to surpass the school achievements of children with lesser endowments, so may we anticipate the degree to which a pupil is able to achieve in critical reading. Nevertheless, slower learners should be encouraged to react to ideas to the extent that they are able to do so. But our expectations of their achievements ought not be as high as for brighter children.

Although intelligence and ability to read critically appear to be related, investigators have found that high performance on an intelligence test does not guarantee equally-high performance in situations which require critical thinking. This fact has prompted many educators to point to the importance of providing instruction directed to improvement of critical thinking.

A second factor associated with ability to do critical reading is background of experiences. If we define critical thinking as comparing what is read with a known standard, then the standard arises from knowledge or understanding. "In general, the more a child knows about the circumstances surrounding a problem, the better his solution will be. Knowledge does not necessarily mean good thinking, but high-order thinking is dependent upon knowledge." [2] Knowledge is identified with concepts, and vague or tenuous ones may not be used as models for comparison. Since many of the ideas with which learners deal are abstract, then it follows that real experiences help to add substance to them. First-hand experiences are usually preferred to vicarious ones and should be provided. The student who is expected to evaluate a newspaper editorial must not only possess some information about the topic, but also understandings based upon his previous experiences.

A third factor which may affect ability to react critically is the attitude of the reader toward the content read. Prejudices toward or against persons, ideas or topics have been shown to interfere with the reader's performance in evaluating printed matter. The results of several investigations have demonstrated that the student's attitude toward the content which he is reading can influence his reactions to it. Among these is the study of Crossen [3] who

[2] *Ibid.*, p. 336.
[3] Helen Crossen, "Effects of Attitudes of the Reader upon Critical Reading Ability." Unpublished Ph.D. dissertation, University of Chicago, August 1946.

reported a positive relationship between adolescents' ability to read material about minority groups critically and their attitudes toward these same groups.

There are indications also that the reader's understanding may be impaired when his attitude toward the subject matter is negative. Kendall and Wolf [4] reported the results of an experiment in which the individuals' predisposition toward the material read interfered with their understanding of it. Readers whose attitudes were favorably identified with the ideas expressed in cartoons were able to react positively to them while others whose views differed with those same ideas misinterpreted them. Psychologists have been categorizing patterns of behavior and have been able to identify persons who are likely to be swayed easily and others who are bound to resist.

## Scope and Sequence

The over-all concept of readiness for learning is inherent in sequential learning. To start with the known, the simple, the concrete are guidelines that each of us may follow.

Although there have not been systematic studies to determine in what order the skills of critical reading should be taught we have been able to extrapolate some hierarchy from the experiences of teachers. These empirical findings, however, remain to be tested under carefully controlled conditions. Students of critical reading have examined different aspects of the major ability in terms of the known and the unknown, the simple and the complex and the concrete and the abstract. Additional data have been drawn from our knowledge of some of the limiting factors that have been described earlier.

Several conclusions have been reached:

1. Some children have learned to think critically before entering school.
2. Critical reading has its earliest beginnings in the primary grades.
3. The level of critical reading achieved is controlled not so much by the nature of the process as it is by the experiences of the reader and his ability to deal with them.

On what skills of critical reading should the minds of six-, seven-, and eight-year-olds be stretched? One of the first might involve the reading of pictures which appear in their books. Illustrations may depict reality accurately or they may take liberties with it. It is not wholly a matter of accepting or rejecting them but rather recognizing them for what they are. Even though we see Jack climbing the beanstalk which towers over everything, we have no hesitation about going along with the story and picture.

Another ability is to select one picture among several, on the basis of its character and relationship to the highlights of the story. An extension of this

[4] Patricia Kendall and Katherine Wolf, "The Analysis of Deviant Cases in Communications Research." In P. Lazarsfeld and F. Stan, *Communications Research*, pp. 152–179. New York: Harper & Bros., 1949.

ability would involve the recommendation of pictures which could be used to accompany original stories and poems.

The ability to accept or reject statements on the basis of authority can begin in the primary grades. A group studying the requirements of proper diet would be led to seek information from the school dietitian rather than from the school custodian. This ability to recognize the reliability of a source of information is built first upon gross discriminations and then finer ones. For example, to choose between the school nurse and school dietitian for authoritative information about food values would be more difficult.

Primary-grade children read fanciful tales as well as factual reports. The ability to discriminate between the two should be developed. Outright rejection may be tempered by tentative acceptance. But, here too, sequence demands simple distinctions first and more difficult ones later.

Children must learn to select sources which yield appropriate information for their purposes. Skilful evaluation of printed materials is reserved for higher levels but second and third graders can learn to choose a book or a magazine which is most likely to contain the knowledge they seek. Sequential learning calls for judgments based in turn upon the pictures, titles, and tables of content.

The development of reading tastes involves discriminatory thinking. Preschool children are capable of making choices on the basis of some standard, and this ability may be strengthened in the primary grades. The ability to compare the worth of books and express a preference for better ones should be on our list of requirements.

Critical reading in the middle grades involves the strengthening and extension of skills that have been built in the primary grades. It also means the introduction of some higher-level skills for which older children are ready. The same type of critical attitude which is fostered in the lower grades will be encouraged in the higher ones; the materials with which the pupils deal, however, will be of a more difficult sort.

It is in the middle grades that wide reading of factual materials in textbooks, magazines and newspapers is encouraged. The solution to curriculum problems demands that children begin to use care in selecting and evaluating information from the above-mentioned sources. To determine the adequacy and accuracy of what purports to be a factual statement is an ability which calls for rather mature insights. Children are bound to meet different reports of the same event and must be prepared to evaluate each in terms of the authors' possible biases and qualifications, the audience for whom the information is intended and the recentness of the content. A viewpoint which depreciates the notion of space travel or the possibility of life on other planets may be seriously questioned in view of current scientific advances.

It would be well to note that most ten- or eleven-year-olds can hardly be expected to recognize biases which are masked by the use of subtle phraseology. But they surely can be taught to identify statements of personal opinion.

Another aspect of critical reading for pupils of this age involves questions of judgment based upon values to which they subscribed. For a child to be able to answer the question, "Was it the right thing to do?" as he studies the westward movement and the ultimate placement of the Indian on reservations requires the accumulation of more facts and fewer opinions and the weighing of issues. Of course he is able to relate such conduct only to his concept of fairness, and no effort should be made to have him struggle with moral issues that are beyond his present reach. But there is no question that this attitude of judging issues should be fed by careful guidance.

An adjunct to this ability is the restraint that should be shown in withholding judgments until the facts are available. It is tempting to base conclusions upon a minimal amount of information, but children must learn to curb this tendency. Later, learning to withhold judgment lays the foundation for dealing with propaganda and its techniques.

If we may assume that elementary school pupils have been participating in a developmental program in which provisions have been made for the sequential development of critical reading skills, the progression should continue through the high school and college. Obviously some students will be more advanced in their ability to react critically than others.

Though we may expect to deal with more complex skills, students' readiness for undertaking them can mean the difference between success and confusion. One would need to ascertain the point at which instruction should be initiated before plunging into areas which challenge even the ability of adults.

The ability to select sources which yield pertinent information and to determine the reliability of them should have been growing in the elementary grades. As students are surrounded by more advanced materials the exercise of these abilities becomes increasingly difficult. Instruction must continue if students are to respond satisfactorily.

Are students able to evaluate conclusions which have been drawn for them? Have they learned to examine the evidence which is cited to support these conclusions? Are they able to recognize that certain "evidence" is difficult to verify? Reading in the content fields provides a challenge to these skills.

Writers may merely present factual reports or they may be sharpening axes. The reader is in a better position to question if he recognizes the intent of the author. Then a written statement by the president of an organization known to have vested interests in an issue will not be viewed as another statement presented by an impartial observer. The reader should be able to answer a simple question: "Who would have me believe this?"

This ability to sense the author's purpose is tied to another one, the ability to discern and evaluate propagandistic or persuasive statements. Although one may not take issue with efforts to indoctrinate—and there are many causes for whose support we work—any attempt at deception or distortion is often regarded as unethical. The term propaganda has taken on these connotations, possibly because efforts to advocate particular practices or ideas have been accompanied by trickery and craftiness.

The techniques of propaganda have been analyzed and are well known. One which needs to receive special attention is the practice of citing quotations that have been deliberately removed from a larger context and as a result mislead the reader to believe what he would not ordinarily accept. A second device calls for truthful but incomplete statements, which cause the reader to react the way the writer desires. Other familiar techniques include the testimonial, band wagon and transfer. Students not only need to be alerted to these devices but also must have opportunities to respond to them as they read. The adolescent has demonstrated his readiness for learning suitable responses to exaggerated claims and partial truths; we must be ready to help him learn them.

The use of language and its influence upon reactions have been studied. There is no question about the power which words can generate. The specialists have responded intelligently: in economics, depressions have become recessions; and in ladies' wear, half-sizes are now B sizes.

Even writers of highly-regarded publications occasionally use words in such a way as to color the facts and influence the reader. A few years ago one of the leading newspapers of the country included a front-page account of the efforts of a "spinster ex-school teacher" to enact social legislation to which many persons were opposed. In this particular case straight factual reporting did not demand revelation of the marital status or previous profession of the bill's sponsor.

The reader must learn to separate words which have the power to produce feelings from words which merely serve to identify referents. The simple act of interspersing emotionally charged words among factual ones has led to reactions which the writer sought to cause. Readers must not be permitted to become slaves to words; our job is to lead readers to be masters of them.

## CONCLUDING STATEMENT

To read critically is to read intelligently. Evidence which has been accumulated over the years reveals that such reading does not occur through osmosis nor does it result from chance. Efforts to develop this ability must be made by each teacher at every level of instruction. Only determined teachers can alter the reading behavior of students by helping each to become a thoughtful careful, and critical reader.

# THE DEVELOPMENT OF
# WORD MEANINGS

## INTRODUCTION

*Some high school teachers tend to underestimate the role of vocabulary in reading. Neither do they understand the effect that vocabulary difficulties have upon their students. Many sentences in high school textbooks are as enigmatic for the average reader in high school as the following sentence is for the average college graduate: "The rawinsonde helped the scientist make quotidian, veridical illations about tropospheric phenomena." Although this sentence is admittedly contrived, it serves to remind the reader that vocabulary problems can serve as formidable obstacles to the development of meanings in reading.*

*The authors of the selections in this part discuss the principles of teaching and learning vocabulary, practical methods and materials for teaching vocabulary, and the implications for teaching of research on vocabulary improvement courses.*

# TEACHING ESSENTIAL READING
# SKILLS—VOCABULARY *

Earle E. Crawford

Someone has called words the counters of experience. Meaning is developed for words by the real and vicarious experiences people have in connection with these words and the language used in referring to these experiences. The development of meanings is one of the key tasks of education. Crawford feels that vocabulary training should "grow out of the pupil's reading experience or other use of words." He discusses various aspects of vocabulary teaching and concept development and provides some useful paradigms for structuring the study of vocabulary in the classroom.

1. Before reading this article, list briefly your approaches to vocabulary improvement.

2. Why might it be a good idea to try the suggestions given here, a few at a time?

3. Of what personal and professional values could a personal program of vocabulary development be?

4. Do you agree with the author's contention that it is wise to give pupils some comprehension of the process involved in contextual analysis and some training in applying it?

5. The author wants the reader to be particularly aware of several very important points in the discussion on "Figurative. . . . Language." Can you infer what these points are?

6. What can be done to improve vocabulary and to retain new vocabulary?

## IMPROVEMENT OF VOCABULARY

TWO CLOSELY related fundamental skills in reading are recognition of words and symbols and an understanding of the language used. Effective instruction in vocabulary building contributes to the pupil's understanding of what is read, to growth in expressing ideas both in oral and in written form, and to an understanding of ideas presented orally.

### A. Background Experiences

Pupils frequently fail to understand what is read because the vocabulary is not within their experience. Therefore, provision for common background experiences to enable pupils to understand many words before they meet them in reading about a problem or a topic helps in overcoming vocabulary difficulties. The following suggestions apply especially to slow readers:

1. Use these general guides for preparing pupils to read a selection:
   a. Provide concrete background experiences.

---

* REPRINTED BY PERMISSION FROM the Bulletin of the National Association of Secondary-School Principals, February 1950, pp. 56–68. Copyright: Washington, D.C.

   b. Use visual aids, such as maps, diagrams, charts, pictures, models, and
   motion pictures.
   c. Use words in conversation and explain specific terms.
2. Provide exercises giving specific helps for developing readiness to read
   a particular selection:
   a. Change the language of the text to one the pupils understand.
   b. Write difficult words in the lesson on the board. After each word, list
   the page on which it is found. In an informal discussion, have pupils
   find each word and tell what it means.
   Select difficult words from the lesson. After each word, write the page
   on which it is found. In another column write a word or phrase that
   has the same meaning.

## B. Development of Vocabulary

The emphasis in vocabulary building should be on meaning. In the best
classroom practice, procedures for improving word recognition and pronunciation and for developing wider meaning vocabulary will be closely related.
In this way, word meaning will be constantly emphasized. Specific exercises
should be given for improving the mechanics of word recognition and pronunciation because ". . . comprehension cannot be raised to a high degree
if the learner is struggling with the mechanics of the reading process." [1]

Although certain types of vocabulary drill are not always successful and
the degree of improvement does not always justify the effort expended to
produce it, the majority of research studies seems to justify well-motivated
vocabulary training which grows out of the pupil's reading experience or other
use of words.

The following suggestions, according to Ruth Strang, have proved to be
of value: [2]

1. Note definitions which frequently follow the introduction of technical words.
The definitions given in the text are often preferable to definitions found in a
standard dictionary.
2. Check lightly unfamiliar words which are not defined in their context, and
later look them up in a dictionary. Write each at the top of a small card. At the
bottom of the card should appear a synonym, and in the middle of the card a
sentence using the word, or a familiar word derived from or giving derivation to
the unfamiliar one. These cards may then be used for individual practice. When
the word is not immediately recognized, the "player" looks down to the "connecting link" in the middle of the card. If this does not bring about the recall of the
meaning, he must resort to the synonym or definition at the bottom of the card.

---

[1] A *Preliminary Survey of a Reading Program for the Secondary Schools*, Bulletin 202.
Harrisburg, Pennsylvania: Department of Public Instruction, Commonwealth of Pennsylvania, 1939, p. 32.
[2] Ruth Strang, with the assistance of Florence C. Rose, *Problems in the Improvement
of Reading in High School and College.* Lancaster, Pennsylvania: The Science Press Printing Co., 1938, p. 84.

Junior-high-school youngsters enjoy playing games with such cards and finding the words in new contexts. Adults find such a method of keeping up their recently acquired vocabulary useful because a knowledge of the range of literal meanings of a large number of words helps the reader to grasp its meaning in context.

Throughout his reading experience, an individual tends to read about things more or less familiar to him. Each new bit of reading increases his fund of ideas, gives him new understandings and wider experiences, often vicarious, all of which builds up a certain ability to infer meanings.

When new words are encountered for the first time, great dependence is placed upon context clues. In fact, familiarity with ideas being expressed gives the reader his first clues to word symbols. In normal reading development, occasional unfamiliar words present little difficulty since meanings can often be derived from the otherwise familiar context. The more remote the subject matter from the reader's background of experience, the less able is he to anticipate or infer meanings. Thus, the poor reader with inadequate skill in word perception goes down under a too heavy load of unfamiliar words encountered in his reading.

Most of the instruction which is directed toward enlargement of students' vocabularies is based upon use of the dictionary. Instruction and practice in dictionary use are often carried to such a point that pupils feel helpless without a dictionary or, as a labor-saving substitute, a teacher who will define unknown words. Since, in practice, mature readers use context clues far more frequently than they use dictionaries in arriving at word meanings, it is highly desirable to give pupils some comprehension of the process involved and some training in applying it. All pupils need some help in this area and less alert ones must have intensive practice in it. To enrich the background and to choose material not too far above the level of the pupil's reading ability are first steps in specific training to use context clues as an aid to word recognition as well as to word meaning.

The next step might well be to help pupils become aware that words and meanings may be guessed, at times. Practice on familiar expressions will serve to awaken pupils to the realization that many words may be read without having been printed in the sentence. This is easily demonstrated by completing the following phrases:

Early in the .....................    His one ...................interest
As light as a .....................    Flew in a straight ................

Other types of clues should be analyzed and taught specifically. Often an unfamiliar word is merely a synonym for a word previously used, as illustrated in the following two sentences:

Today he tells the *property man* what he wants and tomorrow he finds the items waiting on the set. The *property custodian* has become the movie director's Santa Claus.

An unfamiliar word may be an antonym for a known word, for example:.

Water is *seldom* found in the desert, but springs *frequently* occur in the surrounding hills.

Organized and systematic instruction on the use of these and other types of clues should form a part of the reading program throughout elementary- and high-school grades. Awareness of context clues and skill in using them are indispensable for independent and intelligent reading. Pupils must be able to use context clues in various ways:

a. In associating meaning with known word forms.
b. In discriminating between words which are very much alike in sound and form but not in meaning.
c. In checking on pronunciation derived from phonetic analysis.
d. In determining which one of the various sounds of a certain vowel is appropriate in a given word.[3]

## C. *Qualifying Words*

Common qualifying words are important to the meaning of a sentence, yet many pupils fail to understand the idea expressed in a sentence because they pass over the qualifying words. Common qualifying words include *many, no, more, most, less, few, only, almost, always* and *all*. Short phrases and clauses are frequently used in a qualifying manner, and pupils should be trained to notice the way in which such phrases, as well as words similar to the ones listed above, change the meaning of a sentence. The following types of exercises have been found helpful in training pupils to notice how qualifying words or phrases change the meaning of a sentence.

1. Write on the blackboard sentences containing qualifying words or give them orally. Discuss with pupils the way in which the words affect the meaning of the sentence.
2. Write a group of sentences on the blackboard with the instructions to copy these sentences and draw a line through each qualifying word.

   Example: There are *many* apples on the plate.

   a. After the sentences have been discussed and all pupils have drawn a line through each qualifying word, have them rewrite each sentence and substitute another qualifying word for the one used.
   b. Discuss the meaning of these rewritten sentences to show how qualifying words make distinct changes in the meaning of a sentence.
3. Write on the blackboard sentences containing qualifying words or

[3] William S. Gray and Lillian Gray, *Guidebook for Streets and Roads.* Chicago: Scott, Foresman and Company, 1941, p. 29.

phrases. Check the pupils' knowledge of how the words or phrases change the meaning of the sentence by having them answer yes or no to questions about the sentences.

> Example: The old Indian nearly always came to the trading post in the morning
>
> Questions:

1. Did the old Indian always come to the trading post in the morning?
2. Did the old Indian usually come to the trading post in the morning?
3. Is it true that the old Indian seldom came to the trading post in the morning?

Oral discussion is a vital factor in all preceding procedures. It should be used freely.

### D. Words Commonly Overworked

Some words are so badly overworked that they have almost lost their specific meanings. They are the "maids of all work" and are used principally by the language beggars. High-school pupils need to be helped to overcome the tendency to use trite phrases and overworked words. The following exercises have been useful for this purpose.

1. Write on the blackboard from 1 to 15 sentences each containing the word "got." Have pupils substitute a verb with specific meaning for the overworked verb "got" in each sentence.
2. Have pupils develop a list of frequently overworked words, such as asked, awful, divine, fix, grand, great, keen, lovely, neat, nice, perfect, replied, said, swell, take, terrible, thing, want, wonderful.

### E. Figurative and Other Non-Literal Language

How far the teacher can go in teaching junior and senior high-school pupils to understand the various forms of nonliteral writing depends on the same factors which limit teaching in other fields: the intelligence and cultural background of the pupils, the size of the class and the consequent ease or difficulty of conducting class discussions, the availability of good textbooks and of supplementary material, the rigidity of the course of study, and the teacher's own knowledge and love of literature. Every English teacher, however, should feel that he is remiss in his duties if he fails to open to his pupils the door to the infinite wealth of allusion, description, and suggestion which the intelligent writer and reader may enjoy.

Many teachers overlook the fact that figurative language is not confined to poetry, fairy tales and legends, and similar imaginative writing and limit their teaching of figures of speech to these rather limited areas, leaving largely untouched the much wider and more important fields of idiom, satire, irony, and the innumerable symbolically used words and phrases which appear in daily speech, in advertising, and in newspapers, books, and magazines. Pupils are left floundering in a sea of dimly or wrongly understood language. It is small wonder that they do not read more enthusiastically.

A brief consideration of sample passages from a newspaper, a textbook, and from ordinary conversation will show the necessity for teaching pupils to interpret this prosaic type of nonliteral language. The following samples may not appear to the average adult to be figurative at all because they are so familiar:

A thousand bills were thrown into the legislative hopper.
A chorus of protest arose throughout the land.
I almost died laughing.
The winning candidate swept the field.
The United States is a melting pot.
The enemy lines crumbled.

In junior high school it is probably better to explain figures of speech as they arise in regular class work than to present them "cold" as a unit of study unrelated to the rest of the work in literature, composition, and grammar. The teacher should scan carefully all assigned reading for phrases which might offer difficulty in interpretation and should himself bring them up for class discussion if one of the pupils does not do so.

At first, most of the initiative for such discussions will have to come from the teacher. Most pupils hesitate to admit their inability to understand the real meaning of something the surface import of which is clear. Only when they realize that adults, too, need help in interpretation will they bring their problems into the open. The teacher soon finds that sheer ignorance is the cause of many of the difficulties which pupils have. Biblical, historic, legendary, and artistic references can convey no meaning to those who lack a background of knowledge. "As strong as Samson" might just as well be "As strong as George" so far as many contemporary pupils are concerned. "Mars stalked the earth" creates confused astronomical impressions in the minds of pupils who have been deprived of the Greek myths.

Specific instances of this sort give the alert teacher an excellent opportunity to create in his classes an interest in reading some of the basic literature of our civilization. The classroom or school library should, of course, be ready to provide appropriate books for the pupil whose curiosity is thus aroused.

Lack of knowledge in other areas increases the difficulties of interpretation. "The log-roller lost his footing" was interpreted by a pupil as meaning that the man's foot had been amputated; the reader had no idea of the process of log-rolling. The acquisition of knowledge is, obviously, a never-completed process. The teacher can help himself to appreciate his pupil's shortcomings in this respect by thinking of the gaps in his own information.

It is an accepted principle of education that learning takes place best when the learner participates actively in the process. Thus pupils learn to understand the figurative speech of others when they use such figures themselves. At first, they may simply be asked to complete common similes. These are clichés to the adult, but not to the junior high-school pupil. The following list [4] of incomplete similes is suggestive:

| | |
|---|---|
| black as ........................ | quick as ........................ |
| straight as ...................... | light as ........................ |
| wise as ......................... | clear as ........................ |
| brown as ........................ | sharp as ........................ |
| white as ........................ | sober as ........................ |
| busy as ......................... | hungry as ........................ |
| cold as ......................... | sly as ........................ |
| hard as ......................... | happy as ........................ |

If some of the pupils' responses differ from the conventional ones which the teacher expects, these can be used as a point of departure for a discussion of the value of originality and vividness in figurative speech. The next step, of course, is to have some actual writing done by the pupils. The subjects assigned should be simple and of a nature to encourage the use of simile and metaphor. Short, carefully prepared compositions are preferable to long ones. Sample passages dealing with subjects similar to those assigned may be read to furnish pupils with ideas and inspiration. The best compositions may be read to the class, and particularly happy figures of speech may be pointed out and praised. It is easily understood that no public notice should be taken of the inevitable unsuccessful excursions into writing.

Bright pupils enjoy and benefit from learning the names of the various kinds of figures of speech and differences among them. However, merely learning to recognize and name them is a sterile exercise if it does not lead to understanding and appreciation.

Figurative language often offers the inexperienced and perhaps more literal-minded pupils some difficulty in comprehension. The junior high-school pupil can understand onomatopoetic words, alliteration, and similes, but the more complex aspects of figurative language should be developed at the eleventh- and twelfth-grade levels. At the outset the pupil must learn that figurative language occurs more frequently in poetry than in prose. He must be taught some of the basic distinctions between the two forms.

| Prose | Poetry |
|---|---|
| 1. No regular beat or rhythm. | 1. Definitely measured and rhythmical. |
| 2. No particular form. | 2. Definitely shaped and often divided into stanzas. |
| 3. Often low in emotional tone. | 3. Often concentrated and intense in tone. |
| 4. Usually involves facts and information. | 4. Usually involves feelings. |
| 5. Often detailed and precise. | 5. Imaginative and suggestive. |

[4] Adapted from list in Frieda Radke, *Living Words*. New York: The Odyssey Press, 1940, p. 153.

Perhaps the best way to teach the pupil to interpret figurative language is by pattern. Once an easy pattern is established, the pupil can gradually learn to recognize the same type of pattern in his reading. Alliteration and onomatopoeia are so obvious they can be understood without difficulty. The more complex forms require examples, such as the following:

1. Simile (similarity).
   a. *Like* a cloud of fire.
   b. My love is *like* a red, red rose.
   c. My heart is *like* a rhyme.
2. Metaphor (identification transfer).
   a. The moon is a ghostly galleon.
   b. The road is a ribbon of moonlight.
   c. Sarcasm is a dangerous weapon.
3. Personification (having the attributes of a person).
   a. . . . the jocund day, stands tiptoe on the misty mountain top.
   b. Now morning from her orient chambers came and her first footsteps touched a verdant hill.
4. Apostrophe (addressing the dead as living, or the absent as present).
   a. Phoebus, arise and paint the sable skies.
   b. Build me straight, O Worthy Master.
   c. Mother, come back from that echoless shore.
5. Metonomy (associating an object that is closely connected with the idea).
   a. The *pen* is mightier than the sword.
   b. Polly, put the *kettle* on and we'll have tea.
   c. A man should keep a good *table*.
6. Synecdoche (using a part to represent the whole).
   a. She gave her hand in marriage.
   b. I'll not lift a finger.
   c. Fifty sails were seen on the horizon.

The pupil can increase his enjoyment of the daily newspaper by learning to recognize both simile and metaphor as used so frequently in the headlines. He can have fun noticing the clever use of clichés in various radio plays and will discover that these clichés often are similes or metaphors. By training his ear to catch such clichés as "red as a beet," "bitter as gall," and "mad as a hornet," he can immeasurably improve his own speech and writing. Constant alertness on the part of the teacher and the pupil is necessary to enable the pupil to understand the great masterpieces. Nor can this be done in one semester; it must be part of a well-planned English program through the entire secondary school.

## F. Retention of New Vocabulary

In order that words may become a permanent part of a pupil's vocabulary, word study must be vitalized for the individual through purposeful listening and reading so that vocabularies are enriched both for oral and written expression.

EXTENSIVE READING. Wide and extensive reading is necessary if pupils are to develop rich vocabularies and wider interests in the world about them.

Too often a pupil reads only one type of book—an adventure series, or radio magazines. Frequently, as pupils advance through junior high school, other interests take the place of reading; many pupils never read anything, even a magazine, unless required to do so by a teacher.

More extensive reading habits can be developed by the use of reading "ladders" in the case of the one-type reader; that is, suggestions of related books of wider interest or more mature nature. Books or magazine stories germane to the subject matter studied in class or to popular motion pictures, radio programs, and the like may be recommended. A classroom library, attractive displays, bulletin board, reading nook, are all helpful. The pupil should be given *time* to read. Sometimes, as a special treat, the teacher may read aloud a portion of a book from the library, stopping at some interesting point. Pupils will have to read the book themselves to find out the rest of the story.

The teacher himself will have to know books in order to provide a graded vocabulary load. A poor reader cannot acquire a good vocabulary and effective reading habits by being plunged into difficult reading material full of unfamiliar words. Second, the teacher must check the reading by discussion of the problem of the book, the characters, or the author and make use of the new words in conversation and in class.

The most common way of improving one's vocabulary is through extensive and varied reading. The meaning of words is acquired through the recognition and use of words as parts of words of dynamic thought patterns. . . .

. . . It is advantageous, however, for teachers to increase their students' acquaintance with words by using repeatedly in their conversation during a week several important new words in their field.[5]

ENLISTING PUPILS' CO-OPERATION. Teachers should use a variety of procedures to (1) make the below-average pupils conscious of their need of knowing more words to meet everyday problems; (2) stimulate an interest in increasing vocabulary for the average pupil; and (3) help pupils to overcome their adolescent tendency to censure those pupils who use their vocabularies more effectively than others.

FUNCTIONAL VOCABULARIES. The functional vocabulary is the vocabulary which the pupil uses to express himself in writing and in speech. Activities in which pupils of difficult levels of maturity may use this functional vocabulary are suggested below:

1. The *below-average* pupil may talk about actual experiences, such as home, school, and church activities; movies, radio programs, and community affairs. He may also write letters and fill out applications. In his writing, the pupil should strive for short paragraph development.

---

5 Ruth Strang, with the assistance of Florence C. Rose, *Problems in the Improvement of Reading in High School and College.* Lancaster, Pennsylvania: The Science Press Printing Company, 1938, pp. 82–83.

2. The *average* pupil may talk about various experiences gained through reading as well as through actual participation. His vocabulary should show increased maturity and his talks should show greater detailed observation than those of the below-average pupil. The average pupil should engage in considerable writing of an expository or narrative nature and should write letters.

3. The *above-average* pupil should be able to make deductions from listening and reading activities and should participate imaginatively in the experiences about which he is reading. The writing of above-average pupils should show maturity of thought and expression.

RECOGNITION VOCABULARIES. The recognition vocabulary is largely a listening or reading vocabulary. The *below-average* pupil will get general meanings only. He will read the vocabulary of current events. He will learn technical words largely through listening. The *average* pupil should work for more exactness in interpretation of thought through word study. The *above-average* pupil should approximate a more "ultimate" truth: *i.e.*, get implications. Reflection on subjects about which he reads may lead to participation in his chosen field.

DEVICES FOR MAKING PERMANENT THE PUPILS' ENRICHED VOCABULARY. A variety of procedures may be used to help pupils incorporate words into their permanent vocabularies. The following suggestions are offered:

1. Teach pupils to discriminate between the various meanings of words and phrases. Suggestions for below-average, average, and above-average pupils are listed below:

| WORD | BELOW AVERAGE | AVERAGE | ABOVE AVERAGE |
|---|---|---|---|
| root | The root of the plant is large. | The root word comes from Latin.<br>Take the square root of four.<br>A pig roots in the ground. | The root of all evil. |
| ordinary | The ordinary way of doing the home work all right. | It is a very ordinary procedure. | The ceremony was most ordinary. |
| pass | The pass is narrow.<br>Pass the cake. | The hall pass is needed.<br>He was passed to first base. | Things have come to a pretty pass! |
| ground | The apple fell on the ground.<br>The meat is being ground. | This is the ground floor.<br>This is made of ground glass. | He stood his ground.<br>The ground swell is heavy today. |
| see | I see my way.<br>I see a house. | I see what you mean.<br>I shall come to see you. | I see my way clear.<br>He shall never see death. |

2. Teach pupils to learn new words from context and not alone from dictionary definitions:

| WORD | BELOW AVERAGE | AVERAGE | ABOVE AVERAGE |
|---|---|---|---|
| hostile | My enemy is hostile. | He is a hostile witness. | He is hostile to my interests. |
| leg | The boy broke his leg. | The first leg of the journey is over. | He hasn't a leg to stand on. |
| propaganda propagandize | Do not listen to enemy propaganda. | To propagandize is unfair. | Propaganda is often a falsification of news. |
| object objective | Please pick up the object. | I object to your going to the party. | What is your ultimate objective? |
| proof | What is your proof of that statement? | We shall make a proof of the picture. | The proof of the pudding. |

3. Have pupils listen to an auditorium program or a radio speech, listing unfamiliar words and reasoning out their meanings from the contexts.

4. Organize a vocabulary club in the classroom, members of which will be responsible for bringing in words from all subject fields and sharing them with the class.

5. Have pupils classify words for special study from a selected list, noting those foreign in meaning and those they may be using or may be taught to use in formal spoken and written English.[6]

6. Study words in *phrase groupings*, not as isolated vocabulary. Pupils and teachers should use them consciously in later discussions.

7. Increase vocabulary of meanings by learning new words through specifically purposeful meanings for written composition.

8. Point out for special study: (a) powerful verbs, and (b) colorful adjectives with fine discrimination of meanings, as they are discovered in reading.

9. Use the "Word to the Wise" section in *Scholastic Magazine* as a weekly check.

10. Provide exercises on synonyms, with dictionary help.

11. Make vocabulary matching games for drill several times a term.

12. Have pupils deduce meanings of words from good oral reading by the teacher.

13. Have pupils analyze words through detection of familiar stems, prefixes, and suffixes.

14. Encourage pupils to be watchful for new words and their implications in wide and varied reading.

G. *Exercises for Improvement of Vocabulary*

In addition to the suggested drills and exercises which have been given in connection with discussions on the various phases of improvement of vocabulary in the preceding sections, the following specific exercises for identifying and analyzing compounds, finding words within words, developing pronunciation from known parts of known words, and certain kinesthetic techniques may help to strengthen the program.

[6] William M. Tanner, *Correct English*, Vol. I. Boston: Ginn and Company, 1931, p. 408.

COMPOUNDS. Knowledge of the use of compounds and attention to their form is an excellent means of extending vocabularies. Exercises such as the ones given below are effective in this field.

1. Choose from a current reading lesson several solid compound words (not hyphenated) and write them on the board. Ask pupils to examine them for any unfamiliar parts. Point out that either part of each word may be used alone.
2. Let each pupil choose a compound word which he will separate into parts, using each part in a sentence. He then makes a third sentence in which he uses the compound.
3. Have pupils make sentences containing two or more compound words, for example, John's *workshop* was full of model airplanes made from *cardboard.*
4. Illustrate (when pupils are ready for it) the difference between the two big families of compounds: (a) the solids, as bookworm, roadbed; and (b) the hyphenated compounds, as long-eared, old-fashioned.

FINDING WORDS WITHIN WORDS. As an aid to discovering similarities in word forms and, sometimes, word meaning, practice on identifying short words within longer words is helpful. Seeing that *management, carpenter, attendant, etc.,* contain familiar phonetic elements which are words, themselves, is often an awakening to the pupil who has had difficulty with word perception.

Practice in finding small words may be given in the following way: Pupils select from the context being read a list of long words. Small words within these words are then underlined. Caution must be used to prevent the identification of a small word which is not heard as the long word is pronounced; that is, it would be incorrect to underline *as* in *fashion.*

DEVELOPING PRONUNCIATION FROM KNOWN PARTS OF KNOWN WORDS. Young and relatively immature pupils in junior high school may profit from some of the elementary techniques and exercises noted below.

1. Brief drills on consonant digraphs will facilitate recognition of known parts of words. Sight rather than sound should influence the recognition. List five to ten initial digraphs on the board—bl, br, ch, cl, ch, fl, *etc.* After each one write, in parentheses, the remainder of a word—bl (ack); cl (ean). First see that pupils are familiar with the completed words, then ask them to see how quickly they can find additional words having the same beginnings, using a reading selection for the source.
2. Sentences including numerous digraphs offer a challenge. Give a sample sentence, as "The hunters blew *th*eir horns; the hounds *br*ayed, and the *ch*ase was on! The horses *cl*eared the fences, *cr*ossed the meadows and *sp*ed toward the fleeing fox." Have pupils try writing sentences having two or more of the digraphs illustrated.

3. Common phonograms of three or four letters, especially end-phonograms, furnish worth-while association material. Well-rhymed poetry provides good patterns. Have pupils find pairs and mark the endings that rhyme.

4. Write a paragraph on the board containing many familiar word endings, something like this: "W*ake* up, J*ake*; you're an hour l*ate*, now. Sh*ake* yourself and d*ive* into your clothes. I'll dr*ive* you as far as St*ate* Street if your pride won't be hurt by a r*ide* in my old cr*ate*." Ask pupils to see whether they can outdo the teacher by bringing a similar paragraph of their own the next day.

# VOCABULARY DEVELOPMENT TO IMPROVE READING AND ACHIEVEMENT IN SCIENCE *

Ray F. Deck

*Vocabulary load is, of course, an important factor in determining the comprehensibility of reading material; and the technical vocabulary load in the sciences is almost overwhelming. It hardly seems practical to reduce the quantity of technical vocabulary; therefore, a sound and comprehensive approach that will enable teachers and students to learn systematically and well is needed. Deck offers such a rational approach, which is designed to stimulate an interest and desire in reading with comprehension and also to grasp the con-tent of the science material.*

*1. Why do you think the division of science terms into different categories might help improve the effectiveness with which they are taught? Give your own reasons after examining characteristics of the words.*

*2. How does the author make use of learning principles in the development of his unit?*

*3. Do the outcomes of the unit seem logical? In what ways?*

*4. How would you overcome the difficulties of this plan?*

THROUGH experience as a teacher in science the writer has concluded that the inability to read with comprehension accounts for pupils who are interested in science but not interested in the reading of science. This difficulty is largely one caused by the vocabulary of science. Thus there is need for procedures which serve to help them develop an interest and desire to read with understanding and at the same time grasp the content of the science material.

* REPRINTED FROM *American Biology Teacher*, XIV (January 1952), pp. 13–15, by permission of the publisher.

It is all too easy to assume that students have learned through previous experiences the necessary vocabulary for topics in science. Instead we should realize that each field of science has its own technical vocabulary and that we must develop with pupils the terms necessary to understand the basic concepts which the particular unit of science is designed to develop. The nature of the problem is twofold; first, the teacher must identify the words or terms which may be new or difficult. Second, the teacher must discover and arrange learning activities which help pupils develop meanings and facility in the use of technical words.

This article presents procedures used by the writer. To make the procedures specific they are related to a particular unit in biology entitled, "Our Welfare Is Tied up with That of Other Living Things."

## Preliminary Planning

Before introducing the unit to the students the writer made a careful selection of words and terms on which pupil difficulty was anticipated. A list of one hundred thirty-eight words or terms was formed, and each word was studied to see in what way it could best be learned. In selecting the words the writer relied on his experiences with pupils, realizing that more techniques might be used. These words were then segregated into different categories as follows:

1. Those which were considered as key words of the unit, such as pollination, interdependence, nitrification, parasite, and symbiosis.
2. Words that serve as basic stems in the learning of related words; e.g., pollen as the base for pollination, self-pollination, cross-pollination; depend as the base for dependent, independent, interdependence.
3. Terms needed to identify the basic concepts of the unit; e.g., nitrate, nectar, lichen, nodules, terracing, shelter belt, stomach poison, arsenate, public domain.
4. Words which present the possibility of mechanical difficulty; e.g., ichneumon fly, entomology, exploitation, inevitably, exquisite, insectivorous.
5. Words which are new to many pupils but not especially necessary to understand basic concepts; e.g., mongoose, symbionts, seine, lespedeza, plum curculio, cormorants.
6. Words which should be learned by associating them with objects, typical of which are pollen, nectar, legumes, gypsy moth, lichen and termites.
7. Terms which should be learned by experiences or a background of associated activities; e.g., balanced aquarium, balance of nature, biological control, gullying, overgrazing, crop rotation, check dam, green manure.
8. Words to be learned because they are necessary in a world becoming

more dependent upon science; e.g., inoculation, nitrification, shelter belt, contour cultivation, sanctuary, contact poison.

9. Technical scientific words—insectivorous, quarantine line, clean-cultivated crops, close-growing crops, migratory, denitrification.
10. Words demanded by exact biological terminology—pollination, parasites, symbiosis, biological control, limiting element, propagation.

Having segregated these words and terms into the various groups it was recognized that some of them fit into more than one group. This is as it should be and naturally means that the same word or term will be presented and used in its varied different groupings, and undoubtedly will be fixed and learned the better thereby.

## DEVELOPMENT OF THE UNIT

The unit was introduced by relating an interesting account of an interdependence of living things.

The key words pertaining to the first division of the unit were written upon the blackboard and underlined with colored crayon. This list included pollinations, interdependence, and others of this type.

Another list of all the new words on which difficulty of comprehension by the pupils was anticipated was made. This list included pollen, nectar, depend, dependent, independent, and similar words, all of which have a direct relation to interpretation of the key words.

In order to familiarize pupils with these words the following activities were used.

1. Showing actual flowers with their pollen and nectar glands, and making microscopic examinations.
2. Showing pictures of bees and other pollinating insects on flowers.
3. Examining live bees in specimen jars or showing preserved bees and observing means of carrying pollen.
4. Mounting legs of bees and mouth parts on slides and showing on seoscope to pupils.
5. Projecting mounted specimens of lengthwise sections of pistils to observe stages of fertilization of ovules.
6. Asking pupils to read an account of the failure of raising clover seed in New Zealand until the introduction of the bumblebee. This serves to create a stage for the understanding for the word *depend*. Using depend as a stem of a basic word, teach the meaning of *dependent, independent,* and *interdependence*.

In order to clarify and enrich the meanings of the above words, questions such as the following were suggested to stimulate purposeful reading.

1. Why do fruit growers wish for fair weather during the time their fruit trees blossom?
2. Why do apiarists desire to have fields of clover or buckwheat growing close by?
3. Why are night-blooming flowers frequently white?

Reading of certain books and magazines was suggested so that pupils might do some research findings as to discovering some specific cases of interdependence of insects and flowers.

The second division of the unit, namely, the nitrogen cycle, and all other subsequent divisions of the unit were taken up in study in the same procedure. The list of key words of each subsequent division was added to original list until eventually the whole list of key words for the unit was completed and in view on the blackboard. However words from the other classifications were only presented and written on the blackboard as they appeared in the respective divisions and as they were being taught.

Words or terms newly learned can only be remembered and of value to the learner if he has opportunities to use them again and again. In order to gain more experiences with the new vocabulary and assist the pupils in remembering them, many of the following suggestions were done.

1. Pupils may collect specimens of insects and flowers illustrative of pollination and exhibit them.
2. Draw diagrammatic charts of the nitrogen cycle.
3. Model soil-conservation programs.
4. Exhibit models of wildlife preservation practices.
5. Perform experiments on water absorption, run-off, and erosion of soil.
6. Collect exhibits on parasitism.
7. Carry on simple experiments on soil-conservation in gardens or nearby fields and lots.
8. The class make field trips for observations on interdependence of living things.
9. Conduct an exhibit of pictures portraying examples of the key words learned.
10. Conduct forums on United States reclamation services.

Some of the above projects were carried out while the various divisions of the unit were studied, others were used as summations of facts learned. A few served as a splendid means of summarizing the whole unit on the interdependence of living things. The above list of suggestions are obviously incomplete; they may readily be augmented.

### OUTCOMES OF THE UNIT

The procedures mentioned above result in varied outcomes. Some of the specific outcomes may be stated as follows:

1. It is a varied way of vocabulary development using objective and sensory experiences. Vocabulary development need not necessarily be a dull, uninteresting procedure of drill. In fact, if proper methods are followed in vocabulary building, interest will be increased rather than destroyed.
2. Reading the textbook and other reference literature becomes interesting, understandable and easier to the pupil because of a familiarity with the meanings of the difficult words.
3. The pupil is reading to learn while he is learning to read.
4. The concepts of science are learned as a unit of coherent and correlated facts as they are built up around the key words.
5. Studying and learning science is not a coverage of so many pages but a compilation of interrelated causes and their results.
6. Such a procedure may be academic but it will seem purposeful to the pupil and incidentally he is acquiring a proper habit of work which is one of learning through vocabulary building.

## DIFFICULTIES TO OVERCOME

Naturally any conceived plan of instruction is not wholly applicable in any and all cases and therefore difficulties may develop. The number and kinds of difficulties arising would depend on local conditions in the school.

1. Forty-five- or fifty-minute periods of class time is too short for some of the experimental and project work.
2. Where other classes meet in the same room as biology, inadequate blackboard space may be reserved for the biology classes.
3. If there is more than one section of biology, using different textbooks, the plan becomes inconvenient and cumbersome to administer.
4. If there is extreme variation of reading ability amongst the members of the class the plan is not equally effective to all students.

Inasmuch as this plan was used in the development of a unit in biology it does not mean that the procedure is thus limited. I feel certain that it can be equally well adapted in any other field of the content studies.

# RESEARCH AND DEVELOPMENT IN VOCABULARY-IMPROVEMENT COURSES *

George B. Schick

*In this article Schick explains some of the subtle nuances of vocabulary development and then gives an interesting, critical review of the corpus of published material on this topic. The appended bibliography will help the reader locate the research articles and the actual published materials that he may use in helping students develop vocabulary. Not to be slighted in the least, are the stimulating testing techniques that make it possible to probe new dimensions of vocabulary knowledge.*

*1. What advantages might accrue to people who regard words as highly useful utensils?*

*2. Which of the categories of publications on vocabulary teaching appeal to you? Why?*

*3. Consider the avenues of learning-teaching possibilities that might be opened if you were to construct and administer to your students a depth-of-meaning test. (You may wish to consult available tests of this nature.)*

IN THEIR presentations, my colleagues on this panel have set forth specifics for the improvement of teaching, for the development of greater vocabulary among members of academic or adult groups.

A third approach to the problem of instruction in growth of vocabulary is to survey some of the most significant and representative articles, research reports, and textbooks which have been produced within the past decade and to consider possibilities for further research and practical applications of these principles in the predictable future.

Before proceeding to considerations of what has been done and what may be done in the way of practice and research upon which improved vocabulary growth can be fostered, a look at language itself and specifically the English language, its qualities and richness of heritage, may not be amiss. For to bring about true understanding of the use of words, our tools of expression in this complex and hectic world society, it is necessary to appreciate the astonishing wealth with which preceding generations of writers and speakers have endowed English-speaking peoples. On every level of instruction, from primary grades to advanced adult training, the teacher has an unmistakable obligation to impart, simply but with conviction, some realization of the tremendous

* FROM *Problems, Programs and Projects in College-Adult Reading*, Emery P. Bliesmer and Ralph C. Staiger, editors, Eleventh Yearbook of the National Reading Conference. Milwaukee: The National Reading Conference, Inc., 1962, pp. 113–119. Reprinted with permission of George B. Schick and the National Reading Conference, Inc.

power of English words to express not only direct and clear statements but also shades and colorings of meanings, depth of significance, and implications or suggestions beyond the prosaic and straightforward declarative. Not that third or twelfth graders or college students or adults need to be burdened with extensive lectures on the technical or abstruse aspects of the history of the language; rather, they may be stimulated to regard the words which they meet in reading or which they employ in speaking and writing as highly useful utensils which have been developed and adapted and refined by many generations of English-speaking persons. By this means, a creative and active interest in words themselves is developed; without this interest the acquisition of greater word power tends to become sterile drudgery forced upon unwilling minds merely to satisfy some authoritarian's notion of what is necessary for a certain number of credits. The intimate relationship of an extensive vocabulary to the setting forth of complex and subtle ideas which are the outcome of deep thinking need not be dwelt upon here. But it must be emphasized that this interest in vocabulary is vital; it must be induced and nurtured intelligently if true learning is to come about. Moreover, it should follow without further argument that the instructor himself must have a strong and abiding interest in words and their ways if he is to impart real concern for vocabulary growth to his classes.

Now for a critical look at the body of published material on vocabulary improvement. In quantity, comparatively recent articles in professional journals on this subject run into the hundreds. Edgar Dale's two bibliographies of vocabulary studies total some 1500 items in the first volume (11) and more than 3000 items in the second. (13) By far the greatest number of these articles, however, are concerned with the primary and middle grades. Almost as many have to do with secondary school situations. As for college and adult circumstances, relatively few significant papers have appeared, indeed almost none specifically related to the improvement of vocabulary by adults. Nonetheless, quite a few of these reports and research publications have sufficient validity for college people and adults to warrant their consideration. Of the published materials which we may designate as significant in one phase or another, nearly all fall into one of five main categories.

Representative of the affix and root study of words to improve vocabulary control is James S. Brown's "Vocabulary: Key to Communication." (10) Selecting fourteen "master" words which exemplify twenty prefixes and fourteen root elements, Brown adopts a four-step approach illustrated by his forty item diagnostic test which measures performance at the following four levels: memorization, identification, application, and generalization. Brown's analysis of the utility and extensiveness of this method for improving word knowledge is sufficiently detailed to require no further illustration of this first category, although several other articles might be cited.

A second category, for which a great many articles might be enumerated, consists of a word-list approach to the improvement of readers' vocabularies. George C. Kyte's "A Core Vocabulary in the Language Arts" (27) is somewhat typical of this grouping in that the attempt is made to select a complete list of words, mastery of which is essential to success in various instructional programs or areas of the academic curriculum. Popular and useful as any word-list scheme may prove, it has its limitations. It may readily be granted that a consistent drilling on any group of words for any reasonable length of time will produce satisfying results on a final test for knowledge of these particular words. Yet the conscientious teacher will feel strongly forced to go beyond any specific list for word understanding, or feel compelled to admit that this approach is limited in scope and somewhat sterile in its application to the problems of the whole growth of vocabulary for most students.

A third group of publications on vocabulary improvement comprises the exposition of various schemes, devices, games, or specific practices designed to create curiosity and interest in words. Of this category, M. Z. Wiersema's "Ceiling Unlimited!" (52) may be thought of as a representative, but there are many suggestions of this nature in print, and most of them can be quite useful to the teacher who will apply them enthusiastically and intelligently in word study.

Another category of articles is that concerned with the significance of context in word acquisition. Every thinking teacher of vocabulary improvement knows full well that the bulk of every person's vocabulary is achieved by acquaintance with particular words in various contexts and circumstances. But this approach to growth in vocabulary usually requires extensive use of students' time and concerns long-term rather than immediately demonstrable results. Of this group, not at all large in number but surely important to any consideration of vocabulary improvement, two papers may be cited as representative: James D. Young's "An Experimental Comparison of Vocabulary Growth by Means of Oral Reading, Silent Reading, and Listening," (54) and "Teaching College Freshmen to Read" (34) by Arthur S. McDonald and Walter J. Pauk. Within this very year have appeared two college textbooks which seek to develop students' vocabulary clues; they are Paul C. Rogers' *A Word to the Wise* (38) and DeVitis-Warner's *Words in Context* (15). The latter book gives strong emphasis to contextual acquisition of words, probably more so than most of the excellent workbooks now in print.

In a classification of its own is the first in a series of programmed workbooks called *Word Clues* (44) by Arthur McDonald, Stanford Taylor, and the staff of Educational Developmental Laboratories. Utilizing "teaching machine" techniques, the editors have programmed the thirty lessons in this first book so as to present contextual clues, information on derivation, and multiple-choice quizzes for each new word which the student comes upon as he reads the text of a story or essay. Also, there are thirty word-meaning exercises for additional practice on all the words dealt with in each lesson. Since this is, it would seem, almost a pioneer venture into full-scale use of programmed learning techniques as applied to vocabulary development, reports on its use in various circumstances will be most interesting and suggestive.

A fifth category of publications on vocabulary teaching considers the problem of testing. Although not notably large in number, these studies reflect growing awareness that many tests now in use fail to recognize the existence of multiple meanings for English words. But if vocabulary testing instruments are to have any utility beyond a bare score of 98 or 72 or 46, they must demonstrate to the student that thousands of the most used words in the language have more than a single meaning. Were there opportunity, detailed consideration of each of the following reports would be highly provocative. But I shall have to content myself with mere mention of these four: Frederic C. Osenburg's "A 'Qualitative' Vocabulary Test"; (36) "Vocabulary Tests and Depth of Meaning" (17) by E. W. Dolch and Don Leeds; Mildred Berwick's "The Semantic Method for Testing Vocabulary" (6); and "The Synonym Vocabulary Test" (29) by William M. Lepley and Martin L. Zeigler.

Finally, attention should be called to at least two articles which suggestively point to future needs in research and development of improved techniques, instruments, and practices in the teaching of vocabulary growth. E. W. Dolch in "Depth of Meaning" (16) emphasizes that mere quantity in the acquisition of vocabulary is not enough; full understanding of words must never be neglected. In his "Developing Vocabulary: Another Look at the Problem," (14) Lee C. Deighton stresses need for recognition that there are many meanings for a large number of words in the English language, that contextual clues must not be overlooked, that word-analysis gives additional hints for word-meanings, and that meaning—and vocabulary-growth come from continuing experience.

Difficult as the task may be to conduct courses or units of intensive work on vocabulary improvement, the teacher may be genuinely encouraged by the great and popular interest in growth of word power. Newspapers and some of the most widely circulated of national magazines have regular features to enable readers to enlarge their word-stock; soft-cover publications on vocabulary growth sell by tens of thousands. Despite all this continuing interest on the part of the general public, research reports and articles on techniques of adult vocabulary improvement are almost nonexistent. Surely Johnson O'Connor's "Vocabulary and Success," (35) first published in the *Atlantic Monthly* and frequently reprinted, is not to be taken as the final word on matters of training adults to enlarge their vocabularies.

Another area of public interest is shown in recent news and magazine articles (47; 51) which assert that Russian children in the grades are exposed to far more rich and extensive vocabularies than are North American pupils. Extravagant as some of these allegations may seem, the fact remains that the most widely used textbooks in American schools present new words at an alarmingly decelerated rate. In fact, it would seem that many of our textbooks are so constructed that the words used represent only a minimal standard for vocabulary growth, that these words are those which the average pupil should acquire. But what of all those pupils on the upper half of the academic scale?

Are they to be deprived of stimulation to develop their own vocabularies beyond the most basic of needs?

In view of this heightening interest, though not necessarily *enlightened* public awareness, opportunities to study and practice new techniques, to develop instructional aids with wider scope seem to be great. But in the devising of new and improved testing instruments, of workbooks and exercises and teaching devices, of better classroom methods and study guides—all of which must be achieved in the predictable future, certain pitfalls must be avoided. Chief among these are the use of the single definition pattern for teaching and testing, of far too limited word-lists and core vocabularies, of over-emphasis on word derivation or even contextual learning of new terms. For vocabulary growth develops on a very broad front for everyone—to limit training to any one area is seriously to impair the total growth of word power on the part of the student.

SELECTED LIST OF REFERENCES ON
VOCABULARY IMPROVEMENT *

1. ALTUS, W. D., "The Relationship Between Vocabulary and Literacy When Intelligence Is Held Constant," *Journal of Social Psychology*, 31:299–301, May, 1950.
2. ANDERSON, M. A. and R. C. STAIGER, "Language Arts Research, 1956," *Elementary English*, 34:246, April, 1957.
3. AYLESWORTH, T. G., "Teaching Vocabulary in Biology," *Science Teacher*, 26:479–83, November, 1959.
4. BAKER, J. B. J., "Mastery of Vocabulary in History," *Journal of Educational Research*, 50:589–95, April, 1957.
5. BAXTER, F. B., "Vocabulary Development Through the Reading of the Daily Newspaper," *English Journal*, 40:570–1, December, 1951.
6. BERWICK, M., "Semantic Method for Testing Vocabulary," *Journal of Experimental Education*, 28:123–41, December, 1959.
7. BLACK, E. L., "Eight Types of Mistakes in Comprehension," *English*, 11:10–14, Spring, 1956.
8. BLANCHARD, B. E., "Improving Rate, Vocabulary, and Comprehension in Reading by the Inversion Technique," *Journal of Experimental Education*, 26:43–49, September, 1957.
9. BORGATTA, E. F. and R. J. CORSINI, "Quick Word Test," *Journal of Educational Research*, 54:15–19, September, 1960.
10. BROWN, J. I., "Vocabulary: Key to Communication," *Education*, 80:80–84, October, 1959.
11. DALE, EDGAR, *Bibliography of Vocabulary Studies*, Bureau of Educational Research, Ohio State University, Columbus, 1949.
12. ——, "Problems of Vocabulary in Reading," *Educational Research Bulletin*, 35:111–23, May, 1956.

* Acknowledgment of extensive help in the preparation of this selective bibliography is due Martha Curtis Johnson, assistant on the Reading Staff at Purdue University.

13. DALE, EDGAR, and Donald Reichert, *Bibliography of Vocabulary Studies*, Bureau of Educational Research, Ohio State University, Columbus, 1957.
14. DEIGHTON, L. C., "Developing Vocabulary: Another Look at the Problem," *English Journal*, 49:82–88, February, 1960.
15. DEVITIS, A. A., and J. R. WARNER, *Words in Context: A Vocabulary Builder*, Appleton-Century-Crofts, New York, 1961.
16. DOLCH, E. W., "Depth of Meaning," *Education*, 49:562–66, May, 1949.
17. DOLCH, E. W., and DON LEEDS, "Vocabulary Tests and Depth of Meaning," *Journal of Educational Research*, 47:181–89, November, 1953.
18. EDWARDS, T. J., "Context Clues and Word Mastery in the Junior College," *Junior College Journal*, 29:292–98, March, 1959.
19. EICHOLZ, G., and R. BARBE, "Experiment in Vocabulary Development," *Educational Research Bulletin*, 40:1–7, January, 1961.
20. FUNK, WILFRED, *Six Weeks to Words of Power*, New York, 1960.
21. FUNK, WILFRED, and NORMAN LEWIS, *30 Days to a More Powerful Vocabulary*, New York, 1961.
22. GOODMAN, ROGER B., and DAVID LEWIN, *New Ways to Greater Word Power*, New York, 1960.
23. GULICK, S. L., and D. HOLMES, "Vocabulary Tool for the English Teacher," *College English*, 19:214–17, February, 1958.
24. HEINBERG, P., "Experimental Investigation of Measuring Diction," *Journal of Educational Research*, 52:303–6, April, 1959.
25. HUNT, JACOB TATE, "The Relation Among Vocabulary, Structural Analysis, and Reading," *Journal of Educational Psychology*, 44:193–20, April, 1953.
26. JOHNSON, HARRY W., "A Single Procedure for the Development of Meaning Vocabulary, Sight Vocabulary, or Foreign Vocabulary," *Journal of Developmental Reading*, 4:174–83, Spring, 1961.
27. KYTE, GEORGE C., "A Core Vocabulary in the Language Arts," *Phi Delta Kappan*, 34:231–34, March, 1953.
28. LEPLEY, WILLIAM M., "The Rationale, Construction, and Preliminary Try-Outs of the Synonym Vocabulary Test," *Journal of Psychology*, 39:215–25, January, 1955.
29. LEPLEY, WILLIAM M., and MARTIN L. ZEIGLER, "The Synonym Vocabulary Test: Standardization and Validation," *Journal of Psychology*, 41:419–25, April, 1959.
30. LEVIN, JANICE, and CHALMERS L. STACEY, "Awareness of Vocabulary Size: Its Relation to Class Standing and Sex Differences," *Journal of Educational Psychology*, 42:174–84, March, 1951.
31. LEWIS, NORMAN, *Word Power Made Easy*, New York, 1961.
32. MALSBARY, D. R., *et al.*, "Spelling, Vocabulary-Building, and Handwriting Library," *American Business Education*, 16:319–24, May, 1960.
33. MASEK, R., "Vocabulary Testing in Remedial English," *Junior College Journal*, 28:7, September, 1957.
34. McDONALD, A. S., and W. J. PAUK, "Teaching College Freshmen to Read," *Phi Delta Kappan*, 38:104–9, December, 1956.
35. O'CONNOR, JOHNSON, "Vocabulary and Success," Introduction to *English Vocabulary Builder*, Human Engineering Laboratory, Stevens Institute of Technology, Hoboken, New Jersey.

36. Osenburg, F. C., "Qualitative Vocabulary Test," *College English*, 18:91–94, November, 1956.
37. Phillips, M. V., "Methods to Improve Skill in the Use of a Geography Vocabulary at the High School Level," *Journal of Geography*, 55:369–74, November, 1956.
38. Rogers, Paul, *A Word to the Wise*, Prentice-Hall, Englewood Cliffs, New Jersey, 1961.
39. Salling, A., "Essay in Comparative Vocabulary Study," *Modern Language Journal*, 42:222–25, May, 1958.
40. Schubert, D. G., "How College Students Develop Their Vocabularies After High School Graduation," *California Journal of Secondary Education*, 34:328–30, October, 1959.
41. Singleton, Carlton M., "Vocabulary Development for Mature Students," *Research and Education in College Reading*, Ninth Yearbook of National Reading Conference, 72–78.
42. Solomon, Richard L., and Leonard Postman, "Frequency of Usage as a Determinant of Recognition Threshold for Words," *Journal of Experimental Psychology*, 43:195–201, March, 1952.
43. Swineford, Francis, and Peter M. Miller, "Effects of Directions Regarding Guessing on Item Statistics of a Multiple-Choice Vocabulary Test," *Journal of Educational Psychology*, 44:129–39, March, 1953.
44. Taylor, Stanford E., Helen Frackenpohl, Arthur S. McDonald, and Nancy Joline, *Word Clues*, Educational Developmental Laboratories, Huntington, New York, 1961.
45. Thompson, Ernest, "The 'Master Word' Approach to Vocabulary Training," *Journal of Developmental Reading*, 2:62–66, Autumn, 1958.
46. Triggs, Frances O., "The Development of Measured Word Recognition Skills Grade Four Through the College Freshman Year," *Educational and Psychological Measurement*, 12:345–49, Autumn, 1952.
47. Trace, Arthur S., Jr., "Can Ivan Read Better Than Johnny?" *Saturday Evening Post*, May 27, 1961, 30:67–68.
48. Vernon, P. E., "The Estimation of Difficulty of Vocabulary," *British Journal of Educational Psychology*, 20:77–82, June, 1950.
49. Warner, John R., "The Inadequacies of Vocabulary Workbooks," *Journal of Developmental Reading*, 2:54–57, Winter, 1957.
50. Westfall, A., "Can College Students Expand Their Recognition Vocabularies?" *School and Society*, 73:25–28, January 13, 1951.
51. "What Ivan Reads," *Time*, November 17, 1961, pp. 52, 54.
52. Wiersema, M. Z., "Ceiling Unlimited!" *Education*, 80:76–79, October, 1959.
53. Winship, G. P., Jr., "Vocabulary Workbooks," *College English*, 21:538–43, April, 1960.
54. Young, James D., "An Experimental Comparison of Vocabulary Growth by Means of Oral Reading, Silent Reading, and Listening," *Speech Monograph*, 20:273–76, November, 1953.

# USING READING IN RESEARCH-STUDY SITUATIONS

## INTRODUCTION

*The research-study skills are those skills involved in locating, interpreting, evaluating, organizing, and retaining information. The students who will continue their education in college are, by and large, the more able students. They will use the research-study skills for many years. These more able students are often neglected in high school because they generally manage to get their lessons after a fashion. Consequently, they develop poor study habits and reading deficiencies.*

*The research project reported by Moe and Nania points to the reading deficiencies existing among able pupils and to what can be done to help them overcome these deficiencies. Robinson, originator of the SQ3R study approach, shows both the need for teaching study skills to superior students in high school, and how to teach those skills that will help them improve their comprehension and retention of reading material. Finally, Jolly provides various techniques to help students understand the main idea of a paragraph, a key skill in organizing and retaining information for the purposes of writing good themes and examination papers.*

# READING DEFICIENCIES AMONG ABLE PUPILS *

Iver L. Moe
and Frank Nania

*Some teachers select for special help in reading those individuals whose reading skills are below the class or national average. However, a basic question is, "Which individuals should profit most from instruction?" The answer is: those who show the greatest discrepancy between achievement and capacity. Now selection is put on a psychologically sounder basis and individuals selected will be reading below, at, and above average; but they are the ones who need and should be able to profit from instruction.*

*In this article Moe and Nania prove that able pupils do have reading deficiencies and that these pupils can be helped to overcome such deficiencies.*

*1. What are the problems in this study?*

*2. Note the difficulties that are encountered in using standardized tests. How are these difficulties overcome?*

*3. What, basically, does the corrective program attempt to do?*

*4. Why do the authors advocate selective underlining?*

*5. What are the implications of this statement: "Probably few people can read difficult material for both general concepts and detail simultaneously."?*

*6. Is the practice in this book of having you read the questions before you read the selection substantiated by the authors of this article?*

*7. How can you apply the conclusions of the study to your reading and to the reading of your able students?*

PUPILS whose standard reading scores place them well above national norms and whose academic records are exemplary can be, and often are, retarded in reading. "Retardation," as used in this article, describes a situation in which the pupil's development in reading is significantly below a readily accessible potential. In this study, twelve high-achieving junior high school pupils were selected to receive special help in an effort to further develop reading skills. Weaknesses found among these students were concealed from perfunctory view by a smokescreen of exceeded norms and excellent report-card marks. However, an analysis of their performances on standardized and informal tests revealed correctable deficiencies. Two deficiencies, common to all students, were identified: (1) deficiency in study approaches to chapter-length materials, and (2) inflexibility in reading rate. The general inadequacy in their approach to chapter-length materials was established by interviews

---

* FROM the *Journal of Developmental Reading* (Autumn 1959), pp. 11–26. Reprinted with permission of Iver L. Moe and the International Reading Association.

with the students, and inflexibility of reading rate was identified when the students were given an informal test especially devised for this study. Accordingly, this article will focus upon selection of students, analysis of reading development, the corrective program, and the results observed. Technical clinical procedures, complicated statistics, mechanical reading aids, and formal research design were not used. Therefore, the procedures of this study including the devising of a Rate Flexibility Test, can be duplicated in any junior high school where teachers recognize that all pupils—including high achievers —need a continuous, carefully planned, skills program to accompany efforts to provide enrichment of reading experience. This article is intentionally limited to skill development. Growth "in" reading (skill development) is coessential with growth "through" reading.

## SELECTION OF PUPILS

Four criteria were used for selection of pupils: (1) excellent report-card marks, (2) high scores on two different standardized reading tests, (3) an intelligence quotient of 110 or better, and (4) parental and pupil consent. A testing program was administered after which twelve pupils were selected, six boys and six girls. Equal distribution of boys and girls was coincidental.

First, the *Gates Reading Survey*,[1] Form I, was administered. This test purports to measure speed and accuracy, reading vocabulary, and level of comprehension. The complete *Iowa Every-Pupil Tests of Basic Skills*,[2] Form O, was also administered. Only subsection "A" and "B" were used for selecting pupils. These subsections purport to measure reading comprehension, vocabulary, map reading, use of references, use of index, use of dictionary, alphabetizing skill, and ability to read graphs. Form G of the *Kuhlmann-Anderson Test*[3] was used to obtain psychological data.

After the standardized testing program was completed, high scorers were tentatively selected. At a group meeting, the students were informed that data accumulated were generally favorable. It was pointed out that an analysis of standard scores, administration of informal tests, and interviews, would be used to identify deficiencies, if any. The students were then invited to participate in the experiment. All concurred. The next step, therefore, was designed to identify possible deficiencies through the use of procedures described earlier in this paragraph. When the analysis was complete, weaknesses identified, and a tentative corrective program planned, the parents were invited to attend a group meeting at which time a report was given describing the findings to date and the plan of work. All students were represented by at least one parent, all of whom indicated their support. Final selection of twelve eighth-grade pupils from the Campus School at the State University of New York, Teachers College, Cortland, New York, was then made. It was decided that twenty-four forty-minute sessions over a six-week period would be arranged.

## Presentation of Standard Test Data

Following are the data from the tests, in turn, with an analysis for each:
DATA FROM GATES READING SURVEY AND KUHLMANN-ANDERSON TEST.
The Gates test was administered during the first month of the eighth-grade
term. Accordingly, the norm for the test was 8-1 (eighth-grade, first-month).
For convenience, the results of the Gates and Kuhlmann-Anderson tests are
shown in Figure 1.

FIGURE 1

*Scores on Part II of the Gates Reading Survey of the
Kuhlmann-Anderson Intelligence Test*

| | GATES READING SURVEY [1] | | | | KUHLMANN-ANDERSON [2] | | |
| CASE NUMBER | SPEED | VOCAB-ULARY | COMPRE-HENSION | AVERAGE | C.A. | M.A. | I.Q. |
|---|---|---|---|---|---|---|---|
| 1 | 11-8 | 12-6 | 12-0 | 12-1 | 13-5 | 17-0 | 127 |
| 2 | 12-1 | 11-7 | 10-6 | 11-5 | 13-5 | 14-1 | 117 |
| 3 | 11-9 | 11-2 | 10-3 | 11-1 | 13-0 | 15-0 | 115 |
| 4 | 11-3 | 11-5 | 11-1 | 11-3 | 12-10 | 16-5 | 128 |
| 5 | 11-3 | 11-3 | 8-8 | 9-1 | 13-3 | 14-7 | 110 |
| 6 | 10-6 | 10-0 | 10-6 | 10-4 | 13-6 | 15-4 | 114 |
| 7 | 7-1 | 10-6 | 11-1 | 9-6 | 12-2 | 14-2 | 116 |
| 8 | 7-8 | 10-4 | 8-2 | 8-8 | 13-6 | 14-11 | 111 |
| 9 | 7-8 | 10-3 | 10-3 | 9-5 | 13-7 | 17-3 | 127 |
| 10 | 11-0 | 10-8 | 9-5 | 10-4 | 13-5 | 15-0 | 112 |
| 11 | 11-3 | 10-8 | 10-6 | 10-9 | 13-5 | 15-6 | 116 |
| 12 | 10-6 | 9-6 | 11-1 | 10-4 | 13-0 | 14-7 | 112 |

[1] Gates Reading Survey data are expressed in grade equivalents.
[2] Chronological age (C.A.) and mental age (M.A.) are expressed in years and months.

It can be noted in Figure 1, that the high grade-equivalent score in speed
was 12-1 (Case No. 2) and the low score was 7-1 (Case No. 7). The median
score was 11-1, thirty months above the norm. Case Nos. 7, 8, and 9 were the
only students below the norm in speed of reading. It becomes apparent, superficially, that the standard scores in speed were favorable. However, after
closer analysis to be described later, evidence will be presented to indicate
that the selected pupils read materials at an inflexible, habituated, rate irre-
spective of purpose for reading or the relative difficulty of materials being
read.

In the vocabulary subsection of the Gates test, all pupils were above the
norm. The high score was 12-6 (Case No. 1) and the low score 9-6 (Case
No. 12). The median was 10-8, twenty-seven months above the norm. Favorable scores also accumulated from the comprehension subsection of the test,

the high score being 12-0 (Case No. 1) and the low score 8-2 (Case No. 8). The median score in comprehension was 10-6, twenty-five months above the norm. In average reading, the high pupil (Case No. 1) was thirty-nine months above the norm and the low pupil (Case No. 8) was one month above. The median score in average reading was 10-4, twenty-three months above the norm.

THE KUHLMANN-ANDERSON TEST. Results, in Figure 1, show that intelligence quotients were 110 or better. The high quotient (Case No. 4) was 128 and the low score (Case No. 5) was 110. The median intelligence quotient was 116.

## ANALYSIS OF DATA: GATES READING SURVEY

The form of the Gates test used in the experiment is advocated for upper third grade through grade ten. The first subsection purports to be a test of reading speed and accuracy. The experimental pupils scored high as previously indicated. Since the writers believe that standard scores can be misleading unless carefully examined in an effort to determine what the test measures, the structure of the speed subtest was studied. The speed subsection is comprised of thirty-six short, simple paragraphs written at about third-grade level. The paragraphs presented no conceptual or ideational challenge to the experimental students. However, if the speed subsection was given to third-grade pupils, the concept load represented in the thirty-six paragraphs may well represent a different problem. Third-grade children may score low on such a subsection for a variety of reasons. Some younger children may score low because of poor word-recognition skill, or poor comprehension, or low reading rate. However, the speed and accuracy subsection presented only one problem to the selected eighth-grade pupils—speed of reading. The time limit of four minutes was the only obstacle to their reading the thirty-six paragraphs containing approximately 1000 words. It was estimated that if the experimental pupils had read third-grade material at 350 words per minute, ample time would have been provided for reading and answering questions and all would have reached the ceiling for that subsection. However, as shown in Figure 2, no student was able to finish the test. The "number attempted" column in Figure 2 shows the number of paragraphs attempted. The highest number of paragraphs attempted was thirty-four (Case No. 2) and the fewest number of paragraphs read was seventeen (Case No. 7). A further study of Figure 2 indicates that only one student failed to score perfect comprehension on paragraphs read. Case No. 5 attempted twenty-seven paragraphs and scored correct responses in twenty-six paragraphs.

This analysis led to the conclusion that while these students were characteristically above norms (median score 11-1) the speed subsection did not measure practical speed and accuracy well enough to justify generalizing. Some questions remained. Is it reasonable to expect able eighth-grade pupils to read third-grade materials at the rate of 350 words per minute and answer

FIGURE 2

*Scores on the Speed and Accuracy Subtest*
*of the Gates Reading Survey*

| CASE NUMBER | NUMBER ATTEMPTED | RAW SCORE (NUMBER RIGHT) | PERCENT ACCURATE |
|---|---|---|---|
| 1 | 31 | 31 | 100 |
| 2 | 34 | 34 | 100 |
| 3 | 32 | 32 | 100 |
| 4 | 26 | 26 | 100 |
| 5 | 27 | 26 | 96 |
| 6 | 24 | 24 | 100 |
| 7 | 17 | 17 | 100 |
| 8 | 19 | 19 | 100 |
| 9 | 19 | 19 | 100 |
| 10 | 25 | 25 | 100 |
| 11 | 26 | 26 | 100 |
| 12 | 24 | 24 | 100 |

simple multiple-choice questions? If all students had been able to do so, they would have reached the extreme upper limits of the speed subsection. Another question remained. Is it reasonable to expect that competent eighth-grade pupils should be able to vary reading rate according to purpose and content? An attempt to answer these questions will be discussed later.

Examination of the results in the vocabulary section of the Gates test revealed no particular need for further testing. However, the comprehension test was considered to be limited in scope. It is comprised of twenty-one short paragraphs which gradually increase in reading difficulty. The high scores on this subsection seemed to be justified. However, an informal analysis of reading chapter-length materials was considered necessary and later administered.

## PRESENTATION OF DATA: IOWA EVERY-PUPIL TESTS OF BASIC SKILLS

As indicated earlier, the *Iowa Every-Pupil Tests of Basic Skills* was also administered in September. Only results of subtests "A" and "B" are shown in Figure 3. It was decided by the writers that these data were sufficient to establish high achievement levels for the twelve pupils selected. As can be observed in Figure 3, scores in comprehension and vocabulary essentially support the findings of the *Gates Reading Survey*. The median score in comprehension was 10-6 while the median score in vocabulary was 9-5. All pupils were substantially above norms on the comprehension and vocabulary subsections of the Iowa. There were, however, some relatively low scores in map reading (see Case Nos. 2, 3, 4, and 12). Case Nos. 3, 4, 5, 6, 8, 10, and 12 were comparatively weak in the "use of reference" subtest. Scores on index, dictionary, alphabetizing, and graphs were characteristically substantial.

FIGURE 3

*Scores on the Iowa Every-Pupil Tests of Basic Skills* *

| CASE NO. | COMPRE-HENSION | VOCAB-ULARY | MAP READING | USE OF REFER-ENCES | USE OF INDEX | USE OF DIC-TIONARY | ALPHA-BETIZING AND GRAPHS |
|---|---|---|---|---|---|---|---|
| 1 | 11-3 | 10-7 | 10-6 | 9-0 | 9-7 | 10-8 | 10-3 |
| 2 | 10-9 | 10-1 | 7-5 | 9-0 | 8-8 | 9-6 | 8-8 |
| 3 | 11-0 | 10-4 | 8-0 | 8-0 | 8-0 | 10-8 | 9-8 |
| 4 | 10-0 | 9-4 | 7-2 | 8-0 | 9-7 | 10-1 | 10-0 |
| 5 | 10-1 | 9-7 | 8-5 | 5-5 | 8-4 | 8-9 | 8-3 |
| 6 | 9-8 | 9-2 | 11-2 | 6-5 | 9-5 | 10-1 | 9-8 |
| 7 | 11-3 | 8-6 | 9-5 | 8-5 | 9-5 | 10-1 | 10-3 |
| 8 | 10-5 | 8-6 | 10-0 | 6-5 | 8-4 | 8-9 | 9-3 |
| 9 | 10-0 | 8-7 | 10-3 | 8-5 | 10-1 | 9-6 | 9-8 |
| 10 | 10-0 | 10-4 | 10-6 | 7-0 | 9-5 | 8-4 | 9-8 |
| 11 | 10-8 | 10-7 | 10-3 | 9-5 | 9-7 | 8-9 | 10-7 |
| 12 | 10-9 | 8-9 | 8-0 | 7-5 | 8-4 | 10-8 | 8-3 |

* Scores are expressed in grade equivalents.

Space here does not permit recounting the analysis of standard scores on the Iowa test. Weaknesses were noted, as mentioned above, in map reading and use of reference materials. Appropriate notations were made to guide the instructors in formulation of a corrective program.

## INFORMAL TESTING

COMPREHENSION. It is recognized that standard tests of comprehension are necessarily designed to be easily administered and scored. This precludes the possibility of testing comprehension in chapter-length selections in various types of materials. Therefore, a series of individual interviews was arranged in an attempt to assess the students' ability to approach chapter-length materials. All pupils were vague with regard to reading for general ideas, reading for details, and specific study approaches. *Reading was just reading.* It was believed that special work in reading chapter-length materials was indicated.

FLEXIBILITY TEST. In order to augment and clarify the speed subtests of the *Gates Reading Survey,* an informal test of rate flexibility was devised. Materials for the test were selected from the *Reading Laboratory* [4] published by Science Research Associates. The authors, Don H. Parker, *et al.,* have accumulated a great deal of interesting reading material designed for practice in speed and comprehension. The materials are graded as to readibility by the Lorge and Dale-Chall formulas. The materials are divided into speed and comprehension exercises. There are fifteen speed selections and fifteen comprehension selections on each grade level from grade three through twelve.

Selections vary in subject matter and include, among others, materials relating to science, biography, literature, music, art, and history. By experimenting with the graded materials, it was found that all twelve pupils could read and comprehend materials at tenth-grade level or above. With this information, a rate flexibility test was devised.

Reading selections were chosen from third-grade, fifth-grade, seventh-grade, and tenth-grade levels. Each pupil, individually, was then given a rate flexibility test. Each was asked to read silently the graded paragraphs, in turn, from simple to difficult. The reading of each selection was timed with a stop watch and the percent of comprehension recorded when the student responded to the multiple-choice question accompanying each selection. In the interest of simplicity only the rates on easy material (grade three) and difficult material (grade ten to twelve) was placed in Figure 4.

FIGURE 4

*Flexibility Test*

| CASE NUMBER | RATE ON EASY MATERIAL | RATE ON DIFFICULT MATERIAL | FLEXIBILITY INDEX |
|---|---|---|---|
| 1 | 510 | 330 | 180 |
| 2 | 520 | 408 | 112 |
| 3 | 360 | 330 | 30 |
| 4 | 360 | 282 | 78 |
| 5 | 228 | 210 | 18 |
| 6 | 282 | 216 | 66 |
| 7 | 252 | 234 | 18 |
| 8 | 204 | 200 | 4 |
| 9 | 276 | 240 | 36 |
| 10 | 310 | 282 | 28 |
| 11 | 390 | 288 | 102 |
| 12 | 240 | 198 | 42 |

\* All rates are expressed in words per minute.
  Flexibility Index represents the difference in reading rate between easy and difficult materials.

It was noted that Case Nos. 1, 2, and 11 demonstrated superior flexibility as compared with other students. For example, Case No. 1 read and comprehended easy materials at 510 w.p.m. By subtracting the rate in difficult material from the rate in easy material, the flexibility index of Case No. 1 was found to be 180 w.p.m. (see Figure 4). Case No. 2 had a flexibility index of 112 w.p.m. A sharp contrast can be noted by inspecting the flexibility index of Case No. 8. This student read simple material only four w.p.m. faster than difficult material. The median flexibility index for the group was found to be thirty-nine w.p.m. The low flexibility index was four w.p.m., the high 180 w.p.m. The range in flexibility index was 176 w.p.m. which indicates a highly variable characteristic

After the testing period—both informal and standardized—was completed, it was decided to devise an improvement program designed to develop study skills in chapter-length materials using textbook selections with which the students were currently engaged in their regular school program. In addition, the corrective program was directed toward improving the flexibility index in relationship to difficulty of materials read. To put it more concretely, we hoped that the twelve students could be taught to shift gears to the end that easy materials would be read faster than difficult materials. It was further hoped that reading rate could be improved at all levels of difficulty.

## The Corrective Program

STUDY SKILLS. The standard tests results revealed comparatively high grade-equivalent scores in comprehension. However, it is not feasible, in a standard test, to use chapter-length selections for testing purposes. As indicated previously, pupils were vague concerning study approaches in regular school work. Accordingly, a program was devised to improve study approaches.

The pupils were taught how to survey a chapter to discover: (1) the general content of the chapter, (2) the author's plan for presenting material, (3) the location of introductions and summaries, (4) significance of illustrative materials such as maps, charts, pictures, and the like, (5) relationship of the chapter to the book, (6) careful examination of headings and subheadings, and (7) location of glossary, index, and other printed parts of the book. Several types of books were used to familiarize pupils with a variety of organizational patterns and content.

After the survey of the chapter, pupils were asked to read carefully the introduction (if one was included). After reading the introduction, the chapter summary was read where applicable. The survey and the reading of introduction and summary is believed to contribute materially to a reader's general awareness of the content of the entire chapter. The next step is that of changing headings of chapter subsections into question form. This can be done by writing questions or by simply keeping them in mind.

The first reading of the material begins at the first subsection and continues to the end of the subsection. At the end of the subsection the pupil either recites to himself or reflects upon whether his question or questions have been answered. In the first reading pupils were discouraged from underlining, or reading for detail. Each subsection is read in turn as quickly as possible consistent with good comprehension of general ideas.

During the second reading, pupils were encouraged to selectively underline where they believed necessary. Only key words were underlined. An example of selective underlining follows:

What Rights Did The English Colonies Bring To The New World?
The last *stop* in our journey is at the little *home* of *Jonathan Blake* in *Massachusetts Bay Colony*. *Jonathan* was a *free man* when he *came from England* to

*make a better living,* and his *life* in *America* is much *freer than* that of *Fernando* or *Pierre.* He *owns* his *house* and *farm,* which he is *free* to *manage* as he *wishes.* He has a *right* to *share* in the *government* of the *colony.* He may *vote* for *representatives* who become *members* of the *assembly* for the whole *colony.* This *assembly decides* many important *questions, including* the *taxes* which each *colonist* must *pay.* Jonathan *also* has certain other rights. For example, he *cannot be punished* for a *crime unless* he has been *found guilty* by a *group* of his *fellow men* called a *jury.*

It is believed by the writers that selective underlining requires more thinking on the part of the reader as compared with solid underlining of material. Moreover, many pupils have found that, in review reading, it is possible to grasp general concepts through reading only the underlined words.

It should be noted that "key" words are underlined, not "big" words. The little word "but" is often a key word. Other short but important words may be among others, "before," "after," "first," "second," "however," "if," etc. Good selective underlining will vary from pupil to pupil. Each is encouraged to underline as much or as little as necessary to highlight the concept.

Three weeks, four 40-minute periods per week, were given to practice in this technique. Regular textbooks were used for practice material and pupils were encouraged to use the approach while doing homework. It was pointed out to pupils that the approach was to be modified according to pupil purpose and relative difficulty of material.

Details in the chapter were handled differently. After general concepts were familiar, pupils then read for detail. Names, dates, places, events, and the like were thus associated with the general concepts. Some pupils preferred to underline details in a different color. It is believed by the writers that details can often be memorized while concepts need to be understood. Probably few people can read difficult material for both general concepts and detail simultaneously.

FLEXIBILITY TRAINING.   After three weeks of work designed to increase efficiency and comprehension in chapter reading, it was decided to begin work to increase flexibility of rate.

Research regarding the relationship between rate and comprehension is confused. Some are willing to assume that fast readers are always good readers. Therefore, these people assume that a desirable way to improve comprehension is to teach pupils to read faster. Unfortunate consequences may result from assuming that speed and comprehension are so closely correlated. Indiscriminate rate training may often result in teaching the pupil to *miscomprehend more rapidly.* Part of the confusion is due to the fact that results of a speed test cannot be very useful unless the results are coextensive with a test of comprehension. It is very difficult, if not impossible, to devise a standardized test of speed and one of comprehension in such a way that neither score is dependent upon the other. We know that speed without comprehension is useless. Low comprehension scores on tests received by bright pupils can be a result of overcautious procedures probably caused by an unnecessarily slow, inflexible, habituated, rate. While it is not easy to devise and standardize mutually exclusive measures of speed and comprehension, research indicates that efficient readers adjust their rate according to the difficulty of the material and the purpose for which they are reading.

As shown in Figure 4, only three pupils (Case Nos. 1, 2, and 11) demonstrated considerable flexibility in rate between third-grade material and material rated between tenth and twelfth-grade.

All pupils began rate training in third-grade material selected from *Science Research Associates Reading Laboratory*. After a warm-up period, pupils were timed on each exercise. Timing was done with a stopwatch. The instructor placed time in seconds on the blackboard. When a student finished reading, he copied the last number written on the board. Then, without rereading, he answered the questions, scored them by using the key provided, and recorded his comprehension score and rate on his personal data card.

Since pupils had learned earlier in the experiment to formulate questions to guide their reading of chapter-length materials, it was decided to adapt this question-first technique to rate work. Accordingly, pupils were given ample opportunity to study the questions before reading the selection. The procedure of reading the questions first is considered to be sensible even in rate work. Mature readers rarely, by choice, read and then answer questions. It is unfortunate, in the opinion of the writers, that school assignments are often given as follows: "Read the chapter, then answer the questions at the end of the chapter." Inquisitive, participating readers wish to read to answer questions or bring information to bear upon a problem. The reader in this situation is not passive, he makes demands upon the writer as he seeks information. Moreover, it is believed that where pupils read to get answers to questions, rate is increased without loss of comprehension. The procedure of reading questions first seemed to encourage confidence. All of the pupils preferred the question-first technique.

No machines, eye-span exercises, phrase-reading exercises, and the like were used. Pupils were asked to read as quickly as they could and still maintain adequate comprehension. Since the S. R. A. materials are graded as to readability, the twelve pupils were practicing speed reading at many different levels. When they were able to read quickly and effectively at a given level, they asked to try more difficult selections. Pupils exercised good judgment. Careful examinations of the individual data cards were made each day in order to furnish the instructors with information necessary to guide the pupil. From time to time, some were helped to reduce excessive head movement while reading. Early in rate training experience some pupils were helped to overcome lip movement.

All pupils began at third-grade level. They progressed to increasingly difficult material at their own discretion. At the end of the rate training, all were practicing in materials of tenth-grade level, or above. Four pupils were reading at twelfth-grade level.

The final results are shown in Figure 5. By subtracting the rate in column 2 from the rate in column 3, one arrives at the gain (in words per minute). This difference was placed in column 4. As can be seen in column 4, the gain varied from 66 to 630 words per minute. All pupils except Case Nos. 6 and

FIGURE 5

*Gains in Rate on Easy and Difficult
Material and Flexibility* *

| COL. 1 | COL. 2 | COL. 3 | COL. 4 | COL. 5 | COL. 6 | COL. 7 | COL. 8 | COL. 9 |
|---|---|---|---|---|---|---|---|---|
| CASE NO. | RATE ON EASY MATERIAL (NOV. 21) | RATE ON EASY MATERIAL (NOV. 3) | GAIN | RATE ON DIFFICULT MATERIAL (NOV. 21) | RATE ON DIFFICULT MATERIAL (NOV. 3) | GAIN | FLEXI- BILITY (OCT. 12) | FLEXI- BILITY (NOV. 21) |
| 1 | 816 | 510 | 306 | 600 | 330 | 270 | 180 | 216 |
| 2 | 960 | 520 | 440 | 660 | 408 | 252 | 112 | 300 |
| 3 | 510 | 360 | 150 | 396 | 330 | 66 | 30 | 114 |
| 4 | 540 | 360 | 220 | 396 | 282 | 114 | 78 | 144 |
| 5 | 600 | 210 | 390 | 390 | 228 | 162 | 18 | 210 |
| 6 | 360 | 282 | 78 | 330 | 216 | 114 | 66 | 30 |
| 7 | 318 | 252 | 66 | 276 | 234 | 42 | 18 | 42 |
| 8 | 642 | 200 | 242 | 396 | 204 | 204 | 4 | 246 |
| 9 | 480 | 276 | 104 | 300 | 240 | 60 | 36 | 180 |
| 10 | 900 | 310 | ·590 | 390 | 282 | 114 | 28 | 510 |
| 11 | 1020 | 390 | 630 | 500 | 288 | 212 | 102 | 520 |
| 12 | 630 | 240 | 390 | 396 | 198 | 198 | 42 | 234 |

* All figures are expressed in words per minute.
"Easy Material" refers to third-grade level.
"Difficult Material" refers to tenth to twelfth-grade materials.

7, column 4, made substantial rate gains in simple material. The median gain in rate in simple materials was found to be 279 words per minute.

Rates in difficult material are shown in columns 5 and 6. The difference between columns 5 and 6 represents gain in rate and these data are shown in column 7. The smallest gain was 42 words per minute and the largest gain was 270 words per minute in difficult materials. The median gain was 139 words per minute.

Flexibility data were placed in columns 8 and 9. In column 8 are the flexibility data recorded October 12, the beginning of the six-week experiment. Flexibility scores represent the rate differential, in words per minute in simple material as compared with rate in difficult material. Case No. 8, column 8, read simple material only 4 words per minute faster than difficult material. In contradistinction, Case No. 1, column 8, read simple materials 180 words per minute faster than difficult materials.

In column 9 are the final flexibility data. Case No. 11 established a flexibility of 520 words per minute between simple and difficult materials. For

Case No. 6, flexibility was only 30 words per minute. Median flexibility in October was 39 words per minute. Median flexibility in November was 213 words per minute.

Actual rate training *per se* was begun November 3 and completed November 21, during which time twelve 40-minute periods were scheduled. However, it is believed by the writers that preliminary work in chapter reading with practice given in reading for general ideas served as a good foundation for rate work.

## Interviews and Testing After Three Months

Three months after the special teaching had been finished, the pupils were interviewed individually. Each was asked to comment concerning the value of the practice work in chapter-length materials. In general, selective underlining was considered to be the most helpful. Four pupils felt that little value was received from the attempt to improve study approaches as described in this article. All but three pupils reported that the procedures learned during the experiment were currently being used. At least eight of the twelve pupils were enthusiastic concerning their progress.

Finally, each pupil was given a rate flexibility test to determine whether gains made were maintained after the three-months' lapse. Rate of reading in both simple and difficult materials dropped for all but two pupils; however, all pupils maintained a substantial net gain. The highest net gain in difficult materials was 396 w.p.m. The lowest net gain was only 12 w.p.m. Flexibility (difference between w.p.m. in simple and difficult materials) was enhanced as compared with the initial test results. All but three pupils showed a net increase in flexibility. Perhaps the most important gain can be stated thus: *All but three pupils read difficult materials faster (even after three months' elapsed time) than they did simple materials at the beginning of the experiment.*

## Conclusions

1. Correctable deficiencies in reading may exist among pupils whose achievement is high.
2. Skill in paragraph reading, as measured by standardized tests, is not a good measure of whether a pupil can effectively manage chapter-length materials in practical situations.
3. All standard tests results should be carefully analyzed to determine what is being measured and how it is measured.
4. Rate Flexibility Tests are useful diagnostic devices.
5. Pupils tend to read at a given speed regardless of materials or purpose.
6. Rate training should begin with simple materials. Adjustment in rate or difficulty of materials should be made when comprehension consistently drops below 80 per cent.

7. Pupils should take an active part in deciding when they are ready to increase rate.

8. No particular rate can represent the goal for all pupils. The characteristic is highly variable even among able pupils.

9. The goal of rate training is not directed toward set norms but rather toward individual flexibility. Pupils can learn to "shift gears" as materials and purpose change.

10. The typical practice of saving only standard test profiles (outside covers) while destroying the test itself, is contraindicated. The whole test is needed if full benefit is to be derived.

11. Skill development in reading should be taught at all grade levels and include all pupils.

12. Improvement in rate and flexibility were substantially present after three months had elapsed from the end of the teaching cycle.

While this experiment was limited in scope, it presented some evidence that reading problems of able pupils are often unnoticed. Many able pupils are retarded in reading regardless of high achievement established by standard norms. If Johnny is really to grow in reading at a rate commensurate with his potential, teachers on all levels from kindergarten through college have a significant responsibility. The early struggle of the first-grader to build a sight vocabulary and the task of the graduate student in handling an extensive bibliography are all part of the complicated reading process.

REFERENCES

1. *Gates Reading Survey*, Form I. New York: Bureau of Publications, Teachers College, Columbia University.

2. *Iowa Every-Pupil Tests of Basic Skills*, Form O. New York: Houghton Mifflin Company.

3. *Kuhlmann-Anderson Test*, Form G. Princeton, New Jersey: Personnel Press, Incorporated.

4. *Science Research Associates Reading Laboratory*. Chicago, Illinois: Science Research Associates.

# STUDY SKILLS FOR SUPERIOR STUDENTS IN SECONDARY SCHOOL *

Francis P. Robinson

When Robinson points out in this article that even Phi Beta Kappas study quite inefficiently and that their study skills can be improved, he whets our appetite for more information: what research says about developing effective reading-study skills, how academic skills are like athletic skills, and how a special technique is best used to improve comprehension and retention of material.

1. Why is it often difficult to interest superior students in learning better reading skills?

2. What evidence exists for the contention that many students, including superior ones, are inefficient readers?

3. What do authors, publishers, and teachers do to help readers take advantage of what is known about the writing and organizing of textbooks?

4. How would you impress upon your students the value of each of the steps in the SQ3R study approach?

5. Give illustrative examples for the brief points the author lists in his summary.

READING instruction is a regular part of most college programs (4, 8). It deals not only with remediation of reading disabilities but also with instruction in higher levels of reading skill needed for collegiate study. This article will emphasize the value of giving instruction in higher level reading skills to superior high school students, particularly those who may be taking collegiate courses early, or those who want to learn these reading skills in preparation for later college work. It is also obvious that these reading skills can be of value in doing high school work.

Because high schools give much emphasis to remedial work for poor readers and because superior students read so much better than their peers, it is usually difficult to interest these students in learning better reading skills. However, the fact that these higher level skills are needed in college, and are a part there of the regular instructional program, should increase interest of superior students in maximizing their reading skills. In addition, the use of instructional materials specifically written for the college level will help indicate that higher levels of skill are being emphasized rather than remediation.

It will be necessary to show students that their reading skills are actually quite inefficient. Some data obtained from outstanding students in college will be useful here. Studies of Phi Beta Kappa and other honor roll candidates show that their rate of reading is typically little above that of other students

---

* FROM The Reading Teacher (September 1961), pp. 29–33; 37, reprinted with permission of Francis P. Robinson and the International Reading Association.

and that they have quite inefficient study skills (6, 13). Other studies show that superior students given selections with headings in and headings omitted read the former no faster nor comprehend them any better, although evidence indicates that such headings can with training be used to increase speed and comprehension (16). A study made during World War II of superior college students referred for specialized training showed that these students had been making their A's and B's more by strength of intellect than by efficient study skills (14). When these students were asked to read and take notes their "work rate" was only ninety-three words per minute, and the quality of their notes was little better than average.

Other studies show that with a single reading the typical reader gets only about 60 per cent of the ideas asked on an immediate quiz, and with immediate rereadings is able to raise his comprehension score only to about 65 per cent (7). Another study of several thousand high school students showed that there is rapid forgetting after reading: within two weeks after an initial reading only 20 per cent is rememebered of what was known immediately after reading (17).

In brief, the average and superior student in high school and college is inefficient in his reading and study skills; he tends to excell other students in grades mostly because of differences in intellectual ability and not because of better reading and study methods.

Before turning to the nature of some of these higher level reading skills and how they may be taught, two preliminary points need to be made: (a) textbooks should be even better organized to facilitate learning and (b) when students are given better books they will not do much better unless they are taught the necessary reading skills to use the facilitative cues. While modern textbooks are written in many ways to facilitate learning, e.g., use of headings, final summaries, illustrations, etc., there is good evidence that school textbook writers and publishers are still too much bound to the typographical style of ancient papyrus times, e.g., close printed, full line paragraphs in one type size. School textbooks make little use (except in footnotes) of paragraphs printed in different type sizes to indicate degree of importance. They do not use a style (found useful in governmental and industrial publications) of indenting the whole left side of subordinate paragraphs. Academic authors seem unprepared to use pictorial material as the main form of presentation, with prose added as explanation. Few help the reader by starting chapters with summary statements or by putting their headings into question form, etc. A great deal is known that could improve textbooks, and experiments such as trying the scramble order of the recent *Tutortexts* should be encouraged and evaluated.

The second preliminary point is that superior students may not be able to read better when they are given well organized and facilitative material *unless they are given special instruction.* Earlier it was stated that inserting headings into a text does not increase reading speed or comprehension of college students. A more extensive study by Christenson and Stordahl showed similar results and found in addition that adding such cues as underlinings, summary statements, etc., does not help uninstructed adult readers (5). Another study by Newman showed that when material is prepared which forces students to read in a manner which seems to better fit psychological knowledge of how learning takes place, the students actually do better using their own self-derived methods with which they are comfortable (12). Additional studies show that simple explanations of better techniques (either through reading about them or through oral explanation) are not sufficient to bring about better skill (2, 18). However, with supervised practice, as is necessary in learning any skill, there is a definite gain in skill to levels far beyond those attained with self-help methods (2). In brief, what has been discovered in developing optimum athletic and industrial skills applies to learning scholastic skills as well. Research can be used to design new higher levels of skill, and these must be taught in a coaching and practice situation.

What are some of the higher level reading and study skills? One of them is the SQ3R method—a technique devised from research findings for use in studying college textbooks (15). Some of the research will be summarized and the method then described. McClusky divided 118 college students into two equated groups; one group was shown how to skim over headings and summaries and the other was not shown. When these two groups were then given a selection to read, the trained group read 24 per cent faster than, and just as accurately as, the control group (11). Holmes also set up two large equated groups of college students and had them read selections about science and history (9). One group was given twenty questions *before* reading. As might be expected, the group given the questions did better in answering them, but they also did as well or better on additional questions. The advantage was particularly great on tests given two weeks after reading. Still another study by Washburne indicates the best placement for such questions (19). In this study 1,456 high school students were divided into several groups of equal ability. Questions were given to the different groups as follows: at the beginning of reading, at the end of reading, each question just before the material answering it, each question just after the material answering it, and no questions. The test contained questions already provided as well as other questions. Of these different placements two proved most effective: all questions at the beginning of the reading and each question just before it was answered in the material.

These findings, plus the fact that textbook writers regularly use headings, numberings and summaries, provide a basis for designing the first three steps of the SQ3R methods: (1) *survey*, (2) ask a *question* before reading a section, and (3) *read* to answer that question. The reader is taught to quickly survey the headings and read the summaries before he starts to read the text. This gives him an orientation as to what the chapter will present, helps him recall what he already knows about these topics, and facilitates his subsequent readings.

We have already noted that students tend to forget much of what they learn from reading within a very short time, e.g., 80 per cent within two weeks (17). This same study also showed that a testing-type review immediately after reading was very helpful in reducing forgetting, e.g., instead of 80 per cent there was only a 20 per cent loss. Other studies show that readers often do not clearly comprehend ideas as they read along, and the rapid succession of ideas in reading tends to interfere with what is comprehended because of retroactive inhibition. So there is need for a system to check on comprehension while reading and also to help in fixing ideas better in memory. Notetaking can be used for this purpose, but the manner in which most students take notes is of little help. That is, studies show that students do as well with straight reading as they do with trying to read and take notes (1, 18). One reason for this is that students tend to copy down phrases as soon as they find an important idea, and if the phrase is in italics they may write it down without understanding the point. Many students do not like to take notes because they write in complete sentences, which markedly slows down their reading speed.

Thus, a method must be worked out which helps the student check his comprehension as he reads, helps fix the ideas in memory, does not take too long, and is useful for later review. The fourth and fifth steps of the SQ3R method are designed to take care of these needs: (4) after completing a headed section, *recite* by writing a brief phrase from memory, and (5) immediately after reading the whole lesson *review* it by looking over the notes taken and reciting on them from memory. Notes are not taken until *after* a headed section has been read. This enables the student to read to answer his question (step 3) and then check on his comprehension and help fix the material in memory by reciting a brief answer. Waiting until the end of the section means that all of the ideas in that section can be seen in relation to each other and the most important selected; writing the note from memory means that the student has to organize his answer, and if he has trouble he can recall the material as needed; using phrases means that much time is saved in writing, and these cues will be sufficient later on for reminders in review.

The SQ3R method then consists of five steps: (1) *Survey* the headings and summaries quickly to get the general ideas which will be developed in the assignment, (2) turn the first heading into a *Question*, (3) *Read* the whole section through to answer that question, (4) at the end of the headed section stop to *Recite* from memory on the question and jot the answer down in phrases (Steps 2, 3 and 4 are repeated on each succeeding headed section), and (5) at the end of reading the assignment in this manner then immediately *Review* the lesson to organize the ideas and recite on the various points to fix them in mind. This higher-level study skill cannot be learned simply by reading about it, it must be practiced under supervision just as with learning any skill. Modifications of this skill have also been worked out for studying collateral readings, English literature, and charts and tables (15).

While particular attention has been given to the explanation of one particular higher-level study skill, there are many other specialized skills which the superior secondary school student needs in college as well as in high school. Much use is made of specialized graphs, charts, maps, dictionaries, encyclopedias, resource books, etc., in college. A surprising number of college students tend to skip graphs and tables, refuse to use dictionaries and indices, or handle such material in an inefficient manner. Studies of college students' ability to use the library to find assigned books or to use easy short cuts in writing research papers show ignorance of fundamental and simple devices (10). Studies of the manner in which college students go about reading examination questions show that rather than use systematic skills in analysis they usually use a self-taught "jump and guess" system (3). In brief, superior students in high school need to learn many higher-level skills if they are to be highly effective in college work.

Since students going to college move away from their usual surroundings and conditions for study, they also need help with study habits and planning. Irregular class schedules and the need for self-planning of study time leave many students floundering. Both the home and high school usually provide study conditions with a minimum of distraction, but in college there are many places to study, and students often try to combine studying with social possibilities. Finally, many students—even superior ones—go through high school with only vaguely understood adult goals, and go on to college mostly because "everyone in school does." Such motivation is insufficient to help students direct study efforts when so many more fascinating things are possible in college. Youngsters need help in thinking about why they want to go to college so that their college efforts can be more effectively self directed.

Our points, in brief, have been: Superior students in high school are typically inefficient in study methods; they have kept ahead of others through brilliance of intellect. College work will offer them particular difficulties because of greater demands and competition and because of many distractions for poorly controlled individuals. Furthermore, superior students are interested in making outstanding records of achievement and discovery and not simply in excelling others; this demands that they learn research-designed higher-level study skills.

*(F. P. Robinson is a Professor of Education at Ohio State University. His publications include works on effective study and student counseling.)*

REFERENCES

1. ARNOLD, H. F. "The Comparative Efficiency of Certain Study Techniques in Fields of History," *J. Educ. Psychol.*, 33 (1942), 449–457.
2. BARTON, W. A. "Outlining As a Study Procedure," *Teach. Coll. Contri. Educ.*, No. 411, 1930.
3. BLOOM, B. S., and BRODER, L. J. *Problem Solving Processes of College Students.* Chicago: Univ. of Chicago Press, 1950.

4. CAUSEY, O. S., and ELLER, W. (Editors) "Starting and Improving College Reading Programs," *Eighth Yearbook of National Reading Conference.* Fort Worth: Texas Christian University Press, 1959.
5. CHRISTENSON, C. M., and STORDAHL, K. E. "The Effect of Organizational Aids on Comprehension and Retention," *J. Educ. Psychol.,* 46 (1955), 65–74.
6. DANSKIN, D. G., and BURNETT, C. W. "Study Techniques of Those Superior Students," *Pers. & Guid. J.,* 31 (1952), 181–186.
7. ENGLISH, H. B., WELBORN, E. L., and KILLIAN, C. D. "Studies in Substance Memorization," *J. Gen. Psychol.,* 11 (1934), 233–259.
8. ENTWISLE, D. R. "Evaluations of Study-skills Courses: A Review," *J. Educ. Research,* 53 (1960), 243–251.
9. HOLMES, E. "Reading Guided by Questions versus Careful Reading and Re-reading without Questions," *School Rev.,* 39 (1931), 361–371.
10. LOUTTIT, C. M., and PATRICK, J. R. "A Study of Students' Knowledge in the Use of the Library," *J. Appl. Psychol.,* 16 (1932), 475–484.
11. McCLUSKY, H. Y. "An Experiment on the Influence of Preliminary Skimming on Reading," *J. Educ. Psychol.,* 25 (1934), 521–529.
12. NEWMAN, S. E. "Student vs. Instructor Design of Study Method, *J. Educ. Psychol.,* 48 (1957), 328–333.
13. PRESTON, R. C., and TUFTS, E. N. "The Reading Habits of Superior College Students," *J. Exper. Educ.,* 16 (1948), 196–202.
14. ROBINSON, F. P. "Study Skills of Soldiers in ASTP," *School & Soc.,* 58 (1943), 398–399.
15. ROBINSON, F. P. *Effective Study* (Revised edition), New York: Harper and Brothers, 1961.
16. ROBINSON, F. P., and HALL, PRUDENCE. "Studies of Higher Level Reading Abilities," *J. Educ. Psychol.,* 32 (1941), 241–252.
17. SPITZER, H. F. "Studies in Retention," *J. Educ. Psychol.,* 30 (1939), 641–656.
18. STORDAHL, K. E., and CHRISTENSON, C. M. "The Effect of Study Techniques on Comprehension and Retention," *J. Educ. Research,* 46 (1956), 561–570.
19. WASHBURNE, J. N. "The Use of Questions in Social Science Material," *J. Educ. Psychol.,* 20 (1929), 321–359.

# DETERMINING MAIN IDEAS:
# A BASIC STUDY SKILL *

Hayden B. Jolly, Jr.

*Determining the main idea of a reading selection is a key skill underlying the reading-study jobs. Mastery of this skill is necessary for effective reading and writing, and therefore paves the way to better grades in school.*

*In this paper Jolly explains well (1) the value of properly teaching students to master the skills of getting the main idea; (2) which materials are used in teaching these skills; (3) the sequence of main idea skills; (4) how to teach the skills, and (5) the responsibility of all teachers for teaching the skills.*

*1. What evidence exists for the need to teach main idea skills?*

*2. The author suggests certain materials be used in teaching main idea skills. What reasons does he offer for using these materials?*

*3. How can the teacher check the student's ability to use the main idea skills?*

*4. Why is it important to remember that the suggested exercises are teaching tools?*

*5. Explain the importance of teaching the main idea skills in proper sequence.*

*6. Who should teach these skills?*

MEETING my college freshman English class for the second session of a new quarter, I attempted to begin a discussion of their first assignment with a question; the question posed by the title of the assigned essay: "What is Literature For?" by S. I. Hayakawa. In asking that title question I hoped to get from the students some of the essay's main points. I got none; the class was silent. Not to be dismayed, I rephrased the question, trying to make it more specific—but still no answers came. A third question was asked for possible suggestions as to why Mr. Hayakawa wrote the essay and what his purposes might have been. This time a few hands went up but the hesitant answers were vague and unrelated to the thesis of the essay.

I first decided that most of the students had not read the essay, but they answered succeeding questions of detail easily. Most of the students had indeed read the essay; they had simply failed to get from it what I considered most important—the main ideas. They had read, but they had not studied. And even after we listed the details and categorized them, the students had to be led through a painful (to us all) series of questions in order to arrive at generalizations of main points remotely akin to the author's. Even Socrates would have been weary.

This experience is not unique to the college English teacher. Most teachers, regardless of grade level or subject, have had similar ones. What is important,

---

* Written especially for inclusion in this volume.

however, is what the teacher does or thinks after the agony is over. There is some danger that he may conclude that this is an unusually dull class, shrug his shoulders, and move on to more successful endeavors. This would be an injustice to the students, for although it is possible that the class might be a dull one this is probably not the case.

Experience and research point to the fact that even the brightest students have difficulty identifying main ideas. William G. Perry[1] in the *Harvard Educational Review*, describes an experiment conducted on 1,500 freshmen from Harvard and Radcliffe to determine how they approached a study task and how well they identified significant details and main ideas.

The students were assigned a chapter in a history text and simply told to "study the chapter; you will have a test later." After the study period, during which the experimenter observed how they approached the task, the students were given a multiple choice test on details. The results were, according to Perry, impressive. But, he continues, the students had considerably more difficulty identifying the main ideas:

We asked anyone who could do so to write a short statement about what the chapter was all about. The number who were able to tell us . . . was just one in a hundred—fifteen. As a demonstration of obedient purposelessness in the reading of 99% of freshmen we found this impressive . . . after twelve years of reading homework assignments in school they had all settled into the habit of leaving the point of it all to someone else. . . .

If these bright students have difficulty with main ideas, can we expect most other high-school and college students to be more successful? The problem would seem to be universal.

Perry also implies that perhaps too often, rather than go through the agony of trying to elicit main ideas from students or trying to teach them to do it on their own, we teachers simply point them out ourselves and get on to questions of detail. We can usually count on the students to have recognized a few of those.

The value of properly teaching students to master this skill cannot be overemphasized, for it is the foundation of most other study-meaning skills. Karlin[2] and Smith[3] classify the identification of main ideas as the most fundamental of selection and evaluation skills, and point out that efficient use of the organization skills is dependent upon mastery of main idea skills.

If a student cannot identify main ideas he cannot be expected to write a good summary, for a summary is little more than the reduction of an expository selection to its main ideas and supporting details. To be able to outline, the student must be able to identify main ideas and supporting details and arrange them in a form that indicates their relative importance and relationships. Outlining and summarizing are invaluable aids for study and retention. They are simple techniques for the student who has learned the prerequisite skills—and are meaningless rituals to those who have not.

And the organization skills are not the only ones which demand the ability to determine main ideas. Such highly regarded study techniques as the SQ3R or PQRST are psychologically sound methods to encourage thoroughness and retention but are valueless until the student learns in his reading to distinguish what Perry called the "point of it all." The student who would learn to read or skim rapidly with utmost comprehension must be able, from a welter of illustrations, examples, and details, to quickly sort out significant points.

To be able to infer an author's purposes the student must first understand what the author's main points are. Indeed, most problems of interpretation, either in literary or expository material, are matters of drawing conclusions or making inferences after a consideration of main ideas. In short, if a student cannot identify main ideas, he is in danger of missing the most vital meaning in his reading; and his ability to use many valuable study aids is greatly handicapped.

The purpose of this brief article is to examine some of the causes of this widespread problem with main ideas and suggest some guidelines and techniques for more effective instruction in this skill.

## Possible Causes

Because of the complex nature of learning problems causes are always difficult to specify, and authorities seeking causes often disagree. The assumption underlying this paper, however, is that the most common and the most fundamental cause of deficiencies related to main idea skills is educational, and that the cause and the cure lie in the teaching methods and materials. The writer does not rule out the possibility of other contributory causes. Nevertheless, educational problems are the ones with which we teachers are best able to deal.

Observation of teaching practices and the examination of a number of reading and English textbooks suggest that the following weaknesses are largely responsible for the almost universal problems associated with identifying main ideas:

1. Skills prerequisite to the effective mastery of main ideas are often not included in textbooks, or courses of study. When they are included, they are rarely taught in sequence.
2. Identification of main ideas and related skills are usually taught in workbook or composition exercises affecting little transfer to other reading needs.
3. Textbook exercises, which purport to teach main ideas, often simply *test* students' ability with the skill rather than *teach* the skill.
4. Teachers in the content areas, if they consider the problem at all, assume that the responsibility for teaching the skill belongs to the teacher of reading or of composition.

The suggestions and recommendations that follow are based upon a careful consideration of these weaknesses, and upon the assumption that the well-informed teacher in any subject matter area can do much to overcome them with the material he has available.

## MATERIALS FOR DEVELOPING MAIN IDEA SKILLS

Karlin [2] has suggested among his five guidelines for teaching the study skills that, whenever possible, the teaching of these skills be done with materials students are actually using in their subject-matter areas—their textbooks. Apparently, few teachers use textbooks for this purpose; perhaps because they feel that special workbooks are necessary to teach such skills effectively. However, if the teacher will only consider this proposal he will see its practical value. After all, it is the textbooks which we wish the students to study more effectively. It is the main ideas in textbooks that we wish them to identify and understand.

Workbook and English textbook exercises on main ideas and topic sentences follow a familiar pattern: (1) definition; (2) examples, and (3) exercises. They do little teaching. They simply provide sample paragraphs and ask students to find the topic sentence or the main idea. The student does not have the valuable experience of forming his own generalizations. It appears that many textbooks assume that providing a definition of a term or a concept is equivalent to teaching the related skill.

Experience should have taught us otherwise. The typical definition of a topic sentence as "the sentence which states the main idea of a paragraph" is of no value unless the student can already recognize the main idea when he encounters it. We teachers of English should have realized long ago how ineffective this "teaching by definition" is. For years we have defined the sentence as "a group of words expressing a complete thought." This was fine for the student who could already recognize a complete thought. Many students could quote the definition accurately but continued to write fragments. Obviously we cannot depend upon this type of teaching to insure mastery of necessary skills for reading or writing.

The use of students' regular textbooks is particularly appropriate for teaching main ideas. The history book, the science text, and any material with which the student must deal in his regular work, will be far more valuble for the development of these skills than exercises unrelated to his actual reading and study needs. Not only do his textbooks contain a wealth of sentences, paragraphs and longer selections that can serve as vehicles for instruction, but there is also the advantage that, in addition to learning the skill, the student is dealing with information the teacher wishes him to master.

Much incidental teaching of main idea skills can effectively be done with newspapers, magazines, articles in encyclopedias, student publications, student essays and, indeed, any material students normally use at school. Only one caution is necessary: the material used should be at the students' instructional reading level in order that it present no meaning problems other than those related to the skill being taught.

## Sequence of Main Idea Skills

If the student, by the time he reaches high school, is still deficient in basic skills, reason assures us that he is not likely to acquire them suddenly through a surge of intuition. *He must be taught.* The skills he has failed to learn must be developed, beginning with the simplest skill in the sequence which the student has not acquired in progressing through the more complex aspects of the skill. The following list of requisite skills for the identification of main ideas appears to have been rather commonly neglected:

1. Identification of the topic of a sentence.
2. Identification of the topic of a paragraph.
3. Identification of the topic sentence of a paragraph.
4. Identification of the main idea of a paragraph.
5. Perception of the relationships among main ideas in related paragraphs.
6. Identification of thesis statements, and in main ideas in longer selections.

Although the first two of these skills appear to be remarkably simple, the teacher should not assume that all students have mastered them. Such assumptions too often prove false, even for high-school and college students; our facile assumptions about the skills of students are partly responsible for their frequent lack of them. It is certainly natural for the teacher to feel that the student has mastered the skills necessary to have reached his grade level, but it is probably better—until he knows otherwise—for the teacher to assume he has mastered none of them.

An informal check of these skills is quite simple to give either to groups or to individuals. Simply choose several paragraphs and sections from any of their texts and ask them to identify the topics, the main ideas, and the topic sentences. Requesting them to write the main ideas in their own words can be particularly revealing. An examination of their responses will indicate which students need work on particular skills. Also their outlines, or summaries, of text material will furnish clues to the strengths and weaknesses in main idea skills.

## Suggestions for Teaching Main Idea Skills

To locate the topic of a sentence the student must be able to distinguish the subject of a sentence; not the structural subject or the specific substantive, but the topical or notional subject. They are often the same. But, because students' minds often close at the mention of anything which smacks of grammar it is probably wise not to use the term "subject" at all. The bright students will note the parallel on their own. Often however, the topic or notional subject is more inclusive than the simple subject, as in the following example:

There are no billboards or other advertising on the Blue Ridge Parkway.

The structural subjects are the nouns "billboards" and "advertising." The topic is simply "advertising on the Blue Ridge Parkway." That is what the sentence is about.

Perhaps the simplest way to begin teaching this concept is to put several sentences on the board:

The present goal of our space program is to land a man on the moon.

Bluntly stated, Jackson's thesis arouses some skepticism, but as Jackson states it, explaining his basis, it becomes convincing.

It was just twenty years ago that the Supreme Court handed down its famous decision in the *Esquire Case*.

As he presents each example, the teacher should demonstrate the process of identifying the general topic of each. He might reason aloud, considering alternatives and explaining why he rejects some and concludes with topics like these: (1) goal of the space program; (2) Jackson's thesis, or (3) Supreme Court decision in the *Esquire Case*. The problem of terminology will become immediately apparent to the teacher. What else can you call these but topics? It is probably not as important what the teacher calls them so long as he gives adequate illustration of what he seeks and students are led to understand that he has isolated the notional subject.

Bright students may react to such an exercise with the question "Why bother?" After all, the notional subject or topic apart from its predication is a meaningless phrase. Students should be led to understand that this stage is a stage of preparation similar to the initial stages in programmed instruction. Its usefulness may become apparent only after more complex problems are confronted.

Next, students might be provided with sample sentences followed by two or three options from which to choose the topic:

There is hardly an area of modern life—education, industry, agriculture, medicine, etc.—in which computers do not perform some important function.

The topic is:
1. The complexity of modern living.
2. Areas of modern life.
3. Complexity of computers.
4. Computers in modern life.

The teacher should keep in mind that such exercises are teaching tools and not tests. They should be gone over carefully and students who make errors should be aided to see why they were wrong.

After students have demonstrated proficiency with this exercise, direct them to appropriate sentences in any of their textbooks to locate the sentence topics. If they can identify—without assistance—the topics of the sentences selected they are ready for the next phase. If they are still having difficulty more demonstrations are probably in order.

The development of the next stages might proceed in much the same manner. The teacher may present sample paragraphs first, demonstrating how he identifies the topic of the paragraph by examining the sentence topics and details. After his demonstrations he may present the students' paragraphs with several options from which to choose the appropriate one. The following example paragraph from Emerson's "Beauty" illustrates a typical exercise:

Beauty is the quality which makes to endure. In a house that I know, I have noticed a block of spermaceti lying about closets and mantelpieces, for twenty years together, simply because the tallow-man gave it the form of a rabbit; and, I suppose, it may continue to be lugged about unchanged for a century. Let an artist scrawl a few lines or figures on the back of a letter, and that scrap of paper is rescued from danger, is put in portfolio, is framed and glazed, and, in proportion to the beauty of the lines drawn, will be kept for centuries. Burns writes a copy of verses, and sends them to a newspaper, and the human race take charge of them that they shall not perish.

This paragraph is about:
1. A spermaceti rabbit.
2. Beauty.
3. An artist's scrawls.
4. A Burns poem.

By first examining the details with the students and having them search for the most general and inclusive of the topics which can relate to all of the details, the students can be led to choose the correct topic. Following this exercise almost any paragraphs from their texts will provide a challenge to their independent efforts.

The same sample paragraphs will also be suitable for practice in locating the topic sentence. After successfully locating the topic they should have little difficulty locating the topic sentence. Some care may be necessary at this point to help students see the difference between the topic of a paragraph and the topic or thesis sentence. After several exercises they should be led to see that although the topic of a paragraph identifies the subject matter of the paragraph, the topic sentence makes some assertion about that subject.

This will be facilitated by using the same paragraphs for teaching both elements. With the previous example paragraph, for instance, after the students have identified "beauty" as its topic, they should have little difficulty noting the sentence that makes the most general statement about "beauty"—the first sentence.

In the following paragraph, students should be able to determine that the topic is grammar, and that the topic sentence specifies the author's attitude toward that topic:

> The teacher who considers the traditional grammatical rules of English to be sacred and inviolable must be unaware of the true nature of language. The English language is not static. It has never been, despite the attempts of numerous grammarians to make it so. It changes as our technology changes, as new things and new concepts come into being. The fact is that our dictionaries and our grammars are out of date from the moment they come off the press.

The first sentence, the topic sentence, immediately gives us the author's focus and direction but even after identifying it we have not adequately captured the author's main idea. The second and third sentences contribute vital clarification for the first. For this reason it is often appropriate to have students express a paragraph's main idea in their own words.

It is important to be consistent in the types of paragraphs presented for instruction in the early stages. It would be confusing, for example, to present descriptive paragraphs which do not contain topic sentences or inductively organized paragraphs in which the topic sentence is last until students can deal efficiently with the typical expository paragraph. It is advisable also to explain with examples the various types of paragraph structures before requiring students to analyze them. This may require some research on the part of the history or science teacher for adequate material, but if he recognizes the value of guided learning he will see its merit.

It will be also helpful, after students' work with paragraphs choosing options provided by the teacher, to present them with paragraphs from which topic sentences have been removed. Allow them to write topic sentences and compare them with the original. The final test of the effectiveness of this instruction is given when students attempt to identify topic sentences and main ideas unaided in their textbooks.

An expository paragraph is an essay in miniature and, if the skill of identifying the main ideas in paragraphs has been adequately developed, instruction with longer selections should be relatively easy. The teacher need only continue with the same inductive approach. One simple way to begin might be to locate a well-unified selection of several paragraphs in a chapter or essay and have students extract the main ideas from each paragraph. Present them with several choices of topics and main ideas from which to choose the ones appropriate for the selection.

After a few experiences of this kind, students can generally be led to identify the main ideas and thesis statements when guided by proper questions: Do the topic sentences of the paragraphs deal with similar or related ideas or elements? How are they related? What new information does each contribute? Is there one statement which is general enough to include the topics of all the paragraphs?

Through such an analysis students can usually be led to see not only the relationships between the paragraphs but the thesis idea to which each paragraph is related. It is vital that students have guided practice of this kind before they attempt to analyze longer selections on their own.

Some of the following exercises may also be useful in teaching topic sentences and main ideas:

1. Students construct topic sentences for possible paragraphs on subjects suggested by the teacher.
2. Students provide major headings for outlines after being provided with subheadings.
3. Students write headlines for hypothetical articles about school events.
4. From a list of relevant and irrelevant details, students select details related to main ideas provided by the teacher.
5. Students do research to locate facts to support conclusions provided by the teacher.
6. Students locate main ideas in the body of a textbook chapter which parallel ideas restated in the chapter summary.
7. Students synthesize portions of assigned reading into main ideas.
8. Students formulate main ideas for teacher's lecture which provides significant details.

## RESPONSIBILITY OF ALL TEACHERS

It has become almost trite to proclaim to every high-school teacher that he must teach reading. Nevertheless, past pleas for an acceptance of this notion have fallen largely on deaf ears; so the pleas must continue. Until the teachers in every field accept some responsibility for teaching basic reading skills when students need them to achieve in their areas, many gross weaknesses in the study-meaning skills will continue. It is almost a gleeful irony to the reading teacher that one hears the subject matter teachers complaining the loudest about students' inability to study their material effectively.

Granted that the history teacher should not be expected to deal with serious reading problems, there is still much that he can do to contribute to students' study skills. And there are too many fine articles and textbooks available to the teacher today to make any excuse of ignorance about teaching reading an acceptable one.

It seems particularly vital that the subject matter teacher concern himself with main idea skills. Authorities agree that the most effective learning of any skill occurs when the skill is taught as the need for it arises and when students can recognize that need. It is in this regard that the subject matter teacher has a distinct psychological advantage, for his students—particularly those who are in difficulty—are quite aware of their needs. The subject matter teacher has an additional advantage in that his students can be learning significant facts in the area in conjunction with the skill instruction. Also the experience of providing instruction and testing on the skills will give the teacher new insights into the strengths and weaknesses of each student and into the problems each has comprehending the reading material in his subject.

## CONCLUSION

A remedy for any reading skill weakness is likely to be regarded like any suggested remedy for a bad cold. As a prescriptive cure, it is likely to be viewed with doubt and its advocate branded as asinine for not being aware that there are a great variety of cures which might be just as effective, particularly when combined—a sort of eclectic cure. Well, this writer is aware of the danger. And he is aware that any creative teacher who recognizes the need for instruction on main idea skills can certainly add many other suggestions for improving instruction in this skill or create an entirely different approach that might be just as effective. He has hoped to accomplish two ends: to make teachers aware of the vital need for instruction in this skill and, following accepted principles of learning, to provide a prescription—regimented though it appear—that might be used where *no* remedy has been used in the past. Hopefully, if more teachers become aware of the vast need for remedying this ill, they will experiment with prescriptions of their own.

## REFERENCES

1. PERRY, WILLIAM G., JR., "Students' Use and Misuse of Reading Skills: A Report to the Faculty," *Harvard Educational Review*, XXIX (Summer 1959), pp. 193–200.
2. KARLIN, ROBERT, *Teaching Reading in High School*. Indianapolis: Bobbs-Merrill Company, Inc., 1964, pp. 138–148.
3. SMITH, NILA B., *Reading Instruction for Today's Children*. Englewood Cliffs, N.J.: Prentice-Hall, Inc., 1963, pp. 305–351.

# EVALUATION IN READING

## INTRODUCTION

*The teacher who wants to teach well and effectively must discover both the reading instruction needs of his students, and their capacity for profiting from such instruction. These needs and capacities can be determined through the use of appropriate diagnostic and survey instruments. A careful analysis by the teacher of the information provided by such instruments helps him to select materials and methods which, when wisely and assiduously used, will help his students grow in reading and* through *reading.*

*But the teacher faces a problem in the selection of reading tests. The type of test he selects depends upon such factors as the purposes for testing; the validity of a test for those purposes; the number of students to be tested; the time and facilities for testing, and how the test results are to be used.*

*The problems presented by the contemplation of these factors are discussed by the authors of the selections in this unit. These problems are focused in the debate between those individuals who favor informal tests, which require the students to* produce *a correct answer, and those who favor standardized tests, which generally require the students to* recognize *a correct answer. The person who reads these articles critically and thoroughly should be amply rewarded.*

# ABILITY OF STUDENTS TO IDENTIFY CORRECT RESPONSES BEFORE READING *

Ralph C. Preston

*Both objective and subjective types of reading tests have their particular advantages and disadvantages. Because the better objective reading comprehension tests have such advantages as reliability and ease of administration and scoring, they have gained wide acceptance.*

*In this research article Preston investigates the value of one type of reading comprehension test as presently constructed. After asking how more valid measures might be constructed, he explores the possibility of adopting new models of reading comprehension and new procedures for measuring it.*

*1. What is the purpose of this investigation?*

*2. How are students able to recognize correct answers without reading the passages on which the questions are based?*

*3. What suggestions does the author give for developing more valid measures of reading comprehension?*

IMUS, ROTHNEY, and Bear (4) reported that Ophthalm-O-Graph reading comprehension scores of college students were almost as high when the comprehension test on a given passage was taken before the passage was read. Subsequently, the investigator has occasionally given informal tests of reading comprehension to graduate students, requiring them to answer questions about selected passages before they read the passage and again after the reading. Like the Ss of Imus et al., many of the graduate students achieved considerably better than chance.

The present investigation explored this tendency systematically. The following hypotheses were tested: (a) Students as a group score better than chance on a reading comprehension test when deprived of the opportunity of reading the passages on which the items are based. (b) Individual differences in reading comprehension, tested under these conditions, are positively related to reading ability as conventionally measured; academic aptitude as measured by the verbal score of the Scholastic Aptitude Test (V-SAT); scholastic performance as measured by class standing in high school (high-school quintile) and by grade-point average earned during the first semester of college (GPA); and sex.

---

* REPRINTED FROM *Journal of Educational Research*, LVIII (December 1964), pp. 181–183, by permission of the publisher and the author.

## PROCEDURE

The first 30 comprehension items of the Cooperative English Test: Test C2: Reading Comprehension (Higher Level), Form R, were isolated from the passages which the items were designed to test. They were combined to form a test entitled "Information Test." The followed instructions preceded the items: "In taking this test now, you will be 'warming up' for the reading exercises which will follow. Check what you consider to be the correct response to each item. You will have absolutely no basis for knowing the correct answers for some of the items. In any case, make the most of your experience in taking this kind of test, and check what you imagine the test maker is fishing for!" The stem of each item was changed slightly as considered necessary for the sake of clarity. Thus, the original stem of the first item which read: "The main thought of this passage is that" was changed to read: "A certain reading test contains a passage about photography. In all probability the main thought of this passage is that."

The passageless test was administered to 128 freshmen (75 men and 53 women) at the University of Pennsylvania. After taking the passageless test, the students took the same form of the test in its entirety and in the conventional way.

## RESULTS

The first hypothesis concerned students as a group. Since there were five options per item, the expected score on the 30-item passageless test was six. The majority of students (77 percent) achieved scores greater than six, or better than chance. The significance of these scores was tested in two ways. First, the observed mean was compared with the expected mean on the basis of chance. The observed mean was 8.34. This was significantly greater than the expected mean of six ($p < .001$). Second, a count was made of the number of Ss whose scores were significantly greater than chance. Given the expected proportion of .200, an observed proportion of .367 (or a score of 11) was necessary in order to reject the hypothesis for a given individual at the .05 level that a real difference did not exist. Twenty-six of the Ss achieved scores at or beyond this level. The 128 probability figures, ranging from .00005 to .94, were combined by Fisher's method (3). The combined probabilities yielded a Critical Ratio of 10.71. Hence, although 102 of the probability figures were greater than .05, the varying performances considered in the aggregate were considerably better than chance ($p < .001$). The first hypothesis was confirmed.

In testing the second hypothesis, reading comprehension as conventionally measured and speed of comprehension were found to be significantly related to ability to identify correct answers in the absence of the reading passages (see Table 1). Men's scores were significantly greater than women's scores (the mean sex difference, 1.10, was significant at the .05 level). The following variables were not significantly related: reading vocabulary, academic aptitude, and scholastic performance (see Table 1). The variables which were significantly related to high performance on the passageless test also, together with academic aptitude, significantly differentiated the 26 students with the highest passageless scores from the 26 students with the lowest scores. Thus, part of the second hypothesis was confirmed and part was rejected.

## DISCUSSION

Although the obtained differences were small in any absolute sense, this investigation revealed that its Ss were able to recognize correct answers without reading the passages on which the questions are based. How are students able to do this? Imus et al., (4) attributed a part of their Ss' ability in this respect to "inexpert test construction." Such a charge can hardly be brought against the test used in this study. Its sampling of the passage content is excellent and it avoids content which generally is known by college students. Although 16 of the 30 items theoretically could have been answered from previous knowledge of the subject, the accuracy of student performance on these 16 items did not differ significantly from the accuracy of student performance on the entire 30 items. Smith (5), in a hyperbolic but perspicacious vein, described how students respond to multiple-choice items· "As presently prepared, one choice is usually too broad, one is too narrow, one is irrelevant and one is correct. After a few of these, the student no longer needs to look at the paragraph. He simply reads the choices, identifies the broad and narrow, eliminates the irrelevant since it has nothing in common with the other three, and chooses the remaining answer." It seems likely that by some such intuitive analysis, learned through years of

TABLE 1

*Correlation Coefficients Between Passageless Test Scores and Other Measures*

| MEASURE | R | 95% C. L. |
|---|---|---|
| Cooperative English Test | | |
| Level of comprehension, items 1–30 | .20 * | .02–.37 |
| Level of comprehension, all items | .26 * | .07–.43 |
| Vocabulary | .13 | |
| Speed of comprehension | .32 * | .13–.46 |
| V-SAT | .02 | |
| High school quintile | .02 | |
| GPA | .02 | |

* Significant at .05 level.

experience in taking tests and practicing on comprehension exercises, the student acquires test "wisdom." If this speculation is correct, one would probably find that few elementary-school children would perform better than chance on a passageless test.

The practical question remains: How can tests of reading comprehension be constructed so that their scores are more valid measures of reading comprehension? Two needs suggest themselves.

First of all, reading comprehension tests must reflect a sound theory of comprehension. It is not enough that they be built around the nine components of comprehension described by Davis (1), valuable as his analysis is and important as it is historically in having sharpened our concept of the reading process. Future authors of tests of reading comprehension would do well to ponder the model proposed by Smith (6) in which the operations of convergent and divergent thinking were related to products ranging from literal and implied meanings to implications and application. Smith was on solid ground in attributing improvement in reading comprehension to growth in concept formation. Professor Merle W. Tate, University of Pennsylvania, proposed that tests of reading comprehension should focus on measuring concept attainment.

Second, instruments other than the multiple-choice test should be widely experimented with. The "cloze" procedure developed by Taylor (8) deserves particular attention. It not only marks a clean break with the multiple-choice form, but it could be used readily for measuring concept attainment if before-reading scores were obtained on a sample of the passage and an estimate thus obtained of the status of concepts possessed by the student before taking the test. Less radical departures from the conventional test than the "cloze" procedure have been proposed which might also contribute to improved validity. For example, Dressel and Schmid (2) explored several variations of the multiple-choice test which appear promising. In one of these variations the student was directed to mark as many alternatives as needed to be sure he did not omit any correct answers. In another type, the student indicated for each item the degree of certainty with which he felt that his selected answer was the correct one. In still another variation, the student knew that two of the alternatives were correct. Appropriate scoring devices were proposed for each of these types.

The finding that male Ss had significantly higher scores on the passageless test than the female Ss is consistent with a similar finding of Tate, Stanier, and Harootunian (7). Their Best Answer test is similar to the passageless test in its demand for sharply discriminating judgment. Tate has speculated informally that the superiority of his male Ss may be attributable to their broader, less sheltered experiences which in turn may have had a favorable influence upon the development of perceptual skills. The same explanation is a plausible one to consider in attempting to account for the male superiority reported in this investigation.

REFERENCES

1. DAVIS, F. B. "Fundamental Factors in Comprehension in Reading," *Psycho-metrika*, IX (1944), pp. 185–97.
2. DRESSEL, P. L., and J. SCHMID. "Some Modifications of the Multiple-Choice Item," *Educational and Psychological Measurement*, XIII (1953), pp. 574–95.
3. FISHER, R. A. *Statistical Methods for Research Workers*, 8th Edition (London: Oliver and Boyd, 1941), pp. 97–99.
4. IMUS, H. A., J. W. ROTHNEY, and R. M. BEAR. *An Evaluation of Visual Factors in Reading* (Hanover, N.H.: Dartmouth College, 1938), p. 66.
5. SMITH, D. E. P. "Clay Models in the Reading Business," in O. S. Causey and W. Eller (Eds.), Starting and Improving College Reading Programs, *Yearbook of the National Reading Conference*, VIII (1959), 164–70.
6. SMITH, D. E. P. "Reading Comprehension: A Proposed Model," in O. S. Causey and E. P. Bliesmer (Eds.), Research and Evalution in College Reading, *Yearbook of the National Reading Conference*, IX (1960), 21–27.
7. TATE, M. W., BARBARA STANIER, and B. HAROOTUNIAN. *Differences Between Good and Poor Problem-Solvers* (Philadelphia: School of Education, University of Pennsylvania, 1959).
8. TAYLOR, W. L. *Application of 'Cloze' and Entropy Measures to the Study of Contextual Constraint in Samples of Continuous Prose*, unpublished Ph.D. dissertation, University of Illinois, 1954.

# WHAT CAN BE MEASURED? *

Roger T. Lennon

In this article a recognized expert in test construction tackles the problem of sifting through the research to find the components of reading ability that "we may recognize and hope to measure reliably." After explaining what each component of reading ability means, Lennon tackles the problems connected with the measurement of rate of reading and then concludes by explaining why it is quite difficult to conceive a completely objective test that will take into account the nuances of personal interpretation.

1. List some of the misconceptions about what can be measured by reading tests.

2. What are the points of agreement among the various researches reported? —the areas of disagreement?

3. Devise several questions for each of the four components of reading ability that the author hopes we may recognize and hope to measure reliably.

4. Summarize the issues, findings, implications and conclusions of the article. List the three or four truly key ideas developed by the author.

* FROM The Reading Teacher (March 1962), pp. 326–377, reprinted with permission of Roger T. Lennon and the International Reading Association.

W E CAN look back today upon virtually a half-century of experience in the development of objective, standardized tests of a wide variety of reading skills and abilities. Such tests, numbering well into the hundreds have been making their appearance year after year since about 1910; some have enjoyed decades of apparently satisfactory use, others have lapsed into disuse after relatively brief careers. The period since 1910 has witnessed prodigious research activity in the reading field; for the past several decades, an average of a hundred or more publications per year have swelled the literature devoted to this endlessly fascinating topic. Much of this research literature has been concerned with analysis of reading skills, speculation and experimentation concerning the nature and organization of reading abilities, and development and utilization of appropriate instruments. To undertake even the most cursory review of the reading tests that have appeared, or of the implications of the voluminous research with respect to reading measures, is far too ambitious a task, and yet an answer to the proposed question requires at least passing cognizance of some of the history and research.

## THE PROBLEM

*What can be measured?* An unsuspecting student who sought to answer this question from an examination of test catalogs, or of the instruments which they describe, might say, "We can measure paragraph comprehension, word meaning, word discrimination, word recognition, word analysis skills, ability to draw inferences from what is read, retention of details, ability to locate specific information, rate of reading, speed of comprehension, visual perception of words and letters, ability to determine the intent of a writer, ability to grasp the general idea, ability to deduce the meaning of words from context, ability to read with understanding in the natural sciences, in the social sciences, in the humanities, ability to perceive relationships in written material, ability to sense an author's mood, or intent, ability to appreciate poetry, ability to grasp the organization of ideas, ability to read maps, charts, and tables"—The list may be extended, if not *ad infinitum*, at least *ad* some seventy or eighty alleged reading skills and abilities. And this, mind you, from an inspection only of tests that are labeled as reading tests, without any consideration of other tests which look very much indeed like blood brothers to the reading tests, but which mask their familial ties under such beguiling aliases as tests of "critical thinking," of "educational developments," or even —most artful deceivers of all—as tests of "mental ability," "intelligence," or "scholastic aptitude."

Surely, no reader is so naive as to suppose that there really corresponds a separate, identifiable skill or ability to each of the test names. What then may we assume we are actually measuring with the scores and scores of differently named tests?

It is one thing—and a necessary thing—to make a careful analysis of reading ability, to spell out its various supposed components in detail, and to prepare extensive lists or charts of the specific skills or abilities to serve as statements of desired goals or outcomes of the reading program. It is quite another thing to demonstrate that these manifold skills or abilities do, in fact, exist as differentiable characteristics of students; and still a third thing to build tests which are in truth measures of one or another of these skills, and not of some more general, pervasive reading ability.

But if the number of abilities or dimensions of reading is not the seventy or eighty indicated, what is it? And how can we tell? Can we reduce this vast complexity to a single, global measure of reading ability, as some have concluded—or three, or five, or ten? Twenty years ago Dr. Arthur Traxler (14) addressing a conference on problems in measurement of reading, adverted to this same issue, and remarked that "What is apparently needed is a mathematical resolution of the difficulty by means of a thorough-going factor analysis of the abilities which enter into silent reading." Even as Dr. Traxler made his plea, such empirical attacks on the problem were under way, and during the decade or so following, there appeared a series of excellent studies of this kind that shed much light on our topic.

## REVIEW OF RESEARCH

Traxler himself in 1941 (15) reported an analysis of the Van Wagenen-Dvorak Diagnostic Examination of Silent Reading Abilities, one of the most impressive tests of this kind that had appeared up to that time. He sought to ascertain whether the several parts of the test yielded "measures which are independent enough to warrant their separate measurement and use as a basis for diagnostic and remedial work." Studying the results on these tests for a group of 116 tenth-grade students, Traxler concluded that the "measures of Central Thought, Clearly Stated Details, Interpretation, Integration of Dispersed Ideas, and Ability to Draw Inferences appear to be measuring closely related reading abilities. There is at least reasonable doubt concerning whether or not the separate scores contribute anything greatly different from the reading level score." He found most of the parts so highly correlated that diagnosis based on the scores had little real meaning. In fact, when the intercorrelations were corrected for attenuation, most approached unity.

Even before Traxler's call for research, Gans in a 1940 study (5) had analyzed the relation between a specially built measure of "the critical types of reading required in the selection-rejection of content for use in solving a problem," and a reading composite based upon two standardized reading tests, Thorndike-McCall and Gates Silent Reading, and four sections of the California Test of Mental Maturity. (Worthy of note is the fact that Gans justified the composite as a general measure of reading comprehension on the basis that the intercorrelations among the components approached their respective reliabilities—even though the components were as superficially varied as the Thorndike-McCall score, Gates' scores on Appreciating General

Significance, Predicting Outcome, and Noting Details, and California Delayed Recall, Numerical Quantity, Inference, and Vocabulary.) Analysis of the results of a group of 417 intermediate-grade pupils led Gans to conclude that "the abilities [i.e., the reference-reading abilities] are not closely enough related to those in the reading criterion to be measured by tests designed for discovering the criterion abilities," and "the composite which functions in reference reading is made up of a number of variables, with *reading ability*, as measured by the reading criterion one factor, and the selection-rejection pattern another." ". . . another factor operates which possibly includes some function of delayed recall."

A trail-blazing study, and probably still the best known of all the investigations of this type, was that reported by Davis, originally in 1941 (3). Davis sought to identify some of the fundamental factors in reading comprehension and to provide a means of measuring them. On the basis of a comprehensive survey of the literature, he listed nine supposed categories of basic skills of reading comprehension. He proceeded to develop test questions to measure each of these skills, administered the tests to a group of subjects, and computed the intercorrelations among the nine tests. He interpreted a factor analysis of the results as indicating the presence of nine factors, six of them clearly significant. These latter included word knowledge; ability to manipulate ideas and concepts in relation to one another—"reasoning in reading"; ability to grasp the author's expressed ideas; ability to identify the writer's intent or purpose; ability to follow the organization of a passage; and knowledge of literary devices and techniques. Of Davis's nine factors, word knowledge accounted for by far the greatest part of the variance, followed by the so-called "reasoning in reading" and the literal meaning factors.

Davis concluded that at least two factors, the word knowledge and the reasoning factor, were measured in his tests with sufficient reliability for practical use, and that adequately reliable measures of three other factors—literal meanings, inference, and ability to follow the organization of a selection—could be developed as a practical matter.

A re-analysis of Davis's data by Thurstone (13), employing a somewhat different factor analysis technique, led Thurstone to conclude that a single factor was sufficient to account for the obtained correlations. The apparent conflict in interpretation reflects different purposes served by the respective types of factor analysis employed in the two investigations. Davis, reacting to Thurstone's re-analysis of his data, continued to maintain that his first six factors, at least, represented significant dimensions of reading comprehension, though admittedly, several of them accounted for very little variance in reading scores (4).

Langsam in 1941 (9) reported a factor analysis of results of six reading tests, yielding fourteen scores, and one intelligence test yielding seven scores. She identified five factors, labeled respectively a *verbal* factor, concerned with word meaning, a *perceptual* factor, a *word* factor denoting fluency in dealing with words, a *seeing relationships* factor, perhaps concerned with logical organization, and a *numerical* factor. The factors were found to overlap to a considerable degree, beclouding their interpretation.

Conant in 1942 (2) undertook to answer the questions: "Is there a general reading comprehension, or does reading proficiency depend upon skills using a number of different reading techniques? If there are different reading abilities, how are they interrelated?" She developed an outline of a test to measure the following skills: (1) Reading to get in detail the pattern of the author's thought, including comprehension of the main points, comprehension of specific facts which support main points, comprehension of cause-and-effect relations, and comprehension of words in context. (2) Ability to interpret and make a critical evaluation of material read, including selection and organization of facts relevant to a more general idea, and ability to draw inferences.

Conant developed tests designed to measure these skills and administered them, together with the Nelson-Denny Reading Test and American Council Psychological Examination. Intercorrelations among all the measures except five were above .50, leading Conant to state that there was no evidence "that students in general employed relatively independent abilities in this study-type reading." She concluded that the results were largely accountable for in terms of a single factor, tentatively defined as general comprehension. Three other factors appeared, but accounted for extremely small parts of the variance. Conant pointed out that her results by no means precluded the possibility that some individuals may show marked differences in their relative abilities to use different reading techniques.

A doctoral dissertation by Artley in 1942 (1) explored the relationship between general comprehension ability, as measured by the Cooperative C-1 Level of Comprehension test, and hypothesized special reading abilities in the social studies area, measured by the Cooperative Tests of Social Studies Ability, Proficiency in the Field of Social Studies, and Survey Tests in the Social Studies, including ability to obtain facts, to organize, to interpret, to generalize, to perceive logical relations and to evaluate arguments. For a group of two hundred eleventh-grade students, Artley found the correlation between the general comprehension measure and the composite of the specific measures to be .79 (.86 corrected for attenuation). He found also that the correlations of the several specific measures with total reading comprehension all fell within a fairly narrow range, from .6 to .8 and he concluded that one could not "dismiss the possibility that there are a great number of pupils who might profit from a specific type of instruction." Artley interpreted his findings as "evidence that there exists a significant degree of specificity in the measures relating to reading comprehension of the social studies."

Hall and Robinson reported in 1945 (6) an attempt to develop independent measures of various aspects of reading. After analyzing the research and the available tests produced up until the time of their study, and concluding that these tests left very much to be desired from the standpoint of diagnostic potentiality, they developed a battery that included twenty-five measures, many of which were tests of reading of non-prose material. Factor analysis of the results of administration of this battery of tests to one hundred college students yielded six factors, which Hall and Robinson defined as "attitude of comprehension accuracy"; an "inductive" factor; a verbal or word meaning factor; a "rate for unrelated facts" factor; a chart-reading factor; and a sixth undefined factor. In other words, six factors, one of which was quite nebulous, were sufficient to account for the variance in the twenty-five separate reading measures.

Harris in a 1948 study (7) identified seven skills or behaviors called for in comprehension of various types of literature, as follows: recognition of synonyms for uncommon words and groups of words; recognition of words or groups of words that are used figuratively; recognition of antecedents of pronouns, of subjects and predicates in loosely organized statements; recognition of summary of ideas expressed or implied; recognition of summaries and characteristics of persons or characters; recognition of author's attitude toward his characters, of his mood or emotion and of his intent; recognition of relationship between technique and meaning.

After administering a battery of tests designed to yield measures on each of these seven skills to two groups of adults, and factor-analyzing the results, Harris concluded that "(1) one and only one ability is common to the comprehension of these literary passages of different types; and (2) that one general factor is adequate to account for the intercorrelations of the seven variables."

Maney and Sochor in 1952 studies (10, 11) sought to develop tests to measure specific factors in comprehension of science and social studies material. Their tests yielded measures of "literal comprehension" and of "critical interpretation" in these two areas. Administering these tests together with the Gates Survey Test and the Pintner General Ability Tests (Verbal Type) to some five hundred fifth-grade pupils, they found correlations from .61 to .67 between the literal and the critical reading scores; from .60 to .76 between these scores and scores on the Gates test; and from .67 to .75 between these scores and scores on the Pintner tests. The "critical" scores correlated slightly lower with the general reading ability or the intelligence test scores than did the "literal" reading scores. Maney and Sochor interpreted the findings as showing considerable independence between literal and critical reading skills, and between the specific abilities required for critical reading and "general" reading comprehension. In other words, they saw a high degree of specificity in the types of processes involved in different reading situations.

Another 1952 study, the doctoral dissertation of Lyman Hunt (8), represents one of the most competent studies in this area. Hunt sought to determine whether the six factors identified by Davis would reappear in an independent investigation, or, more generally, whether reading comprehension is made up of aspects sufficiently specific to be measurable as independent variables. Hunt developed tests to measure each of the six factors, taking great pains to insure that every item included as part of the test for a given factor

was judged with very high consistency by competent consultants to be measuring the ability in question. For a group of 585 college students he first
compared item-discrimination values for every item with respect to each of
the six postulated factors. Despite the fact that the items had been constructed specifically to measure a carefully defined aspect of reading ability,
and had been judged by qualified consultants to be measuring that particular
ability, Hunt found that in general the items classified in any given area—as,
for example, vocabulary items, or items intended to measure reasoning—
correlated no higher with the total score on the ability they were supposed to
measure than with the score on any of the other abilities. That is to say, there
was no evidence in the item-discrimination statistics that the items possessed
any differential validity as measures of one aspect of reading comprehension
rather than another. Factor analysis of the scores led to the same general
conclusion—that, except for the vocabulary test, the other measures "may be
measuring much the same function of reading comprehension." Comparing
the factor structure revealed in his study with that reported by Davis, Hunt
reports emergence of a first factor somewhat resembling Davis' reasoning
factor, a second factor similar to Davis' word knowledge factor, though appearing much less important than it did in the Davis study. He found a third
factor like Davis' organizing ability, but it accounted for only 8 per cent of
the total variance. He also found three other factors, all probably not significant.

A later study by Stoker and Kropp (12) reported a factor analysis of results
of Iowa Tests of Educational Development administered in 1959 to a sample
of ninth-grade students. Three sub-tests of the Iowa are concerned respectively
with ability to interpret reading materials in the social studies, in natural
science, and literary materials. Stoker and Kropp found intercorrelations
(uncorrected for attenuation) among these three parts from .67 to .76. A first
factor, identified by them as "general mental ability," had extremely high
loadings on these three sections and on the Verbal section of the Scholastic
Aptitude Test; no other factor contributed significantly to the variance on
these parts of ITED. They concluded, therefore, that there were no differentiable reading abilities in the three areas, at least as measured by ITED.

Most of the references cited above have to do with the state of affairs that
exist at the secondary or college level. We may very well ask whether reading
ability has not become so highly organized at this stage that an individual's
performance on all kinds of reading tasks is pretty much of a piece, defying
diagnosis or differentiation. It is certainly conceivable that at lower grade
levels reading ability is much less highly organized than it is at the high
school, college, and adult levels. We may readily suppose that in the beginning stages of reading, emphasis is on the perceptual and mechanical aspects
of the task to a greater extent than on central thought processes; and that,
since the requisite perceptual skills are being acquired at varying rates by children, there may exist among pupils more readily differentiable degrees of
proficiency in various components of reading ability. Such a conclusion seems

probable, but it should be said, too, that this belief is buttressed by no such amount of experimental data as are available concerning the nature and organization of reading abilities at the higher levels—and, indeed, there is some contrary evidence, as in the intercorrelations among the subtests of the Gates Primary Batteries, or the several reading tests of the Metropolitan Achievement Tests. Virtually all of the tests of lower-level reading abilities that purport to be diagnostic are based upon *a priori* identifications of the various reading skills; and however expert one may consider the analysis and the identification, it nevertheless remains true that we still have little experimental evidence about the reality of the distinctions that are made among the various reading abilities and about the validity of supposed diagnostic profiles of reading skills. In the realm of vocabulary, for example, we have measures that are labeled tests of "word recognition," or of "word discrimination," or of "phonetic analysis skill," all of which characteristically yield quite substantial intercorrelations relative to their reliabilities.

## IMPLICATIONS

The studies cited above are not the only ones bearing upon the organization of reading comprehension ability, but together they comprise a representative sample of the research in this area. Even from brief recapitulations, one can sense a lack of consistency in the findings with respect to the generality or specificity of comprehension abilities. What are we to make of it all? Shall we conclude that the reading experts, with their lengthy lists of objectives, of finely differentiated, ever more specific skills, have simply been spinning a fanciful web that bears no relation to the realities of the nature of reading ability? Or shall we charge the test makers with a lack of ingenuity in devising test exercises to provide reliably differentiable measures of the several skills, with a failure to provide instruments that will match in their comprehensiveness and sensitivity the goals elaborated by the reading experts? The truth, it seems to me, is to be found between the two extremes. The following discussion is an attempt to make sense of the research findings, and to suggest their implications for the question, "What can be measured in reading?"

One generalization seems to emerge with very considerable support. With distressing sameness, or with gratifying consistency, depending upon one's point of view, the studies agree that most of the measurable variance in tests of reading competence, however varied the tests entering into the determination, can be accounted for in terms of a fairly small number of factors, certainly not more than six being required to account for better than 90 per cent of the variance. One investigator after another has launched his battery of tests, with all segments neatly labeled, carefully segregated and packaged in separate if not watertight compartments, only to have the vessels founder on the shoals of hard data, with the cargo jumbled together in a single heap, or in a few mixed-up collections. It seems entirely clear that numerous superficially discrete reading skills to which separate names or titles have been attached are, in fact, so closely related, as far as any test results reveal, that we must consider them virtually identical.

It would seem that we may recognize and hope to measure reliably the following components of reading ability: (1) a general verbal factor, (2) comprehension of explicitly stated material, (3) comprehension of implicit or latent meaning, and (4) an element that might be termed "appreciation."

The "verbal factor" in this context is intended to connote word knowledge: breadth, depth, and scope of vocabulary. Every investigation shows vocabulary to be substantially related to other measures of reading ability. Extensive word mastery, or fluency in handling words, is almost a prerequisite to attainment of high competence in any type of reading skill. We are well equipped for reliable measurement of this factor at virtually every level.

Under "comprehension of explicitly stated material" is included such skills as the location of specifically stated information, comprehension of the literal meaning of what is written, and ability to follow specific directions set forth in what is read. Many reading tests are available that measure these skills acceptably; probably the most widely used tests measure this type of reading ability to a greater extent than any other.

The third component, "comprehension of implicit meanings," embraces all of those outcomes that we tend to label as "reasoning in reading." Included here would be the ability to draw inferences from what is read; to predict outcomes; to derive the meaning of words from context; to perceive the structure of what is read—the main idea or central thought, and the hierarchical arrangement of ideas within a selection; to interpret what is read, as manifested either by applying the information to the solution of a problem or by deriving some generalizations or principles from it; in a word, all those abilities that demand active, productive, intellectual response and activity on the part of the reader. The research, in my opinion, does support the belief that this type of reading ability can be differentiated from the ability to comprehend what is explicitly stated, though we should always expect to find the two correlated because the ability to get at the implicit meaning of what is read presupposes the ability to understand the explicit or literal meaning.

Test makers have been, and are, devoting more effort to the measurement of the inferential, interpretive abilities, and such abilities are well represented in the reading tests produced in recent years. It is perhaps not inappropriate to comment in passing on what seems to be a false issue that has sometimes been raised by those who object that reading tests which stress this factor are too much like intelligence tests. My view is that the intellectual operations or processes that it is common now to include in the notion of reading as a thinking process are indistinguishable from at least some of the operations and processes that we define as comprising "intelligence." In other words, it is inconceivable that a good test of reading as reasoning should not also be a valid measure of some aspects of the complex we term intelligence.

Finally, we have the factor termed "appreciation." By this is meant such things as sensing the intent or purpose of an author, judging the mood or tone of a selection, perceiving the literary devices by which the author accomplishes his purposes, etc. Existence of these types of outcome as distinct from the ones enumerated above seems less clearly established by the research findings, but here some of the blame may perhaps be laid at the feet of the test makers, who have, by and large, been less concerned with the development of suitable instruments in this area than in the three general areas suggested above. We may reasonably hope that more satisfactory measures of outcomes of this kind will be produced.

## SPEED

Thus far the measurement of our old friend, rate or speed, has been neglected. That speed of reading is an important and desired outcome of reading instruction goes without saying. Evidence concerning the extent to which a pupil is improving in rate of reading is highly desirable in any evaluation of a reading program. Our assessment of rate, however, leaves much to be desired, though paradoxically enough, we are better off today because we have a keener appreciation of the limitations of our speed measures than we were twenty-five or thirty years ago, when it was not uncommon to encounter the belief that measurement of rate was a fairly simple, straightforward operation.

Our problems in the measurement of rate stem from the fact that we are never really concerned with pure speed—that is, with just the rapidity with which the subject can move over a given number of words or lines of written material. Rate is only meaningful as it defines the rapidity with which the reader covers material at a particular level of comprehension. We are all now well aware that an individual's rate is a function of the level of difficulty of the material being read; and some would say also of the type of material, though the experimental data on this question are inconsistent. Indeed, this ability to change rate of reading is accepted as one of the desired outcomes of reading instruction; we want the student to adapt his reading to the demands of the particular material, to move as rapidly or as slowly as the requirements of the material and his own purposes in reading dictate. The question of the relation of speed and comprehension is a perplexing one, to which the experimental data give no single clear-cut answer.

We are troubled also in the measurement of rate by the fact that the test situation poses quite a different motivation for the reader than does the normal, unsupervised reading situation. Unfortunately, from the standpoint of validity the difference between the test situation and the normal reading situation, as far as motivating property is concerned, varies from one subject to another, and our interpretation of rate of reading scores derived in test situations must, therefore, always be subject to some reservation—at least in the case of rate measures obtained when the subject is aware that his speed of reading is being appraised.

Nevertheless, our measures of rate are not without usefulness. For the estimation of change or development, rate measures derived from the same test are quite serviceable. Research, moreover, suggests that while rate measures are not perfectly correlated by any means, there is an appreciable community among the various measures. We thus may identify with a good deal of confidence those readers who are excessively slow; and this is perhaps the most important use of rate measures.

## CONCLUSION

As important as what *can* be measured in reading, perhaps, is what *cannot*. There remains the uneasy feeling that no matter how excellent our measure of comprehension, whether of explicit or latent meanings, no matter how clever our techniques for assessing "critical" reading skills may become, our evaluation still leaves much to be desired. Whence this dissatisfaction? Is it sensible to anticipate that we can develop wholly adequate objective measures for "reading ability"? Consider what reading is, or should be. Not only do we read what we read; in the layman's peculiarly apt term, we read *into* what we read—that is, we read something of ourselves into the written word. We bring to bear on the material we are reading our total experience, background, interests, understandings, purposes, and so on. The response that each person makes to a given piece of reading matter, therefore, is necessarily and desirably a unique, personal kind of response. When we set before a student an exercise in arithmetic, or a word to be spelled, or a problem in algebra, there is only one response that is desired and that is to be considered correct. When we are concerned with appraisal of a person's ability to read insightfully and meaningfully, we almost assume that there will be many different but equally acceptable responses to the stimulus material. Under these circumstances it looms as a very difficult task to conceive a completely objective test that will permit us to assess the quality or richness or correctness of each person's interpretation of a given selection.

"Reading," is the words of Francis Bacon, "maketh the full man"—and this neatly epitomizes the goal of reading instruction. It is important for people to learn to read because reading can enrich their lives so enormously. We want people to be able to read the sign that says "Stop," so that they will not endanger themselves and others at crossings. We want people to be able to read the directions, simple or complicated, that enable them to comply and cooperate with the practices necessary for getting along with others. We want them to read because in no other manner can they so readily share in the experiences of the rest of mankind that will inform and ennoble them. For these purposes, surely *what* a person reads is as important as how well he reads it; but I am afraid that we have no measures of the wisdom with which persons make their choices of reading matter, nor have we any measures of the extent to which they profit from their reading in the manner suggested above; and I for one am dubious that we shall ever have such measures.

Like many other students who have considered reading tests, I have suggested that the labels on the tests are perhaps poor indicators of the jobs the tests actually perform. I am less dismayed by this fact than some critics have been, for I feel that it does not preclude the possibility of considerable usefulness and value in these measures. Insofar as uncritical acceptance of test names as representative of their contents leads to erroneous descriptions and improper diagnosis, such names are, of course, harmful. But, in a fortunate way, the very difficulty that surrounds our efforts to develop differentiating measures of various reading skills becomes our salvation in the instructional program. If these abilities are substantially related and overlap to the extent that the various studies make it appear, then it is entirely likely that efforts devoted to improving one or another of the types of skill will carry over to improvements in the other types of skill. There is nothing in the research reports which would lead us to believe that it is fruitless to attempt to set up varied types of goals or outcomes, to prepare exercises calculated to develop power in these several skills, and even to use these analyses as bases for developing tests. Indeed, in no other way can we sensibly plan or conduct the instructional program.

REFERENCES

1. ARTLEY, A. S. "A Study of Certain Relationships Existing between General Comprehension and Reading Comprehension in a Specific Subject Matter Area." Unpublished doctoral dissertation, The Pennsylvania State College, 1942; and in *Journal of Educational Research*, 37 (1944), 464–473.

2. CONANT, MARGARET M. *The Construction of a Diagnostic Reading Test.* New York: Teachers College, Columbia University. Contributions to Education No. 861 (1942).

3. DAVIS, FREDERICK B. "Fundamental Factors of Comprehension in Reading." Unpublished doctoral dissertation, Graduate School of Education, Harvard University, 1941; and in *Psychometrika*, 9 (1944), 185–197.

4. DAVIS, FREDERICK B. "A Brief Comment on Thurstone's Note on a Reanalysis of Davis' Reading Tests." *Psychometrika*, 11 (1946), 249–255.

5. GANS, ROMA A. *A Study of Critical Reading Comprehension in the Intermediate Grades.* New York: Teachers College, Columbia University. Contribution to Education No. 811 (1940).

6. HALL, W. E., and ROBINSON, F. P. "An Analytical Approach to the Study of Reading Skills." *Journal of Educational Psychology*, 36 (1945), 429–442.

7. HARRIS, C. W. "Measurement of Comprehension of Literature: II Studies of Measures of Comprehension." *School Review*, 56 (1948), 332–342.

8. HUNT, LYMAN C. "A Further Study of Certain Factors Associated with Reading Comprehension." Unpublished doctoral dissertation, School of Education, Syracuse University, 1952.

9. LANGSAM, ROSALIND. "A Factorial Analysis of Reading Ability." Unpublished doctoral dissertation, New York University, 1941. Abstract in *Journal of Experimental Education*, 10 (1941), 57–63.

10. Maney, Ethel Swain. "Literal and Critical Reading in Science." Unpublished doctoral dissertation, Temple University, 1952.

11. Sochor, E. Elona. "Literal and Critical Reading in Social Studies." Unpublished doctoral dissertation, Temple University, 1952.

12. Stoker, Howard W., and Kropp, Russell P. "The Predictive Validities and Factorial Content of the Florida State-Wide Ninth-Grade Testing Program Battery." *Florida Journal of Educational Research*, 1960, 105–114.

13. Thurstone, L. L. "Note on a Reanalysis of Davis' Reading Tests." *Psychometrika*, 11 (1946), 185–188.

14. Traxler, Arthur E. "Problems of Measurement in Reading." *Proceedings of the 1941 Invitational Conference on Testing Problems* (mimeo.). American Council on Education, pp. 65–73.

15. Traxler, Arthur E. "A Study of the Van Wagenen-Dvorak Diagnostic Examination of Silent Reading Abilities." *Educational Records Bulletin*, No. 31. New York: Educational Records Bureau, January, 1941. Pp. 33–41.

# THE DETERMINANTS OF READING COMPREHENSION *

## Philip E. Vernon

*In this article Vernon admits his bias against contemporary tests of educational abilities and his affinity for the essay examination as a means of eliciting such factors as the understanding of principles and the ability to apply knowledge and to think critically. Using various types of objective and subjective reading tests, he explored eight unusual hypotheses in the hope of providing answers regarding certain purported values of these kinds of tests. Some conclusions are expected, others unexpected. By any standards, the results are interesting and important.*

*1. What is the purpose of this investigation?*

*2. Try to relate what the various tests purport to measure to the hypotheses that were made.*

*3. When interpreting the results of the study, try to keep in mind which tests require a multiple-choice response and which require a creative response. (See Table 2.)*

*4. Which hypotheses were supported?*

*5. Which student academic-work situations resemble the situation in which he will use his training in professional or in daily life?*

*6. What are the implications of this research for your teaching for your professional development?*

---

* REPRINTED FROM *Educational and Psychological Measurement* (Summer 1962), pp. 269–286, by permission of the publisher and the author.

CONTEMPORARY tests of educational abilities are far more sophisticated instruments than the new-type attainment tests of the 1920's and '30's. At the high school and college levels they avoid questions relating to straight-forward factual knowledge and skills, since these have been found to stimulate undesirable methods of study. Instead, as Brownell (1946), Dressel (1954) and Bloom (1956) point out, their aim is to elicit understanding of principles, ability to apply knowledge, critical thinking, judgment, and other educationally valuable qualities.

The present writer, however, brought up in a European educational system which still relies primarily on the essay examination for eliciting these higher educational qualities from its students, is inevitably struck by certain weaknesses in such tests. Whatever the subject matter—English, social studies or natural sciences—they tend to take the form of complex reading comprehension tests, and they therefore appear to depend partly on the students' facility in understanding the instructions and copying with multiple-choice items. While admitting that fluency and legibility in essay writing unduly affects the students' performances in any European examinations, he wonders whether new-type test sophistication does not equally distort assessments of abilities in the American setting (Vernon, 1958). These suspicions are confirmed by a study of the experimental literature and of test manuals, from which it appears that the correlations between tests aimed at different mental functions or different school subjects are extremely high. For example, the mean intercorrelation for five of the Iowa Tests of Educational Development among 9th and 12th grade students is quoted as .716, where the mean reliability is .905; yet these tests are supposed to measure such different abilities as: 1. Basic Social Concepts, 5. Reading in Social Studies, 6. Reading in Natural Science, 7. Interpreting Literary Materials, and 8. Vocabulary. A battery of this kind is highly inefficient for differential predictive purposes, and it is noteworthy that, in Horst's (1959) extensive studies of differential prediction, the tests which generally contribute most to the regression equations are the more factual ones such as Scientific Vocabulary, Mathematical Concepts, together with specific high school grades and Strong or Kuder interests. Though several investigations have claimed to show good differentiation among tests in different subjects (e.g., Shores, 1943), far too often there is no indication of the extent to which score differences may not be due merely to the imperfect reliability of the contrasted tests.

Evidence regarding the measurement of different levels, or types, of ability is somewhat contradictory. Davis (1944) attempted to measure nine skills hypothesized in reading, but Thurstone (1946) claimed that all the intercorrelations could be attributed to a single vocabulary + comprehension factor. Derrick (1953) suggests that a significant bipolar factor separates these two aspects, and many other studies have shown reading rate, vocabulary, and comprehension to be at least partially distinct. In Derrick's own research, three types of item—factual, inferential and judgmental—(classified by expert judges) and three lengths of reading passage were compared. Factor analysis yielded no reliable differentiation either according to function measured or to length of passage. However, a study of his mean intercorrelations indicates some distinction between factual and more complex items (scarcely any between inferential and judgmental); also between scores on a 50,000 word passage studied beforehand and performance at short and medium passages.

By contrast, Howard (1943) extracted five subtests of items representing different levels of complexity (*not* of difficulty) from a 160-item General Science test. The intercorrelations clearly show that the more complex subtests measure a somewhat different ability from the simpler. Again Horrocks (1946) describes a test of the ability of psychology students to apply their knowledge of adolescent psychology to the interpretation of case studies, which correlated far below the reliability coefficients with ordinary course marks.

The writer would contend that a major reason for high correlations between tests aimed at somewhat different abilities is their common item-form and their dependence on the students' sophistication. In the same way essay examinations in different subjects, or marked for different qualities, are apt to intercorrelate highly, but to show lower correlations with new-type tests in the same subject. Both test-content or function and test-form or method are highly complex, but a possible analysis (partly derived from Thorndike, 1949) is in Table 1.

Educationists and psychometrists, in their concern over Content and Error, have paid little attention to the Method category; and even if its influence on test or examination performance is small, we should at least attempt to investigate its components more fully. Though correlational factor analysis can help, there is always the danger of interpreting the nature of a factor in terms of content, which really derives more from common method components. (For example, the distinction often drawn by factorists between I—inductive, and D—deductive, reasoning may arise more because most I-tests are based on non-verbal, numerical or letter material, most D-tests on verbal material, than because they involve different kinds of thinking.) A Fisherian type of factorial design would therefore be more appropriate for studying content and method variances simultaneously. The same conclusion was reached by Campbell and Fiske (1959) in the field of personality: "Method or apparatus factors make very large contributions to psychological measurements"; and they advocate the Multitrait-Multimethod Matrix to overcome this.

## DESIGN OF INVESTIGATION

An investigation was carried out among 108 male students in a British Training College for Teachers. The time available for testing, and the students' patience, permitted the exploration of only a few of the factors listed in Table 1. However, the value of the study was greatly enhanced through its repetition with a group of 75 American college students, for which Dr. W. Coffmann of the Educational Testing Service and Professor D. L. Cook of Purdue University were responsible.[1]

TABLE 1

*Sources of Variance in Educational Test Scores*

CONTENT

Level of integration—interpretation, understanding vs. knowledge of concepts and operations
Different functions at a given level, e.g., evaluation, application to new problems, retention, etc.
Technical bias—scientific, historical, literary, etc.

METHOD

Factors attributable to the medium or material of the test (verbal, symbolic, visual, performance, etc.) irrelevant to its purpose
Type of presentation—oral, visual, verbal; questions asked simultaneously or subsequently
Difficulty level and speed conditions, which may modify factor content
Response-type—multiple-choice, matching, etc.; short-answer (in student's own words), oral, essay (restricted time), dissertation (unrestricted)
Attitudes and motivations induced by the tester and testing conditions
Sophistication—knack in coping with these types of item, recognizing unsuspected clues, guessing and using time wisely, etc.
Sets arising from the student's understanding (or misunderstanding) of the instructions or transferred from previous tests; adaptations in the course of doing the test
Other response sets, e.g., tendency to guess, to choose extreme responses, etc.
Speed and accuracy in recording answers on answer sheets; speed and legibility in written answers

ERROR

Sampling variance between the passages or questions set
Fluctuations in moods, attention, fatigue and health of students
Scoring errors in objective tests
Variance between markers in essay or other non-objective assessments

Several tests were constructed, or adapted, in two parallel forms, to cover various content and method differences in the area of verbal comprehension. Half of each group were given the first form during the first of two 2-hour

[1] The views expressed in this article must not, of course, be attributed to my collaborators. I am further indebted to the Educational Testing Service for the loan of certain test materials and for payments made to the American students; and above all for a grant which enabled me to study current developments in educational testing at Princeton, N. J., during 1957.

sessions, the second form at another session a week or two later; half took them in the reverse order. This enabled practice effects, and fluctuations associated with the session or occasion, to be controlled. The order of application was arranged to provide variety. Numbers of items and time limits are listed in Table 2.

### Tests

1. Vocabulary A and B. Definitions to be written by the students in their own words, either synonyms or short phrases.

2. Vocabulary C and D. Multiple-choice.

3. Sentence Completion A and B. Filling gaps in sentences, multiple-choice.

4. Reading Comprehension A and B. Answering questions on 200–400 word passages, in own words.

5. Reading Comprehension C and D. Ditto, multiple-choice.

6. Reading Comprehension E and F. In each test two passages of 400–500 words were presented, to be read in 3–4 minutes without seeing the questions; thereafter questions were given to be answered without consulting the passages, one lot in own words, the other multiple-choice.

The questions in Tests 4–6 were further cross-classified, half of them being based primarily on factual information given in the paragraphs, half requiring more inference or judgment. Thus each pair of tests could be alternatively scored for factual or inferential abilities.

7. Reading Comprehension G and H. This was a published, multiple-choice test which aims particularly to measure inference from social studies materials.

8. The British group only was given a multiple-choice test of comprehension of tables and graphs, referring mainly to medical and psychological statistics.

9–11. The American group had previously taken the Nelson-Denny Reading Test (Vocabulary and Comprehension) and an Entry English Test, two-thirds of whose items dealt with sentence-structure, punctuation and spelling, the remaining third with vocabulary and reading. The numbers of available subjects dropped to 67 and 62, respectively.

12. An external criterion of intellectual competence, in the form of grade-point averages, was available for the American students. British students wrote essays on educational themes during the year and took an essay examination in education two months later. As their papers were marked by various lecturers, the marks were expected to be weak in reliability. Fourteen months later they took a more thorough, and uniformly marked, examination; but its results were published only in the form of very coarse, and therefore also unreliable, grades.

The scoring of the "own-word" or "creative-response" tests, Nos. 1, 3 and half of 6, was done by the writer alone. However, acceptable and unacceptable answers were listed, and it is believed that no greater subjectivity was involved than in scoring, say, Terman-Merrill vocabulary.

The main hypotheses which can be tested by the above battery are listed in an order following that of Table 1:

I. Tests at different levels (Reading A-H versus Vocabulary A-D) involve partially distinguishable abilities. Sentence completion should be intermediate.

II. Tests of different functions, such as factual versus inferential, will show some distinction, though this may be small. For the classification of items was made by the writer alone, and Derrick (1953) has shown that interjudge consistency is not high.

III. The Table and Graph Reading test involves verbal and numerical questions and responses; but as these refer to visual material, it should measure a somewhat different ability from the verbal tests.

IV. Type of presentation: Reading Tests E and F, in which students cannot search for the answers in the paragraphs, will measure a different ability from conventional reading tests, and will show a higher validity against an examination criterion.

V. Form of response: Tests responded to in own words will correlate more highly among themselves, also multiple-choice tests among themselves, than own-word with multiple-choice.

VI. American students will do relatively better at reading tests, to which they are far more accustomed, than British students, and their responses to multiple-choice tests will be more structured and consistent.

VII. British students, but not American, will improve with practice at these same tests.

VIII. There will be a small but appreciable sessional effect, that is, higher correlations within than between sessions.

## RESULTS

Both groups of students were mostly in their early twenties. The British were all male, but the American included 32 men and 43 women. No appreciable difference between the sexes could be observed, except in the Entry English test; thus no distinction was made in analyzing the results.

Table 2 gives the main information about each test in each group. It will be seen that American students were generally allowed longer times since it was thought that they were somewhat less highly selected than the British. Clearly, direct comparisons of means not legitimate. Nevertheless it is obvious that the British are at least $1\sigma$ superior on both vocabularly tests, despite their shorter time, and yet they obtain much the same scores on reading tests. It might conceivably be argued that British students receive much less training in reading at school, and thus perform less well than might be expected in view of their good vocabulary. But it seems much more likely that

American students do relatively well at reading tests because of their familiarity with such tests and their expertise in coping with this item-form. The
British would have had virtually no experience of new-type tests (except
possibly some eight years earlier when they entered high school). This is
confirmed by the fact that the British show larger and more consistent gains
in score from the first to the second occasion on all reading tests, but not on
vocabulary. On the combined tests the British rise of .30 sigma units is highly

TABLE 2

*Numbers of Items in Combined Tests, Total Times, Means, and*
*Score Increases from First to Second Sessions*

| TEST | FORM OF RE-SPONSE | NO. OF ITEMS IN BOTH PARTS | TIME (MINS) | | MEAN SCORES | | STANDARD DEVIATIONS | | SCORE GAINS | |
|---|---|---|---|---|---|---|---|---|---|---|
| | | | AMER. | BRIT. | AMER. | BRIT. | AMER. | BRIT. | AMER. | BRIT. |
| Vocabulary AB | cr[1] | 40 | 16 | 14 | 6.1 | 12.7 | 5.72 | 6.66 | −0.17 | +0.49 |
| Vocabulary CD | mc | 56 | 16 | 12 | 21.7 | 31.4 | 7.69 | 8.12 | −0.05 | −0.31 |
| Sentence Completion AB | mc | 36 | 20 | 20 | 19.9 | 24.1 | 6.40 | 5.20 | +0.02 | +0.07 |
| Reading AB | cr | 33 | 34 | 30 | 16.5 | 16.2 | 4.16 | 3.88 | +0.14 | +0.60 |
| Reading CD | mc | 32 | 30 | 30 | 20.3 | 21.6 | 4.94 | 4.15 | +0.33 | +0.28 |
| Reading EF | (i) cr | 16 | | | 9.6 | 9.4 | 2.88 | 2.39 | | |
| | | | 34 | 30 | | | | | −0.08 | +0.31 |
| | (ii) mc | 15 | | | 9.0 | 8.9 | 2.67 | 2.51 | | |
| Reading GH | mc | 34 | 30 | 27 | 23.8 | 23.6 | 4.01 | 5.00 | +0.13 | +1.08 |
| Tables & Graphs | mc | 50 | — | 40 | — | 29.7 | — | 6.09 | — | — |
| N-D Vocabulary | mc | 100 | 10 | — | 42.2 | — | 14.15 | — | — | — |
| N-D Reading | mc | 36 | 20 | — | 45.7 | — | 10.72 | — | — | — |
| Entry English | mc | 225 | 65 | — | 78th percentile | — | — | — | — | — |

[1] cr = creative response, written in own words. mc = multiple-choice.

significant; the American rise only slightly exceeds its standard error. Hypothesis VII, and the first half of Hypothesis VI, are therefore confirmed.

The low scores, particularly among American students, on creative-response
Vocabulary are noticeable. Clearly the test was made much too difficult.
However, the four vocabulary lists, A, B, C, and D, were drawn from a
common pool of words, and they were known from previous item-analysis
data to be of closely similar difficulty. Thus the differences between the means
for Vocabulary CD and Vocabulary AB provide an indication of how much
easier it is to recognize than to formulate a correct concept. Similarly Reading
CD is easier than Reading AB, though not so markedly.

*Sessional Variance*

All 14 part-scores from the seven main tests were intercorrelated in each
group by the tetrachoric method, taking splits close to the tertiles and averag-

ing the two coefficients so obtained. Changes from one session to the other in students' motivation, or general adaptation to the testing situation, will be shown by contrasting the correlations of different tests at the same and at different sessions.

TABLE 3

*Mean Correlations Showing the Sessional Effect*

|  | AMER. | BRIT. |
|---|---|---|
| 42 correlations within sessions | .534 | .427 |
| 42 correlations between sessions | .487 | .408 |

The difference is appreciable in both groups, the average correlation being 5 to 10 per cent higher within the same occasion than between occasions. Doubtless this difference would increase with a longer time interval. Much the same effect could have been shown by contrasting the Kuder-Richardson and the repeat reliabilities of the seven tests. For the British group these averaged .697 and .626, respectively.

There is no obvious technique for testing the significance of differences between mean tetrachorics. However, if the distributions of coefficients themselves are compared, the American within-session mean exceeds the between-session mean at the .001 level. The British difference is not significant. Over-all, it would seem that Hypothesis VIII is confirmed.

*Factual versus Inferential Questions*

When the scores on Reading Tests AB, CD, and EF for factual and inferential questions are separated, their tetrachoric intercorrelations yield the means shown in Table 4. Also listed are the correlations of both types of score with Reading Test GH, most of whose items are strongly inferential.

TABLE 4

*Mean Correlations Showing Effects of Function Tested*

|  | AMER. | BRIT. |
|---|---|---|
| 6 correlations within factual or within inferential | .535 | .385 |
| 6 correlations between factual and inferential scores on different tests | .437 | .397 |
| 3 inferential scores with Reading GH | .563 | .415 |
| 3 factual scores with Reading GH | .482 | .313 |

The American, but not the British, results confirm Hypothesis II. However, in both groups the correlations with Reading GH are confirmatory. Though there is no satisfactory test of the significance of differences between mean correlations, it would appear that functions in reading can be differentiated rather more readily than Derrick believed, and they may contribute some 10 per cent of variance. But it should be noted that, in this investigation (unlike Davis's and Derrick's), the two types of questions referred to different passages; and it might be argued plausibly that the difference is not so much one of psychological function as of technical bias (cf. Table 1). Thus the passages yielding inferential questions were all of a philosophical, psychological, or aesthetic nature, whereas the passages yielding factual ones were more descriptive—scientific, geographical, or historical.

### Retentive Reading versus Immediate Comprehension

The experimental design was inadequate for covering Hypothesis IV. Nevertheless Table 5 provides a little evidence, and more will emerge in Table 10. Here, all tetrachoric correlations are between multiple-choice and own-word scores, that is, item-form is held constant.

The correlations within Immediate Comprehension tests (AB, CD) are no higher than between these and the Retentive tests (EF). However, the

TABLE 5

*Correlations Within and Between Retentive and Immediate Comprehension Tests*

|  | AMER. | BRIT. |
|---|---|---|
| 4 correlations within Immediate Comprehension Tests | .485 | .328 |
| 8 correlations between Immediate and Retentive Tests | .535 | .359 |
| 1 correlation within Retentive Tests | .60 | .47 |

single correlation within the two halves of the Retentive test is higher in both groups, indicating that type of presentation may have some influence.

### Multiple-choice versus Creative (Own-Word) Responses

The scores on the two forms of each test were now combined, and the product-moment correlations between all tests are shown in Table 6. The coefficients for American students are above the diagonal. Kuder-Richardson Formula 20 reliability coefficients are shown along the diagonal. Some of these are very low, particularly for Reading test EF, where the creative and multiple-choice scores were based on only 15 or 16 items. But the tests were intentionally kept short to avoid over-taxing the students' patience, and there is no reason to suppose that longer tests, containing more carefully pre-tried items, would not reach acceptable levels of reliability.

A comparison of all the multiple-choice and creative-response correlations does not appear to bear out Hypothesis V. For example, Vocabulary AB does not correlate more highly with Reading AB (both creative) than with Reading CD (multiple-choice). Table 7 shows the mean coefficients.

TABLE 6

*Intercorrelations of All Tests (American Group Above, British Group Below the Diagonal), and Kuder-Richardson Reliabilities*

| | VOC. AB | VOC. CD | SENT. COMP. | RDG. AB | RDG. CD | EF CR | EF MC | RDG. GH | N-D VOC. | N-D RDG. | ENTRY ENGL. | TAB. GRA. |
|---|---|---|---|---|---|---|---|---|---|---|---|---|
| Vocabulary AB | .892 / .874 | .770 | .578 | .477 | .483 | .393 | .457 | .484 | .783 | .669 | .702 | — |
| Vocabulary CD | .844 | .834 / .847 | .726 | .575 | .539 | .448 | .528 | .487 | .759 | .646 | .648 | — |
| Sent. Completion | .702 | .687 | .826 / .758 | .656 | .689 | .587 | .707 | .711 | .642 | .718 | .610 | — |
| Reading AB | .488 | .406 | .591 | .626 / .600 | .690 | .586 | .601 | .587 | .651 | .680 | .461 | — |
| Reading CD | .498 | .434 | .621 | .504 | .785 / .708 | .719 | .679 | .657 | .590 | .696 | .522 | — |
| Reading EF cr | .476 | .431 | .501 | .499 | .495 | .622 / .490 | .568 | .572 | .531 | .641 | .422 | — |
| Reading EF mc | .346 | .331 | .435 | .416 | .413 | .389 | .591 / .516 | .643 | .474 | .569 | .478 | — |
| Reading GH | .567 | .521 | .567 | .569 | .436 | .388 | .456 | .619 / .779 | .604 | .710 | .458 | — |
| N-D Vocabulary | — | — | — | — | — | — | — | — | .899 / — | .737 | .678 | — |
| N-D Reading | — | — | — | — | — | — | — | — | .867 / — | — | .569 | — |
| Entry English | — | — | — | — | — | — | — | — | — | — | — | — |
| Tables & Graphs | .105 | .046 | .192 | .233 | .191 | .125 | .394 | .090 | — | — | — | .711 |

A further examination was made of the residual correlations after removing the Content factors by factor analysis (see below). A majority of these tended to be positive for within-item-form coefficients, negative for between-item-

TABLE 7

*Mean Correlations Within and Between Multiple-Choice and Creative-Response Tests*

| | | AMER. | BRIT. |
|---|---|---|---|
| 6 correlations within multiple-choice | | .595 | .432 |
| 3 correlations within creative | | .484 | .488 |
| | Mean | .558 | .451 |
| 11 correlations between multiple-choice and creative (omitting Vocab. AB with Vocab. CD) | | .562 | .455 |

form, but not to a significant extent. If any variance is attributable to this difference in item-form, it can hardly amount to more than 1 or 2 per cent. It is unfortunate that a wider difference, as between essay-form and multiple-choice form, could not readily be investigated. Nevertheless some further evidence will emerge in the factor analysis.

### Comprehension of Visual Items

The correlations of the Table and Graph Reading test with the seven verbal tests in the British group are clearly very low and irregular (Table 6), thus apparently confirming Hypothesis III that test medium or material makes an important difference. However, it will be seen that the coefficients are highest for Reading tests AB and EF (multiple-choice), lowest for Reading GH and Vocabulary. Unfortunately EF and AB happened to include more passages with a natural science content, whereas GH was based wholly on social science materials. Thus the obtained differentiation probably arises as much, or more, from what was labeled Technical Bias in Table 1, as from test medium.

### Level of Integration: Vocabulary versus Comprehension

All eleven verbal tests were factor analyzed by the centroid method in the American group, and the eight tests (omitting Tables and Graphs) in the British group. No significant variance remained in either matrix after two factors had been extracted, hence factorization was stopped and the calculations repeated until the guessed communalities coincided with the obtained values (median discrepancy .002, maximum .006).

As shown in Table 8, the second factor clearly differentiates reading comprehension tests from vocabulary tests, in both groups. Hence rotation was carried out, passing the first axis through the center of gravity of the two vocabulary tests. The second factor then yielded loadings for the Comprehension tests approximately as great as their Vocabulary loadings (cf. Table 9).

This confirms our first hypothesis and thus contradicts Thurstone's verdict on Davis' tests. Sentence Completion is intermediate between the Vocabulary and the Comprehension tests, and Nelson-Denny Reading shows almost the same composition, presumably because its reading passages are simpler than those used in the writer's tests and it is more highly speeded. The Entry English test, consisting mainly of questions about words or separate phrases, obtains a near-zero Comprehension loading.

In the American analysis almost all the specificities (Kuder-Richardson reliabilities minus communalities) are near zero, except those for the Nelson-Denny tests, which probably results from this test being given several months previously.[2] The picture is very different in the British analysis. The communalities for all Reading Comprehension tests are lower, and the specificity is especially large in the multiple-choice tests, CD, EF (mc), and GH. Clearly the responses of British students to these tests were less organized, more

[2] Vocabulary CD also shows a suspiciously large specificity. Possibly this arises because the multiple-choice responses were chosen by the writer, and many of them might represent English, rather than current American, interpretations of word-meanings.

## TABLE 8

### Factorial Analysis of Verbal Tests

| | UNROTATED FACTORS | | | | | | ROTATED FACTORS | | | | | |
|---|---|---|---|---|---|---|---|---|---|---|---|---|
| | AMERICAN | | | BRITISH | | | AMERICAN | | | BRITISH | | |
| | I | II | H² | I | II | H² | VOC. | COMP. | SPEC. | VOC. | COMP. | SPEC. |
| Vocabulary AB | .771 | .503 | .847 | .829 | .364 | .820 | .916 | −.093 | .045 | .902 | .074 | .054 |
| Vocabulary CD | .796 | .307 | .728 | .791 | .513 | .889 | .849 | .093 | .106 | .939 | −.074 | −.042 |
| Sentence Completion | .855 | −.083 | .738 | .840 | .030 | .707 | .722 | .467 | .088 | .752 | .374 | .051 |
| Reading AB | .763 | −.160 | .608 | .709 | −.279 | .581 | .605 | .492 | .018 | .490 | .583 | .019 |
| Reading CD | .815 | −.299 | .753 | .677 | −.123 | .473 | .588 | .638 | .032 | .536 | .431 | .235 |
| Reading EF (cr) | .704 | −.290 | .580 | .628 | −.153 | .417 | .492 | .581 | .042 | .479 | .434 | .073 |
| Reading EF (mc) | .733 | −.254 | .602 | .554 | −.275 | .383 | .534 | .563 | −.011 | .356 | .506 | .133 |
| Reading GH | .761 | −.252 | .643 | .698 | −.068 | .492 | .560 | .573 | −.024 | .581 | .392 | .287 |
| N-D Vocabulary | .839 | .275 | .777 | | | | .871 | .140 | .122 | | | |
| N-D Reading | .855 | −.038 | .732 | | | | .743 | .427 | .135 | | | |
| Entry English | .714 | .290 | .594 | | | | .767 | .070 | | | | |
| Percentage Variance | 69.1 | | | 59.5 | | | 50.3 | 18.8 | | 43.6 | 15.9 | |

random, than those of Americans, whereas in the own-word or creative tests —Reading AB and EF (cr)—the two groups were confronted with equally unfamiliar forms of response and show much the same specificities. Had the experiment included ordinary written essays, we may infer that the American

## TABLE 9

### Mean Variances of Five Complex Reading Tests

| | VOCABULARY FACTOR | COMPREHENSION FACTOR | TOTAL COMMUNALITY |
|---|---|---|---|
| American analysis | 31.1 | 32.6 | 63.7 |
| British analysis | 24.4 | 22.5 | 46.9 |

students would have shown greater specificities on these. A possible alternative explanation might be that the American students are more heterogeneous in reading capacity; but this is contradicted by Reading GH, where the British variance and reliability are higher.

### External Validation

The correlations with academic grades, shown in Table 10, are quite low among the British students, partly because of the low reliability of their education marks, but partly also because these grades were based on essay-

TABLE 10

*Correlations with Academic Grades*

|  | AMERICAN | BRITISH |
|---|---|---|
| Vocabulary AB | .272 | .163 |
| Vocabulary CD | .341 | .198 |
| Sentence Completion | .421 | .128 |
| Reading AB | .281 | .039 |
| Reading CD | .296 | .085 |
| Reading EF (cr) | .225 | .276 |
| Reading EF (mc) | .434 | .203 |
| Reading GH | .295 | .081 |
| Tables and Graphs | — | .218 |
| Nelson-Denny Vocabulary | .129 | — |
| Nelson-Denny Reading | .237 | — |
| Entry English | .340 | — |

type examinations, whereas in the American group objective course examinations would have been generally applied.[3] Several of the predictors were amalgamated and multiple correlations calculated, with the results shown in Table 11. In the British group, Vocabulary, retentive reading (particularly the creative form), and Tables and Graphs all contribute to the prediction. But apparently the ordinary reading tests, whether in multiple-choice or creative form, are so unlike normal student reading activity that their beta-weight is strongly negative. Even in the American group these reading tests are again the least valid and so yield a negative beta-weight. The objective form of retentive reading contributes most, followed by Sentence Completion, the Entry English test, and Vocabulary. Note that all three creative-response tests are slightly less predictive than their multiple-choice parallels among students who are more accustomed to the latter.

While it would be possible to calculate the validities of Vocabulary and Comprehension factor scores, it is simpler, and as effective, to obtain the combined validities of Vocabulary AB + CD and of Reading AB + CD + GH by Correlation of Sums, and then to find the partial validity of the latter, holding the former constant. The results are given in Table 12.

---

[3] Correlations with the further criterion of achievement, one year later, are not quoted here since they were even lower. However, they followed just the same pattern.

TABLE 11

*Multiple Correlations*

| AMERICAN | BETA COEFFICIENTS |
|---|---|
| Vocabulary ABCD | .0259 |
| Reading ABCDGH | −.1672 |
| Sentence Completion | .2332 |
| Reading EF (mc) | .3218 |
| Entry English | .1169 |
| $R_m = .480$ | |

| BRITISH | |
|---|---|
| Vocabulary ABCD | .2017 |
| Reading ABCDGH | −.2682 |
| Sentence Completion | −.0630 |
| Reading EF (cr) | .2924 |
| Reading EF (mc) | .1241 |
| Tables and Graphs | .1847 |
| $R_m = .392$ | |

We may deduce that the Comprehension factor can make a small but useful contribution to prediction of educational achievement among American students, over and above Vocabulary, but that it actually possesses a small negative validity among British students.

TABLE 12

*Validities of Combined Tests*

| | AMERICAN | BRITISH |
|---|---|---|
| Vocabulary ABCD × Criterion | .326 | .188 |
| Reading ABCDGH × Criterion | .333 | .083 |
| Vocabulary × Reading | .616 | .617 |
| Reading × Criterion with Vocabulary constant | .177 | −.042 |

## Conclusions

All our specific hypotheses except V (and possibly III) are borne out. But the general trend of the results goes against our initial argument, in that it suggests that what were called Content factors (particularly "Level" and "Technical Bias") have a much stronger influence than Method factors.

Nevertheless, the superior validity of reading tests which employ an unconventional method, that involving retention, suggests that Method variations would be worth further investigation. A similar test, called Directed Memory, was developed by Coffman and Papachristou (1955) and is now incorporated in the E.T.S. Law Schools Admission test, where it shows good validity, over and above ordinary reading comprehension.

Although the clearly demonstrated Comprehension factor, orthogonal to Vocabulary, would seem at first sight to reflect the difference between comprehending connected arguments and comprehending isolated concepts, it must be viewed with considerable suspicion in view of the British students' weak and poorly organized performance, particularly at multiple-choice tests. Apparently there is an important element of facility or "know-how" in the typical Reading Comprehension test, though presumably the great majority of American students have become so accustomed to it that, in their case, it contributes to the measurement of a valuable study skill. Others who are less sophisticated cannot so readily translate their understandings of the passages into terms of its conventions; hence for them the Comprehension component (as distinct from the Vocabulary component) has no predictive validity whatever.

More generally it would follow that, in the evaluation of complex skills and understandings, it is desirable to employ techniques which will resemble as closely as possible the ways in which these understandings will be ultimately expressed. Neither the objective test, nor the essay examination where the student has to muster all his knowledge and communicate it by answering a few questions in a limited time, much resemble the situation in which he will use his training in professional or in daily life. Probably the oral and clinical examination of the doctor, or the dissertation written and revised by a student in his own time with access to books and notes, both come much nearer to this ideal, since they involve less distortion by Method variance (though admittedly they may be more subject to Error variance). Similarly, in assessing the effectiveness of an educational film, or radio or television program, it is doubtful how far the conventional multiple-choice test of the knowledge retained by the viewer or listener provides an adequate criterion of the total impact of these media on his thinking and behavior.

## SUMMARY

1. Assessments of the understanding of complex concepts, whether by objective tests, written essays, oral or other methods, are affected not only by the level and type of concepts tested, but also by many factors arising from the method of testing, and the subject's facility in handling it. Certain weaknesses in current new-type achievement tests, such as their poor differential predictive capacity, may result from neglect of such method components.

2. An investigation was designed to elicit the relative variance of certain test-content, method, and error components, and was carried out among 108

British and 75 American college students. The former group was more highly selected and was much superior in vocabulary tests; but its lack of superiority in reading comprehension tests, and its significant improvement with practice, illustrate the importance of facility or sophistication at such tests.

3. Parallel forms of seven specially constructed tests of vocabulary and reading were applied in two sessions. A sessional or "Occasion" effect was demonstrated by the higher correlations among tests within than between sessions, particularly in the American group.

4. Three reading tests included passages and questions, some of which called for relatively factual, others for more inferential, comprehension. Higher correlations were obtained within than between these types of comprehension, in both groups. However, the difference may reflect the technical bias of the respective passages rather than the psychological functions aimed at.

5. A test in which the questions were not seen or answered until after the completion of the reading of the passages (i.e., involving retention) appeared to measure a somewhat different ability from the conventional immediate-comprehension test, and it was found to be considerably more valid than the latter in the prediction of academic achievement.

6. The writing of responses to vocabulary and reading questions by students in their own words (creative type) did not, as had been hypothesized, involve a different ability from the objective or multiple-choice type of response. However the scores of British students on multiple-choice reading tests showed very high specificity, reflecting their unsophisticated and relatively unorganized approach to these tests.

7. Centroid factor analyses revealed a strong Comprehension factor, orthogonal to the Vocabulary factor, among both groups in the reading tests. The validity of this factor in predicting achievement among American students is positive (though lower than that of Sentence Completion, Retentive Comprehension, and English Usage tests). Among British students its validity is slightly negative.

REFERENCES

Bloom, B. S. *Taxonomy of Educational Objectives.* New York: Longmans, Green & Company, 1956.

Brownell, W. A., *et al. The Measurement of Understanding.* Forty-Fifth Yearbook of the National Society for the Study of Education. Chicago: University of Chicago Press, 1946.

Campbell, D. T. and Fiske, D. W. "Convergent and Discriminant Validation by the Multitrait-Multimethod Matrix." *Psychological Bulletin,* LVI (1959), 81–105.

Coffman, W. E. and Papachristou, J. "Experimental Objective Tests of Writing Ability for the Law School Admission Test." *Journal of Legal Education,* VII (1955), 388–394.

DAVIS, F. B. "Fundamental Factors of Comprehension in Reading." *Psychometrika*, IX (1944), 185–197.

DERRICK, C. *Three Aspects of Reading Comprehension as Measured by Tests of Different Lengths*. Princeton, N. J.: Educational Testing Service, RB 53–8, 1953.

DRESSEL, P. L., et al. *General Education: Explorations in Evaluation*. Washington, D. C.: American Council on Education, 1954.

HORROCKS, J. E. "The Relationship Between Knowledge of Human Development and Ability to Use Such Knowledge." *Journal of Applied Psychology*, XXX (1946), 501–508.

HORST, P. *Differential Prediction of Academic Success*. Seattle: University of Washington, 1959. ONR Contract—477(08).

HOWARD, F. T. *Complexity of Mental Processes in Science Testing*. New York: Teachers College, Columbia, Contributions to Education, 1943, No. 879.

SHORES, J. H. "Skills Related to the Ability to Read History and Science." *Journal of Educational Research*, XXXVI (1943), 584–593.

THORNDIKE, R. L. *Personnel Selection: Test and Measurement Techniques*. New York: John Wiley & Sons, 1949.

THURSTONE, L. L. "Note on a Reanalysis of Davis's Reading Tests." *Psychometrika*, XI (1946), 185–188.

VERNON, P. E. *Educational Testing and Test-form Factors*. Princeton, N. J.: Educational Testing Service, RB 58–3, 1958.

# CONCERNING OBJECTIVE READING TESTS, A MINORITY OPINION *

F. C. Osenburg

*In this article Osenburg reports the results of informal studies which, hopefully, will set the reader to thinking seriously about his assumptions regarding the value of objective tests of reading compared with subjective tests. In the objective test, the student selects the correct answer from among a group of alternative possibilities. In the subjective test he must see a number of relationships, make his own inferences, and produce his own answers. The reader might find it educationally profitable to conduct similar studies.*

*1. Why did the author write this article?*

*2. What does the author mean by the phrase "brainwashed by Statistical Divination"?*

*3. How does the author make his claims regarding the shortcomings of objective reading tests?*

*4. What was the purpose of the first study?*

* FROM the *Journal of Developmental Reading* (Summer 1962), pp. 275–279, reprinted with permission of F. C. Osenburg and the International Reading Association.

5. To what would you attribute the inability of the students to perform well on the informal tests?

6. Are the author's contentions supported by the opinions of others? the research of others?

S OME READING teachers use the multiple-choice objective reading test because they believe it to be a useful and valid measurement of the results of important training. Others use it because it is convenient to administer and easy to score. But still others will admit that they use it mainly because its statistically derived scores can bewilder into silence those students who regard grades as prizes in a battle to be won by constant harassment of the teacher.

Teachers who give the first reason are possibly the more professionally minded, but teachers who give the latter two are probably the more realistic. As it becomes increasingly evident that the test-makers' claims of validity are more than merely exaggerated, the test would seem to serve more efficiently in the same sort of capacity as a baby's pacifier—an article which has no nutritional value, however thoroughly chewed upon, but which does keep the infant occupied and quiet.

The reading teacher who has not been brain-washed by Statistical Divination will meet over the years any number of students who have been labeled by the Test as "superior" but who seem never to be able to remember from what they have read anything but the incidental, the superficial, or the irrelevant. And every reading teacher who has called for a written interpretation will remember some really exotic compositions that had so little relationship to the subject assigned that they would have seemed to be clear cases of faking had the teachers not known that the writers had actually read the passages. Yet, to challenge the validity of the test, to suggest that too frequently it seems to be passed with great success by students whose only claims to distinction are good short-term memories, keen eyesight, and a capacity to recognize the obvious when it is put clearly before them is to become embroiled in a controversy the nature of which will be concealed by a rhetoric as obscure as the oracles of Delphi.

For the stubborn heretics who will not accept all objective tests as valid simply because they can be graded by electronic machines, that is, for the teacher who has been wondering why his reading tests so often label as *good* or even as *superior* some students who he has suspected are only *fair* or even downright *poor*, the following studies might prove of interest. Although the investigations were limited and the conclusions tentative, they do suggest that there is to the testing of reading something which possibly cannot be done successfully with objective tests, and that perhaps that something is even more important than what the tests and the machines do measure. They might even reinforce a growing suspicion that the kind of "reading" that is tested by objective tests is not the disciplined, mental activity that teachers like to require of students but something much less important, something comparable to what people do while sitting in front of detective stories, confession magazines, and comic books.

The first study was intended to examine the assumption that students who are identified by objective tests as superior readers must of necessity also be in possession of the other mental powers for comprehending and explaining what they have read. It would be reasonable, therefore, to expect that a *superior* reader be able to do more than just recall, immediately after having read a very short passage, the facts contained in it; he should also be able to state in his own words, and without clues, suggestions, or strong hints, what the facts implied. A student who cannot explain a passage, cannot draw inference, even though he might be able to recall all the facts in it, can hardly be regarded as a good reader—unless good reading is defined as nothing more than just that. And if it is, a great deal of time has been wasted measuring something very unimportant.

In the first set of tests several groups of superior readers were given a short passage to read and then required to explain it in their own words and without the assistance of suggested answers. The readers selected were high school seniors enrolled in the accelerated English programs of four high schools. All of the students had been rated by nationally used, standardized objective reading tests in the top fifteen percentiles. The passage read was Emily Dickinson's "I Like to See It Lap the Miles," a poem of sixteen lines. The students were asked only to identify the subject of the poem and to explain their answers. As the subject was not named in the poem described by some thirteen characteristics, some vague, some even ambiguous, the problem was to keep all the facts in mind and select a subject to which all and not just some would apply. To anticipate any objection that an unusual ingenuity was being called for or perhaps a special sort of creative imagination, the poem was given to several seventh-grade classes, but with the exception that they were permitted to discuss it. They seem to have encountered little difficulty.

Of the high school students taking the test, forty-six per cent identified the subject incorrectly, and though this percentage is startlingly high, it is of even less significance than the fact that most incorrect answers resulted from careless reading or from an inability to draw logical inferences or from both. Some students jumped to their conclusions apparently after having read only a part of the poem, either skimming over the remainder or ignoring it entirely. Others seem to have drawn their conclusions from some of the more picturesque or image-suggesting characteristics, pretending that the less picturesque were either unimportant or meaningless. Still others, possibly unable to make anything of the poem as a whole, chose from the data a homogenous group of characteristics which could support a conclusion:

It seemed that in the first stanza there was some animal running around and stopping occasionally to pause for a drink. The fourth stanza led me to believe it might be a horse because of the word "neigh." (Perhaps four characteristics were sufficient!)

I think it is the wind because the wind covers much country and blows in all places. It blows over valleys and mountains and water. It howls and also chases itself. It stops at sundown. (These are compatible characteristics. The incompatible have been ignored.)

"It" is the sun, because as it is explained in the first verse, "it" completely covers the earth, except where there is an obstacle to make a shadow. "It" goes around mountains, because it has to go in a straight path. The sun crawls between the obstacles and peers through windows and doors of the shanties. When "it" stops at its own stable door, the sun has set. (References to *hooting* and *neighing* have been excluded—or overlooked.)

Only a few students, but at this level of reading ability even a few should be too many, ignored the description more or less and used the passage as a point of departure from which to produce what can only be described as an original composition which owed little or nothing to the passage read:

"It" is the symbol of tourists. Tourists, as the poem explains, have a knack all of their own which enables them to become different from their "real selves." They travel at fast rates, stopping only to feed themselves. They take the shortest routes, which means side-stepping mountains. When they arrive at their destinations, they, if visiting a foreign country, become "natives" and try to "live as the natives live," but one soon finds them unhappy and complaining. So, they pack their belongings and travel homewards. Upon reaching their homes they "neigh like Boanerges" to their neighbors about their wonderful trips, and soon settle down to becoming docile and omnipotent.

It might also be noted that some of the correct answers were supported by even poorer reasons than were some of the incorrect answers:

The attributes of a train seem to be present in the poem. The "hooting" in the third stanza and the description of its route all seem to point to a train.
I think "it" is a train. It chases itself down a hill. It can make a noise and also be quiet.

To explore further some of the implications of this experiment, a second one was devised, this time to examine the variations between objective test scores and subjective evaluations of student performances. A somewhat larger and more heterogeneous group of students was chosen—about four hundred, distributed in high school accelerated and regular senior English classes and in university freshman composition and sophomore literature survey classes. The first half of the experiment consisted of repeating the previous test. The second half consisted of taking an objective test of ten items, including besides the right answer, eight of the most frequently occurring wrong answers drawn from previous subjective tests, and, as item 10, "something not listed above." Because of the tenth item and because the other nine contained about ninety-five per cent of the answers that would be found on the subjective tests, there was no question of the students having their thinking channeled or the correct answer flagrantly isolated among a number of im-

EVALUATION IN READING

228

possible ones. The less than five per cent who would not find their subjective answer among the nine items would include those who had produced original fantasies rather than correct answers, and they of course could check number 10.

The ratio of correct answers on the subjective test to the correct answers on the objective test was 1.00:1.75. Seventy-five per cent more students could select the right answer from a list of suggested answers than could think of that answer without assistance. In this particular case, then, forty-three per cent of the students who got the right answer in the objective test did not know the answer but only could recognize it!

As stated above, just what these experiments *prove* might be debatable, though what they suggest is rather obvious. They might suggest, for instance, that what the multiple-choice objective reading tests measure may not be reading at all, but a sort of familiarizing oneself with terms, details, facts, etc., in order that when one sees them again a few minutes later he will be able to distinguish them from terms, details, and facts with which he has not familiarized himself. Then, they might suggest that students, after repeated testing, might condition their reading to this sort of measuring and instead of developing their reading as a kind of mental discipline convert it into a game of Right Answers, which is about as intellectually useful as Parchesi or Old Maid. And, finally, they might suggest that objective test-makers and test-givers, seduced by the belief that all knowledge is measurable and that the unmeasurable, because it is outside of knowledge, is non-existent, have, in the matter of reading, limited themselves to the measurement of something that is only incidental to reading and not always very important.

Teachers who have been bewildered by the inability of some "good" readers to explain anything in their own words might suggest that these experiments indicate to them that some test-makers are obviously attempting to measure something which they themselves do not quite understand.

# READING, LEARNING, AND HUMAN DEVELOPMENT

## INTRODUCTION

*Man is a complex being. He is able to initiate ideas, to see how ideas are related, and to make decisions about these ideas. He is not an automaton that follows a predetermined sequence of instructions; on the contrary, he has some choice about what he is going to do and how he is going to do it. Yet the plans that he makes and is able to carry out have a dimension of contingency, i.e., these plans and their chances for successful execution are affected by such factors as his abilities, his interests, and his past decisions and accomplishments.*

*How a child will accomplish his many developmental and learning tasks depends, in part, on whether he is permitted to work on the tasks that suit his abilities, and his needs and interests. He will have a chance (1) to complete tasks (such as reading) successfully; (2) to grow, and (3) to learn—if his teachers and parents utilize what the various disciplines tell us about how children develop and learn.*

*In this group of articles the authors draw upon the findings of research to explain how reading instruction can profit from what is known about the principles of human development and learning. The authors show how teachers can enhance the probabilities that children will learn successfully and enjoy learning. They show how the wise teacher arranges optimal conditions for learning, and then utilizes known principles of human development and learning in teaching pupils how to read well.*

229

# READING AND HUMAN DEVELOPMENT *

Albert J. Harris

A growing number of educators and psychologists believe that certain innovations in the development of educational curricula, methods, and materials do not take cognizance of research findings in educational psychology or child psychology. These individuals object to such practices as treating the child like a learning machine whose sole function is the learning of fractionated S-R sequences or insisting that because a child might be taught to learn to read by the time he is four or five years of age, he should do so regardless of the consequences for his total psychological development.

In this article Harris performs a valuable service by systematically reviewing research on reading and human development, and drawing implications for the teaching of reading which can help place various educational practices in proper perspective.

1. How can the "pacing" idea in reading be misused?

2. Why should the secondary teacher know about reading readiness?

3. What incorrect teaching practices might a person engage in if he did not have an adequate understanding of intellectual development?

4. What major implications for the teaching of reading do we find in the discussion on perceptual development?

5. Compare the aspirations of your students, or other people whom you know, with the aspirations of: a. lower-class parents, b. middle-class parents.

ONE OF the progressive trends in modern education is manifested in the effort of leading members of the teaching profession to make full use of what is known about the nature of human development. As the knowledge about human development has expanded, those concerned with the teaching of reading have eagerly sought for applications of the new knowledge and have made changes in practice in accordance with this knowledge.

## CHARACTERISTICS OF CHILD DEVELOPMENT

### Meaning of Development

Development means a sequence of related, progressive changes which follow one another in an organism from its origin to maturity and lead to a higher degree of differentiation and complexity.[1] Development and growth are some-

[1] Horace B. English and Ava C. English, A Comprehensive Dictionary of Psychological and Psychoanalytical Terms. New York: Longmans, Green & Co., 1958.

---

* REPRINTED FROM Development In and Through Reading, Nelson B. Henry, editor, Sixtieth Yearbook of the National Society for the Study of Education, Part I. (Chicago: Distributed by the University of Chicago Press, 1961), pp. 17–34, by permission of Albert J. Harris and the National Society for the Study of Education.

times used as synonyms, although development was originally used to indicate qualitative changes while growth signified quantitative changes. It has been customary to divide the life span into more or less arbitrary periods according to chronological age. However, the observed overlapping of these age periods suggests that individual differences in rate of development are significant.

## Principles of Child Development

CONTINUITY OF GROWTH. One of the striking characteristics of the development of the child is its continuity. Whether it is a physical trait, such as height, or a psychological one, such as intelligence, curves of growth tend to be continuous, and the approach to maturity is so gradual that it is practically impossible to determine when growth ceases.

GROWTH CYCLES. Continuity does not imply straight-line growth, nor does it negate the possibility of cycles in the growth process. In the analysis of physical growth curves, Shuttleworth concluded that there are two major growth cycles, each with an accelerating and a decelerating phase.[2] The degree to which psychological development occurs in similar cycles is still a debatable issue, but it is well established that the mental-growth curves of children are uneven.[3]

MATURATION AND LEARNING. Development involves the complex interplay between a maturing organism and its environment. That is, maturation means "those developmental changes that take place more or less inevitably in all normal members of the species so long as they are provided with an environment suitable to the species. In this concept, the normal environment is conceived as playing a supportive or permissive, rather than a determining, role in development." [4] Learning, on the other hand, is "a highly general term for the relatively enduring change, in response to a task-demand, that is induced directly by experience. . . ." [5]

The relative importance of maturation and learning is a matter of dispute. In general, those who have had the most influence on reading instruction have tended to take a middle position on the issue. On the one hand, they have recognized clearly the magnitude of individual differences in rate of development and have explored many ways of adapting reading instruction to these differences. On the other hand, they have tended to maintain the importance of a carefully planned sequence of guided learning activities and to emphasize the desirability of diagnostic and remedial efforts when children do not learn according to their capacities.

[2] Frank K. Shuttleworth, *The Physical and Mental Growth of Girls and Boys Age Six to Nineteen in Relation to Age at Maximum Growth*. Monographs of the Society for Research in Child Development, Vol. IV, No. 3, Serial No. 22. Lafayette, Indiana: Child Development Publications, 1939.

[3] Nancy Bayley, "Mental Development," in *Encyclopedia of Educational Research*, pp. 817–823. Edited by Chester W. Harris. New York: Macmillan Co., 1960 (third edition).

[4] English and English, *op. cit.*, p. 308.

[5] *Ibid.*, p. 289.

THE TOTAL GROWTH OF THE CHILD. It has been taken almost as a basic axiom in some educational writings that education must be geared to the needs of the child as a whole. Generally this has been interpreted to mean that not only intellectual but physical, emotional, and social development as well must be considered.

The concept of *organismic age*, developed by Olson, attempts to provide a quantitative base for measuring a child's total development. In computing organismic age, Olson averages together the child's mental age, reading age, and several measures of physical growth such as dental age, height age, weight age, grip age, and metacarpal age (maturity of the small bones of the wrist).[6] The organismic age is heavily weighted in the direction of physical development. Olson believes that children's progress in reading is more closely related to organismic age than to mental age and that retardation in learning to read is simply one aspect of a general retardation in organismic development.

The organismic-age concept has been subjected to severe criticism. Anderson has questioned the propriety of averaging together various dissimilar measures with differing reliabilities into a single scale with equal weights.[7] Stroud and his associates have challenged the basic validity of the concept. They have pointed out that all growth processes require time, and this relationship to time in itself makes necessary a certain relatedness in various growth functions. They have brought together the results of several research studies in which correlations were found between reading and the various measures that are included in organismic age. The practically uniform conclusion of these studies is that there is a substantial correlation between reading and mental age, and the addition of a variety of measures of physical growth, singly or in combination, increases the correlation by only a negligible amount.[8]

Nevertheless, many educators have been strongly impressed by the implications that Olson has drawn for educational practice. Emphasis is placed upon "pacing" the child in the early stages of reading instead of "forcing" him; readiness for learning is emphasized, and the need for systematic instruction is minimized. The policy is favored of waiting for the child to display an interest in reading and then allowing him to set the pace of the program and to select his own reading materials.[9] Skepticism is expressed that differences in method of instruction can produce important differences in quality of reading, and remedial instruction is judged to be of questionable value.[10] Olson's point of view provides a theoretical rationale for a highly individualized ap-

[6] Willard C. Olson, *Child Development*, chap. vii. Boston: D. C. Heath & Co., 1959 (second edition).

[7] John E. Anderson, "Methods of Child Psychology," in *Manual of Child Psychology*, p. 8. Edited by Leonard Carmichael. New York: John Wiley & Sons, Inc., 1954 (second edition).

[8] Paul Blommers, Lotus M. Knief, and J. B. Stroud, "The Organismic Age Concept," *Journal of Educational Psychology*, XLVI (1955), 142–150.

[9] Olson, *op. cit.*, p. 160.

[10] *Ibid.*, p. 166.

proach in the teaching of reading and for a largely *laissez faire policy* with regard to reading instruction.

## ASPECTS OF DEVELOPMENT SIGNIFICANT FOR READING

### Reading Readiness

The concept of reading readiness, first given prominence in 1925 in the Report of the National Committee on Reading,[11] has had a profound influence on reading instruction. Readiness has been defined as a state of maturity which allows a child to learn to read without great difficulty. It assumes that the child's response to instruction is strongly influenced by his level of development.[12]

Although entrance into the first grade in most school systems is based entirely on the child's chronological age, recent evidence indicates that chronological age in itself has no significant relationship to success in learning to read.[13] Age is significant because it is a dimension in which both maturation and learning take place; when these are equated, younger children do as well as older ones. The implications of this for policy concerning entrance into the first grade have generally been ignored, probably because from an administrative standpoint it is far easier to apply and to defend an admission policy based solely on age.

Studies of sex differences in readiness have rather consistently shown earlier readiness for girls than for boys. Although this fact has caused some to advocate a higher first-grade entering age for boys than for girls,[14] the amount of overlapping between the sexes, with many boys far above the average for girls, seems a valid reason why this proposal has not received much support.

The substantial relationship generally found between intelligence test scores and success in beginning reading has led many writers to state that a mental age of six or six-and-a-half is a minimum requirement. When instruction is geared to the abilities of the children both in method and in rate of progress, average five-year-old children can achieve success in learning the beginnings of reading, as has been amply demonstrated in Great Britain.[15] On the other hand, beginning systematic reading instruction at the age of seven, as is done in Sweden, does not seem to reduce greatly the percentage

[11] *Report of the National Committee on Reading.* Twenty-fourth Yearbook of the National Society for the Study of Education, Part I. Chicago: Distributed by the University of Chicago Press, 1925.

[12] Albert J. Harris, *How To Increase Reading Ability*, p. 26. New York: Longmans, Green & Co., 1956 (third edition).

[13] Donald D. Durrell, "First-Grade Reading Success Study: A Summary," *Journal of Education*, CXL (February 1958), 5.

[14] Frank R. Pauly, "Should Boys Enter School Later than Girls?" *N.E.A. Journal*, XLI (January 1952), 29–31.

[15] W. W. Inglis, "The Early Stages of Reading: A Review of Recent Investigations," *Studies in Reading*, Part I, pp. 1–92. Publications of the Scottish Council on Research in Education, XXVI. London: University of London Press, 1948.

of children who experience difficulty.[16] It has yet to be demonstrated that there are lasting advantages in either an early or a late start for most children, and the age of six at which most children begin reading in the United States seems to be reasonably in line with what we know about the mental growth of children. Some, however, are ready for reading at a considerably younger age, and others would probably find the beginnings of reading much easier if they could be introduced to it somewhat later.

There is general agreement that readiness should be studied and assessed, but the idea that one can "build" readiness has been attacked and the point of view advanced that "drills and exercises cannot do the job that only growth and maturation and living can do." [17] Research seems to indicate, however, that children who have had kindergarten experience have an advantage in the first-grade program over those with no kindergarten experience,[18] and that certain types of specific training designed to enhance readiness for reading are beneficial.[19]

## Intellectual Development

THE MEANING OF INTELLIGENCE. Although psychologists have not been able to agree on a definition of intelligence, the three ideas that occur most frequently in definitions are that it involves ability to deal effectively with abstractions, to learn, and to respond appropriately in new situations.[20]

Whether intelligence is essentially unitary or is better conceived as a composite of interrelated but separate primary abilities is still in dispute. Most intelligence tests are based on the unitary concept, but tests of "primary abilities" are available from the primary grades up. Interrelations of different abilities tend to be high in early childhood and to decrease as adolescence is approached. During the teens, differences in verbal, numerical, spatial, and reasoning abilities are significant for guidance.[21]

The intelligence tests which correlate substantially with progress in reading and other school work have been shown to be weighted with cultural factors. On the other hand, tests which come closer to being culture-free have such low correlations with scholastic success as to be of little use for academic prediction.[22] There is an increasing tendency to use the term "scholastic aptitude

[16] Eve Malmquist, *Reading Disabilities in the First Grade of the Elementary School*, pp. 322–328. Stockholm: Almqvist & Wiksell, 1958.

[17] James L. Hymes, Jr., *Before the Child Reads*, p. 17. Evanston, Illinois: Row, Peterson & Co., 1958.

[18] Willis E. Pratt, "A Study of the Differences in the Prediction of Reading Success of Kindergarten and Non-Kindergarten Children," *Journal of Educational Research*, XLII (March 1949), 525–533.

[19] R. W. Edminston and Bessie Peyton, "Improving First-Grade Achievement by Readiness Instruction," *School and Society*, LXXI (April 15, 1950), 230–232.

[20] English and English, *op. cit.*, p. 268.

[21] Florence L. Goodenough, "The Measurement of Mental Growth in Childhood," in *Manual of Child Psychology*, *op. cit.*, chap. viii.

[22] Kenneth W. Eells, *Intelligence and Cultural Differences*. Chicago: University of Chicago Press, 1951.

tests" for those commonly used in schools, avoiding the implication of measuring native abilities.

THE NATURE OF MENTAL GROWTH. Mental growth, as measured by intelligence tests, tends to increase steadily from birth to maturity. The rate of growth during early childhood is generally thought to be more rapid than that attained during the elementary-school years, and the beginning reader, aged six, probably has completed at least half of his total mental growth. The exact shape of the average mental growth curve has not been established. During middle and late childhood, mental growth tends to proceed at a fairly steady rate, begins to slow down as adolescence is reached, and on Binet-type tests reaches adult status between the ages of sixteen and nineteen.

Most intelligence tests are scored in terms of mental age (M.A.) and intelligence quotient (I.Q.). The M.A. is a measure of the level of mental maturity achieved at a particular time; it, therefore, increases fairly steadily as the child gets older. The I.Q. is a measure of rate of mental development, with the average rate set at the value of 100, and tends on the average to remain fairly constant as the child gets older. The meaning of both measures varies somewhat according to the test used. Intelligence quotients computed by the "deviation" method tend to vary less from year to year than those computed by the older method of dividing mental age by chronological age.[23]

INTELLIGENCE AND READING. The degree of correlation between measured intelligence and reading performance varies with the tests used as well as with the ages of the children. Individual verbal tests, such as the *Stanford-Binet*, tend to correlate with reading success in the neighborhood of .60 to .70. The primary-grade I.Q. tests, which utilize oral directions and have a high verbal content but use pictures in order to avoid reading, tend to have correlations with reading scores about like those of the Binet. Verbal group mental ability tests from the fourth grade up tend to have higher correlations with reading scores, ranging from .70 to about .85, while the so-called nonverbal or nonlanguage group tests have much lower correlations with reading tests, generally ranging between .20 and .40.[24] Obviously, the verbal group tests have much in common with reading tests; not only the linguistic and reasoning skills necessary for solving the problems but also the reading skills needed to find out what the questions ask. For this reason, verbal group tests above the primary grades do not distinguish between mentally slow children and those with reading disabilities; often the latter are mistakenly categorized as intellectually retarded.

In estimating the potential reading capacity of a child, one compares his measured potentiality (mental ability or listening comprehension) with his present attainment in reading; if the former is significantly higher, a reading disability may exist. The methods of estimating a reading disability range from the simple and direct comparison of reading age with mental age to the

[23] Goodenough, *op. cit.*, pp. 470–477.
[24] Arthur E. Traxler and Agatha Townsend, *Eight More Years of Research in Reading*, p. 65. Educational Record Bulletin, No. 64. New York: Educational Records Bureau, 1955.

use of formulas in which mental age is combined with chronological age (or with chronological and arithmetic ages) or in which I.Q. is combined with the number of years of instruction. The comparison is facilitated when the tests for potentiality and present attainment have been standardized on the same population.

The fact that beginning reading is successfully taught at the age of five in Great Britain, age six in the United States, and age seven in certain other countries was noted in the discussion of reading readiness. The association of the visual perception of a word symbol with its heard and spoken equivalents is a relatively simple form of associative learning and may not require much intelligence. As the reader progresses, recognition becomes a prerequisite to understanding and reasoning about the content. As understanding and reasoning become increasingly complex and difficult, the significance of intelligence in determining the child's optimum level of reading becomes greater.

INDIVIDUAL DIFFERENCES IN INTELLIGENCE AND READING. The closer schools come to helping each child read in accordance with his mental ability, the wider become the differences in reading achievement. If we consider only the middle 80 per cent of the child population (those with I.Qs from 80 to 120), at the beginning of the second grade the expected reading range is from beginning first grade to third grade; at the beginning of sixth grade, from third to eighth grade.[25] If the school is one in which the child who does poorly is not promoted, there will be fewer pupils with low reading scores in each grade but a corresponding number of over-age pupils. Effective reading instruction does not produce more uniform achievement but, rather, helps the very bright to achieve at a superior level and aids the slow to progress successfully but slowly.

Adapting reading instruction to this wide range of normal differences is one of the most difficult and challenging problems. Nearly all teachers recognize the existence of these differences, yet in practice the teacher's main goal often seems to be to try to get all his pupils up to grade level—an impossible and frustrating goal for the genuinely slow, and an unstimulating one for the bright. Since teachers have such difficulty, considerable improvement can be expected when the teacher receives help from a curriculum consultant, reading consultant, or remedial teacher.

### Language Development

The ability to communicate with others by means of verbal symbols is the most distinctively human characteristic. Speaking and writing are active phases of communication; listening and reading are receptive phases. All phases depend upon a common structure of language, which in turn depends upon a base of common experiences. In the development of civilizations, the attainment of a complex spoken language has been necessary before reading

[25] Harris, *op. cit.*, p. 123.

and writing could be developed to a substantial degree and before the individual needed to learn reading and writing.[26]

VOCABULARY. One of the most significant aspects of language development is the growth of vocabulary. Starting off slowly in the first half of his second year, the child tends to increase his vocabulary rapidly during the second half of that year and from then on. Early estimates of vocabulary size have been greatly increased in more recent studies; M. E. Smith estimated an average vocabulary at age six of about 2,500 words,[27] while M. K. Smith's corresponding estimate is 23,700.[28] All research has relied on small samples drawn from the entire vocabulary of the language, and the sampling techniques used and types of questions asked have had marked influence on the results obtained. Vocabulary grows not only with respect to words whose meaning is understood but also in the precision of meanings, the number of alternative meanings known for a word, the ability to apply the word correctly, and the ability to think of the word when needed. Listening and speaking vocabularies develop during the preschool period and provide a base for the development of reading vocabulary, which becomes about equal in size to the listening and speaking vocabularies when word recognition skills have been mastered; writing vocabulary lags somewhat behind.[29]

SENTENCE STRUCTURE. By the first grade the very short and grammatically incomplete sentences of the preschool period have developed into complete sentences of several words. Templin's data suggest that sentence length has increased in recent years; the mean sentence length which she found for six-year-olds in the 1950's (6.6 words) was higher than that for nine-year-olds in the 1930's.[30] Both sentence length and sentence structure show progressive development throughout the school period. Compound and complex sentences make up less than one-tenth of first-grade sentences, while more than half of the sentences in college compositions are complex.[31]

CONCEPT DEVELOPMENT. The words children can use and understand give us a good insight into the development of their concepts and ideas. Usually the first words a baby learns deal with the concrete objects and

[26] Dorothea McCarthy, "Language Development in Children," in *Manual of Child Psychology, op. cit.*, pp. 492–630; and "Research in Language Development: Retrospect and Prospect," in *Proceedings of the Fortieth Anniversary of the Iowa Child Welfare Research Station*, pp. 3–24 (Child Development Monographs, Vol. XXIV, Serial No. 74, 1959).

[27] Madorah E. Smith, *An Investigation of the Development of the Sentence and the Extent of Vocabulary in Young Children.* University of Iowa Studies in Child Welfare, III, No. 5, 1926.

[28] Mary K. Smith, *Measurement of the Size of General English Vocabulary through the Elementary Grades and High School.* Genetic Psychology Monographs, XXIV (November 1941), 311–345.

[29] *Ibid.*, pp. 343–344.

[30] Mildred Templin, *Certain Language Skills in Children, Their Development and Interrelationship.* University of Minnesota Institute of Child Welfare Monograph Series, No. XXVI, 1957.

[31] McCarthy, *op. cit.*, pp. 551–562.

activities in his environment. The common adjectives, such as "big" and "good," are used by children at an early age, but their meanings are highly specific at the beginning. The understanding of class names, such as "animal," and of words like "because," which cannot be concretely pictured, develops slowly and is frequently overestimated by parents and teachers. Children often use such words with only a very incomplete and limited understanding of their meanings.

CLARITY OF SPEECH. The ability to pronounce sounds correctly increases steadily during the preschool period, and approximately 90 per cent of all sounds are given correctly by most children at the age of six years. Consonant sounds are mastered somewhat later than vowel sounds, and consonant blends and final consonants tend to be perfected last. The degree to which articulation defects are due to poor auditory perception on the one hand or to muscular incoordination on the other is still an open question. Accuracy of articulation is strongly related to most other aspects of proficiency in speech, such as word usage, sentence length, sentence completeness, and complexity of sentence structure.[32]

INTERRELATIONS AMONG COMMUNICATION SKILLS. Since listening, speaking, reading, and writing all deal with recognition, comprehension, and organization of language patterns, it would be surprising if there were not a substantial relationship among them. Although some children who have trouble with reading do not show other language problems, a great many of them are also poor in spelling, and problems of penmanship and speech defects are significantly prevalent. For some of these children, it would be more proper to speak of a generalized language disability than to indicate one area of linguistic functioning as the focus of the problem.[33] For the child who has such a general language disability, it is desirable to provide a modified reading program paced according to his linguistic development; this may be considerably below his general intellectual level. Help should be given in listening and in oral self-expression as well as in reading and writing.

### Perceptual Development

PERCEPTION AND READING. Perception is meaningful experience brought about by sensory stimulation. What one perceives is determined not only by the stimulation received from the external object situation but also by one's background experience which provides possible meanings and by the immediate mind set or anticipatory attitude. Teachers should strive to help pupils acquire a wide experiential background and to provide guidance in the anticipation of meanings.

Basic to success in reading are the following: (a) sufficiently clear visual perception to be able to distinguish the printed form of a word from other

[32] Ibid., p. 575.

[33] A. Sterl Artley, "A Study of Certain Factors Presumed To Be Associated with Reading and Speech Difficulties," Journal of Speech and Hearing Disorders, XIII (December 1948), 351–360.

word forms; (*b*) sufficiently clear auditory perception to be able to distinguish a spoken word from similar sounding words; (*c*) simultaneous attention to the printed and spoken word, allowing the formation of a learned association; (*d*) increasingly clear perception of letters and letter groups within the total word configurations; (*e*) increasingly clear perception of the sound elements within the spoken word; (*f*) association of the sound elements with their printed equivalents; and (*g*) functional use of the perceived parts as aids in the perception of the words, either in immediate recognition, or, failing that, through a combination of analysis and synthesis.

VISUAL PERCEPTION. Current methodology in the teaching of reading assumes that it is easier and faster for a child to learn to respond correctly to the appearance of a word as a whole than to perceive it part by part and put the parts together. This viewpoint originated from pioneer work of Cattell, who demonstrated that, on the average, words could be recognized in a shorter time than single alphabet letters. This was reinforced by eye-movement photography, which showed that, in good reading, words are perceived as units or in groups, and was given a theoretical base by Gestalt psychology, which emphasized the primacy of the whole over the parts. The development of perceptual skill starts in infancy with perception of a rather vague whole against a dim background and progresses toward increasingly sharp and clear apprehension both of the quality of the whole and of its details.

According to Vernon, young children tend to see things as a whole, but this is dependent upon the "goodness" of the shape; whether it is a coherent whole with a clear outline and fairly obvious structure or consists of a complicated mass of details without obvious interrelations. Some children have great difficulty with reading because they are less likely to see words as wholes than as meaningless jumbles of details. Other children have trouble because they react to the word as an undifferentiated whole with insufficient attention to the features which distinguish one word from another.[34] To be successful in word recognition, the child must be able to perceive both the whole and the distinctive parts.[35]

Research studies have shown that certain tests of visual perception skills are significantly related to success in beginning reading. Every reading readiness test has at least one subtest which purports to measure visual perception. Published readiness materials contain many exercises designed to improve visual perception. Using these with all beginners is questionable because many children are already well advanced in perceptual skill when they enter school and do not need them, while others find these materials too difficult. It is probable that direct practice in the discrimination and comparison of letter shapes and words is more useful than practice with pictures of objects or geometrical designs.

[34] M. D. Vernon, *Backwardness in Reading: A Study of Its Nature and Origin*, chap. ii. Cambridge: Cambridge University Press, 1957.

[35] Jean T. Goins, "Visual and Auditory Perception in Reading," *Reading Teacher*, XIII (October 1959), 9–13.

The problem of reversals in the perception of words and letters has been recognized as a fascinating one for many years. Inability to distinguish between shapes which are mirror images of each other is quite common among five-year-olds but decreases rapidly with the training in perception and in the left-right direction that is ordinarily given in kindergarten and first grade. In a small minority of children, directional confusion persists for several years and is a serious impediment to progress in reading. This problem of reversed orientation in reading perception has become confused with left- and right-sidedness, but it is becoming clear that the major question for reading is the presence or absence of directional confusion rather than which hand or eye is preferred. Directional confusion, in some cases, seems to be a symptom of a special kind of immaturity and, in others, seems related to changed-handedness. Children with directional confusion can usually respond to instruction which stresses left-right sequence.[36]

AUDITORY PERCEPTION. Although auditory perception requires adequate acuity of hearing, it may develop slowly in children whose acuity for sounds is normal. Much development takes place during the preschool years. Since children tend to pronounce words as they hear them, the gradual disappearance of immature pronunciations (*muvver* for mother, *wothe* for rose) indicates a corresponding sharpening of auditory perception. A school child's indistinct enunciation is often the first clue to poorly developed auditory perception.

Research indicates that initial consonants are easiest to perceive, followed by final consonants, long vowels, short vowels, and consonant combinations. Training in auditory perception—in listening to words and comparing their beginning sounds, middle sounds, and final sounds—is likely to be valuable to children whose initial scores in auditory perception tests are low.[37] Practice in hearing sounds within words, sometimes called "ear training," improves readiness for phonic instruction, and the first step in introducing a new phonic element should be practice in hearing the sound. For children whose auditory perception remains poor in spite of training, instruction in phonics is likely to be ineffectual.

### Physical Development and Reading

The most easily observed aspects of physical growth—height and weight—show rapid growth during infancy, slower but steady increase during most of childhood, acceleration during preadolescence, and a slowing-down after the attainment of puberty. Specific parts of the body show a variety of quite different growth patterns. Correlations among measures of different aspects of physical growth tend to be low or of moderate size. Growth is based largely on hereditary determiners but is markedly influenced by nutrition and disease. The growth process is governed by hormones, particularly those of

[36] Vernon, *op. cit.*, pp. 27–30, 81–110; Harris, *op. cit.*, pp. 249–260.
[37] Donald D. Durrell and Helen A. Murphy, "The Auditory Discrimination Factor in Reading Readiness and Reading Disability," *Education*, LXXIII (May 1953), 556–560.

the pituitary, thyroid, and sex glands. Girls tend to reach physical adolescence and maturity a year or two earlier than boys, but differences in rate of physical maturing are large within both sexes.

The idea that a composite or average measure of physical growth is closely related to reading development and determines its course has been discussed with some skepticism earlier in this chapter. It seems more promising to attempt to relate reading development to aspects of physical development which appear to have a more direct bearing upon progress in reading, such as visual acuity, health, and, particularly, neurological development.

The relationship between brain functioning and reading has become a subject of renewed interest, and it seems fairly certain that some kind of neurological deviation is present in many cases of severe reading disability.

Brain damage caused by birth injury, encephalitis, or anoxia may be accompanied by various degrees of physical impairment, from severe paralysis to mild clumsiness, or may be evidenced only in deviant psychological functioning and behavior. Brain-injured children show special difficulties in perception and tend to be very distractible. Educational recommendations for them include the elimination of distracting stimuli and very concrete teaching materials and methods.[38]

There are also some children whose neurological development seems to be uneven, with some abilities developing normally and others lagging behind. Bender has proposed the term "developmental lag" to describe the condition in children whose good general intelligence is at variance with a severe reading disability, in which directional confusion and immature perceptual skills are prominent and whose response to remedial help improves as they approach adolescence.[39] There is a close correspondence between this concept of delayed and irregular maturation and that of "strephosymbolia" developed by Orton.[40]

It has been proposed that reading disability is the result of deviations from the normal concentrations of two chemicals involved in the transmission of nerve impulses.[41]

The neurological requirements for success in learning to read are still mainly unknown, and both the diagnostic techniques for identifying specific neurological deviations and the educational procedures appropriate for neurologically deviant children are still in a very early stage of development.

[38] See A. A. Strauss and N. C. Kephart, *Psychology and Education of the Brain-injured Child*, Vol. II (New York: Grune & Stratton, 1956), and William M. Cruickshank, Harry V. Bice, and Norman E. Wallen, *Perception and Cerebral Palsy* (Syracuse: Syracuse University Press, 1957).

[39] Lauretta Bender, "Specific Reading Disability as a Maturational Lag" (Review of a lecture given at the 1956 annual meeting of the Orton Society), *Bulletin of the Orton Society*, VII (1957), 9–18.

[40] Samuel T. Orton, *Reading, Writing, and Speech Problems in Children*. New York: W. W. Norton & Co., 1937.

[41] Donald E. P. Smith and Patricia M. Carrigan, *The Nature of Reading Disability*. New York: Harcourt, Brace & Co., 1959.

*Sociocultural Factors and Reading*

HOME CONDITIONS.  The educational level reached by a child's parents, their occupational status, and the number of books in the home are significantly related to the progress the child is likely to make in reading. Milner, studying the relation between social status and the reading readiness of children, concluded that middle-class children tend to have a warmer, pleasanter family atmosphere and more verbal interaction with adults than lower-class children, giving them advantages in adult-controlled learning situations.[42]

CULTURAL DIFFERENCES IN ATTITUDES TOWARD SCHOOLING.  The particular accomplishments which are expected of a child as he grows up vary greatly from one culture to another. "A *developmental task* is a task which arises at or about a certain period in the life of an individual, successful achievement of which leads to his happiness and to success with later tasks, while failure leads to unhappiness in the individual, disapproval by society, and difficulty with later tasks." [43] One of the major groups of developmental tasks for children is the development of fundamental skills in reading, writing, and calculating. Of these, reading is particularly central because of the need to use it as a way of learning in most other curriculum areas.

The degree to which reading is central varies according to cultural setting. Lower-class attitudes tend to place little importance on educational accomplishment or on reading. Neighborhood influences may be strongly anti-intellectual, particularly when child society is organized along gang lines. Parents of low sociocultural status may be quite indifferent to their children's success or lack of it in school. Those parents who have middle-class aspirations and standards tend to place a great deal of emphasis upon success in school, and the parental attitude enhances the importance of reading skills in the eyes of children. Sometimes parental ambition for the child is so great that the child becomes tense and reacts unfavorably to the pressure.

Whether the parents and children recognize its importance or not, reading is truly a developmental task for children because success or failure in reading is intimately related to success or failure in the entire educational career of the child. Many studies have shown clearly that reading ability is a necessary prerequisite for success in the middle-elementary grades and in secondary school. Even when intelligence is held constant, substantial relationships remain between reading and general achievement. School success, in turn, to a large extent governs the occupations one can enter, the friends one can make and hold, and the cultural groups in which one is found acceptable.

In New York City, reading proficiency has been recognized as the most

42 Esther Milner, "A Study of the Relationship between Reading Readiness in Grade-One School Children and Patterns of Parent-Child Interaction," *Child Development*, XXII (June 1951), 95–112.

43 Robert J. Havighurst, *Human Development and Education*, p. 2. New York: Longmans, Green & Co., 1953.

important single requirement for success in secondary school. As of September, 1959, a reading grade of 5.0 or better is required for admission (without repeating Grade VI) to junior high school; for entering senior high school (Grade X) programs, a reading grade of 7.0 or better is required.

### Personality Development and Reading

CHARACTERISTICS OF PERSONALITY DEVELOPMENT.   At present there are too many theories concerning the nature of personality and its development to make possible anything more than a descriptive statement of developmental trends.

As a child grows up, he changes in many ways. Some of the significant trends in personality development are the following:

1. From helplessness to self-help with consequent reduction of frustration and fear.
2. From dependence on others to self-reliance.
3. From living in the immediate present to wider grasp of the past and future.
4. From parent-centered to peer-centered to a wide-ranging social interest.
5. From all-or-none emotional reactions to control over one's emotional responses.
6. From self-centered egotism toward satisfaction in sharing and giving.
7. From low frustration tolerance toward ability to endure tension and to function effectively despite anxiety.
8. From emotional attachment to parents to interest in the same sex during middle childhood to heterosexual responsiveness and love in adolescence and maturity.[44]

EMOTIONAL MALADJUSTMENT AND READING.   Success in reading may be one phase of a healthy and richly varied adjustment; on the other hand, it may be used as an avenue of escape from social contacts. Failure in reading is sometimes a result of emotional difficulties which were well established before the child entered school and which prevent him from engaging naturally in classroom learning activities. In other cases, a happy, contented child gradually develops symptoms of emotional distress as his failure in reading becomes more frustrating and its effects spread out.

The search for a type of personality characteristic of the poor reader has demonstrated that such a type does not exist. Some poor readers are overactive, some sedentary; some are talkative, some are taciturn; some are hostile and aggressive, some are submissive; some are emotionally volatile, some are stolid. From the standpoint of dynamics of causation, many theories have been advanced. This writer holds a pluralistic view and has described ten

[44] Arthur T. Jersild, "Emotional Development," in *Manual of Child Psychology, op. cit.*, p. 861.

different patterns which can be discerned in the performance of children with reading disabilities.

The teacher of reading should not be afraid to try to teach a child who is showing signs of being somewhat maladjusted. A friendly relationship with a kind and helpful teacher is itself a therapeutic experience for many children. The experience of some success in learning tends to alleviate feelings of inadequacy and inferiority and to lessen anxiety so that more efficient learning can take place. Increased self-confidence may make it possible for the child to behave more adequately in other types of situations. For many children, successful response to special help in reading is accompanied by a variety of favorable personality changes.

This does not imply that all teachers can obtain such results; expertness in diagnosis and in remedial teaching is very important. Nor does it imply that all children with reading difficulties can respond to an educational approach; some are so blocked emotionally that psychotherapy is a needed preliminary before remedial efforts can succeed. But it does mean that an educational approach based on an understanding of the individual child's needs can quite often achieve valuable results.

# READING READINESS AT THE HIGH-SCHOOL AND COLLEGE LEVELS *

## Ned D. Marksheffel

*In any field of human endeavor, in any age, individuals have been able to arrange conditions which either facilitate or hinder further efforts.*

*Weaknesses in strategy, tactics, logistics, materials, or personnel reduce the chances of successful completion of a task whether the task be an attack on enemy troops, an attack on disease or slums, or an attack on the printed page. Leaders on the battlefield, in the scientific laboratory and in city government, insist on and help to develop conditions*

*of readiness which facilitate successful completion of their respective tasks. Can the classroom leader, the teacher, do any less?*

*Marksheffel shows how classroom leaders train their charges to do battle successfully with the printed page.*

*1. Before reading this article, state in a column your ideas of reading readiness at the high-school or college level.*

*2. In an adjacent column list the author's ideas on readiness. Compare and contrast your ideas with his.*

---

* REPRINTED FROM *Education* (January 1961), pp. 269–272. Copyright, 1961, by The Bobbs-Merrill Company, Inc., Indianapolis, Indiana.

HIGH-SCHOOL teachers and college professors are becoming alarmed at the "poor" reading skills of some of their otherwise more capable students. They are asking, "How can I get students to 'read between the lines'? Why don't they improve their vocabularies? Do students ever read for a purpose?"

There is no one answer to all of these questions. There is, however, an answer which is basic to all other answers—professors, teachers, and students must be ready for reading before any appreciable progress is made in learning through reading.

The secondary teacher or college professor can make an immediate and valuable contribution to student learning if he will do the following: (1) recognize that reading readiness is a prerequisite to learning in subject-matter areas; (2) provide for a reading readiness period.

## ASSIGNMENT PERIOD

The much-abused assignment period is the key to reading readiness. Few teachers take advantage of this time to develop student interest in the reading, to introduce "new" vocabulary, to broaden concepts, or to set purposes for the reading.

Inadequate use of the assignment period is not a new idea. Over twenty-five years ago, Yoakam (10) and others were criticizing the inadequacy of secondary-teacher lesson assignments. Betts (1), and Gray (6), and others give evidence that there was, and is, a lack of understanding of the value of the assignment period. Burton (2) condemns the "meager, vague, unanalyzed, wholly inadequate type of assignment which persists in the secondary schools." McKee (8) calls such practices "hide-and-seek education."

## INADEQUATE ASSIGNMENTS

During the past year the writer questioned over one thousand experienced secondary teachers from the western states, Alaska, and Canada on how they assigned lessons in their subject-matter fields. With few exceptions they replied that they wrote the assignments on the board or told the students to "take the next chapter," or to "read pages 317–399 for tomorrow and be ready to answer questions." A few teachers used duplicate sheets of questions which the student was to answer, or had the students answer the author's questions at the end of the chapter. A "mere handful" of the teachers followed a method that could be termed sound and conducive to learning.

This "crude" sampling of teacher methods of assigning lessons does not lend itself to valid conclusions. It does, however, indicate that (1) many teachers receive little or no guidance as to the importance of the assignment period; (2) teachers need help in learning how to give assignments; and

(3) some teachers are receiving such instruction, but they are relatively few in number.

When assigning a lesson, the teacher needs to keep in mind certain important factors which will be discussed in detail. They are as follows: (1) time for assigning lessons; (2) introducing "new" vocabulary; (3) purposes for reading; (4) concept development; (5) teacher use of questions.

## Time and the Assignment Period

It is suggested that assignments be given at the beginning of the class period. When this plan is followed, as much time as is needed may be taken so that the student is aware of his obligations and the intent of the assignment. When the teacher has completed the assignment, the student should know enough of what is expected from him so that he can ask intelligent questions pertaining to any vague portions. He must know the objectives of the assignment and be capable of setting additional purposes as he reads. He must know what he is expected to do, when he should do it, how he should do it, and some of the "why it should be done."

## Introducing "New" Vocabulary

"New" vocabulary should be introduced orally and in context. The words need to be written on the chalkboard and pronounced clearly by the teacher. The pronunciation as well as the meaning behind the written symbol will be entirely new to some students. When two factors to be learned are introduced simultaneously, the student needs all the help he can get from the teacher.

The student must be taught that a previously accepted definition of a word may not apply in a different setting. It is no secret that high-school and even college students sometimes express amazement upon "discovering" that a word may imply many and varied meanings. Until a student understands that words shift in meaning according to context, his reading may be superficial and lacking in reality.

## Setting Purposes for Reading

By asking specific as well as general questions, the teacher can direct student reading onto paths which lead toward definite and established goals. The successful achievement of goals in a sequential pattern tends to urge the student forward in his reading. He must, and can be taught to set his own goals for reading. This, however, is a gradual process which calls for teacher guidance.

Once the student has learned to set his own goals for reading, he can adjust his rate of reading to the type of material being read and according to his own background of experience. When he can do this, the student has developed a skill which will take him far. It is a skill in which so many high-school and college students are lacking.

## CONCEPT DEVELOPMENT

In a highly industrialized, atomic-age civilization, no one person can possibly be prepared for, nor engage in, all the direct experiences he will need for living in "tomorrow's" world. As the student progresses through the grades and into higher levels of learning, he gets farther and farther away from direct experiences. His learning becomes more dependent upon vicarious experiences such as reading, listening, and televiewing. He must consciously and continually improve his ability to deal with printed and spoken words lest his concepts become faulty, warped, or totally inadequate. The more complex the concept, the more abstract are the symbols for understanding. It is vital that each student recognize the necessity of, and the obligation for, learning and using spoken and printed symbols.

Concept development and vocabulary go hand in hand. Advanced learning is dependent upon one's ability to comprehend and use words. Precise use of words clarifies problems, saves time, and increases one's ability to think. Students can acquire new vocabulary and develop concepts when they participate in guided student-teacher-student discussions. Sufficient discussion of "new" words *before* reading will enhance the student's understanding of the material that he reads.

## TYPES OF QUESTIONS TO USE

Teachers need to know and to use various types of questions. Too much emphasis has been placed upon fact-typed questions. As a consequence, high-school students are quite adept at finding answers based upon facts. When confronted with inference-type questions based upon the same facts, they flounder and give up with a baffled, "The book didn't say." They need to be taught to "dig out" inferred meanings. Even the brilliant student develops the habit of seeking and remembering facts for but one purpose—to answer teacher questions.

Questions based upon vocabulary should not be slighted. Gray (6) said that "meaningful vocabulary correlates more closely with comprehension in reading than any other (factor), excepting intelligence."

During the assignment period, key vocabulary words should be introduced by the teacher. He cannot assume that the student will "look them up in the dictionary." In order to insure student understanding of new words, the teacher should use questions based upon knowledge of these new words. By providing for student use and review of the new vocabulary, the teacher is teaching reading and subject matter.

Every possible clue and device should be used to insure student mastery of vocabulary. Context clues, picture clues, charts and graphs, teacher-student discussion, explanation, structural clues, root words and affixes, and the use of the dictionary—all are means of helping the student to arrive at the meaning of words. This is teaching reading—this is teaching subject matter.

## Summary

Teachers should not assume that all college and high-school students are ready to read assignment materials. Student readiness for reading at all grade levels is a prerequisite for optimum learning. Students can develop readiness for reading when teachers prepare them for it by introducing some of the difficult vocabulary, and by asking thought-provoking questions which lead students to read "deeply" rather than to "soak up" information or to "gather" facts.

### REFERENCES

1. BETTS, EMMETT A. *Foundations of Reading Instruction* (rev. ed.; New York: American Book Co., 1957).
2. BURTON, WILLIAM H. "Implications for Organization or Instruction and Instructional Adjuncts," *Learning and Instruction*, Forty-Ninth Yearbook, Part I, of the National Society for the Study of Education (Chicago: University of Chicago Press [Distributor], 1950), p. 227.
3. BURTON, WILLIAM H. *Reading in Child Development* (Indianapolis: The Bobbs-Merrill Co., Inc., 1956).
4. DURRELL, DONALD D. "Learning Difficulties among Children of Normal Intelligence," *Elementary School Journal*, Vol. 55 (December, 1954), pp. 201–208.
5. GATES, ARTHUR I. *Improvement of Reading* (rev. ed.; New York: The Macmillan Co., 1947).
6. GRAY, WILLIAM S. *Reading in the High School and College*, Forty-Seventh Yearbook, Part II, of the National Society for the Study of Education (Chicago: University of Chicago Press [Distributor], 1948), p. 98.
7. GRAY, WILLIAM S., and LARRICK, NANCY (eds.). *Better Readers for Our Times*, International Reading Conference Proceedings, Vol. I (New York: Scholastic Magazines, 1956).
8. McKEE, PAUL. *The Teaching of Reading in the Elementary School* (New York: Houghton Mifflin Co., 1948), p. 548.
9. STRANG, RUTH; McCULLOUGH, CONSTANCE M.; and TRAXLER, ARTHUR E. *Problems in the Improvement of Reading* (2d. ed.; New York: McGraw-Hill Book Co., 1955).
10. YOAKAM, GERALD A. *The Improvement of the Assignment* (New York: The Macmillan Co., 1934).

# WHAT CURRENT RESEARCH SAYS ABOUT POOR READERS IN HIGH SCHOOL AND COLLEGE *

Arthur S. McDonald

*Each year a number of enterprising teachers set out to organize a high-school or college reading improvement program. Too often their first question is "What materials shall I use?" They might well inquire into the nature of the population they are going to serve and what the research says about the success of programs designed to help similar populations with similar needs.*

*In this article McDonald discusses the problems that have confronted researchers who delve into the problem of reading disability at the high-school and college level. Although adhering to the principles of multiple causation in reading difficulty and interaction of the factors that affect reading performance,*

*he discusses the factors separately in the interest of simplifying the presentation. His conclusions set forth fundamental guidelines that reading teachers must observe if they expect to help poor readers.*

*1. Why are the results of research studies concerned with reading disability at the high-school or college level often contradictory?*

*2. Relate the deficiency symptoms listed to the findings in other sections of the article. What problems do you encounter in this endeavor?*

*3. What do you think the author wants you to remember as you work with students who have reading problems?*

THE RESULTS of research studies concerned with reading disability at the high school and college level are often contradictory. A number of possible causes for such disagreement may be noted. Frequently, an adequate definition of achieving and disabled readers was lacking, or there was considerable difference among investigators in the standards used for classifying reading ability.[45] In many cases, there was no comparison of disabled readers with control groups of able readers. Only a few studies took into account the effect of the school "press" or the effect of the teaching situation.[39, 55]

Pace and Stern have asserted that failure of assessment studies of achievement is often due to inadequate description of environments in which assessed modes of behavior were supposed to occur. In their view, the students must face and deal with the press of the school environment. Thus, the total pattern of congruence between personal needs and environmental press may be more predictive of achievement, growth and change than any single aspect

* FROM the *Journal of Developmental Reading* (Spring 1961), pp. 184–196, reprinted with permission of Arthur S. McDonald and the International Reading Association.

of either the person or the environment.[39, 66] It has also been shown that different personality types respond best to different teaching environments.[41, 54]

Certain other factors serve to complicate adequate research. Many of the most grossly handicapped readers have dropped out of or have been eliminated from school by high school and college age. Furthermore, there is considerable variance in the holding power of high schools [46] so that the proportion and type of disabled readers vary greatly from school to school. College admission standards differ greatly. Some colleges admit practically any student with a high school diploma; others are highly selective. Consequently, types of reading disability cases will vary greatly in accordance with the college selection program. In addition, the type and extent of reading disability found in a college population will depend on the ability of the school to provide special services as well as on the faculty's philosophy in this regard.[26]

Traxler has pointed out the difficulty of adequately measuring reading ability, showing the variance among tests in their measurement of various components of the reading process.[68] Other studies have shown that personality dimensions, method of test administration, and type of test may interact to produce spurious indications of reading disability.[35] In part, this problem of assessment lies at the base of much of the inconsistency of the research. Inadequate definition of disabled readers, overemphasis on one factor or viewpoint, and limitations of environment, time and available subjects have led often to biased populations, designs, or results. This may be the explanation for the failure of the studies to be conclusive with respect to the effect of environmental, social, emotional, personal, educational, and other factors on reading performance.

Despite these and other conflicts and disagreements, the consensus among researchers, however, is that no single cause or factor can be held solely responsible for reading difficulties. The principle of multiple causation applies here as in other areas of human behavior. A constellation of related factors is practically always found in cases of reading disability if the research study has been adequately designed and executed. Therefore, although factors affecting reading performance will be discussed separately in the interest of simplifying the presentation, it should be kept in mind that they always interact.

## Physical Factors

The research literature shows no conclusive study indicating that physical factors are significantly related to reading disability at the high school and college level.[10, 61] Nevertheless, recent research carried on by Smith and his associates has suggested that some types of severe reading disability may result from faulty mediation of nerve impulses in synaptic transmission due to chemical imbalance.[53]

## Intellectual Factors

Psychological theory and practice have established relative functional independence of at least two large sectors of intellectual abilities: *non-verbal factors*, the ability to deal effectively and precisely with quantities as contrasted with *verbal factors*, the ability to deal with less precise, often affectively toned verbal constructs.[1, 9, 73] Several studies, resting on the use of the A.C.E. Psychological Examination, have found that disabled readers often have high measured intellectual abilities in the non-verbal or performance area and poor measured abilities in the linguistic area.[33, 69, 75]

We administered the WAIS to fifty disabled readers of high school age and fifty disabled readers at the college level and got results similar to those reported by Spache for elementary school children.[58] The high school group was approximately average in intelligence: Verbal 101 (9.5), Performance 108 (10.9). The college group was in the bright-normal range: Verbal 110.5 (10.9), Performance 118 (14.5). For the two groups, 30% of the students were higher on Verbal, 65% were higher on Performance, and 5% had similar scores on the two. Using a deviation of 3 from the student's scale average, plus deviations were greater on Comprehension, Similarities, Picture Completion, Picture Arrangement, and Object Assembly. Minus deviations were significantly greater in Arithmetic, Digit Span, and Digit Symbol. Information, Vocabulary, and Block Design had insignificant deviations. These results may be interpreted to mean that disabled readers did better in tasks involving social comprehension, ability to recognize relationships between verbal concepts (when presented orally), in attention to details, and in simple manipulative tasks than they did in tests reflecting attention, concentration, fluency, and freedom from distraction.

## Deficiency Symptoms

A number of overtly expressed deficiencies characteristic of high school and college disabled readers have been identified:

1. General vocabulary lacks.
2. Poor spelling.
3. Deficiencies in word sense.
4. Weakness in word recognition and structural analysis.
5. Self-concept of being a poor reader.
6. Desire for more speed.
7. Lack of retention.
8. Inability to concentrate.
9. Tendency to give equal stress and value to every word.
10. Search for the *one* best way to read.
11. Procrastination and cramming.
12. Reading causing nervousness, restlessness, fatigue, etc.

Ephron has termed most of these "surface patterns." Raygor, however, has suggested that such self-reports may be used in diagnosis of reading disabilities.[42]

## HOME INFLUENCES

A number of researchers have reported that inadequate home-family situations were found in a majority of reading disability cases. It may be pointed out that deficiences in interfamilial relationships are often closely related to inadequate emotional development.[44, 45, 61]

## EDUCATIONAL FACTORS

In regard to schools there are a number of practices in the educational system which tend to produce defective readers.[61, 64] Some of these are inadequate preparation for the work-type reading in content fields necessary at high school and college levels; lack of training in mature reading; the absence of true reading instruction in many high schools; and educational policies which keep the high school student *in* his group but fail to make him a member *of* his group.

## EMOTIONAL FACTORS

Increasing attention has been given to the relationship between reading and emotional status. Many writers have pointed out that reading disabilities are accompanied by more or less severe personality difficulties.[4, 8, 10, 11, 12, 13, 14, 16, 19, 20, 21, 25, 28, 32, 34, 37, 38, 42, 44, 45, 46, 48, 51, 52, 53, 54, 55, 57, 58, 59, 60, 61, 63, 64, 72, 75, 76, 77] On the other hand, there are some researchers who did not find reading to be significantly related to personal adjustment of students.[2, 3, 22, 24, 29] Holmes concluded that, for his samples of college students, the data did not support the hypothesis that a strong relationship exists between reading disabilities in either speed or power of reading and any particular syndrome of personality traits.[23, 24]

Disabled readers at the high school and college level often manifest definite emotional maladjustments.[44] It has been emphasized that every person who deals with poor readers must be alert to the presence of complicating emotional problems which have repeatedly been shown to interfere with learning. Ephron reports that all the "surface patterns" of reading disability (mentioned previously) are various expressions of fear: fear of taking chances, of making mistakes, of succeeding, etc.[12] Woolf noted the presence of fear together with evidence of many symptoms associated with frustration: stereotypy, insecurity, undifferentiated self-concepts, etc.[76] Raygor and his associates found that college students with reading disabilities differ in what they say and feel about reading from the achieving college students. Such reports were significantly negative in tone and affect.[42] Students who significantly improved their reading by means of work in a reading clinic manifested a general trend of personality change in the direction of decreased anxiety and increased emotional stability and self-confidence.[41]

MMPI responses for disabled readers at the college level were found to be significantly different from responses for achieving readers. Poor readers also showed a lack of self-understanding and a delay in identification with adults of the same sex as well as indications of low morale, lack of self-confidence, extreme anxiety, and rigidity for the disabled readers.[75] Poor readers also manifested less orientation to achievement and greater need for deference than good readers. Disabled readers found it very difficult to organize a situation.[76] Another study found marked discrepancies among the ideal-self concept, the self-concept, and the concept of others in a group of poor readers at the college level.[34] These students, as determined by TAT and diagnostic interviews, manifested strong needs for abasement and deference. They lived in a press of coercion and rejection.

In another investigation we compared the TAT protocols of twenty-five college students who were rated as poor readers with the protocols of twenty-five college students who were able readers. The poor readers evidenced high needs for abasement, succorance, sentience, and deference. They manifested low needs for autonomy, achievement, aggression, and dominance. The poor readers exhibited much greater tendency toward stereotypy in their stories. They evidenced some uncertainty in sex role identification. Many of them exhibited characteristics similar to the pattern which Rosen found for the category which he termed the *over-inhibited person*.[47] In comparison, the good readers manifested high needs for achievement, dominance, autonomy, and cognizance. Similar findings have been reported by Middleton and associates.[38] These investigators point out that personality factors may be associated with achievement in a complex pattern of subgroupings in each of which groupings different relationships between syndromes and achievement exist.

To conclude this discussion of the relationship of emotions to reading disability, it may be well to note some of the difficulties in carrying out research with this factor. Some of these are

1. Biased populations available to the researcher.
2. Approach to the research with a possibly biasing attitude toward the importance of educational or psychological factors.
3. Paucity of means for adequately controlling within-group variability while comparing to inter-group variability on a number of variables.
4. Superficial evaluations of personal adjustment.
5. Inadequate determination of reading status.
6. Failure to take into account the environmental press of the educational institution.
7. Failure to equate groups on basis of emotional factors for comparison on reading achievement.

Johnson's conclusions from her study of the research seem in point: [30]

1. There is no single personality trait or combination of traits invariably associated with either success or failure in reading. Variability of personality structure will be great within groups of both achieving and disabled readers.
2. Personal maladjustments which lead to inability to attend and concentrate will have a negative effect on the development of reading ability.
3. The presence of the very serious symptoms of personal maladjustment is more frequently associated with failure in reading than with success in reading.
4. Emotional problems and reading disability, when they occur together, are likely to aggravate each other. Both must be considered in the treatment of the whole problem.
5. The influence of home conditions is strong in determining both personal adjustment and achievement in reading.

## USE OF LEISURE TIME

A coded survey of the leisure time pursuits of fifteen hundred high school and college students in the Milwaukee area showed that those students ranking lowest in reading ability resorted more to activities making lesser demand on the intellect than did the students ranking in the upper quarter on reading ability. Students with low reading ability claimed to spend a mean of twenty hours per week viewing television. The programs listed were stereotyped, low-demand, immediate reward type. Students of high reading ability claimed to spend a mean of seven hours per week viewing TV. A high proportion of programs listed by these students demanded a rather purposeful, intellectual approach. The poor readers listed a mean of three times the number of movies attended as did the good readers. Claimed leisure-time reading habits, as might be expected, differed significantly both in regard to time spent and type of reading reported. The poor readers claimed very little voluntary reading. Most of this was of the ephemeral, low-demand type. Television, movies, and reading activity were significantly more purposeful, intellectual, and more often of a delayed reward type for the good readers than for the poor readers. No difference was found between the groups with regard to social and athletic pursuits.

## SUMMARY AND CONCLUSIONS

The research findings indicate that reading disability is the result of a constellation of inhibiting factors varying with different students and with different institutional environments. Most of the factors considered in this paper may act at different times either as predisposing or precipitating factors. Usually, a single factor will become functional in reading disability only in connection with other factors as part of a constellation.

Because multicausal factors and psychological functions underlie reading disability in high school and college students, because reading is a function of the whole personality and is one aspect of the growth of the individual (Olson), the ultimate goal of reading instruction must be the modification of the personal and social adjustment of the student wherever such adjustment impedes reading ability. Spache has observed that gains in reading skills by students really reflect better adjustment and adaptation to high school and college demands.[59, 60]

The student in his reading, as in his behavior generally, perceives in accordance with his needs, goals, defenses, and values. Ephron has pointed out that an instructor who attempts to change and improve reading habits is really trying to change a great deal more and must act accordingly.[12] Snygg and Combs have observed[56] that the process of education is fundamentally a process of change in the person's phenomenal field. They assert that the important thing in the determination of behavior is the meaning which objects, facts, and settings have for the person through their relationship to the self. Material forced upon students without consideration of their present needs and immediate goals tends to acquire a negative connotation. This is no less true even though the material be labeled "remedial" and administered in a clinical setting. To be effective, reading instruction will have to accept the task of dealing as necessary with the whole phenomenal field of the individual, of planning to bring about changes in his self-perception as well as in his perception of his environment. Since behavior must be appropriate to the phenomenal self, changes in this self are invariably followed by changes in behavior.[12, 56, 75]

## BIBLIOGRAPHY

1. ALTUS, WILLIAM D. "Q-L Variability, MMPI Responses and College Males," *Journal of Consulting Psychology*, XXII (1958), 367–371.

2. ANDERSON, M., and KELLEY, M. "An Inquiry into Traits Associated with Reading Disability," *Smith College Studies in Social Work*, II (1931–32), 46–63.

3. BENNETT, CHESTER C. *An Inquiry into the Genesis of Poor Reading. Contributions to Education*, No. 755. New York: Bureau of Publications, Teachers' College, Columbia University, 1938.

4. BURFIELD, LEONE M. "Emotional Problems of Poor Readers among College Students," *Clinical Studies in Reading I*, Supplementary Educational Monograph No. 68, Chicago: University of Chicago Press, 1949.

5. BUSWELL, GUY T. "The Relationship between Perceptual and Intellectual Processes in Reading," *California Journal of Educational Research*, VIII (1957), 99–103.

6. COHEN, JACOB. "The Factorial Structure of the WAIS between Early Adulthood and Old Age," *Journal of Consulting Psychology*, XXI (1957), 283–290.

7. ——. "The Factorial Structure of the WISC at Ages 7-6, 10-6, and 13-6," *Journal of Consulting Psychology*, XXIII (1959), 285–299.

8. CHANSKY, NORMAN M. "Threat, Anxiety and Reading Behavior," *Journal of Educational Research*, LI (1958), 333–340.
9. DAVIS, PAUL C. "A Factor Analysis of the Wechsler-Bellevue Scale," *Educational and Psychological Measurement*, XVI (1956), 127–146.
10. DECHANT, EMERALD. "Some Unanswered Questions in the Psychology of Reading," *Eighth Yearbook*, National Reading Conference. Fort Worth: Texas Christian University Press, 1959, pp. 99–112.
11. DOTSON, ELSIE J. "The Reading Improvement Program at the University of Texas," *Sixth Yearbook*, Southwest Reading Conference. Fort Worth: Texas Christian University Press, 1957, pp. 32–43.
12. EPHRON, BEULAH K. *Emotional Difficulties in Reading*, New York: Julian Press, 1953.
13. FEINBERG, H., and REED, C. L. "Reading Level of a Group of Socially Maladjusted Boys," *Journal of Social Psychology*, XII (1940), 31–38.
14. FENDRICK, PAUL, and BOND, GUY L. "Delinquency and Reading," *Pedagogical Seminary and Journal of Genetic Psychology*, XLVIII (1936), 236–243.
15. FRENKEL-BRUNSWIK, ELSE. "Intolerance of of Ambiguity as an Emotional and Perceptual Personality Variable," *Journal of Personality*, XVIII (1949), 130–134.
16. GANN, EDITH. *Reading Difficulty and Personality Organization*. New York: King's Crown Press, 1945.
17. GARRETT, H. E., and SCHNECK, M. R. *Psychological Tests, Methods, and Results*. New York: Harpers, 1933.
18. GATES, ARTHUR I. *Improvement of Reading*, revised edition. New York: Macmillan, 1947.
19. ———. "The Role of Personality Maladjustment in Reading Disability," *Journal of Genetic Psychology*, LIX (1941), 77–82.
20. GOODSELL, J. G. "A Study of Reading Ability as Related with Physical, Mental, and Personality Traits in Senior High School Students," *American Journal of Optometry*, XIX (1942), 399–404.
21. GRAU, ALBERT F., S. J. "The Emotional World of the Non-achiever," *Journal of the American Optometric Association*, XXVIII (1957), 523–531.
22. HOLMES, JACK A. "Occupational Aptitudes of Delinquents," *Journal of Genetic Psychology*, LXXVIII (1951), 47–54.
23. ———."Factors Underlying Major Reading Disabilities at the College Level," *Genetic Psychology Monographs*, XLIX (1954), 3–95.
24. ——— "Personality Characteristics of the Disabled Reader," *Journal of Developmental Reading*. Delivered at APA Symposium, 1959.
25. HOPKINS, J., MALLISON, N., and SARNOFF, I. "Some Non-intellectual Correlates of Success and Failure among University Students," *British Journal of Educational Psychology*, XXVII (1958), 25–36.
26. IFFERT, ROBERT E. *Retention and Withdrawal of College Students*. U. S. Educational Bulletin, 1958, No. 1.
27. JENSEN, M. B. "Reading Deficiency as Related to Cerebral Injury and to Neurotic Behavior," *Journal of Applied Psychology*, XXVII (1943), 535–543.
28. JENSEN, VERN H. "Influence of Personality Traits on Academic Success," *Personnel and Guidance Journal*, XXXVI (1958), 497–500.

29. Johnson, D. M., and Reynolds, F. "A Factor Analysis of Verbal Abilities," *The Psychological Record*, 1941, 183–195.
30. Johnson, Marjorie S. "Factors Related to Disability in Reading," *Journal of Experimental Education*, XXVI (1957), 1–26.
31. Jones, Leonard. "Frustration and Stereotyped Behavior in Human Subjects," *Quarterly Journal of Experimental Psychology*, VI (1954), 12–20.
32. Kunst, Mary S. "Psychological Treatment in Reading Disability," *Clinical Studies in Reading I*, Supplementary Education Monographs, No. 68. Chicago: University of Chicago Press, 1949.
33. Levy, Jerome. "Readability and Test Performance," *Journal of Educational Psychology*, XLIX (1958), 10.
34. McDonald, Arthur S., Zolick, Edwin S., and Byrne, James A. "Reading Deficiencies and Personality Factors: A Comprehensive Treatment," *Eighth Yearbook*, National Reading Conference. Fort Worth: Texas Christian University Press, 1959, pp. 89–98.
35. McDonald, Arthur S., "Factors Affecting Reading Test Performance." *Ninth Yearbook*, National Reading Conference (in press).
36. McKillop, Anne S. *The Relationship Between the Reader's Attitudes and Certain Types of Reading Responses*. Doctoral dissertation, University of Michigan, 1951.
37. Mann, Helen P. "Some Hypotheses on Perceptual and Learning Processes with their Applications to the Process of Reading: A Preliminary Note," *Journal of Genetic Psychology*, XC (1957), 167–202.
38. Middleton, George, Jr. and Guthrie, George M. "Personality Syndromes and Academic Achievement," *Journal of Educational Psychology*, L (1959), 66 ff.
39. Pace, C. Robert, and Stern, George G. "An Approach to the Measurement of Psychological Characteristics of College Environments," *Journal of Educational Psychology*, XLIX (1958), 269 ff.
40. Penty, Ruth C. *Reading Ability and High School Drop-outs*. New York: Bureau of Publications, Teachers' College, Columbia University, 1956.
41. Raygor, Alton L. "College Reading Improvement and Personality Change," *Journal of Counseling Psychology*, VI (1959), 211–217.
42. Raygor, Alton L. and Vance, Forrest L. "The Diagnosis and Treatment of College Reading Difficulties Using Patterns of Symptomatic Statements," *Journal of Developmental Reading*, III (1959), 3–11.
43. Rapaport, David. *Diagnostic Psychological Testing*. Vol. I. Chicago: Yearbook Publishers, Inc. 1946.
44. Robinson, Helen M. "Emotional Problems Exhibited by Poor Readers: Manifestations of Emotional Maladjustment." *Clinical Studies in Reading I*, Supplementary Educational Monographs, No. 68. Chicago: University of Chicago Press, 1949.
45. ——. "Problems of Corrective Reading in American Schools," Supplementary Educational Monographs, No. 79. Chicago: University of Chicago Press.
46. ——. "Some Poor Readers have Emotional Problems," *Reading Teacher*, VI (1953), 25–33.
47. Rosen, Sidney. "An Approach to the Study of Aggression," *Journal of Social Psychology*, XLVI (1957), 259–267.
48. Russell, David H. "Research on Reading Disabilities and Personality Ad-

justment," *Improving Educational Research*, American Educational Research Association, official report, 1948, pp. 10–13.

49. SEGEL, DAVID and SCHWARM, OSCAR J. *Retention in High Schools in Large Cities*. U. S. Office of Education Bulletin, 1957, No. 15.

50. SHAW, MERVILLE C. and BROWN, DONALD J. "Scholastic Underachievement of Bright College Students," *Personnel and Guidance Journal*, XXXVI (1957), 195–199.

51. SHERMAN, MANDEL. "Emotional Disturbances and Reading Disability," *Recent Trends in Reading*, Supplementary Educational Monograph, No. 49. Chicago: University of Chicago Press, 1939.

52. ——. "Psychiatric Insights into Reading Problems," *Clinical Studies in Reading I*, Supplementary Educational Monographs, No. 68. Chicago: University of Chicago Press, 1949.

53. SMITH, D. E. P. and WOOD, R. L. "Noncognitive Personality Dimensions as Indices of Reading Improvement at College Level," *American Psychologist*, 1953, 438 ff.

54. SMITH, D. E. P., WOOD, R. L., and CARRIGAN, PATRICIA. *Manual for the SA-S Senior and Junior Scales*. University of Michigan: Bureau of Psychological Services, 1956.

55. SMITH, D. E. P., WOOD, R. L., DOWNER, J., and RAYGOR, A. "Reading Improvement as a Function of Student Personality and Teaching Method," *Journal of Educational Psychology*, XLVII (1956), 47–58.

56. SNYGG, DONALD, and COMBS, ARTHUR W. *Individual Behavior*. New York: Harpers, 1949

57. SOLOMON, RUTH H. "Personality Adjustment to Reading Success and Failure," *Clinical Studies in Reading II*, Supplementary Educational Monographs, No. 77. Chicago: University of Chicago Press, 1953, pp. 64–82.

58. SPACHE, GEORGE D. "Personality Patterns of Retarded Readers," *Journal of Educational Research*, L (1957), 461–469.

59. ——. "Psychological Explanations of Reading," *Fifth Yearbook*. Southwest Reading Conference. Fort Worth: Texas Christian University Press, 1956, pp. 14–22.

60. ——. "Reading Improvement as a Counseling Procedure," *Eighth Yearbook*. National Reading Conference. Fort Worth: Texas Christian University Press, pp. 125–130.

61. ——. "Factors which Produce Defective Reading," *Corrective Reading in the Classroom and Clinic*, Supplementary Educational Monographs, No. 79, 1953, pp. 49–57.

62. STAUFFER, RUSSELL G. "Certain Psychological Manifestations of Retarded Readers," *Journal of Educational Research*, XLI (1948), 436–452.

63. STEWART, ROBERT S. "Personality Maladjustment and Reading Achievement," *American Journal of Orthopsychiatry*, XX (1950), 410–417.

64. STRANG, RUTH, MCCULLOUGH, CONSTANCE M., and TRAXLER, ARTHUR E. *Problems in the Improvement of Reading*. 2d ed. New York: McGraw-Hill, 1955.

65. STRANG, RUTH and BRACKEN, DOROTHY. *Making Better Readers*. Boston: D. C. Heath, 1957.

66. THISTLETHWAIT, DONALD L. "College Press and Student Achievement," *Journal of Educational Psychology*, L (1959), 183–191.

67. Trapp, E. Philip and Kausler, Donald H. "Test Anxiety Level and Goal Setting Behavior," *Journal of Consulting Psychology*, XXII (1958), 31–33.

68. Traxler, Arthur E. "Critical Survey of Tests for Identifying Difficulties in Interpreting What Is Read," Supplementary Educational Monographs, No. 74. Chicago: University of Chicago Press, 1951, pp. 195–200.

69. Triggs, Frances O. "Appraisal of Reading Skills in Relation to Effectiveness of Teaching and Learning Techniques," *Fifth Yearbook*, Southwest Reading Conference. Fort Worth: Texas Christian University Press, 1956, pp. 65–72.

70. Trow, William C. *Educational Psychology*. Boston: Houghton, Mifflin, 1941.

71. Van Gilder, Lester. *Study of Effect of Communications Media on College Academic Success*. M. A. thesis, Marquette University, 1957.

72. Vorhaus, Pauline. *A Manual on the Use of Selected Psychological Tests in Certain Aspects of the Diagnosis of Reading Problems*. Doctoral Project, Teachers' College, Columbia University, 1950.

73. Wechsler, David. *The Measurement and Appraisal of Adult Intelligence*. Baltimore: Williams and Wilkins Co., 1958.

74. Weigand, George. "Adaptiveness and the Role of Parents in Academic Success," *Personnel and Guidance Journal*, XXXV (1957), 518–526.

75. Woolf, Maurice D., and Woolf, Jeanne A. *Remedial Reading*. New York: McGraw-Hill, 1957.

76. Woolf, Maurice D. "Is Linguistic Ability Related to Personality Traits?" (in press).

77. Worell, Leonard. "Level of Aspiration and Academic Success," *Journal of Educational Psychology*, L (1959), 47–54.

# PSYCHOLOGICAL CORRELATES OF THE READING PROCESS *

Katrina de Hirsch

*To de Hirsch reading is a perceptual and an intellectual act that can be explained best in a framework of Gestalt psychology. The various psychological correlates of reading such as language growth, perception, ego development, spatial and temporal organization, and sensory modalities are discussed within this framework of Gestalt psychology. In the conclusion de Hirsch draws implications of these findings for the teacher of reading.*

* from *Challenge and Experiment in Reading*, J. Allen Figurel, editor, International Reading Association Proceedings, VII (New York: Scholastic Magazines, 1962), pp. 218–226, reprinted with permission of Katrina de Hirsch and the International Reading Association.

1. What are the basic issues discussed in this article?

2. Why is it important for a teacher to have an adequate understanding of the reading process?

3. How is Gestalt theory applied throughout the discussion of the topics up to and including Temporal Organization and Oral Language?

4. What are the different sensory modalities?

5. How might your approach to the teaching of reading be altered as a result of reading this article?

I SHALL TRY in this paper to discuss some of the structures and processes involved in the reading act in the light of Gestalt psychology and shall then try to apply some of the general concepts to children who are learning to cope with printed words.

## DEFINITION

Reading is the successful response to the visual forms of language. The goal of reading is the understanding of graphically fixed language units.

## VISUAL ASPECTS

Reading is obviously more than and different from seeing. More is involved than simple ocular functioning. The visibility of letters is not the same as their readability. Dyslexic children do see letters but they do not grasp their symbolic significance. Reading is not only a matter of perception, it is, in the last instance, an intellectual act.

There are, of course, some reading disabilities which are related to visual problems. Robinson and Cleland refer to farsightedness and lack of binocular vision, to difficulties with visual fusion and depth perception which contribute to reading problems.

The 1940 report of the Los Angeles County Medical Association takes a different stand. "If the visual activity is reduced 50%, the child will have difficulty in interpreting symbols he does not see well. Except in farsightedness and astigmatism of a marked degree, the child's power of focusing is sufficient to give adequate though not perfect vision. Crossed eye with normal vision in one eye has little effect on reading ability."

The discussion whether or not faulty eye movements are responsible for reading difficulty is still going on. Orton and Tinker deny the significance of faulty eye movements in the etiology of reading disorders. Research has shown that the difference in number of eye fixations in excellent and poor readers is surprisingly small. The Los Angeles report quoted above says: "So-called faulty eye movements, as judged by regressions, depend primarily on poor understanding of the subject matter read, and not on uncoordinated eye muscles; not the eye but the brain learns to read."

Kainz also maintains that the number of eye movements is a function of ability to grasp meaning and not the other way around. In other words, visual processes in reading are largely of a central rather than of a peripheral nature.

## CORTICAL FUNCTIONS

Earlier concepts of the central processes pertinent for reading have undergone considerable modification. Neurologists no longer believe that precisely pinpointed brain areas are responsible for specific performance. We do know that in lesions of the angular gyrus the interpretation of printed material is impaired or lost. We also know that the areas adjacent to the angular gyrus do subserve processes involved in reading. However, we no longer believe that we deal with separate and summative cortical excitations. Rather, we assume the existence of highly complex activities involving the whole brain. We know that in aphasic patients who suffer from severe receptive speech disturbances, reading is often impaired as well.

## RELEASE OF MEANING

The fact that in cases of language pathology loss of speech is usually accompanied by difficulties with reading comprehension has important implications. For the beginning reader the visual and the auditory structure of the word are intimately bound up with each other and the graphic sign has to be translated silently or aloud into auditory verbal form. The printed word "mat" —a series of letters seen—a sequence in space—is transformed overtly or in inner speech into a series of sounds heard—a sequence in time—which in turn release the concept of "mat." Schilder found an increase of electrical activity of the vocal muscles in slow readers.

While Kainz believes that the highly skilled reader proceeds directly from the printed symbol on the page to the underlying concept, that the printed word itself is a carrier of meaning, many studies show that even the fluent reader evokes the auditory and motor images symbolized by letters, but that these images are so fleeting and of so short a duration that the individual is not necessarily aware of them. Even the practiced reader will resort to vocalization when he meets an unknown word or tries to understand a difficult passage. Inner speech phenomena are probably never entirely eliminated. How many vocal clues are needed may be a matter of reading proficiency.

## PARTIAL PERFORMANCES INVOLVED IN THE READING PROCESS

However, evoking the auditory image of the word during reading is only part of the total performance. Kainz, in analyzing the reading process, finds a number of partial performances: there is the perceptual grasping of letter and word configurations, there is their evocation in inner speech, there is the comprehension of syntactical relationships, the construction of anticipatory schemata as to what the sentence is going to say, there is finally the assimilation of content into an already existing framework. All of this constitutes an integrated performance, each part influencing the others. It is only in unsuccessful reading experiences—as when someone reads a text aloud but does not grasp its significance—that one can separate out partial performances.

## GLOBAL VS. SYNTHETIC READING

One of the basic problems in reading research is the question whether the skilled reader adds letter to letter or rather sound groups to sound groups in order to comprehend the word, or whether the printed word is experienced globally. An answer to this question is obviously pertinent in terms of the battle now raging between the people who teach reading in a global fashion and those who believe that words should be broken up into their phonetic elements and then blended into larger units.

The philosophical foundation for the global approach is based on Gestalt psychology, and it is thus imperative to discuss briefly how this theory influenced the different systems of teaching reading.

## SOME GESTALT CONCEPTS

Gestalt psychology, as originally conceived by Wertheimer, defines Gestalt as that function of the organism which responds to a given constellation of stimuli as to a whole. There is an innate tendency in human beings to experience whole configurations. We respond to a given series of separate musical tones as to a tune—a melody—even when it is transposed into a different key. The single element—the separate notes—are different, but the essence of the configuration stays constant, the "figure" as Wertheimer calls it, the tune, in this particular case—remains the same. We respond to an arrangement of pencil strokes as to a square even if the square is presented at a different angle. As defined by Gestalt psychology, visual forms obey certain laws:

1. Form is characterized by being separated and standing out from the ground.
2. The whole and its parts mutually determine each other's characteristics.
3. The various parts of a form have different values, some are indispensable if wholeness is to be retained, others are relatively unnecessary.

These are only a few of the Gestalt laws.

## APPLICATION OF GESTALT CONCEPTS TO READING

The original Gestalt experiments were done with simple visual forms like circles and squares. Although letters are, of course, more complex—quite apart from the fact that they have symbolic significance—much of what is true for simple forms, is also true for letters and words. We do not see all the single elements in a word, we see its characteristic features. Words have a physiognomy, derived from the particular relationship between the whole and its parts. This physiognomy makes it possible to recognize these words no matter whether they are printed large or small, black or red, whether the print is good or relatively poor. We know that if one tears a word apart and prints it in separate syllables it takes 66% longer to read, because, as a result of the syllable division, the Gestalt quality gets lost. In one of his experiments Korte presented words from a long distance so that they were at first quite indistinct and diffused. The first impression of the word was a global one, including Gestalt qualities like length, density, and so forth. The second phase of recognition began with the moment when characteristic details were recognized as physiognomic and as definitely influencing the total Gestalt.

Because fluent readers are global readers, educators and psychologists have concluded that the best way of learning to read is by the global approach. However, it is only the proficient reader who sees words in a structured and organized way. The beginning reader does not—his ability to differentiate and to integrate is as yet undeveloped and as a result he often cannot cope with long and complex configurations in the form of words. Shorter configurations as represented by letter and letter groups are often easier to take in for the beginning reader. A letter, of course, is a Gestalt also, a partial Gestalt it is true, but possessing, nevertheless, the same qualities as do whole words. We see the single elements in a letter as little as we see the single elements in a word—we only see characteristic features which enable us to recognize the letter as such—whether printed in black or in red, written in one handwriting or in another. Like a word, the letter also has a Gestalt in the sense that it is separate, that it stands out.

What it amounts to is this: There is no essential difference between the recognition of letters and that of whole words. The process is the same: letters as well as words are grasped on the basis of their determining features. Proficient readers tend to take in more complex Gestalten, but even if they grasp them as wholes, they still must be able to analyze them quickly and reliably into their elements. Reading requires both integrative and analyzing competence.

Thus, the dichotomy between the reading of parts and the reading of wholes is largely an artificial one. In normal reading the grasping of complex configurations and the integration of partial ones goes forward simultaneously. It is the combination of both which makes for good reading. The approach depends largely on the age of the reader and on the reading goal. A research paper is read differently from a light novel. When one has to read a large number of newspapers one takes in only the essential words. However, the beginning reader is unable to "skim"—this is a technique he still has to learn. Integrative and differentiating functions develop only slowly. In the light of this statement what happens to the young child who is first confronted with the printed word?

## READING READINESS

Reading readiness is a much discussed concept and has numerous facets. Language growth—and reading is one aspect of such growth—is closely related to the climate of the home. The quality of the mother-child bond is a significant factor in early ego organization and thus basic to verbal communication.

Some children fail in reading because of severe psychopathology, much of their psychic energy is blocked off and not available for learning of any kind. Diffuse anxiety, extremes of aggression and submissiveness, psychological infantilism, may all result in a learning disability. Some children are so passive, so phantasy-ridden, that they have little to invest in academic work. However, these children will tend to do poorly in *all* subjects, not in reading only; their difficulties are usually non-specific.

In some homes there is little verbal communication. The cultural level is low, there are few, if any books available, the children are never read to; theirs is an environment deprived of important verbal experiences. For such children language is not a comfortable tool and reading is likely to present problems.

The correlation between intelligence quotient and reading readiness has been discussed extensively and it has been shown that intelligence is by no means always a reliable indicator of future reading performance. Lately the concept of mental age has been stressed rather than that of I.Q. Most investigators feel that the child must have attained a mental age of between six and six and one-half years in order to successfully deal with printed words.

However, by no means all children with a mental age of six and one-half years are able to cope with visual verbal forms. Our guidance clinics, our schools, and our private offices are filled with youngsters whose mental age is ten years or older and who fail in reading, writing, and spelling for a variety of reasons.

The author feels that "developmental age" is a better yardstick for reading prediction than either intelligence quotient or mental age. There are many lively, reasonably well-adjusted youngsters with excellent reasoning ability, whose developmental age is low. These children suffer from what Bender calls "maturational lags." Language growth and development do not exist apart from organismic growth. Learning to read depends more on maturation than on I.Q., although these two are, up to a point at least, related. Dyslexic children are often neurophysiologically immature. In order to integrate successfully the visual and spatial patterns as they are represented to the child on the printed page, physiological functions underlying such complex activities as reading, writing, and spelling must have reached a degree of maturation.

## MOTILITY

There is, to begin with, the youngster's motility patterning. A young child's movements involve the total organism, they are random and little organized.

The ability to move isolated parts of the body develops later out of this generalized pattern. Young children are normally immensely active, their postural reflexes and their tonus reflect a primitive state of C.N.S. organization. They respond to external stimuli in an undifferentiated, global, and sometimes explosive way. Learning to pattern motor and behavioral responses, however, is required in first grade where the youngster is expected to sit still for a considerable length of time.

## FINER MOTOR CONTROL

Orton was the first to point to dyspraxic features in dyslexic children. Rabinovitch refers to their non-specific awkwardness and clumsiness. Movements require patterning. A skilled motor act, as Gestalt theory points out, is not merely a summation of isolated events; a series of separate movements will not necessarily result in a fluid rhythmic performance. To hold a pencil and learn the rudiments of writing requires a degree of finer motor control which not all children have reached at the age of six and a half years. Youngsters with severe writing difficulties lack the control needed for the rhythmic flow of pressure and release required in the writing act. Indeed, we find many older dyslexic children whose written compositions look like those of youngsters who have just begun to write. Their letters are crudely executed and in some severe cases we find continuing difficulties not only with spacing, but with the formation of the letters themselves.

## PERCEPTION

Not only the formation but the very recognition and identification of letters is difficult for some children. Perception starts out as an only crudely differentiated process and becomes more precise as time goes on.

Intact sensory equipment is not all the young child needs in learning to speak and read. It is not sufficient for the three-year-old to *hear words*, he has to differentiate between a bewildering variety of phonemes. In the same way, it is not enough for the six-year-old to *see* letters and words. His peripheral and central visual apparatus must be mature enough to discriminate between minute differences in the shapes of letters and words.

For some children nothing on the printed page stands out—in Gestalt terms the "figure" and the "ground" are fused, and as a result, the printed page looks like an undifferentiated and meaningless design.

Beginning readers and immature older children do not perceive words as structured wholes, but as a jumble of details lacking organization. As Langman puts it, "they do not perceive the complex and distinct internal designs of words, nor do they respond to their general shape and outline." Young children are often unable to grasp the physiognomic features of words, the specific relationship between the whole and its parts which, according to Gestalt theory, makes a word or a letter look familiar. They sometimes recognize a word in one situation, perhaps in heavy black print against the background of a white card. However, the perceived Gestalt is unstable and the child might fail to recognize the same word when it is embedded in a page. For successful reading the youngster's perceptions must be mature and stable enough to allow him to transpose the word or letter configuration into different situations, so that he can differentiate between a *t* and an *f* or a *d* and a *b*, whose only discriminating feature is orientation in space.

## SPATIAL ORGANIZATION AND PRINTED LANGUAGE

Since reading is a pattern laid out in space, it is pertinent to discuss briefly spatial organization in young children. The point of origin for all spatial relationships is the child's body image. His own body is the frame of reference. Between the age of three and four the child's image of his body—its parts and their relationship to each other—still is fairly undifferentiated. Body image is determined by laws of growth and development. It unfolds in the course of a maturational process by integration of the child's sensory, motor, emotional, and social experience. Spatial organization in the pre-school youngster still is at a primitive level. Many five-year-olds are unable to see the difference between the picture of an object and its mirror image. Furthermore, the child acquires only slowly the verbal concepts expressing spatial experiences. He has to learn what "upside down" or "right side up" means. As a matter of fact, acquisition of these verbal labels helps to fix the relationships themselves.

Laterality implies an internal awareness of the two sides of the body, directionality is the ability to project this awareness into extrapersonal space.

Ambiguous laterality is frequently found in combination with disturbances in understanding and formulating of spoken and printed language. Most young children are ambidextrous and only slowly develop a functional superiority of one hand over the other. Thus it is of interest that Subirana reports that E.E.G.s of strongly right-handed children are more mature than those of ambidextrous ones. This would tend to prove that laterality has maturational aspects as well as genetic ones as emphasized by Orton. Zangwill resolves the apparent dichotomy between a genetic and a maturational point of view by postulating a constitutionally determined maturational weakness in children whose laterality continues to be ambiguous.

Some researchers feel as does Harris that failure to develop a superiority of one hand over the other may result in difficulty with consistent left to right progression which is essential for reading, writing, and spelling in our culture.

## VISUO-MOTOR ORGANIZATION

One of the ways we judge spatial organization is by means of the Bender Gestalt test, which is designed to evaluate visuo-motor organization. The evolution of visuo-motor Gestalten is primarily a developmental process, and the youngster who is expected to cope with reading and writing must have visuo-motor experiences similar to the adult's. The Bender Gestalt test correlates highly with existing reading readiness tests and it has been shown that the visuo-motor competence of poor readers is inferior to that of good ones. Difficulty with arrangement of the Gestalten on paper, tendency to rotation, and verticalization all bespeak the dyslexic child's troubles with spatial patterning.

### TEMPORAL ORGANIZATION AND ORAL LANGUAGE

Language in its different forms is organized in a time-space pattern. Chesni and Simon say that dyslexia is a disturbance in spatio-temporal organization, which consists, according to Hardy, in failure to "perceive and reproduce the serial order of auditory and visual information." As discussed earlier, oral language, which demands sequential organization in time, is intimately linked to reading.

Disorders of auditory memory span and difficulties with auditory discrimination interfere not only with speech, but also with reading and spelling. In spelling the simple recognition of visual configurations is not sufficient. Spelling requires reproduction of these configurations, and if temporal representation is inadequate, spelling difficulties are bound to follow. Vernon says that bad spelling reflects a lack of phonetic appreciation. Reversals of sounds in speech show up in reading reversals. Trouble with the intonational and melodic aspects of oral language are usually reflected in arrhythmic and non-fluent reading. It is quite possible that the same basic disturbance in temporal patterning underlies the rhythmic disorders of both reading and speech.

There is an abundance of literature dealing with the relationship between poor articulation and dyslexia. It is less well known that inadequate inner language structure and grammatical deficits will tend to interfere with the formation of anticipatory schemata in reading.

Another aspect which has been largely overlooked, and which we have long felt is an important factor in dyslexia, is word-finding difficulties. The child who has trouble evoking familiar word concepts when presented with pictures, is bound to have difficulties with the printed symbols representing these words. Rabinovitch feels, as does the author, that anomia—word-finding difficulty—is a significant and often neglected cause of reading disabilities. Dyslexic children's vernacular may be adequate, but they are frequently unable to remember not only the letters of the alphabet, but also the names of weeks and months. Since naming is a conceptual function, difficulty with naming would reflect problems of a categorical nature.

Another and very important speech disturbance is cluttering, which is characterized by extremely fast, arrhythmic, and disorganized verbal output and is frequently associated with severe spelling disabilities. The clutterer's reception and reproduction of auditory configurations is usually diffused and poorly structured—he will tend to say "monstry" for "monastery," and this is the way he will spell the word. His poor auditory discrimination is directly reflected in his inferior spelling.

### Individual Endowment in the Different Modalities

We know that normal individuals' endowment differs in terms of the various sensory modalities. I now refer to the auditory, visual, and motor types described by Charcot and discussed by Freud in his paper on Aphasia in 1886.

Children vary enormously in ability to deal with the various sensory modalities. Some show excellent competence in the visual-spatial area, in striking contrast to their weakness in the auditory-motor realm. Others show a different pattern: excellent auditory ability while visual-spatial performance lags.

We are now testing approximately 100 children by means of a battery of 37 maturational tests for a reading prediction study on the kindergarten level,* and we are trying to get an impression of each child's maturational pattern in the various modalities and in the following areas: motility, gross and fine muscular coordination, laterality, visuo-motor organization, body image, figure-ground discrimination, auditory competence, receptive and expressive aspects of oral language, and matching ability. So far we have observed a number of phenomena:

1. There is a striking difference in children's performance from month to month, between the ages of five and six, before they have been exposed to formal learning. Apparently this age span is a crucial one in terms of maturation.
2. Some of the children's maturational patterns are bizarre in the sense that they are far advanced in one modality and quite slow in another one.
3. Some youngsters seem to mature slowly in all modalities in spite of good reasoning ability. One gets the impression that they have trouble with the structuring of Gestalten on different levels and in various areas. Their immature motor patterning, their trouble with organizing auditory and visual stimuli into sharply and clearly delineated configurations, their primitive perceptual and motor experiences, and their difficulty with reception and expression in oral speech seems to reflect some basic Gestalt weakness—perhaps as Bender and Subirana suggest—some inherent maturational deficit.

### Implications for Teaching

What then are the implications for the teaching of reading? Most children learn to read regardless of the method of teaching. They learn to integrate

---

* Grant from the Health Research Council of the City of New York, Contract No. U-1270. The preliminary report will be published by Harper and Row in October 1966.

short configurations into larger ones and analyze wholes into their determining parts, simply by being exposed to them over a period of time and by being given some organizational principle to help them unscramble printed patterns. The majority of bright youngsters learn to integrate and differentiate toward the middle or end of first grade, and as time goes on they acquire a stable enough perceptual organization to enable them to maintain a "linguistic Gestalt."

However, there are many other children for whom specific teaching approaches will make a world of difference. And only if we study the various sensory modalities differentially will we find out what type of learning a child can use best. The work done by Hardy and Wepman in the auditory realm and the very important new investigations done by Birch in the area of auditory-visual integration have significant implications for learning of both normal and handicapped children.

Since, as the author tried to show, reading requires both the grasping of wholes and the analyzing of parts, there is no real dichotomy between the teaching of whole configurations and that of separate units which are blended into larger entities. What method is best depends entirely on the individual child, his specific competence and weakness, and his differential maturation in the various modalities.

The youngster who has "physiognomic" troubles, as it were, for whom words do not easily become familiar even after many exposures, the child whose visual-spatial competence is lagging, will do better with phonics, which involves temporal rather than spatial organizational principles. If the child's auditory ability is adequate, phonics will make it easier for him to link the visual with the auditory structure of the word. Moreover, since the learning of smaller units reduces the complexity and length of Gestalten, such a child will find it easier to cope. Phonics does not, of course, mean the simple adding of sound to sound—after laboriously blending short units, there comes a moment when the process changes qualitatively and the Gestalt "jells"; only from that moment on the child is actually reading.

On the other hand, there are children who cannot possibly be taught by phonics. Children, for instance, who have trouble with analysis and synthesis, whose intellectual potential is low, whose auditory competence is weak, whose frustration level is too low to build up words slowly and patiently from their determining parts, will undoubtedly do better with the whole word approach.

It is not easy for the overburdened classroom teacher to investigate each child's competence and weakness. On the other hand, awareness that avenues of approach are not necessarily the same for all children, has significance for all teaching, not only for reading. Such awareness is especially important in dealing with those children whose maturational pattern is markedly uneven. Much time and effort could be saved by careful study of the differential maximal learning modality in children.

Kofka says any perceived Gestalt is a product of organization and maturation and is promoted by training. Such training contributes to the formation of essential sensory-motor patterning in the Central Nervous System. We know from animal experiments that the non-use of a function leads to atrophy. Thus, the emphasis on maturation should not be understood to mean that one should sit back and let development do the rest. The clinician's and educator's task is to study carefully the maturational level of the different modalities in each child who has difficulties. Thus, in the framework of a warm and supportive relationship the teacher can help the child perform at the highest level of his potential.

## To Sum Up

Reading is one segment of the interrelated skills which we call language. It requires a relatively high degree of integration and differentiation. If viewed as immaturity of Gestalt functioning, many of the correlates of reading difficulties like reversals, poor auditory discrimination, figure-ground difficulties, and poor oral speech become a comprehensible part of the total picture.

Differential study of the maturational level of the various sensory modalities will prove to be helpful not only for remedial work, but will also, in the last instance, provide another avenue for exploration of educational tools and methods.

# CONCRETE THINKING AS A FACTOR IN READING COMPREHENSION *

James Jan-Tausch

*There are individuals who do not read well; and if they had a choice in the matter, many of them would rather work with their hands and deal with concrete, specific objects than read. In listening to these people speak we notice that they talk about objects and events in their immediate environment and usually in boring detail. They seldom come to a well-ordered generalized conclusion about the state of affairs in the world.*

*Jan-Tausch throws light on some of*
*these problems as he discusses concrete thinking as a factor in reading comprehension.*

*1. Compare and contrast the author's concept of reading with that of de Hirsch.*

*2. Why do people who are largely limited to concrete thinking experience have difficulty with reading?*

*3. What advantages might the tests of concrete-abstract thinking have over typical group intelligence tests?*

*4. State the article's key ideas.*

* FROM Challenge and Experiment in Reading, J. Allen Figurel, editor, Internationl Reading Association Proceedings, VII (New York: Scholastic Magazines, 1962), pp. 161–164, reprinted with permission of James Jan-Tausch and the International Reading Association.

EDUCATORS have long been concerned and perplexed by the children of normal or superior intelligence who do not seem to be able to profit from instruction in the field of reading. Much has been written about the diagnosis of reading difficulty, and much has been done to improve the tools used to measure the factors involved in the reading process. Materials for use in the reading process have become more and more plentiful and methods of instruction have come under close scrutiny by the lay public as well as by the professional educators. Despite the advances made in the past half century there still remain ten to twenty-five per cent of the school population who have varying degrees of reading disability.[1] The diagnostician has frequently found, after gathering evidence of a child's vision, hearing, intelligence, experiential background, emotional stability, and ego development, that he has not arrived at a satisfactory answer to his problem. The missing factor (or factors) is still being sought.

That the missing factor is constitutional in nature and may be found in the neural development of the child or the brain damage of the child, is more than a mere possibility, Delacato reported his findings in this area to this very conference in 1960. That such lack of development or damage exists and produces an effect which limits the child to concrete behavior, has been demonstrated by Goldstein and Scheerer and others in studies started as far back as the 1930's. To be able to prove that behavior limitation of a concrete nature is an important factor in reading retardation could possibly contribute to the discovery of an important elusive missing factor in reading retardation diagnosis.

The reading act requires facility in comprehending symbols. To comprehend symbols the child must acquire methods of abstracting meaning through the use of experience, context clues, thought phrasing, recognition of semantic variations, and story organization. "The mind is assailed by every word in a paragraph. It must select, repress, soften, emphasize, correlate and organize, all under the right mental set." [2] Growth in reading then depends upon the child's ability to build thought units from sight words, to analyze the structure of words, to see relationship and common properties in words, phrases, and sentences.

Finally, reading may be thought of as a complex response to symbol-stimuli. It is made by the total organism and involves many mental processes. The interests, values, and attitudes of the organism may determine the particular response to any specific reading situation.

The study I report to you is concerned with the influence of a particular attitude, *concrete thinking*, upon the reading response.

[1] Guy L. Bond and Miles A. Tinker, *Reading Difficulties*. New York: Appleton-Century-Crofts, Inc., 1957, p. 7.
[2] Edward L. Thorndike, "Reading as Reasoning: A Study of Mistakes in Paragraph Thinking," *Journal of Educational Psychology*, 8:329, June 1917.

## I. The Problem

The purpose of the study was to determine the relationship, if any, existing between reading comprehension and concrete thinking as measured by standardized reading achievement tests and by selected parts of the Goldstein-Scheerer battery of abstract and concrete thinking tests.

*Abstract attitude or behavior* is interpreted in this study of the terms of Goldstein and Scheerer as conscious activity in the sense of reasoning, awareness, and self-accounting of one's doing: the transcending of the immediately given situation, the specific aspect or sense impression; the deriving of common from particular properties; the orientation of action by a rather conceptual viewpoint, be it a category, a class, or a general meaning under which the particular object falls; the detaching of one's self from the given impression, and the individual thing representing an accidental sample or representative of a category.

There are various degrees of abstract behavior corresponding to the degrees of ideational complexity which the performance in question involves. For instance, the highest degree of abstract behavior is required for the conscious and volitional act of forming generalized and hierarchic concepts or of thinking in terms of a principle and its subordinate cases and to verbalize these acts. Another instance of similar abstract behavior is the act of consciously and volitionally planning or initiating insightful behavior without a distinct awareness or self-accounting of every phase of its further course. As a special instance of the latter degree, the understanding of symbols or metaphoric thinking and intelligent behavior in everyday life may be considered. Here it is mostly the directional act which is abstract and the ensuing performance runs off on a concrete plane—until difficulties arise. Then the required shift again calls into play the abstract, anticipatory deliberation, and so on.

A gradation applies just as well to concrete behavior. The most concrete way of dealing with situations or things, is to react to one aspect of them exclusively; i.e., reacting to one global impression or to one color alone, to a particular form of an object, to one property of it, as, for example, its practical usage. A less concrete approach is indicated when the person is unreflectively embracing in his scope the total, palpable configuration of an object or situation, and is not determined in his response by any one impressive peculiarity of it. An unreflective variation of perspective toward the situation is less concrete than a rigid fixation to one aspect of it.

It would seem, therefore, that a child's learning progress in reading, provided he has the necessary intellectual capacity, follows closely his freedom from the limitations of concrete thinking.

Specifically, there should be an increase in the reading comprehension achievement of the child as the ability of the child to think abstractly increases, and a retardation in reading comprehension as the child is limited to more concrete levels of thinking. There should be a positive statistical relationship between performance on the Goldstein-Scheerer tests of abstract and concrete thinking and the reading comprehension results as measured by a standardized reading comprehension test. It is also assumed that the child cannot behave in reading in a more mature manner than his level of capacity to think. It is further assumed that reading comprehension is essentially a thinking process which requires ability to manipulate verbal symbols.

One hundred seventy children were chosen for the study, all of whom were pupils of the public schools of Springfield, New Jersey. The intelligence quotients of the children ranged from 79 to 133. Two-thirds of the group had I.Q.'s ranging between 90 and 115 as measured by the California Short Form Test of Mental Maturity.

There were 32 children from the fourth grade, 40 from the fifth grade, 46 from the sixth grade, and 52 from the seventh grade. At each grade level half the number were boys and of each sex half were advanced readers and half were retarded readers as measured by the California Reading Tests Form CC of the Elementary series for the children in grades 4, 5, and 6, and Form AA of the Intermediate series for the children in grade 7.

Each child was administered the Color Form Sorting Test and the first six designs of the Cube Test in strict adherence to the instructions given in the respective manuals. These tests are designed (a) to detect impairment of abstract behavior and assess degree and extent to which different performance fields have thereby suffered, and (b) to provide diagnostic criteria of pathological concreteness. The tests are performance tests in which the use of language is not essential, though verbal responses are not excluded. The tests present tasks where proper solution requires an abstract approach manifested in the performance and failure or errors reveal abnormal concretization.

The resultant data was assembled and separate studies were made according to sex, age, and intelligence, in addition to a grade level and total group study of the concept attitude and reading achievement results.

The evaluative procedure recommended by the authors of the tests was examined for criteria by which levels of success or failure on each item could be recorded.

Data were compiled in the form of "yes" or "no" on each test by each pupil. These and other pertinent data were analyzed according to *chi*-square formulas for statistical significance.

## CONCLUSIONS

1. An over-all comparison of performance showed that a significant difference in abstract and concrete behavior was found to exist at the one per cent level of confidence between the advanced and the retarded readers when concept attitude was measured by the Color Form Sorting Test and the first design of the Cube Test.

2. Advanced readers with but few exceptions are also abstract thinkers. The exceptions may be due to validity error in the Goldstein-Scheerer tests, in faulty administration or scoring of the tests or the exceptions may be

erroneous categorizing of the advanced reader. The exception may also be due to factors unknown.

3. Retarded readers are retarded because of limitation to concrete thinking but the data tends to bear out many previous studies that indicated as causes of reading retardation such other factors as vision,[3] hearing,[4] poor ego development,[5] and poor instruction.[6]

4. Girls tend to behave more abstractly than boys. This may be a clue to why boys have a higher incidence of disability in all phases of language than do girls.

5. The significance of the relationship between concept attitude and reading achievement tends to become greater in the higher grades. This suggests the possibility that reading comprehension at higher levels takes on more abstract qualities.

6. Although intelligence testing almost always includes tests of concept attitude, it is possible to have similar intelligence quotients and dissimilar reading achievement when age and grade are held constant. As intelligence scores are usually the average or sum of several factor scores, it is possible that similar I.Q.'s may in one case include an abstract attitude and in another case the abstract attitude would be missing.

7. The results of this study reject the null hypothesis that there is not a significant difference in ability to behave abstractly between advanced and retarded readers.

[3] C. A. Selzer, "Lateral Dominance and Visual Fusion," *Harvard Monographs in Education, No. 12.* Cambridge: Harvard University Press, 1933.

[4] G. L. Bond, *The Auditory and Speech Characteristics of Poor Readers.* New York: Bureau of Publications, Teachers College, Columbia University, 1935.

[5] L. K. Barber, *Immature Ego Development as a Factor in Retarded Ability to Read.* Unpublished Ph.D. Thesis. University of Michigan, Ann Arbor, 1952.

[6] L. Cole, *The Improvement of Reading.* New York: Farrar and Rinehart, Inc., 1938.

# DEVELOPING FLEXIBILITY— THE ABILITY TO READ FOR DIFFERENT PURPOSES

## INTRODUCTION

*Flexibility is a characteristic of the mature, healthy, creative personality. Rigidity is a characteristic of the immature, unhealthy, and imitative personality. Flexibility is characteristic of a Leonardo Da Vinci; rigidity is exemplified by an Adolf Hitler.*

*Just as there are behavioral differences within a species, there are also behavioral differences across the broad spectrum of species represented among living organisms. The flexibility-rigidity dimension is related to differences in personality characteristics among humans, and also to differences among behavioral characteristics between higher level and lower level organisms.*

*Generally speaking, the lower an organism is on a scale of complexity, the more limited the range of activities it is able to perform; the less complex are these activities, the more rigidly it performs the activities, and the shorter the time until the organism reaches developmental maturity. The progression is easy to see if we compare the behavior of organisms as we go up the complexity scale from earthworm to cat to chimpanzee to man. Flexibility is seen as a characteristic of the human personality and mentality; and within the species Homo sapiens, flexibility is a characteristic of the creative, effective personality; for example, the creative musician and architect, the creative writer, the creative reader!*

*Just as we shift gears and drive at different speeds to accomplish such varying purposes as threading our way through traffic, turning a corner, driving up a mountain road, or passing a car on a four-lane highway, so must we "shift gears" to accomplish our various purposes for reading. If a person uses a wrong speed and approach to accomplish a particular driving task, the result can be deleterious. In like manner, the individual who uses an incorrect speed and approach to accomplish a particular task or purpose in reading will reap equally disastrous results.*

*A key to creative, effective reading, then, is flexibility—adjusting the reading speed and approach to the difficulty of the material, and the purposes for which it is read. The authors of the articles in this unit generally agree with this thesis. Spache explores the scientific possibilities of a "potential breakthrough of the limits of reading skills imposed by current training methods." Letson clarifies some of the basic problems in the area of testing speed and comprehension in reading and points to the need for flexible approaches in reading. Fisher shows the teacher how to overcome some of the limitations associated with the use of reading training machines. And, in the last paper, Sister M. Herculane investigates the ability of junior high-school students to adapt rate of reading to reading purpose.*

# IS THIS A BREAKTHROUGH IN READING? *

George D. Spache

Anyone who has taught a course in reading improvement has been beleaguered by those who want to know if "you teach that speed reading." Extravagant claims about the merits of certain commercial ventures in teaching speed reading have been aided by a few testimonials from national figures, and traveling exhibitions of speed reading by graduates of these courses who apparently are extremely intelligent individuals.

In this report Spache succeeds in restoring a balanced view to the matter of speed reading by analyzing the claims of one of the commercial speed reading ventures. His analysis consists of (1) examining claims in the light of scientific facts about reading, and (2) performing an experiment with graduates of one of the speed reading institutes.

1. To what basic problems does the author address himself?

2. Why would the resolution of these problems be of interest to teachers?

3. Of what importance is the distinction that is made between skimming and reading?

4. To what conclusions did the author come as a result of the demonstrations? What are your reactions to the entire matter?

IN THE *Reading Teacher* of November 1960 the methods of the Reading Dynamics Institute of Washington, D. C., were mentioned as possible indications of a potential breakthrough of the limits of reading skills imposed by current training methods. This article is written to explore the scientific possibilities of such a breakthrough. The problem is well stated by Dr. Howard N. Walton:

Within the past few years numerous reports have appeared describing the phenomenally high speeds achieved by students of speed reading training programs. Reading rates ranging from 2,000 to 8,000 words per minute are often reported. One newspaper article told of an individual reading at 30,000 words per minute. Information of this nature is being disseminated by various journals, magazines, brochures and circulars, with radio and television joining the chorus. We often hear people speak of other reading feats, these being performed by mental giants, who are capable of reading a page at a glance and those, with a more "limited span," grasp complete paragraphs with a single fixation. Since these reports are being circulated, it would seem desirable to conduct scientific inquiry concerning their validity (7).

---

* FROM *The Reading Teacher* (January 1962), pp. 258–263, reprinted with permission of George D. Spache and the International Reading Association.

Recent reports which are typical of those to which Dr. Walton alludes are the following quotations:

From the Tampa *Tribune*, March 26, 1961:

The picture of reading at 10 times today's speeds with better comprehension was painted by Mrs. Evelyn Neilson Wood, a reading specialist working on half a dozen U.S. campuses weekly as well as for the Air Force Academy.

and several paragraphs farther on:

She said once the system is perfected that the entire page can be seen at a glance—and understood completely—and that speeds of more than 12,000 words a minute are possible for the best of those who work to perfect their reading.

and still farther on:

She contacted scores of people in all parts of the nation who read at 1,500 words or so a minute and studied their habits.

"They all read straight down the page," she told the USF audience, "and they told me they saw whole groups of words, groups totaling as much as half a page at a time."

and again:

A 12-week study session, Mrs. Wood said, with two hours of class work weekly and another hour a day in practice can bring average reading speeds of between 2,000 and 3,000 words a minute with full comprehension.

Out of a class of 25 or so, several will get no better than 1,800 words a minute and several more will push beyond 6,000 words a minute, she told the USF faculty and students (4).

Or this statement from *Family Weekly:*

If you are average, you are reading this page at a speed of about 250 words a minute. If you will work an hour a day for 12 weeks and attend classes for 30 hours, Evelyn Neilson Wood of the Dynamics Reading Institute in Washington, D. C., can teach you to increase your speed by 10 times, to 2,500 words. And if you are a rare person, with an affinity for rapid reading, you can learn to cruise through a book at the "impossible" speed of 25,000 words a minute (3)!

Or, more recently, from the New York *Times:*

The operators of this particular speed reading system called reading dynamics say they do not feel satisfied if their pupils are reading fewer than 1,000 to 2,500 words a minute at the end of the twelve-week course.

If a student is particularly adept and does his homework—at least an hour a day —he may, it is claimed, come to read 6,000 or more words a minute. The pace of the average college graduate is 350 words.

But if you let your eye sweep over it, say from top to bottom, you grasp the idea of it quickly.

So you turn the pages with your left hand and run your right hand down them with a gently caressing motion, letting your eye follow the right hand from top to bottom instead of reading across the lines from left to right (6).

These quotations consistently repeat certain statements as though they were common knowledge. These claims might be summarized as follows:

1. Reading speeds as great as several thousand words a minute are obtainable after special training. Speeds ranging from 1,000 to 25,000 words per minute are mentioned in these various articles.

2. These reading speeds are attained not only without loss in original reading comprehension, but are accompanied by improved comprehension.

3. These extraordinary reading speeds apparently result from abandoning the usual eye movements in reading line-by-line and substituting vertical movements down the page, guided or paced by a rapid vertical movement of the free hand. Large groups of words, perhaps as much as half a page, are read with one fixation.

4. On numerous occasions, former students of the Reading Dynamics Institute have apparently demonstrated their ability to read at these exceptional speeds, with good ability to recall and discuss the material read.

If these claims can be substantiated, then practically all present methods of training intended to improve rate of reading are, by comparison, antiquated and ineffectual. It is imperative, then, that these claims be examined scientifically.

1. *Is it physiologically possible to read at speeds of thousands of words per minute?* The answer to this question hinges, of course, on the definition of the word "reading." If we interpret the term in the common understanding of reading most of the words on a page, *it is impossible to read faster than 800 to 900 words per minute.* This fact derives from the amount of time necessary for (1) the shortest fixation (approximately 1/6 to 1/5 of a second) during which reading occurs, (2) for the sweep or saccade to the next fixation (1/30 to 1/255 of a second), (3) for the return sweep to the next line (1/30 to 1/25 of a second), and (4) the maximum number of words that the eye can possibly see with a single fixation during continuous reading (probably 2.5 to 3 words). Obviously, these estimates of average adult performances, first established by Javal in 1878 and reconfirmed by Buswell (1), Walton (7), and many others, may be modified by the degree of complexity of the material and the comprehension demanded. However, the figures do not vary considerably; even in tasks in which practically no comprehension is demanded, as Walton has shown, the fastest average time for a fixation was 1/6 of a second.

Gilbert (2) has shown that processing (reading) two-word phrases requires .17 to .18 second, while a three-word phrase demands over .25 second. The conditions of his experiment did not demand continuous reading, which usually requires longer fixations for apprehension. Moreover, Gilbert's students read tachistoscopically, rather than at reading distance, thus permitting a larger span of perception than in the usual act of reading. Thus, Gilbert's data confirm that the shortest possible fixation in reading two or three words is at least 1/5 to 1/4 of a second.

Expressing these figures in different form, it is apparent that the minimum time to read a ten-word line of four inches is approximately .66 second, assuming that it is possible for the shortest duration to co-exist with the largest span.

| | |
|---|---|
| 3.3 fixations (.166 sec.) | .547 sec. |
| 2.5 saccades (.033 sec.) | .083 sec. |
| 1   return sweep (.033 sec.) | .033 sec. |
| | .663 sec. |

A number of European and American researchers have shown that at reading distance the maximum possible span of apprehension of the human eye is about two inches (approximately 5 or 6 words). Letters outside of this span cannot be distinguished. Even all the letters or words within this span are not clearly visible and must be deduced by context. Only words within a span of one inch (2.5 or 3 words) are seen with greater than 50 per cent acuity.

But, assuming that the reader can recognize and comprehend the maximum span of three words per fixation, and that there are *no* regressions, the line of ten words is read in .66 of a second, or at a rate of approximately fifteen words per second or nine hundred words per minute. Any speed greater than this involves omitting lines, the technique recognized by most authorities as skimming, not "reading." It is apparent that the upper speeds suggested as feasible in these various newspaper articles are not possible in the act of reading as here defined, but must be characteristic of such performances as skimming or scanning, in which relatively large portions of the reading material are skipped.

Tinker (5) similarly concludes from his review of eye-movement studies that "any rate of over 800 words per minute can only mean that the reader is skimming rather than reading all the material." He also bases his calculations on three fixations in a ten-word line.

Granting that the special techniques taught by the Reading Dynamics Institute could not result in extraordinary speeds of reading, as that term is commonly understood, but rather in some sort of skimming or scanning technique brings us to the second question.

2. *Is comprehension at the normal levels of 70–80 per cent present when using the Institute's special method of "reading"?* It is interesting to note that according to this author's knowledge students trained at the Reading Dynamics Institute usually refuse to answer questions on the material they have read. They also believe that current reading tests cannot possibly measure their speed and comprehension and, therefore, decline to take such tests.

Thus, to our knowledge, no scientific test of the improved comprehension claimed to result from this special training has previously been available. At least, there has been no publication of data which would substantiate this claim of improved comprehension, of which this author is aware.

To secure such data, we began a year ago the collection of records of the eye movements of students before and after their training by instructors of the Institute. These graphs were recorded on the latest eye-movement camera, the Reading Eye. Two kinds of records were obtained, one in the act of reading one of the test selections which are supplied for use with the camera; and second, the act of skimming the pages of a book. Comprehension checks by true-false questions accompanied both types of reading. Inspection of these graphs reveals the following:

1. As a result of the special training these students showed a small average gain in rate, approximately 20 to 25 per cent in various groups.

2. In the test selections no students showed exceptional speeds of reading, the average for various groups falling in the 400–600 words per minute category. The fastest rate recorded was about 900 words per minute.

3. In the skimming records various groups covered 1800–2400 words per minute.

4. Comprehension in the test selections was normal (70 per cent or better) before and after training. The gain in comprehension after training averaged less than 5 per cent.

5. Comprehension in skimming was weak, averaging about 50 per cent after training.

3. *Are the usual eye movements, present in reading line-by-line, replaced by vertical eye movements down the page when using the Institute's special method of "reading"?* Does the reader recognize large portions of the page in a single fixation when trained by this special method? The eye-movement records cited earlier again refute the belief that the students of the Institute succeed in reading large portions of the page at a single fixation. While skimming, the students made approximately one fixation per line, then moved vertically to the next fixation on the next line or two. Occasionally, the graphs show some tendency to read horizontally for a fixation or two.

Few eye-movement records of individuals skimming are available for comparison. But, as most reading teachers will recognize, the Institute's trainees were using a normal skimming pattern, similar to that taught in many reading manuals and clinics under such titles as skimming, surveying, previewing, etc. The rates achieved in this skimming are not very high, and, if we may judge by the comprehension achieved, neither is the skimming very effective.

4. *What do the demonstrations by former students of the Institute, in which they apparently "read" at exceptional speeds, mean?* The author was privileged to see such a demonstration conducted and directed by Mrs. Wood at Texas Christian University. The demonstration was given by three of her pupils before a meeting arranged during the sessions of the National Reading Conference. It was witnessed by perhaps two hundred persons who were

either attending the conference or came especially for the demonstration.

The Institute's pupils were permitted to select from a number of college textbooks. Each chose the book he would "read." He then made an intensive survey of the contents of the book, and particularly the chapter he intended to "read." The pupil took notes, or made an outline, memorized a few statistics, facts or simple quotations, as he chose. The time necessary for this pre-reading study, extending to perhaps five or so minutes, was not considered as part of the pupil's "reading."

When the pupils had finished their survey to their own satisfaction, they signified their willingness to begin "reading." A three-minute time limit was agreed upon. During these three minutes the pupil turned with one hand the pages of the book he had previously studied, while pacing his skimming down the page with the other hand. At the end of three minutes, one student had "read" ninety-three pages, another, more than seventy-pages, and the third probably "read" a comparable amount.

The students declined to answer direct questions on the material, on the plea that they were not trying to demonstrate a memory stunt, but simply showing the results of their reading. They volunteered to discuss what they had read, and each did so for approximately five to ten minutes, or until the chairman requested him to stop.

During this discussion each pupil cited approximately the few statistics or quotations he could have previously memorized during the pre-reading survey. He also demonstrated an excellent background of information in the field of the book he had selected to "read," by allusions to other comparable materials.

If we assume that each pupil's post-"reading" report was based on the skimming he did, this would be a most impressive demonstration. It is this author's opinion that the pupils' facile oral reports were based (1) on the information gained during the pre-"reading" survey or (2) on their previous familiarity with the field of the book they "read."

This article is not written to disparage the efforts of the Reading Dynamics Institute or any of its personnel, for it is apparent that they do produce some degree of reading improvement in their pupils. Rather, we have tried to examine scientifically some of the newspaper and magazine reports regarding the Institute's unusual methods and results.

## REFERENCES

1. BUSWELL, GUY THOMAS. *Fundamental Reading Habits: A Study of Their Development.* Supplementary Educational Monograph, No. 21. Chicago: University of Chicago Press, 1922.
2. GILBERT, LUTHER C. "Speed of Processing Visual Stimuli and Its Relation to Reading," *Journal of Educational Psychology,* 55 (Feb. 1959), 8–14.
3. MITCHELL, CURTIS. "She Can Teach You to Read 2500 Words a Minute," *Family Weekly,* February 5, 1961, pp. 18–19.

4. "Ten Times Present Speeds—Specialists at U(niversity) S(outh) F(lorida) Teases Professors with Promise of High Speed Reading," *Tampa Tribune*, March 26, 1961.

5. TINKER, MILES A. "Recent Studies of Eye-Movements in Reading," *Psychological Bulletin*, 55 (1958), 4.

6. "12 Lawmakers Go to Reading Class," *New York Times, Sunday*, June 11, 1961.

7. WALTON, HOWARD N. "Vision and Rapid Reading," *American Journal of Optometry and Archives of American Academy of Optometry*, 34 (Feb. 1957), 73–82.

# TESTING SPEED AND COMPREHENSION IN READING *

Charles T. Letson

*It has been said that getting the right answers requires asking the right questions. Many right answers are needed in the field of testing speed and comprehension in reading. Some of the right questions are: Can we safely assume there is only one reading speed, or one kind of reading comprehension? Which tests will measure the kinds of speed and comprehension that we are interested in measuring? Are criteria available for selecting such tests? What practical tips are available for helping students improve in reading? These are the questions. The answers are found in this article by Letson.*

*1. In the introductory remarks the author makes several assumptions. What happens if we grant these assumptions?*

*2. Do you agree that the limiting factor of speed, or timing, should not be included in a good test of comprehension? What reasons are adduced for this practice?*

*3. Examine several tests of reading rate to see how they meet the eight criteria for rate tests set up by the author.*

*4. Try to arrange the "cautions" in descending order of importance.*

J UST BEFORE the turn of the century, certain discoveries in eye movements called attention to the element of speed in reading. This added a new dimension to the concept of reading ability so that it became a composite of comprehension *and* speed. No one will disagree that the ultimate aim of all

---

* FROM *Changing Concepts of Reading Instruction*, J. Allen Figurel, editor, International Reading Association Proceedings, VI (New York: Scholastic Magazines, 1961), pp. 225–228, reprinted with permission of Charles T. Letson and the International Reading Association.

reading is better understanding—or comprehension. However, we must recognize that, in an age where the demands of time are so pressing, the comprehension should be accomplished in as short a time as possible. There are those who question the importance of speed and feel that it is being overemphasized. On the other hand, there are those who realize the need for faster reading and feel that it should occupy an important place in reading instruction today.

Before examining the testing of speed and comprehension in reading, it is necessary to know what is meant by the two terms. Any testing that involves silent reading undertakes a difficult task, for silent reading is a personal experience that is performed behind closed doors, as it were. It is impossible to know what takes place in the mind of the reader, and any attempt to do so only interrupts the reading act. This imposes restrictions on the testing and limits the resulting information.

## The Nature of Speed and Comprehension

Speed and comprehension are, to begin with, general terms. Each one is influenced by a number of related factors. Comprehension, for example, means generally to understand what has been read; *but* does this mean ability to recall ideas and facts, or to draw inferences, or to recognize the author's intent, or to criticize the thought, or to appreciate the style? In the instance of speed, we also encounter a number of related factors. Do we mean rapid reading of easy or of difficult material? Do we mean prolonged, uninterrupted reading, or do we mean reading short, unrelated passages? Is the reading for recreation, for mastery, for the general idea, or for any of a hundred other purposes?

It is little wonder then that the relationship of speed and comprehension is beset with a certain amount of confusion. If it were possible to test each of these factors separately without influence from the other, our job would be somewhat simplified. We would give a test of comprehension, for example, and include no time element whatsoever, thus obtaining what is referred to as a "pure" measure of comprehension, or power. This, of course, can be done, provided unlimited time is available. But when we come to test speed, it is impossible to omit comprehension. We must know something about how well the material was read—indeed, that it was read at all.

Thus, we see that whereas comprehension can be measured without time, speed cannot be measured without some kind of comprehension check. This leads to the conclusion that a test which measures both speed and comprehension is essentially measuring speed; comprehension, serving as a check, becomes secondary in importance.

From this we may conclude that the best tests of comprehension are those in which the limiting factor of speed, or timing, is not included. The Gates reading survey tests fall into this classification. We may further conclude that the best tests of speed are those in which the limiting factors are kept at a minimum. Laycock[1] states that "The purest (speed) test comes with passages which make practically no demands on intelligence or prior knowledge." Gulliksen[2] defines a pure speed test as a "test composed of items (questions) so easy that the subjects never give a wrong answer to any of them."

These suggest that in tests where rate of reading is the prime concern, neither the material nor the questions should be of such difficulty "as to cause the reader to interrupt his rate of reading to reread involved, complex or profound ideas such as one might expect to find in tests whose chief objective is to measure comprehension or in tests of critical thinking."[3]

## SELECTING AN APPROPRIATE TEST

A reading test should measure those aspects of reading found in the course of study, and subsequent instruction should be directed at improvement in the areas tested. In order to select a rate of reading test that will be appropriate, we must first determine *what kind of speed* we wish to measure. There are a number of kinds of speed, and different tests measure different kinds. For example, the reading section of the *Cooperative English Test*, one of our better-known tests, yields scores in three areas: *vocabulary, speed of comprehension,* and *level of comprehension.* For purposes of convenience these are usually reduced to the single-word terms of *vocabulary, speed,* and *comprehension.* This means that the *speed* score, which includes time spent in reading, rereading, thinking, and answering questions, is not a rate of reading score but rather a rate of working score. A reading test that includes a *speed* score should, therefore, be examined to find out what kind of speed is being measured and to make sure the test is an appropriate one. For instance, in a class where instruction is on rapid reading of longer selections, a test that measures time spent on reading *and* answering questions would not be measuring the kind of reading being taught. For this, the survey section of the *Diagnostic Reading Tests* contains a rate of reading score that measures speed of continuous, uninterrupted reading and would therefore be appropriate.

Complete information relative to the various kinds of reading tests, together with critical reviews by leading authorities, may be found in Buros' *Mental Measurement Yearbooks* (Gryphon Press).

Other factors that influence speed and comprehension in reading should be considered in the selection, or construction, of reading tests, include: difficulty level of the material, interest appeal and familiarity of the material, the purpose of the reading, and the method of measuring the performance.

---

[1] Frank Laycock, "Incorporating Flexibility into Reading Rate," *The High School Journal*, 39:134–140, December 1955.

[2] Harold Gulliksen, *Theory of Mental Tests.* New York: John Wiley & Sons, Inc., 1950, p. 230.

[3] Charles T. Letson, "Speed and Comprehension in Reading," *Journal of Educational Research*, 52:49–53, October 1958.

Authorities in the construction of tests whose primary objective is to measure rate of reading have recommended the following principles:

1. Continuous, uninterrupted text is preferable to short, unrelated passages.
2. Longer selections yield more reliable rate scores.
3. Difficulty level of the material should be appropriate to the purpose.
4. Interest level of the material should be reasonably high.
5. Material that is of a neutral nature and does not favor any subject area is preferable.
6. Time taken to answer questions should not be included in the rate of reading score.
7. Questions should be answered untimed and without recourse to the text.
8. Questions should be of appropriate kind and level of difficulty.

## INFORMAL TESTING

So far all references have been to standardized tests of reading which yield data that is general but necessary to any program of instruction. For the teacher who wishes to carry out further diagnosis of reading problems in the classroom, informal tests will take over where the standardized tests leave off. These enable a teacher to check quickly and frequently pupil progress in the skill being taught.

To test speed and comprehension informally, the teacher chooses from texts, readers, magazines, or any available source, an appropriate selection for silent reading and prepares a set of comprehension-check questions. In this way, the difficulty level of the material and the questions is entirely at the discretion of the teacher who knows best the immediate needs of the pupils in the group.[4]

For the teacher who wishes to test speed and comprehension regularly on graded materials, such sources as Simpson's SRA *Better Reading Books 1, 2, and 3*, (Science Research Associates), will provide selections and questions for classroom use, as well as graphs for charting daily progress in both speed and comprehension.

## CAUTIONS

Because of the numerous variables present, the area of testing, and instructing, in speed reading, harbors a number of problems that teachers should be aware of:

*First*, speed is a kind of refinement, to be encouraged only after the mechanics of reading have been mastered. It is mainly for the able, better readers. Any attempt at making the poorer, handicapped readers read faster can only result in frustration for both pupil and teacher.

[4] Charles T. Letson, "Building an Informal Flexibility Test," *Education*, 80:537–539, May 1960.

*Second,* a popular misconception is that speed reading is applied to everything read. This is farthest from the truth. The speed should be according to the purpose and the difficulty of the material. There are times when a good reader reads rapidly and times when he reads carefully and slowly. The important thing is that he is able to read fast when the occasion demands.

*Third,* many teachers and authorities want to know when to begin instruction in reading faster. Good teachers start as early as possible; they do not emphasize speed; but as their pupils make the transition, for example, from oral to silent reading, they point out the differences and encourage them to read more rapidly in their silent reading.

*Fourth,* the level of material suitable for instruction in rapid reading is often misunderstood. Pupils learn to read faster and gain fluency of eye movements on easier materials. As improvement occurs, the difficulty level of the materials may be increased.

*Fifth,* and lastly, overemphasis of speed should be avoided. Pupils sometimes are inclined—and encouraged—to work for impossible gains. This is, of course, absurd, and the proper use of comprehension checks should prevent this tendency.

### CONCLUSION

There can be no doubt that speed occupies an important place in the program of reading instruction and therefore in testing. Together with proficiency in comprehension, it constitutes the highest achievement in effective reading. But like dynamite, like atomic power, it must be handled with knowledge and caution.

# TRANSFER TECHNIQUES IN READING IMPROVEMENT COURSES *

Joseph A. Fisher

*There are many problems connected with the use of specialized equipment in reading improvement programs. In this article Fisher points to the need to re-evaluate both materials and teaching methods if federal monies available for materials, such as reading machines, are to be spent wisely. It is Fisher's view that certain limitations associated with the use of these machines can be attributed to the way they are used by the teacher rather than to the machines themselves. The basic purpose of this paper is to explain proven tech-*

---

\* Written especially for inclusion in this volume.

*niques whereby "transfer of the mechanically induced improvement of reading skills to the normal reading situation" can be effected.*

1. *What are some of the problems connected with the use of specialized equipment in reading improvement programs?*

2. *How can the two major problems associated with intensive pacer work be solved?*

3. *What is the "reading score"?*

*What are the advantages of using the reading score?*

4. *How can the teacher "wean" students from the pacer?*

5. *How does one justify the use of the tachistoscope in reading improvement work?*

6. *How are progress charts used to best advantage?*

7. *What can be done legitimately to insure increases in comprehension scores?*

THE AVAILABILITY of federal monies for establishing and equipping reading improvement programs has done much to alleviate the age-old problem of finances that has traditionally plagued school systems considering such programs in the past. In order to insure that the money be wisely spent, it is reasonable to expect that it should also serve to stimulate considerable re-evaluation of teaching methods and materials as well. It is not surprising, then, to find many schools taking long hard looks at the specialized equipment being offered by various manufacturers as adjuncts to reading improvement programs in a serious effort to assess their true value.

In all likelihood, not all such reviews will be equally critical or motivated by the same needs. No doubt there will be found some newly-appointed program development committees, composed of members largely ignorant of the more subtle aspects of remedial teaching, who will eagerly welcome the advice and guidance of equipment manufacturer salesmen in the selection and use of equipment and materials. Without questioning the sincerity of either party, this probably amounts to a delegation of the committee's responsibility in most cases. Others too, recognizing that it will probably be difficult—if not impossible—to employ a fully-trained reading specialist to conduct the program will, unconsciously at least, expect the equipment and materials purchased to compensate for the lack of training in the teacher. For them the purchase of such equipment represents a kind of insurance against failure of the teacher to achieve the sort of minor miracle that the generous financing of such a program commonly envisions.

However the decision to purchase equipment is reached, and regardless of the motivation that originally prompted it, in most cases the sizeable capital investment such equipment represents will be justified ultimately on the grounds that it will make a positive contribution to the development of new and presumably better reading skills in those who use them. Although research findings have not yet quite justified blind confidence in all such equipment, it must be admitted that the machine approach can offer certain unique advantages.

Such devices do provide a welcome variety to the approaches open to the teacher; they regularly afford much needed motivation for students; they make it possible to effectively handle a larger group of students at one time; and they undoubtedly offer new hope for reading improvement in cases where reading is excessively slow because of bad habits, lack of confidence, or a certain compulsion to perfectionism on the part of the student. They proved effective where other methods have failed. Yet one must bear in mind that machines cannot be used successfully with all students and certainly should not be used indiscriminately with any students. These devices do not and cannot teach a child to read; they serve only as aids to the teacher in teaching the child by providing a special kind of control over certain facets of the reading process.

It will not be surprising, then, to find that many of the limitations associated with the use of such machines are not really inherent in the devices themselves but can be attributed to the manner in which they are used by the teacher. To be really effective, the training these devices afford must be transferred to the normal reading situations in which the student does his everyday reading. By using a pacer device it is quite possible to train a student to achieve quite high reading rates with good comprehension, only to learn that he is unable to read at even half that rate when unassisted. The unusually wide recognition spans which students learn to use effectively in tachistoscope work are almost impossible to find in use in the normal reading situation of those same students. There is, therefore, a valid basis for the criticism of reading improvement statistics based directly on skills employed while using various reading improvement devices. They are only measures of the student's success in learning to read with the device, and are not necessarily valid measures of the improvement that will be shown in normal reading situations. Teachers must not confuse learning to read *with* a machine with learning to read *from* a machine.

The procedures or techniques used to affect the transfer of the mechanically-induced improvement of reading skills to the normal reading situation thus becomes the central problem in the effective use of equipment for improving reading skills. The purpose of the present discussion is to explain several proved techniques whereby such transfer can dependably be achieved for each of the more commonly used types of devices employed in machine-oriented reading improvement programs.

## READING ACCELERATORS OR PACERS

Reading rate is perhaps the most readily measured phenomenon associated with reading and, because it appears to be dependent upon habit to a large extent, it has proved to be the most easily-improved reading skill. Devices which have been designed most specifically to improve rate of reading are generally referred to as reading accelerators or pacers. Regardless of type, whether driven by spring, gravity, or electricity, and whether the pressure to read faster is derived from a moving shutter, a bar, or a beam of light, all are designed to place the reader in a position in which he must read at a rate fast enough to outdistance a moving object or find it either impossible or inconvenient to see the reading material.

Student motivation for pacer work is usually quite high and is not noticeably affected by the usual factors of sex, age, or intelligence. Probably this motivation is founded on the feeling of accomplishment or success that one receives when beating the pressure mechanism to the bottom of the page. This page-end reward is immediate and recurrent, two characteristics of reinforcement having known validity in establishing new habits. Because of the unquestionably objective evidence the pacer affords that he is performing effectively at a given speed, the student is more willing to set new standards with confidence.

Two major problems are associated with intensive pacer work. First, there is danger that the student will become so fascinated with the challenge of beating the shutter to the bottom of the page that he will begin to neglect his comprehension. Younger children particularly seem to become satisfied with very superficial reading comprehension when they are allowed to work too long with pacers, but almost any student will give some evidence of this if he is not properly supervised. This problem is readily controlled, and may even be eliminated entirely by providing frequent comprehension checks over all material read with the pacer. Probably no more than twenty minutes should ever be devoted to pacer work in a given class period, but even during this twenty-minute period several comprehension tests should be taken. Students who achieve below the 70 per cent level on such tests should not be allowed to increase their reading speed further until their comprehension scores improve to at least this minimum level.

A second problem arising in connection with pacer work is not so easily avoided. The very interest and support such devices afford tend to make students dependent on them. After a few weeks of practice it is not unusual to find students who can read quite rapidly and with satisfactory comprehension while using the pacer and yet be unable to read at more than half that speed with comparable comprehension without it. Frequent comprehension checks and specific transfer exercises are essential prerequisites to intelligent and beneficial pacer usage, especially in these cases.

One very effective way to provide for this transfer is to have students, after only a few periods of training, shut off the drive mechanism when beginning the fourth page of pacer reading and require them to read the remainder of the page without external pressure. The pressure should be applied again at the beginning of the following page, and the same procedure repeated again with every fourth page thereafter.

The technique is easy to implement in the classroom, if all the students are required to read the same material at a rate set by the teacher. Because the pacers will control their reading rates and the teacher knows exactly where the group will be reading at all times, it is possible to signal the students to read without pressure when the proper page has been reached. Later, after students learn the technique themselves, they can be held responsible for reading every fourth page without pressure. Since this may entail a certain amount of distracting page counting by the students, it is recommended that students mark every fourth page of their pacer reading material before beginning work. The procedure is very effective in making students aware that they must be able to use the higher reading rates they are developing on the pacer, independently of the machine.

Another very effective procedure for achieving transfer of pacer speed is to require students to take a timed reading at the end of their pacer work period. A timed reading is an article of some fifteen hundred words which students read, keeping a record of their reading time. It is always followed by a comprehension check. The procedure can be simplified considerably if all students are required to begin reading on a signal from the teacher, and the time lapsed is recorded in five-second intervals on the blackboard by the teacher. To determine his reading rate, the student need only note the time on the board when he finishes reading and refer to a conversion table prepared by the teacher. By comparing his pacer scores with his timed reading scores, both teacher and student can see how much transfer has taken place.

In all evaluations of reading improvement mentioned thus far, two figures have been employed. When both of these vary in the same direction, it is a simple matter to interpret their meaning; unfortunately, there are frequent occasions in which one may rise and the other drop. When a student reads 200 wpm at 70 per cent on one occasion and on another reads at 300 wpm with 80 per cent, he has undoubtedly improved. But when a student reads at 200 wpm with 80 per cent, and then finds that he reads 300 wpm with 70 per cent comprehension, he is less certain about his improvement. To eliminate such doubt it has been found useful to compute a single score that will make it easier to evaluate improvement by eliminating concern over whether increases in speed were justified by the loss of comprehension or vice versa. This figure is called a reading score, and it is computed by multiplying the reading rate in words per minute by the comprehension score in percentage form.

The reading score is easy to compute and provides a simple means of assessing overall growth of improvement, but it has other advantages which are not apparent until it has been used for some time. Reading rate and comprehension scores may vary widely from day to day, depending on a variety of circumstances; but the reading score, because it combines the two variables, is less effected by changes in either and tends to be more stable. Also, because it tends to weight comprehension more when speed rises and rate more when comprehension drops, it makes comparisons between easy and hard reading material more meaningful. By affording ready means of comparing pacer and independent reading, and difficult and easy materials, the reading score should be preferred as a measure of improvement over either rate or comprehension in most cases, especially where improvement graphs are employed to sustain motivation.

As work with the pacer progresses, the teacher should take active steps to wean students away from it entirely. This can be achieved by increasing the "off pacer" reading time systematically. When the student reaches the stage where he is able to read with the pacer about twice as fast as he reads without it and has adequate comprehension, or is found to be reading more than 500 wpm with the pacer with good comprehension, the weaning process should be initiated. This is accomplished in stages by requiring the student to read three pages with the pacer and the fourth without it for about one week; then the ratio is changed to three with and two without the pacer for another week or so. When this becomes comfortable, the student should begin reading two pages with the pacer and two without for another week. Then the off-pacer time is increased again so the student reads one page with it and three without it for a few sessions.

In the final stages of weaning the student uses the pacer only for a few minutes in the beginning of the period, and reads without it until the last few minutes of the practice period. Using and not using the pacer in the manner described develops a sense for speed in the student, because if his speed slackens between pacer usages the student immediately becomes aware of the change when he returns to the pacer. Used in this way the student literally learns to read from the pacer instead of learning to simply read with the pacer.

## TACHISTOSCOPE

There is considerable controversy over how valid tachistoscopic training is in improving reading skills. But because of the close relationship between reading and perception, it is possible that it has more than motivational value. There is evidence that most poor readers spend much more time than is necessary to adequately perceive what is seen in a single fixation, and anything that can even motivate readers to reduce this fixation time would be accounted valuable in improving reading efficiency.

The tachistoscope is considered by many to be a means of developing word-grouping skills which can be applied to the printed page and result in rhythmical eye movements very conducive to accuracy of perception as well as speed. The increased visual span that such training is intended to develop is probably most readily transferred if the work is inserted between pacer practice sessions. During time allotted to pacer work, the students may be interrupted for a five-minute drill with the tachistoscope. After presenting five or ten 2-word phrases flashed at 1/25th of a second, a number of 3-word phrases may be presented at the same speed. It is important that the phrases increase in length as the exercise progresses. But extending phrases much beyond four words or about fifteen characters is probably unnecessary.

Toward the end of the training program phrases of different length may be intermixed. Time can be saved in this sort of drill if the student is not required to write out the phrases, but shown the phrase and immediately given the correct response. Then he need only check with a mark to see whether he was correct or not. To be correct, it must be entirely accurate. His score is the per cent correct. The time exposure is often reduced to 1/100th of a second, but it is unlikely that reducing exposure rate below 1/10th of a second is ever actually transferred to normal reading conditions. Since it does not follow that a student who is able to read three words in 1/100th second using the t-scope will be able to read at a speed of 1,800 wpm—which is what this comes to in words per minute—it is difficult to imagine how such skill can be transferred to normal reading conditions. Hence there is little justification for developing it as a reading skill.

One feature of t-scope work deserves special attention, namely, the adaptability of this sort of drill to individual needs. The device is of considerable value in setting up a success pattern in students who have become discouraged about their progress or who possess a defeated attitude at the outset of their training program. In such cases number recognition drills seem to have a decided advantage over words or phrases, at least in the beginning. The student should be assigned to flash a series of 20 five-digit numbers only once at half-second speed. When he succeeds in correctly identifying 16 out of 20, he can reduce exposure time to one-fourth second. When necessary, in successive practice periods, higher speeds can be used to build the student's confidence even further. There is no real advantage in increasing the number of digits beyond about five because the drill is primarily designed to provide self-confidence. In working with numbers the student should write them before checking his work because of the danger of transposing digits.

When the student has overcome his defeated attitude, he may be given work with phrases instead of numbers and proceed much as the group work does. Since the value of such work lies in the tangible evidence it gives the student confidence that he can improve both in accuracy and speed of perception, there is no need to attempt a direct transfer of the skills so developed —except perhaps that with this conviction the student should be able to profit from the usual reading improvement program.

## Reading Films and Filmstrips

Reading films and filmstrips is essentially a mechanization of tachistoscopic exposure with the added dimension of rhythm and return sweep. Because of the pressure created by the sequential exposure of continuous material, these also share certain characteristics of the accelerator or pacer devices described earlier. The elimination of the time lag between successive exposures of phrases and the continuous character of the material makes the reading film much closer to a normal reading situation than is possible with the tachistoscope. This is an important attribute because it somewhat reduces the problem of transfer.

Because of common psychological foundations, transfer techniques suitable for pacer training will be suited to reading films or filmstrips as well. Just as the speed of reading developed with use of pacer devices often exceeds speed in reading without such pressure, so after using a film or filmstrip there will very likely be a dropping off in reading speed and for identical reasons. Just as the reading speed developed under pacer pressure was transferred to normal reading by following pressure periods with short unassisted reading periods, so films and filmstrips may be employed before reading short articles to increase normal reading rate.

This can be achieved by having the class set up for a timed reading as described earlier, then turning off the lights and showing a part of a reading film. After the group has become accustomed to the reading rate imposed by the film, the lights may be turned on and work begun on the timed reading. Since it is advisable to avoid unnecessarily sharp contrasts in lighting conditions, the room should not be entirely darkened when the film is shown.

## PRINTED READING MATERIALS

Though it is possible to conduct a very effective reading improvement program by employing any of the mechanical adjuncts described earlier, it would be quite difficult to imagine an effective reading program that did not make considerable use of printed materials. Because they are such an essential part of the program, the teacher should be aware of techniques which will insure that these materials are used to the maximum advantage.

Because of the premium it seems necessary to place on rate and comprehension in the measurement of reading proficiency, extensive use is made of articles for which word counts have been made and conversion tables prepared which make it possible for the student to determine his reading rate at a glance if he knows how long it took him to read it. These articles are always followed by a comprehension test the student corrects himself and determines a percentage score. Although the primary purpose of such exercises is to measure reading efficiency, a careful record of performance in the form of a graph serves the additional purpose of motivation by providing the student with visual evidence of his improvement with each successive entry. These graphic records of performance, called progress charts, are excellent motivational devices. However, it is imperative that the charts indicate a general upward trend if they are to sustain student motivation, and therefore the teacher must be careful not to allow prolonged plateaus—or continuous drops—to develop in these graphs.

To convince the student of his potential, when these discouraging points develop, the teacher could use several variations of procedure. The student may be allowed to complete such a reading using only the even-numbered questions as a comprehension check. Then, after encouraging him to exert still greater efforts at speed, he may be allowed to read the same article a second time using the odd-numbered questions as his comprehension check. This approach is effective because it allows the student to concentrate on his speed feeling that he already knows the content of the selection. The true objective of such an exercise is to increase reading speed without resorting to mechanical aids. This constitutes a transfer of speed arising from the confidence built up by a previous reading.

Less dramatic, but perhaps more generally valid, increases in speed can be achieved by having students read two articles in succession. Care must be taken in this case that the two readings assigned are of equal difficulty, or that the second is somewhat easier than the first.

Increases in comprehension scores can also be highly motivating. These can often be insured by allowing the students to skim selections before reading them. Two approaches are available. In one, the students arc allowed to read the first and last paragraphs of the article and the first sentence of each of the intervening paragraphs. Then the student is asked to pause and formulate questions for himself which he will keep in mind while reading the same article under timed conditions. This seems to enhance the student's power of concentration by providing him with a clear purpose for reading. The effect of the increased attention is revealed in proportionately higher comprehension scores for most students. An exercise of this kind is particularly valuable in cases where the student is discouraged by persistently low comprehension scores. A variation on this approach is to allow students a minute—more or less—depending on the length of the article, for skimming and having them read it under timed conditions.

Another method useful in raising comprehension scores is to allow students to read the comprehension questions before reading the article. The student should be urged to read only the questions, not the answer choices in this procedure. This type of exercise assists the student in the formulation of questions for which he should seek answers in his reading. It is particularly useful with students who find it difficult to frame valid questions prior to reading, or who have difficulty remembering them as they read. The exercise is really practice in directed reading.

As soon as the plateau or drop in the student's progress graph is improved, these crutches can be eliminated. Meanwhile, the student has been occupied with developing useful supplementary reading skills.

Undoubtedly, other effective techniques of transfer will occur to the enterprising teacher who takes time to analyze the nature of the equipment with which he works. The degree to which the teacher succeeds in achieving such transfer determines the training value of the specialized equipment at his disposal. To this same degree he will succeed in improving the reading skills of his students.

# A SURVEY OF THE FLEXIBILITY OF READING RATES AND TECHNIQUES ACCORDING TO PURPOSE *

Sister M. Herculane

*How flexible are people in problem-solving? Studies utilizing the Wechsler Intelligence Tests and certain projective techniques tell us that many individuals will not modify their plan of attack on a problem. Common sense observation also reveals those who will not experiment to find a better way of attacking a problem or accept alternative plans that are suggested. Such inflexibility in the approach to reading means inefficiency and waste of time.*

*In this research report Sister M. Herculane probes the ability of eighth graders to adapt rate of reading to reading purpose. The implications of this research are important for education.*

*1. The term "true efficiency" is used in the introductory paragraph. What does it mean?*

*2. What were the most important findings of the study?*

*3. How do you account for the performance of the pupils on the various tests?*

*4. What are the implications of this study for classroom teachers for education in general?*

D URING the past twenty years reading specialists have been stressing the need for varying the reading techniques and rates according to the difficulty of material and purpose of reading. This refined skill affects true efficiency and is definitely needed to meet the increasing demands of both extensive and intensive reading today.

The greatest stress on flexibility in reading has been in the adult and college reading courses with present emphasis on this important skill at the high school level. A survey of available literature reveals that little is being done at the elementary level.

However, since the program of instruction at the elementary level stresses the development of the fundamental skills of reading (the two principal ones being word-recognition and comprehension), the junior high school level seems to be the best suited to the formal introduction of and stress on this skill. This would mean that children entering the secondary school should have some initiation in adapting rate and technique to purpose of reading and difficulty of material.

A recent study was made to ascertain the extent to which pupils in the eighth grade vary their reading rate and technique of reading to the purpose

* FROM the *Journal of Developmental Reading* (Spring 1961), pp. 207–210, reprinted with permission of Sister Mary Herculane and the International Reading Association.

of reading. A group of 102 eighth-grade pupils, whose intelligence and reading ability were average or above average, was selected. These pupils came from three schools in a midwestern city. Since the three schools were all in the same educational system, they followed the same reading curriculum which was a sequential basal reading program with the enrichment materials commonly used in schools: supplementary books, reference material, and weekly magazines.

The schools represented different sections of the city, allowing for considerable variation in backgrounds. This variation of backgrounds included children in low as well as high socio-economic areas. They were children of professional and factory workers. As reported by the children, two-thirds of the parents were engaged in manufacturing in near-by factories. A greater percentage of them had come from a bilingual home environment.

The specific objectives of the study were:

1. To find out how much knowledge the eighth-grade pupils have acquired of various rates and techniques according to the purpose of reading.
2. To determine whether pupils are able to change their techniques of reading according to the purpose of reading.
3. To ascertain if pupils actually make the application of several reading techniques in the content fields according to the purpose of the assignment.
4. To discover whether pupils actually change their rate according to the purpose of the assignment.
5. To compare the number of words per minute for the different techniques of reading at the eighth-grade level.

To measure the flexibility of reading rate and technique, objective testing was employed. Three selections with purpose and test questions designed for three reading rates and techniques—skimming, rapid, and thorough reading—were employed. The selections, varying from 1500 to 1900 words in length, were evaluated by the Dale Chall formula for difficulty level to avoid introduction of a second variable because the study was focused on variation of rate and technique according to purpose only. During the tests, the pupils were carefully timed, and comprehension was checked. A comparison of the means and standard deviations for the tests for the three techniques of reading was made. To determine the variation of speed, the flexibility index was calculated by finding the ratio between the different techniques of reading: thorough vs. skimming, thorough vs. rapid, and rapid vs. skimming. The Pearson-Product-Moment coefficient of correlation was used to see if there was any relationship between speed used and the comprehension on the three types of reading.

After calculation of the results for the group as a whole, comparisons of the same factors for the three types of reading were made between the group which scored highest in comprehension and the group which scored lowest in comprehension.

To compare the pupils' knowledge of flexibility with the result obtained on the tests, two other research tools were used: a questionnaire on the choice of rate and technique and practices in flexible reading; a tape-recorded group-interview with the pupils participating in the study.

The data were analyzed to determine the pupils' reading power, the adjustment of rate and technique of reading to the purpose for each particular selection, and finally the ratio between the different rates of reading for the different techniques and purposes.

From the three instruments of research used in this study, it was possible to evaluate actual practices of the students, their own ideas of what they did while reading, and the knowledge they possessed of the important skill of flexibility in reading at the eighth grade level. That the pupils in this survey were unable to change rate and technique according to purpose was quite evident from a comparison of the mean comprehension and the mean rate, the ratios between the different techniques, and from the study of individual pupil performance as well as a study of the differences, which were very insignificant, between those who were high and those who were low in comprehension skills.

The findings of this investigation present the following conclusions:

1. The pupils of the eighth grades tested had a very insignificant variation in speed and technique according to the purpose of reading. The results show a difference of only a few words. Evidently the pupils had not acquired the ability at this level to adjust the rates and techniques necessary for the various purposes of reading.
2. No pupil was capable of defining or explaining the concept of flexibility of reading rate accurately.
3. Approximately ninety per cent of the pupils are aware of the need to determine the purpose and speed, but in actual performance in reading, they did not make this knowledge sufficiently functional.
4. The group had a general idea of the nature of skimming, rapid, and thorough reading; however, there was evidence of insufficient practice in changing rates in accordance with the purpose.
5. The pupils performed best in rapid reading which approximates the type most often used in classroom reading programs. Much of the material is narrative and emphasis is on securing the idea of the story.
6. Skimming was the weakest of the three techniques both in rate and comprehension.
7. Few pupils knew their rate in silent reading, and for these there was no definite agreement in their responses with actual rate of reading manifested in the tests.
8. The findings from the interview corroborated the answers of the questionnaire.
9. This survey agrees with the research studies that indicate there is a

definite lack among the eighth-grade pupils in flexibility of reading rate and technique according to the purpose of reading.

The questionnaire indicated that the pupils had some elementary knowledge of the factors of flexibility although they were very inconsistent in their responses, in practices before and during reading. The most reliable responses were in a selection of a particular technique for a specified purpose. This selection of proper technique seemed to be the aspect of flexibility best understood by the pupils.

The interview corroborated the findings secured by the use of objective measurement and the questionnaire. All the data emphasized the vagueness of the knowledge concerning flexibility of rate and technique which has evidently been introduced but has not yet been made clear to the pupils. Consequently, there is little functional knowledge of flexibility at this grade level in the particular groups participating in this study.

Implications resulting from this study show that there is a need of reevaluating the reading program at the upper elementary level to study the need for greater emphasis on the development of flexibility in reading. Furthermore, because of the recent stress at the upper levels of education on the flexibility of reading, children should have some preliminary ideas of adapting rate and technique of reading to purpose.

There are indications that teachers and pupils are unaware of this important phase of reading which affects true efficiency and is definitely necessary to meet the increasing demands, in this Age of Space, of both intensive and extensive reading.

Likewise there is definite need for pupils' evaluation of the flexibility in reading because by doing so pupils could be motivated to greater effort in developing this reading skill to the maximum. Since studies have proved that flexibility in reading is capable of being measured, teachers should demand instruments for assessing this important key to efficient reading.

Apparently, success in reading quantitatively and qualitatively is impossible without the consistent habit of adjusting reading rate and technique to the various purposes of reading. Hence there should be provision for time and place in the elementary curriculum for the development of flexibility in reading.

Section **10**

# READING IN THE CONTENT AREAS

## INTRODUCTION

*The important goals of reading instruction are growth in reading and growth through reading. This growth does not stop, but it can be slowed down because of lack of adequate reading instruction at the time when it is needed—the high school years!*

*As the student advances through junior and senior high school, the reading materials increase in complexity and difficulty. In addition, new, higher-level purposes for reading place greater demands upon the reader. Since the subject matter teacher has the responsibility of teaching his students to think more effectively about the ideas in his subject—and reading is a thinking process—it follows that the subject matter teacher bears much responsibility for helping his students to improve their reading skills.*

*The nature of this help is two-fold. First, the teacher helps the students apply the basic reading skills to the reading task. (How these skills are taught initially was discussed in the first nine units.) Secondly, these teachers teach their students the specialized reading skills and modes of inquiry that are specific to their particular subjects. How the basic skills are applied in the content areas is discussed in some of the articles in unit ten. Most of the articles are devoted to explaining how to teach the specialized reading skills needed to master a subject.*

# READING AND INDUSTRIAL ARTS; INTERVIEW *

Gordon Funk

*Reading plays a vital role in developing competence in the industrial arts. Funk discusses the nature of this role and how industrial arts teachers can capitalize on what is known about helping students improve their reading skills. He shows how the ten basic reading skills can be applied specifically to industrial arts.*

*1. List in descending order of importance the ten most important concepts discussed in this article.*

*2. Evaluate, in terms of these ten concepts, the reading instruction aspects of an industrial arts class, or program, with which you are familiar.*

*3. What basic steps would you take to implement the initiation of reading*
instruction in industrial arts classes?

*4. State the article's key ideas.*

*The belief that industrial arts—as a phase of general education—has a role in fostering improved ability in reading —as the basic facet of the three "R's" —indicates that I-A instructors should re-examine their teaching practices in this area.*

*The following report questions Gordon Funk, supervisor of industrial education for the Los Angeles, Calif., City Schools on: (1) the modern concepts of presenting reading and how they should be incorporated into industrial arts education; and (2) how, specifically, the ten basic skills of reading are presentable in the typical I-A program.*

Q. *Mr. Funk, why would you say, first of all, that the reading program has special implications for industrial arts?*
A. The role of industrial arts in the total pattern of general education in the secondary school certainly implies an objective for our field of reinforcing and expanding the three "R" skills. And I believe there are two reasons why industrial arts educators should expand their practices in the methods used to teach and to develop the first "R," reading. First, many secondary students, who have a deeper interest in industrial arts than in academic subjects, have achieved reading levels no higher than the intermediate elementary grades and need additional reading practice which can be gained through this motivation. Secondly, methods used to develop basic reading skills have special applications to the development of reading ability in the highly technical subject matter of industrial arts.

---

* REPRINTED FROM *Industrial Arts and Vocational Education*, L (October 1961), pp. 24, 25; 45. Copyright, 1961, The Bruce Publishing Co.

Q. *In illustrating this role, wouldn't the changing concepts in the modern reading program provide a basis for discussion?*
A. Very definitely. Before industrial arts instructors will acknowledge the point of view which involves their acceptance of an expanded responsibility for reading instruction, they must become aware of, and accept, the modern concept that there is no subject matter of reading; that all teachers in secondary education share in the responsibility for teaching reading; that the elementary school does not have the sole charge for teaching reading skills. And beyond that, the I-A instructor must accept the concept that a reading program conducted within his specialized field, is not only beneficial to the reading program but also to the subject field.

Q. *What is the status of research in this area?*
A. To my knowledge there is no published research available with regard to the results of a reading program in industrial arts; however, research by Kathleen B. Rudolph [1] definitely established that a reading program in the social studies area helped the student master the subject more adequately, while improving in reading skills and increasing reader comprehension. As a result of this reading instruction, pupils improved in such reference skills as notetaking, outlining, and summarizing, as well as in the ability to comprehend written materials.

Q. *And you would say that this has direct applications in industrial arts?*
A. It is reasonable to assume that a high degree of basic reading ability, supplemented by specific instruction in the reading skills pertinent to industrial arts, would find that there was growth in overall reading ability as well as a quickening of abilities in the mechanical areas. And Rudolph's study implied that such superiority in social studies content achievement can be accomplished in a similar manner in regular industrial arts instruction patterns without additional class time or additional expenditure for reading instruction.

Q. *How, then, can and should industrial arts contribute specifically to reading?*
A. First, let's identify the reading skills most needed by learners. Then we can demonstrate how these skills can be developed in the I-A program. A widely accepted list is that organized by Simpson in her manual, *Helping High School Students Read Better:* [2] (1) developing reading readiness; (2) reading to get the main idea; (3) reading to get important details; (4) reading to answer a specific question; (5) reading to evaluate; (6) applying what is read; (7) developing vocabulary; (8) outlining and summariz-

[1] Rudolph, Kathleen B., *The Effect of Reading Instruction on Achievement in Eighth Grade Social Studies* (New York: Bureau of Publications, Teachers College, Columbia University, 1949).
[2] Simpson, Elizabeth A., *Helping High School Students Read Better* (Chicago: Science Research Associates, Inc., 1954).

ing what is read; (9) reading for implications; and (10) increasing the reading rate.

Q. *And industrial arts has responsibilities for the development and application of all ten of these reading skills?*
A. In varying degrees, of course. This variance is in accord with the relationship of basic reading abilities to the content field, since all subject areas do not require the same reading abilities.

Q. *How does industrial arts help develop the first skill, reading readiness?*
A. As used in elementary school, readiness means the organization of the instructional program in reading to accommodate the individual pupil's physical, social, emotional, and mental development and to help this pupil acquire the understandings, skills, and attitudes necessary to master the reading material presented. Reading readiness, applied on the more mature secondary school level, promotes growth in basic reading abilities and develops skills in specialized reading areas.

Q. *And what techniques in industrial arts will accomplish these reading readiness goals?*
A. In *labeling,* tools are identified by labels at the beginning of the semester. In *identifying* as an orientation device, such as a floor plan of the shop with equipment located and numbered, is given to the student on his first day in class. Each piece of equipment in the shop has a printed identification sign conspicuously attached. Eager to become familiar with the equipment, the student completes a numbered sheet with the name of the piece of equipment listed opposite the number corresponding to that on the floor plan. In *demonstrating,* the teacher uses the technical names of all tools, material, and equipment during each demonstration. He writes the new name on the chalkboard and uses the name in context. In *technical illustration,* a pictorial representation of tools and equipment, parts are labeled.

In addition to these techniques, reading readiness is promoted in industrial arts by the very nature of the materials and tools used. When a teacher talks about a jack plane, for example, he has one in his hand and he points out and demonstrates its function and how it differs from other planes. When the teacher discusses the wood used for building a shoeshine box, he shows samples of white oak, white pine, and mahogany. The student handles each piece and notes its color, weight, grain characteristics, strength, workability, etc. These examples for nurturing reader readiness are part of the fiber of the everyday teaching process in industrial arts. Let's go on to the second reading skill, reading to get the main idea.

Q. *Does industrial arts contribute to this skill also?*
A. To develop this ability, students are taught to vary their reading rates. The speed-up reading rates used to select the main ideas are known as skimming and speeded reading. This important skill is promoted in industrial arts through the use of a textbook and supplemental books.

Q. *What are illustrations of this?*

A.  One example of this is a student in auto mechanics bringing his 1954 Plymouth into the shop. He reports to the instructor that he is getting poor mileage and has difficulty starting the car when it is cold. After trouble shooting, under the instructor's direction, the student determines that the carburetor needs to be overhauled. Before the student undertakes the job, he is questioned by the instructor as to his general knowledge about carburetion, and is referred to the section in his text which deals with this subject. His assignment is to skim the article, report back on the main idea—the function of the carburetor in the fuel system, of an automobile. Thus, through individual questioning, the instructor builds the need for the skill of skimming for the main idea.

Another example of the development of this skill consists of the student who, under instruction, determines that a wood project ready for finishing, needs three coats of semi-gloss enamel, and wants the color to be mellow ivory. To select a can of paint to meet the two specifications of color and degree of gloss, the student must skim the information on the label of the paint can to obtain the pertinent information which indicates how closely the paint meets the above specifications.

Q.  *The third reading skill, reading to get important details, would seem to have a very direct application in industrial arts. How would you illustrate this?*

A.  By going back to the paint can label. I believe we can show how success in developing this skill is important in, and directly related to industrial arts. This skill enables the student to follow specific directions, to organize work on an orderly step-by-step basis, and to be successful in using material according to directions. The paint can label supplies necessary directions which the student must understand in order to finish his project successfully. Outlines, according to the manufacturer's directions, are drying time, area of coverage (does he have enough paint to do the job?), preparation of surface to be painted, and safety instruction.

Again, this reading for specific information is handled by the teacher on an individual basis at the time of need; repeated questioning elicits the specific information and the student, in most cases, verifies the information he has read by inspection, measuring, and testing.

Q.  *The fourth skill, reading to answer a specific question, seems quite broad. How is this applied specifically to industrial arts?*

A.  This skill involves a combination of the second and third basic reading abilities, I would say. Reading to answer a specific question is concerned with locating the information which requires skimming or speed reading, the use of an index, understanding a table of contents, the importance of footnotes, alphabetizing, etc. Through the use of textbooks and reference material, the I-A instructor reinforces and provides practice in the use of the standard means of locating information. After this first step, the second phase, finding the answer to a specific question, is identical to the third skill of reading for important details.

It is in the first part of this fourth skill that the instructor has specific responsibilities for reading instruction. The reference books used regularly in I-A classes have such an unusual organization that for their correct use students need specific instruction.

Q.  *What are some examples of these specialized reference materials which require the exercise of this reading skill—accomplished, of course, on an individual basis at the time of need and in answer to a specific question?*

A.  Well, there is the *Machinery's Handbook*, which is organized in a typical reference manner, and *Chilton's Automobile Repair Manual*, which is an example of the complexity of organization of auto repair manuals. It has the table of contents arranged by topic of the separate car section and not by page number.

However, let's consider *The Radio-Electronic Master*,[3] the official buying guide of the industry. It is an example of a specialized I-A reference book which requires specific instruction in its use. The use of this specialized reference material is an example of one of the extensions of reading skills developed in Industrial Arts. As are many shop reference materials, this buying guide is not organized according to standard reference practices. It can be confusing, therefore, unless specific instruction for its use is given. Instead of an index at the back of the book, it has three separate indices: (1) alphabetical index of manufacturers, (2) general index, and (3) outlines index of display pages. These are in the front of the book and occupy the same place as the usual table of contents. The pages are not numbered consecutively, but are organized in sections A–U and numbered within each section.

In using such a reference work, students read to answer a specific question by locating the information and reading for important details. This area of reading instruction is one perhaps, which many instructors have not recognized as a contribution to their students' reading skills. Students certainly are not aware that they are acquiring reading skills.

Q.  *And the fifth skill, reading to evaluate; how does that gear with I-A instruction?*

A.  This skill enables the student to differentiate between statements of fact and statements of opinion. They also check the basis of authority for making a statement. The time that a statement was made is important, since it might have been made prior to the discovery of some new data. Students learn to evaluate by comparing statements made by different authorities and then to check these authorities whenever possible by direct experience and research.

Q.  *And how is this accomplished in industrial arts instruction?*

A.  This is, perhaps, the least used reading skill in Industrial Arts, but on

[3] *The Radio-Electronic Master*, 20th ed. (New York: The United Catalog Publishers, Inc., 1955).

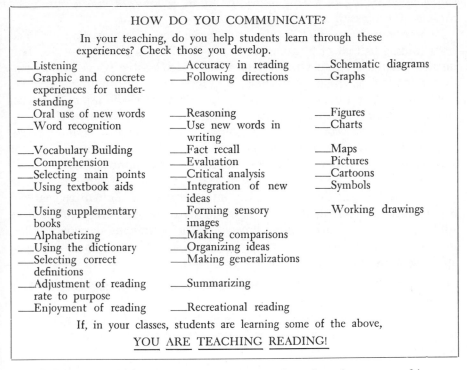

HOW DO YOU COMMUNICATE?

In your teaching, do you help students learn through these experiences? Check those you develop.

___Listening
___Graphic and concrete experiences for understanding
___Oral use of new words
___Word recognition

___Vocabulary Building
___Comprehension
___Selecting main points
___Using textbook aids

___Using supplementary books
___Alphabetizing
___Using the dictionary
___Selecting correct definitions
___Adjustment of reading rate to purpose
___Enjoyment of reading

___Accuracy in reading
___Following directions

___Reasoning
___Use new words in writing
___Fact recall
___Evaluation
___Critical analysis
___Integration of new ideas
___Forming sensory images
___Making comparisons
___Organizing ideas
___Making generalizations

___Summarizing

___Recreational reading

___Schematic diagrams
___Graphs

___Figures
___Charts

___Maps
___Pictures
___Cartoons
___Symbols

___Working drawings

If, in your classes, students are learning some of the above,

YOU ARE TEACHING READING!

*Above: a check sheet used to prove to teachers that they are teaching reading—albeit not with a drill or formalized approach.*

an advanced level, the student with experience and skill, evaluates design information, construction procedure, etc. The reading of schematic diagrams, working drawings, etc., need to be evaluated particularly those in some of the hobby magazines.

Q. *Let's go on to the sixth skill, applying what is read. This would seem to have a direct relation to I-A instruction.*
A. Absolutely. It's most important in our field and every instructor should include the teaching of this skill as a regular part of his program while using the three common methods of communication: (1) oral instruction, (2) working drawings which include some writing, and (3) written instructions. The good teacher balances, of course, these three methods of imparting information.

Q. *And what are examples of how these methods of instruction are ultilized to help students apply what they read?*
A. First, in making a job card, a sequential list of operations in building a project, the student, from reading instructions, is required to write the operations in order. (This technique parallels development of reading charts in

the elementary school.) This individual effort follows, of course, from the making of a job card as a class project.

Another operation which involves the application of information obtained from reading, is that of planning a "routing bill" for a production job. This involves planning production stations for the step-by-step operations of cutting, fastening, assembling, finishing, packaging, and distributing.

The reading of dimensions, the selection of materials, the use of fasteners, the selection of drills and taps, and the setting of a form: all involve reading followed by application. Of course, simpler examples consist of interpreting such safety signs as "place only rags here," "observe safety lines," "do not use this piece of equipment without the instructor's approval," etc.

I would say the important factor in the application of what is read in industrial arts is that the results of the interpretation of the written material is immediately apparent. It is the responsibility of the I-A instructor to have students use written material as directed, to help students develop abilities in this type of reading, and to challenge the able students with problems in applying what they read to complex situations.

Q.  *Has the seventh skill, developing a vocabulary, a high degree of application in industrial arts?*
A.   Instructors with industrial arts training have made, I would judge, more progress in the development of vocabulary than any of the other basic reading abilities.

Although there has been some recent literature published concerning the vocabulary needs for the different activities by grade level—as well as lists appearing in study guides—there is a need for basic research in the vocabulary of industrial arts subjects. The principal areas which seem to need investigation are: (1) the level of vocabulary of secondary school textbooks; (2) basic vocabulary lists developed by activities and grade levels in oral and reading and writing functions; and (3) the words which have industrial arts meanings differing from their common usage, for example, "tolerance."

But, to go on, instructors promote the development of vocabulary by labeling, by the use or completion quizzes, by captions on bulletin boards and other displays. Instructors must realize that it is not enough for them to say a word. In order for students to learn new words, they must hear it, see it, use it, and review it.

Q.  *And the eighth reading skill?*
A.   Before we go on to that, I would like to interject a few devices which the instructor must use to further the seventh skill. One commonly used practice is to have students develop a vocabulary list in a notebook. Another is to have a "word-of-the-week" sign in which the letters can be changed to follow a schedule to highlight important words. By including this series of words in shop demonstration and in "quickie" quizzes, the teacher helps underline the importance to students of adding technical words to their vocabulary.

The elementary school technique of using flash cards is highly adaptable here. Many teachers are using flip charts for instructional purposes with carefully prepared and labeled illustrative material; this labeling makes it easy for the teacher to coordinate oral and visual stimuli so necessary for vocabulary building.

In addition, I'm eager to learn the results of using a dictionary box. This has a series of 5 by 8 cards with an important word printed in the upper left-hand corner of each card. Immediately under this is the word divided by syllables with accent for pronunciation. Pictures and sentences illustrate the word. On the reverse side of the card will be a definition of the word. This dictionary box is essential when used by students writing job cards, bills of material, and other written reports; by amplifying dictionary information, it extends learning and increases student independence.

Q.  *And how does the eighth skill, outlining and summarizing what is read, apply to industrial arts?*
A.  Let's consider the last three skills together: the eighth; the ninth, reading for implications; and the tenth, increasing the reading rate.

Outlining and summarizing what is read facilitates organizing of important and valid information according to a purpose in mind—a study technique, according to research, which helps the learner retain more information than merely reading and rereading assigned material. This skill does have limited application in industrial arts. When we discussed the use of the job card for the sixth reading skill, we noted that this card is one form of an outline, or a step-by-step organization of doing activities.

Reading for implication, the ninth skill, is again, of relatively little importance in our field. In consumer education, though, students are taught to question material published in advertisements. Statements such as "brass finished" and "walnut finished hardwood" are analyzed.

And the tenth skill, increasing the reading rate, is approached when students are taught to adjust their reading rate from skimming to locate needed material to reading slowly to find important details.

Q.  *What would you say, then, that the Industrial Arts teacher might do by way of furthering reading skills in his instruction?*
A.  Well, on the secondary level in the Los Angeles City Schools, students are encouraged to do free reading in I-A classes. Each shop has a small library —approximately 50 books, plus magazines which apply to the area of instruction. Several magazines are supplied in classroom sets. Research has shown that there is a high interest factor, I might add, in mechanical and technical magazines and students are taught to read these for enjoyment. Above all, I-A teachers need to be aware of their role and responsibilities in reading instruction.

Q.  *Finally, Mr. Funk, would you care to suggest what might be done on different levels by way of accelerating the role of industrial arts in teaching reading?*
A.  Teacher training programs must include at least a survey course in principles and purposes of the reading program. School districts should establish

in-service training programs to enlighten industrial arts instructors about their responsibilities.

The importance of the role of industrial arts in the development of basic reading abilities is clearly evident. It must be apparent also that there are specialized reading skills peculiar to industrial arts. Our instructors should be alerted to the contribution to, and responsibility for developing this basic skill. An analysis of the more successful teachers' techniques reveals many areas where reading instruction is taking place—and it is taking place without the teacher designating the instruction as reading, in his own thought or in that of the students.

The most significant contribution that the discipline of industrial arts can make to reading is in the area of development of meaning! In the industrial society in which we live we need to understand the language of industry. In order to be an educated man in this civilization, one must have an understanding of the world of industry. Basic to this understanding is reading. And basic to all reading is meaning!

# HOW TO PROVIDE BETTER ASSIGNMENTS
## FOR IMPROVED INSTRUCTION *

John W. Struck

*What do assignments have to do with reading? Practically everything! To a large extent the nature of the reading approaches employed reflect directly the nature of the assignment given. Struck discusses various aspects of assignment making, and relates them to reading in industrial arts. These ideas have applications in other fields, also.*

*1. How important is the assignment in teaching?*

*2. Evaluate the course assignments that you have made or that have been given to you during the last week in terms of the characteristics of good assignment making.*

*3. Write three questions of each type of question for some specific material and a specific class.*

*4. In view of the many suggestions for improving reading instruction in industrial arts, criticize the adage, "Teachers are born, not made."*

*As the "starting point in guiding learning," assignments can be an effective teaching technique; this discussion tells how to use them, with information on types, characteristics, and so on.*

How many of us have fallen into the habit of making class or shop assignments in a matter-of-fact, perfunctory manner? Or worse yet, have we come to the point where assignments of homework, reports, and other

* REPRINTED FROM *Industrial Arts and Vocational Education*, LI (November 1962), pp. 24, 25. Copyright, 1962, The Bruce Publishing Co.

in-school or out-of-school work has been relegated to such an unimportant role so as to be virtually nonexistent? In both our industrial arts and our vocational—industrial classes, are we *really* challenging our students? Are we really developing minds parallel to and equal with the development of manipulative skills? Certainly we must admit to overemphasis of the manipulative phases of training at times; we must also recognize that in this modern industrial and technical world, the mental development of students is not among the least important reasons for the very existence of industrial education.

## SIGNIFICANCE OF ASSIGNMENTS

Educationally, assignments are of far greater importance than commonly recognized. As far as organized school instruction is concerned, the assignment is the starting point in guiding learning. With increased emphasis being placed upon attitudes in learning and upon the prime importance of interest, it can be seen that the assignment can, and should, become the means for a right start.

Though not intending to minimize teaching methods and organization, it has been held by many experienced teachers that (1) the desire to learn is more important than are methods of teaching, and (2) the student's attitude toward learning is more important than well-organized courses of instruction. It is precisely for these reasons that assignments are so educationally important. Through them, the teacher has many opportunities to so influence student attitudes that effective learning will result.

## RELATION TO INDIVIDUAL DIFFERENCES

All teachers recognize the existence and extent of individual differences, and assignments provide an opportunity to do something about it. The teacher can modify the assignment in amount, quality, difficulty, sequence, and type. Such changes take into account personality traits, previous experience, capacity, and other factors that must be considered in fitting work to individual requirements.

Other differences may likewise serve as guideposts in making assignments. There are differences between individuals, and also between schools and communities, such as differences in resources, equipment, facilities, public opinion, occupational opportunities, etc.

## TYPES OF ASSIGNMENTS

So important are proper assignments to today's effective teaching and so different from yesterday's type, that brief mention should be made to illustrate this point. The "old-type" assignments were usually made on the basis of pages, paragraphs, topics, chapters, or questions. Today's "new-type" form of assignments more often stresses the development of original thinking and of more carefully directed learning.

Weaver and Cenci list a variety of student assignments, such as "reports, observations, experiments, readings, investigations, shop work to be done, notebooks to be expanded, or problems to be solved." [1] Other assignments may be made on the basis of job sheets, units, projects, contracts, or work orders.

## ESSENTIAL CHARACTERISTICS

While assignments differ greatly from class to class and individual to individual, most are characterized by a number of rather essential elements. Check the various assignments you now make to see if they meet most of the following suggested characteristics:

1. THE ASSIGNMENT SHOULD BE RELATED TO PREVIOUS LEARNING. An old principle of starting with the known and proceeding to the unknown is involved here. An old, time-worn suggestion, but still excellent and worthwhile.

2. THE ASSIGNMENT SHOULD BE CLEAR AND DEFINITE. Use some of the rules of a good, concise newspaper report by indicating *what* is to be done, *when* it is to be done, *how* it is to be done, and *how well* it is to be done. It is possible for poor assignments to be definite, yet not clear to the students. Don't use hazy phrases or unfamiliar technical terms, words, or expressions. Use concrete and specific examples where possible.

3. GOOD ASSIGNMENTS INDICATE SOURCES. Save students time by mentioning specific references, materials to be used, tools and equipment needed. With more mature students, teachers may be justified in giving less detailed or specific sources in order to develop students' abilities in finding sources.

4. GOOD ASSIGNMENTS STIMULATE INTEREST. Well made assignments call into play both emotional and intellectual responses so that the problem or job will be begun with zeal. In making assignments, interest may be destroyed by too much talking, whereas demonstrations and specific examples used to illustrate what is wanted and expected from an assignment are often very effective motivators. Show students what to look for, what parts to study. Use thought-provoking questions to stimulate curiosity and a desire. Interest is also developed by appealing to desirable forms of competition and rivalry to the inherent urge of constructiveness and curiosity.

5. GOOD ASSIGNMENTS GUIDE LEARNING. Good assignments should give certain suggestions, should ask for certain information, and should lead to thought-provoking activity. It should not be so detailed that it

---

[1] Gilbert G. Weaver, and Louis Cenci, *Applied Teaching Techniques* (New York: Pittman Publishing Corp., 1960), p. 50.

requires little more ability than to do as one is told. Neither may it be so general that students must guess as to what is expected. Good assignments should not do all the thinking for the student; neither should they lack suggestions for a good approach. Assignments can direct attention to possible points of difficulty and can make suggestions concerning them.

6. ASSIGNMENTS SHOULD BE SUITED TO GOALS AND CIRCUMSTANCES. When assignments are made in industrial arts where tryouts, exploration, and guidance are important factors in the outcomes desired, they should definitely encourage student growth in these directions. But when assignments are given with specific trades or vocational objectives in mind, the procedure needs to be different.

All assignments should enable students to be successful in completing them with reasonable effort. Problems and tasks should increase in difficulty from week to week in order to challenge students. Success breeds interest, confidence, additional effort, and more success. Make each assignment appropriate to the individual concerned and the objectives desired.

## Questions Motivate and Guide

Both oral and written questions serve as excellent guides to study and many a student has been motivated to do intensive reading and searching as a result of well-timed, pinpointing questions by his instructor. Several types of questions serve well to achieve this goal:

1. FACTUAL QUESTIONS. These often call for facts secured through memorization or through more thoughtful learning.
2. RECALL QUESTIONS. Should involve not only memory, but also selective thinking.
3. QUESTIONS REQUIRING REASONING AND SELECTIVE THINKING. This involves thought processes of a higher order than in the two preceding ones. Explanations of processes and principles are often called for in this type. Can be quite involved. Excellent practice and training.
4. QUESTIONS CALLING FOR APPRECIATION OR INTERPRETATION. One may know much and still lack appreciation. An assignment can be made more meaningful through questions that ask for evaluation or interpretation.

Many other types of questions also serve well. For purposes of motivating assignments, first one, then another, will serve best. A varying combination of types is also often helpful.

## Other Motivators

TRADE LITERATURE. All alert teachers in the various phases of industrial education know of the interest and appeal to students that information concerning new tools, materials, and processes holds. A wide range of educationally valuable trade literature is readily available from manufacturers and magazines. Technical advances within recent years have been rapid, affecting particularly materials which are now available. Assignments of reports and readings can be most interesting and stimulating.

INDUSTRIAL, TRADE, AND TECHNICAL TERMS. New words and terms arouse interest, and many varied and interesting assignments involving this work can be made. Simply distributing a list of technical terms together with definitions for the students to learn can be quite deadening. To explain in a class discussion what various tools are called or parts are named, and having the *student* make up a definition *which he can best remember*, is much more stimulating from the student's point of view.

BLUEPRINT READING. Assignments asking questions concerning blueprints, shop drawings, or manufacturers' schematics is like challenging students with a game or puzzle. Judicial use of such assignments offers many advantages. By asking students to make shop sketches in connection with the blueprint reading, the teacher combines muscular participation together with practice in mastering blueprints. Skills thus developed through the use of several senses, together with high interest, are likely to be more permanent.

JOB SHEETS, WORK ORDERS. Assignments of this type should not provide all decisions, but should be designed so as to give the student practice in planning and making decisions. The objective must be stated clearly, but students (except rank beginners) should plan materials to be used, estimate costs, determine order of procedure, etc. Only through practice do people learn to plan and make good decisions. It is through interesting assignments that teachers can hope to achieve these aims of their teaching.

CONTRACT ASSIGNMENTS. Probably educators borrowed the term *contract* from the field of business or industry. Just as a contract is usually made for service of considerable extent, so the contract in educational work is a large-unit assignment. In form and content, the contract should vary greatly in order to be suited to its purpose. Outcomes sought may be either highly specialized or broad in scope. The contract must not be a standardized form of school work. Flexibility is the keynote here. Relatively long-time assignments such as these have the advantage of promoting the co-ordination of learning. Various areas of learning, such as mathematics, science, and drawing, may be needed. Completion of contract assignments often cuts across traditional, academically determined boundary lines just as do life experiences. While the term *contract* is not often heard in today's industrial education shops, laboratories, and classes, it is a teaching tool well worth using.

## OPEN YOUR TOOLBOX

Good teachers, just as good mechanics, must have the best of tools to do a good job. There are *many* fine tools in the creative teacher's tool kit—each with its own special or general purpose. Among these are the various types of assignments just mentioned. Each is used to help achieve a certain objective, to get a certain job done.

Let's open our tool kit of teaching tools, dust them off, oil them up a little, and start putting these specialized tools to work. A good mechanic would never try to use an adjustable crescent wrench for everything. Neither do good teachers rely upon only a very few techniques of teaching to do the best job. With your next assignments, put some planning and thought into them—and good results will surely be yours.

# SOLVING READING PROBLEMS IN VOCATIONAL SUBJECTS *

Isidore N. Levine

*In this extensive report Levine identifies very specific reading problems that occur in vocational subjects. He gives detailed suggestions for helping the student overcome these reading problems, and he expresses a definite attitude about who is responsible for giving this instruction.*

*1. Who should help solve reading problems in vocational subjects? Why?*

*2. Do you agree with the various assumptions of the author regarding experiential backgrounds of English teachers? (See also Point Two in the summary.)*

*3. How might "English" teachers and "vocational arts" teachers work together to solve the problem raised in this report?*

*4. State the article's key ideas.*

MANY TEACHERS of trade subjects in the vocational high schools are convinced that their students can't read. The pupils show their inadequacies by being unable to cope with the texts provided for them. They indicate their limitations by their failures on the final written examinations. They are unable to read the job sheets that can be crucial in daily shop work. Every teacher would like to see some improvement in this deplorable situation.

Some shop teachers feel that reading is the job of the teacher of English. He teaches spelling, composition, vocabulary and literature—all the elements comprising the study of reading. Why doesn't the English teacher do his job well enough to solve the reading difficulties the students experience in other subjects? Perhaps the language arts teacher would assume such responsibility if he were certain he could do the work required. However, mere will-

* REPRINTED FROM *High Points*, XLIII (April 1960), pp. 10–27, by permission of the publisher.

ingness to teach "reading" does not solve special problems to be met in instructing pupils in the art of getting meaning from a page of trade information.

## Specialized Vocabulary

What are some of those problems? Suppose we take electric wiring as a possible trade subject for teaching reading. The class in English is taught to recognize the words "splice," "junction," "tap," "tee," "knotted," "pigtail," and "Western Union." The dictionary definitions of these words are as follows:

*splice*—joining of ropes or timbers by overlapping.
*junction*—joining or being joined, station.
*tap*—(1) strike lightly (2) a stopper or plug (3) tool for cutting internal screw threads.
*tee*—a mark from which a golf player starts, a little mound of sand and dirt.
*knotted*—(1) joined (2) tangled. (There are eight other definitions the teacher of English could rule out as being unrelated to electrical work.)
*pigtail*—braid of hair hanging from the head.
*Western Union*—a telegraph company.

The final electrical wiring examination includes this typical question:

To make a splice in a junction box where a number of wire leads are to be joined, the best splice to use is the (a) tap or tee (b) knotted tap (c) pigtail (d) Western Union.

No combination of definitions will yield a solution to the problem for the ambitious teacher of English. We can go farther and say that even accompanying illustrations for each of these splices would still leave the language arts instructor feeling that he was teaching an unfamiliar language.

Lest some teachers suppose that the electrical trades have the only occupational information the English teacher cannot read, we will take an example from the radio and television field. A recent final test in that subject carried this question:

In a 100% modulated AM transmitter the modulator varies the carrier (a) from zero to the strength of the carrier, (b) from zero to twice the strength of the carrier, (c) from zero to half the strength of the carrier, (d) does not vary.

As an English teacher, the writer cannot help admiring any pupil who has the knowledge and understanding to read the above intelligently—not as an academic studies teacher would read it, that is, with correct pronunciation, phrasing, inflection and emphasis, but with the meaning necessary to arrive at a correct answer and to be able to explain the reason for such selection.

As a matter of fact, the above passage takes the writer back to his high school Latin study days, when he could "read" the orotund phrases of Caesar's Commentaries with little inkling as to what that ancient was trying to communicate. In the case of radio and television, there is no Latin "pony" to help understand the above question. We can go farther here and state that no application of the thousand and one skills of reading so exhaustively described in the new Board of Education Curriculum Bulletin, "Reading Grades 7-8-9. A Teacher's Guide to Curriculum Planning," can be of any help here. Reading the above properly means studying the subject.

Perhaps other examples from the trade subjects will make this situation even clearer. In the pamphlet on "Machine Shop Practice for Vocational High Schools" (Curriculum Bulletin #10—1954-1955 Series) on page 82, we find the following in part:

Unit—How to Turn Tapers by the Offset Tailstock Method
Topic—Checking Offset with Dividers
1. Set the legs of the dividers to the required offset. Adjust set-over screws until the distance between the index line on the base and the index line on the tailstock body corresponds to the setting of the dividers.

Here the teacher of English is not too puzzled since the number of technical references is limited and there is an accompanying series of illustrations with the directions. But after calling out the words and studying the drawings we are still far from a complete understanding of this first step. These directions are not meant to be read and discussed. They are useless without the equipment to which they can be applied as far as instruction is concerned.

Another illustration from still another trade will throw light on still another facet of this problem. In the course of study called "Hairdressing and Cosmetology for Vocational High Schools" (Curriculum Bulletin #8—1952-1953 Series) we note the Instruction Sheet on page 85 includes this series of steps:

### FACIAL MASSAGE

STEPS IN FACIAL

1. Apply cleansing cream
2. Give manipulation for cleansing
3. Remove cream
4. Apply massage cream
5. Give massage manipulation
6. Remove massage cream
7. Apply astringent
8. Apply powder base
9. Apply makeup

### POINTS TO REMEMBER

Apply cream with an upward and outward movement.
To remove cream dab at it lightly with tissues.

As a male teacher of English it might be a little embarrassing to study this with a class of girls, but there would be little difficulty in interpreting and understanding the words. Here at last is a trade sheet we can read. But, would it be wise to take the time in the English classroom for this? Like Shakespeare's plays, these directions are not meant to be read aloud only. They are supposed to be *acted* out and certainly not in an English room except in pantomime. And further, the trade of cosmetology has its own foreign language. Among the terms to be studied by a language-arts teacher determined to give proper reading guidance in this occupation are included:

free edge, keratin, lunula, nippers, oil glove, pledget, French twist, effilating, sebum, bias wave, reverse roll, cuticle of hair

and hundreds of others which take years to learn properly.

## Vocations and the Language Arts

We have not discussed some of the implications of the English teacher's efforts to teach the reading of vocational subjects in the language-arts class. The woodworking boy who wants to know why his English teacher is taking the time to have his students read the expressions below would be compelling us to reexamine our goals in vocational education:

Explain how to make a mortise on a leg.
List the first five steps in squaring a piece of wood to size.
Draw a marking gauge.
Name five different types of lines used in making a drawing.
Give three uses of the hack saw.
Draw a combination square.

Do we want our vocational students to have a restricted curriculum involving trade experiences exclusively? Would any teacher of English accept appointment to a vocational high school knowing that he would be expected to familiarize himself sufficiently with the trades taught in that school to be able to teach the reading matter of those shops?

In desperation some shop subjects chairmen might suggest that the English teacher should interest himself in the trades of the school. They may not be impressed with the argument that the teacher of English selected his subject just as the trade teacher did, that is, because of a personal interest or talent in that field of study. Nor may it be important that the language arts instructor spent many years studying and preparing for the teaching of literature and composition. However, we may well ask such chairmen whether we have the right to deprive the vocational high student of his share of appreciation of the cultural products of writers in every field of literary expression.

The shop teacher presented with this situation might adopt one or both of the attitudes below:

1. The English teacher should teach pupils to recognize words, not teach the meaning of the words in a technical sense.

2. The English teacher should teach pupils the general skills of reading, such as selecting main ideas in a paragraph, reading for details, skimming, reading in phrases, reading with a purpose, reading to understand and follow directions, and many others; in sum, to develop those skills which some experts claim can be transferred from one type of reading matter to another.

## Word Recognition in Context

In answer to the first view, teachers of English claim that they are doing their utmost to assist students to use the various skills of word recognition when these skills are needed in the reading of literature in the language arts classes. For example, in the study of O. Henry's short story, "Gift of the Magi," the pupil meets the phrase "imputation of parsimony" in the first paragraph. The teacher will help the students analyze the parts of each difficult word (*im-pu-ta-tion*) (*par-si-mony*) where such analysis is needed. Then he will go on to discuss with the class the meaning of this phrase in the complete picture of that first paragraph. He will select as many such word groups for study as he thinks are material for the appreciation of an O. Henry story, with the hope that the student will be stimulated to look up such phrases as, "instigates the moral reflection," "with sniffles predominating," "on the lookout for the mendicancy squad," and numerous others.

If the trade instructor were to suggest that the English teacher take the opportunity to teach such word recognition skills using the technical terms of the shops, the answer would be that this learning activity would be a waste of time for teacher and student. As we have seen above, the English teacher does not merely analyze the word elements in "imputation of parsimony." What is more important is that he spends valuable class time discussing the meaning of the words as used in *that paragraph* of the story. If the teacher of English were merely to attempt analysis of the oral elements of the technical terms, he would be giving little assistance to the shop teacher anxious to have his students read for understanding. The pupils could call out the words from the examination of radio as smoothly as the teacher and still be no farther into reading the question than when they first started the analysis of words like "modulating."

## Transfer of Training

Going on to the suggestion that the English instructor train students in the general skills of reading other than word recognition, it can be said that such practice is given in most English classes in the vocational high schools. Most schools are equipped with reading workbooks which are used to develop the general reading skills used in informational reading. However, it has yet to be determined that any such training can be carried over into the other fields of study included in the vocational school curriculum.

Let us take an example from such workbooks to reveal the possibilties of transfer of training in reading. One of the many such used in the high schools is the Scott, Foresman text called "Basic Reading Skills for High School Use" (Revised Edition, 1958). Included in this text are 18 sections, each devoted to a different reading skill such as Main Idea, Summarizing and Organizing, Word Analysis, Phrase and Sentence Meaning, etc. Suppose we turn to the section called Relationships (cause-effect, sequence). Within this section are included twelve reading selections varying in length from 150 to 1,700 words. The titles of these passages indicate that two of them are stories (A Fish Story, Old Three Toes), nine are informational essays (The Dust Storm, The Flood, The First Basketball Game, Fire-Boats to the Rescue, It's the Ham in Them, The Giants of the Galapagos, Who Is Handicapped?, and Collecting Animal Tracks) and one is a biographical sketch (Thirteen). Students are asked to read these selections and answer questions specially prepared to develop the ability to see cause and effect relationship and sequence of ideas in stories.

It is doubtful that a student who has read all these selections and scored a high percentage of correct answers is any nearer to understanding his trade text or has become more skillful in seeing cause-effect relationships in his radio work. The thinking processes to be used in these selections are not the same reasoning skills to be applied to the trade subjects. To be specific, a reading of the most technical of these essays, "It's the Ham in Them," which is concerned with amateur radio operators, is followed by such non-technical deductions as these:

1. Why might a shut-in enjoy operating a "ham" radio outfit as a hobby?
2. Why would "ham" radio operators be valuable in any community in an emergency?
3. Why might being a "ham" be valuable to you as an individual?

Compare these questions with the following appended to chapters from the text "Elements of Radio" by Abraham and William Marcus (Prentice-Hall, 1952):

1. Why cannot the magnetic field of an electromagnet be used to send wireless messages in a practical manner?
2. Why must a reproducer be used in a radio receiver?
3. Why must a receiver have a detector?

The first set of questions can be answered without reading the text if one knows, as is explained in the first sentence of the paragraph, that a "ham" is an amateur radio operator. The latter set of questions carries no clue to the answer without the reader's having some previous knowledge and information to be obtained only in a graded course of study such as a trade subject curriculum provides.

The writer believes that most authorities who assume transfer of training in reading skills fail to take account of the cumulative knowledge of technical words and phrases needed to draw meaning from a paragraph in a textbook.

To be specific, when an English teacher uses a workbook such as "Unit Drills for Reading Comprehension" by R. Goodman (Keystone Education Press, 1955) with its 45 paragraphs and accompanying thought test questions, he is supposing that the student brings to each selection only a general knowledge of things. In fact, the pupil is expected to confine his thinking to the items in the paragraph. Thus, in the paragraph below (Paragraph 2, page 27):

If you watch a lamp which is turned very rapidly on and off, and you keep your eyes open, persistence of vision will bridge the gaps of darkness between the flashes of light, and the lamp will seem to be continuously lit. This optical afterglow explains the magic produced by the stroboscope, a new instrument which seems to freeze the swiftest motions while they are still going on, and to stop time itself dead in its tracks. The magic is all in the eye of the beholder.

The thought questions bearing on this selection are:

The "magic" of the stroboscope is due to (1) continuous lighting, (2) intense cold, (3) slow motion, (4) behavior of the human eye, (5) a lapse of time. "Persistence of vision" is explained by (1) darkness, (2) winking, (3) rapid flashes, (4) gaps, (5) afterimpression.

We will note two points here. First, the author has included no technical terms or phrases which he has not explained, or which could not be found in an ordinary dictionary. Second, there is no graded block of knowledge on which this paragraph depends for clarity of understanding.

Turning to a textbook in the trade, the above-mentioned text on elements of radio, let us study some typical paragraphs:

All the above methods of communication suffer from one common fault; they are useful only over comparatively short distances, a few miles at best. (p. 1)

Having mastered the theory of the crystal receiver, we are now ready to go ahead. If you have constructed the receiver described here and "listened in" on it, you must be aware that the crystal detector has shortcomings. First of all, it is difficult to manipulate. Not every spot will work. You must move the catwhisker about for some time before you touch a spot which enables you to hear radio signals in your phones. (p. 100)

The problem, therefore, is to devise a system that will build up the signal before it reaches the detector. (p. 200)

But corresponding points on each vertical arm are struck simultaneously and, therefore, the electrons are set flowing in these arms in the same direction at the same time (*up* in Fig. 199) and with equal pressure. Since the electron streams in each of the vertical arms are equal and flow toward each other, these streams cancel themselves out; hence we have no electron flow into the receiver, and, therefore, nothing can be heard. (p. 300)

You will notice in Figure 281 that in both curves the electromotive force and current reach their maximum in the same direction at the same time and are likewise at zero at the same time. When the electromotive force and current have this relationship to each other, we say that they are *in phase*. (p. 400)

On the other hand, the further up we go, the rarer the air gets—that is, there are fewer molecules in any volume. Beyond a distance of 200 miles from the earth's surface, there probably are so few molecules that ionization is virtually nil. So we see that the ionosphere is a layer or region beginning at about 60 miles beyond the surface of the earth and extending about 200 miles beyond the surface of the earth. (p. 500)

If some of the voltage from the bottom end of the coil is fed through a small variable capacitator (Cn), called a neutralizing capacitator, onto the grid of the tube, neutralization is achieved. The neutralizing capacitator controls the amount of voltage so fed to insure that it is just enough to neutralize that arising from the capacitance of the electrodes. Since this neutralizing voltage comes from the plate circuit, this method is called *plate neutralization*. (p. 600)

This continues until a whole series of bright spots, corresponding to the outline of the shore, have appeared on the screen of the tube. Since the screen of the cathode-ray tube is of the high-persistence type, the bright spots will remain for some time after the sweep has moved on to other angular positions. The result then would be a picture of the area surrounding the ship, whose position is indicated by the center of the screen. (p. 689)

Certain points should be made with respect to these paragraphs. The first paragraph is a sentence which has meaning only when read with the previous related sentences. The second paragraph notes the existence of a body of knowledge which must be brought to bear on subsequent pages for proper understanding. The third paragraph is again a sentence which states a problem developed at some length in previous paragraphs. It has little meaning in isolation, but is necessary for summation. Paragraph four refers to an illustration and demands a special type of reading rarely found in workbooks used in the English class. Here, the pupil's eyes and thoughts must shift from print to picture, a skill developed by comicbook readers but not usable for this text even by the most avid devotee of this art form. The fifth paragraph develops a technical term which may be the key to future pages in the book. Unfortunately the authors do not include this item in the index. Paragraph six leads the reader to believe that the authors are no longer discussing elements of radio. It contains a number of concepts which are clear only to a student of previous pages. The seventh paragraph would probably be double talk to most students in their third year of science. The last paragraph appears easy to understand, but it has a few terms which may or may not be keys to proper understanding of the passage: *e.g.*, "cathode ray tube," "high persistence type," "sweep" and "angular positions." The writer is not sufficiently conversant with the ideas to decide whether those technical words are the solution to the meaning of the paragraph. He is in the same position as an individual who has read a paragraph in a novel and attempts to compare his understanding of it with that of a person who has read the complete narrative. A typical example of this would be the following:

Tom went to bed that night planning vengeance against Alfred Temple; for with shame and repentance Becky had told him all, not forgetting her own treachery; but even the longing for vengeance had to give way soon to pleasanter musings, and he fell asleep at last with Becky's latest words lingering dreamily in his ear—"Tom, how could you be so noble!"

A junior high school pupil who has read *Tom Sawyer* with understanding would be able to explain that paragraph more clearly than a college student who had never taken the opportunity to follow the adventures of that Mark Twain hero. There is little to indicate the true age, character, or motives of the individuals mentioned. The college student would not know what Becky's "treachery" encompassed, or what "planned vengeance" included.

## GUIDED GROWTH IN READING

If then, we come to the conclusion that the English teacher cannot help teach reading in the trade subjects, what other solutions are there to our problem? Let us examine the conclusions of some authorities on the subject.

1. Mr. Herman Hall in his book, *Trade Training in School and Plant* (Century Company, 1930) has this to say about the problem:

As far as the writer knows there are few if any textbooks that are likely to be of service to the trade instructor in his teaching. There are many books which may be valuable if used as reference books for occasional use in connection with some definite job.

The academic instructor in the high school has all too often "gotten by" in his work with the help of a well-written textbook used as a sort of crutch to hold him up. Such instructors are prone to assign "pages so-and-so for tomorrow's lesson." If the instructor himself learns those pages, or even contrives to have them before him, he can sample his learner's ability to repeat the material contained in the pages. Such teaching will not meet the objectives of trade instruction.

. . . Textbooks as such have little place in trade education . . ."

2. "Guideposts in Vocational High School," a pamphlet issued by the Board of Education in 1946 states:

Teachers of all subjects, especially English, should guide the student's growth in reading. (As we have seen above, teachers of English in most vocational high schools have taken practical steps to follow that suggestion.)

3. *Methods of Teaching Industrial Subjects* (Gerald B. Leighbody, Delmar Publishers, 1946) decries this practice:

Some teachers follow the practice of assigning pages in text or reference books to be studied outside of regular school hours. The mere reading of material is no guarantee of comprehension or retention.

4. In the bulletin of June 1952 entitled, "Instruction in English and Speech," (page 57) it is stated that,

It is the opinion of the committee, however, that the problem of reading cannot be solved by the teacher of English in isolation. English is to a degree a tool subject; so to a degree are other subjects. It cannot be assumed that because teachers of English teach vocabulary, pupils will know the meaning of all words, or will understand the special vocabulary and concepts of other subjects. All departments must know the factors involved in the reading process and must take direct application of the skills which are taught in the English class.

5. The authors of "Machine Shop Practice for Vocational High Schools," Board of Education Curriculum Bulletin #10, 1954–55 Series, have this to say about the problem:

The systematic use of instruction sheets helps students learn to read and follow written directions. (page 71)

Mention of references is one means of stimulating curiosity about the subject matter and of leading pupils to subject matter that will supplement instruction. However, on the instruction sheet or otherwise, the teacher should suggest only reading that is available and within the student's comprehension. (page 81)

It is necessary to bear in mind that many pupils have difficulty in getting information and direction from the printed page; they prefer to depend on spoken language. However, the ability to follow written material is an important part of the equipment of the machine shop worker. . . .

Show the pupils exactly how to use the various instruction sheets. For example, if you are conducting a demonstration, have a pupil read aloud the steps of the operation while another pupil performs each step. (page 87)

The writer is of the opinion that we should reject the advice to use little or no reading in the shops. On the other hand, few trade instructors have the time or energy to become reading experts.

## Shop Teacher and Reading

For the shop teacher, fundamental reading tasks are involved in the job sheets which guide the pupil's work from day to day. Such instruction sheets can be made the subject of reading instruction with profit to both teacher and student. As to when such instruction can take place, it seems wise for such purposes to use the shop information period when demonstrations, lectures and discussions are an important part of the procedure.

There cannot be a blueprint for every type of reading lesson in shop subjects, or academic studies, for that matter. However, it seems to the writer that a carefully thought out lesson should contain some or all of the following steps:

1. Motivation for reading.
2. Study of difficult words and concepts.
3. Oral reading of the selection.
4. Discussion and questioning for understanding.
5. Application of knowledge gained.

Let us apply these steps to the teaching of the job sheet on page 82 of the Board of Education Bulletin "Machine Shop Practice for Vocational High Schools." (The first paragraph of that job was quoted previously.)

After the teacher has explained and demonstrated the required processes orally with the use of appropriate equipment, the attention of the class is turned toward the blackboard where the teacher has written the key words of the job. Among these would be included such phrases as the following:

1. required offset
2. set-over screws
3. corresponds to the setting
4. tailstock body
5. index line
6. tailstock assembly
7. toward the headstock
8. adjust set-over screws
9. amount of offset
10. inside caliper
11. caliper setting
12. secure the tool post
13. compound rest
14. extends far enough
15. lighten spindle lock

The meaning of each of these phrases may be checked by student demonstration or verbalization. Thus in teaching set-over screws, the instructor might have the pupil point to the equipment part and give its function if that is an important part of the learning. This helps concentrate attention on the appearance and spelling of key words. The teacher can take one or two of these words for study of correct spelling by erasing them and having a student write them in again. The rest of the class can be ready for corrective work if necessary.

After these are studied, the teacher reads the sheet orally, or has a capable student read it while the rest of the class follows the reading on their own sheets. Despite the emphasis on silent reading in our schools today, there are immediate values to be derived from reading the job sheets aloud. Just as in the study of a poem the English teacher dwells on the oral reading of the verses for rhythm, color and expression, similarly the trade instructor can read for pronunciation, phrasing and emphasis.

The lesson can be closed with a series of questions designed to develop various reading skills. Many job sheets have such prepared questions, but the teacher may wish to use his knowledge of the needs and capacities of his students to formulate his own tests of understanding. The teacher might thus ask his students,

1. Where would the caliper setting be taken from?
2. How far should the set-over screws be adjusted?

It is possible that neither of those questions would be of concern to an instructor. The writer cannot claim a knowledge of the subject sufficient to decide the points of emphasis on this particular job.

The results of this learning period can be tested through the use of a short quiz given perhaps before the next job is begun. The quiz might include objective questions requiring one-word or one-phrase answers, and one or two essay questions to be answered in two or three sentences if possible. Such quizzes have value in preparing students for final or midterm examinations. In most cases they can be marked by pupils who are provided with key answers.

## DEVELOPMENTAL LESSON AN AID

Two things should be noted concerning this lesson. First, this training in reading skills closely parallels the developmental lesson which is the stock-in-trade of every teacher. Second, this procedure follows the steps taken in learning a language. We begin with listening and go on to speaking, reading and writing. If it is argued that the difficult words and phrases can be explained through the use of a technical dictionary, it should be understood that mere definition too often means substituting one set of unknown words for another set. For example, the definition of a set-screw as given in the glossary of W. L. Shaaf's *The Practical Outline of Mechanical Trades* reads, "A screw, usually hardened, which is used to lock a machine part in position by pressure on the point." However, when a set-screw is actually shown to a class and its function observed, its definition can be derived by the pupils themselves. In fact, preparing a clear definition of a term may be a test of knowledge in shop subjects. Such facility with trade language may not mean the making of a good workman, but all things being equal, a worker who can handle the language of his trade in reading and writing will probably be the more efficient mechanic.

Authorities on the subject of reading list a number of skills which should receive attention in developing the ability to following directions. Thus, in the bulletin "Reading—Grades 7-8-9" previously mentioned, such achievements as these are listed:

1. Recognizing need for preliminary reading.
2. Care for complicated or confusing statements.

3. Recognizing need for understanding the purpose of each step.
4. Recognizing need for second reading.
5. Visualizing steps during re-reading.
6. Need for final review before applying directions.

Most of these excellent skills will be acquired during the process of learning to read the job sheets as outlined above.

After some success with the job sheet, the instructor might attempt to use the text or periodical for reading purposes. An arrangement might be made with the school librarian to borrow appropriate trade magazines from her files to be read, studied and discussed in class.

The writer attempted to stimulate an interest in trade periodicals through the procedure mentioned above when he taught English in a vocational high school. However, the report formulated below, one of many, to be used as a basis for oral discussion, lacked vitality because there was no authority present to evaluate the relevance of the facts or their significance to the trade.

Electrical Construction and Maintenance
Vol. 55 No. 5                  May 1956

Questions on the Code – – – – – Page 295
by B. A. Mcdonald, G. Powell and B. Z. Segall

Wiring for a Service Station

If a device had to be 18 inches or more above the floor level in order to comply with the Code, is it OK to install sealing fittings as close to the floor as possible?

The Code answers this question by stating that it permits the sealing fitting to be located on either side of the boundary where the Conduit run passes from a more hazardous to a less hazardous location. The answer means that you can if the pipe or other material that you are using comes out from an ordinary run and has to pass through a room of high explosives. It must be completely sealed and as tight as the sealing fitting can go.

If we were installing lights at a baseball field, could we run No. 14 wire circuits for individual light outlets which will be lamped with 1500 watt light?

We can use No. 14 wire if we limit the load on a branch circuit to 80% at 12 amps. But if you don't want to limit the load you can use No. 12 wire, which is a safer investment.

The teacher of English never did get around to asking the electrical shop teachers whether that written report made by an eighth-term student was related to the work in the shop. However, it seems that this library lesson was profitable because many boys did testify that they learned something therefrom. The English teacher did not have time in his program to include many such periods.

What is accomplished by using the assistant to teaching afforded by a job sheet, text or trade periodical? A student who uses printed sheets or textbooks in school really has two teachers: the living instructor with his foibles and sympathies, and a silent teacher who has no psychological reactions to every-day student activities. The first implements the program of learning which the curriculum envisages for the years the student will remain in school. The second will ready our student to continue to learn long after he has left school. Neither teacher can be very effective without the other. The pupil who uses no printed matter in his shop is almost at the same disadvantage as the student who takes home study courses. If we wish to train our students to take their places in the social-economic world, we cannot deny them the reading skills and habits needed to progress with the movements in industrial development.

## SUMMARY

To sum up we have tried to sketch the following points in this paper.

1. Vocational students need training in reading trade subjects.
2. The English teacher is willing but unable to provide such reading instruction.
3. The vocabulary, idioms and language of the trades demand special language arts instruction to be provided only by one who is familiar with that trade.
4. Even where language is not a barrier, reading the trade subjects requires application and activity appropriate only to a shop room.
5. The tendency to compel the English teacher to solve such problems will compel us to change our objectives in vocational education.
6. The reading skills taught in the English classroom cannot be used profitably in the trade subjects.
7. A trade text or series of job sheets accumulates a host of concepts which must be mastered to make further reading possible.
8. There are solutions to this problem which are not entirely realistic.
9. Shop teachers should attempt a sample reading lesson in their trade and make such changes in procedure as their experiences dictate.
10. Such reading lessons will have educational perquisites which will facilitate attainment of our vocational high school objectives.

James Joyce in his novel "Portrait of the Artist as a Young Man," illustrated one of the fundamental concepts of this essay in these words (Modern Library Edition—Page 221):

The language in which we are speaking is his before it is mine. How different are the words "home," "Christ," "ale," "master," on his lips and on mine! I cannot speak or write these words without unrest of spirit. His language, so familiar and so foreign, will always be for me an acquired speech. I have not made or accepted its words. My voice holds them at bay. My soul frets in the shadow of his language.

As long as students regard their trade texts with the same feeling as the person speaking above views his teacher's language, we as instructors have failed to prepare our boys and girls for vocational competency after their school days are over.

# Science and Mathematics

## METHODS AND MATERIALS
## FOR TEACHING READING
## IN SCIENCE *

### George G. Mallinson

*In this selection Mallinson begins by discussing the two basic aims of studies on the problems of reading in science. He then lists the four major difficulties hampering the development of reading materials for science and concludes by explaining what steps are being taken to eliminate these difficulties.*

*1. What are some of the problems unique to the field of science that interfere with reading development?*
*2. How do writers make science texts more readable?*
*3. What are the "built-in" qualities in science texts and how can they be used to best advantage?*

THE PROBLEMS associated with reading in the content areas have been studied more extensively for science than for any other subject-matter field. Among the earlier studies was the major investigation by Curtis [1] in which he summarized the results of more than one hundred investigations in the problems of vocabulary related to science teaching. The findings of his investigation were supplemented by those from a series of studies by Mallinson et al. [2] in which other dimensions of reading difficulty in science books, in addition to vocabulary load, were analyzed. More recently, the studies of Herrington [3] and the reviews of research on problems in reading by Mallinson

[1] Francis D. Curtis, *Investigations of Vocabulary in Textbooks of Science for Secondary Schools.* Boston: Ginn & Co., 1938.
[2] George Greisen Mallinson, "Textbook and Reading Difficulty in Science Teaching," *Science Teacher,* XXV (December 1958), 474–475.
[3] Roma Lenore Herrington, "An Investigation of the Consistencies with Which Readability Formulas Measure and Reading Experts Estimate the Reading Difficulty of Materials for Elementary Science," pp. iii–41. Unpublished Master's thesis, Western Michigan College, Kalamazoo, Michigan, May 1956. Roma Lenore Herrington et al., "An Investigation of Two Methods of Measuring Reading Difficulty of Materials for Elementary Science," *Science Education,* XLII (December 1958), 385–390.

* REPRINTED FROM *Sequential Development of Reading Abilities,* Helen M. Robinson, editor, Supplementary Educational Monographs, No. 90, pp. 145–149, by permission of The University of Chicago Press. Copyright, 1960, by the University of Chicago Press.

and Lockwood [4] have enabled textbook authors and publishers to be more effective in developing textbooks of science with levels of reading difficulty appropriate for the students for whom the books are designed.

All these studies were concerned, directly or tacitly, with two basic aims: (a) the development of science vocabularies suitable for the science topics being studied, and (b) the sequential growth of reading skills for better understanding of science. The efforts of the workers, however, were beset by problems, unique to the field of science, that produced results considerably less rewarding than had been sought.

## PROBLEMS WITH READING IN SCIENCE

The preparation of reading materials for science, and the development of methods for using the materials, are hampered by four major difficulties:

1. The recent explosive growth in the fields of science has accelerated the obsolescence of scientific vocabulary. Annually vast numbers of terms drop from common scientific use and many new ones are added. Thus lists of scientific vocabulary need constant modification.

2. One of the major concerns with science teaching is the overlap of science topics that are taught at different grade levels. Also, from one grade level to another, as well as from one specialized science subject to another, there is little continuity. Hence, the development of sequence in reading with science material is severely handicapped. Obviously, subject matter that suffers from lack of sequence is not conducive to the development of materials and methods for sequence in reading subject matter.

3. The sophistication of the materials of science with which students have contact is increasing daily. The scientific ideas that interest the students are becoming increasingly complex. It is indeed difficult to utilize a "one-syllable-word" vocabulary for developing a "ten-syllable" science concept.

4. There is great disagreement among authors and publishers concerning the level of reading difficulty with which science books should be written. Some espouse the viewpoint that the development of sequential reading skills with these materials should be congruent with growth in science knowledge and in the understanding of science concepts. Thus a textbook designed for science courses at the ninth-grade level should have a ninth-grade level of reading difficulty.

Others believe that the efforts of a student in using science materials should be devoted to "learning the science" and not dissipated in struggling with the problems of developing reading skills. The lack of resolution of these conflicting viewpoints is evidenced by analyses of the reading difficulty of different science textbooks. The findings indicate that competing textbooks are written with levels of reading difficulty below, at, and above the grade levels of the students for whom the books are produced.

---

[4] George G. Mallinson and J. Bryce Lockwood, "Reading Skills for Effective Learning in Science: Research on Problems in Reading Science," *Reading for Effective Living*, International Reading Association Conference *Proceedings* (1958), III (edited by J. Allen Figurel), 172–173.

Despite the foregoing problems publishers do seek to surmount these obstacles and "build sequence" in the reading materials they market for courses in science.

## Technical Versus Non-technical Vocabulary

The words that are used in writing textbooks of science fall in two categories. In the first category are those words that are part of the common vocabulary of the student. They are regularly used whether or not the material in question is scientific in nature. These terms constitute the nontechnical vocabulary. Among such words would be "the," "begin," "house," and "follow." In general, except where it is impossible to do otherwise, authors and publishers use only non-technical words whose grade levels of difficulty are below that of the students for whom the book is designed. In general, it is assumed that the student has learned the terms prior to studying the science content. Such words are found in many of the well-known word lists. If it is necessary for an author to use a *difficult* non-technical word, for example, "incapacitate," in a sixth-grade science textbook, the word is treated like a term in the technical vocabulary.

The second category of words, namely the technical vocabulary consists of those terms that are unique to science and which are used for developing scientific understandings. Such words may or may not be difficult, depending on whether they have been introduced and used in earlier science courses. Ordinarily students will not use such terms in their conversation or encounter them in general reading materials. Among such words are "mammal," "photosynthesis," "proton," and "convection."

The technical vocabulary may be handled in several different ways:

It is well-known that the ability to learn new words increases with maturity. Thus, the vocabulary load of technical terms in science books increases as the grade levels of the books increase.

In books designed for the third grade or below, the number of scientific terms introduced is ordinarily 40 or less. The material in books for the lowest level is practically non-verbal. Technical terms are introduced only where they are clearly related to illustrations and their meanings are evident. In the upper elementary grades, from 50 to 75 new technical terms are introduced at each grade level. In the seventh and eighth grades the number increases to about 125, and in the ninth and tenth grades, to about 175. In books designed for juniors and seniors, as many as 250 technical terms may be introduced. There is little tangible research evidence that such increases in vocabulary load are justifiable. Apparently the logic is based on empirical evidence.

Beginning with Grade IX, a new dimension of vocabulary is found in some textbooks. In addition to the "essential," "key," or "required" vocabulary, a second group of "desirable" terms may be included with illustrations, supplementary activities, or in sections that are optional. The number of desirable terms may equal those in the "essential" list.

Nearly always, the technical terms are brought to the attention of the students when they first appear in the text. This may be accomplished by using boldface type, by italicizing the term, or by footnoting. If the term is difficult, or above the level of the students, in addition to being technical, its phonetic spelling may be included following the term in the text or in the footnote. If the meaning of the term is not completely explained in the text, its definition may also be included in the footnote. For example, the word "microscopic" is technical, and at a certain grade level, may be difficult for the students. Since it is an adjective and ordinarily would not be explained in the text, the definition might be included in the footnote. A difficult nontechnical word appearing in the text is usually treated in the same way as a difficult technical term.

In most textbooks for science the technical terms, and the difficult nontechnical terms appear in lists at the end of the chapters in which they are introduced and in the glossary with their definitions.

In general, the newer vocabulary lists are prepared by modifying and reanalyzing some of the earlier lists such as those prepared by Curtis[5] and Mallinson.[6]

## The Gestalt of Reading Difficulty

Although the measures taken for developing graded vocabulary lists for science, for keeping the lists up-to-date, and for properly introducing technical terms are indispensable they alone are not sufficient to provide for the sequential development of reading skills, or assure the proper level of reading difficulty of the text material. The pattern, or *Gestalt*, of the presentation is equally significant.

A sentence consisting of ten non-technical, easy words is obviously not difficult to understand. However, a sentence of fifty non-technical, easy words, with several dependent clauses, and obtuse phrases is likely to be more difficult than one that contains a few technical terms. With such difficult sentences, it is unlikely that sequence can be attained.

Authors and publishers of science textbooks seek to eliminate these road blocks to sequence. The obtuse phraseology, or just plain "bad writing," is ordinarily eliminated in the standard editing procedure. The length and complexity of the sentences are controlled by continuous inspection of the material as writing progresses. In general, the materials are measured for these dimensions of reading difficulty with one of the common reading formulae.

[5] Curtis, *op. cit.*

[6] George Greisen Mallinson, "The Development of a Vocabulary for General Physical Science," *Twelfth Yearbook of the National Council on Measurements Used in Education*, Part II, 1955, pp. 6–8.

Generally, the publishers seek to establish the level of reading difficulty on the basis of *Gestalt*, about one-grade level below the students for whom the book is designed. Measurements of books published recently compared with those of books published about ten years ago indicate some improvement with respect to this aspect of reading difficulty. However, many publishers have not been able to resolve the problem of increasing the level of sophistication of science materials without increasing the reading difficulty of their materials. In some cases, the reading difficulty has increased markedly.

## USING MATERIALS TO DEVELOP SEQUENCE OF READING SKILL

The extent of attainment of direct, compared with that of concomitant, objectives has been sufficiently established to warrant little or no discussion here. However, suffice to say, the less direct the efforts are toward exploiting the attributes of a material, the less it is likely that a student will profit from using the material. If the "built-in" qualities of reading materials for science are to be optimally useful, both the teacher and the student must be aware of the qualities and use the materials accordingly. A few suggestions are here made.

In nearly all science textbooks there are introductory sections called "To the Student," "To the Teacher," or some similar name. In these sections are discussed the ways in which the technical and non-technical vocabularies are treated. These sections should be considered initial assignments for the students. In general, without such attention, students are likely to be unaware of, or prone to ignore, bold-faced or italicized terms, phonetics, definitions, and other similar devices designed for sequence in growth of reading skills.

Training should be given to the student in examining all emphasized terms, in using the phonetics and in checking the glossary in which the meanings of the terms are further amplified.

The lists of key words at the ends of the chapters should not be studied *before* the materials in the chapter are covered. Otherwise, the student will acquire a number of atomistic definitions that are out of context. The relationships between words and their contexts and the development of reading skills need no amplification here. These lists may well be suitable for post-testing, but hardly for pre-study.

The process of reading the science materials, however, demands some examination. There have been a few, not completely conclusive studies undertaken that suggest that certain special skills beyond the general reading skills, need to be developed in order to read science materials with understanding.

In general, these studies indicate that extensive reading of science material in and of itself does not yield significant increments in learning science. However, these studies indicate also that where direction and effort is applied in such reading toward the development of science understandings, there is a significant increase.

The implementation of such general findings is best expressed by Culver in this statement:

> Certainly the student should not expect to read a science textbook as rapidly as he reads a book of science fiction or simply written biography. Neither should he expect to read a textbook for the purpose of finding the steps for proving an experiment as rapidly as he reads a textbook just for pleasure. Nevertheless, many a student makes little adjustment in his reading rate. Of all content fields, science requires the most accurate reading. There are, of course, times when skimming may be utilized, as in locating specific items of reference, and rapid reading is usually preferable in reading science fiction or biography of scientists. When, however, a student reads to find details, to learn the steps for an experiment, or to locate information to help him form a generalization, he must read at a rate which will allow him to be accurate.
>
> The science teacher can help a student vary his reading rate by providing class drills which will show the appropriate rate for various materials. To point up the difference between skimming and a slower rate of reading required for accuracy, follow the skimming exercise with one in which the student reads a selection and is then given a detailed comprehension test.[7]

## CONCLUDING STATEMENT

It may be said that one of the best criteria for the development of reading skill using science materials is growth of understanding of the science material. Measurements of the accumulation of scientific facts may serve some objectives. However, the results of the measurements are not indications of understanding any more than the ability to parrot dictionary definitions is a measure of general reading ability. Thus, since a criterion of the development of reading skill is the students' level of understanding of the science, evaluation in science should take cognizance of this dimension.

[7] Mary Kay Culver, "Materials and Procedures To Develop Reading Efficiency in the Sciences: In Grades Seven through Nine," *Promoting Maximal Reading Growth among Able Learners*, pp. 111–112. Edited by Helen M. Robinson. Supplementary Educational Monographs, No. 81. Chicago: University of Chicago Press, December 1954.

# SCIENCE INSTRUCTIONAL MATERIALS FOR THE LOW-ABILITY JUNIOR HIGH-SCHOOL STUDENT *

Arnold J. Moore

*The upsurge of technological development has increased the demand for adequately-trained personnel in many fields of science and technology. Not all of these personnel will be scientists and engineers; some will be technicians. These technicians are classified into several grades according to their knowledge and skills. Some of the lower-grade technicians can be drawn from the ranks of persons with less than average intelligence. Their training is facilitated by their ability to read scientific and technical materials.*

*Moore devotes this article to explaining the need for special science materials written for low-ability junior high-school students and showing how to write such materials.*

*1. List the problems encountered by the teacher who selects science texts for his classes.*

*2. What guidelines for the construction of special materials for students with below average ability does research provide?*

*3. List the psychological traits of low-ability students that authors should consider when writing special science materials.*

*4. Relate the suggestions given for writing special materials to the actual sample of specially written material provided.*

## INTRODUCTION

THE RECENT accomplishments of Soviet Russia in man's efforts to overcome the obstacles of space have caused the American educational system to be subjected to increasing scrutiny. One of the adverse effects of this assessment, according to Tanzer, is that, in our eagerness to raise standards for the average and above-average student, we may lose sight of the needs of a large segment of our pupil population—the low-ability students (13). The increasing growth of the comprehensive high school with its heterogeneous population complicates the problem of providing equal learning opportunities for all youth. Concentrated efforts by professional educators and citizens of our communities to increase the holding power of our schools, to reduce the drop-outs, and to promote students on the basis of social and chronological growth have increased the complexity of the task of teaching secondary school pupils. Naturally, increased holding power and social promotion have extended the range of individual differences at the

---

* REPRINTED FROM *School Science and Mathematics*, LXII (November 1962), pp. 556–563, by permission of the publisher.

lower extreme and increased the number of pupils in this category. These and other factors have contributed to the problem of providing desirable instruction to students with widely diverse interests and capacities.

For the purposes of this article, the low-ability student is defined as a student whose measured intelligence quotient is ninety-five or below. Under normal conditions this type of student will continue to lag behind more intelligent youth in academic attainments. The more he advances in the typical secondary school, the greater will be the differences between his academic skills and knowledge and those of brighter pupils. Due to the fact that the student with limited ability has difficulty understanding and recalling the verbal concepts which are common in the academic curriculum, he requires careful guidance and a more concrete, and often individualized type of instruction which is time consuming both for the teacher and the student. Most of the instructional materials that have been produced by publishing companies, because of commercial factors, have been developed to meet the needs of students who have average or above average ability.

The problem of reading difficulty, with its related facets, long has been recognized as one of the most important problems in the field of education. In his extensive investigations of the vocabularies of science textbooks, Curtis found, among other things, that both the technical and non-technical vocabularies of general science textbooks were too difficult for the pupils for whom the books were written (3). Due to numerous requests and inquiries, a recent study of the reading difficulty of science textbooks was undertaken by Mallinson, Sturm and Mallinson (7). They state:

Recent textbooks do not seem to be easy. If the level of reading difficulty of a textbook should be one grade level below that of the students for whom it is designed, few can be considered suitable. . . . It would seem that recent textbooks in science are as variable and are likely to cause as much difficulty as their predecessors which were analyzed in early studies. . . . It is obvious that no matter how well organized, a book is not likely to be of much value to students if they cannot read it with sufficient ease to understand it.

If our science textbooks are too difficult for the average students in the class, it is little wonder that our low-ability students become frustrated in their futile attempts to read the science textbook.

It is important that instructional materials provided for the low-ability junior high school students be written at their reading level so that they can understand them. However, it is equally imperative that such materials also be on their level of interest and maturity. Textbooks written for fifth or sixth grade pupils may be easy enough for low-ability junior high school students to read, but the subject matter or manner of presentation probably will be of such a nature as to cause these students to reject the books. Pittler found that most junior high school basic textbooks do not meet the needs of the reader whose ability is below the average of the group, nor do books written for the elementary school child, even though the readability of the books is appropriate (9).

Using as criteria the data obtained from research studies and the opinions of recognized educators, it would seem safe to conclude that low-ability junior high school students need specially prepared science instructional materials. Perhaps Flesch's contention that textbooks are written for teachers, not for students, has greater implications than textbook authors and educators are willing to admit (5).

In order to overcome the difficulty of reading encountered in many of the science text materials, several people have suggested that the same textbook be written at different levels of reading difficulty. Thus, the same basic areas and content would be included, but the manner of presentation and level of understanding required would be differentiated for the different levels of student abilities. Conant recommends that students in the ninth grade, who read at a level of the sixth grade or below be provided with special types of textbooks (2). Mallinson says that theoretically this is a fine plan, but publishing three versions of the basic textbook would triple the costs of publication and tend to raise the costs of textbooks to prohibitive levels (6). However, some publishing companies have accomplished this feat in subject matter areas other than science. Consequently, it would seem that the people in the science education field will need to increase the intensity and persistency of their demands if the needs of the low-ability junior high school student are to be met.

Most of the science instructional materials for schools are designed for average students and are found easily by examining catalogues, indexes, and book lists (6). Unfortunately germane materials for the low-ability student either have not been prepared in any quantity, or are not accessible, with the former premise probably being more true. Consequently, the burden of obtaining appropriate instructional materials falls on the teacher, who seldom has either the time or the facilities for such a task. These facts, however, do not suggest that nothing can be done about the plight of the low-ability student.

Is it possible to write suitable science text materials for the low-ability junior high school student? Using research evidence as a criterion, it would appear that the answer to the preceding question is yes. Prichard, when unable to locate any science instructional materials for the low-ability student, developed four units for students in the seventh grade (12). He was able to demonstrate that his units, written at the reading grade level of the experimental classes, with high interest, concrete and concise, were far better for the low-ability student than the traditional textbook materials. He also learned that the interests of the below average student were no different than those of the average student. In a similar study, another investigator prepared text-type units for low-ability ninth grade students (8). Data obtained from this study demonstrated that it was possible to compose instructional materials having a degree of readability commensurate with the capabilities of the low-ability student, as well as being equal to or superior to standard textbooks with respect to scope of science concepts. In addition, it was found that the special materials were more effective than standard textbooks in enhancing the low-ability student's achievement of science concepts.

## PREPARING SPECIAL MATERIALS

In teaching the student with below average ability, several learning concepts are pertinent. Perhaps the one that is most important is to keep the language composition at a level that is not beyond the capacity of most of the students. Data from research studies indicate that the average low-ability junior high school student has a reading level at least two grades below that of his grade classification. Due to the fact that many experts maintain that text materials should have a level of reading difficulty one grade level below that of students for whom they are designed, congruous instructional materials for low-ability ninth grade students would have a sixth grade level of reading difficulty.

Since one of the incessant criticisms of science text materials has been the use of non-scientific vocabularies which are too difficult, it is important to use easier synonyms of difficult words. For example, one ninth grade textbook describes lightning as a spectacular exhibition of static electricity. If the words "spectacular exhibition" were replaced by "great display," the level of reading difficulty of the sentence would be greatly reduced without adversely affecting the validity of the concept or appeal to the ninth grade student. One wonders if the use of such words as incredible, permissible, innumerable, bleakest, brilliantly, injurious, severity, words which currently are being used, can be justified in a ninth grade science textbook when easier synonyms could readily be substituted. Such sources as *The Teacher's Word Book of 30,000 Words* (14), and the vocabulary lists compiled by Curtis (3), Powers (10), and Pressey (11) are extremely valuable in preparing instructional materials at an appropriate reading level. Other graded vocabulary lists are also quite helpful.

Authors of science instructional materials should be mindful of the fact that in addition to difficulty, diversity is an important part of vocabulary load. Data from most studies indicate that the fewer the different words, the easier the material is to read. Unfamiliar words, both scientific and non-scientific, should be defined when introduced. As an aid to comprehension these unfamiliar words should be redefined in a variety of contexts. It seems paramount that only those words that are absolutely essential in presenting a concept and are to be utilized in the presentation of subsequent information should be introduced.

Thorndike's recommendation that one difficult word in two hundred running words seems reasonable. Yet in many science textbooks unfamiliar words occur more frequently than one in fifty. Although the extension of the reader's vocabulary is important, it should be secondary to the acquisition of science concepts. Comprehension should not be jeopardized in an attempt to augment the vocabulary of the reader. Difficult science text materials usually can be simplified by substituting more concrete and familiar words for unfamiliar and abstract words.

According to Chall there is a significant relationship between sentence structure and comprehension difficulty, with the most popular method of estimating sentence structure being sentence length (1). For the most part, longer sentences make comprehension more difficult. However, it does not follow that all long sentences are hard to read and understand. In fact, there are some very short sentences which are more difficult to comprehend than longer ones. But, conversely, many of the instructional materials are difficult to comprehend because the words used are unnecessarily abstract and the sentence and paragraph structure needlessly complex.

What about sentence structure in frequently used ninth grade science text-books? An examination of these texts reveals that, in general, the sentences are unduly long with the average sentence length in several books being about seventeen words. Many of the sentences vary in length from about thirty to forty-five words. Some even longer. For example, in ten random samples from selected textbooks, this writer discovered a sentence containing fifty-nine words. In writing text materials, the use of sentences whose average length is about ten to twelve words and whose structure is simple rather than complex would tend to make the materials easier to read. However, some concepts are difficult to describe because the ideas are intricate. It may be impossible to simplify the description of these kinds of ideas. These intricate concepts will need to be re-interpreted which may involve an extensive amplification of the concepts or a reduction in the total number of concepts presented.

Another trait of the low-ability student is a short attention span. It is possible to make provisions for this characteristic by varying the materials and learning activities as much as possible, and by making a concerted effort to relate the content and activities to previous experiences of the students. In order to enhance understanding, the concepts should be presented in several ways so that through repetition, comprehension might be increased. An effort should be made to make the explanations explicit and precise as well as including frequent summaries and self-evaluations.

Pupils characterized as low-ability students are often those who learn more readily from overt and direct experience than from reading. The student with below average mental ability also encounters considerable difficulty comprehending abstract concepts. However, such pupils often do well in science work which involves experimentation and laboratory-type experiences. Therefore, materials designed for this type of student should include activities which call for a modicum of reading. Student interest in and a need for reading as a means of gaining additional information can be developed and fostered by the project type activities just suggested.

The student who belongs in the category being discussed can write a little about what he has done, observed, and read, but he cannot project with much success. Instructional materials which establish a greater similarity between what the low-ability student does in the classroom and what he does or sees other people do outside the school are more meaningful to him. Activities should be made concrete by basing them on tangible features of the student's environment.

There is reason to believe that the low-ability students require more cues in the way of details to stimulate thought. Consequently, for these students the simplification of instructional materials will often necessitate their expansion to include much necessary detail and illustrative material. In writing special instructional materials, the teacher should be cognizant of the fact that the meagerness of treatment accorded many concepts makes them difficult to comprehend. For the low-ability student this means that the number of principles presented probably should be reduced with the depth of understanding remaining as nearly constant as possible.

According to Mallinson, the selection and utilization of reading materials in science for slow learners should be based on the premise that the level of social and cultural sophistication of these students is well above their levels of intelligence and/or reading ability (6). He says this premise is often ignored by educators. After having observed low-ability secondary school students using elementary school textbooks, Mallinson concluded that the students were not interested in such a naive approach and ultimately rebelled at being treated as juveniles. Tanzer also feels that the use of elementary school textbooks by junior high school students will often result in violent rejection because of the undesirable psychological effect (13). These opinions, and previously cited research data, provide cogent arguments for guidelines in the preparation of special materials.

Previous research has indicated that evaluations of the levels of reading difficulty of instructional materials should be accomplished by use of reading formulae rather than by inspection. Of the many formulae devised to measure the reading difficulty of materials, the one developed by Dale and Chall has been shown to be highly reliable and easily applied (4). This formula takes cognizance of the percentage of unfamiliar words and the average sentence length. Although this or similar readability formulae should be used to indicate the relative levels of reading difficulty, these formulae should not be used as rules in writing. Chall maintains that the more mechanically a readability formula or any readability factor is used in simplifying material, the smaller will be the effect on either comprehension or readership (1).

The following excerpt from special instructional materials is given to illustrate a type of textual material which has been used quite successfully with low-ability ninth grade students (8). Other examples of this kind of material can be found in the original source. Although the very nature of excerpts tends to destroy continuity and eliminates preliminary background information, it is hoped that some guidelines for writing special materials are demonstrated. Most of the factors previously given as important aspects in the simplification of instructional materials are included in this passage. The use of many personal references and "active" verbs as techniques in the simplification of instructional materials is also demonstrated in this excerpt. Using the Dale-Chall Readability Formula as the criterion, the grade-level classification of this excerpt is fifth-sixth grade. The grade-level classification indicates the grade at which the material can be read with understanding by average children in that grade.

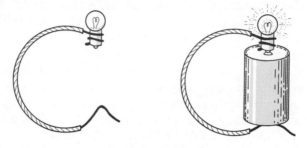

FIGURE 1.

*A simple electric circuit.*

*You can best understand electric circuits by working with some circuits. It will be easy for you to make the simple circuit shown in Fig. 1. Wrap the end of a short piece of bell wire around the screwlike base of a flashlight bulb. Be sure the wire is wrapped tightly around the base of the bulb. Bend the rest of the wire in the shape of the letter C. Next place the tip of the flashlight bulb on the flashlight cell as is shown in Fig. 1. Adjust the free end of wire so that it will be against the bottom of the cell. If the connections are tight, the bulb should light. Any flashlight bulb should operate when connected in this way. However, a bulb for a single cell flashlight will give a brighter light.*

*Turn the cell upside down and reverse the connections. The bulb will be pressed against the bottom of the cell. Does the lamp still operate? It should. The electrons move through the wire and the bulb in the opposite direction now. However, the electrons always move from the negative post to the positive post. An electric current always flows from the negative to the positive. Make a drawing showing the path and direction of the current. In the dry cell the zinc can is the negative post. The carbon or the center post is the positive post.*

*Let's see how a switch works. Bend the bell wire as shown in Fig. 2a. Now fasten it to the dry cell with a rubber band as shown in Fig. 2b. Adjust the wire so that the tip of the bulb touches the center post. Now use the free end of the wire as a switch. The bulb will not light unless the wire is pressed against the bottom of the cell. No current can flow through the circuit as it is shown in Fig. 2b. This is an open or incomplete circuit. Your switch makes a gap in the circuit. Electrons cannot move across this gap. Now complete the circuit by pressing the wire or switch against the cell. This closes the gap and provides a bridge for the electrons to use.*

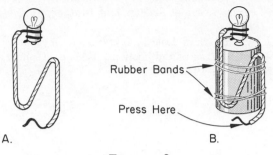

FIGURE 2.

*An electric current is controlled by a circuit and a switch.*

REFERENCES

1. CHALL, JEANNE S., *Readability: An Appraisal of Research and Application*, Bureau of Educational Research Monographs, No. 34, Ohio State University, Columbus, Ohio, 1957.
2. CONANT, JAMES B., *The American High School Today*, McGraw-Hill Book Company, New York, 1959.
3. CURTIS, FRANCIS D., *Investigations of Vocabulary in Textbooks of Science for Secondary Schools*, Ginn and Company, Boston, 1938.
4. DALE, EDGAR, and CHALL, JEANNE S., *A Formula for Predicting Readability*, Bureau of Educational Research, Ohio State University, Columbus, Ohio, 1948.
5. FLESCH, RUDOLPH, *The Art of Plain Talk*, Harper and Brothers, New York, 1946.
6. MALLINSON, GEORGE G., "Science for Slow Learners and Retarded Readers," *Materials for Reading;* Annual Conference on Reading, University of Chicago, Supplementary Educational Monographs, No. 86, December, 1957.
7. MALLINSON, GEORGE G., STURM, HAROLD E., and MALLINSON, LOIS M., "The Reading Difficulty of Some Recent Textbooks for Science," *School Science and Mathematics*, 57, May, 1957, pp. 364–366.
8. MOORE, ARNOLD J., *The Preparation and Evaluation of Unit Text Materials in Science for Low-Ability Junior High School Students*, Unpublished Doctoral Dissertation, State University of Iowa, Iowa City, Iowa, 1961.
9. PITTLER, FANNIE, *An Analysis of the Relationship between the Readability of Textbooks and the Abilities of Students in a Junior High School*, Unpublished Doctoral Dissertation, University of Pittsburgh, Pittsburgh, 1956.
10. POWERS, S. R., "The Vocabulary of Scientific Terms for High School Students," *Teachers College Record*, 28, November, 1926, pp. 220–245.
11. PRESSEY, LUELLA COLE, "The Determination of the Technical Vocabularies of the School Subjects," *School and Society*, 20, July, 1924, pp. 91–96.
12. PRICHARD, L. BRENTON, *Science for the Slow-Learner*, Unpublished Doctoral Dissertation, University of Denver, Denver, Colorado, 1957.

13. Tanzer, Charles, "Utilizing Our Total Educational Potential: Science for the Slow-Learner," *School Science and Mathematics*, 60, March, 1960, pp. 181–186.
14. Thorndike, Edward L. and Lorge, Irving, *The Teacher's Word Book of 30,000 Words*, Bureau of Publications, Teachers College, Columbia University, New York, 1952.

# IMPROVING READING IN THE LANGUAGE OF MATHEMATICS— GRADES 7–12 *

Harold H. Lerch

*The confidence of an individual to pursue the study of a subject is increased if he develops facility in using the language of the subject. This facility, in turn, is developed by meaningful, correctly-paced exposure to this language. In this article, Lerch explains how to teach students the distinct vocabulary for the language of mathematics and its unique form of symbolization. He discusses certain instructional procedures for increasing reading skills which can be used with the poor reader who suffers with disabling difficulties as well as with the better readers of the language of mathematics.*

*1. What are some factors that complicate the meaningful interpretation of the symbols used in writing the language of mathematics?*

*2. What are some of the major causes of reading difficulty cited by the author?*

*3. How does one ascertain the student's readiness to read mathematical materials?*

*4. List several principles to follow in developing mathematics concepts.*

*5. How can individuals be helped to read the language of mathematics in short form?*

*6. How can teachers encourage students to read mathematical materials?*

*7. State the article's key ideas.*

## Mathematics as a Language

THERE IS some validity to the argument that there is a distinct language of mathematics. This validity is built not upon the idea that many students have a great deal of difficulty in the area of mathematics and regard pages of mathematical materials as "Greek" to them, but upon the fact that there is a distinct vocabulary for the language of mathematics and a unique form of symbolization. Even though many of the terms of mathematical

---

* Written especially for inclusion in this volume.

language are abbreviations for and have meanings similar to words and phrases in the regular vocabulary of the speaker or reader of the language, there are words and signs unique to the language of mathematics.

For those students and former students who have been somewhat unsuccessful in their study of mathematics, the language of mathematics is quite often thought of as cold, impersonal, too precise, inconsistent, and highly inflexible. To others, the language is much more meaningful because an understanding of the mathematical concepts described or used has been developed. In actuality, the language of mathematics has inconsistencies in its vocabulary and in its symbolization. To those who thoroughly understand the topic of mathematics under discussion, these inconsistencies do not really hinder communications or growth in the topic.

The means of communicating mathematical ideas or concepts are much the same as they are for communicating other ideas—speaking, listening, reading. It has been said that the process of reading the language of mathematics is the same as the process of reading English or any other language. However, it should be noted that the language of mathematics is actually written not only with words or verbal symbols but also with mathematical symbols. These symbols or signs are used to represent not only words, but also concepts or phrases with meanings much more complex than the meaning of a single word.

As the student studies mathematics he proceeds from the use of a simple sign used to represent a rather simple concept to the use of more complex symbolization, often involving combinations of signs representing concepts which are also more complex or difficult to understand. Consider, for example, quantitative symbols and the student's study and use of such signs as $3$, $\frac{1}{2}$, $5\frac{1}{4}$, $-4$, $\sqrt{2}$, $x$, $y^2$, $3n$, and $\sum\limits_{x=2}^{n}$ . In order to interpret the meaning of these symbols, the student must understand the meaning of each singular sign in its relationship to the total symbol, and combine the meanings into a mathematical concept. In addition to quantitative symbols, the student must also deal with symbols representing comparative ideas, operational ideas, descriptive or definitive ideas, and other mathematical abbreviations.

The meaningful interpretation of the symbols used in writing the language of mathematics is somewhat complicated by the fact that the reader must know the meaning of both words or verbal symbols and the meaning of the signs, both singularly and in combination. It is further complicated by the fact that a singular sign may have somewhat different meanings or interpretations in different situations. The symbols, both English words and mathematical signs, must be meaningfully interpreted for the reader to receive the ideas to be communicated. An analysis of the mathematical materials to be used in the junior and senior high schools will indicate that English words are used in explanations, giving directions, descriptions, and in word problems, and that mathematical signs are also used in much the same way in explanations, illustrations, examples, and descriptions.

## The Mathematics Teacher as a Teacher of Reading

There is little doubt that the teacher of mathematics must also be a teacher of reading, insofar as the language of mathematics is concerned. Virtually every teacher of mathematics at every level wants his students to be able to read the language of mathematics and to use this reading skill as a self-learning tool. The problem then, for teachers of mathematics, is two-fold. They must help students learn to read mathematical materials, and they must help them read to learn mathematical concepts.

In helping students learn to read mathematical materials, teachers of mathematics must be concerned with developing mathematical concepts and comprehensive speaking and reading vocabularies of mathematical terms and mathematical signs. They must also be concerned with developing skills in identifying unfamiliar words; developing speed and fluency in the reading process; helping students grasp the major idea of concept in sentences and paragraphs; helping students read to find details or facts; to follow a logical presentation or sequence of ideas, and to develop the ability to follow written directions.

In helping students to develop the ability to read to learn mathematical concepts, mathematics teachers must be concerned not only with developing the previously mentioned skills, but also in helping students to find and use such materials as may be appropriate or necessary. This would include the use of reference materials such as the dictionary, the encyclopedia, pro- grammed instructional materials, and other discourses related to the topic or area of mathematics being considered. They must also be concerned with developing skills in the reading of problems, maps, charts, and graphs; with developing abilities to select the materials needed; and, with developing abilities to organize what is read.

## Difficulties in Reading the Language of Mathematics

Before discussing suggestions for improving reading in the language of mathematics, perhaps it would be well to cite certain causes of reading diffi- culties in this area. In general, students having difficulties in reading other materials will also have difficulties with reading the language of mathematics. In addition, other mathematics students at the junior and senior high-school level will come to the mathematics class with a distinct lack of prerequisite learnings necessary to read and to understand the mathematical content presented.

They may be lacking in the necessary understandings or knowledge of mathematical concepts which would enable them to comprehend the mate- rials being presented. They may not have the desirable speaking or reading vocabulary in terms of mathematical reference. They may also be somewhat confused as to the meaning of some of their vocabulary in regard to its mathematical reference and a different reference or meaning in its regular

English usage. They might also lack the necessary reading vocabulary of the mathematical signs to be used in a particular program.

This is especially true of students who have moved from one mathematics program or school system to another mathematics program and, quite possibly, because of the fact that there are inconsistencies in the symbolism used by mathematicians preparing the material to be studied. Although the variations in notation may be minor, they could very well lead to frustration on the part of the student.

Another major cause of reading difficulty for students may be that they lack clarity of purpose in their reading. In the mathematical materials of the junior and senior high schools, students are often required to read to obtain a main idea. In other sections of these materials they may be asked to follow a logical presentation, assimilating ideas as they go or as they proceed in order to make an inference or to come to some conclusion. In any case, the nature of reading to accomplish one purpose is different from the type of reading required for other purposes.

Closely related to the causes of reading difficulties, and adding to the complexity of the problem, is the poor self-concept held by students who are unable to read adequately the language of mathematics and are unsuccessful in their mathematics classes. The poor attitudes they have developed toward their own abilities to read and to understand mathematical content are detrimental to the development of those skills. At the junior and senior high-school level these attitudes are rather firmly entrenched and no amount of telling such pupils that they can learn to read mathematical materials will bring about a noticeable change. Poor self-concepts in regard to achievement can be improved only through success on the part of the individual student.

## Increasing Reading Skills

Whether the student is a poor reader suffering with some of the disabling difficulties previously cited, or whether he seems to be a good and able reader of the language of mathematics, there are certain instructional procedures which the teacher of mathematics can and should use to increase reading skills. The specific nature of these procedures is dependent upon the reading and mathematical ability levels of the students, but the general suggestions given here are applicable to all levels.

### Ascertaining Readiness

Asking a student to read mathematical materials which are beyond his ability will almost certainly cause him to fail in this endeavor and will probably contribute negatively to an already poor self-concept. The concept of readiness for reading is as applicable at the junior and senior high-school level in regard to reading the language of mathematics as it is for developing reading skills at the first grade. Ascertaining students' readiness to read mathematical materials dealing with a specific area of content should involve:

1. Checking the students' knowledge of the mathematical concepts which are prerequisites to understanding the new concepts to be introduced and developed. Teachers of mathematics cannot assume that students possess the necessary prelearnings, and attempts to develop new learnings upon poor or nonexistent previous learnings will be unsuccessful.

2. Checking the students' speaking and reading vocabulary that is to be used in developing the new concepts and to develop larger vocabularies. It is impossible to communicate effectively ideas or concepts in mathematics unless the teacher and students have common meanings and understandings for the terms being used. For example, in modern programs of mathematics a set approach is used to great advantage. The importance of the set concept in clarifying mathematical ideas is great, and it is therefore helpful to use the language of sets.[1] However, if students are unfamiliar with the language of sets, the teacher's attempts to utilize a set approach to clarify mathematical ideas will be unsuccessful.

3. Checking students' understanding and use of the mathematical signs to be employed in the study of the new concepts. This idea is closely related to that of checking the speaking and reading vocabulary. The mathematical signs used must be precise and correct and in common usage between teacher and students. Kenner, Small, and Williams[2] in a chapter on "Equations and Inequalities" list the following as important symbol conventions which students should know before beginning study of the unit: $x < y$; $2x$; $mx$; $\{2, 3, \ldots, n \ldots\}$; and $\{5, 6, \ldots, 105, 106\}$.

Ascertaining readiness to read the language of mathematics is not an activity to be conducted only once or twice during the academic year. Rather it is a continuing activity in which the teacher repeatedly checks and rechecks the use students make of concepts, vocabulary, and signs and in which he attempts to determine the extent of their understandings. Activities used by the teacher to ascertain student readiness are quite varied. They may involve teacher-made-inventories or pretests, question-and-answer sessions, discussions, or some other review activity.

In any case, aspects of readiness are to be determined as objectively as possible, are to involve both good and poor students, and are to be directed toward ascertaining individual abilities and understanding rather than those of a group. If it is determined that certain students are not ready to study particular mathematical materials, the teacher must insert into his teaching plan those activities which will develop the necessary prerequisite concepts, vocabulary, and use of symbolism.

*Developing Concepts*

After student readiness to begin the study of certain mathematical materials has been established, the mathematics teacher's concern in increasing

[1] Mervin L. Keedy, *A Modern Introduction to Basic Mathematics.* (Reading, Massachusetts: Addison-Wesley Publishing Company, Inc., 1963), p. 84.

[2] Morton R. Kenner, Dwain E. Small, and Grace N. Williams, *Concepts of Modern Mathematics,* Book 1 (New York: American Book Company, 1963), p. 52.

reading skills should be that of helping students develop clear and precise concepts which will be presented in the material to be read. The student's interpretation of the materials he reads will be a function of the concepts he possesses and his understanding of those concepts. In modern programs of mathematics these concepts are to be developed meaningfully, using instructional procedures which emphasize student participation in discovering or recognizing patterns and relationships upon which conclusions and generalizations can be based. In most instances, initial activities in the instructional procedures should involve practical situations and visual instructional aids such as models, mock-ups, diagrams, illustrations, and should be conducted without reference to textual materials.

Suppose, for example, that the objectives for a unit of work concern student acquisition of knowledge and understandings of certain relationships between the size of angles and the length of sides in right triangles. The teacher might initiate study with models of similar right triangles (having equal angles, unequal sides) on a pegboard using pegs and string, or with drawings or diagrams of similar right triangles. Pupil participation in the measurement of angles and sides of several similar right triangles, in establishing the desired ratios, in discussing the relationships of sides and angles in one triangle with the relationships of sides and angles in similar triangles, and in developing the desired generalizations will help to develop the conceptual foundations necessary for the meaningful interpretation of textual materials. The fact that the measurements are not exact and that the derived ratios will only be approximate should not hinder development of the general concept.

It should be noted that activities such as these would be appropriate whether the teacher was trying to develop concepts of the Pythagorean theorem, or whether he was trying to develop the concepts concerning sine, cosine, or tangent. Similar activities would be helpful in developing concepts of other geometric relationships or trigonometric functions. Conceptual foundations developed in this manner will contribute to the effectiveness of the students' reading of textual materials as resource or reference aids which will further develop and reinforce concepts in a formal approach and provide exercises and examples to strengthen the students' understandings of the concepts through practice.

### Developing Speaking and Reading Vocabulary

An integral part of that aspect of the instructional program concerned with developing mathematical concepts through active participation is an emphasis upon further development of the students' speaking and reading vocabularies. As these learning experiences proceed, the teacher and students will be questioning and discussing the mathematical concepts being developed. The teacher will be able to interject orally new terms in context in such a way that meanings of the terms will be implied or intuitively understood. Students should be encouraged to use the new terms in their verbalization or participation in the learning activities. The term "hypotenuse" (the side of a right triangle opposite the right angle) may be introduced in this manner when students are studying the characteristics of right triangles. Many other mathematical terms could be similarly introduced and used.

At times it may be appropriate to try to incorporate terms into the students' speaking and reading vocabularies simultaneously. This should be done through procedures which will assist students in attacking new words encountered in materials to be read. After a new word has been introduced in the context of oral discussion, the word could be written on the chalkboard and an appropriate kind of word analysis used. Thus, contextual clues and structural analysis of the word are combined to help students develop skills in pronunciation and recognition and to develop meanings and understandings. The form of structural analysis used to develop these skills is somewhat dependent upon the word being considered.

The most generally useful form of structural analysis is syllabication [3] which involves dividing a word into syllables and helping students pronounce the word syllable by syllable. This method seems very appropriate for helping students with such terms as "hy-pot-e-nuse," "re-cip-ro-cal," and "pa-rab-o-la." Syllabication is also useful in combination with other forms of structural analysis and in helping students learn to spell. Another form of structural analysis that becomes important when polysyllabic words are met with some frequency is the technique of looking for familiar prefixes, root words, and suffixes.[4] In many instances the meaning of the part of the word being considered will have to be reviewed, and reference should be made to other words containing the same prefix, root word or suffix. For a simple example using a prefix in this manner, consider the terms *trihedron, trinominal, triangle, trilateral, trisect, trillion, tripod,* and *tricycle.* The root word "nominal" referring to a single name or term could be used in developing understanding of *monomial, binomial,* and *trinomial.*

If an approach utilizing the oral development of the language of mathematics is used with techniques of structural analysis, not only will students' speaking and reading vocabularies be increased but they will also be more likely to apply skills such as looking for contextual clues and structural analysis when they are reading to learn mathematical content and encounter unfamiliar terms.

In addition to developing speaking and reading vocabularies of words or terms, students must also learn to read the language of mathematics in its "short form" as it is written with signs. No amount of skill in reading word sentences or paragraphs will enable students to interpret meaningfully such expressions as $+3 < x < +8$ or $\overline{AB} \cong \overline{CD}$ or to distinguish between the meanings of the parentheses in the expressions $x(x+2)$, $f(x)$, and $(a, b)$. In the language of mathematics certain symbols are deliberately allowed a

---

[3] Albert J. Harris, *How to Increase Reading Ability*, Fourth Edition, revised (New York: David McKay Company, Inc., 1961), p. 340.

[4] *Ibid.*, p. 340.

wide variety of interpretations.[5] Skills in reading such symbolism must be developed sequentially and meaningfully. It cannot be assumed that students will assimilate skills in recognition, meaning, and use of the signs without direct efforts on the part of the teacher. New signs should be introduced; old signs should be reviewed; and the appropriateness of the symbolism should be discussed with students when concepts are being meaningfully developed.

### Encouraging Students to Read Mathematical Materials

Persuading students to read mathematical materials is a difficult task for teachers. Students will not be encouraged to read if they have not developed the abilities which have been briefly discussed. Only the practice of reading and an appreciation for the materials being read will develop speed and fluency in the reading desired of students. It would be ideal if mathematics students wanted to read more mathematical materials than the textual materials specifically required of them in mathematics classes, and to read for purposes other than being able to solve problems and exercises for homework and for tests. Students may be more encouraged to read mathematical materials if teachers help them (1) to clarify their purposes in reading; (2) to understand that most mathematical materials cannot be read in the same manner as less concise materials; (3) to find mathematical materials that are enjoyable, interesting, and informative, and (4) to use their mathematical reading skills to study and organize content in other academic areas.

The purposes for which a student reads mathematical materials may be as distinct as reading to (1) obtain or reinforce a major idea; (2) gather pertinent facts or details; (3) acquire general information; (4) collect data from which an inference or a conclusion is to be drawn; (5) logically follow directions until a task has been completed, and (6) derive satisfaction or enjoyment. Or, the objective may be a combination of these purposes. In any case the mathematics teacher can help students clarify the purpose of their reading by discussing with them the nature of the material and what they are supposed to achieve by reading it. He can also help students by making suggestions as to how they might read the material.

The conciseness of mathematical materials is such that most of it must be read at a slower and more exacting pace than materials in other academic areas. Skipping a symbol or word when rapidly reading some materials may not deter students from achieving their goals or obtaining precise meanings; but skipping a symbol or word in mathematical content may alter the derived meaning drastically. Students must be made to understand that they cannot be careless in reading mathematical materials and that they may have to slow their reading speed. In other instances they may have to use special kinds of reading skills suitable to the presentation of the content such as

[5] M. Evans Munroe, *The Language of Mathematics* (Ann Arbor: The University of Michigan Press, 1963), p. 8.

in formulas, tables, and graphs. By using appropriate reading skills and reading speed in accordance with purpose, students will be more successful in their reading endeavors—and few things are as encouraging as success.

In too many instances the junior and senior high-school student's reading in the language of mathematics is limited to the basic textbook used in his mathematics class. This limitation could be very stifling to his growth in mathematical understandings and to his development of reading skills in the language. One way of broadening the scope of the mathematical content to be read is for the mathematics teacher to work co-operatively with teachers in other academic areas such as chemistry, physics, geography, history, and industrial arts to co-ordinate efforts in developing reading skills in the content of those areas which is presented in mathematical terminology. Another way of broadening the scope of materials in the language of mathematics is to provide either in the school library or in the mathematics classroom suitable supplementary materials of need or of interest to the students.

An encouraging trend in the field of mathematics is an increasing amount of resource, reference, programmed instruction, trade books, and other supplementary materials appearing on the market. These materials can be used both to stimulate interest in mathematics and to broaden mathematical understandings. Accompanying this trend is a willingness on the part of school systems to financially support the acquisition of such materials. The following references are only a few examples of the available materials that may stimulate interest and encourage students to read more in the language of mathematics.

ADLER, IRVING. *Magic House of Numbers.* New York: The John Day Company, Inc., 1957.

ASIMOV, ISAAC. *Quick and Easy Math.* Boston: Houghton Mifflin Company, 1964.

BARR, STEPHEN. *Experiments in Topology.* New York: Thomas Y. Crowell Company, 1964.

CLARK, FRANK. *Contemporary Math.* New York: Franklin Watts, Inc., 1964.

JUSTER, NORTON. *The Dot and the Line: A Romance in Lower Mathematics.* New York: Random House, Inc., 1963.

LERCH, HAROLD H. *Numbers in the Land of Hand.* Carbondale, Ill.: Southern Illinois University Press, 1966.

MUNROE, M. EVANS. *The Language of Mathematics.* Ann Arbor, Michigan: The University of Michigan Press, 1963.

# TEACHING LEVELS OF LITERARY
# UNDERSTANDING *

### John S. Simmons

*Do boys in high school develop a dislike for poetry because it is a "sisssy activity" or because they do not understand poems? It is the latter reason, according to Simmons. Boys do develop a taste for poetry if they understand it. A teacher can be more successful in helping students understand poetry if he applies techniques germane to the reading of poetry, rather than techniques developed for reading an essay.*

*The main part of the paper is devoted to showing the English teacher how to help students differentiate their approaches to the reading of drama, poetry, and prose fiction. In addition, Simmons explains how certain specific, sequential steps must be taken if the teacher is to succeed in establishing literature as a basis for good reading instruction.*

*1. What are the two responsibilities for the teaching of reading that secondary school teachers have?*

*2. What intellectual demands are made on students as they study literature?*

*3. What reading problems does one encounter when reading drama?*

*4. How can the teacher help students develop adequate meanings as they read poems?*

*5. How does the reading of modern prose fiction differ from reading fiction written in the traditional narrative patterns?*

*6. What steps should the teacher take to help students read literature skillfully?*

*7. State the article's key ideas.*

A SOURCE of frustration to secondary school teachers imbued with the "reading point of view" may well be found in their unsuccessful attempts to promote developmental reading through the use of literary selections. Often it is not that the task cannot be done but that the wrong approach is taken with the materials used. That is, teachers are sometimes guilty of attempting to employ selections of imaginative literature as vehicles for certain reading exercises when in fact the forms of the selections do not fit the exercises in question.

My first premise in this matter is that all secondary school teachers, re-

---

* FROM *English Journal*, 54 (February 1965), pp. 101, 102; 107; 129, reprinted with permission of the National Council of Teachers of English and John S. Simmons.

gardless of their field, have the dual function (among countless others, of course) of *extending* certain reading abilities among their students, and *developing* others. Those aspects of the reading act taught and reinforced in elementary school should be extended in the more mature and complex environs of high school reading material. Those reading abilities which are, relatively speaking, unique to high school should be developed. Literature study, it would seem, is largely the function of the secondary school English teacher. Within this study lie special kinds of reading approaches, those infrequently and (no malice intended) superficially handled in most elementary schools.

In the study of literature, students are taught and/or guided in the interpretation, analysis, and appreciation of a variety of selections. For many students such demands are largely unfamiliar; they must learn to perform a task which is new to them. Teachers require a series of reactions to the literature read, both in speaking and in writing. In this they are asking for *critical* reading, a task which should be central to reading assignments in all secondary content areas. Students must go beyond mere passive acceptance, or *comprehension*; they must do something with what they read. In evoking a critical response, English teachers are moving students toward more mature, sophisticated reading activities.

The teacher of literature could also hope for a degree of involvement by her students with the selections they read. Since most selections studied will present conflicts in human ideals, or desires, offer moral choices, or identify ways to the good life, it would be hoped that some works would have an effect on the *attitudes* of the great majority of students. Research gathered to date suggests that this goal is not achieved as frequently as we would like, but this does not make the desire to affect students' personal feelings through literature study less desirable or less popular with most teachers. Most important to this discussion, however, is that in the study of literature, secondary English teachers are asking students to deal with "new" kinds of materials.

From the point of view of most instructors of "general reading abilities," the essay and the biography, together with some conventional selections from prose fiction, represent the kind of material most suitable for certain reading exercises: developing rate, improving comprehension, increasing vocabulary, finding main ideas in paragraphs, identifying key facts and the relationship among sentences, and the like. Actually, it must be made clear that in the study of imaginative literature, the teacher *must depart from these kinds of activities*. The process of comprehending literature demands other approaches. One of the major reasons for this needed modification is that the nature of imaginative literature is quite different from the typical materials used to develop reading skills and is thus not suited for developing the kinds of reading skills indicated above. To amplify this assertion, I will call attention to some of the special considerations involved in reading drama, poetry, and prose fiction.

## READING DRAMA

As a form to be read silently, drama takes about as big a structural departure from "regular developmental" reading materials as one could imagine. The play tells a story but not along familiar narrative lines. The main portion of the narrative is written in the form of speeches of one or more characters; thus, no one is really *telling* the story. Both action and setting are largely supplied by stage directions, usually italicized, which are vitally important to the understanding of the play but are often understated. These directions also serve to break up the dialogue, making the following of a sequence of events more difficult.

Another dimension of drama which causes reading problems is the "simultaneous action" within the play. Drama has been written chiefly to be acted, not read silently. Therefore, several things are meant to happen at once during a presentation. A character may be walking, gesturing, making facial expressions while he is speaking. At the same time, other characters may be doing the same things, and some of them may even be speaking as well. To perceive the total situation of the play, the student must be able to do more than *comprehend*; he must *visualize*. As reader, he must intuitively sense that certain things are happening or are about to happen that will cause certain inner reactions from various members of the cast. Such reading calls for imagination, guidance, and experience. It is not provided for in basic reading instruction and thus demands another kind of *readiness* on the part of the reader.

## READING POETRY

Poetry offers at least as large a number of structural problems as does drama. Lines of poetry obviously do not conform to prose "reading" models. They are long, short, and have little to do with typical sentence structure. Syntax in poetry is highly irregular, with phrases, clauses, and unusually placed single modifiers jutting out all over the place. Students often have trouble finding not only the end of a sentence, but its subject and verb as well. The juxtaposition of words for intellectual, emotional, and aesthetic effect further complicates the issue. The poet is frequently working for audial effects of various kinds and does this by the conscious selection of certain words (often unusual) and certain constructions (often irregular) to effect the exact intonation or balance. The student who searches for even surface meaning in poetry must adjust to all of these manipulations.

Another kind of reading readiness of an extraordinary nature must be built by the teacher of poetic selections. Many poems, including a fair proportion of those often taught to high school students, either tell a story or relate a fact in the denotative sense. They may create an impression (Pound, "In a Station of the Metro"), a mood, an observation on the human situation. They may tell a story in a most oblique manner (Robinson, "Eros Turannos"), or they may reveal only the barest of details. Metaphor is a fundamental, vital ingredient, and the reader must be ready to pursue relationships among unusual entities to clarify and intensify his perception of meaning. In reading poetry, that is part of the game.

Finally, and obviously, in poetry much is compressed into a few words. The poet habitually speaks volumes in a few lines. Consider the first two and a half lines of the third stanza of Yeats' "Leda and the Swan":

A shudder in the loins engenders there
The broken wall, the burning roof and tower
And Agamemnon dead.

A reader who has no more than a slight background in classical mythology misses the idea as well as the *sweep* of those lines.

I have suggested here only a few of the problems that poetry presents to the student who has not been taught to read in a "special" way. Certainly such problems are not met in basic reading instruction at any level. They must be dealt with by a teacher who is trained to read and to *teach the reading* of poetry. A contention which I have harbored for years is that many high school boys dislike poetry because it is effeminate. They do not like it, because they are not competent enough to *read* it.

## READING PROSE FICTION

It would seem that prose fiction offers the most fertile ground in a literature class for the teacher who would develop the reading skills mentioned earlier. Although this is in part true, many fictional selections, important in the high school curriculum, offer reading problems of a most unusual nature.

I feel, or at least I *hope,* that it is safe to assume that there is a perceptible trend in the curriculum away from the *Silas Marner, Ivanhoe* preoccupation to an interest in considering works of more recent vintage. If this is true, some pitfalls await the unsuspecting reader. Novels and short stories, particularly those of the twentieth century, are replete with structural and stylistic involvements for which the typical high school reader is not necessarily prepared.

Modern prose fiction characteristically deviates from traditional narrative patterns. The more frequent uses of limited point of view, in which the reader views the situation through the eyes of one of its participants, brings about some unusual sequences. When, as in Faulkner, reality is viewed through the eyes of a Benjie Compson, some most irregular structures result; stream of consciousness, interior monologue, and abrupt shifts in the identity of the narrator demand flexibility on the part of the reader.

The ease of following the chronological sequence was once a big selling point of the novel or short story as a reading exercise. In much significant fiction, however, the writer has tampered with his clock, as E. M. Forster might say. Irregular placing of events, lengthy and unusually developed flashbacks, and rapidly shifting locales often make following the plot a chore. A reader not aware of such stylistic jockeying can soon become confused and frustrated.

The opening and closing of many significant works of prose fiction deserve careful attention. In *The Return of the Native*, the opening chapters develop a setting, Egdon Heath, slowly and painstakingly. This description must be read and fully perceived, because much of the characterization and plot structure that follows depends directly on such understanding. In the beginning passages of a large number of short stories, vital events, and propositions of human experience are developed with such a sparseness of detail as to demand minute analysis. In Poe's "Cask of Amontillado," it is virtually impossible to follow the narrative intelligently unless the personality of Montresor, self-described at the outset, is clear.

Restraint in use of detail in the presentation of key actions is characteristic of today's prose fiction, as are abrupt, anticlimactic conclusions. When the untrained reader is left up in the air, he tends to become confused. Such a reader must be taught to examine the text more carefully so that such endings will not be so obscure of intent. Throughout all subtle fiction, it must be realized that the paragraph, and even the sentence, are not the functional elements they are in conventional reading exercise materials. Teachers should not expect students to search for "main ideas" in structures where none in fact exists.

The forms of literature represent material for which special and mature reading abilities are required. Teachers who would teach students to read literature skillfully should first settle on specific areas of competence to be developed. They should next find selections appropriate to these purposes. Before assigning the selections, they should find and prepare devices that insure *honestly critical* responses from the students (and these do *not* include memorization, teacher's critical pronouncements, or long "background" lecture assignments). If we are to move adolescent readers toward *appreciation*, we must remember that they must perceive symbolic meaning in order to discriminate, that they must develop the ability to relate symbol to referent, within the structurally difficult, on their own and with no heavy-handed prompting. Literature becomes the basis for good reading instruction when it becomes a vehicle for individual critical insight and true aesthetic revelation. This kind of instruction must be both mature and sophisticated. It cannot be done in the early stages of high school reading instruction.

# AWARENESS OF GRAMMATICAL STRUCTURE AND READING COMPREHENSION *

Roy O'Donnell

*Not only is structural linguistics a magic word in these times but new claims for the powers of grammar have been made in its name. In this study O'Donnell investigates these claims and provides an answer that comforts both the believers and the disbelievers in its magical powers. Rather than making the reader feel comfortable, it should move him to inquire how the basic structural relationships of words in sentences might be taught so as to improve reading comprehension.*

*1. What is the purpose of this study?*

*2. How did the author force the readers in his study to depend upon signals of syntactic structure?*

*3. Can you mentally picture in scattergram form the correlations obtained?*

*4. Would the statistical results of this study justify the attempt to increase reading comprehension scores through the teaching of grammatical structure?*

*5. How does the author go on to explain to a reader the value of the knowledge of grammar? Do you agree with his explanations? Explain.*

THE QUESTION of what relationship exists between knowledge of a grammar and the communication skills is one that has been frequently debated, and it has been the subject of a number of statistical studies. Although most of these studies have indicated low statistical correlations between grammar and reading and writing, the idea has persisted that knowledge of grammar is necessarily related to skill in expressing and interpreting ideas.

One of the first studies in this area was made in 1906 by Franklin S. Hoyt (2). It was the purpose of Hoyt's study to test two assumptions that many grammar teachers had made: (1) that a knowledge of grammar leads to the use of better English in oral and written expression; and (2) that a knowledge of grammar aids in the interpretation of written English. He administered tests in grammar, composition, and interpretation to 200 first-year high school students. Using the Spearman formulae, he calculated the correlations of the tests with each other. His findings indicated a probable true correlation of grammar with composition of .30 and of grammar with interpretation of .35. Comparing the scores on these tests with scores made in other subjects, Hoyt found about the same relationship apparently existing

* REPRINTED FROM *The High School Journal* (February 1962), pp. 184–188, by permission of the University of North Carolina Press.

between grammar and composition and between grammar and interpretation of language as exists between grammar and totally different subjects, such as mathematics and history.

In 1907, Louis W. Rapeer repeated Hoyt's study by giving the same tests to a different group of students (4). The results of Rapeer's investigation were essentially the same as those of Hoyt's study, and both investigators concluded that the relationship of the factors tested was not statistically significant. Other studies made at various times and on various grade levels have produced similar results. In the light of these findings, many English teachers abandoned the teaching of formal grammar on the assumption that it produced no practical results.

In recent years, however, the study of structural linguistics has contributed to a new interest in grammar, and new claims have been made about the value of knowledge of grammar. Advocates of structural linguistics readily accept the lack of high correlation between knowledge of traditional grammar and ability in reading and writing, because they regard the traditional grammar as inaccurate and unrealistic. Many of them assume, however, that there is necessarily a high degree of relationship between grammar properly defined and described and the communication skills.

Recognizing the possibility that the tests used in earlier studies might have been concerned with a body of knowledge of dubious value, the writer began an investigation in 1959 of the relationship between awareness of grammatical structure and ability in reading comprehension (3). From several textbooks taking the structural linguistics approach to English grammar, a list of basic structural relationships was compiled. These basic structural relationships include the relationships between (1) subject and predicate verb, (2) predicate verb and complement, (3) modifier and element modified, (4) coordinate elements, and (5) pronoun and antecedent. It will be noted that traditional grammar includes these same grammatical relationships; however, the typical grammar test includes a great deal of material other than these basic relationships.

A test was constructed to measure ability to recognize the basic structural relationships of words in English sentences. Since no instruction in either traditional or structural grammar was part of the investigation, it seemed desirable to arrange the test items so that no direct use of grammatical terminology of any kind would be necessary. In order to avoid the direct use of grammatical terminology, items containing a pattern sentence followed by three option sentences were used. Two different elements were underlined and numbered separately in the pattern sentence of each item, and the students were asked to select the option sentence in which a similar relationship was indicated. They were not asked to tell what the underlined elements were; ability to recognize similarity of the indicated relationships was the only requisite to successful performance on the test.

In order to minimize reliance on semantic or lexical meaning, and to force reliance on signals of syntactic structure, non-sense words were used in the option sentences. These words were arranged in normal English word order, and English prepositions, conjunctions, auxiliaries, articles, etc., were used. Regular English inflectional and derivational affixes were used. Presumably, students would have to rely on these structural signals to recognize the grammatical relationships between the marked elements, and it seems evident that any student who failed to recognize the structural relationships involved could not achieve a high score on the test. Reliability of the test was established by standard statistical methods.

The structure test and the Cooperative *Test C1: Reading Comprehension* were given to 101 high school seniors in the spring of 1960. Separate scores were obtained for vocabulary and level of comprehension on the reading test. A traditional grammar test, the *Iowa Grammar Information Test*, was given for the purposes of comparison. The scores were submitted to statistical treatment and the following correlation coefficients were obtained: level of comprehension and awareness of structure, .44; level of comprehension and knowledge of grammar, .46. The correlation of vocabulary and structure scores was .46, and the correlation of vocabulary and grammar scores was .90. Vocabulary and level of comprehension scores had a correlation of .76.

A comparison of the correlation coefficients obtained seems to indicate that the degree of relationship between awareness of structure and reading ability is slightly lower than that of knowledge of traditional grammar and reading ability. Since the correlation between vocabulary and grammar scores is a great deal higher than that between vocabulary and structure scores, however, and since there is a high correlation between vocabulary and level of comprehension, it seems likely that knowledge of vocabulary accounts for a considerable amount of the correlation between grammar and reading scores. Application of a partial correlation formula to "partial-out" knowledge of vocabulary shows that knowledge of vocabulary does account for most of the relationship between reading and grammar test scores and supports the conclusion that awareness of structure is related to reading comprehension in a higher degree than knowledge of traditional grammar is. However, the fact remains that the degree of relationship is not high enough to justify the teaching of grammatical structure as a major means of developing reading comprehension.

The data obtained in this study indicate that knowledge of vocabulary is a great deal more important as a factor in reading comprehension than awareness of grammatical structure is. But are we to conclude that awareness of structure is of no importance? Such a conclusion may seem to be justified by the statistical data, but it is doubtful that the data demand such an interpretation.

Anyone who has had the experience of learning to read a foreign language is aware of the fact that knowledge of vocabulary alone is not sufficient. There must be some awareness of how the words are related to one another in the sentence. It is true that a reader who knows something of the general context can get a reasonably accurate translation if he knows the lexical meaning of all the words in a passage. But he cannot be absolutely certain of the accuracy of his translation unless he is able to recognize the syntactic relationships of the various elements of the sentence. In a language such as Latin these syntactic relationships are indicated largely by the inflections of the words. While it is true that modern English does not depend to any great degree on inflections, it is hardly possible to assume that awareness of syntax is less important in English than in Latin. Functions formerly performed by inflectional endings in English are now performed by word order, prepositions, auxiliaries, etc., but the distinction between subject and object is still of fundamental importance in interpreting the meaning of a sentence. The reader whose native language is English may not be able to intelligently discuss the syntactic structure of his language, but it seems that he would have to have some awareness of the varying functions of different elements of a sentence if he is to accurately interpret what he reads.

The absence of a high statistical correlation between awareness of grammatical structure and ability in reading comprehension is probably accounted for, not by the unimportance of awareness of structure but by the fact that there are numerous factors in reading not directly related to grammatical structure. Sentences combine to form paragraphs, and paragraphs combine to form large units. Reading tests are necessarily concerned with units larger than the sentence, and the relationship that one sentence has to another or that one paragraph has to another is something different in kind from the relationship between a subject and a verb or a verb and a complement. Then too, there are usually some test items concerned with inferences from the context and even with the tone and style of writing. These are legitimate concerns in reading, but again they are apparently unrelated to awareness of syntactic structure. Of the nine separate factors in reading ability listed by Frederick B. Davis, only "Ability to follow the organization of a passage and to identify antecedents and references in it" appears to have any direct relation to basic structural relationships (1). Even this ability to identify antecedents and references may depend on knowledge of vocabulary more than on awareness of structure.

It is possible that a factor analysis study using an accurate measure of awareness of grammatical structure would show that such awareness is of basic importance in reading. Up to this time, however, no statistical evidence is available to conclusively prove that mastery of grammar, traditional or structural, will guarantee success in reading. On the other hand, there are probably few teachers who would be willing to assume that a student could become a good reader without some awareness, whether conscious or unconscious, of the basic structural relationships of words in sentences.

REFERENCES

1. DAVIS, FREDERICK B. "Two New Measures of Reading Ability," *Journal of Educational Psychology*, XXXIII (May, 1942), 365–372.

2. Hoyt, Franklin S. "Grammar in the Elementary Curriculum," *Teachers College Record*, VII (November, 1906), 467–500.
3. O'Donnell, Roy C. "The Relationship Between Awareness of Structural Relationships in English and Ability in Reading Comprehension." Unpublished Ph.D. dissertation, George Peabody College for Teachers, 1961.
4. Rapeer, Louis W. "The Problem of Formal Grammar in Elementary Education," *Journal of Educational Psychology*, IV (March, 1913), 125–137.

# HOW TO READ A VICTORIAN NOVEL *

Betty M. Bivins

*"Time is of the essence" in our complex, fast-moving, industrial society. Technological advancement is predicated on and results in timesaving devices and processes. Life moves so rapidly and passes in review so swiftly that we have developed habits of sampling our environment and of skimming over and hitting the highlights of things which come within our purview. Such habits ill prepare us for viewing in depth and at a leisurely pace the detailed descriptions of life in another era.*

*In this article Bivins tells how to approach the reading of a Victorian novel so that we can savor the beauty and flavor of the detailed, intimate descriptions of life in that era.*

*1. Why do many high-school students approach the reading of Victorian novels reluctantly?*

*2. What advantages are cited for a more leisurely approach to life?*

*3. What are the four suggestions for reading a Victorian novel? State at least one reason for each suggestion given.*

Many high school students, regardless of grade or ability, approach the reading of Victorian novels with a great deal of reluctance. And no wonder! Most novels of the Victorian era dawdle along at an extremely slow pace, overwhelm the reader with voluminous detail couched in elaborate language, and amble off frequently into digressions, characteristics that can only leave the unaccustomed reader feeling that if there is a point to the story it is so buried under "irrelevancies" as to be not worth the time and trouble necessary to unearth it.

A few years ago, after trying various techniques designed to involve my students in the era and subject matter of particular novels, I came to the conclusion that such devices, while valuable, are not enough to overcome that initial reluctance. What is needed first is a bridge of some kind to

* REPRINTED FROM the *English Journal*, 54 (November 1965), pp. 741–743; 747, reprinted with permission of the National Council of Teachers of English and Betty M. Bivins.

help students close the gap that is sometimes called cultural distance. Therefore, I prepared, for my students, an informal introduction and the four suggestions which follow. The class time required for the entire presentation is about thirty minutes, time that seems to be well spent, for, during the three years I have been using this approach, many students have said they understand and enjoy Victorian novels for the first time.

## Introduction to the Victorian Novel

Frequently you can better understand and enjoy the literature of a given period if you know something of the society from which it emerged and some of the ways in which that society differed from ours, particularly since literature often reflects its society in style as well as subject matter. A basic difference between the Victorian Age and ours is the pace of daily existence. Where we use the automobile, the Victorians walked or rode horseback; where we travel at speeds ranging from 70 to several hundred miles an hour in cross-country buses, diesel trains, and jet planes, they traveled at ten to perhaps 30 miles an hour in horse-drawn carriages and old fashioned, steam-powered trains. Victorian novels reflect this difference; one of their basic characteristics is the *leisurely pace* at which the story unfolds, a pace that was undoubtedly comfortable for the Victorian reader, but one that can be irritating to the unprepared modern reader.

A simple comparison—between driving two blocks and walking the same distance—can illustrate that slower pace, and, at the same time, explain the origin of two other major characteristics of the Victorian novel: *detailed descriptions* and *digressions*. Let's say you set out to get a coke at the drug store two blocks away. If you travel by automobile, you will get there quickly but see little along the way. You will be conscious primarily of other traffic on the street, and, though you may get a glimpse of people in other cars when you stop at a traffic signal, and a quick view of other stores as you drive along, you will see almost nothing in detail and are not likely to stop for a closer look.

If, however, you walk the same route, you will enter what might be called, without much exaggeration, another world altogether. For one thing, the people you pass on the sidewalk stand out much more sharply as individuals. And one reason for this is that, because you are moving slowly, you see them in greater detail. You might be amused by a woman wearing a crazy pink straw hat decorated with yellow sunflowers. Or, you might be struck by the obvious pleasure an old man at the corner takes in selling his newspapers, and wonder how anyone with crutches and such shabby clothes can find enjoyment in life. The author of a Victorian novel does much the same thing. In a sense, he walks instead of rides and, as he does, he takes the reader with him. In this way the reader is made acquainted with the scenes the author sees—and in the same detail.

Another thing you will probably do on your way to the drug store is window shop. If you pass a jeweler's, you might stop to look at platinum wrist watches, diamond engagement and wedding rings, or jade cuff links set in gold. And, if you have a normal amount of imagination, you are likely to visualize yourself as the owner of something you like, and even daydream of a future in which you are successful and wealthy. Or, if you see a sporting goods shop and stop to admire an expensive surfboard or an elaborate ski outfit, you might imagine yourself as a daring surfer or a champion skier. Does this mean you've lost sight of your original errand—to get a coke? Of course not. All you've done is take a little time out to think of other things. In other words, you have digressed, temporarily, from your major purpose. And this, too, the Victorian novelist does. He doesn't forget the thread of his main story; he merely digresses from it occasionally to offer the reader an idea or a scene that he considers interesting.

Let me read to you an excerpt from a Victorian novel first published in 1857, *Tom Brown's Schooldays* by Thomas Hughes. In this section the author has left his story for a moment and is speaking to the reader. It is a good example of a digression, and, at the same time illustrative of one purpose of a digression. Also, as I read, you will see why I chose this particular selection; there are some echoes in it of what I have just been saying to you and of what I am going to suggest to you in a few minutes:

I only know two English neighbourhoods thoroughly, and in each, within a circle of five miles, there is enough of interest and beauty to last any reasonable man his life. I believe this to be the case almost throughout the country, but each has its special attraction, and none can be richer than the one I am speaking of and going to introduce you to very particularly; for on this subject I must be prosy; so those that don't care for England in detail may skip the chapter.

"Oh, young England! young England! You who are born into these racing railroad times, where there's a Great Exhibition, or some monster sight, every year; and you can get over a couple of thousand miles of ground for three pound ten, in a five weeks' holiday; why don't you know more of your own birthplaces? You're all in the ends of the earth, it seems to me, as soon as you get your necks out of the educational collar, for mid-summer holidays, long vacations, or what not. Going around Ireland with a return ticket in a fortnight; dropping your copies of Tennyson on the tops of Swiss mountains; or pulling down the Danube in Oxford racing boats. And when you get home for a quiet fortnight, you turn the steam off, and lie on your backs in the paternal garden, surrounded by the last batch of books from Mudie's library, and half bored to death. Well, well! I know it has its good side. You all patter French more or less, and perhaps German; you have seen men and cities, no doubt, and have your opinions, such as they are, about schools of painting, high art, and all that; have seen the pictures at Dresden and the Louvre, and know the taste of sour kraut. All I say is, you don't know your own lanes and woods and fields. Though you may be chock-full of science, not one in twenty of you knows where to find the wood-sorrel, or bee-orchis, which grow in the next wood or on the down three miles off, or what the bog-bean and wood-sage are good for. And as for the country legends, the stories of the old gable-ended farmhouses, the place where the last skirmish was fought in the civil wars, where the parish butts stood, where the last highwayman turned to bay, where the last ghost was laid by the parson, they're gone out of date altogether.

Hughes, then, even during the Victorian period itself, was distressed by what he thought of as an increasingly fast pace of living. He obviously felt that quantity of ground covered and a broad view of many different things was not as valuable as a deeper, more detailed knowledge of less territory and fewer things, a viewpoint that might lead you to some reflections of your own. Is it enough to get a quick glimpse of things and people as we whirl by each other in automobiles, or is there some value in slowing down occasionally to take a closer look at the human scene? In fact, is it possible that just because we do live in a high speed, high pressure society, we *need* to escape from it once in a while? If so, then perhaps it is valuable for us to read the Victorian novels that give us a more detailed picture of humanity, and permit us to travel for a while at a more relaxed pace. This is certainly one of the reasons that I enjoy Victorian novels. I look forward with pleasure, each time I open one, to stepping into a world where people do not seem to be in such a tearing hurry that they can't stop long enough to say more than "Hi" to each other!

### Suggestions for Approaching Victorian Novels

You can easily see now, I think, that the contrast between the Victorian society and ours is great. And, as a result, the modern reader, accustomed both to a rapid pace of living and to novels that frequently move at the same rate of speed, can find some parts of Victorian prose exceedingly difficult. But does this mean that you are poor readers, or that the novels aren't worth reading? Not at all! All you really need is a new approach to something so different from what you are used to. Therefore, let me offer a few suggestions that will help.

1. Take a deep breath—and slow down! Keep in mind that as you open a Victorian novel you are entering another, much more leisurely world.

2. Don't read with a dictionary at your elbow. If the author uses four or five adjectives to describe something, you'll probably know at least two of them, and that's enough to understand most of what he's saying. If you interrupt your reading every few minutes to look up a word, not only will you be unable to follow the thread of the story, but you will probably turn what could be fun into a dreary chore. However, if a word you don't know is repeated several times, then it would be wise to look it up. Caution: Remember that this advice applies only to Victorian novels. It is not advisable to read poetry, textbooks, or other technical material without looking up all words you don't know.

3. Take time to join the author. Don't read in stretches of 15 or 20 minutes; plan to allow at least an hour at a time. Otherwise you'll accumulate only a series of scattered, largely meaningless impressions.

366 READING IN THE CONTENT AREAS

4. Do, on occasion, skim through the author's little lectures and asides rather than read them word for word. Sometimes the author is obliging enough to warn you when he is about to digress—as in the excerpt from *Tom Brown's Schooldays*—and it is always the reader's privilege to join the author on his side excursions or skip them and go ahead with the story. However, please note that I said "on occasion." If you seldom or never stay with the author during his digressions, you will lose part of the pleasure and value of what he has to offer. For example, at one point an author, in the course of describing a cricket match, may digress to talk about the character building qualities of cricket or sports in general. One reader, a sports fan, may read that section out of interest; another who dislikes sports might consider reading it to get a new viewpoint on sports; a third who already knows a great deal about the values of sports may skim the section. Thus, the question of whether or not to skim is largely a matter of individual judgment based on preferences and previous knowledge.[1]

As you see, there's no magic, no trick, not even a special technique in these suggestions; they're more common sense ideas than anything else. But if you try them on the novel we're about to begin reading, perhaps you will find some of the great pleasure I have found in Victorian novels, especially in the books of Charles Dickens, George Eliot, and William Thackeray.

[1] Sometimes teachers are reluctant to advise skimming for fear students will take too much advantage of the privilege. But, in my experience the reverse has been true, partly, I suspect, because of the contrariness of human nature—if they have permission to skim, the temptation to do so isn't nearly as strong. And, the idea of exercising their own judgment is a powerful appeal to their maturity, one that teenagers are very likely to respond to.

# ANTIDOTE FOR APATHY—ACQUIRING READING SKILLS FOR SOCIAL STUDIES *

### Helen Huus

The social studies are generally considered an important part of the school curriculum. Therefore any hint that these studies are not being taught as well as they might be taught is a cause for concern.

In this selection Huus comments on apathy in our social studies classrooms. There are students who approach social studies in a way that is not conducive to developing the concepts, skills, and attitudes they need to be adequate citizens. Huus explains her antidote for apathy and details the prescription under three categories.

1. What is the apathy to which the author refers in the title of her article?

2. Pronunciation skills can be taught deductively or inductively. Does the author suggest which method to use?

3. Can you see any advantages or disadvantages in teaching some of these skills to individuals or small groups of students before attempting them with larger groups? Explain.

4. At your first opportunity, examine a social studies text and list particular examples under the headings listed under "Inference" in this article, e.g., "cause-effect implications," etc.

5. Develop and write out an argument for not neglecting the teaching of application skills in social studies. Subject it to the criticism of others.

WHILE school keeps in thousands of classrooms throughout our country and while a generation of pupils grows up to take their turn at running the world, time does not stand still. Europe busies herself with the Common Market, Algeria has an uneasy truce, trouble crops up in Indonesia, Argentina, or Syria, and our children study school and community, state and nation, often in a half-hearted, mechanical way, and dull their senses by rote memory, a multitude of proper names (many unidentified), and a lack of zest for the whole idea. Why an apathy for social studies, when it is constantly teeming with action, people, adventure, and daring—all aspects that interest the elementary school child? Why, indeed?

The answer lies, perhaps, in three directions—the pupils' own skills, the

* FROM Challenge and Experiment in Reading, J. Allen Figurel, editor, International Reading Association Proceedings, VII (New York: Scholastic Magazines, 1962), pp. 81–88, reprinted with permission of Helen Huus and the International Reading Association.

materials available, and the teacher's enthusiasm and know-how. The anti-dote for apathy, as for any evil, lies in counteraction—in working against, and since the opposite of apathy is interest, feeling, activity, and excitement, the obvious way to counteract it is to promote these opposites.

While there are many and varied ways in which such skills might be analyzed, they have been organized into the three general categories of pro-nunciation, meaning, and application for purposes of this discussion. Each of these will be treated in turn.

### Pronunciation Skills

MULTISYLLABIC WORDS.  Whenever a reader faces new material, his first responsibility is to decipher the symbols into meaningful units. In social studies, as in any subject area, the reader applies the skills of phonetic anal-ysis, structural analysis, and context clues that help him arrive at the pro-nunciation and ultimate recognition of the words he must read. Since many of the words in social studies are multisyllabic words, the reader needs the ability to apply the generalizations dealing with words of this type. Following are five useful generalizations for this purpose:

1. When a word has a double consonant (or two consonants) following a vowel, divide the word between the consonants, such as: Hit-tite, Mis-sis-sip-pi, Ham-mer-fest, col-lec-tive, Ap-pian, Bren-ner, and tun-dra, Mos-lem, mon-soon, or-bit, or Den-mark.
2. When a vowel is followed by a single consonant in a word of more than one syllable, the division is made *before* the consonant, as in: A-ra-bi-an, A-so-ka, as-tro-labe, co-lo-ni-al, Hai-fa, Rho-de-sia, So-viet, and ve-to.
3. When a word ends in "le," the preceding consonant belongs with the unaccented ending, as in: Bi-ble, mid-dle, Con-stan-ti-no-ple, and mar-ble.
4. When a word contains a consonant blend, the blend is usually not divided, as in: West-min-*ster*, Rem-*brand*t, man-u-*scripts*, Liv-ing-*stone*, and Ca-sa-*bla*n-ca.
5. A word may be composed of a root plus a prefix and/or a suffix. Com-mon prefixes that should be learned are: *un, ex, pre, ab, ad, com, en, in, re, de, sub, be, dis, pro*. Common suffixes include: *ment, tion, tive, ly, less, ance, ness, ful, ship*.

Unless pupils are given practice in using syllabication skills, both in the reg-ular developmental reading class and as applied in social studies and other classes, they do not acquire the needed ease of recognition that allows them to read material of difficulty with interest, and simply plodding along can become a deadly bore.

FOREIGN WORDS.  Even a student who may have acceptable skills in word recognition will almost certainly encounter difficulty when he tries to apply those he knows with some of the words he finds in his social studies reading—words derived from foreign languages that have kept certain elements intact, and proper names that have retained the original pronunciation and have not been Anglicized.

In the first category are such words as: *plateau, saga, mesa, fief, kaiser, hotelier, veld, apartheid, fjord, atrium,* and *ballet,* while in the latter are the French Renaissance, Marseilles, Versailles, St. Chapelle, and Basque, but Paris (not Paree); the German Roentgen, Gutenberg, Bach, Beethoven, Wagner, Worms, and Frankfort am Main (not Maine); the Italian da Vinci, Verdi, Rossini; the Indian Brahman and Buddha; the African Leopoldville, Afrikaner, or Nkrumah; or other difficult pronunciations like Goteberg, the Louvre, and Popocatepetl or Port Said. At any rate, children who learn correct pronunciation of the many proper names in social studies have a small beginning toward becoming multilingual.

USE OF THE DICTIONARY. Knowing the basic generalizations for getting words independently will help, but there comes a point when even the mature reader needs the verification that can be found only in an authoritative source. Is it Himälaya or Himalaya? Hamburg or Hämburg? Istanbul or Istambul? Yucatan or Yucatän? Edinburg or Edinboro? The dictionary or glossary should tell, but the difficulty lies in checking the pronunciation initially so that incorrect forms are not practiced and thus become difficult to eradicate.

## MEANING SKILLS

TECHNICAL WORDS. In addition to the pronunciation problems already described, the number of technical words used in social studies promote apathetic reaction. The technical words may be unique to the field or may be words for which the student already has one meaning. In the former category are words like *latitude, longitude, Constitution, Declaration of Independence, dictatorship, consumer, transportation,* and so on. In the latter are such words and phrases as *compass rose,* the *Gold Rush, world trade, the world market, diet* (as in Diet at Worms), *man power, raw materials, fixed salary,* and others equally obscure.

ABSTRACT WORDS. Social studies also abounds in abstract words like *democratic, loyalty, dignity, appreciation, interdependence, conservation, Dark Ages, industrial revolution, capital and labor,* the *Iron* or *Bamboo Curtain,* the *Cold War,* and the *New Frontier.*

The antidote for getting meaning into these technical and abstract words lies in tapping the pupils' own experiences by first relating the unknown word to some similar concept within his knowledge—location by latitude and longitude, for example, could be related to the location of buildings at a street intersection. Explanation is another way, and easy, or a study can be made of the word itself by first stripping off the prefix and suffix, as in the word *transportation,* leaving only the root word. Some pupils may already relate the root *port* to other words like *porter* or *portable* and make their own generalization about its meaning. When the prefix meaning of *across*, and the suffix meaning of *the act or state of* are added, pupils arrive at a meaning for *transportation* as "the act or state of carrying across." By substitution in the sentence, pupils clinch the idea and learn its use.

Of course, first-hand experience is the best teacher, and pupils who have been to Sutter's Mill have heard vivid tales of the Gold Rush; first-hand experience with maps will soon clarify what a compass rose is. Excursions are by far the most fruitful techniques for developing vocabulary easily, quickly, and permanently. Students learn new vocabulary naturally as they use the proper terminology for describing a place, an object, a method, or a product. A visit to a mill, for example, clarifies such words as *millwright, grist, rollway, undershot, mill race, vats, roving, carding, spinning jenny, sawyer, turbine, penstock,* or *sluicegate.*

The maps, diagrams, pictures, and other types of illustrations found in abundance in many social studies texts are there for a purpose—to help children visualize the scenes, to help them grasp relationships of rainfall, products, income, taxes, or time. Meaning is certainly enhanced when a diagram or photograph accompanies a description of locks on a canal, water wheels or ladders for fish, when a graph shows the distribution of rainfall for a certain area according to seasons or months, or when a time line puts the Age of Exploration into proper relationship with the Viking Era and the present. To make time really meaningful, let children put their own dates of birth on the line and let them see how short a span their life up to the present actually is.

For those pupils who simply cannot keep up, even with expert help, Fry recommends "glossing" as an aid to comprehension. This means "simply reading to students from the text, stopping frequently to explain concepts and terms." [1] At best, the teacher makes the page come alive by supplementing from his extensive background and, when coupled with enthusiasm, is guaranteed to capture the interest of even the most apathetic.

ORGANIZATION SKILLS.    Inherent in the total complex of skills in comprehension lies those related to the organization or structure of the material. The "cluster" of skills, as Robinson calls them, related to organization includes reading for details and main ideas, changing main ideas to topics and details to sub-topics, then labeling them in outline form. He presents three steps as a practical approach: (1) locating key words in sentences, (2) finding the key sentence in a paragraph, and (3) determining the main thought in a paragraph.[2]

1 Edward B. Fry, " 'Glossing,' An Ancient Method to Aid Social Studies Teachers with Reading Instruction," *California Journal of Secondary Education*, XXXII (February 1957), pp. 90–92.
2 H. Alan Robinson, "A Cluster of Skills: Especially for Junior High School," *The Reading Teacher*, XV (September 1961), pp. 25–28.

While pupils may be able to see the structure of a sentence or a paragraph, they must be able also to obtain the larger view of a section or a chapter—yes, even of a total book—if they are to place historical events in proper perspective or obtain an international rather than a national or regional view alone. This means a constant shifting of position as additional information is obtained, and seeing these new relationships may require help. Modern textbooks provide useful aids in their varied type faces, side headings, and sectional titles, and teachers help pupils use outlines. One practical way is to have topics set down without numbers or letters, but using indentation instead to show relationship between main and subordinate levels. Then, as the story unfolds, these outline parts can be rearranged and literally lifted out and placed in the new frame of reference in its proper location.

Certain words act as "cue words" to help readers define organization and relationships, or shifts, and transitions. Such words include: *on the other hand, furthermore, nevertheless, in addition, moreover, since, because, for, but,* and the obvious *first, second, third,* and *finally.* These indicate transition, connection, and relation, and give warning that such will occur. Teachers can give added practice in heeding these signals by concocting exercises where pupils fill in missing connectives or change meaning by substituting other connectives. Another technique is to have pupils locate words clues in their textbooks and other reading materials.

Besides the logical organization embodied in the main idea-detail structure of writing, other types encountered in social studies include chronological organization, with pertinent events related in the order they occurred, or the fictional approach sometimes used in the lower grades, where events lead up to the climax of the story. Time lines help give the proper chronological perspective, as do two-dimensional charts that place topics like "economics," "political history," "geography," "invention," and "trade" along the top of a chart and the names of various countries along the side. Each row then shows one country in relation to each topic, while each column shows the status of that topic in the various countries listed. Such charts can be made for a decade, a century, or even an era, but reducing organization to visual form has the added advantage of sensory appeal. Picture charts serve a similar purpose and catch the interest of some students who might not be enticed by the abstract approach.

Understanding the over-all pattern of a subject area, such as social studies, provides a background and a Gestalt for further learning. While this pattern is complicated by the staccato presentation of facts without expansion, by the introduction of many names and terms, and by the remoteness to pupil experience, it has the advantage of providing many new learnings and enough "top" for even the brightest, as well as a certain exotic flavor inherent in eras past and places distant.

SIMPLE COMPREHENSION. Anderson makes a plea for the constant use of the "unseen question" as a stimulus for students to read and comprehend.

He emphasizes the importance of the reader's purpose, that he set his own, and that he then answers what he started out to find.[3] While it may not always be practical for pupils to set their own purposes, teachers can arouse interest and, together with their pupils, set the purposes for reading. The SQ3R technique (survey, question, read, recite, review) is a similar method couched in catchy terms, but useful nonetheless.

Once purpose is set, pupils need to choose a speed of reading commensurate with the job to be done. For the survey, skimming to locate key words and headings, to see the over-all job, and to obtain an overview will suffice. For the answering of questions, a more careful reading than before is needed. For the review following the recitation, a quick cursory reading will be sufficient. Being able to shift speed gears smoothly is a mark of the mature reader, and students need practice under supervision in order to accomplish this task.

INTERPRETATION SKILLS. The intricate "cluster" of skills comprising thoughtful interpretation cannot be discussed fully here; only two will be mentioned—inference and evaluation.

*Inference* refers to those ideas implied but not explicitly stated and which are acquired by reasoning or concluding. The contents of social studies texts are replete with cause-effect implications, time relationships, generalizations about exploration, the effect of terrain on development, the organization of governments, the influence of imperialism or a thousand other ideas. How to teach becomes a problem, for, of necessity, the making of inferences requires the use of higher mental abilities—to see two ideas, to note common elements and make a connection between the two, then adapt the new idea to the unknown—and slow learners will need explicit help in having the points of similarity and relationship specifically cited while fast learners are already applying the method to new content.

The first question that might well be asked in *evaluation* relates to the author and his purpose. "Who wrote this material? Is he qualified to do so?" In an article entitled "The Power and the Glory of the Word," Nance makes the following statement about authors in general:

The writer is a human being and a citizen. The scope and content of his material will be conditioned by his major interests, his outlook on life, his responses to life, and his experience, knowledge, abilities, and opportunities. . . .[4]

The competency of the author becomes particularly important when facts disagree, or when different works place different interpretations on the same series of events, or when events are presented from different points of view. Finding pertinent information about living authors is sometimes difficult,

[3] A. W. Anderson, "Directing Reading Comprehension," *The Reading Teacher*, XIII (February 1960), pp. 206–207, 211.

[4] E. C. Nance, "The Power and the Glory of the Word," *Vital Speeches*, XXIII (April 1, 1957), p. 381.

but students can look at the book jackets, the comment column in a periodical, or the blurbs from the publisher. The reputation of a publishing house can lend dignity and prestige to an unknown author until he makes his mark. At any rate, readers must be taught to consider the source.

Related questions, "Why did the author write on this topic? Was it to advertise, to propagandize, to present information, to present a point of view?" must also be given attention. Nance comments on purposes for writing by saying:

> Writers throughout the centuries have had many different goals: To recover the past, to record and conserve for the future, to interpret, comment, report, arouse, condemn, defend, entertain, annoy or to obtain personal or institutional publicity.[5]

Certainly if there are hidden or ulterior motives, students should be able to locate the signals and analyze the material accordingly. The use of sweeping generalizations not backed by data or examples, the "snob appeal" so rampant in advertising, the pseudo-scientific surveys often quoted, the testimonial or "everyone believes" technique, or the use of emotionally tinged words like *fellow traveler, anarchy, slave, imperialistic, dictatorial,* or *beneficent, philanthropic, generous, handsome, immense proportion,* or *gigantic, colossal, stupendous, magnificent,* reach various people in different ways. It becomes important to create in readers a studied wariness that aids them in objective judgment: to paraphrase *caveat emptor,* "Let the reader beware!"

The second question in evaluation ought to be, "Is the information true?" In part, a reputable author's word is taken, but skeptical readers and careful scholars check to see if facts agree and decide if enough facts are presented. Here is where the student's knowledge and background come into play, for his incidental or systematic learning serves as a backboard against which to bounce the ideas of the author, as well as to raise questions about facts that seem somehow to ring not quite true. Checking against other references— encyclopedia, atlas, almanac, or any number of handbooks and general works —becomes necessary, and through practice and guidance students become proficient in locating the right source and finding within that source the material needed.

A third aspect of evaluation relates to the quality of writing exhibited by the author. For illustration, the following excerpt from an article entitled, "Hong Kong Has Many Faces," in a recent issue of *National Geographic* describes Hong Kong's rise as an industrial city:

> For decades . . . Hong Kong was the front door for the great China market. Sitting astride the world's trade lanes, the city endlessly shuttled goods in and out of its busy warehouses, bound from China to the world, and from the world to China. Then came the Korean War. The United Nations voted an embargo on trade with China, and Hong Kong—the old Hong Kong—sickened.

[5] *Ibid.*

The city might have died if another "disaster" had not come along at almost the same time. The years of the refugee were 1949 to 1951, when men poured out of Red China in the hundreds of thousands.

"Fortunately," he said, "that problem arrived with a built-in solution, for the refugees were not all poor men. . . .

"Here, in one place, were capital and labor, eager to work together." [6]

Figures of speech like *the front door, sitting astride, sickened . . .* and *might have died, men poured out,* and *a built-in solution,* add meaning through the imagery and relationships implied. Certain of the words connote a tone that transcends the description. These words create a feeling of greatness and strength, as implied in the phrases *front door for the great China market, sitting astride the world's trade lanes,* and *endlessly shuttling.*

The style of writing—the figurative, picturesque, and connotative aspects— influences the reader's understanding and reaction to what he reads. A lack of awareness of the subtleties of style will result either in gullibility or lack of accurate perception.

The acquisition of complete meaning, therefore, lies in the reader's ability to understand the technical and abstract vocabulary, to grasp the structure and organization of the whole, to interpret the ideas implied but not directly stated, and to evaluate not only the author's competency and the validity of his statements, but his style of writing as well.

## Application Skills

PROBLEM SOLVING. The third reading skill to be emphasized here is reacting to and using the ideas and impressions gained through reading. The highest level of reaction and application is the actual integration of the concepts, attitudes, and appreciations into the reader's own life so that what he reads becomes a part of him forever. For each person, there could be compiled, perhaps, a list of "Reading that changed my life." And is not this, after all, the ultimate goal of education—social studies, too—to change people from illiterate to literate, from uncultured to cultured, from irrational to rational? When reading materials in the social studies serve this goal, they are powerful agents indeed.

Students may react to their reading about Hong Kong, for example, by changing or forming opinions about the city itself, the people who live there, or they may do further research in order better to understand this complex city.

EXTENDED READING. What other use can the student make of his new found skills in reading? Merely keeping up with textbook assignments keeps some students busy, but even they should have an opportunity to use some

[6] John Scofield, "Hong Kong Has Many Faces," *The National Geographic Magazine,* CXXI, No. 1 (January 1962), pp. 9–10.

of the beautiful, interesting, up-to-date books about our own and other countries, about historical eras, geographical areas, and the function and operation of government. The hundreds of books for children published each year contain a wealth of information; teachers need but to make them available to the right children at the right time.

Teachers stimulate extended reading when they take time for current events, for even elementary school children are interested in weather, sports, space, royalty, and the President and his family. Keeping up to date with the news is a good way to establish the habit of news reading with young children.

But it is in books that many children find their identification with heroes of another age or of another culture. Serviss recommends that teachers "help children find books convincing in portrayal, vivid in sensory imagery, reasonable and alive in characterization, discerning in the revelation of universal traits." [7]

Library books contribute in various ways to make the social understandings meaningful and interesting to children. They paint images in depth and detail, for one paragraph in the text can be amplified by extended treatment. They clarify concepts and expand reasons only briefly mentioned in the text, and they put the breath of human life into historical characters and people who live in other countries.[8]

In choosing books to counteract the pallid fare or pulp material so easily available to children, first ask, "What do children of this age *like* to read?" If the group is young, they like stories of children their own age, animals, slapstick humor, pictures with clear colors and not too much detail, and simple plots with repetition and refrain. A book like *Nu Dang and His Kite* not only tells of Siam (Thailand) as Nu Dang paddles up the long river to look for his kite, but also contains the gloomy refrain, "But nobody had seen it. Nowhere. No kite at all." Fortunately the kite is at home when Nu Dang arrives, for the wind had carried it there; so the ending is most satisfying to young readers. Children sympathize with Ping, the duck who runs away rather than being last on the boat and getting the spank he knows will come, for they, too, know that "fair is fair." But they rejoice when he escapes, and they realize that after all, a spank is nothing much compared to what Ping has survived.

Children learn about the world of work through such books as Lois Lenski's *Farmer Small*, *Cowboy Small*, and *Pilot Small*, or through Burton's *Mike*

---

[7] Trevor, K. Serviss, "Reading in the Content Areas," *Elementary English*, XXX (October 1953), p. 359.

[8] See Helen Huus, *Children's Books to Enrich the Social Studies: For the Elementary Grades*, Bulletin 32 (Washington, D. C.: The National Council for the Social Studies, 1961), p. 196.

The World History Bibliography Committee of NCSS, Alice W. Spieseke, chm., *World History List for High Schools: A Selection for Supplementary Reading*, Bulletin 31 (Washington, D. C.: National Council for the Social Studies, 1959), p. 119.

*Mulligan and His Steam Shovel,* or Bate's *Who Built the Bridge?* While
some of these books personify machines, nevertheless the power and importance of their work is clearly portrayed. Children get gentle nudgings about
manners from Munro Leaf, and through the charming books of Tasha Tudor
they follow the seasons and the calendar, learn to count, and recite the
alphabet in order. Holidays give a chance for biography—the colorful picture
books by the D'Aulaires of Lincoln and Washington, Franklin, and Columbus—or for stories like *The Thanskgiving Story* and *The Fourth of July Story,*
by Alice Dalgliesh, or *The Egg Tree,* that won the Caldecott Award, and
*Patrick and the Golden Slippers,* that tells about Philadelphia's annual New
Year's Day Mummers' Parade. (Yes, there are many books that appeal to
younger children.)

The middle-graders love adventure and mystery, exploration and invention,
and girls begin to look for romance. All of these can be found in books that
enhance the social studies. Biography is fun when there is *Ben and Me* to
compare with the facts, or *Mr. Revere and I.* History becomes contemporary
when *Adam of the Road* contains the story of a budding wandering minstrel,
an eleven-year-old boy who has lost his beloved dog, even though the story
begins in the year 1294. Geography is really people when preadolescents
follow Big Tiger and Christian, who get caught on a troop train just because
they tried to fly their kites from an empty box car. Their adventures through
Mongolia and Sinkiang include robbers, bandits, a lama, and soldiers, and
the responsibility of carrying a secret message. Geography is people when
Young Fu has grown gradually into a capable coppersmith craftsman, and
when Li Lun, Lad of Courage, plants seven grains of rice on the highest
mountain, then tends the last grain so that it survives to bear rice heads.
Thus he shows his people a new way to combat hunger. Geography is people,
too, when Momo, a little Tibetan girl, follows the trail of her stolen golden
Lhasa terrier, Pempa, from her home in the hills to the busy city of Calcutta.
Even boys will thrill to the suspense in this story, and all who read it will
learn about the people of the mountains and about their customs and country.
Pearl Buck's story of Japan, *The Big Wave,* Armstrong Sperry's *Call It Courage* and Elizabeth Lewis' *To Beat a Tiger* are other books that show the
character, traditions, and problems of peoples of the Far East.

Older boys and girls can find in books stories that contain the drama and
daring of yesterday and today—books like those of Roman Britain by Rose-
mary Sutcliffe or *The Byzantines* by Thomas Chubb, which begins during
the Fourth Crusade in 1203 and describes the wealth and culture of this
great empire at the crossroads of the world. *Engineers Did It!* contains interesting accounts of feats like Roman aqueducts and roads, the flying buttresses
of the cathedral at Amiens, and the laying of the Atlantic cable, while modern adventures are depicted in books like *Kon Tiki,* or Quentin Reynolds' *The
Battle of Britain.*

These are but a few of the exciting, well-written, vivid tales that transport
the reader for a time into another era, another place, another culture, and

allow him to identify himself with these heroes to obtain vicariously some of the emotions, the grandeur, the problems of a different age, a different sphere. When he returns to reality, he will be more knowledgeable, more insightful, more understanding, and more thoughtful than before his flight of fancy, and this, in itself, is reward enough.

## SUMMARY

And so it becomes evident that pupils who have the skills of pronunciation and recognition, who can put meaning into words, see order in the content, delve beneath the written word and look at the total with a studied appraisal have acquired the reading skills that make social studies an enjoyable experience. Then when pupils have, in addition, books and books that let them rove through the world and down the centuries, vicariously experiencing the triumphs and disappointments of people who really lived or might have done so, then teachers can say, "We tried to teach them about people. We taught them to read and think. We gave them books and time to read. We helped them when they asked and prodded them when they would be complacent. It remains for the future to tell how well we have succeeded."

# MATERIALS FOR THE UNIT PLAN IN SOCIAL STUDIES *

Jean Fair

It is a commonly accepted fact among educators that the unit plan of teaching is effective because the learner can set many of his own goals and work on problems that interest him. A second advantage of the plan is that it allows the learner to work with materials that interest him and are at his ability level. Finally, the unit plan permits experiences to be organized in a way that brings out meaningful generalizations, facilitates seeing inter-relationships among the experiences, and allows the learner to see the wholeness or the unity of these experiences.

In this article Fair shows how materials are used to best advantage in teaching the social studies unit so that the purported values of the unit method can be experienced.

1. For what purposes are various types of social studies materials used?

* REPRINTED FROM *Materials for Reading*, Helen M. Robinson, editor, Supplementary Educational Monographs, No. 86, pp. 158–162, by permission of The University of Chicago Press. Copyright, 1957, by The University of Chicago Press.

2. *What can you infer about the author's attitude toward the importance of developing mature readers?*

3. *The author is cognizant of psycho-* logically sound teaching-learning principles. Can you infer what these principles are?

4. *State the article's key ideas.*

A UNIT PLAN implies that students are to organize some wholeness or unity out of many aspects of their experiences. A unit plan usually calls for the development of several kinds of behavior, understanding, beliefs and attitudes, interests, skills, and thinking, in content areas appropriate for individual students. The topic or problem on which the content is centered is frequently, although not necessarily, structured in some other fashion than that of the conventional subject field. Since a unit plan is usually expected to organize several weeks of student time, some careful decisions must be made about definitions of, and priorities among, objectives, with mere coverage for its own sake ruled out. Student purposes take on great importance, and materials and experiences need to have maximum meaning. Learning activities must be chosen with an eye to what students are to learn, and these activities must be ordered to facilitate organization of experiences.

## MATERIALS TO PROMOTE A VARIETY OF OBJECTIVES

Let us turn to the kinds of reading materials required in a unit plan of study. It is obvious that we shall need a wide variety; no one book is likely to permit the development of the several kinds of behaviors appropriate for the purposes of a particular group of students. Textbooks are useful for giving information about, and understanding of, topics and problems. Many teachers and students limit what can be learned by relying almost exclusively on such books. Others go to the needless trouble of finding the necessary discussions in a cumbersome variety of sources, when equally useful, and sometimes more suitable, treatments could be found more efficiently in classroom textbooks. The helpfulness of textbooks is increased when several are available and when students free themselves of the mind-set that textbook information can be used only in the organizational structure of the textbook itself.

Still, textbooks alone are not likely to be sufficient. Students also need encyclopedias appropriate for their reading ability; reference books, from the common almanacs to the less often used, but frequently more efficient, *Statistical Abstracts* (U.S. Government Printing Office), maps, atlases, gazeteers, biographical dictionaries, and the like; pamphlets; magazines suitable for readers of different abilities (to be saved over a period of years to increase sources); and books. We are all aware of the variety of sources which promote understanding.

However valuable these may be, they are usually not the most useful materials for involving students' feelings and so developing meaningful understandings, attitudes, and interests. Novels can help here. Consider, by way of illustration, Lewis' *Young Fu of the Upper Yangtze* (Winston, 1937) and Pearl Buck's classic, *The Good Earth* (World Publishing Co., 1952), for a unit dealing with China. Short stories are helpful; how valuable in a study of civil rights is a story such as Shirley Jackson's "The Lottery." [1] Plays are useful, for example, Miller's *Death of a Salesman* (Viking, 1949), for showing the values of modern society. Titles from biography and poetry will occur to all of us. We sometimes forget, however, the non-fiction articles and books. Think of the power of "The Blast in Centralia No. 5" [2] in a problem unit on how to improve conditons of labor; John Hersey's *Hiroshima* (Knopf, 1946) in a topical unit on World War II or a problem unit on what to do about national defense; or James Michener's *The Bridge at Andau* (Random, 1957) in a study of present American policy toward Europe. There are classic documents, too: Webster's "Reply to Hayne," Bryan's "Cross of Gold" speech, and many more. A collection of such materials, while not sufficient in themselves, do represent a needed type.

Many of these can be used also for the development of abilities in critical and creative thinking. Textbooks should be used to obtain comparisons of authors' points of view and for documents, graphs, and tables for interpretation. However, students will frequently need materials, other than textbooks, specifically chosen to permit questions like these: "What is the problem discussed?" "To what kind of audience does the author intend to speak?" "What are his assumptions or conclusions?" "Is his argument consistent?" "Are his facts relevant, accurate, and adequate?" "How does this interpretation compare with that interpretation?" "What difference does it make whether we adopt one or the other interpretation?" "What other solutions are possible?"

For able students, several sets of materials are particularly useful in units on American history. The Amherst series of "Problems in American Civilization" (Heath), which range over many significant problems (for example, "Slavery as a Cause of the Civil War" and "Loyalty in a Democratic State"), help students define problems and analyze and compare arguments in both contemporary statements and interpretations by later historians. Similar remarks might be made about Leopold and Link's *Problems in American History* (Prentice-Hall, 1952) and other excellent collections. Somewhat less difficult are the three pamphlets dealing with American foreign policy toward China, Russia, and Germany, recently published under the auspices of the North Central Association of Colleges and Secondary Schools (Science Research Associates, 1957). The series in the yearly "Reference Shelf" (H. W. Wilson) on such problems as federal taxes and national defense can also be mentioned. Such materials as these, which offer help in defining problems and choosing among alternative solutions, are particularly valuable in unit

[1] Shirley Jackson, "The Lottery," *Fifty Great Short Stories*, pp. 175–185. Edited by Milton Crane. New York: Bantam Books, 1952.

[2] John Bartlow Martin, "The Blast in Centralia No. 5," *Harper's Magazine Reader*, pp. 38–89. New York: Bantam Books, 1953.

plans where individuals or small groups are working on aspects of a problem independently.

Students will need what we often call "documents." Some of the classics ought not to be overlooked. The *Declaration of Independence* and Number Ten of *The Federalist Papers* are easily available arguments for some units. Analyses of contemporary materials, such as quotations from Churchill and Hitler, may be needed in a unit on the origins of modern war. Eye-witness accounts are helpful when properly criticized or skimmed for a point of view. While there are fewer such accounts suitable for world-history units, a wealth of such material is available to us in other areas. Moreover, accounts of current events are readily obtained from newspapers and magazines.

Controversy is inherent in almost any meaningful social-studies unit, whether the content comes from the past or the present. In a unit on problems of improving law and justice, the concepts of justice embodied in Hammurabi's Code can provoke controversy when applied to cases of modern wrongdoing. Contemporary materials from books, magazines, and newspapers will be needed both for units on recurring issues in human affairs and for those dealing with specific present-day problems. Articles in magazines of opinion and editorials will be integral parts of plans for a unit; they are to be criticized, evaluated, and compared, and used as statements of alternatives in decision-making.

Graphs and tables, too, are helpful, particularly when they encourage interpretation. Those of the National Industrial Conference Board, "Road Maps of Industry" (The Board, New York), a regular and easily obtained series, fit into many units dealing with recurring issues. They present enough data to compare trends, question predictions, and check the accuracy of many other materials.

Students will need, then, materials which allow the development of a range of behaviors in content flexibility structured to meet their particular purposes.

## Meaning in Materials

Young people must also have meaningful materials, for they cannot organize what does not carry meaning. I will do little more here than call attention to the use of audio-visual materials and the study aids, pictures, and the like found in textbooks and pamphlets. We might help students by taking advantage of many excellent television programs which can contribute meaning to the reading materials used. Picture magazines, both those current and those saved from past years, are useful at many ability levels.

Some special mention may well be made of the kind of pamphlet material which contains enough of what we may call "case material" to put meaning into often empty generalizations. The "Life Adjustment Series" (Science Research Associates), by way of example, includes more than fifty titles, some at two maturity levels, on such topics as *Relations with Parents, Leisure Time,* and *Unions*, which are of particular use in problem units dealing with the family, recreation, working, and the like.

Documents like the Magna Charta can often be rewritten by able students and used by the less able in units such as one centered on the growth of democratic government.

*Life* magazine has done some heavily illustrated series on general topics, such as "The World's Great Religions" (Time, 1957), which, by drawing matters together, promote meaning in topics of broad sweep. Cartoons like Burr Shafer's "Through History with J. Wesley Smith," which have appeared frequently in the *Saturday Review*, can clarify, in a memorable way, the meaning of many an important point.

### RELATIONSHIPS AMONG MATERIALS

Students also need materials selected with particular reference to the organization planned for in the unit. To develop, within a unit centered on the American West, the generalization that frontier life influenced the growth of American democracy, students might read a variety of novels for pictures of western life and compare them in group discussions. Just any novels set in the West will not do; students need those which actually present pictures of democratic living. Rölvaag's *Giants in the Earth* (Harper, 1927), for example, contains enough material for students to work from; Willa Cather's *Death Comes for the Archbishop* (Knopf, 1927) does not, even though this book has much merit in itself and may be useful in other kinds of units. To enable students to discuss the control of wealth, excerpts taken from the writings of Jefferson, Hamilton, Bryan, M. Dooley, Andrew Carnegie, and Franklin D. Roosevelt must be carefully selected; selections from just any of their writings and speeches will not do. Teachers and students are often bewildered about the use of a variety of reading materials in group learning activities, partly because the variety of materials gathered have only a tenuous connection with the hoped-for organization.

Moreover, students need enough materials to arrive at sound conclusions. Learning activities sometimes have not borne fruit because students have not read enough. Concretely, the weekly current-events paper or even two or three well-selected pieces of material may be insufficient to permit students to apply the concept of the balance of power, which has been developed, let us say, in an international relations unit in a panel discussion on "Should We Revise NATO?"

Reading materials must be capable of fitting into some sort of sequence within the unit. Some materials are first rate for the beginnings of units; think of the power of Irwin Shaw's short story "Preach on the Dusty Roads" [3] for raising questions about citizens' responsibilities in foreign affairs. We have

---

[3] Irwin Shaw, "Preach on the Dusty Roads," *Best American Short Stories of 1943.* Edited by Martha Foley. Boston: Houghton Mifflin Co., 1944.

already mentioned the value of materials which define problems. While controversial materials may also be used to raise questions and to define problems, students are not likely to be able to analyze and interpret the reading until they have had opportunities to read materials which give them information and understanding. The excellent chapter on the Constitution in Bragdon and McCutchen's *The History of a Free People* (Macmillan, 1954) is usually more suitable for developing understanding in a unit on the development of American government than for the beginning or the concluding activities. Materials to be interpreted or skimmed for a point of view very often fit best after students have some information and understanding. Maps are likely to be most useful, too, when students are developing understanding, although I can think of times when they might be used as summary materials. Teachers will be wise, also, to consider as reading materials the sources which enable students to locate the information they need. Forum discussions are useful for comparing points of view, generalizing, and summarizing.

Moreover, our unit plans need to permit sequence among units within a course and, for that matter, among courses. If students in a course on problems of democracy are to relate various concepts of democratic method, some collection of such materials as Stuart Chase's short article, "Zoning Comes to Town";[4] a more difficult article, "A New Attack on Delinquency,"[5] and Vern Sneider's *Teahouse of the August Moon* (Putnam, 1951) will be useful. An article like Kouwenhoven's "What's American about America?"[6] is fine material for extracting common elements from several kinds of American-history units.

## CONCLUDING STATEMENT

There is a wealth of reading material for the kinds of unit plans that high-school students need. Some clear ideas of what the students need materials for and some imaginative thinking help both teachers and students to find them.

[4] Stuart Chase, "Zoning Comes to Town," *Reader's Digest*, LXX (February 1957), 129–133.

[5] John Bartlow Martin, "A New Attack on Delinquency," *Harper's Magazine*, CCI (May 1944), 502–512.

[6] John Kouwenhoven, "What's American about America?" *Harper's Magazine*, CCXIII (July 1956), 25–33.

# THE PROBLEM OF UNDERSTANDING HISTORY *

John R. Palmer

The citizens of a country are faced with the problem of making critical judgments about contemporary domestic and international social and political problems. Most teachers of history in the secondary schools feel that the insights one can gain from the reading of history can be applied to understanding these problems. However, the sophistication with which teachers, as well as students, approach the reading of history varies widely. Palmer discusses factors which affect the individual's approach to history and the depth of understanding that he will be able to gain from it.

1. What does it mean to think historically?
2. Discuss the problem that readers face in making accurate inferences and generalizations on the basis of text materials of the type cited in the article.
3. What problems complicate the explanation process in teaching history?
4. Why is it difficult to establish generalizations in history and to apply the generalizations appropriately?
5. What are two major problems that must be considered if the teaching of history is to lead to an understanding of society? How can the teacher of history successfully cope with these problems?

THE LAY reader often approaches a history book as he would a novel. He expects to be carried along by the rapid succession of events, the drama of war, intrigue, the conquering hero, turning the rascals out, and so forth. Some historians are content with this view of history as an interesting story and nothing more. Most, however, are not. If history is merely a colorful story, then we should read a few selections from historical writing in English courses as one example of narrative form and be done with it.

Part of the historian's job, of course, is to tell a story and tell it as accurately as possible. W. B. Gallie recently defended again the history-is-a-story point of view and in so doing suggested an interesting analogy between following a story (the "story" of the past, for example) and following a game.[1] Consider the different perspectives brought to a game by the expert observer as compared to the youngster attending one of his first matches. In explaining the moves of the players, the expert brings them under certain relevant generalizations or principles. After assimilating and appreciating the expert's explanation, the younger spectators are in a position to follow more fully the

[1] W. B. Gallie, "The Historical Understanding," *History and Theory*, III, No. 2 (1963), 149–202.

* REPRINTED FROM *The Educational Forum*, XXX (March 1966), pp. 287–294, by permission of Kappa Delta Pi, An Honor Society in Education, owners of the copyright.

progress of the game. The need of explanation in this sense shows that following a game always admits of degrees of fullness or depth of understanding. We naturally presume that the spectators, like the audience in a theater or those listening to a story, are able to follow in a sufficient degree. There is a question, of course, as to what are the minimum or basic qualifications for following a game at all; and arising from this is the question of how further experience and practice, and more particularly the comments and explanations we receive from others, can help us to improve that basic capacity.

Knowing the rules of the game (the commonly understood and accepted generalizations, if you will) is essential for following the game but not sufficient. Following a game also presupposes some sense of the point and purpose of the game, what makes it "go," what makes it move to a climax, what counts most from the point of view of the pleasure of playing it, and so on. What is required is a much-more-than-legal appreciation of such notions as winning or losing a game and playing a good or worthwhile game. In the study of history these are counterparts of the value problem, the moral issues, the questions involving "ought," which, although frequently very difficult to get hold of, are so very important. To think historically, to exercise historical understanding, always includes the appreciation of human aims, choices, valuations, efforts, deeds—things that are to be attributed exclusively to individual men, whether acting on their own or in concert, whether on their own personal behalf or as representatives of their group or cause or nation.

Our concern here, of course, is not with games but the study of the past. While the analogy between the two breaks down at many points, the task of "following" (which I take to mean understanding or making sense of) an historical account and the peculiar situation of the novice with respect to this task raise some interesting problems.

What is required to "follow" this selection from Stavrianos' A Global History of Man, a recent and very carefully prepared world history textbook?

We come here to an important difference between Western Europe and Russia. In Western Europe, serfdom existed in the Middle Ages and disappeared in modern times. In Russia it was the other way around—serfdom did not exist in the Middle Ages but appeared in modern times. The explanation for this difference is that in the medieval period there was too much land and too few people in Russia to make serfdom possible. So long as there was plenty of land on all sides, no Russian peasant would stand for any abuse from his landowner. A peasant simply picked up his belongings and moved off to the empty lands of the nearby frontier.

However, a remarkable change took place in modern times with the coming of rulers such as Ivan the Terrible and Peter the Great. These men wanted to make Russia strong and to do this they needed a big army and plenty of money. But they could get neither so long as the peasants were free to run off to the frontier whenever they saw a recruiting officer or a tax collector. So the government cooperated with the nobles in forcibly tying the peasants to the land they tilled.

Laws were passed which steadily took away the peasant's freedom of movement. . . .

This system of serfdom is very important because it helps us understand why Russia fell behind the West with the coming of the Industrial Revolution. . . . One of the main reasons for this lag is to be found in serfdom. After all, the Industrial Revolution was nothing more or less than the invention and use of machinery in order to save labor. But there was no need for labor-saving machines in Russia at this time because there were plenty of serfs who could be ordered to do any work. . . .

For these reasons Russia during the nineteenth century fell far behind the West in her economy and technology. This became clear when Russia fought the Crimean War against France and England in 1855–1856. . . .

Russia lost the war but learned a lesson. During the following years the government initiated a number of basic changes. The most important were the abolition of serfdom and the pushing of industrialization.[2]

We have little difficulty in following the rapid transitions that occur in this passage, but consider what we bring to the account that really isn't there. We are well acquainted with the situation of the serf in Western Europe during the Middle Ages. Our knowledge of the concept "serf" as well as the attributes and attitudes of the peasant in various societies contribute to our understanding. Probably the Turner thesis flashes across our mind for an instant, and we toy with the notion of possible comparisons between our own frontier and that of Russia. Is the author making use of some generalization in the first paragraph concerning availability of land and a sense of independence? If so, certainly the next paragraph suggests the need for qualifying the generalization, for it appears that strong rulers can overcome the desire for independence despite the availability of land. Are the actions of Ivan and Peter accountable on the grounds of nationalism, the lust for power, or was it a matter of balance of power and the threat of outside domination? The concert between the nobles and the government which served the self-interest of each raises interesting questions about the use of power, the organization of governments, and the exercise of power by various classes.

The next causal leap takes us into the area of economics—the relationships which exist among the availability of cheap labor, the need for more consumer goods, and the effect of technological advances. We feel certain the author knows that when one asserts that serfdom caused the lag in Russian industrial development a key factor is being considered but hardly the complete picture.

The narrative shifts quickly to the Crimean War. It is suggested that somehow technological advancement and success in war are closely related. A number of examples, perhaps the use of the cross-bow in the Hundred Years War or our own explosion of the atomic bomb in World War II, come to mind. The aftermath of the Crimean War brings the story full circle. Ap-

[2] Leften S. Stavrianos, *A Global History of Man* (Boston: Allyn and Bacon, 1962), pp. 342–343.

parently the author feels that nations, like people, frequently learn from their mistakes, for after a miserable showing in the Crimean conflict the Russians abolished serfdom and promoted industrial growth. Perhaps the author has in mind here a situation of challenge and response in the manner of Arnold Toynbee. Now the story of Russian serfdom is before us from beginning to end.

It is impossible in a short time to suggest all the nuances of meaning and interpretation that one might develop from this passage. Indeed, they are almost endless. The reader can be said to have "followed," to have understood the narrative, however, without being aware of every possible referent. But it certainly is necessary, if one is to follow this account, to be somewhat of an expert, to know the rules of the game, to sense what the game is all about without having to be told at every turn, to have the knowledge and experience necessary to make sense out of the narrative.

The words written by the author constitute, to use Hempel's expression, a mere sketch of a succession of explanations that form a causal chain.[3] If the reader—and we are thinking particularly of the high school student—is to follow this very sparse narrative, a great deal of filling out is required. He will need an expert sitting at his elbow to interpret the plays for him. I have already suggested a number of aspects of the narrative that may need attention and will call for the exercise of the student's critical powers: examining the value problems, clarifying concepts, and establishing the pertinent ideological forces that may have been present. I shall discuss only one aspect crucial to the reader's understanding—the explanation process.

The essential elements in an explanation are (1) a description of the situation or circumstances which are relevant to the thing to be explained and (2) one or more generalizations or hypotheses asserting relationships among these prevailing factors that produced the occurrence in question. Obviously textbooks prepared for survey courses only begin to provide the context in which events have taken place. When more details are needed, we provide outside readings, use multiple texts, or prepare lectures. A number of critical thinking tasks accompany the building up of context: determination of relevancy, assessing the accuracy of the source, and so forth.

Establishing the pertinent generalizations or hypotheses appears to present great difficulties. Every characteristically human action involves a tacit reference to other actions, and not simply to such other actions as actually have taken place or will take place. To talk, to think, to promise, to trade, even to fight requires references to what *any* person subject to certain conditions or answering to a certain description would do or can be expected to do. In other words, characteristic human actions are performed and interpreted as expressions of generally accepted institutions, beliefs, routines, and norms. With land available, the peasants acted in a predictable manner. The Tsars and

---

[3] C. G. Hempel, "The Function of General Laws in History," *Journal of Philosophy,* XXIX (1942), 33–48.

the nobles calculated moves in accordance with their own self-interest as we would expect them to do.

In order to construct a narrative and relate events sequentially the historian must draw on all manner of general knowledge about life in society, from traditional truisms to the theorems and abstract models of the social sciences. He presumes that the reader, like the spectator at the game, is well enough acquainted with these generalizations, hypotheses, and models to follow the narrative at a satisfactory level of understanding. My experience indicates that most elementary and high school students are unable to follow the typical history textbook in this sense without a great deal of assistance.

The Stavrianos material quoted earlier will serve as an example. Generalizations, both stated and implied, abound in this passage. We are not certain, of course, whether the author expects all or even any of these to be learned, but almost any reader will take note of some of them. But just how valid are they? Shouldn't they be pulled out of the passage and examined more closely? If not, there is a dual danger. The student may accept those he picks out by chance as truisms that apply in all times and places, or he may overlook many that provide genuine insight into the actions of men and nations. In any case, is it the teacher's place to call attention to such generalizations and provide a classroom situation such that they can be examined, clarified, qualified, rejected, accepted, or whatever?

The following is a slightly abbreviated version of an explanation used by Stavrianos:

This system of serfdom is very important because it helps us understand why Russia fell behind the West with the coming of the Industrial Revolution. . . . One of the main reasons for this lag is to be found in serfdom. After all, the Industrial Revolution was nothing more or less than the invention and use of machinery in order to save labor. But there was no need for labor-saving machines in Russia at this time because there were plenty of serfs who could be ordered to do any work. So why should the nobles spend their money on machines and factories when all their needs were taken care of by the serfs? Why should anyone in Russia offer prizes for labor-saving inventions as was being done at this time in England? Not only were there plenty of workers, but also there was no need to turn out more and more goods because Russia did not have the world-wide markets that England did. . . . And the market in their own country was very small, since almost all Russians were serfs who could buy almost nothing.[4]

It was suggested earlier that the historian bases his explanations and assertions of causal relationships on commonly understood uniformities in social behavior. This is often true, but it is a dangerous assumption. It undoubtedly leads the student to think he is getting much more out of a history course than he really is. In the passage above the author has supplied more detail than for most of the explanations in the book. Perhaps he surmised that commonly understood generalizations were not enough to enable the reader

---

[4] Stavrianos, *loc. cit.*

to follow his narrative at this point. This attempt to account for variations among nations in economic development is much more complete than most such accounts one finds in high school textbooks, but it still assumes a great deal of economic understanding on the part of the reader. The Industrial Revolution is grossly over-simplified. What does the way the nobles spent their money have to do with economic development? How is economic growth related to the labor supply and the development of domestic and foreign markets? Is this example of lag purely an economic matter or are there ideological or value aspects that are crucial? In any case, a number of generalizations developed in the area of economics have been presumed by the author that may not be clear to the student or understood by him. If this is the case, he can read the passage, learn it in a relatively meaningless manner if that is required, but certainly he will not follow the explanation in the sense we have been using the term.

In most explanations found in history textbooks some concepts, generalizations, or models are used from one or more of the social sciences. In the instance just cited, much of the knowledge required for the explanation came from economics. This reliance on the social sciences can be either a virtue or a vice in the education of the student. It is a virtue when the generalizations and concepts of the social sciences are brought into the history class, examined and related to historical situations, and are understood by the students. However, when the crucial role of the social sciences in historical explanation is not recognized, the student may learn to be content with superficial and vague explanations that tend to distort his understanding of social reality and the process of social change. This affects not only his understanding of the past but also his understanding of current and future happenings.

There is space to make only brief mention of a number of aspects of historical explanation that appear to have a bearing on the reader's ability to understand historical writing and thus need to be taken into account in the teaching of history.

There is little place at present in any area of knowledge, except possibly mathematics, for universal truths, the sort of generalizations that may be stated in the form "If and only if. . . ." We must recognize and learn to be emotionally content with probabilistic generalizations that are continually subject to revision and the possibility of exception.

It appears that the historian generalizes at a number of levels. Terms or concepts are grouping words and therefore a type of generalization. Nouns such as "serfdom," "nation," "freedom," and "industrialization" or verbs like "subdue," "revolutionize," and "cooperate" are examples. At another level there are groupings of statements about events. "So long as there was plenty of land on all sides, no Russian peasant would stand for any abuse from his landowner." This statement contains a number of assumptions about the Russian peasant, social psychology, history in general, and so forth. The sentence generalizes in a way that covers possibly thousands of individual cases over decades or even centuries. The historian, as historian, is not primarily interested in what he may be implying about the nature of history, or the peasant, or social psychology. It seems, however, that for purposes of general education these matters are more important than the statement of fact taken at face value.[5]

The historian also brings to his data one or more generalized schema which play a significant role in the shaping of his narrative. These may be dealt with in terms of structure and process. Process involves a coherent theory of change through time as implied by such terms as "urbanization," "adaptation," and "industrialization." Structure is concerned with an analysis of a slice of time with respect to the economic, sociological, political, ideological, and other factors which existed in a given situation. Clearly this approach assumes a degree of regularity and orderliness in the social realm. It brings us again to the application of hypotheses, techniques, and models from the social sciences to historical events.[6]

One further matter should be mentioned. Some of the claims made for the study of history emphasize the value of students' knowing about the past, while other claims require that the student, through the study of the past, gain a better understanding of the present and the future. Hypotheses which are valid only if stated in the past tense may assist in the fullfillment of the first set of objectives but not the second.[7] "But there was no need for labor-saving machines in Russia at this time because there were plenty of serfs who could be ordered to do any work." This statement suggests the hypothesis: "There was an abundant supply of cheap and readily available labor in Russia during the first half of the Eighteenth Century so few labor-saving machines were introduced." This assertion is limited in application to one particular time and place. But change the tense of the verb and the hypothesis becomes: "If there is an abundant supply of cheap and readily available labor in a society, the introduction of labor-saving machines is relatively slow." Now the statement suggests that it is true at the present time and has wide applicability. It must be determined, of course, whether or not it is valid at present, if it is true only in societies at a certain level of technological development, and so forth. If we actually mean to use the study of history to increase the student's understanding of the present, it seems crucial to rephrase generalizations so they are stated in the present tense and then test their validity on this basis.

It is in the explanation process that the historian makes use of generalizations and hypotheses stating relatively stable societal relationships. Very often these are not stated directly but are implied in historical narrative. The narra-

---

[5] Ernest Nagel, *The Structure of Science* (New York: Harcourt, Brace and World, Inc., 1961), Chapter 15 and H. Stuart Hughes, "The Historian and the Social Scientist," *American Historical Review*, LXVI (October 1960), 20–46.

[6] *The Social Sciences in Historical Study*, Social Science Research Council, Bulletin 64 (New York: Social Science Research Council, 1954), Chapters 4 and 5.

[7] Lawrence E. Metcalf, "The Reflective Teacher," *Phi Delta Kappan*, XLIV (October 1962), 17–21.

tive may make very interesting reading for the student even though he is unaware of these generalizations. However, if we are concerned for developing proficiency in following historical (as well as the contemporary) narrative, "knowing what the game is all about" and comprehending it as the expert does, it is necessary to expose these generalizations and hold them up for scrutiny. In so doing students will be called upon to exercise a wide variety of critical skills necessary in the analysis of historical situations. This poses serious obstacles to the teaching of history in the elementary and secondary schools, unless the objectives of such teaching are limited to entertainment and the inculcation of certain attitudes associated with love of country and adoration of national heroes.

There are at least two major problem areas with respect to the teaching of history that must be dealt with if it is to lead to an understanding of society, whether it be past, present, or future society. An appreciation of human aims and values must be continually considered in the process of social education. The second broad area consists of the cognitive social understandings: the information, concepts, and generalizations that are used in the writing of history. Can the teacher of history systematically deal with both of these broad domains of content? To do so leads one into virtually an infinite regress which traverses much of the total human culture. This is obviously an impossible task. But how does the history teacher stop short of this? What reasonable and workable criteria establish the limits of historical study? The answers, of course, depend to a large extent on what one perceives as the purpose of studying history. If the history that is being taught in the schools is not to be "followed" or "understood" in the manner suggested earlier, then what is its purpose? And where in the curriculum are the very significant learnings essential to such understanding to be dealt with?

# Business Education

# THE READING PROBLEM IN TEACHING BOOKKEEPING *

Vernon A. Musselman

*How much of a problem is reading in bookkeeping? What are the three elements that combine to aggravate the reading problem in bookkeeping? After discussing the nature of these problems, the author gives some excellent suggestions for overcoming them.*

*1. How can you know your students as individuals?*

*2. What three factors complicate the reading problem in bookkeeping?*

*3. Can you infer from the discussion several principles regarding the teaching of bookkeeping vocabulary?*

*4. How would you use suggestions four, five, and six to make your bookkeeping class an instruction period?*

*5. State the article's key ideas.*

IT HAS become popular to remain in school and complete at least a high school education. As we have increased the percentage of those who stay and finish we have widened the range of individual differences in the student body. Any group of boys and girls which elects to study bookkeeping is anything but homogeneous. The students vary from one another in mental ability, family background, interests, hobbies, skill in reading, skill in computation, habits of workmanship, and attitudes. They even vary in reasons why they choose to study bookkeeping.

During recent years a great deal of attention has been focused on the problems of meeting individual differences adequately. Some students make good grades in all of their school subjects; others make low grades in all. Some like to study and have good study habits; others find studying difficult and have not yet really learned how to study. Some are good in reading comprehension or in arithmetical ability; others are poor. Each member of your bookkeeping class varies from all other members in many ways.

## KNOW STUDENTS AS INDIVIDUALS

First of all we must learn to know our students as individuals and find out what the differences in students are. Some personal information may be

* REPRINTED FROM *Business Education Forum*, XIV (December 1959), pp. 5–7, by permission of the National Business Education Association, a department of the National Education Association.

obtained through informal class discussion and reports. Brief questionnaires may be used to gather additional data desired by the teacher. Many schools have records of the mental abilities of their students. Many schools also have indexes of student abilities in such skills as vocabulary, reading comprehension, spelling, and arithmetic. Where cumulative records are kept, all of this information is available in one place. In schools where cumulative records are not in use, it may be necessary to administer achievement tests to secure all of the data one needs. Valid and reliable tests are available at a very small cost per student. In addition to test results that are of interest to all high school teachers, the business teacher may wish to use some type of clerical ability test such as the *Detroit Clerical Aptitude Examination, Minnesota Vocational Test for Clerical Workers,* or the *Turse Clerical Aptitude Test.* These tests give a measure of abilities basic to successful performance in various types of clerical work.

## THE READING PROBLEM

Students who can read with understanding have less difficulty with bookkeeping than do those who are retarded in their ability to read with comprehension. Bookkeeping teachers have been aware for many years that many students have difficulty with their reading, but what to do about it has long been a question of utmost concern. In bookkeeping there very definitely is a reading problem, but there are also several things that can be done and that have been done about it.

How serious is this problem of reading high school bookkeeping? Wayne House, in his study of some of the factors that affect student achievement in bookkeeping, focused our attention on the seriousness of the problem: His conclusions as they pertain to reading are: [1]

The technical vocabulary load in beginning bookkeeping is extremely heavy, particularly in the early parts of the course.

Beginning bookkeeping students vary in reading ability from a level comparable to the *lowest* 5 percent of seventh-grade students to a level comparable to the highest 5 percent of twelfth-grade students.

When measured by standardized tests, there is a significant relationship between achievement in beginning bookkeeping and reading ability.

There is a significant relationship between achievement in beginning bookkeeping and reading ability examined by questionnaire responses and personal interviews.

There are three elements that combine to aggravate the reading problem in bookkeeping: (a) the extremely heavy "vocabulary load," (b) the high level of difficulty of textual materials, and (c) the wide range of reading abilities of the students in any class.

[1] F. Wayne House, *Factors Affecting Student Achievement in Beginning Bookkeeping in the High School.* Oklahoma Agricultural and Mechanical College, Stillwater, Okla.: 1953, p. 89.

## THE VOCABULARY LOAD

Because of its technical nature, bookkeeping carries an extremely heavy "vocabulary load." This load consists of two types of terms: technical bookkeeping terms and common terms that have a special bookkeeping connotation. Most high school bookkeeping textbooks contain well over 200 technical bookkeeping terms. House found that in one textbook there were 33 such terms in the first chapter alone. He also found that approximately 30 percent of the questions on tests covering the early parts of the bookkeeping course are specifically designed to test the student's knowledge of technical bookkeeping terms.[2]

COMMON WORDS WITH SPECIAL MEANINGS. There are a number of common words that are already a part of the vocabulary of many students but that have a special bookkeeping meaning frequently quite different from the meaning the student normally associates with the word.

These common words may represent a greater learning barrier than the new technical terms. This results from the natural tendency on the part of both the teacher and the student to assume that an understanding of these terms exists. A partial list of such words includes:

| | | | |
|---|---|---|---|
| abstract | credit | post | ruling |
| capital | extend | prove | statement |
| charge | footing | register | terms |

If you will analyze the words in the list, you will observe that each word has more than one meaning. For example, "charge" has a meaning on the football field and quite another in the bookkeeping classroom. "Abstract," when used in the term, "abstract of accounts receivable," has a meaning different from its meaning when used to refer to the condensation of a story.

The vocabulary problem is further complicated in that a number of bookkeeping terms are used interchangeably. A few of these terms are given in the following list. Some of these terms have different precise meanings, but few teachers are aware of the difference and there is a tendency to interchange the terms freely in class discussion.

Analysis paper, work-sheet paper, working paper.
Bad debt, bad account, uncollectable account.
Cash on hand, cash balance, balance on hand.
Proprietorship, net worth, capital.
Minus asset, valuation account, reserve account.
Principal of note, face of note.
Profit and loss statement, operating statement, income statement, income
    and expense statement.
Liabilities, debts, obligations.

[2] F. Wayne House, "Are You Solving the Reading Problem in Bookkeeping?" *Business Education World*, 33:291; February 1953.

READING DIFFICULTY OF MATERIALS. Sentence length and syllabic intensity are two commonly used measures of reading difficulty. The longer the sentence and the higher the syllabic intensity, the more difficult the reading.

A common goal in business-letter writing is to have 70 percent of the words one-syllable words. Such magazines as *The Saturday Evening Post* and the *Ladies Home Journal,* which are written for a wide range of adult readers, strive to maintain an average sentence length of less than 12 words and a low syllabic intensity.

A study of two high school bookkeeping textbooks shows that the average sentence length was 21.6 words in one textbook and 16.9 words in the other. The syllabic intensity of both textbooks was found to be approximately 1.6. When these data are plotted on Flesch's "Reading Ease Chart," the textbook material scores as "Fairly Difficult." It is equivalent to the reading difficulty of such magazines as *Harper's, New Yorker,* and *Business Week.* The material is beyond the reading ability of over 50 percent of the high school students.

This reading difficulty is further verified by House who found from interviewing bookkeeping students that nearly one-half of the students reported they did not finish reading textbook assignments because they could not understand what they were reading.

RANGE OF READING LEVELS OF STUDENTS. The students in any bookkeeping class represent a wide range of reading levels. House found that 62 percent of the 357 students included in his study were below the average tenth-grade student in vocabulary proficiency as measured by the *Co-operative Reading Comprehension Test* and 60 percent were below the average tenth-grade student in reading comprehension. He states: [3]

Since a tenth-grade reading level is considered essential for comprehending material that is "Fairly Difficult," *only 40 percent of the students possessed enough reading ability to read and comprehend satisfactorily the subject matter in bookkeeping.*

## SUGGESTIONS FOR OVERCOMING THE PROBLEM

1. APPLY SOUND PRINCIPLES OF LEARNING TO THE VOCABULARY BUILDING. Memorization of word lists and definitions has been rather generally discredited as a means of developing vocabulary. Memorization, devoid of association with real, purposeful experiences, is but temporary learning. Words become a permanent part of the vocabulary of an individual only when they are given meaning through experiences or association with experiences.

For example, the word "assets" and its definition, "things owned which

[3] F. Wayne House, "Are You Solving the Reading Problem in Bookkeeping?" *Business Education World,* 33:292; February 1953.

have a money value," has little meaning to the student until it is associated with things that are real and meaningful, such as a bicycle, radio, wrist watch, and clothing. When the term is associated for the boy who works in the filling station with such things as tires, gasoline, oil, auto supplies, or delivery truck, it becomes meaningful.

The term "auditing the sales slips" becomes meaningful when the class makes a field trip to the office of a store and observes an office clerk checking the accuracy of the calculations on the sales slip. The term "dividends" takes on meaning when, through dramatization, the class has set up a corporation and has participated in the dramatized situation to determine the amount to be paid to stockholders from profits.

The answer to the vocabulary problem, therefore, is (a) to give the students as many direct and indirect experiences as possible through the in-school learning situation and (b) to assist them in associating terms with those experiences which they have had or are having outside the classroom.

2. PREPARE VOCABULARY LISTS. Analyze each chapter or unit before it is presented and prepare a list (a) of technical bookkeeping terms that are introduced for the first time in the chapter, and (b) of common words or phrases that have a special bookkeeping connotation. Such a list identifies the words that must be emphasized and considered in the lesson planning.

In planning for the lesson, each term should be studied by the teacher to determine what experiences the students have had that might be associated with the term. It is for this reason that, early in the course, the teacher should obtain as complete an inventory as possible of the students' work and business experiences and of the occupation of the parents. It is possible through this information to associate the new bookkeeping terms with experiences the students already understand.

Common words or phrases that have a special bookkeeping connotation also should be emphasized in the planning. Care must be taken to point out the distinction and relationship between the meaning of the term as it applies to bookkeeping and its other meanings. For example, pointing out the relationship between the use of the word "overhead" when referring to the ceiling and then when referring to bookkeeping, helps the student to understand the term better.

3. AVOID CONFUSION, BY BEING CONSISTENT IN TERMINOLOGY. A number of terms that are used interchangeably in bookkeeping have been pointed out. Confusion can be avoided if the teacher is consistent in the terminology used in the introductory weeks of the course. Such interchangeable terms as "account period" and "fiscal period," or "account sales," "credit sales," "sales on credit," "charge sales," and "sales on account," should be explained and used interchangeably before the completion of the course. However, to use these multiple-terms when the student is first being introduced to the topic increases the learning problem.

4. MAKE THE BOOKKEEPING CLASS PERIOD AN INSTRUCTION PERIOD IN PLACE OF RECITATION AND TESTING PERIOD. Many teachers follow

the practice of assigning new material to be read and studied from the textbook. The following days class period is devoted primarily to questioning and testing the student's understanding of the assigned reading. Such a plan is certain to result in low class morale and a high dropout and failure rate, for this procedure completely ignores the vocabulary and reading problem.

After a topic has been explained, illustrated, and visualized in the classroom, after new bookkeeping terms have been carefully presented, students may then profitably turn to the textbook for further study and clarification. The textbook then becomes a valuable and intelligible reference source for the student.

5. TAKE TIME TO EXPLAIN TO THE STUDENTS HOW TO READ AND STUDY THE TEXTBOOK. Bookkeeping requires a different reading pattern from that to which most students are accustomed. Most bookkeeping textbooks are well illustrated. The illustrations are keyed to the reading and must be included as part of the reading pattern. Daily oral reading demonstrations, therefore, are an essential part of the lesson plans for the first few days of the bookkeeping course.

Those students who have the greatest difficulty in reading might be encouraged to use a blotter or a sheet of paper as a reading guide.

6. USE STUDY GUIDES AS A LEARNING AID AND NOT AS A CHAPTER TEST. The workbooks that accompany most bookkeeping textbooks provide study or learning guides for each unit or chapter. When these study guides are used as chapter tests, which is frequently the case, the student is being denied a valuable learning aid.

When correctly used, the student completes the guide as he reads the textbook. The guide focuses the student's attention on the textbook material; thus, it aids the student in his reading. Again, class demonstration must be used to show the student how to use the study guides correctly.

The heavy vocabulary load, the reading difficulty of the textbook, and the low reading level of students represent barriers to the learning of bookkeeping. These barriers become formidable to many students when the bookkeeping course is kept largely on the "verbalized level," as opposed to the "experience level." Reading drill and rote memorization of definitions are not enough.

The solution is to tie bookkeeping vocabulary to the direct experiences the students have had and to provide as part of the bookkeeping course, as many direct and indirect purposeful experiences as possible. This can be done through in-school and out-of-school work experience, through dramatizations, through field trips, through effective demonstration, through visual aids, and through well-organized practice materials.

# TEACHING ACCOUNTING STUDENTS
# HOW TO READ *

L. J. Harrison

A *subject matter teacher does well to devote classroom time to overcoming reading deficiencies in order to increase the competence of his students in the subject. In this brief report Harrison explains the procedures he used to help students and reports on the success of those procedures.*

1. *Before reading the article, make a short outline of procedures that you would use to improve the reading of accounting students.*

2. *Compare your ideas with those of the author.*

3. *What basic reading principles did the author use with his class?*

BASED UPON writings in the journals and panel discussions at professional meetings, there seems to be general agreement among business educators that one of the greatest hindrances to effective learning is the inability of a large number of students to read textbook material with comprehension. My experiences with teaching college courses in accounting lead me to agree that this is a problem which the teacher faces all too frequently.

Recently, my instructional efforts with a class of prospective teachers in a course in intermediate accounting seemed to be yielding unusually poor results. The students experienced great difficulty in completing their regular problem assignments, and their scores on examinations were much below acceptable standards.

## ACTION WITHOUT THOUGHT

After nine weeks of very little progress, an analysis of the difficulties appeared to point toward weaknesses in reading abilities. It became apparent that quite a number of the students did not understand what information was given in a problem, the instructions relative to what was to be done, and the steps to take in solving the problem. One common fault was reading a problem hastily and carelessly. Without knowing what was required or what steps to take, students then took up paper and pencil and made a start. This tendency to spend very little time thinking about the problem but to hurry to get something down on paper was very noticeable. Needless to say, this resulted in many false starts and waste of time.

Even though aware that perhaps I was invading the domain of reading

---

* REPRINTED FROM the *Journal of Business Education*, XXXV (January 1960), pp. 169, 170, by permission of the publisher. Copyrighted by Robert C. Trethaway.

experts, I decided to see what an accounting teacher could do to help the students improve their ability to read and comprehend textual and problem material. At the same time, I was aware that to devote much of the class period to work on the reading deficiencies would mean that the class would not "cover" the material outlined for the course. Still, the sacrifice of "accounting time" to "reading time" might be beneficial in the long run.

Two principal procedures were adopted for the class reading sessions. One technique was to have the students read over an assigned problem in class. Then, individual students were called upon to express in their own words the general information given. Next, they were asked to tell in detail the instructions for solving the problem. Finally, students were asked to present a step-by-step procedure for solving the problem without using any figures at all. Thus, before attempting to solve a problem, students were encouraged to spend some time determining the information given, the requirements of the problem, and mentally outlining the steps to be used in solving it. The teacher tried to emphasize the thought that a problem which is well understood is half-solved, and that the more time spent on this "mental" phase means less time spent on the "activity" phase.

## STUDENTS STUDY COMPREHENSION PROBLEMS

The idea for the second type of reading exercise came from an article in *The American Business Education Yearbook* which reported what Ball State Teachers' College had been doing for a number of years in order to sharpen the reading habits of its accounting students.[1] For every new unit of work students spend ten to twenty minutes in class reading a few significant paragraphs concerning the particular topic. Then, a short quiz is given on the material covered. For my class, the paragraphs to be read generally came from the textbook, and it did not matter whether the particular material had been previously assigned or not. After reading the material once, the students were given a quiz and the papers checked. Then, they were given an opportunity to study the paragraphs again and to make changes in their answers if found to be incorrect. The papers were graded again, a record of the two scores being kept for each of reading exercises.

An example of the type of material read in class and the quiz given appears on this page.

### NATURE OF TEMPORARY INVESTMENTS

A company with an excess of available cash may deposit such funds as a time deposit or under a certificate of deposit at a bank, or it may purchase securities. Income will thus be produced that would not be available if cash were left idle. Investments made during seasonal periods of low activity can be converted into cash in periods of expanding operations. Asset items arising from temporary conversions of cash are commonly reported in the current asset section of the balance sheet under the heading, Temporary Investments. Temporary investments are frequently limited to only marketable securities.

[1] *The American Business Education Yearbook*, Vol. VIII, 1951, pp. 30–33.

Securities that are purchased as temporary investments should actually be marketable on short notice. There should be a day-to-day market for them, and the volume of trading in the securities should be sufficient to absorb a company's holdings without considerably affecting the market price. While there may be no definite assurance that the securities will be disposed of without loss, it is essential that any possible loss resulting from such disposal be kept at a minimum. Securities that have a limited market and fluctuate widely in price are not suitable for temporary investments. The prices of United States government securities tend to be relatively stable and the market for these securities is quite broad. Because of these factors, short-term government securities are particularly favored despite their relatively low interest rates.

### COMPOSITION OF TEMPORARY INVESTMENTS

Investments qualify for reporting as temporary investments as long as (1) they are readily available for conversion into cash and (2) it is management's intent to sell them to take care of cash requirements. Such investments may be converted into cash within a relatively short period after being acquired, or they may be carried for some time. In either case, however, since they represent a ready source of cash, they are properly shown under the current heading. The following types of investments do not qualify as marketable securities, and should not be included in the current section: (a) reacquired shares of the company's own stock, (b) securities held in subsidiary companies, (c) securities held for maintenance of business relations, and (d) other securities that cannot be used or are not intended to be used as a ready source of cash.[2]

### INTERMEDIATE ACCOUNTING 311
### READING COMPREHENSION EXERCISES
#### Chapter 5—Temporary Investments

Name  ...................................

Score  ...................................

1. Check the items below which may be included in temporary investments.
   - \_\_\_\_\_ Idle land
   - \_\_\_\_\_ Time Deposit at a bank
   - \_\_\_\_\_ Marketable Securities
   - \_\_\_\_\_ Treasury Stock
   - \_\_\_\_\_ Investments in Subsidiary Companies
   - \_\_\_\_\_ Certificate of Deposit
   - \_\_\_\_\_ Mortgage Bonds
2. Short-term government securities are of doubtful value as temporary investments. — Yes — No
3. All stocks and bonds should be classified as temporary investments. — Yes — No
4. Temporary investments provide a means of putting idle funds to work. — Yes — No
5. Temporary investments should be reported on the balance sheet under **current assets**. — Yes — No

[2] *Intermediate Accounting* (Standard Volume), 3d Edition. Karrenbrock and Simons, South-Western Publishing Co., pp. 133–134.

It would be good to report that all members of the class showed marked improvements and that the procedures were highly successful. With only nine weeks left in the semester such a possibility is highly improbable. However, there was sufficient evidence of improvement on the part of many of the students to justify a continuation of such experiments. Also, it appeared that once some of the students learned to be more careful in their reading habits they would continue to make an effort to further develop their reading ability and skill in problem solving.

From the teacher's standpoint, the greatest benefit derived was the stimulation of having tried to wrestle with a perennial problem and coming to the conclusion that through a systematic plan and a little special effort business students may be assisted in overcoming special weaknesses.

# Foreign Language

## GIVE THE STUDENT TIPS ON HOW TO GET THE MOST FROM FOREIGN LANGUAGE BOOKS *

Ralph C. Preston

*The foreign language student gets bogged down quickly in his reading if he is required to read materials that are too difficult for him. As in reading one's native language, there are many, if not more, problems in reading a foreign language. If one is to make progress in reading a foreign language, specific obstacles to progress must be identified and dealt with systematically.*

*Preston gives general and specific suggestions for helping a student increase his proficiency in reading foreign language material.*

*1. What are the three basic steps for overcoming problems in foreign lan-*

*guage reading?*

*2. Which teaching of reading principles has the author applied to the area of building a more substantial vocabulary?*

*3. Do the injunctions regarding the mastering of the grammar of a language seem plausible to you?*

*4. What does "syntax" mean?*

*5. How can the foreign language notebook-dictionary be used as an auto-instructional device?*

*6. What can the student do to help himself read in terms of ideas and phrases?*

*7. State the article's key ideas.*

A STUDENT who studies a foreign language or who must read extensively in foreign language references in connection with his courses often spends unduly large amounts of time in extracting the meaning from a comparatively short passage. Most of his woes in this task can be overcome through (1) building a more substantial vocabulary in the language, (2) mastering the grammar, and (3) acquiring the ability to think in the language. Correct study procedures in learning a foreign language are of especial importance.

1. BUILDING A MORE SUBSTANTIAL VOCABULARY. The student should be persuaded to test his basic sight vocabulary by examining the vocabulary list in the back of a first-year foreign language textbook to see if he can instantaneously and accurately identify the meaning of at least a hundred

---

* REPRINTED FROM *Teaching Study Habits and Skills* (New York: Rinehart and Company, Inc., 1959), pp. 34–37, by permission of the publisher.

of the words. If he cannot do this, he may assume that his stock of sight words is deficient. Using the same book, he may read aloud its simple sentences and stories—repeatedly if necessary—until he knows them well. This method is more effective than trying to memorize word lists.

However, this is a mere beginning. It is doubtful if he will be able to read the language with fluency and adequate understanding unless he knows over 95 per cent of the running words at sight. This means he must set about to expand his vocabulary vastly. Systematic reading of interesting material—stories, newspapers, and the like—should be carried on apart from regular class assignments. In fact, language teachers often make such reading a part of the regular assignment to ensure its being done. In this recreational reading, it is not essential that all unknown words be looked up in a dictionary. The student should be encouraged to utilize as fully as possible the clues offered by the context. New words supplied by the clues will be gradually added to the student's vocabulary. Where context is insufficient, examination of the unfamiliar word may help through recognition of cognates (e.g., Spanish "concerto," French "concert," and German "Konzert") or through structural analysis (e.g., in German, "Strassenbahnhaltestelle" = Strasse (street) + Bahn (railway) + Halt (stop) + Stelle (place) = "streetcar stop"). There are always those words, of course, which have to be looked up.

Important words, or words that the student finds he is looking up more than once, he should be advised to keep in his own notebook-dictionary for recording words and idioms, and perhaps he should also make flash cards, as suggested on page 50. To clinch the difficult words and idioms, the student should be instructed how to recite them to himself through using them orally and in writing sentences, through repeating them from memory, and through reading them aloud.

2. MASTERING THE GRAMMAR OF THE LANGUAGE. Although much grammar is learned through a program emphasizing wide reading and vocabulary building, many constructions in a student's reading continue to have a fuzzy meaning for him if he has no firm understanding of the language's structure. Each language has its peculiar syntax, which is described in beginning textbooks and in grammars. They are sufficiently different from English to cause trouble in reading comprehension until they are thoroughly grasped. The rules of sentence structure are not numerous and can be briefly summarized. The best test of having mastered them is the student's ability to give his own examples of sentences representing each type of sentence order. Aside from syntax, each language has its peculiar conjugations. Each student seems to have his own particular difficulties with grammar. He can be helped to identify them and to focus his study upon them.

The nomenclature of foreign grammars often constitutes a hurdle for the student. He should be provided with a book of English grammar and helped to see parallels between English forms and those of the language he is learning. Through making such comparisons he will inevitably identify

| WORD | PHRASE IN WHICH IT OCCURRED | TRANSLATION | OTHER MEANINGS | A |
|---|---|---|---|---|
| | | | | B |
| anstellen | Wenn ich mich gut anstelle... | set about a thing | pretend<br>make a fuss | |
| Abschnitt | ... im ersten Abschnitt. | paragraph | section<br>era<br>segment | |
| beobachten | ... den Flug eines Adlers zu beobachten. | observe | examine<br>execute<br>obey an order | |
| Ankunft | ... die Ankunft des Zugs. | arrival | advent | |

*From a student's foreign language notebook-dictionary.*

many distinctive and important features of the foreign language. For example, he will discover the French use of the comparative form of adjectives in connection with superlative expressions as in *mon meilleur ami* (my dearest friend); and the German use of adjectives as adverbs as in *sie singt schön* (she sings beautifully). Incidentally, it is advisable that the student be told that translating English sentences into the new language in connection with each grammatical concept will be more helpful than the learning of rules and conjugations, although that has its value, too.

3. ACQUIRING THE ABILITY TO THINK IN THE LANGUAGE. As long as the student's reading comprehension depends upon literal translations from the foreign word to the English word before forming the image for which the word stands, reading in the foreign language will be a tedious experience for him. Furthermore, such a word-by-word approach, whether in his native tongue or in the foreign language he is learning, interferes with fluent, accurate comprehension. The teacher can assist him in drawing parallels between his successful reading in English and his lumbering reading of the foreign language in order that he may pattern the latter after the former, orienting himself to the author and trying to anticipate the author's plan and thoughts. When the student succeeds in doing this, he will find himself reading in terms of phrases and ideas as he reads, and thinking ahead. It will take abundant practice before such reading becomes habitual. Unfortunately, instructors who emphasize literal translation in class inhibit this growth toward truly participating and thinking in a foreign language. Students should never be permitted to be satisfied with literal translations in their reading, but should be urged to get an image directly from the foreign words and phrases without the intermediary of the corresponding English words and phrases.

# ENCOURAGING READING
# INTERESTS AND TASTES

## INTRODUCTION

*Reading interests and tastes are important topics. It is probably an over-statement to say that they are the key topics in education, but they are matters of great import, to be sure. Evidence of the concern educators and parents have for interests and tastes is found in the educational aphorisms we widely quote: "Success breeds interest." "Give a child a book that interests him." "You need to get the right book together with the right child at the right time." "Tastes are caught, not taught." If interests in general and reading interests in particular are such important facets of education, it might be well to ask which factors seem to condition or determine what a person will read. The following factors singly or in combination seem to condition what a person will read and the avidity with which he will read it:*

1. *The availability of reading material.*
2. *The difficulty of the material.*
3. *The style in which the material is written.*
4. *What he has read previously.*
5. *How much he depends on others (or allows others) to solve his problem of reading choice.*
6. *The feeling of hope or fear or satisfaction that he experiences when reading a given type of material.*
7. *What he has done before when confronted with the choice of reading versus not-reading.*
8. *His self concept as a reader.*

*In reading the articles in this section, the reader should check to see which of the eight points listed as determining factors are borne out by the experiences and contentions of the authors. Above all, the reader should take advantage of the insights the authors offer regarding the discovery, development, and utilization of reading interests and tastes.*

# WHAT DO TEEN-AGERS READ? *

Richard H. Rice

and James E. Sellers

*In this pilot study Rice and Sellers explore the question of what teen-agers read on their own. Although the number of students sampled is admittedly small, certain insights are obtained which can be used to guide development of curricular materials in religious education.*

*1. What were the authors hoping to discover from the results of their questionnaire?*

*2. What are the implications of their findings for the development of literature for teen-agers?*

HISTORICALLY, Protestants have relied on the written word as one of the means by which individuals find faith. With the coming of mass communications, however, the written word has changed in its function and even its nature. Because there is now much more to read, we do not read deeply. Because there are many other ways to communicate, we do not read much. In a questionnaire given to Congregational Christian churches, about three-fourths of the senior high teachers who responded reported that students did little or no reading of curriculum materials.[1] This study, we believe, is representative.

What do these changes in reading habits indicate? On the one hand, they mean that the historic Protestant use of the written word as a means of faith is now in a serious decline. On the other hand, they mean that Protestant educators have not kept up with the times. People have not *quit* reading; they have merely turned to new kinds of written materials. The reading we ask our students to do often does not serve their needs.

## STUDENTS ANSWERED A QUESTIONNAIRE

We planned a survey to seek clues about the new reading habits of teen-agers. A short questionnaire was designed to obtain objective data:

[1] *Questionnaire on Use of Church and Home Series and Pilgrim Series* (Board of Christian Education and Publication of the Evangelical and Reformed Church and the Division of Christian Education, Board of Home Missions, Congregational Christian Churches, 1957).

* REPRINTED FROM the *International Journal of Religious Education*, XXXVII (October 1960), pp. 6, 7; 38, by permission of the National Council of Churches of Christ in the U.S.A. and the authors.

1. If you could read only three magazines, which ones would they be?
2. Have you read any of the above three magazines in the past two weeks? Name them.
3. List the subjects of articles or portions of articles you read.
4. If you did not read any magazines in the past two weeks, describe other ways in which you secured news or information (not counting school work).
5. What was the last book, other than books assigned at school, you remember reading?

Age ——— Sex ——— Occupation of Father ———————————

All five questions pertain to unassigned reading. We were not concerned about the influence of assigned reading except as it had become a part of the internal motivation of the teen-agers. Our hope was that answers would indicate some teen-age attitudes toward printed materials and, perhaps more important, certain needs and interests, conscious and unconscious. We wanted answers to this question: What does the teen-ager want to read and go to the trouble to read when there is no adult standing over him with an assignment?

"Questions About Reading" was given in March, 1960, to a tenth-grade class of six students and a senior class of eight at Belmont Methodist Church, Nashville, Tennessee. Our idea in working with such small groups was not to make a rigorously defensible statistical analysis, but rather to gain whatever clues we could.

## They Prefer Life and Mad

Results of the test show that *Life* and *Mad* are the magazines the Belmont teen-agers are reading and looking at. *Reader's Digest* tied with *Mad* for second place in the older group. Other magazines mentioned were *Saturday Review, Motive, Natural History Magazine, American Heritage, Sports Illustrated, Together, Time, Saturday Evening Post, Seventeen, The New Yorker, Hot Rod, Esquire, Playboy,* and *Ladies Home Journal.*

Only two of these—*Motive* and *Together*—are church periodicals. Perhaps it is significant that no curriculum periodicals were listed. Teen-agers may see them as textbooks, to be read only if there is a class assignment; or as dull, not well related to things of interest.

*Life* is a magazine that teen-agers enjoy along with adults, whereas *Mad* is strictly a teen-age magazine. *Mad* is so incisive in its satiric comments on adult society that it may well be, indirectly, a more "adult" publication than the solidly middle-class *Life.* Most of *Mad's* criticisms are purely negative— in fact, a positive note would probably rob the humor of its bite. *Reader's Digest* is well known for its sparkling style and heavy stress on human interest.

We are under no illusions that the test exacted fully candid answers. Only one boy listed a magazine that could be described as catering principally to sex (*Playboy*). No girl listed a romance or movie magazine. Yet we have observed some of these students leafing through such fare in a drugstore.

The subjects of articles read fall roughly into these categories: history, current events, hobbies and sports, fiction, humor, sex and dating. One senior described the fiction she read as "true-to-life stories"—probably romances and confession stories. One implication is immediately apparent: these interests are not, as a rule, prominent in our curriculum materials. For example, we do little in the category of humor. The usual curriculum materials, by their very nature, virtually preclude attention to current events. Our point is not that these various interests should simply be repeated in curriculum materials. Rather, we would suggest that whatever understanding of faith the teen-ager develops will have to come by way of these interests.

## Books Have Limited Appeal

Twelve students listed the last book they had read as follows: *Have Space Suit—Will Travel, 1984, Come My Beloved, Fifty Years at Ringside, War Birds, Jane Eyre, Newspaper Lady, The Last Cruise of the Nightwatch, Anne of Green Gables, The Egg and I, Point of No Return, Angel Unaware.*

Several implications may be commented upon. The presence of a few outstanding books in the list indicates that teen-agers can handle serious reading if they are motivated. The large number of titles in the "less significant fiction" category was to be expected. Yet some of the rather nondescript titles may indicate that students do little or no book-reading and have to grope for a title. *War Birds* and *Newspaper Lady* sound like books they read when they were seventh and eighth graders. Only one book on the list, *Angel Unaware*, has a discernible religious motif.

Our general impression is that books are a much less live option for teen-agers than are contemporary periodicals.

## Mad Satirizes Adult Society

In the April 1960 issue of *Mad*, a cartooned take-off of the television program "Father Knows Best" not only illustrates one type of sick humor but also provides a clue to teen-age reaction to typical "family life" units in our curriculum.

In the first panel, father is arriving home "after a grueling eight-hour day at the office." (*Mad* uses this cliché ironically; in curriculum periodicals we would probably use it or a similar one with utter seriousness.) His wife suggests that he "help the children with their average everyday teen-age problems." Father agrees, and asks his daughter, "What typical teen-age problem can I help you with in my usual level-headed and intelligent manner?"

What is the point of the humor here? The joke is obviously on the adults, who think themselves masters of all problems but, from the teen-ager's point of view, don't know what the problems are. The teen-age frustration at this situation is symbolized by the daughter's reply: "I'm expecting a baby, my husband ran off to Australia, and I'm drinking an awful lot lately." Adult illusions are again satirized in well-adjusted father's solution: he coolly suggests that these problems aren't serious, passes them off, and advises her on the kind of dress to wear.

Surely teen-agers crave this material for more reasons than amusement. It offers them an outlet for hostility against those who hand them easy answers, or answers to questions they aren't asking. It strikes back at the sober adult framework which we insist they submit to for learning about life. It condemns us for failing to correlate their real problems and point of view with the gospel we attempt to proclaim to them as the answer.

## Life Is a Panorama of Life

Let us examine briefly a recent issue of *Life* (March 7, 1960). The cover features a dramatic picture of a woman's face with fixed, bulging eyes, one illuminated by a doctor's flashlight. In the lower right corner are the words "The Use of Hypnosis to Cure Mental Illness." This is enough to make a reader pick up the magazine and, in a few minutes of looking and reading, get in the "know" about hypnosis.

Inside the issue are enough action photos and stories to fascinate a teen-ager for half an hour or more. There is a story, with twenty-five photos, on the "Seventeen-Year Mystery of the Lady Be Good." In World War II an airplane disappeared in a North African desert; recently the plane and the remains of the flyers were found. In many captions active verbs in the present tense make the reader feel a sense of motion, action, life.

*Life's* stories are the kind that will be read and looked at. Can curriculum builders for the senior high learn from *Life's* journalism? Life as it is savored and lived; life's glamor and grandeur and its sordidness and misery—here is where the teen-age reader is alert and teachable.

This article reports and interprets findings from a small sampling of high school students. Mr. Rice and Dr. Sellers are planning to continue this study with a much larger number of students. If readers of the Journal are moved to use the test in studying the reading interest of groups of high school students the authors of this article will appreciate receiving reports of their findings, whether they agree or disagree with the results reported in this article.

## Curriculum Needs Are Implied

We also administered the questionnaire to a class of five eleventh- and twelfth-graders at Love's Chapel Methodist Church in a rural area north of Nashville. *Life* and *Saturday Evening Post* were the leading choices. *Mad* was not mentioned by a single student, a fact which indicates an absence of "sophistication," we think, rather than a contradictory finding. Can one church school periodical bridge the gap between students with such varied preferences? Or should we try to meet the problem by issuing several kinds of periodicals, each aimed at a different teen-age audience?

From these observations we have come to several conclusions about our curriculum materials for teen-agers:

1. There is not enough similarity between the curriculum materials we produce and the reading teen-agers do on their own initiative.

2. We suspect that curriculum builders turn away from concrete, sensible experiences of teen-agers, so eager are they to thrust before young people easily recognizable ideals of the church. Thus many materials may be planned primarily from a middle-class adult point of view (adults who put in "a grueling eight-hour day at the office").

3. Printed materials that attract teen-agers are pictorial in character, focused on human beings rather than ideal types. Too often human interest in curriculum materials expends itself in stereotyped images.

4. We would like to see exploration of new literary ventures that appeal to young people's interests—humor, hobbies, current events, all treated pictorially. Such a program would not mean a departure from theological, biblical, and ethical instruction, but rather the relation of these disciplines to the real world of teen-agers.

5. A danger to be avoided would be that of identifying the gospel with popular culture. We would have to search constantly for ways of pointing to the Christian faith as a *rescue* from the fallen existence of everyday life.

6. If the written word has ceased to be a vital Protestant instrument, it is largely the fault of the church. Perhaps teen-age readers could be won if we provided materials that keep up with their interests. Otherwise our senior high students will turn elsewhere for what they read.


# MEETING REALITY IN
# THE CLASSROOM *

Carl A. Brown

"Culture comes slowly at best but it does not come at all to a person who never contacts it on a level that he can understand," contends the author of this article. In an effort to bring his students into contact with culture on a level they can understand, Brown and his students analyzed various facets of a first-rate popular adult magazine; they also devoted time to "perceiving values more apparent in better materials." Through these procedures an effort was

---

* FROM the English Journal, XLIX (January 1960), pp. 41–43, reprinted with permission of the National Council of Teachers of English and C. A. Brown.

made to improve the tastes of the students and to deepen their understanding and appreciation of the culture represented in this magazine.

1. What problem does the author pose?

2. How do you think the quality of reasons listed by teenagers for reading a magazine compares with the general quality of magazines read by them?

3. Do you think adoption of the plan recommended would entail a reorganization of pedagogical and philosophical values on your part? In what ways?

4. How might you adapt this program to your situation? To other situations you know?

MANY ENGLISH teachers have come to realize that there is very little relation between the literature they teach and the material which many students will read after graduation. Sometimes this gap is so large that it is never bridged and the student's school experiences have no relation to his real life. In other words, for every adult who continues to read the type of literature to which he is introduced in high school, there are probably several hundred who, in their adult life, read nothing but popular paperbacks and magazines.

Habits of reading certain specific publications are often fixed even before high school age. It seems more logical to start where the student IS, and then work up from there instead of always to talk about an unobtainable dream castle in the skies which is too fairylike and unreal to have any connection with the actual events of his future everyday life.

With this in mind we conducted at Northern High a unit devoted to the study of available current magazines. The results of this unit were not only enlightening but amazing.

It was noticeable that some of the most disinterested students were avid readers of lurid and sensational "pulp" magazines which were often the only reading material available in their homes, sometimes even lovingly provided by the parents for the children on the theory that they furnished needed moral and sex education.

The following information revealed by the one hundred eleventh grade students participating was astonishing to the more cloistered members of the teaching staff and would, no doubt, raise a few eyebrows at the P.T.A.

| MAGAZINES READ 50% OR MORE REGULARLY | NO. OF READERS |
|---|---|
| Jet | 58 |
| This Week (and similar Sunday supplements) | 57 |
| True Story | 28 |
| Look | 20 |
| Ebony | 20 |
| Down Beat | 19 |
| Life | 19 |
| True Confessions | 17 |
| Confidential | 17 |

| MAGAZINES READ 50% OR MORE REGULARLY | NO. OF READERS |
|---|---|
| Modern Romance | 17 |
| Post | 16 |
| Rhythm and Blues | 14 |
| TV Guide | 14 |
| Jive | 14 |
| Seventeen | 13 |
| Reader's Digest (sold in school) | 12 |
| Bronze Thrill | 11 |
| Vogue | 11 |
| Secrets | 11 |
| Time | 10 |
| Playboy | 10 |
| Esquire | 10 |
| Field and Stream | 9 |
| Watch Tower | 9 |
| Escapade | 9 |
| Photoplay | 8 |
| Harper's | 6 |
| Science and Mechanics (All titles combined) | 6 |
| Low Down | 6 |
| Family Circle | 5 |
| Billboard | 3 |
| American Legion | 3 |
| Photography (All titles combined) | 3 |
| Modern Teens | 3 |
| Duke | 2 |
| Crisis | 2 |

This list was obviously NOT prepared by the English teachers.

The next step following the survey was to hold a discussion in the participating classes. Students were asked to think carefully and then list their own personal reasons for reading any magazine, including those they had used so far. Reasons listed were combined and condensed into the following list:

News—domestic and foreign.

Entertainment—just to "kill" time.

Information.

Skills.

Imaginative experiences.

Understanding of other people.

Help in forming opinions.

Advice in solving social problems, personal and group.

Self help to better health, success, and vocational advancement.

Illustrations were brought out during the discussions showing how these aims could be realized in specific situations.

The next step was to distribute to all members of the classes a copy of a recent *Post* magazine. (The *Post* was selected for this study because, even though it is a recognized adult publication, it seems to have a wide variety of features which appeal to the genuine interests of the high school students and also because it is consistently free from the cheaper type of humor and questionable advertising.) The class period was then used to list the various types of materials which go into the make-up of the magazine.

These were discussed and listed as follows: Cover Art, Index, Cost as related to value received, Stories and Articles by qualified authors, Advertising, Poetry, Illustrations for stories and articles, Jokes, Cartoons, and Special Features. In each case both quality and variety were considered.

### INTENSIVE STUDY

Next a period was devoted to the selection of one sample story for intensive study. Then an article of special interest was read and studied. After this a variety of other editions were distributed and other samples were read and discussed with emphasis on the scope and variety of interests and materials covered. Many students borrowed copies to continue their reading after school entirely of their own accord.

Advertising was the next study undertaken. The tricks and skills of the advertising writers were observed by selecting various illustrations of ways used to sell a product such as: originality, integrity, color, brevity, humor, slogans, catch phrases, single feature emphasis, beauty and luxury appeal, safety emphasis, and the inclusion of necessary information.

To provide active, creative participation, students were assigned the task of writing a magazine advertisement for a new product not yet on the market (an invention of the teacher). This actual attempt to produce an "ad" made the problems of advertising much more real and gave the teacher a chance to point out the ethics of false and elaborate claims that are all too common in the "pulp" materials many of them had been reading.

Other periods were devoted to reading and sharing orally the humorous special features, listing new words added to vocabularies, discovering new and broader interests, and perceiving values more apparent in better materials.

As a test all students were asked to rate the two best magazines, in their own opinions, considering all the features listed previously, and to explain why they selected any favorite one. These comments showed a marked increase in analytic skill and frequently a change of attitudes and interests. Some individual conferences were held with those who needed extra help to overcome special prejudices.

Culture comes slowly at best but it does not come at all to a person who never contacts it on a level that he can understand. I have long believed that the ancient literary masters are likely to be a little mouldy for the young readers of today, who live in a modern city and have only a very limited relation to an historical English background. For these, the historical approach is a poor starting point for arousing interest.

Students are not necessarily "stupid" because they are more interested in a star baseball player's successful technique than in Romeo's antique methods of "pitching woo." For every English teacher who dotes on the story of Prometheus, a thousand modern youngsters want to know the thrilling story of the satellites. Should we insist that they wade through a million pages of mythology before they read one word about modern medicine or the conquest of the Arctic by a modern *Nautilus*?

Should we help them to take one real step forward, or concentrate entirely on moving them from our own cloud nine to cloud ten, assuming that we can get them to that cloud nine in the first place?

# "SURF'S UP"—AND SO IS
# READING INTEREST *

### Sister William Paul, O.P.

*Can reading compete with surfing? In this article Sister William Paul explains how the English Department of her school, located near a good surfing area, convinced students that "reading is as important as surfing—and in its own way, just as exciting."*

*1. What problems faced the teacher*
*in the English Department of this high school?*

*2. What steps did they take to solve these problems?*

*3. Why, in your opinion, was the "Reading in Depth" program successful? How might you adapt the program to your teaching situation?*

IT IS a wonderful experience to teach in a high school located near the Atlantic Ocean, especially when the local beach happens to be one of the best surfing areas along the coast. The only difficulty is that frequently the teacher is in competition with six-foot waves! The problem that confronted us in the English Department was just that: how does one convince students who are needlessly retarded readers that reading is as important as surfing— and, in its own way, just as exciting.

Last September, when we surveyed the reading situation in our school, we found that approximately one-fourth of the student body was below grade. As a beginning step, four basic reading classes were included in the daily curriculum. Interested and enthusiastic teachers held several impromptu meetings to select appropriate remedial reading material. It was decided that they would begin by using the Globe series of graded readers, the SRA diag-

* FROM *English Journal*, 55 (January 1966), pp. 93, 94, reprinted with permission of the National Council of Teachers of English and Sister William Paul, O.P.

nostic kits and the *Reader's Digest* selections. Strong emphasis was to be placed on individualized reading. Standardized tests were to be used to check student progress throughout the year.

Slowly the groundwork was laid. A Language Arts Assembly was held in late September. The theme of the convocation was "Read Today—for a Better Tomorrow." Junior and senior students' Chamber Drama presentations of *John Brown's Body* and *Our Town* were enthusiastically received by the entire student body. The highlight of the assembly was the inauguration of a "Reading in Depth" program for all students who wished to participate. In essence this meant that anyone interested would meet once a month at night to discuss the book of his choice. (This plan of allowing students to choose the book for discussion was modified as the year went along. A better plan replaced it: to have the teacher present three or four choices and ask the students to select one.) Afterwards refreshments were to be served.

The response to the "Reading in Depth" series was astonishing. Seventy-nine teen-agers in Grades 9–12 agreed to come back to school at night to discuss books which interested them. The meetings were usually held from 7:00–8:00 p.m. Students were divided into three groups: freshmen in one; sophomores in another; and juniors and seniors in a joint session. Some of the topics covered in the junior-senior division were as follows: Hemingway's use of irony in his sketch, "On the Quai at Smyrna"; the satire in George Orwell's *Animal Farm*; Hardy's philosophy of determinism as evidenced in *The Return of the Native*. At the January meeting the choral director explained impressionism in the works of Debussy and Ravel; then students were introduced to the paintings of the French Impressionists. This session demonstrated how music and art are related to literary impressionism. At another session, the symbolism in Golding's *Lord of the Flies* was studied and compared with Conrad's use of symbolism in *Heart of Darkness*.

Sophomore selections included Mark Twain's *Adventures of Huckleberry Finn*, Homer's *Iliad*, Stephen Crane's *The Red Badge of Courage*, Nathaniel Hawthorne's *Scarlet Letter*, George Eliot's *Silas Marner*, and John Steinbeck's *The Pearl*. Freshmen completed the study of Jules Verne's *Journey to the Center of the Earth*, Jack London's *Call of the Wild*, Harper Lee's *To Kill a Mockingbird*, and others.

Interest in the "Reading in Depth" program grew. Allusions were made in English classes to material which had been discussed at the evening sessions. Our daily paper, *The News Tribune*, heard of the project and printed a full page story, giving a detailed description of the venture. In early spring one senior girl was awarded first prize in *The News Tribune*'s Liberal Arts Contest, open to high school and junior college students and judged by author Philip Wylie, for her essay on the problem of evil in *Lord of the Flies*. The idea for her essay grew out of the February session, at which time Golding's book was discussed. In all, the program was judged to be so effective that a similar plan was introduced in the junior high school.

The English teachers who volunteered their time to the "Reading in

Depth" program experienced moments of deep satisfaction when students, who formerly had never enjoyed reading, stopped to say how much they were benefiting from the series. And several senior students, who will be attending nearby Indian River Junior College in the fall, asked if they could be allowed to return in September for another year's sessions of "Reading in Depth."

At the Honors Convocation, as a natural outgrowth of their participation in the reading program, students enacted scenes from three novels they had studied during the year: freshmen presented excerpts from *To Kill a Mockingbird*; sophomores portrayed sections from *The Pearl*; juniors depicted significant passages of *Animal Farm*. At this assembly certificates were awarded to those who had participated in the "Reading in Depth" series. Then a summer reading program was introduced, and the students learned that those involved in the summer program would receive recognition at the September Arts Assembly.

Encouraged by the enthusiastic response to this year's reading program, the English department has future plans to include not only English teachers, but also those teaching in other content fields. A Developmental Program, which will include remedial and individualized reading, will be offered to all students during seventh period. In the face of such wholehearted cooperation from students, faculty, and community, the teacher trying to interest students in reading no longer has to cast a reproachful eye at the surf board jutting out of the junior boy's car window. After all, the "surf's up"—but so is reading interest!

# HELPING DISADVANTAGED AND RELUCTANT READERS

## INTRODUCTION

*In their book* Compensatory Education for Cultural Deprivation, *Bloom, Davis, and Hess pointed out that by the time the typical culturally disadvantaged student begins high school he is reading at a level about three and one-half years below grade level. He is not happy with school and approaches his learning tasks in quite a lackadaisical manner. Such a person needs help so that he can develop hope for the future and become motivated to learn and to develop clear vocational goals.*

*In this section both Lighthall and Spiegler describe further the pitiful problems of the culturally disadvantaged student in the secondary school. Lighthall emphasizes the importance of overcoming the weak informational backgrounds of such students and shows how this can be done. Spiegler explains how he has helped culturally deprived students to develop genuine interest in reading. The article by Hafner and Karlin describes a "three-layered" program for improving the reading skills of young men whose reading-achievement scores range from grade four level to beyond the eighth-grade level.*

# PROCEDURES AND MATERIALS FOR THE CULTURALLY DISADVANTAGED READER: IN GRADES NINE THROUGH FOURTEEN *

Nancy Lighthall

*Only a teacher who has worked with students who are culturally-disadvantaged and probed into their informational backgrounds realizes how conceptually handicapped such students are. Lighthall's discussion provides some insights into the nature of this handicap and what the teacher can do to offset it.*

*1. What does the author mean by the phrase "intellectual vacuum" in reference to culturally disadvantaged students?*

*2. What is the twofold task of the teacher who would help the culturally-disadvantaged student?*

*3. How can a teacher use the short stories of Hemingway, Michener, Aiken, and Lardner to advantage in working with culturally-disadvantaged students?*

*4. The author suggests certain pamphlets and periodicals which the students might read. What advantages are there to using these materials? How would you prepare students to read these materials?*

THE ACADEMIC achievement of culturally disadvantaged students in grades nine through fourteen is likely to be closer to a fifth- or sixth-grade level; at the same time, because of having been held back or because of having been temporary dropouts along the way, they may well be several years older than the average student. The situation confronting the teacher of such a group, then, is this: in interest, experience, motivation, maturity, and general wisdom about the ways of the world, the class is an adult one; but in achievement (including reading achievement) and, equally important, in the realm of general information, the class is a slow, incredibly childlike one.

No matter what his age, there are certain bits of background information that the severely culturally disadvantaged student can be depended upon not to possess. For example, he probably will not know what Congress is, even though he may already be of voting age. He may have heard of the Civil War, but he won't know what it was about or when it occurred. It is possible that he will have heard of the United Nations, but the chances are that he will not have the slightest idea as to what its functions are. And at

---

* REPRINTED FROM *Meeting Individual Differences in Reading,* Supplementary Educational Monographs, No. 94, pp. 155–159, by permission of The University of Chicago Press. Copyright, 1964, by the University of Chicago Press.

least one student of the writer's acquaintance did not know, until the matter came up in class, that the earth is round.

In short, then, the level of reading achievement of such a class requires not only that the teacher provide material which, though mature in content, is readable in terms of vocabulary and sentence structure but, in addition, that the presentation of the material must be made with care. If, for example, the class is to read a story dealing with a group of soldiers stationed somewhere in England in 1944, the teacher must first be absolutely sure that the class knows why these men were where they were in this particular year. He cannot take it for granted that they will read the opening lines and immediately know that this is a World War II story.

Why this intellectual vacuum exists is not the subject for discussion in this paper. But it does exist, and this fact is of extreme pertinence to the work of the teacher of culturally disadvantaged students. If he does not recognize and appreciate this sad fact, he is beaten before he starts.

The task confronting him, then, is basically twofold. First, he must select his material with care, making sure that it is both fast-moving and adult in content but not unreasonably taxing to the reading skills of the class. And, second, he must be sure that his introduction of the material includes enough background information so that the assignment will make sense; and after the reading, he must fill in with a skilful discussion which will lead the students to a meaningful interpretation and appreciation of the material.

## SUGGESTED READINGS IN LITERATURE

Much of Hemingway is ideal material for such a group, and some of his early short stories, dealing with the adventures of Nick Adams, a thinly disguised, youthful Hemingway, make an excellent starting point. Short, with simple sentences, an easy vocabulary, and familiar situations, these stories move swiftly from opening scene to climax. Violence, though rarely described, is often suggested, frequently hovering just below the surface and lending an air of intangible excitement to the story. Most famous among the Nick Adams stories is, of course, "The Killers," [1] a story which moves with incredible swiftness from the initial exposure of the hired gunmen to the tragic despair of the Swede who lies in his room facing a violent, inevitable death. In class, the students can be encouraged to look more deeply into the story: Why was the Swede to be killed? Was there any chance that he might escape death? What about men who kill for money? What effect might his own involvement in this tragedy have in the life of young Nick Adams? Other Hemingway stories popular with such a group include "Indian Camp," [2] in which a much younger Nick is introduced simultaneously to the horrors of a primi-

[1] M. Edmund Speare, ed., *A Pocket Book of Short Stories* (New York: Washington Square Press, Inc., 1959), pp. 1–10.

[2] Ernest Hemingway, *In Our Time* (New York: Charles Scribner's Sons, 1958), pp. 15–21.

tive birth and a violent death, and "The Battler," [3] in which Nick becomes briefly involved in a strange, but somewhat touching, relationship between an ex-fighter and his companion.

Although not so easy to read, James Michener's story "The Cave" [4] is well worth the extra effort. This story concerns a group of navy men stationed on a little island in the Pacific during the height of World War II. On this island, some of the men have found a cave where they go whenever there is a moment of quiet to drink, to talk, or just to forget; and from these brief re- treats to the cave, the men find a new courage which helps them to face battle. Near the end of the story, Michener spells out his symbolism with meticulous care. Each of us, he says, has a cave within us to which we retreat and from which we get courage whenever the going gets tough. Some sort of a goal is the thing which keeps us together, which helps us meet our day- to-day experiences. No student will miss the point of this story. For each one of them, there is a "cave," a dream of respectability, of education, of being someone; and it is this cave within him which brings him to school and which, if it is strong enough, will keep him coming. Months after they have read it, I have had students refer to and want to discuss this story again.

"Impulse," by Conrad Aiken, concerns a young, middle-class man who impulsively decides to try to shoplift a razor in a drugstore.[5] When he gets caught and sentenced to jail, his wife, who was not too happy with him any- way, decides that this is an excellent opportunity for her to leave him. A story like this, which deals sympathetically with the plight of a shoplifter, is vir- tually always successful in a class of culturally disadvantaged students. For those who, at one time or another, have themselves succumbed to such a temptation (and there may be several in such a class), it is apparently a per- fect description of the mental processes which precede and follow a sudden impulse to shoplift. For those who have been caught, the wife's behavior afterward is sadly typical of those on whom one should have been able to depend.

Ring Lardner is always appealing to such a class, although sometimes his tongue-in-cheek style is a little difficult for them to grasp. However, a careful discussion of Jim, Lardner's antihero in "Haircut," [6] will bring the class to the realization that the author must have intended us to look beyond the superficial analysis given by the dim-witted barber. "Champion," [7] another Lardner story written in the same vein and also concerning a scoundrel, is always popular, partially, at least, because it deals with boxing, a favorite sport among many members of such a class.

So far our discussion has centered around the assignment of short stories,

[3] Ibid., pp. 65–79.

[4] Orville Prescott, ed., Mid-Century: An Anthology of Distinguished Contemporary American Short Stories (New York: Pocket Books, Inc., 1958), pp. 289–320.

[5] Robert Penn Warren and Albert Erskine, eds., Short Story Masterpieces (New York: Dell Publishing Co., 1954), pp. 15–28.

[6] Speare, op. cit., pp. 165–176.

[7] Philip Van Doren Stern, ed., The Pocket Book of Modern American Short Stories (New York: Washington Square Press, Inc., 1954), pp. 95–116.

which most students can complete in an hour or so of careful reading. It is also possible, however, for the class to tackle longer works, such as novels and plays, providing that the selections are chosen with care and the teacher is prepared to devote a number of class sessions to each work. Lorraine Hansberry's play *A Raisin the Sun*,[8] for example, is a fast-moving, absorbing study of some of the problems besetting a Negro family in today's urban culture. Arthur Miller's *Death of a Salesman*,[9] though dealing with problems less familiar to the culturally disadvantaged student, has enough universality in its tragic theme to cut across social class lines. John Steinbeck, who writes with sympathy and understanding of the problems of the underdog, is a favorite with these students. In spite of its length, *The Grapes of Wrath*[10] is always worth the many weeks it takes a class to complete it; the students will become completely absorbed in the Joad family's familiar struggle with poverty, discrimination, and exploitation. Considerably shorter but almost as popular is *Of Mice and Men*,[11] Steinbeck's moving story of two homeless men. Ernest Hemingway's *The Old Man and the Sea*,[12] with its short sentences, simple vocabulary, and totally masculine theme, is also a popular selection.

In the field of poetry, two poems by Carl Sandburg come to mind. One of them is "Chicago," and the other "The Hangman at Home."[13] Although both will be well received, the latter can be depended on to stimulate discussion. The identity of the hangman, the part of his guilt we share, Sandburg's real feelings about capital punishment, and the students' real feelings about capital punishment are some of the topics which will arise during discussion of this controversial poem. Robert Frost is always popular with such a class, and good starting points for Frost are "Stopping by Woods on a Snowy Evening" and "The Road Not Taken."[14] Later, the class may want to tackle one of Frost's longer poems, such as "Birches."[15] "Richard Cory,"[16] by Edwin Arlington Robinson, often makes good reading. Its unexpected twist at the end and its implicit suggestion that money and happiness do not always go together can be depended on to arouse interest and discussion.

## SUGGESTED PAMPHLETS AND PERIODICALS

In addition to literary selections, there are other sources of materials one should consider. For example, well-chosen pamphlets often make interesting

[8] New York: New American Library, 1959.
[9] New York: Viking Press, 1958.
[10] New York: Viking Press, 1958.
[11] New York: Bantam Books, 1958.
[12] New York: Charles Scribner's Sons, 1952.
[13] Gerald D. Sanders and John H. Nelson, eds., *Chief Modern Poets of England and America* (New York: Macmillan Co., 1950), pp. 596, 608–609.
[14] *The Pocket Book of Robert Frost's Poems* (New York: Washington Square Press, 1956), pp. 194, 223.
[15] *Ibid.*, p. 89.
[16] Sanders and Nelson, *op. cit.*, p. 494.

and informative reading for this kind of class. In Chicago, the police department puts out a pamphlet entitled *Know the Law*. This pamphlet describes types of crimes, laws regarding automobiles, and reasons for arrest. Other pamphlets which make good reading are some of those put out by banks describing their services and those put out by the Social Security Administration describing some of the benefits of Social Security. All of these pamphlets are available in quantity to the teacher without charge.

In the field of periodicals, there are two which bear mentioning. One of these is *Consumers' Reports*, with its unique evaluation of products as well as its introduction to the idea of co-operatives. The other is *Time*, each issue of which will contain some sections of interest. It goes without saying, however, that selection of reading assignments in either of these magazines must be made with care because there will be large parts which will be beyond the reading comprehension of students. Both magazines are available at classroom rates.

Newspapers offer good reading practice. However, since a newspaper becomes obsolete so quickly, it can be used with real effectiveness only if the reading assignments are made and carried out within the classroom situation.

For the teacher who wishes to supplement his program with a more structured type of material, there are a few fairly good workbooks available. The main problem with workbooks, of course, is to find material at a low enough academic level that is also sufficiently mature in content to be interesting. Good examples of such workbooks are *How To Read Better* and *Progress in Reading*,[17] which, although written at the fifth- and seventh-grade levels, respectively, both contain material that will be of interest to the older student.

Surprisingly enough, the Bill of Rights makes an excellent classroom reading assignment. That there are actually some rights which are guaranteed to each citizen of the United States is a new and intriguing idea for these students, and as they get into those amendments which are particularly pertinent to their lives, most of them will read and begin to interpret with lively enthusiasm.

Finally, there is the material produced by the students themselves. One of my own favorite assignments is to have each student write an autobiography. This is a long-term assignment providing practice not only in writing skills but also in outlining and planning a longer paper. Behind every culturally disadvantaged student, there is, inevitably, a story; and for those who feel like sharing it, it can be a fascinating one. The teacher who is looking ahead will hold on to the best of these, copy them, correct the spelling and grammar, disguise the identity of the writer, type the polished version on stencils, and use them for reading in next year's classes.

---

[17] Harley A. Smith and Ida Lee King, *How To Read Better* (Austin, Texas: Steck Co., 1956); Ullin W. Leavell and William Leonard Gardner, *Progress in Reading* (Austin, Texas: Steck Co., 1957).

# A SUGGESTED CURRICULUM FOR TEACHING READING SKILLS TO YOUTHS WHO ARE RELUCTANT READERS *

Lawrence E. Hafner

and Robert Karlin

A largely experiential approach to improving the functional reading skills of youths is described in this article. Although originally designed to serve as a guide for experienced teachers who are teaching young men enrolled in the Job Corps, it is easily adaptable to teaching high-school students who are reluctant readers and who, for one reason or another, were not able to profit from previous reading instruction.

This program is not a highly-detailed, closed program that would inhibit flexibility and creative innovation. It is rather a flexible framework designed to encourage and stimulate the creative teaching of reading.

1. The ability to read is a key that unlocks many doors. What does this statement mean according to the program described in the article?

2. Comment on the strengths of the various activities in terms of accepted learning-teaching principles.

3. Develop in further detail several of the suggested techniques for teaching the various skills such as phonics and syllabication skills, comprehension and interpretation skills, organizational skills, and so on.

## COMMUNICATIVE SKILLS PROGRAM

### Lower Level (Grades 4–5)

POINT OF VIEW. In these days of change, progress, and challenge the ability to read is almost synonymous with the ability to obtain a better job; to become a better-informed person; to contribute to the well-being of one's country, and to move with greater confidence among one's associates and society.

The purpose of this reading program is to further the development of reading skills and attitudes of the trainees and thereby develop their resourcefulness, and instill in each one a feeling of dignity in his learning. These skills are on a continuum, and aspects of any given skill will be taught at each level; however, the emphasis will vary as more complex materials are introduced.

---

* REPRINTED FROM Suggested Curriculum for the Job Corps Training Center, Camp Breckenridge, Kentucky, a Federal Retraining Project, 1964, Office of Economic Opportunity, Contract 103.

The procedures, activities, techniques, and materials are designed to aid the teacher accomplish these goals and are intended for students whose reading-achievement scores are at the fourth and fifth-grade level.

The basic teaching-learning approach for this level is the *experience method*. Briefly stated, the experience approach utilizes materials based on the experiences of the trainees, thus capitalizing on their goals and interests. Advantage is taken of the interrelationships of the language arts, and therefore the speaking, listening, and writing aspects are incorporated into the reading activities.

DIAGNOSTIC EVALUATION. Trainees will be placed in instructional groups appropriate to their present level of reading achievement and instructed at an appropriate rate in materials they can handle. To assist in the proper placement for reading instruction the total population of trainees will be screened through the use of standardized reading tests:

1. *Gates Reading Survey* (Grades 3–10), published by the Bureau of Publications, Teachers College, Columbia University. This contains subtests of word meaning, speed, level of comprehension and accuracy.
2. *California Reading Test* (Elem., Grades 4–6), published by California Test Bureau, Madison, Wisconsin. Vocabulary and comprehension are stressed in the various subtests.
3. *Botel Reading Inventory*, by Morton Botel. A standardized instrument used to determine functional levels.

Individual and small group evaluation using standardized and informal instruments will determine functional levels, independent reading levels, and instructional reading levels for each student. Informal instruments will be constructed by the teachers. Skills to be measured are auditory discrimination skills, word identification skills, comprehension-interpretation skills, and study skills. The basic criterion for inclusion in this group is an instructional level of 4.0–5.9 as determined by the functional reading inventories.

PROGRAMS AND MATERIALS OF INSTRUCTION. Components of the program will consist of the following: The experience approach using such themes as Getting a Job, My Favorite Sport, Taking Care of a Car, Developing a Code to Live By; specific trade books on such topics as space and science, the level of difficulty of which is appropriate for instructional purposes and recreational reading, and programmed and laboratory material for additional aid in overcoming individual reading weaknesses through individual concentrated practice and reinforcement of learnings.

In the experience approach the emphasis is on the reading of experience selections, signs, notices, campus publications, and letters. In the important instructional phase the reading of experience selections—stories based on the individual and group experiences of the students, and orally related by them to the teacher—will be written on a chalkboard and/or tape-recorded. The story will be recorded on a chart and/or duplicated and given to members of the class. Instruction in vocabulary development and phrase and sentence reading will be based on the story.

The experience approach has several advantages for these trainees over a basal reading program with prescribed materials. Among these advantages are the use of goals and interests which are of greater concern to the students than the activities of outside groups and material based on their own past experiences and background. In the discussion and writing activities, speaking, listening, and writing reinforce the learning of reading and thereby aid language development. Stories relating to campus life and colored slides with subtitles can be developed for use with slide projectors.

Trainees will be helped to develop a daily log (using a mimeographed form) for the purpose of writing new words and phrases; listing vocabulary and spelling demonstrations to work on each day; noting memoranda (someone's name and address or other information such as reminder notes or name of a movie); and for listing functional phrases to be used in letter-writing. Vocabulary, word-identification, comprehension-interpretation, and study skills will be emphasized through the use of experience reading, the reading of trade books and the use of programmed and laboratory materials.

*Techniques*

1. *Word Meanings.* In the development of word meanings and sight vocabulary use will be made of the following activities and materials:

    a. Experience stories—for the purpose of developing sight vocabulary in a meaningful context.

    b. Linguistic blocks (plastic blocks with a word on each side)—for the purpose of developing sight vocabulary through matching of words and sentence-building. Following directions through the use of action games in which the teacher presents to the class or individual signs with directions (such as "White Sox fans raise your hands." "Raise your pencils slowly.").

    c. Writing of personal letters in order to reinforce new words through writing.

    d. Reading signs in the classroom and throughout the campus or reading campus unit newspapers; using the Language Master device (utilizing a card for printing words or phrases and an attached piece of tape for recording the words).

    e. Using the Language Master for reinforcement through dictation practice in which Language Master cards are inserted in the device without looking at the written part. After the phrase is played and the student has written the phrase he checks the card for feedback.

    f. Developing individual spelling improvement booklets using words growing out of the experience stories and other materials used by the trainees. Further aids to word-identification are found in the skills of structural analysis using context clues, phonetic analysis, and use of the dictionary.

2. *Phonics and Syllabication.* A strong syllabication sense will be built by breaking into syllables known words that have been spelled on magnetic boards. Inductive development of recognition and meaning of prefixes, suffixes, roots, and syllables will be facilitated through use of a variety of games using the magnetic board.

Developing the ability to recognize phonic elements such as vowel digraphs and consonant digraphs will be aided through searching for words in a story and classifying them under headings such as *oa, ee, ai, wh, ch, ph.* The inductive development of phonic elements will be facilitated and made more interesting by the use of the overhead projector and by the occasional use of such devices as colored chalk to emphasize the phonic element being taught.

3. *Vocabulary.* In order to reinforce vocabulary learnings through supplementary practice materials use will be made of the vocabulary lessons in materials such as *Lessons for Self-Instruction in Reading* Series C (grade 5), Madison, Wisconsin: California Test Bureau, 1963; the new *Rochester Occupational Reading Series* Level I, Chicago: Science Research Associates, and selected exercise drawn from materials such as *Be a Better Reader* I, Englewood Cliffs, N. J.: Prentice-Hall.

4. *Comprehension and Interpretation.* Practice in word identification skills will be obtained through use of word-analysis lessons in the SRA *Reading Laboratory* IIIa (reading achievement levels 3.0–12.0) Chicago: Science Research Associates. *Phonetic Analysis* I and II and *Context,* New York: Center for Programmed Instruction.

In the development of the comprehension-interpretation skills of getting the main idea, understanding supporting details, seeing cause-and-effect relationships and drawing conclusions, use will be made of activities and material (basically the experience materials) such as discussions to probe the deeper meanings of passages; oral questions requiring the student to identify the main idea of a selection and to bring forth details to support an idea; written questions presented before reading requiring the student to write an answer in a word or phrase; partner-learning, in which two students cooperatively or individually work out answers to various types of questions requiring unaided responses and then discuss why certain responses are correct; reading letters carefully to make accurate inferences; writing a sentence that requires the student to state a cause-effect relationship and tell what a paragraph or selection is mainly about or state the answer to a literal or inferential question; writing questions for a selection; discussing the appropriateness of a response; reading directions for doing an experiment in a trade book.

In order to reinforce the learning of comprehension skills through supplementary practice materials use will be made of materials such as the interpretation and following direction lessons in *Lessons for Self-Instruction in*

*Reading* Series C (grade 5), Madison, Wisconsin: California Test Bureau, 1963; *Reading Skill Builders* (Level Four, parts 1, 2 and 3; and Level Five, parts 1, 2 and 3), Pleasantville, New York: Reader's Digest Services, 1960; *Help Yourself to Improve Your Reading* (Part One, level 5), Reader's Digest Services; *SRA Reading Laboratory* (IIIa, reading-achievement levels 3.0– 12.0), Chicago, Illinois: Science Research Associates; and *The New Rochester Occupational Reading Series* (Level I, topics include: truck farming, super-markets, bakeries, restaurants and cafeterias and gas stations), Chicago: Science Research Associates.

5. *Study Skills.* An important aspect of any program designed to develop proficiency in reading and associated skills is the teaching of study skills. The over-all purpose of teaching study skills is to develop proficiency in locating, evaluating and organizing material and retaining it. At this level, these basic skills in locating information and organizing ideas will be stressed: using a table of contents, using an index, identifying and writing the main idea of a paragraph, and writing a paragraph summary.

6. *Locational Skills.* In the development of the locational skills, use will be made of activities and materials, e.g., listing a topic, for example, baseball, and developing subcategories or subtopics including leagues, teams, and players and playing Twenty Questions to help develop a sense of sequence and order in going from large abstract categories to lesser more concrete categories in order to develop the rationale needed in using an index; answering written questions that require a person to locate in an index the page on which a topic or subtopic is discussed; writing a list of topics that might go into an index for a short mimeographed selection or a very short trade book; checking the tables of contents of eight or ten related books to see if a given broad topic is discussed in any of the books; writing a summary paragraph telling what a book is about after reading the table of contents; writing a table of contents for a folder of experience stories.

7. *Organizational Skills.* In the development of the organizational skills, use will be made of activities and materials such as stating a sentence in one's own words to show an understanding of the main idea; finding, and writing topic sentences for paragraphs that do not contain topic sentences to develop the skill of identifying the main idea of a paragraph; writing a summary sentence for each of several paragraphs in a selection such as an experience story, campus newspaper story, or short chapter in a trade book and combining these summary sentences into a summary paragraph, or listening to a paragraph and writing the main idea. Factual materials will be taken from trade books such as Gallant's *Exploring the Planets* and textbooks such as *Your Country and Mine* by Tiegs. Further practice and reinforcement of study skills will be obtained through the use of the reference skills lessons in such material as *Lessons for Self-Instruction in Reading* Series C (grade 5), California Test Bureau.

RECREATIONAL READING. Not all experiences need be direct experiences; some are vicarious. Reading is an excellent source for vicarious experiences. Many reading experiences are pleasurable as well as profitable; however, reading for pleasure is recreational reading.

In order to fulfill the expectations of a recreational reading program materials of great variety and scope and appropriate to the reading ability and varied interests of the trainees will be required. Supplementary materials such as trade books on a large variety of topics interesting to these young men, campus newspapers, magazines, bulletins, letters, and local newspapers will make the reading process both profitable and pleasurable. In order to facilitate the learning reinforcement possibilities in the interrelationships of the language arts the sharing of information and discussion of books read will be encouraged. Featured in such activities will be the relating of favorite incidents, exchanges of opinions, comparison of views, and critical analysis of material read. Choral reading and dramatization activities such as group play reading will be expected to reinforce language learning, improve expression in oral reading, develop the aesthetic sensibilities, and provide profitable, pleasurable recreation.

PROGRESS AND EVALUATION. In the post-training evaluation, alternate forms of the standardized reading tests and informal inventories of reading will be used to assess growth in the reading skills. Students of average intellectual ability on general population norms who achieve a reading grade placement in the 4.0–5.9 range on pretraining evaluations (using standardized tests) might reasonably be expected to increase those scores at the rate of approximately one and one-half year's growth for every six months of reading instruction.

Students of lesser ability will be expected to show somewhat lesser amounts of growth, and students of greater ability will be expected to show greater amounts of growth. Every two months inventories assessing word-recognition abilities, reading-comprehension abilities and abilities to write dictated sentences correctly will be administered to determine new functional levels, independent reading levels, and instructional reading levels in order to assure that reading instruction is based upon new levels of achievement.

## COMMUNICATIVE SKILLS PROGRAM

### Middle Group (Grades 6–7)

POINT OF VIEW.[1] This phase of the program is designed for students whose reading achievement scores are at the sixth and seventh-grade levels.

The teaching of reading skills at this level will be based on the use of interesting trade materials: stories, special illustrated science books, adventure, social studies, humor, sports, and exploration. Certain functional aspects of the experience approach—the reading of campus newspapers, letters, and

---

[1] For a statement relating the demands of society on the individual, his opportunity to serve society, and the purpose of the reading program, please see p. 11. Point of View in the suggested course in reading for the Lower Level Group.

student-composed materials and the reading of job-related materials will be included as useful auxiliary parts of the program. This useful and interesting approach will capitalize on the ambitions and interests of the students. Speaking, listening, and writing aspects of the language arts will be incorporated into the reading activities.

DIAGNOSTIC EVALUATION.[2] Trainees assigned to this group will have been evaluated by standard reading tests as well as specialized, standardized, and informal reading inventories. The basic criterion for inclusion in this middle group is an instructional level of 6.0–7.9, as determined by the functional reading inventories.

PROGRAMS AND MATERIALS OF INSTRUCTION. Components of this program will consist of the following: the trade materials approach to such topics as exploration, humor, adventure, sports, social studies, and science; modification of the experience approach, considering in depth such themes as Managing Personal Relations, Famous Personalities, Choosing a Career, and Improving Personal Appearance; and programmed and laboratory material for use in overcoming individual reading weaknesses through concentrated personalized practice and reinforcement of learning.

In the interesting trade materials approach emphasis will be on the reading of books, pamphlets, and bulletins from the real world of living. Instructors will clarify purposes and set goals in reading books in order to increase comprehension and encourage efficient reading. They will guide the students in applying word-identification skills to solving the pronunciation and meaning of problem words, and teach the trainees how to apply study skills in locating, organizing, and retaining information. Vocabulary, word-identification, comprehension-interpretation, and study skills will be emphasized through the reading of interesting materials, the use of experience reading,[3] and the use of programmed and laboratory materials.

TECHNIQUES. In the development of word meanings and sight vocabulary, use will be made of activities and materials such as syllabicating names of important people and celebrities (Skel-ton, John-son, Ker-ner, Bern-stein, Mu-si-al, Co-la-vito, Win-ters, and others); finding suffixes in names of famous people (Ga-*ble*, Bea-*tles*, Man-*tle*); finding words with given prefixes from mimeographed selections to see who can locate and place first under these or form-headings words containing given prefixes; classifying words from various reading materials according to phonics and structured elements and putting them into categories on an individual basis; building vocabulary notebooks (class and/or individual) in which words are defined, respelled phonetically, illustrated and used in sentences; writing phonetically-respelled jokes and distributing them to the class or printing them on large pieces of

---

[2] For the complete statement on the pretraining evaluation, please see pp. 12–13. Diagnostic Evaluation in the suggested course in reading for the Lower Level Group.

[3] For an explanation of the experience approach and a discussion of its values, please see p. 13. Programs and Materials of Instruction in the suggested course in reading for the Lower Level Group.

poster board (this idea might be applied judiciously to the development of certain signs and notices);[4] writing sentences and developing context clues (e.g., explanatory words and phrases and contrasting elements) in order to explain difficult words and show students how to recognize and use context clues to meaning.

Furthermore, discussion of concepts and the attempt to develop precision in the use of vocabulary terms will be aspects of the various oral language activities, including discussions, conversations, and informal debates. The inductive development of phonic and structural elements will be facilitated and made more interesting by the use of the overhead projector and by the occasional use of such devices as colored chalk to emphasize the phonic element. Students and teachers will collaborate in the making of slides to be used in teaching phonic and structural elements. Scripts to accompany the slides will be tape-recorded.

In order to reinforce vocabulary learnings through supplementary practice materials, use will be made of the vocabulary lessons in *Lessons for Self-Instruction in Reading* Series D (grade 6) and Series E (grade 7), Madison, Wisconsin: California Test Bureau (to be published); and selected exercises drawn from materials such as *Be a Better Reader* II, Englewood Cliffs, New Jersey: Prentice-Hall. Practice in word identification and vocabulary skills will be obtained through of word analysis and vocabulary lessons in the SRA *Reading Laboratory* IIIa (reading achievement levels 3.0–12.0) Chicago: Science Research Associates; and selected exercises drawn from materials such as *Be a Better Reader* II, Englewood Cliffs, New Jersey: Prentice-Hall.

In the development of comprehension-interpretation skills, use will be made of activities[5] and materials such as discussions prior to group reading of an article to facilitate understanding of concepts and to set purposes for reading, written questions (inserted into some of the articles that have been placed in a folder) to direct reading for the purpose of increasing comprehension and retention of material read; choosing the right headline for a picture that represents a familiar scene in order to aid discriminative thinking and the ability to read sentences; writing of questions for short articles in individual folders; writing "commercials" to be taped and replayed in class or used in skits to furnish a creative outlet and provide practice in problem-solving; writing in a column one author's ideas on a topic and in another column a different author's ideas on the same topic in order to compare and contrast ideas; predicting outcome of a story after reading a given amount of it in order to stimulate the use of clues in the development of inference-making abilities; writing captions to cartoons; discussing critically the adequacy of oral or written responses to questions based on material read; drawing conclusions about the character of individuals in a story and the adequacy of the character's solutions to problems in order to help students

---

[4] In addition, many of the ideas for developing word identification skills listed in the suggested course for the lower level can be adapted to use at this intermediate level.

[5] Most of these activities will be done by the trainees rather than the teachers.

see relationships and make more accurate inferences; discussing figures of speech used by the students, for example, "ready to crawl the wall" (state of agitation or desperation); providing the background of experience, real or vicarious, to understand specific useful figures of speech which are largely unknown to the students, for example, "ship of the desert" (camel), "diamond in the rough" (person with potential); finding "guiding" words, i.e., transitional words and words leading to the conclusion in order to develop accuracy of interpretation.[6]

In order to reinforce the learning of comprehension-interpretation skills through supplementary practice materials, use can be made of the interpretation and following-directions lessons in materials such as *Lessons for Self-Instruction in Reading* (Series D, grade 6 and Series E, grade 7), California Test Bureau, 1963; SRA *Reading Laboratory* IIIa (reading achievement levels 3.0–12.0), Science Research Associates; the *New Rochester Occupational Reading Series* (Level II, topics: truck farming, supermarkets, bakeries, restaurants and cafeterias, and gas stations); and selected exercises drawn from materials such as *Be a Better Reader* (II and III), Prentice-Hall.

In addition to the skills previously discussed, other special functional skills will need to be emphasized at this level: writing informal functional notes in a standard form, reading arithmetic word problems and reading in order to prepare a short talk. Because the level of proficiency of these students in the study skills is not likely to be much greater than that of the students at the lower level, it is suggested that the more fundamental study skills from the lower level course of study be known before advancing to more difficult skills.

At this level will be introduced the locational skills of using the index to almanacs, such as the *World Almanac* and *Information, Please*; indexes to the easier encyclopedias, such as the *World Book*; card catalogues; mail order catalogues; organizational skills of outlining; previewing a chapter in a text, such as *Learning with Science* by Craig, to gain an overview of it. In addition, attention will be given to developing different rates of reading— scanning (very fast rate), skimming (rapid rate), and study reading (a slower rate).

In the development of the locational skills, use will be made of activities and materials such as checking the interesting covers of magazines, e.g., *Look, Life, Newsweek, Time*, and locating basic information about topics featured on the cover through use of the table of contents in the study guide of encyclopedias, for example, *Compton's* and *Britannica Junior*; checking in the almanacs (via the index) to see which students were closest in stating the world's record in various sporting events; who won the World Series in a given year or the names of the ten largest cities in the world in order to develop facility, confidence and interest in the use of almanacs; helping

---

[6] In addition to these suggestions, many of the ideas for developing comprehension-interpretation skills listed in the suggested course for the lower level can be adapted for use at this intermediate level.

students find favorite kinds of books through use of the subject card file; finding more books by a favorite author through use of the author card file, and
locating a book by title in order to develop skill and interest in using the card
catalogue to locate information and to increase the breadth and depth of the
students' reading.

In the development of organizational skills, use is made of activities and
materials such as completing partially-completed outlines of short, interesting
articles on such topics as Famous Personalities or Improving Personal Appearance; previewing the introductions, headings, pictorial material, and
summaries of such texts as Tiegs' *Your Country's Story* for the purpose of
gaining an overview of the structure of the chapters in order to establish
worthwhile purposes for reading and to aid in the retention of material read.

In developing different rates of reading, use is made of such activities and
materials as looking rapidly for a single fact (without actually reading the
text containing the fact) in an article from a magazine, such as *Reader's
Digest*, or an almanac, such as *Information, Please*, in order to develop the
skill of scanning; looking for the name of a friend in the campus newspaper
in order to develop the skill of scanning; reading rapidly, ignoring unimportant words, a letter, a bulletin or a selected article from a magazine, such as
*Reader's Digest*, or a story in a trade book in order to develop the skill of
skimming; looking for the answers to questions in textbook materials, such
as *Experiments in Science* by Craig, to develop the study skill.

Further practice and reinforcement of study skills will be obtained through
the use of the reference-skills lessons in materials, such as *Lessons for Self-
Instruction in Reading* (Series D, grade 6 and Series E, grade 7), California
Test Bureau; and the *Study Skills Library*, Huntington, New York: Educational Developmental Laboratories.

RECREATIONAL READING.[7]   Instructors will be encouraged to familiarize
themselves with the fundamental principles of bibliotherapy (using reading
to further personal adjustment) in order to capitalize on the opportunities
for blibliotherapy presented in the recreational reading programs. Materials
used in bibliotherpay work will include such books as *City for Lincoln* by
Tunis (in which a baseball coach does something about juvenile delinquency); *Hot Rod* by Felsen (about a speed-crazy boy); and *Abraham Lincoln* by Felt (a story dealing with the problem of size). Interesting books for
recreational reading at this level include such titles as *Space Satellite* by
Wells Breeland; *Behind the Silver Shield* by Floherty, and *All America* by
Tunis. In addition to these, materials such as campus newspapers and magazines such as *Reader's Digest* and *Look* will be read by students at this level.

PROGRESS AND EVALUATION.   In the post-training evaluation, alternate
forms of the standardized reading tests and informal inventories of reading
will be used to assess growth in the reading skills. Students of average intel-

---

[7] The basic discussion of the nature and values of a recreational program and general
activities may be found in the suggested course of study for the Lower Level group.

lectual ability on general population norms who achieve a reading grade placement in the 6.0–7.9 range on pretraining evaluations using standardized tests will reasonably be expected to increase those scores at the rate of approximately one and one-half years' to two years' growth for every six months of reading instruction. Students of lesser ability will be expected to show somewhat lesser amounts of growth, and students of greater ability will be expected to show greater amounts of growth.

Every two months, inventories assessing word-recognition abilities, reading comprehension-interpretation abilities, ability to write dictated sentences correctly, and ability to write summary paragraphs will be administered in order to determine new functional levels, independent reading levels, and instructional reading levels in order to provide reading instruction based upon new achievement levels.

## COMMUNICATIVE SKILLS PROGRAM

### Advanced Group (Grade 8 and above)

POINT OF VIEW.[8] This phase of the program is designed for students whose reading achievement scores are at the eighth-grade level and above. The teaching of reading skills at this level will be based on the use of a wide assortment of reading materials. This approach capitalizes on the ambitions and interests of the students and is designed to familiarize them with a wide array of materials, thereby stimulating an ever-growing interest and competence in reading and, through precept and example, actually *developing* this interest and competence in reading in greater depth and breadth. Speaking, listening, and writing aspects of the language arts will be incorporated into the reading activities.

DIAGNOSTIC EVALUATION.[9] Students assigned to this group will have been evaluated by the standardized reading tests and the specialized standardized and informal reading inventories. The basic criterion for inclusion in this advanced group is an instructional level of 8.0+ as determined by the functional reading inventories.

PROGRAMS AND MATERIALS OF INSTRUCTION. Components of this program will consist of the following: use of a wide assortment of published reading materials, newspapers, weekly and monthly general interest and news magazines, special interest magazines, reference works, trade books, vocational and technical manuals and texts, how-to-do-it books, guidance booklets, appropriate religious and devotional materials, biographies, novels, plays, gov-

---

[8] For a statement relating the demands of society on the individual, his opportunity to serve society, and the purpose of the reading program, please see p. 11, Point of View, in the suggested course in reading for the Lower Level group.

[9] For the complete statement on the pretraining evaluation, please see pp. 12 and 13, Diagnostic Evaluation, in the suggested courses in reading for the Lower Level group. See also Appendix.

ernmental booklets and forms, industrial books, brochures and forms; a modification of the experience approach, and programmed and laboratory material.[10] In the wide-reading approach emphasis will be on the reading of a variety of materials—published, teacher and student-made, campus-produced —to stimulate, teach, and guide trainees in a variety of ways.

Instructors will clarify purposes and set goals in reading various kinds of materials in order to increase comprehension and encourage efficient reading, guide the students in applying word-identification skills in solving the pronunciation and meaning of problem words encountered in the material, and teach the students how to apply study skills for the purpose of locating, evaluating, organizing, and retaining information. The evaluation of material will be covered in critical reading.

In the development of word meanings and sight vocabulary, use will be made of activities and materials such as the developing of specialized glossaries in booklet form, including syllabication of words, phonetic respelling, meanings, terms used in context and pictorial illustration where feasible, finding words developed from a given root and listing them in a column and inductively developing the meaning of the root.[11] In addition, discussion of concepts and the attempt to develop precision in the use of vocabulary terms should be an aspect of oral language activities including discussions, conversations, symposia, and debates.

In order to reinforce vocabulary learnings through supplementing practice materials, use will be made of the vocabulary lessons in *Lessons for Self-Instruction in Reading* (Series F, grade 8), Madison, Wisconsin: California Test Bureau (to be published); and selected exercises drawn from materials such as *Be a Better Reader* (IV, V, VI), Englewood Cliffs, New Jersey: Prentice-Hall. Individual practice in word-identification and vocabulary skills will be obtained through use of word analysis and vocabulary lessons in the *SRA Reading Laboratory* (IIIb, reading achievement levels 3.0–12.0), Chicago: Science Research Associates; and the lessons in *Word Clues*, Huntington, N. Y.: Educational Developmental Laboratories.

In the development of comprehension-interpretation skills, use will be made of activities and materials such as group discussion of problem phrases in governmental brochures (job descriptions, health and guidance bulletins) and forms (e.g., income tax forms, job application forms); interpreting descriptions of items in mail-order catalogues of companies, such as Sears and Wards; discussing problem sentences in technical manuals used in popular science magazines, such as *Mechanics Illustrated* and *Popular Science*; paraphrasing sentences; grading magazine articles by difficulty from such magazines as *Look, Science Digest* and *Reader's Digest* and classifying them according to interest areas, and placing them in individual folders with

[10] For further information on these facets of the program see pp. 21 and 22, Programs and Materials of Instruction, in the suggested course in reading for the Middle Group.

[11] Numerous additional suggestions for developing word-identificatian skills are to be formed in the suggested courses of study for the Lower Level and for the Middle Group.

guided reading questions; writing actual functional arithmetic problems (as they occur in real or vicarious experience) as word problems.[12]

In order to reinforce the learning of comprehension-interpretation skills through supplementary practice materials, use can be made of the interpretation and following-directions lessons in *Lessons for Self-Instruction in Reading* (Series F, grade 8), California Test Bureau, 1963; SRA *Reading Laboratory* (IIIb, reading achievement levels 3.0–12.0), Science Research Associates; *Reading for Understanding* (reading achievement levels 3.0–14.0), Science Research Associates; and selected exercises drawn from materials such as *Be a Better Reader* (IV, V, VI), Prentice-Hall. Because the level of proficiency of these students in the study skills is likely to vary considerably, the more fundamental study skills from the previous courses of study (Lower Level and Middle Group) will be taught to those found deficient in these skills before advancing to more difficult skills.

At this level will be introduced the locational skills of using the *Reader's Guide* and also using specialized indexes; the organizational skills of writing a complete original outline and making a bibliography or writing a literary paper, and the evaluative skills pertaining to critical reading: checking the author's qualifications to write in a given field, identifying the assumptions of the author, separating fact from opinion, identifying loaded words and writing critical reviews. Attention will also be given to developing different rates of reading, such as scanning (very fast rate), skimming (rapid rate) and study reading (a slower rate).

In the development of the locational and organizational skills, use will be made of activities and materials such as writing a radio script on some topic— Personalities in the News, Famous People of the Sixties, Developing a Code to Live By, or Managing Personal Relations. In order to develop the ability to locate articles in the *Reader's Guide to Periodical Literature* trainees will write a short outline, make a short bibliography, and write a paper based on this material. This work may be broken into segments in which outlines are mastered before proceeding to bibliographies or before work for each script may be carried through to completion. The approaches will vary with the abilities of the students. Modifications of the procedures just given will be used in preparing talks, notes for forums, and debates.

In the development of the evaluative skills of critical reading, use will be made of such activities and materials as reading advertisements and editorials in order to identify assumptions of the writer; making a bulletin-board display on which are listed false assumptions along with a brief explanation of the error involved (a catchy heading could be used for this such as "Ones That Didn't Get Away" or "They Wouldn't Believe Me"); making charts, booklets, and displays in which are listed false claims and opinions found in

[12] In addition to these suggestions, many of the ideas for developing comprehension-interpretation skills listed in the suggested courses on the Lower Level and the Middle Group can be adapted for use at this Advanced Level.

written materials opposite the facts uncovered in reference works or other authoritative materials.

These could be given headings, such as "You're Putting Me On" or "Try Again, Charlie"; and writing short book reviews in which the reviewer states the scope of the book and whether the goals of the book listed in the preface are carried out (the books selected should be in area of the reviewer's interest and growing competence), and compiling a list of loaded words (such as "carped" used for discussion, or "antics" used for actions found in newspaper editorials, stories, and magazines). Further practice and reinforcement of study skills will be obtained through the use of the reference skills lessons in materials, such as *Lessons for Self-Instruction in Reading* (Series F, grade 8), California Test Bureau, and the *Study Skills Library*, Educational Development Laboratories.

In developing different rates of reading, use is made of such activities and materials as looking rapidly for a single fact (without actually reading the text containing the fact) in an article from a magazine, such as *Look* or *Popular Mechanics* to develop the skill of scanning; reading rapidly—ignoring unimportant words—a letter, a bulletin or a selected article from a newspaper, such as the *Evansville Courier*, or a magazine, such as *Newsweek* in order to develop the skill of skimming for the main idea, and looking for answers to questions in textbook materials such as Commager's *Our Nation* in order to develop the skill of study reading.

RECREATIONAL READING.[13]    In order to fulfill the expectations of a recreational reading program materials of great variety and scope appropriate to the reading ability and varied interests of these students will be required. Use will be made of such materials as newspapers, for example, *Evansville Courier*, *St. Louis Post-Dispatch*; weekly general interest and news magazines, such as *Life, Look, Newsweek, Time, Saturday Evening Post*; special interest magazines such as *Mechanics Illustrated, Science Digest*; Catholic, Protestant and Jewish religious and devotional materials such as *Our Family, Information, America, This Day, Portals of Prayer, Lutheran Layman, Presbyterian Life, United Church Herald, Together, Union Prayer Book* and *Jewish Post and Opinions*.

PROGRESS AND EVALUATION.    In the post-training evaluation, alternate forms of the standardized reading tests and informal inventories of reading will be used to assess growth in the reading skills. Students of average intellectual ability on general population norms who achieve a reading grade placement of 8.0 or above on pretraining evaluations using standardized tests will reasonably be expected to increase those scores at the rate of approximately two years' growth for every six months of reading instruction. Students of lesser ability will be expected to show somewhat lesser amounts of growth,

[13] The basic discussion on the nature and values of a recreational program and general activities may be found in p. 19, Recreational Reading, in the suggested course of study for the Lower Level groups. An introductory statement regarding bibliotherapy may be found in p. 27, Recreational Reading in the suggested course of study for the Middle Group.

and students of greater ability will be expected to show greater amounts of growth.

Every two months inventories assessing word recognition abilities, reading comprehension-interpretation abilities, ability to write dictated sentences correctly, and ability to write summary paragraphs will be administered in order to determine new functional levels as well as independent and instructional reading levels so that instruction and materials will be adjusted to new reading levels.

# GIVE HIM A BOOK THAT HITS HIM WHERE HE LIVES *

Charles G. Spiegler

*Reluctant readers in the schools provide the teachers with a real problem: How do you get someone who treats a book like a hand grenade with the pin pulled to get interested in reading?*

*Spiegler's article relates his experiences in helping the "sons and daughters of 'blue-collar' America" to develop positive attitudes toward books and book reading by providing these individuals with books that "hit them where they live."*

*1. How did the author succeed in getting Barry to read books?*

*2. There are at least two reasons why the author is glad the Barry Saltzes are learning to read. What are those reasons?*

*3. What effects did the book fair have on the reading attitudes and habits of the students?*

*4. How important is the teaching of "dialmanship"?*

*5. What are the children's guidelines for authors who want to write books that appeal to them?*

CULTURALLY, he is bounded on the north by comic books, on the south by the pool parlor, on the east by the racing form, on the west by neighborhood small talk. Born into a home at cultural ebb tide, often raised midst turmoil and trauma, living in an intellectual ghetto, he sits in my classroom—annoyed to the point of hostility. I have asked him to read a book—any book—for a first report of the term.

The "he" I mean is no figment of my imagination. He is Barry Saltz, a 16-year-old future butcher of America (one of many such in my classroom);

* REPRINTED FROM *Improving English Skills of Culturally Different Youth*, Bulletin 1964, No. 5, Doris V. Gunderson, editor, U. S. Department of Health, Education, and Welfare.

a present reluctant reader (one of many such in my classroom). Despite his 20/20 vision, it dismays him not an iota that he has never read a book cover to cover in all his 16 years, that he has never spent a rainy afternoon browsing in the library.

Scan the printed page? Not he!

I search my brain for a *book* that may appeal. "How about *Questions Boys Ask*," [1] I recommend ever so naively, as I brandish a copy I own.

"Naaah. . . ."

I try sports, hobbies, deep-sea fishing—everything from prehistoric man of 5 million years ago to the stars millions of light years away. But I get a look that warns me—"Mister, you're wasting your time."

I am beginning to lose heart when one day it happens! I find the link I need to help move Barry Saltz from the desert island of ignorance about books he has for so long inhabited to the mainland of written words and ideas. It is a tiny link—no bigger than the cluster of warts on Barry's index finger.

Those warts really worry Barry, butcher-to-be, because as he put it, "They're gonna drive away my customers." So I ask him one day, "Why don't you get rid of them?" and learn, to my surprise, that he has an *idée fixé* about warts. They come from touching frogs, and maybe will vanish one day by magic, if you're lucky.

Sensing how deep his superstition about warts really is, I recommend a book, *Superstitious? Here's Why!* [2] urge him to read the section on warts, and agree to accept this as a report.

The result? *Mirabile dictu!* Barry Saltz practically memorizes that paragraph on warts and reads the book through cover to cover in one 4-hour sitting. Moreover, having finally gone to a library, he has now become aware of some very readable books about health and strength—a major interest. Before the semester is over, Barry Saltz can tell you all about *The Wonders Inside You* [3] by Cosgrove, *Magic Bullets* [4] by Sutherland, and *Boy's Book of Body Building* [5] by Pashko. True, he still refers to de Kruif's *Hunger Fighters* as "Hunger Pains"! Who cares! Barry Saltz is on his way!

Does it matter? Does it really matter that the Saltz nose now goes between the covers of a book? Is this a "summum bonum" commensurate with the effort expended? Yes, indeed! For, of all youth's divine rights during that precious period we call "The school years," I place very high the enjoyment of books. Learning how to earn a living is one thing; but in an age of steadily increasing leisure, learning how to live—joyously—is, to me, prime. And learning how to do it, among other ways, through books—is quintessential.

[1] David W. Armstrong, *Questions Boys Ask*. New York: E. P. Dutton & Co., 1955.

[2] Julie Forsyth Batchelor and Claudia De Lys, *Superstitious? Here's Why!* New York: Harcourt, Brace & World, 1954.

[3] Margaret Cosgrove, *The Wonders Inside You*. New York: Dodd, Mead & Co., 1955.

[4] Louis Sutherland, *Magic Bullets*. Boston: Little, Brown & Co., 1956.

[5] Stanley Pashko, *Boy's Book of Body Building*. New York: Grosset & Dunlap.

Perhaps no one has said it for me better than Paul Bueter, a 17-year-old senior who, after viewing *A Night to Remember* [6] on TV, was one of dozens who had remembered it vividly enough to ask for the Walter Lord original. Queried on why he wanted the book, having just seen the TV version, he gave what seems to me the classic answer to those who see TV as the substitute for reading—"Sure, it was good," he says of the TV performance, "but I don't know . . . I didn't really get the feeling of how it was on the *Titanic* on that black night. . . . How could you, with all those camera lights on the people?" In order for Paul to "really get the feeling" of that black night to remember, he needed more than brilliant camera lights. He needed the glow of his own imagination.

Yes, I'm glad I got Barry Saltz to read for other reasons. Just as we learn to write by writing, we learn to read by reading. It's not always that "Johnny doesn't read because he can't." It's often that "Johnny can't read because he doesn't." [7]

Yes, I'm glad I got Barry Saltz to read because I know that the meat upon which our Caesars feed is anti-intellectualism, "know nothingism." In the growing struggles between freedom and authoritarianism, it is better for us all that the Barry Saltzes be thinking, questioning, probing citizens—not vacuums or vegetables. Though there are many paths towards this end, I respect reading as one of them. I'm glad I got Barry Saltz to read.

As chairman of an academic subjects department in a New York City vocational school (from 1956 to 1961), I have had the chance to study hundreds upon hundreds of Barry Saltzes in their raw, untutored state. Coming from homes where the bedtime story at twilight had never been heard and where the television set had replaced the reading lamp, they sat in our classrooms with all the symptoms of cultural blight. Their median IQ score was 85, their reading scores were poor, and their practice of the language arts was unique. One boy who was asked at an assembly to read from Proverbs in the *Bible* prefaced his oral reading with the announcement that he would read some "proud verbs" in the *Bible.* Youngsters asked to write on the "Star-Spangled Banner" began with "Oh, say can you sing by the doors early light?" A lad, reporting on a TV show he liked insisted that the hero was "Quiet Earp." Once in a discussion, I used the term *bachelor of arts* and asked for a definition—"He's a a guy who got away by staying single."

Family ties, as the ordinary middle-class youngster enjoys them, were *terra incognita* to many of my boys. Fully 20 percent lived at home with but one parent, the second having vanished, run off, or died. I had boys who had never been served a warm breakfast by mother since they could remember. I had boys who had never had a heart-to-heart talk with father. Yet let mother or father be called to school, on some matter disciplinary, and we

---

[6] Walter Lord, *A Night to Remember.* New York: Holt, Rinehart & Winston, 1955. Bantam Paperback, 1962.

[7] Estelle H. Witzling, "Johnny Can't Read Because He Doesn't," *High Points*, 38:52–59, January 1956.

were often invited to "Hit him! Whack him! I mean treat him like he was your own!" [8]

Spawned in such homes, the Barry Saltzes never go much beyond talking of "Who's gonna win the fight next week?" watching crime shows on TV, going to the movies with their dates, ogling the girlie magazines. Of the 900 boys at my city vocational school, no more than 20 ever found it worthwhile to take in a Broadway play or a concert at Carnegie Hall even though both are little more than an hour from any boy's home. "That's for eggheads," Billy Brenner, 16, tells me when I offer him a ticket. "It's too far, anyhow. You come home too late." Yet two nights a week, religiously, instead of sitting down with his homework, he marches to the bowling alley where, until midnight, he enjoys a few short beers and the thrill of crashing a 16-pound bowling ball against the varnished pins.

Small wonder, then, that when we talk to them of *Silas Marner* they hear us not. Their ears are tuned to the change-of-period bell. We may appeal to them with a lovely print of an English landscape. They see it not; their eyes are on the clock. Desperate, we bring out ,the great, beloved classics which are on the world's permanent best-seller lists. With pomp and ceremony, with a laying-down of red carpets, with a lighting of candelabra, we introduce children to these classics. But we leave them unmoved. So, in quiet resignation, we affix to them the label "retarded readers"; and that great cultural divide between the middle-class teacher (reared on Shakespeare and Browning and Eliot) and the sons and daughters of "blue-collar" America (so often raised on comics, the movies, and television) becomes deeper and wider.

We've got to heal that breach, and we can! But this can be done only with understanding—the understanding that the Barry Saltzes are, as the late Elizabeth Rose of New York University put it "allergic to print"; that much of what we, his teachers, choose for him to read is not only *not* a cure for this allergy but also an *extension* of it; that only the book which "packs a wallop for him" may hope to effect a cure. The remedy? Begin with a book that hits him where he lives! [9]

I learned this back in 1954 when, as a new departmental chairman, I walked into the middle of a cold war between most of the 900 students in the school and most of the English teachers. The issue at first was books, *required* books for classroom study. The battleground was the bookroom piled high with *Silas Marner* and *Giants in the Earth* (grand books for college-bound youth, but sleeping pills for vocation-bound youngsters). There was a curtain dividing pupil and teacher, which, though made only of paper and print, was no less formidable than today's Iron Curtain. You walked into classes where teachers were devoting a full term to *Silas Marner*, and you saw children with heads on desks and eyes shut. You walked into the library and rarely saw a youngster except with a prescribed booklist based on the

[8] Charles G. Spiegler, "A Teacher's Report on a 'Tough School,'" *The New York Times Magazine*, Nov. 24, 1957.

[9] Elizabeth Rose, "Literature in the Junior High School," *English Journal*, 44:141–147.

predilections of his teacher. The long and short of it was that children were not reading, and teachers had thrown in the sponge with the excuse, "They can't!"

I believed they could, if we would but give a boy a title, a book jacket, a theme that rang true; if we could but talk to him colorfully about the world of books! Don't limit him to the confines of prescribed booklists or restrictive formulas for making book reports. Let the world and its infinite wonders be the subjects he may choose from, I begged. Let him begin with what he likes, appeal to his interests—and he will read.

When we inaugurated a 3-day book fair, displaying 2,000 books dressed in jolly jackets and written on hundreds of lively subjects I was sure youngsters liked, there was a shaking of heads among some members of the faculty. "I'll bet you won't sell a hundred books," one asserted smugly. "All these kids want is comics and girlie books. They won't buy anything decent!"

But they did. For 3 days, while English classes were cancelled, children browsed, read at random, bought or not as fancy struck them. And when the fair was over, we knew that these were the 3 days that had shaken our smug little world. The Johnnies who would buy "only comics and girlie books" had dug into their after-school-odd-job savings to take home 1,123 good books. Granted, Bill Stern's *My Favorite Sports Stories* and *The Real Story of Lucille Ball* were best sellers, but not far behind were the *Burl Ives Song Book*, *The Red Pony*,[10] and books of science fiction. And higher than anyone dared predict were *The Cruel Sea*[11] and *Mutiny on the Bounty*.[12]

Though no teachers were panting down the students' necks to "read this!" they did guide student choice. Some, like the big, broad-shouldered lad who was about to buy *The Scarlet Letter*[13] because he thought it was a football story, needed guidance. Some, like the nature lover who was about to buy *A Tree Grows in Brooklyn*[14] because he thought it was on target for a report he was making on trees, needed guidance. Others passed by the proffered help, however, and bought many books with vocabulary loads somewhat beyond their level. It didn't matter. "Interest," George Norvell, former New York State Supervisor of English, has said, "leaps over all reading barriers, including vocabulary."[15]

Johnny wasn't sleeping through "Lit" class by now. We relegated *Silas Marner* to a basement storeroom and gave the youngsters livelier fare. Booker T. Washington in his struggles for an education became a far more genuine superman to them than the comic book man with wings. It was *Kon-Tiki*[16]

10 John Steinbeck, *The Red Pony*. New York: Viking Press, Inc., 1959.
11 Nicholas Monsarrat, *The Cruel Sea*. New York: Alfred A. Knopf, Inc., 1951.
12 Charles Nordoff and James Norman Hall, *Mutiny on the Bounty*. Boston: Little, Brown & Co., 1932.
13 Nathaniel Hawthorne, *The Scarlet Letter*.
14 Betty Smith, *A Tree Grows in Brooklyn*. New York: Harper & Row, 1947.
15 George W. Norvell, *The Reading Interests of Young People*. Boston: D. C. Heath & Co., 1950.
16 Thor Heyerdahl, *Kon-Tiki*. Chicago: Rand McNally & Co., 1950.

on the perilous Pacific that replaced Eliot's nineteenth-century England. You could now walk into a class studying *Kon-Tiki* and see Jimmy Kolofney at the blackboard writing a letter of congratulations to Thor Heyerdahl. While he is expressing his admiration for the Skipper and "that crazy, wonderful thing you done," seven boys are rehearsing in two separate corners of the room: three of them in one corner play the crewmen of the *Kon-Tiki*; the other four make up a TV panel that will ask the intrepid voyagers all about the dangers, the thrills, the uncertainties of their venture.

Before long all eyes are focused on Jimmy's letter on the blackboard, to correct it—because "You can't send junk to a big shot like that." Later the class turns to the TV panel, which raises some incisive questions on the madness, the glory, and the thrill of adventure dear to any boy's heart. It also raises a question or two that better-bred boys might not ask: "Didja ever 'chicken out'?" "Hey, didja miss girls?" The end-of-period bell rings in the nick of time.

By the end of the year, the majority of our 900 students were reading at least a book a month. Many were doing far better. Library circulation had gone from 600 to 1,500.

Neither "climax" nor "denouement" cluttered up book reports now. As make-believe salesmen, kid critics, Hollywood producers, television panelists, they reported in terms they knew. "I like," "I love," "I hate," "I get mad," "It's great," "exciting," "heartwarming"—these terms indicated how books hit them. "I love that book because it suits my taste," wrote Johnny Gallardo about *Lives of a Bengal Lancer*.

Whatever the individual taste, we had given each of those 900 students a sporting chance to satisfy it. Now that the fair was over and the appetite whetted, I began to observe, ever so occasionally, especially after lunch, a paperback under the arm of a lad or two where earlier in the day there had been a lunch bag. Boys were beginning to walk off their hero sandwiches with short strolls to the neighborhood paperback gallery, sometimes bringing back a sample or two. Soon we discovered the Teen Age Book Club [17] whose titles caught the fancy of many. We were beginning to establish a rapport between children and books, helping many of our boys buy them cheaply, start their own libraries, and see for themselves how "even the smallest library is a veritable Treasure Island that takes no *Hispaniola* to reach—its buried riches no pirate's chart to locate."

This is not to boast that success was absolute and universal. We still had lots of lads like Lenny Kalter who equated the carrying of books with the role of the sissy. It wasn't until Miss Isenberg (public librarian assigned to visit our classes regularly to bestir the reluctant dragons) had introduced young Master Kalter to Henry Gregor Felsen's *Hot Rod* [18] that Lenny could

[17] Teen Age Book Club, sponsored by *Scholastic* magazine.
[18] Gregor Felsen, *Hot Rod*. New York: E. P. Dutton & Co.

identify with a character in a book—in this instance Bud Crayne, *Hot Rod*'s hero, and lover of speed. Lenny borrowed the book, devoured it, then became so avid a reader on the subject that *Street Rod* [19] (also by Felsen), *Mexican Road Race*,[20] *Thunder Road*,[21] and *The Red Car* [22] were finished within 2 weeks. Then he began searching the stacks all over the city for "anything by Mr. Felsen." When he heard that we were planning to invite an author to visit our assembly and set the keynote for our next Book Fair, he volunteered to write the first formal letter of invitation he had ever written in his life—you guessed it—to Gregor Felsen.

Last, but hardly least, let me suggest how television far from proving a menace to reading, as is so often alleged, proved a boon. My major premise here is that culturally deprived youngsters limit their horizons to the four walls of the home, the four corners of the neighborhood, and, as with many of my boys, the six pockets of the pool table. Television is their new window to the world. Through it they find the fullest, richest array of new interests man has ever known. Where or when, for example, in all recorded history could so many Americans in the year 1962 with a flip of the dial take an hour-long journey through the White House, with its gracious First Lady as hostess and guide?

My minor premise is that interest is the key to reading. My conclusion follows naturally. Television, by creating interest, can become the road to wider reading.

I saw it strikingly one morning in April of 1956. I was sitting in my office composing my weekly bulletin when the door burst open and two of my boys came dashing in.

"Got sump'n by Ogden Nash?" came the breathless query.

Slowly I raised my head.

"Who?"

"Ogden Nash—you know," they exclaimed, "the guy wid dose crazy rhymes."

My pen dropped; my ears perked up. Surprised, indeed delighted, that my boys were interested in reading one of America's most literate creators of verse, I asked: "You boys doing a book report on Mr. Nash?"

"Nope!" they parried, "no book reports—we just wanna read sump'n by him. We went to the library, but the other guys beat us to it. *You* got sump'n?"

Happily I had. And happily, Tommy Gorman, a 15-year-old butcher-to-be, and Peter de Stefano, a 16-year-old baker-to-be, walked off with every copy I owned of *I'm a Stranger Here Myself*.[23] When you realize that before this

---

[19] Gregor Felsen, *Street Rod*. New York: Random House, 1953.

[20] Patrick O'Connor, *Mexican Road Race*. New York: Ives Washburn, 1957.

[21] William Campbell Gault, *Thunder Road*. New York: E. P. Dutton & Co., 1952.

[22] Don Stanford, *The Red Car*. New York: Funk & Wagnalls Co., 1954.

[23] Ogden Nash, *I'm a Stranger Here Myself*. New York: Little, Brown, 1941.

day the closest Tom and Peter had come to voluntarily exposing themselves to rhythms and rhymes was the "popular song sheet," you realize what a move forward they had made.

This did not erupt full grown from the head of Zeus. It happened at a time when their English teacher found the going rough as he started a unit on poetry. So he looked for help. Since television was not a dirty word in our school, he looked to see how that week's TV programing could help. And lo, that Sunday Ed Sullivan could! For Sullivan had invited Noel Coward to read from the works of Ogden Nash to the background of music of Saëns, as played by Andre Kostelanetz. So the homework assignment for that Sunday said, "Watch Sullivan"—not just the song, not just the dance—but *all* of it! With the results we have seen.

Teach a little "dialmanship" and TV can become an Aladdin's lamp far more wondrous than the Arabian original. Our librarian, too, recognized that and arranged a bulletin board entitled *IF YOU WATCH: WHY NOT READ*. If you watch the the weather spots, why not read *Weathercraft* [24] by Spilhaus, for example? If you watch Leonard Bernstein, why not read *Leonard Bernstein* [25] by David Ewen?

If, in fact, we really want to introduce the culturally deprived youngster to books he can read on subjects he wants to read about, we are living in an age of huge abundance. For, in truth, this is the Golden Age of Writing for Youth, with many magnificent series available to them; with real writers (Quentin Reynolds, Dorothy Canfield Fisher, John Gunther, to name but a few) writing for them.

I cannot begin to tell you of the many, many hundreds of "juveniles" I have read myself with admiration, and been privileged to review and annotate, with a very high respect for what they can mean to children, and, with genuine appreciation for what they have meant even to ancient old ME.[26]

The job of preparing the proper materials for the customer we are talking about is, however, far from complete. So formidable, indeed, is this task, with both the textbook and the trade book, I would take a leaf from the book of the Ford Foundation man who recently recommended a *Vice-President-in-Charge-of-Heresy* for every school system—by proposing a *Vice President-in-Charge-of-Searching-for-and-Finding-Materials-Written-So-That-the-Children-We-Are-Concerned-With-Will-Read-Them-With-Interest*. As my first piece of advice to said VPI, I would urge: "Listen to the children you are serving." Here are their answers:

1. The subject has to be worth it to us. We like books about animals, aviation, careers, hobbies, sports, the sea, westerns. We love lots of adventure, plenty of excitement, slews of interesting facts about science and things.

[24] Athelstan Spilhaus, *Weathercraft*. New York: Viking Press, 1951.
[25] David Ewen, *Leonard Bernstein*. Philadelphia: Chilton Books, 1960.
[26] The reviews of the books under this category appear in the section called "Books You May Like," in Marion Monroe, Gwen Horsman, and William S. Gray, *Basic Reading Skills*. Chicago: Scott, Foresman & Co.

2. Don't treat us like babies. We may not be such "hot" readers, but that doesn't mean if you give us an easy book about ducks on a farm we'll cackle over it gleefully. We had that stuff in the third grade, remember?

3. Give us lots of good pictures, good drawings, and big print. As one of the fellows said, "I can't read when the print on the pages is so small. After a while I lose my eyesight."

4. You have to know how to write. Maybe the fellow who likes to read a lot will stand for some boring parts, but not us. If you want us to read don't beat around the bush but come to the point. Give us a story that pushes us to go on to the next page and the next page—and we'll stay with it.[27]

Let us search out the books which, as Robert Lawson has put it, will give these kids ". . . the chuckles . . . the gooseflesh . . . the glimpses of glory" they love. The books are here, now, asking to be discovered and enjoyed.

Books and reading are a staple in such a program not only for the well-endowed, but also for *all* the children of *all* the people. Only in the faith that there are no "second-class" citizens in our schools, a faith conceived, nurtured, and cherished in pride for nearly two centuries, can we hope to rise to the urgent tasks ahead. I am supremely confident that we shall.

[27] Charles G. Spiegler, "Reading Materials for Retarded Readers," *Materials for Reading*, Supplementary Educational Monographs, No. 6. Chicago: University of Chicago Press, 1957.